LPIC-1®
Study Guide
Fifth Edition

LPIC-1®

Linux Professional Institute Certification

Study Guide

Fifth Edition

Christine Bresnahan

Richard Blum

SYBEX®
A Wiley Brand

Copyright © 2020 by John Wiley & Sons, Inc., Indianapolis, Indiana

Published simultaneously in Canada

ISBN: 978-1-119-58212-0
ISBN: 978-1-119-58209-0 (ebk.)
ISBN: 978-1-119-58208-3 (ebk.)

Manufactured in the United States of America

For general information on our other products and services or to obtain technical support, please contact our Customer Care Department within the U.S. at (877) 762-2974, outside the U.S. at (317) 572-3993 or fax (317) 572-4002.

Wiley publishes in a variety of print and electronic formats and by print-on-demand. Some material included with standard print versions of this book may not be included in e-books or in print-on-demand. If this book refers to media such as a CD or DVD that is not included in the version you purchased, you may download this material at http://booksupport.wiley.com. For more information about Wiley products, visit www.wiley.com.

Library of Congress Control Number: 2019950102

Acknowledgments

First, all glory and praise go to God, who through His Son, Jesus Christ, makes all things possible, and gives us the gift of eternal life.

Many thanks go to the fantastic team of people at Sybex for their outstanding work on this project. Thanks to Kenyon Brown, the senior acquisitions editor, for offering us the opportunity to work on this book. Also thanks to Stephanie Barton, the development editor, for keeping things on track and making the book more presentable. Thanks Steph, for all your hard work and diligence. The technical editor, David Clinton, did a wonderful job of double-checking all of the work in the book in addition to making suggestions to improve the content. Thanks also goes to the young and talented Daniel Anez (theanez.com) for his illustration work. We would also like to thank Carole Jelen at Waterside Productions, Inc., for arranging this opportunity for us and for helping us out in our writing careers.

Christine would particularly like to thank her husband, Timothy, for his encouragement, patience, and willingness to listen, even when he has no idea what she is talking about. Christine would also like to express her love for Samantha and Cameron, "May God bless your marriage richly."

Rich would particularly like to thank his wife, Barbara, for enduring his grouchy attitude during this project, and helping to keep up his spirits with baked goods.

About the Authors

Christine Bresnahan, CompTIA Linux+, started working with computers more than 30 years ago in the IT industry as a systems administrator. Christine is an adjunct professor at Ivy Tech Community College where she teaches Linux certification and Python programming classes. She also writes books and produces instructional resources for the classroom.

Richard Blum, CompTIA Linux+ ce, CompTIA Security+ ce, has also worked in the IT industry for more than 30 years as both a system and network administrator, and he has published numerous Linux and open source books. Rich is an online instructor for Linux and web programming courses that are used by colleges and universities across the United States. When he is not being a computer nerd, Rich enjoys spending time with his wife Barbara and his two daughters, Katie and Jessica.

Contents at a Glance

Contents

Chapter	4	**Managing Files**	**181**

Chapter   10   Securing Your System   523

Table of Exercises

Introduction

Linux has become one of the fastest-growing operating systems used in server environments. Most companies utilize some type of Linux system within their infrastructure, and Linux is one of the major players in the cloud computing world. The ability to build and manage Linux systems is a skill that many companies are now looking for. The more you know about Linux, the more marketable you'll become in today's computer industry.

The Linux Professional Institute (LPI) has developed a series of certifications to help guide you through a career in the Linux world. Its LPIC-1 certification is an introductory certification for people who want to enter careers involving Linux. The exam is meant to certify that you have the skills necessary to install, operate, and troubleshoot a Linux system and are familiar with Linux-specific concepts and basic hardware.

The purpose of this book is to help you pass the LPIC-1 exams (101 and 102), updated in 2019 to version 5 (commonly called 101-500 and 102-500). Because these exams cover basic Linux installation, configuration, maintenance, applications, networking, and security, those are the topics that are emphasized in this book. You'll learn enough to get a Linux system up and running and to configure it for many common tasks. Even after you've taken and passed the LPIC-1 exams, this book should remain a useful reference.

Why Become Linux Certified?

With the growing popularity of Linux (and the increase in Linux-related jobs) comes hype. With all the hype that surrounds Linux, it's become hard for employers to distinguish employees who are competent Linux administrators from those who just know the buzzwords. This is where the LPIC-1 certification comes in.

With an LPIC-1 certification, you will establish yourself as a Linux administrator who is familiar with the Linux platform and can install, maintain, and troubleshoot any type of Linux system. LPI has created the LPIC-1 exams as a way for employers to have confidence in knowing their employees who pass the exam will have the skills necessary to get the job done.

How to Become Certified

The certification is available to anyone who passes the two required exams: 101 and 102. The current versions of the exams are version 5 and are denoted as 101-500 and 102-500.

The exam is administered by Pearson VUE. The exam can be taken at any Pearson VUE testing center. If you pass, you will get a certificate in the mail saying that you have passed. Contact (877) 619-2096 for Pearson VUE contact information.

To register for the exam with Pearson VUE, call (877) 619-2096 or register online at www.vue.com. However you do it, you'll be asked for your name, mailing address, phone number, employer, when and where you want to take the test (i.e., which testing center), and your credit card number (arrangement for payment must be made at the time of registration).

Who Should Buy This Book

Anyone who wants to pass the LPIC-1 certification exams would benefit from this book, but that's not the only reason for purchasing the book. This book covers all of the material someone new to the Linux world would need to know to start out in Linux. After you've become familiar with the basics of Linux, the book will serve as an excellent reference book for quickly finding answers to your everyday Linux questions.

The book is written with the assumption that you have a familiarity with basic computer and networking principles. Although no experience with Linux is required in order to benefit from this book, it will help if you know your way around a computer in either the Windows or macOS world, such as how to use a keyboard, use optical disks, and work with USB thumb drives.

It will also help to have a Linux system available to follow along with. Each chapter contains a simple exercise that will walk you through the basic concepts presented in the chapter. This provides the crucial hands-on experience that you'll need, both to pass the exam and to do well in the Linux world.

While the LPI LPIC-1 exams are Linux distribution neutral, it's impossible to write exercises that work in all Linux distributions. That said, the exercises in this book assume you have either Ubuntu 18.04 LTS or CentOS 7 available. You can install either or both of these Linux distributions in a virtual environment using the Oracle VirtualBox software, available at https://virtualbox.org.

How This Book Is Organized

This book consists of 10 chapters plus supplementary information: an online glossary, this introduction, and the assessment test after the introduction. The chapters are organized as follows:

- Chapter 1, "Exploring Linux Command-Line Tools," covers the basic tools you need to interact with Linux. These include shells, redirection, pipes, text filters, and regular expressions.

- Chapter 2, "Managing Software and Processes," describes the programs you'll use to manage software. Much of this task is centered around the RPM and Debian package management systems. The chapter also covers handling shared libraries and managing processes (that is, running programs).

- Chapter 3, "Configuring Hardware," focuses on Linux's interactions with the hardware on which it runs. Specific hardware and procedures for using it include the BIOS, expansion cards, USB devices, hard disks, and partitions and filesystems used on hard disks.

- Chapter 4, "Managing Files," covers the tools used to manage files. This includes commands to manage files, ownership, and permissions, as well as Linux's standard directory tree and tools for archiving files.

- Chapter 5, "Booting, Initializing, and Virtualizing Linux," explains how Linux boots up and how you can edit files in Linux. Specific topics include the GRUB Legacy and GRUB 2 boot loaders, boot diagnostics, and runlevels. It also takes a look at how to run Linux in a virtual machine environment.

- Chapter 6, "Configuring the GUI, Localization, and Printing," describes the Linux GUI and printing subsystems. Topics include X configuration, managing GUI logins, configuring location-specific features, enabling accessibility features, and setting up Linux to use a printer.

- Chapter 7, "Administering the System," describes miscellaneous administrative tasks. These include user and group management, tuning user environments, managing log files, and setting the clock.

- Chapter 8, "Configuring Basic Networking," focuses on basic network configuration. Topics include TCP/IP basics, setting up Linux on a TCP/IP network, and network diagnostics.

- Chapter 9, "Writing Scripts," covers how to automate simple tasks in Linux. Scripts are small programs that administrators often use to help automate common tasks. Being able to build simple scripts and have them run automatically at specified times can greatly simplify your administrator job.

- Chapter 10, "Securing Your System," covers security. Specific subjects include network security, local security, and the use of encryption to improve security.

Chapters 1 through 5 cover the 101-500 exam, and Chapters 6 through 10 cover the 102-500 exam. These make up Part I and Part II of the book, respectively.

Each chapter begins with a list of the exam objectives that are covered in that chapter. The book doesn't cover the objectives in order. Thus, you shouldn't be alarmed at some of the odd ordering of the objectives within the book. At the end of each chapter, you'll find a couple of elements you can use to prepare for the exam:

Exam Essentials   This section summarizes important information that was covered in the chapter. You should be able to perform each of the tasks or convey the information requested.

Review Questions   Each chapter concludes with 20 review questions. You should answer these questions and check your answers against the ones provided after the questions. If you can't answer at least 80 percent of these questions correctly, go back and review the chapter or at least those sections that seem to be giving you difficulty.

> The review questions, assessment test, and other testing elements included in this book are *not* derived from the actual exam questions, so don't memorize the answers to these questions and assume that doing so will enable you to pass the exam. You should learn the underlying topic, as described in the text of the book. This will let you answer the questions provided with this book *and* pass the exam. Learning the underlying topic is also the approach that will serve you best in the workplace—the ultimate goal of a certification.

To get the most out of this book, you should read each chapter from start to finish and then check your memory and understanding with the chapter-end elements. Even if you're already familiar with a topic, you should skim the chapter; Linux is complex enough that there are often multiple ways to accomplish a task, so you may learn something even if you're already competent in an area.

Additional Study Tools

Readers of this book can access a website that contains several additional study tools, including the following:

> Readers can access these tools by visiting www.sybex.com/go/lpic5e.

Sample Tests   All of the questions in this book will be included, along with the assessment test at the end of this introduction and the 200 questions from the review sections at the end of each chapter. In addition, there are two 50-question bonus exams. The test engine runs on Windows, Linux, and macOS.

Electronic Flashcards   The additional study tools include 150 questions in flashcard format (a question followed by a single correct answer). You can use these to review your knowledge of the exam objectives. The flashcards run on both Windows and Linux.

Glossary of Terms as a PDF File   In addition, there is a searchable glossary in PDF format, which can be read on all platforms that support PDF.

Conventions Used in This Book

This book uses certain typographic styles in order to help you quickly identify important information and to avoid confusion over the meaning of words such as on-screen prompts. In particular, look for the following styles:

- *Italicized text* indicates key terms that are described at length for the first time in a chapter. (Italics are also used for emphasis.)

- A monospaced font indicates the contents of configuration files, messages displayed at a text-mode Linux shell prompt, filenames, text-mode command names, and Internet URLs.

- *Italicized monospaced text* indicates a variable—information that differs from one system or command run to another, such as the name of a client computer or a process ID number.

- **Bold monospaced text** is information that you're to type into the computer, usually at a Linux shell prompt. This text can also be italicized to indicate that you should substitute an appropriate value for your system. (When isolated on their own lines, commands are preceded by non-bold monospaced $ or # command prompts, denoting regular user or system administrator use, respectively.)

In addition to these text conventions, which can apply to individual words or entire paragraphs, a few conventions highlight segments of text:

A note indicates information that's useful or interesting but that's somewhat peripheral to the main text. A note might be relevant to a small number of networks, for instance, or it may refer to an outdated feature.

A tip provides information that can save you time or frustration and that may not be entirely obvious. A tip might describe how to get around a limitation or how to use a feature to perform an unusual task.

Warnings describe potential pitfalls or dangers. If you fail to heed a warning, you may end up spending a lot of time recovering from a bug, or you may even end up restoring your entire system from scratch.

EXERCISE

Exercise

An exercise is a procedure you should try on your own computer to help you learn about the material in the chapter. Don't limit yourself to the procedures described in the exercises, though! Try other commands and procedures to really learn about Linux.

Real World Scenario

Real-World Scenario

A real-world scenario is a type of sidebar that describes a task or example that's particularly grounded in the real world. This may be a situation we or somebody we know has encountered, or it may be advice on how to work around problems that are common in real, working Linux environments.

The Exam Objectives

Behind every computer industry exam you can be sure to find exam objectives—the broad topics in which exam developers want to ensure your competency. The official exam objectives are listed here. (They're also printed at the start of the chapters in which they're covered.)

Exam objectives are subject to change at any time without prior notice and at LPI's sole discretion. Please visit LPI's website (www.lpi.org) for the most current listing of exam objectives.

Exam 101-500 Objectives

The following are the areas in which you must be proficient in order to pass the 101-500 exam. This exam is broken into four topics (101–104), each of which has three to eight objectives. Each objective has an associated weight, which reflects its importance to the exam as a whole. Refer to the LPI website to view the weights associated with each objective. The four main topics are:

Subject Area

101 System Architecture

102 Linux Installation and Package Management

103 GNU and Unix Commands

104 Devices, Linux Filesystems, Filesystem Hierarchy Standard

101 System Architecture

101.1 Determine and Configure hardware settings (Chapter 3)

- Enable and disable integrated peripherals.
- Differentiate between the various types of mass storage devices.
- Determine hardware resources for devices.
- Tools and utilities to list various hardware information (e.g., lsusb, lspci, etc.).
- Tools and utilities to manipulate USB devices.
- Conceptual understanding of sysfs, udev, hald, dbus.
- The following is a partial list of the used files, terms, and utilities: /sys, /proc, /dev, modprobe, lsmod, lspci, lsusb.

101.2 Boot the System (Chapter 5)

- Provide common commands to the boot loader and options to the kernel at boot time.
- Demonstrate knowledge of the boot sequence from BIOS/UEFI to boot completion.
- Understanding of SysVinit and system.
- Awareness of Upstart.
- Check boot events in the log file.
- The following is a partial list of the used files, terms and utilities: dmesg, journalctl, BIOS, UEFI, bootloader, kernel, init, initramfs, SysVinit, systemd.

101.3 Change runlevels/boot targets and shutdown or reboot system (Chapter 5)

- Set the default run level or boot target.
- Change between run levels/boot targets including single user mode.
- Shutdown and reboot from the command line.
- Alert users before switching run levels/boot targets or other major system events.
- Properly terminate processes.
- Awareness of acpid.
- The following is a partial list of the used files, terms and utilities: /etc/inittab, shutdown, init, /etc/init.d, telinit, systemd, systemctl, /etc/systemd/, /usr/lib/system/, wall.

102 Linux Installation and Package Management

102.1 Design hard disk layout (Chapter 3)

- Allocate filesystems and swap space to separate partitions or disks.
- Tailor the design to the intended use of the system.
- Ensure the /boot partition conforms to the hardware architecture requirements for booting.
- Knowledge of basic features of LVM.
- The following is a partial list of the used files, terms and utilities: / (root) filesystem, /var filesystem, /home filesystem, /boot filesystem, swap space, mount points, partitions, EFI System Partition (ESP).

102.2 Install a boot manager (Chapter 5)

- Providing alternative boot locations and backup boot options.
- Install and configure a boot loader such as GRUB Legacy.
- Perform basic configuration changes for GRUB 2.
- Interact with the boot loader.
- The following is a partial list of the used files, terms, and utilities: /boot/grub/menu .lst, grub.cfg and grub.conf, grub-install, grub-mkconfig, MBR.

102.3 Manage shared libraries (Chapter 2)

- Identify shared libraries.
- Identify the typical locations of system libraries.
- Load shared libraries.
- The following is a partial list of the used files, terms, and utilities: ldd, ldconfig, /etc/ld.so.conf, LD_LIBRARY_PATH.

102.4 Use Debian package management (Chapter 2)

- Install, upgrade and uninstall Debian binary packages.
- Find packages containing specific files or libraries which may or may not be installed.
- Obtain package information like version, content, dependencies, package integrity and installation status (whether or not the package is installed).
- Awareness of apt.
- The following is a partial list of the used files, terms, and utilities: /etc/apt/sources .list, dpkg, dpkg-reconfigure, apt-get, apt-cache.

102.5 Use RPM and YUM package management (Chapter 2)

- Install, re-install, upgrade and remove packages using RPM, YUM, and Zypper.
- Obtain information on RPM packages such as version, status, dependencies, integrity and signatures.
- Determine what files a package provides, as well as find which package a specific file comes from.
- The following is a partial list of the used files, terms, and utilities: `rpm`, `rpm2cpio`, `/etc/yum.conf`, `/etc/yum.repos.d/`, `yum`, `zypper`.

102.6 Linux as a virtualization guest (Chapter 5)

- Understand the general concept of virtual machines and containers.
- Understand common elements virtual machines in an IaaS cloud, such as computing instances, block storage and networking.
- Understand unique properties of a Linux system which have to changed when a system is cloned or used as a template.
- Understand how system images are used to deploy virtual machines, cloud instances and containers.
- Understand Linux extensions which integrate Linux with a virtualization product.
- Awareness of cloud-init.
- The following is a partial list of the used files, terms, and utilities: Virtual machine, Linux container, Application container, Guest drivers, SSH host keys, D-Bus machine ID.

103 GNU and Unix Commands

103.1 Work on the command line (Chapter 1)

- Use single shell commands and one-line command sequences to perform basic tasks on the command line.
- Use and modify the shell environment including defining, referencing and exporting environment variables.
- Use and edit command history.
- Invoke commands inside and outside the defined path.
- The following is a partial list of the used files, terms, and utilities: bash, echo, env, export, pwd, set, unset, type, which, man, uname, `history`, `.bash_history`, Quoting.

103.2 Process text streams using filters (Chapter 1)

- Send text files and output streams through text utility filters to modify the output using standard UNIX commands found in the GNU textutils package.

- The following is a partial list of the used files, terms, and utilities: bzcat, cat, cut, head, less, md5sum, nl, od, paste, sed, sha256sum, sha512sum, sort, split, tail, tr, uniq, wc, xzcat, zcat.

103.3 Perform basic file management (Chapter 4)

- Copy, move and remove files and directories individually.

- Copy multiple files and directories recursively.

- Remove files and directories recursively.

- Use simple and advanced wildcard specifications in commands.

- Using find to locate and act on files based on type, size, or time.

- Usage of tar, cpio, and dd.

- The following is a partial list of the used files, terms, and utilities: cp, find, mkdir, mv, ls, rm, rmdir, touch, tar, cpio, dd, file, gzip, gunzip, bzip2, bunzip2, xz, unxz, file globbing.

103.4 Use streams, pipes and redirects (Chapter 1)

- Redirecting standard input, standard output and standard error.

- Pipe the output of one command to the input of another command.

- Use the output of one command as arguments to another command.

- Send output to both stdout and a file.

- The following is a partial list of the used files, terms, and utilities: tee, xargs.

103.5 Create, monitor and kill processes (Chapter 2)

- Run jobs in the foreground and background.

- Signal a program to continue running after logout.

- Monitor active processes.

- Select and sort processes for display.

- Send signals to processes.

- The following is a partial list of the used files, terms, and utilities: &, bg, fg, jobs, kill, nohup, ps, top, free, uptime, pgrep, pkill, killall, watch, screen, tmux.

103.6 Modify process execution priorities (Chapter 2)

- Know the default priority of a job that is created.
- Run a program with higher or lower priority than the default.
- Change the priority of a running process.
- The following is a partial list of the used files, terms, and utilities: nice, ps, renice, top

103.7 Search text files using regular expressions (Chapter 1)

- Create simple regular expressions containing several notational elements.
- Understand the difference between basic and extended regular expressions.
- Understand the concepts of special characters, character classes, quantifiers, and anchors.
- Use regular expression tools to perform searches through a filesystem or file content.
- Use regular expressions to delete, change, and substitute text.
- The following is a partial list of the used files, terms, and utilities: grep, egrep, fgrep, sed, regex(7).

103.8 Basic file editing (Chapter 5)

- Navigate a document using vi.
- Understand and use vi modes.
- Insert, edit, delete, copy and find text in vi.
- Awareness of Emacs, nano, and vim.
- Configure the standard editor.
- The following is a partial list of the used files, terms, and utilities: vi, /, ?, h, j, k, l, i, o, a, d, p, y, dd, yy, ZZ, :w!, :q!, EDITOR.

104 Devices, Linux Filesystems, Filesystem Hierarchy Standard

104.1 Create partitions and filesystems (Chapter 3)

- Manage MBR and GPT partition tables.
- Use various mkfs commands to create various filesystems such as: ext2, ext3,ext4, XFS, VFAT, and exFAT.

- Basic feature knowledge of Btrfs, including multi-device filesystems, compression, and subvolumes.
- The following is a partial list of the used files, terms, and utilities: fdisk, gdisk, parted, mkfs, mkswap.

104.2 Maintain the integrity of filesystems (Chapter 3)

- Verify the integrity of filesystems.
- Monitor free space and inodes.
- Repair simple filesystem problems.
- The following is a partial list of the used files, terms, and utilities: du, df, fsck, e2fsck, mke2fs, tune2fs, xfs tools (such as xfs_repair, xfs_fsr, and xfs_db).

104.3 Control mounting and unmounting of filesystems (Chapter 3)

- Manually mount and unmount filesystems.
- Configure filesystem mounting on bootup.
- Configure user mountable removeable filesystems.
- Use of labels and UUIDs for identifying and mounting file systems.
- Awareness of systemd mount units.
- The following is a partial list of the used files, terms, and utilities: /etc/fstab, /media/, mount, umount, blkid, lsblk.

104.4 (Removed)

104.5 Manage file permissions and ownership (Chapter 4)

- Manage access permissions on regular and special files as well as directories.
- Use access modes such as suid, sgid and the sticky bit to maintain security.
- Know how to change the file creation mask.
- Use the group field to grant file access to group members.
- The following is a partial list of the used files, terms, and utilities: chmod, umask, chown, chgrp.

104.6 Create and change hard and symbolic links (Chapter 4)

- Create links.
- Identify hard and/or soft links.
- Copying versus linking files.

- Use links to support system administration tasks.
- The following is a partial list of the used files, terms, and utilities: ln, ls.

104.7 Find system files and place files in the correct location (Chapter 4)

- Understand the correct locations of files under the FHS.
- Find files and commands on a Linux system.
- Know the location and propose of important file and directories as defined in the FHS.
- The following is a partial list of the used files, terms, and utilities: find, locate, updatedb, whereis, which, type, /etc/updatedb.conf.

Exam 102-500 Objectives

The 102-500 exam comprises six topics (105–110), each of which contains three or four objectives. The six major topics are:

Subject Area
105 Shells and Shell Scripting
106 User Interfaces and Desktops
107 Administrative Tasks
108 Essential System Services
109 Networking Fundamentals
110 Security

105 Shells, Scripting and Data Management

105.1 Customize and use the shell environment (Chapter 9)

- Set environment variables (e.g., PATH) at login or when spawning a new shell.
- Write Bash functions for frequently used sequences of commands.
- Maintain skeleton directories for new user accounts.
- Set command search path with the proper directory.
- The following is a partial list of the used files, terms, and utilities: ., source, etc/bash.bashrc, /etc/profile, env, export, set, unset, ~/.bash_profile, ~/.bash_login, ~/.profile, ~/.bashrc, ~/.bash_logout, function, alias.

105.2 Customize or write simple scripts (Chapter 9)

- Use standard sh syntax (loops, tests).
- Use command substitution.
- Test return values for success or failure or other information provided by a command.
- Execute chained commands.
- Perform conditional mailing to the superuser.
- Correctly select the script interpreter through the shebang (#!) line.
- Manage the location, ownership, execution and suid-rights of scripts.
- The following is a partial list of the used files, terms, and utilities: for, while, test, if, read, seq, exec, ||, &&.

106 User Interfaces and Desktops

106.1 Install and configure X11 (Chapter 6)

- Understanding of the X11 architecture.
- Basic understanding and knowledge of the X Window configuration file.
- Overwrite specific aspects of Xorg configuration, such as keyboard layout.
- Understand the components of desktop environments, such as display managers and window managers.
- Manage access to the X server and display applications on remote X servers.
- Awareness of Wayland.
- The following is a partial list of the used files, terms, and utilities: /etc/X11/xorg.conf, /etc/X11/xorg.conf.d, ~/.xsession-errors, xhost, xauth, DISPLAY, X.

106.2 Graphical Desktops (Chapter 6)

- Awareness of major desktop environments.
- Awareness of protocols to access remote desktop sessions.
- The following is a partial list of the used files, terms, and utilities: KDE, Gnome, Xfce, X11, XDMCP, VNC, Spice, RDP.

106.3 Accessibility (Chapter 6)

- Basic knowledge of visual settings and themes.
- Basic knowledge of Assistive Technologies (ATs).
- The following is a partial list of the used files, terms, and utilities: High Contrast/Large Print Desktop Themes, Screen Reader, Braille Display, Screen Magnifier, On-Screen Keyboard, Sticky/Repeat keys, Slow/Bounce/Toggle keys, Mouse keys, Gestures, Voice recognition.

107 Administrative Tasks

107.1 Manage user and group accounts and related system files (Chapter 7)

- Add, modify and remove users and groups.
- Manage user/group info in password/group databases.
- Create and manage special purpose and limited accounts.
- The following is a partial list of the used files, terms, and utilities: /etc/passwd, /etc/shadow, /etc/group, /etc/skel, chage, getent, groupadd, groupdel, groupmod, passwd, useradd, userdel, usermod.

107.2 Automate system administration tasks by scheduling jobs (Chapter 9)

- Manage cron and at jobs.
- Configure user access to cron and at services.
- Understand systemd timer units.
- The following is a partial list of the used files, terms, and utilities: /etc/cron.{d, daily,hourly,monthly,weekly}, /etc/at.deny, /etc/at.allow, /etc/crontab, /etc/cron.allow, /etc/cron.deny, /var/spool/cron/, crontab, at, atq, atrm, systemctl, systemd-run.

107.3 Localization and internationalization (Chapter 6)

- Configure locale settings and environment variables.
- Configure timezone settings and environment variables.
- The following is a partial list of the used files, terms, and utilities: /etc/timezone, /etc/localtime, /usr/share/zoneinfo, environment variables (LC_*, LC_ALL, LANG, TZ), /usr/bin/locale, tzselect, timedatectl, date, iconv, UTF-8, ISO-8859, ASCII, Unicode.

108 Essential System Services

108.1 Maintain system time (Chapter 7)

- Set the system date and time.
- Set the hardware clock to the correct time in UTC.
- Configure the correct timezone.
- Basic NTP configuration using ntpd and chrony.
- Knowledge of using the pool.ntp.org service.

- Awareness of the ntpq command.
- The following is a partial list of the used files, terms, and utilities: /usr/share/zoneinfo, /etc/timezone, /etc/localtime, /etc/ntp.conf, /etc/chrony.conf, date, hwclock, timedatectl, ntpd, ntpdate, chronyc, pool.ntp.org.

108.2 System logging (Chapter 7)

- Basic configuration of rsyslogd.
- Understanding of standard facilities, priorities, and actions.
- Query the systemd journal.
- Filter systemd journal data by criteria such as date, service, or priority.
- Delete old systemd journal data.
- Retrieve systemd journal data from a rescue system or file system copy.
- Understand the interaction of rsyslogd with systemd-journald.
- Configuration of logrotate.
- Awareness of syslog and syslog-ng.
- The following is a partial list of the used files, terms, and utilities: /etc/rsyslog.conf, /var/log, logger, logrotate, /etc/logrotate.conf, /etc/logrotate.d/, journalctl, systemd-cat, /etc/system/journal.conf, /var/log/journal/.

108.3 Mail Transfer Agent (MTA) basics (Chapter 7)

- Create e-mail aliases.
- Configure e-mail forwarding.
- Knowledge of commonly available MTA programs (postfix, sendmail, qmail, exim) (no configuration).
- The following is a partial list of the used files, terms, and utilities: ~/.forward, sendmail emulation layer commands, newaliases, mail, mailq, postfix, sendmail, exim.

108.4 Manage printers and printing (Chapter 6)

- Basic CUPS configuration (for local and remote printers).
- Manage user print queues.
- Troubleshoot general printing problems.
- Add and remove jobs from configured printer queues.
- The following is a partial list of the used files, terms, and utilities: CUPS configuration files, tools and utilities; /etc/cups; lpd legacy interface (lpr, lprm, lpq).

109 Networking Fundamentals

109.1 Fundamentals of internet protocols (Chapter 8)

- Demonstrate an understanding of network masks and CIDR notation.
- Knowledge of the differences between private and public "dotted quad" IP-Addresses.
- Knowledge about common TCP and UDP ports (20, 21, 22, 23, 25, 53, 80, 110, 123, 139, 143, 161, 162, 389, 443, 465, 514, 636, 993, 995).
- Knowledge about the differences and major features of UDP, TCP and ICMP.
- Knowledge of the major differences between IPv4 and IPV6.
- Knowledge of the basic features of IPv6.
- The following is a partial list of the used files, terms, and utilities: /etc/services, IPv4, IPv6, subnetting, TCP, UDP, ICMP.

109.2 Persistent network configuration (Chapter 8)

- Understand basic TCP/IP host configuration.
- Configure Ethernet and wi-fi configuration using NetworkManager.
- Awareness of systemd-networkd.
- The following is a partial list of the used files, terms, and utilities: /etc/hostname, /etc/hosts, /etc/nsswitch.conf, /etc/resolv.conf, nmcli, hostnamectl, ifup, ifdown.

109.3 Basic network troubleshooting (Chapter 8)

- Manually configure network interfaces, including viewing and changing the configuration of network interfaces using iproute2.
- Manually configure routing, including viewing and changing routing tables and setting the default route using iproute2.
- Debug problems associated with the network configuration.
- Awareness of legacy net-tools commands.
- The following is a partial list of the used files, terms, and utilities: ip, hostname, ss, ping, ping6, traceroute, traceroute6, tracepath, tracepath6, netcat, ifconfig, netstat, route.

109.4 Configure client side DNS (Chapter 8)

- Query remote DNS servers.
- Configure local name resolution and use remote DNS servers.
- Modify the order in which name resolution is done.
- Debug errors related to name resolution.

- Awareness of systemd-resolved.
- The following is a partial list of the used files, terms, and utilities: /etc/hosts, /etc/resolv.conf, /etc/nsswitch.conf, host, dig, getent.

110 Security

110.1 Perform security administration tasks (Chapter 10)

- Audit a system to find files with the suid/sgid bit set.
- Set or change user passwords and password aging information.
- Being able to use nmap and netstat to discover open ports on a system.
- Set up limits on user logins, processes and memory usage.
- Determine which users have logged in to the system or are currently logged in.
- Basic sudo configuration and usage.
- The following is a partial list of the used files, terms, and utilities: find, passwd, fuser, lsof, nmap, chage, netstat, sudo, /etc/sudoers, su, usermod, ulimit, who, w, last.

110.2 Setup host security (Chapter 10)

- Awareness of shadow passwords and how they work.
- Turn off network services not in use.
- Understand the role of TCP wrappers.
- The following is a partial list of the used files, terms, and utilities: /etc/nologin, /etc/passwd, /etc/shadow, /etc/xinetd.d/, /etc/xinetd.conf, /etc/inetd.d/, /etc/inetd.conf, systemd-socket, /etc/inittab, /etc/init.d/, /etc/hosts.allow, /etc/hosts.deny.

110.3 Securing data with encryption (Chapter 10)

- Perform basic OpenSSH 2 client configuration and usage.
- Understand the role of OpenSSH 2 server host keys.
- Perform basic GnuPG configuration, usage, and revocation.
- Use GPG to encrypt, decrypt, sign, and verify files.
- Understand SSH port tunnels (including X11 tunnels).
- The following is a partial list of the used files, terms, and utilities: ssh, ssh-keygen, ssh-agent, ssh-add, ~/.ssh/id_rsa and id_rsa.pub, ~/.ssh/id_rsa and id_rsa.pub, ~/.ssh/id_dsa and id_dsa.pub, ~/.ssh/id_ecdsa and ecdsa.pub, ~/.ssh/id_ed25519 and id_ed25519.pub, /etc/ssh/ssh_host_rsa_key and ssh_host_rsa_key.pub, /etc/ssh/ssh_host_dsa_key and ssh_host_dsa_key.pub, /etc/ssh/ssh_host_ecdsa_key and host_ecdsa_key.pub, /etc/ssh/ssh_host_ed25519_key and host_ed25519_key.pub, ~/.ssh/authorized_keys, /etc/ssh_known_hosts, gpg, gpg-agent, ~/.gnupg/.

Assessment Test

1. Which of the following are names of shell programs? (Choose all that apply.)

   A. Bash

   B. Korn Shell

   C. Born Shell

   D. Dash

   E. Z Shell

2. You are a system administrator on a CentOS Linux server. You need to view records in the `/var/log/messages` file that start with the date May 30 and end with the IPv4 address 192.168.10.42. Which of the following is the best grep command to use?

   A. `grep "May 30?192.168.10.42" /var/log/messages`

   B. `grep "May 30.*192.168.10.42" /var/log/messages`

   C. `grep -i "May 30.*192.168.10.42" /var/log/messages`

   D. `grep -i "May 30?192.168.10.42" /var/log/messages`

   E. `grep -v "May 30.*192.168.10.42" /var/log/messages`

3. Which of the following commands will determine how many records in the file `Problems.txt` contain the word `error`?

   A. `grep error Problems.txt | wc -b`

   B. `grep error Problems.txt | wc -w`

   C. `grep error Problems.txt | wc -l`

   D. `grep Problems.txt error | wc -w`

   E. `grep Problems.txt error | wc -l`

4. Which of the following conforms to the standard naming format of a Debian package file? (Choose all that apply.)

   A. `openssh-client_1%3a7.6pl-4ubuntu0.3_amd64.deb`

   B. `openssh-client-3a7-24_86_x64.rpm`

   C. `zsh_5.4.2-3ubuntu3.1_amd64.deb`

   D. `zsh_5.4.2-3ubuntu3.1_amd64.dpkg`

   E. `emacs_47.0_all.dpkg`

5. What does placing an ampersand sign (&) after a command on the command line do?

   A. Disconnects the command from the terminal session.

   B. Runs the command in foreground mode.

   C. Runs the command in background mode.

   D. Redirects the output to another command.

   E. Redirects the output to a file.

6. If you are using the `tmux` utility how do you create a new window?

   A. `screen`

   B. `tmux create`

   C. `tmux ls`

   D. `screen -ls`

   E. `tmux new`

7. What type of hardware interface uses interrupts, I/O ports, and DMA channels to communicate with the PC motherboard?

   A. USB

   B. GPIO

   C. PCI

   D. Monitors

   E. Printers

8. What directory does the Linux FHS set aside specifically for installing third party programs?

   A. `/usr/bin`

   B. `/usr`

   C. `/opt`

   D. `/usr/sbin`

   E. `/tmp`

9. Which command allows you to append a partition to the virtual directory on a running Linux system?

   A. `mount`

   B. `umount`

   C. `fsck`

   D. `dmesg`

   E. `mkinitramfs`

10. The system admin took an archive file and applied a compression utility to it. The resulting file extension is `.gz`. Which compression utility was used?

   A. The `xz` utility

   B. The `gzip` utility

   C. The `bzip2` utility

   D. The `zip` utility

   E. The `dd` utility

11. Before the umask setting is applied, a directory has a default permission octal code of which of the following?

A. 111

B. 755

C. 666

D. 777

E. 888

12. You need to locate files within the /tmp directory or one of its subdirectories. These files should be empty. Assuming you have super user privileges, what command should you use?

A. `find / -name tmp`

B. `find /tmp -empty`

C. `find /tmp -empty 0`

D. `find /tmp/* -name empty`

E. `find / -empty`

13. Where does the system BIOS attempt to find a bootloader program? (Choose all that apply.)

A. An internal hard drive

B. An external hard drive

C. A DVD drive

D. A USB flash drive

E. A network server

14. Which firmware method has replaced BIOS on most modern IBM-compatible computers?

A. FTP

B. UEFI

C. PXE

D. NFS

E. HTTPS

15. Which of the following are system initialization methods? (Choose all that apply.)

A. `/sbin/init`

B. `/etc/init`

C. SysVinit

D. systemd

E. `cloud-init`

16. The Cinnamon desktop environment uses which windows manager?

    A. Mutter

    B. Muffin

    C. Nemo

    D. Dolphin

    E. LightDM

17. Your X.org session has become hung. What keystrokes do you use to restart the session?

    A. Ctrl+C

    B. Ctrl+Z

    C. Ctrl+Q

    D. Ctrl+Alt+Delete

    E. Ctrl+Alt+Backspace

18. What folder contains the time zone template files in Linux?

    A. /etc/timezone

    B. /etc/localtime

    C. /usr/share/zoneinfo

    D. /usr/share/timezone

    E. /usr/share/localtime

19. Which field contains the same data for both a /etc/passwd and /etc/shadow file record?

    A. Password

    B. Account expiration date

    C. UID

    D. GID

    E. User account's username

20. What facility and priority setting would log kernel messages that are warnings and higher severity?

    A. kern.=warn

    B. kern.*

    C. *.info

    D. kern.warn

    E. kern.alert

21. Which of the following can implement NTP on Linux? (Choose all that apply.)

    A. Exim

    B. ntpd

    C. Sendmail

    D. Postfix

    E. chronyd

22. Which network layer uses the Wi-Fi Protected Access (WPA) encryption?

   A. network

   B. physical

   C. transport

   D. application

23. Which two commands set the IP address, subnet mask, and default router information on an interface using the command line?

   A. netstat

   B. ping

   C. nmtui

   D. ip

   E. route

24. What tool allows you to send ICMP messages to a remote host to test network connectivity?

   A. netstat

   B. ifconfig

   C. ping

   D. iwconfig

   E. ss

25. Which Bash shell script command allows you to iterate through a series of data until the data is complete?

   A. if

   B. case

   C. for

   D. exit

   E. $()

26. Which environment variable allows you to retrieve the numeric user ID value for the user account running a shell script?

   A. $USER

   B. $UID

   C. $BASH

   D. $HOME

   E. $1

27. When will the cron table entry 0 0 1 * * myscript run the specified command?

    A. At 1AM every day.

    B. At midnight on the first day of every month.

    C. At midnight on the first day of every week.

    D. At 1PM every day.

    E. At midnight every day.

28. Which of the following utilities allows you to scan a system and see what network services are being offered or used via the files that are open?

    A. fuser

    B. lsof

    C. nmap

    D. netstat

    E. ss

29. Which of the following OpenSSH directives should you review in order to ensure the public-facing system's users are employing SSH securely?

    A. Port directive

    B. Protocol directive

    C. PermitRootLogin directive

    D. AllowTCPForwarding directive

    E. ForwardX11 directive

30. Which of the following is true about gpg-agent? (Choose all that apply.)

    A. It starts a special agent shell, so you don't have to re-enter passwords to authenticate to remote systems.

    B. It manages GPG secret keys separately from any protocol.

    C. It is managed by either SysVinit or systemd, depending on your system's initialization method.

    D. It keeps previously used private keys in RAM.

    E. If it needs a private key that is not in RAM, it asks the users for the passphrase protecting the key.

Answers to Assessment Test

1. A, B, D, E. The shell names in options A, B, D, and E are all legitimate shell program names, and thus are correct answer. There is no Born shell (you may have confused that name with the original Bourne shell), so option C is an incorrect choice.

2. B. Option B is the best command because this grep command employs the correct syntax. It uses the quotation marks around the *PATTERN* to avoid unexpected results, and uses the .* regular expression characters to indicate that anything can be between May 30 and the IPv4 address. No additional switches are necessary. Option A is not the best grep command, because it uses the wrong regular expression of ?, which only allows one character to exist between May 30 and the IPv4 address. Options C and D are not the best grep commands, because they employ the use of the -i switch to ignore case, which is not needed in this case. The grep command in option E is an incorrect choice, because it uses the -v switch will display text records that do not match the *PATTERN*.

3. C. To find records within the Problems.txt file that contain the word error at least one time, the grep command is employed. The correct syntax is grep error Problems.txt. To count the records, the grep command's STDOUT is piped as STDIN into the wc utility. The correct syntax to count the records, is wc -l. Therefore, option C is the correct answer. The command in option A is incorrect, because its wc command is counting the number of bytes within each input record. Option B is a wrong answer, because its wc command is counting the number of words within each input record. The command in option D has two problems. First its grep command syntax has the item for which to search and the file to search backwards. Also, its wc command is counting the number of words within each input record. Therefore, option D is a wrong choice. Option E is an incorrect answer, because its grep command syntax has the item for which to search and the file to search backwards.

4. A, C. Debian package files following a standard naming format of *PACKAGE-NAME-VERSION-RELEASE_ARCHITECTURE*.deb. Therefore, options A and C are correct answers. The package file name in option B has the .rpm file extension, which immediately disqualifies it from following the Debian package file standard naming format. Thus, option B is a wrong answer. Options D and E use .dpkg as their file extension, so they are incorrect choices as well.

5. C. The ampersand sign (&) tells the shell to run the specified command in background mode in the terminal session, so Option C is correct. The nohup command is used to disconnect the command from the terminal session, so Option A is incorrect. The fg command moves a command running in background mode to the foreground, so Option B is incorrect. The pipe symbol (|) redirects the output from the command to another command, so Option D is incorrect. The greater-than symbol (>) redirects the output from the command to a file, so Option E is an incorrect choice as well.

6. E. The tmux new will create a new window. Therefore, option E is the correct answer. The GNU Screen utility employs the screen commands to create a new window. Thus, option A is a wrong answer. The tmux create is a made-up tmux command, and therefore option B is also a wrong choice. The tmux -ls will display detached windows, but not create them, so option C is a wrong choice. The screen -ls command will display any detached GNU screen widows, so option D is an incorrect choice as well.

7. C. PCI boards use interrupts, I/O ports, and DMA channels to send and receive data with the PC motherboard, so Option C is correct. USB devices transmit data using a serial bus connected to the motherboard and don't use DMA channels, so Option A is incorrect. The GPIO interface uses memory-mapped specialty IC chips and not interrupts and I/O ports, so option B is incorrect. Monitors and printers are hardware devices and not hardware interfaces, so Options D and E are incorrect.

8. C. The /opt directory is designated for installing optional third party applications, so Option C is correct. The /usr/bin directory is designated for local user programs, not third party programs, so Option A is incorrect. The /usr directory is designated for standard Linux programs, not third party programs, so Option B is incorrect. The /usr/sbin directory is designated for system programs and data, not third party programs, so Option D is incorrect. The /tmp directory is designated for temporary files that are commonly erased when the system reboots, not third party programs, so Option E is incorrect.

9. A. The mount command allows you to specify both the partition and the location in the virtual directory where to append the partition files and directories. The files and directories contained in the partition then appear at that location in the virtual directory. The umount command (option B) is used to remove a mounted partition. Option C, the fsck command, is used to fix a hard drive that is corrupted and can't be mounted, it doesn't actually mount the drive itself. The dmesg command in option D is used to view boot messages for the system , which may tell you where a hard drive is appended to the virtual directory, but it doesn't' actually to the appending. Option E, the mkinitramfs command, creates an initrd RAM disk, and doesn't directly handle mounting hard drives to the virtual directory.

10. B. The gzip utility compresses data files and gives them the .gz file extension. Therefore, option B is the correct answer. The xz, bzip2, and zip compression utilities compress a data file and give it a different file extension, so options A, C, and D are wrong answers. The dd utility is not a compression program. Therefore, option E is also a wrong choice.

11. D. Before the umask setting is applied, a directory has a default permission octal code of 777. Thus, option D is the correct answer. The 111 octal code in option A does not apply to any created files or directories, prior to the umask setting being applied. Therefore, option A is a wrong answer. The 755 octal code is the typical resulting directory permission setting *after* a umask setting of 0022 is applied. Thus, option B is a wrong choice. The 666 octal coded is the default permission octal code for files prior to applying the umask setting. Thus, option C is an incorrect answer. The 888 octal code does not exist, so option E is an incorrect choice.

12. B. The find /tmp -empty command will locate files within the /tmp directory or one of its subdirectories, which are empty. Therefore, option B is the right answer. The find / -name tmp command, starts at the root directory, instead of the /tmp directory, and searches for files/directories whose names are tmp. Thus, option A is a wrong answer. The find /tmp -empty 0 command adds an incorrect additional argument, 0, at the end of the command, so option C is also an incorrect answer. The find /tmp/* -name empty command searches for files/directories whose names are tmp, and adds an unnecessary wildcard, *, to the directory name to search. Thus, option D is also a wrong choice. The find / -empty command starts at the root directory instead of the /tmp directory. Therefore, option E is an incorrect choice.

13. A, B, C, D, and E. The BIOS firmware can look in multiple locations for a bootloader program. Most commonly it looks at the internal hard drive installed on the system, however, if none is found, it can search other places. Most systems allow you to boot from an external hard drive, or from a DVD drive. Modern systems now also provide the option to boot from a USB memory stick inserted into a USB port on the workstation. Finally, many systems provide the PXE boot option, which allows the system to boot remotely from a network server.

14. B. The UEFI firmware method has replaced the BIOS in most IBM-compatible computers, so option B is correct. FTP, PXE, NFS, and HTTPS are not firmware methods, but methods for loading the Linux bootloader, so options A, C, D, and E are all incorrect.

15. C, D. SysVinit and systemd are both system initialization methods. Thus, options C and D are the correct answers. The init program can live in the /sbin/, /etc/, or /bin/ directory, and while it is used by the initialization methods, it is not a method itself. Thus, options A and B are wrong answers. The cloud-init program is a tool that allows you to create VMs out of system images locally or cloud images on an IaaS platform. However, it is not a system initialization method. Therefore, option E is an incorrect answer as well.

16. B. The Cinnamon desktop environment uses the Muffin windows manager. Therefore, option B is the correct answer. Mutter is the windows manager for the GNOME Shell desktop environment, though Muffin did fork from that project. Thus, option A is a wrong answer. Nemo is the file manager for Cinnamon, and therefore, option C is a wrong choice. Dolphin is the file manager for the KDE Plasma desktop environment. Thus, option D is a wrong choice. LightDM is display manager for Cinnamon, and therefore, option E is also an incorrect choice.

17. E. The Ctrl+Alt+Backspace will kill your X.org session and then restart it, putting you at the login screen (display manager.) Therefore, option E is the correct answer. The Ctrl+C combination sends an interrupt signal, but does not restart an X.org session. Thus, option A is a wrong answer. The Ctrl+Z keystroke combination sends a stop signal, but it will not restart the X.org session. Therefore, option B is also an incorrect answer. The Ctrl+Q combination will release a terminal that has been paused by Ctrl+S. However, it does not restart a X.org session, so it too is a wrong choice. The Ctrl+Alt+Delete keystroke combination, can be set to do a number of tasks, depending upon your desktop environment. In some cases, it brings up a shutdown, logout, or reboot menu. However, it does not restart the X.org session, so option D is an incorrect choice.

18. C. Both Debian-based and Red Hat-based Linux distributions store the time zone template files in the /usr/share/zoneinfo folder, so option C is correct. The /etc/timezone and /etc/localtime files contain the current time zone file for Debian and Red Hat-based systems, not the time zone template files, so options A and B are incorrect. The /usr/share/timezone and /usr/share/localtime folders don't exist in either Debian-based or Red Hat-based Linux distributions, so options D and E are also incorrect.

19. E. The user account's username is the only field within a /etc/passwd and /etc/shadow record that contains the same data. Therefore, option E is the correct answer. While both files have a password field, they do not contain the same data. The password can only exist in one of the two files, preferably the /etc/shadow file. Thus, option A is a wrong answer. The account expiration date only exists in the /etc/shadow file, so option B is also a wrong choice. The UID and GID fields only exist in the /etc/passwd file, so options C and D are also incorrect answers.

20. D. The rsyslogd application priorities log event messages with the defined severity or higher, so Option D would log all kernel event messages at the warn, alert, or emerg severities, so it is correct. The Option A facility and priority setting would only log kernel messages with a severity of warning, so it is incorrect. Option B would log all kernel event messages, not just warnings or higher, so it is incorrect. Option C would log all facility type event messages, but include the information or higher level severity, so it is incorrect. Option E would log kernel event messages, but only at the alert or emerg severity levels, not the warning level, so it is also incorrect.

21. B, E. Both ntpd and chronyd can implement network time protocol client services on Linux, so options B and E are correct. Exim, Sendmail, and Postfix are all mail transfer agents (MTAs) for use on Linux, so options A, C, and D are incorrect choices.

22. B. The Wi-Fi Protected Access (WPA) encryption protocol protects access to wireless access points. The wireless network operates at the physical network, so option B is correct. The network level uses addressing protocols such as IP to send data between systems on the network, buy doesn't interact with the wireless signal, so answer A is incorrect. The transport layer uses ports to direct network traffic to specific applications, running at the application layer, so options C and D are both incorrect.

23. C and D. The nmtui command provides an interactive text menu for selecting a network interface and setting the network parameters, and the ip command provides a command line tool tool for setting network parameters, so both Options C and D are correct. The netstat command displays information about network connections, but doesn't set the network parameters, so option A is incorrect. The ping command can send ICMP packets to a remote host, but doesn't set the local network parameters, so option B is incorrect. The route command sets the routing network parameters, but not the IP address or subnet mask, so option E is incorrect.

24. C. The ping command sends ICMP packets to a specified remote host and waits for a response, making option C the correct answer. The netstat command displays statistics about the network interface, so it's incorrect. The ifconfig command displays or sets network information, but doesn't send ICMP packets, making option B incorrect. The iwconfig command displays or sets wireless network information, but doesn't handle ICMP packets, making option D incorrect. The ss command display information about open connections and ports on the system, so option E is also incorrect.

25. C. The for command allows you to iterate through a series of data one by one until the data set is exhausted, so Option C is correct. The if-then and case statements perform a single test on an object to determine if a block of commands should be run, they don't iterate through data, so Options A and B are incorrect. The exit command stops the shell script and exits to the parent shell, so Option D is incorrect. The $() command redirects the output of a command to a variable in the shell script, it doesn't iterate through a series of data, so Option E is incorrect.

26. B. The $UID environment variable contains the numeric user ID value of the user account running the shell script, so Option B is correct. The $USER environment variable contains the text user name of the user account running the shell script, not the numerical user ID value, so Option A is incorrect. The $BASH environment variable contains the path to the executable Bash shell, so Option C is incorrect. The $HOME environment variable contains the location of the home directory of the user account running the shell, so Option D is incorrect. The $1 positional variable contains the first parameter listed on the command line command when the shell script was run, so Option E is incorrect.

27. B. The cron table format specifies the times to run the script by minute, hour, day of month, month, and day of week. Thus the format 0 0 1 * * will run the command at 00:00 (midnight) on the first day of the month for every month. That makes Option B correct, and Options A, C, D, and E incorrect.

28. A, B. The fuser and lsof utilities allow you to see what network services are being offered or used via files that are open. Therefore, options A and B are correct answers. While the nmap, netstart, and ss utilities will allow you to see the various network services being offered (or used) on your system, they do not do so via files that are open. Thus, options C, D, and E are incorrect choices.

29. A, B, C. The Port directive determines what port the OpenSSH daemon (sshd) listens on for incoming connection requests, so any public-facing systems should have it changed from its default of 22. Therefore, option A is a correct answer. The Protocol directive determines what SSH protocol is used, and to ensure OpenSSH 2 is employed, it should be set to 2. Therefore, option B is another correct answer. The PermitRootLogin directive does just what it says — permits or denies the root account to login via OpenSSH, and you do not want to permit the root account to use ssh to log into the system, so option C is also a correct choice. The AllowTCPForwarding directive toggles whether or not OpenSSH port forwarding is allowed, and the ForwardX11 toggles whether or not X11 commands can be forwarded over an OpenSSH encrypted tunnel, which can enhance security in those cases, but don't need to be reviewed, unless those features are desired. Thus, options D and E are incorrect choices.

30. B, D, E. The gpg-agent manages GPG secret keys separately from any protocol, keeps previously used private keys in RAM, and if it needs a private key that is not in RAM, it asks the users for the passphrase protecting the key. Therefore, options B, D, and E are all correct answers. The gpg-agent does not start a special agent shell (that's something the ssh-agent does), so option A is a wrong answer. The gpg-agent is not managed by SysVinit or systemd, but instead is started automatically by the gpg utility. Thus, option C is a wrong choice as well.

Exam 101-500

Chapter

1

Exploring Linux Command-Line Tools

OBJECTIVES

✓ **103.1** Work on the command line

✓ **103.2** Process text streams using filters

✓ **103.4** Use streams, pipes, and redirects

✓ **103.7** Search text files using regular expressions

✓ **103.8** Basic file editing

In the original Linux years, to get anything done you had to work with the *Gnu/Linux shell*. The shell is a special interactive utility that allows users to run programs, manage files, supervise processes, and so on. The shell provides a prompt at which you can enter text-based commands. These commands are actually programs. Although there are literally thousands of these programs, in this chapter we'll be focusing on a few basic commands as well as fundamental shell concepts.

Understanding Command-Line Basics

While it is highly likely that you have had multiple exposures to many of the commands in this chapter, you may not know all of them, and there may be some shell commands you are using in an ineffective manner. In addition, you may have incorrect ideas concerning distributions. Thus, we'll start with the basics, such as distribution differences, how to reach a shell, the various shell options available, how to use a shell, and so on.

Discussing Distributions

Before we look at shells, an important topic to discuss is distributions (also called *distros*). Although it is tempting to think that Linux distributions are all the same and only a few differences exist between them, that is a fallacy. Think of the Linux kernel as a car's engine and a distribution as the car's features. Between manufacturers and models, car features are often different. If you use a rented car, you have to take a few minutes to adjust the seat, view the various car controls, and figure out how to use them prior to driving it. This is also true with different distributions. While they all have the Linux kernel (car engine) at their core, their various features are different, and that can include differences at the command line.

If would like to follow along and try out the various commands in this book, it is helpful to know which distros to use. Because the LPIC-1 V5.0 certification exam is not going to change after its release, it is best to use a selection of Linux distributions that were available during the exam's development. It is incorrect to think that using a distribution's latest version is better. Instead, it is fine to use the same distributions we did while writing the book, which were the CentOS 7 Everything, Ubuntu Desktop 18-04 LTS, Fedora 29 Workstation, and openSUSE 15 Leap distros.

Reaching a Shell

After you install your Linux system or virtual environment distro, set it up, and boot it, you can typically reach a command-line terminal by pressing the Ctrl+Alt+F2 key combination (which gets you to the tty2 terminal), and log in using a standard user account (one without super user privileges). Typically, you create a standard user account when installing a Linux distribution.

If you want to use your Linux distribution's graphical user interface (GUI), you can log in and then open a terminal emulator to reach the command line via the following:

- On an Ubuntu Workstation distro, press Ctrl+Alt+T.

- On a CentOS 7 Everything and a Fedora 29 Workstation distro, click the Activities menu option, enter **term** in the search bar, and select the resulting terminal icon.

- On an openSUSE 15 Leap distro, click the Application Menu icon on the screen's bottom left side, enter **term** in the search bar, and select one of the resulting terminal icons.

Exploring Your Linux Shell Options

When you successfully log into a tty terminal (such as tty2) or open a GUI terminal emulator program to reach a command-line prompt, the program providing that prompt is a shell. While the Bash shell program is the most popular and commonly used by the various Linux distributions, there are a few others you need to know:

Bash   The GNU Bourne Again shell (Bash), first released in 1989, is commonly used as the default shell for Linux user accounts. The Bash shell was developed by the GNU project as a replacement for the standard Unix operating system shell, called the Bourne shell (named for its creator). It is also available for Windows 10, macOS, and Solaris operating systems.

Dash   The Debian Almquist shell (Dash) was originally released in 2002. This smaller shell does not allow command-line editing or command history (covered later in this chapter), but it does provide faster shell program (also called a *script*) execution.

KornShell   The KornShell was initially released in 1983 but was proprietary software until 2000. It was invented by David Korn of Bell Labs. It is a programming shell compatible with the Bourne shell but supports advanced programming features, such as those available in the C programming languages.

tcsh   Originally released in 1981, the TENEX C shell is an upgraded version of the C Shell. It added command completion, which was a nice feature in the TENEX operating system. In addition, tcsh incorporates elements from the C programming language into shell scripts.

Z shell   The Z shell was first released in 1990. This advanced shell incorporates features from Bash, tcsh, and KornShell. Advanced programming features, shared history files, and themed prompts are a few of the extended Bourne shell components it provides.

When looking at shells, it is important to understand the history and current use of the /bin/sh file. Originally, this file was the location of the system's shell. For example, on Unix systems, you would typically find the Bourne shell installed here. On Linux systems, the /bin/sh file is now a symbolic link (covered in Chapter 4) to a shell. Typically the file points to the Bash shell (bash) as shown in Listing 1.1 on a CentOS distribution via the readlink command.

Listing 1.1: Showing to which shell /bin/sh points on a CentOS distribution

```
$ readlink /bin/sh
bash
$
```

It is always a good idea to check which shell the file is linked to. In Listing 1.2, you can see that the /bin/sh file is a symbolic link to the Dash shell (dash).

Listing 1.2: Showing to which shell /bin/sh points on an Ubuntu distribution

```
$ readlink /bin/sh
dash
$
```

To quickly determine what shell you are using at the command line, you can employ an environment variable (environment variables are covered in detail later in this chapter) along with the echo command. The echo command allows you to display data to the screen. In Listing 1.3, on a CentOS distro, the environment variable (SHELL) has its data (the current shell program) displayed by using the echo command. The $ is added prior to the variable's name in order to tap into the data stored within that variable.

Listing 1.3: Displaying the current shell on a CentOS distribution

```
$ echo $SHELL
/bin/bash
$
$ echo $BASH_VERSION
4.2.46(2)-release
$
```

Notice in Listing 1.3 that the current shell is the Bash (/bin/bash) shell. You can also show the current version of the Bash shell via the BASH_VERSION environment variable as also shown in the listing.

While you are exploring your shell environment, you should learn information about your system's Linux kernel as well. The uname utility is helpful here. A few examples are shown in Listing 1.4.

Listing 1.4: Displaying the current shell on an Ubuntu distribution

```
$ uname
Linux
$
$ uname -r
4.15.0-46-generic
$
$ uname -a
Linux Ubuntu1804 4.15.0-46-generic #49-Ubuntu SMP Wed Feb 6
09:33:07 UTC 2019 x86_64 x86_64 x86_64 GNU/Linux
$
```

When used by itself, the uname command displays only the kernel's name (Linux). If you want to know the current kernel version (called the *revision*), add the -r command option, as shown in Listing 1.4. To see all system information this utility provides, such as the processor type (x86_64) and operating system name (GNU/Linux), tack on the -a option to the uname command.

Using a Shell

To run a program from the shell, at the command line you simply type its command, using the proper syntax, and press Enter to execute it. The echo command, used earlier, is a great program to start with. Its basic syntax is as follows:

echo [*OPTION*]… [*STRING*]…

In the echo command's syntax structure, [OPTION] means there are various options (also called *switches*) you can add to modify the display. The brackets indicate that switches are optional. The [STRING] argument allows you to designate a string to display. It too is optional, as denoted by the brackets.

An example is helpful to understand the echo command's syntax. In Listing 1.5 the echo command is employed with no arguments or options and simply displays a blank line. In its second use, the command shows the string provided as an argument to the echo program.

Listing 1.5: Using the echo command

```
$ echo

$ echo I Love Linux
I Love Linux
$
```

Quoting Metacharacters

The echo command is handy to demonstrate another useful shell feature: shell quoting. Within the Bash shell are several characters that have special meanings and functions. These characters are called *metacharacters*. Bash shell metacharacters include the following:

```
* ? [ ] ' " \ $ ; & ( ) | ^ < >
```

For example, the dollar sign ($) often indicates that the characters following it are a variable name. When used with the echo command, the program will attempt to retrieve the variable's value and display it. An example is shown in Listing 1.6.

Listing 1.6: Using the echo command with a $ metacharacter

```
$ echo $SHELL
/bin/bash
$
$ echo It cost $1.00
It cost .00
$
```

Due to the $ metacharacter, the echo command treats both the $SHELL and $1 as variables. Since $1 is not a variable in the second echo command and has no value, in its output echo displays nothing for $1. To fix this problem, you can employ *shell quoting*. Shell quoting allows you to use metacharacters as regular characters. To shell quote a single character, use the backslash (\) as shown in Listing 1.7.

Listing 1.7: Using the echo command and shell quoting a single metacharacter

```
$ echo It cost \$1.00
It cost $1.00
$
$ echo Is Schrodinger\'s cat alive or dead\?
Is Schrodinger's cat alive or dead?
$
```

While the backslash is handy for shell quoting a single metacharacter, it can be tiresome when you have multiple ones. For several metacharacters, consider surrounding them with either single or double quotation marks, depending on the situation. A few examples of this shell quoting method are shown in Listing 1.8.

Listing 1.8: Using the echo command and shell quoting multiple metacharacters

```
$ echo Is "Schrodinger's" cat alive or "dead?"
Is Schrodinger's cat alive or dead?
$
```

```
$ echo "Is Schrodinger's cat alive or dead?"
Is Schrodinger's cat alive or dead?
$
$ echo 'Is Schrodinger's cat alive or dead?'
> ^C
$
```

Notice the first two quoting methods work in Listing 1.8. The last one does *not* work. When the metacharacter to be shell quoted is a single quotation mark, you will need to employ another shell quoting method, such as the backslash or double quotation marks.

Navigating the Directory Structure

Files on a Linux system are stored within a single directory structure, called a *virtual directory*. The virtual directory contains files from all the computer's storage devices and merges them into a single directory structure. This structure has a single base directory called the *root directory*, often simply called *root*.

When you log into the Linux system, your process's *current working directory* is your account's *home directory*. A current working directory is the directory your process is currently using within the virtual directory structure. Think of the current working directory as the room you are currently in within your home.

You can navigate through this virtual directory structure via the cd command. A helpful partner to cd is the pwd command. The cd command moves your working directory to a new location in the virtual directory structure, and the pwd program displays (prints) the current working directory. A few examples are shown in Listing 1.9.

Listing 1.9: Using the cd and pwd commands

```
$ pwd
/home/Christine
$
$ cd /etc
$ pwd
/etc
$
```

It is vital to know your current working directory, especially as you traverse the virtual structure. By default, many shell commands operate on the current working directory.

When using the cd command, you can employ either absolute or relative directory references. *Absolute directory references* always begin with a forward slash (/) in reference to the root directory and use the full name of the directory location. Listing 1.9 contains absolute directory references.

Relative directory references allow you to move with the cd command to a new position in the directory structure in relation to your current working directory using shorter directory arguments. Examples of relative moves are shown in Listing 1.10.

Listing 1.10: Using the cd command with relative directory references

```
$ pwd
/etc
$
$ cd cups
$ pwd
/etc/cups
$
$ cd ..
$ pwd
/etc
$
```

In Listing 1.10 the current working directory is /etc. By issuing the cd cups command, which is a relative directory reference, you change the current working directory to /etc/cups. Notice that pwd always displays the directory using an absolute directory reference. The last command (cd ..) is also a relative move. The two dots (..) represent the directory above the current directory, which is the parent directory.

> You can also employ the single dot (.) directory reference, which refers to the current working directory. Although the single dot is not used with the cd command, it is commonly employed for tasks such as copying or moving files.

The cd command has several other shortcuts you can employ besides just the two dots. For example, to change your current working directory to your user account's home directory, use one of the following:

- cd
- cd ~
- cd $HOME

You can also quickly return to your most recent working directory by employing the cd - shortcut command. An example is shown in Listing 1.11.

Listing 1.11: Using the cd - shortcut command

```
$ pwd
/etc
$
```

```
$ cd /var
$ pwd
/var
$
$ cd -
/etc
$ pwd
/etc
$
```

Understanding Internal and External Commands

Within a shell, some commands that you type at the command line are part of (internal to) the shell program. These internal commands are sometimes called *built-in commands*. Other commands are external programs, because they are not part of the shell.

You can tell whether a command is an internal or external program via the type command. A few examples are shown in Listing 1.12.

Listing 1.12: Using type to determine whether a command is external or internal

```
$ type echo
echo is a shell builtin
$
$ type pwd
pwd is a shell builtin
$
$ type uname
uname is /usr/bin/uname
$
```

Notice in Listing 1.12 that both the echo and pwd commands are internal (built-in) programs. However, the uname command is an external program, which is indicated by the type command displaying the uname program's absolute directory reference within the virtual directory structure.

A command may be available both internally and externally to the shell. In this case, it is important to know their differences, because they may produce slightly different results or require different options.

Using Environment Variables

Environment variables track specific system information, such as the name of the user logged into the shell, the default home directory for the user, the search path the shell uses to find executable programs, and so on. Table 1.1 shows some of the more commonly used environment variables.

TABLE 1.1   Commonly used environment variables

Name	Description
BASH_VERSION	Current Bash shell instance's version number (Chapter 1)
EDITOR	Default editor used by some shell commands (Chapter 1)
GROUPS	User account's group memberships (Chapter 7)
HISTFILE	Name of the user's shell command history file (Chapter 1)
HISTSIZE	Maximum number of commands stored in history file (Chapter 1)
HOME	Current user's home directory name (Chapter 1)
HOSTNAME	Current system's host name (Chapter 8)
LANG	Locale category for the shell (Chapter 6)
LC_*	Various locale settings that override LANG (Chapter 6)
LC_ALL	Locale category for the shell that overrides LANG (Chapter 6)
LD_LIBRARY_PATH	Colon-separated list of library directories to search prior to looking through the standard library directories (Chapter 2)
PATH	Colon-separated list of directories to search for commands (Chapter 1)
PS1	Primary shell command-line interface prompt string (Chapter 1)
PS2	Secondary shell command-line interface prompt string
PWD	User account's current working directory (Chapter 1)
SHLVL	Current shell level (Chapter 1)
TZ	User's time zone, if different from system's time zone (Chapter 6)
UID	User account's user identification number (Chapter 7)
VISUAL	Default screen-based editor used by some shell commands (Chapter 1)

You can display a complete list of active environment variables available in your shell by using the set command, as shown snipped in Listing 1.13.

Listing 1.13: Using set to display active environment variables

```
$ set
[…]
BASH=/bin/bash
[…]
HISTFILE=/home/Christine/.bash_history
[…]
HISTSIZE=1000
HOME=/home/Christine
HOSTNAME=localhost.localdomain
[…]
PS1='$ '
PS2='> '
[…]
SHELL=/bin/bash
[…]
$
```

 Besides the set utility, you can also employ the env and printenv commands to display variables. The env and printenv utilities allow you to see locally defined variables, such as those created in a shell script (covered in Chapter 9) as well as environment variables.

When you enter a program name (command) at the shell prompt, the shell will search all the directories listed in the PATH environment variable for that program. If the shell cannot find the program, you will receive a command not found error message. Listing 1.14 shows an example.

Listing 1.14: Viewing how PATH affects command execution

```
$ echo $PATH
/usr/local/bin:/usr/bin:/usr/local/sbin:/usr/sbin:
/home/Christine/.local/bin:/home/Christine/bin
$
$ ls /home/Christine/Hello.sh
/home/Christine/Hello.sh
$
$ Hello.sh
bash: Hello.sh: command not found…
$
```

Notice in Listing 1.14 that program Hello.sh is in a directory that is not in the PATH environment variable's directories. Thus, when the Hello.sh program name is entered at the shell prompt, the command not found error message is displayed.

To run a program that does not reside in a PATH directory location, you must provide the command's absolute directory reference when entering the program's name at the command line, as shown in Listing 1.15.

Listing 1.15: Executing a program outside the PATH directories

```
$ /home/Christine/Hello.sh
Hello World
$
```

The which utility is helpful in these cases. It searches through the PATH directories to find the program. If it locates the program, it displays its absolute directory reference. This saves you from having to look through the PATH variable's output yourself, as Listing 1.16 shows.

Listing 1.16: Using the which utility

```
$ which Hello.sh
/usr/bin/which: no Hello.sh in (/usr/local/bin:/usr/bin:
/usr/local/sbin:/usr/sbin:/home/Christine/.local/bin:/home/Christine/bin)
$
$ which echo
/usr/bin/echo
$
```

Notice that the which utility does not find the Hello.sh program and displays all the PATH directories it searched. However, it does locate the echo command.

If a program resides in a PATH directory, you can run it by simply entering the command's name. If desired, you can also execute it by including its absolute directory reference, as shown in Listing 1.17.

Listing 1.17: Using different references to run a command

```
$ echo Hello World
Hello World
$
$ /usr/bin/echo Hello World
Hello World
$
```

You can modify environment variables. An easy one to change is the variable controlling your shell prompt (PS1). An example of changing this variable is shown in Listing 1.18.

Listing 1.18: Setting the PS1 variable

```
$ PS1="My new prompt: "
My new prompt:
```

Notice that to change the environment variable, you simply enter the variable's name, followed by an equal sign (=), and then type the new value. Because the PS1 variable controls the shell prompt, the effect of changing it shows immediately.

However, you can run into problems if you use that simple method of modifying an environment variable. For example, the setting will not survive entering into a subshell. A *subshell* (sometimes called a child shell) is created when you perform certain tasks, such as running a shell script (covered in Chapter 9) or running particular commands.

You can determine whether your process is currently in a subshell by looking at the data stored in the SHLVL environment variable. A 1 indicates you are *not* in a subshell, because subshells have higher numbers. Thus, if SHLVL contains a number higher than 1, this indicates you're in a subshell.

The bash command automatically creates a subshell, which is helpful for demonstrating the temporary nature of employing the simple environment variable modification method, shown in Listing 1.19.

Listing 1.19: Demonstrating a subshell's effect on the PS1 variable

```
My new prompt: echo $SHLVL
1
My new prompt: bash
$
$ echo $PS1
$
$ echo $SHLVL
2
$ exit
exit
My new prompt:
```

Notice that the SHLVL environment variable is set to 1, until a subshell is entered via the bash command. Also note that the PS1 environment variable controlling the prompt does not survive entering into a subshell.

To preserve an environment variable's setting, you need to employ the export command. You can either use export when typing in the original variable definition, as shown in Listing 1.20, or use it after the variable is defined, by typing **export *variable-name*** at the command-line prompt.

Listing 1.20: Using export to preserve an environment variable's definition

```
My new prompt: export PS1="KeepPrompt: "
KeepPrompt:
KeepPrompt: bash
KeepPrompt:
KeepPrompt: echo $SHLVL
2
KeepPrompt:
KeepPrompt: PS1="$ "
$ export PS1
$
```

Notice in Listing 1.20 that the first method used the export command on the same line as the PS1 environment variable setting and that the definition survives the subshell. The second change to the PS1 variable defines it first and then employs the export command, so it too will survive a subshell.

If a variable is originally set to nothing (blank), such as is typically the EDITOR environment variable, you can simply reverse any modifications you make to the variable by using the unset command. An example of this is shown in Listing 1.21.

Listing 1.21: Using the unset command

```
$ echo $EDITOR

$ export EDITOR=nano
$
$ echo $EDITOR
nano
$
$ unset EDITOR
$
$ echo $EDITOR

$
```

Use caution when employing the unset command. If you use it on environment variables, such as PS1, you can cause confusing things to happen. If the variable had a different definition before you modified it, it is best to change it back to its original setting instead of using unset on the variable.

Getting Help

When using the various utilities at the command line, sometimes you need a little extra help on a command's options or syntax. While a search engine is useful, there may be times you cannot access the Internet. Fortunately, Linux systems typically have the *man pages* installed locally. The man pages contain documentation on a command's purpose, various options, program syntax, and so on. This information is often created by the programmer who wrote the utility.

To access a man page for a particular program—for example, the uname command—just type in **man uname** at the command line. This text-based help system will take over the entire terminal display, allowing you to read through the documentation for the chosen command.

By default, the man pages use the less pager utility (covered later in this chapter), allowing you to go back and forth through the display using either the PageUp or PageDown key. You can also employ the arrow keys or the spacebar as desired.

If you use the man pages to read through a built-in command's documentation, you'll reach the General Commands Manual page for Bash built-ins. It can be tedious using keys to find a command in this page. Instead, type / and follow it with the command name. You may have to do this two or three times to reach the utility's documentation, but it is much faster than continually pressing arrow or PageDown keys.

A handy feature of the man utility is the ability to search for keywords in the documentation. Just employ the -k option as shown snipped in Listing 1.22.

Listing 1.22: Using the man -k command to search for keywords

```
$ man -k passwd
[…]
passwd (1)            - update user's authentication tokens
[…]
passwd (5)            - password file
[…]
smbpasswd (5)         - The Samba encrypted password file
[…]
$
```

Instead of man -k, you can use the apropos command. For example, enter **apropos passwd** at the command line. However, man -k is easier to type.

Notice in Listing 1.22 that several items are found in the man pages using the keyword search. Next to the utility name, the man page section number is displayed in parentheses. The man pages have nine sections that contain various types of documentation. Type **man man** at the command line to view help information on using the man pages as well as the different section names.

Although it is a nice feature that the man pages contain more than just documentation on commands, it can cause you problems if a utility has the same name as other items, such as a file in the case of passwd. Typically the man command follows a predefined search order and, in the case of duplicate names, will show you only the utility's man page. If you need to see a different page, use the section number along with the item's name. There are a few methods for doing this, using as an example the passwd file documented in section 5:

```
man -S 5 passwd
man -s 5 passwd
man 5 passwd
```

> If you use the man utility and receive a message similar to nothing appropriate, first check the spelling of the search term. If the spelling is correct, it's possible that the man utility's database has not been updated. You'll need to use super user privileges and issue the makewhatis command (on older Linux distributions) or the mandb command.

Besides getting help from the man pages, you can get help from your *command-line history*. The shell keeps track of all the commands you have recently used and stores them in your login session's history list. To see your history list, enter **history** at the shell prompt, as shown snipped in Listing 1.23.

Listing 1.23: Using the history command to view recent commands

```
$ history
[…]
915   echo $EDITOR
916   export EDITOR=nano
917   echo $EDITOR
918   unset EDITOR
919   echo $EDITOR
920   man -k passwd
[…]
$
```

Notice that each command is preceded by a number. This allows you to recall a command from your history list via its number and have it automatically executed, as shown snipped in Listing 1.24.

Listing 1.24: Reexecuting commands in the command history

```
$ !920
man -k passwd
[…]
passwd (1)              - update user's authentication tokens
[…]
passwd (5)              - password file
[…]
$
```

Note that in order to rerun the command, you must put an exclamation mark (!) prior to the number. The shell will display the command you are recalling and then execute it, which is handy.

 If the history command does not work for you, your user account may be using a different shell than the Bash shell. You can quickly check by entering **echo $SHELL** at the command line. If you do not see /bin/bash displayed, that is a problem. Modify your user account to use /bin/bash as your default shell (modifying users' accounts is covered in Chapter 7). You'll need to log out and back in again for the change to take effect.

To reexecute your most recent command, enter !! at the command line and press Enter. A faster alternative is to press the up arrow key and then press Enter. Another advantage of this last method is that you can edit the command as needed prior to running it.

The history list is preserved between login sessions in the file designated by the $HISTFILE environment variable. It is typically the .bash_history file in your home directory, as shown in Listing 1.25.

Listing 1.25: Viewing the history filename

```
$ echo $HISTFILE
/home/Christine/.bash_history
$
```

Keep in mind that the history file will not have commands you have used during your current login session. These commands are stored only in the history list.

If you desire to update the history file or the current history list, you'll need to issue the history command with the correct option. The following is a brief list of history options to help you make the right choice:

- -a appends the current history list commands to the end of the history file.
- -n appends the history file commands from the current Bash shell session to the current history list.
- -r overwrites the current history list commands with the commands stored in the history file.

If you want to remove your command-line history, it is fairly easy to do. First, clear your current history list by typing **history -c** at the command line. After that, wipe the history file by issuing the **history -w** command, which copies the now blank history list to the .bash_history file, overwriting its contents.

Editing Text Files

Manipulating text is performed on a regular basis when managing a Linux system. Whether you need to modify a configuration file or create a shell script, being able to use an interactive text file editor at the command line is an important skill.

Looking at Text Editors

Three popular Linux command-line text editors are

- emacs
- nano
- vim

The nano editor is a good text editor to start using if you have never dealt with an editor or have used only GUI editors. To start using the nano text editor, type **nano** followed by the file's name you wish to edit or create. Figure 1.1 shows a nano text editor in action, editing a file named numbers.txt.

FIGURE 1.1   Using the nano text editor

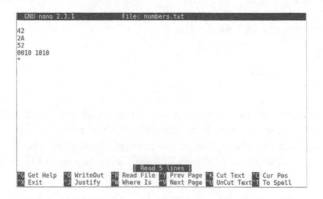

The shortcut list is one of the nano text editor's most useful features. This list at the window's bottom displays the most common commands and their associated shortcut keys. The caret (^) symbol in this list indicates that the Ctrl key must be used. For example, to move down a page, you press and hold the Ctrl key and then press the V key. To see additional commands, press the Ctrl+G key combination for help.

Within the nano text editor's help subsystem, you'll see some key combinations denoted by M-k. An example is M-W for repeating a search. These are metacharacter key combinations, and the M represents the Esc, Alt, or Meta key, depending on your keyboard's setup. The k simply represents a keyboard key, such as W.

The nano text editor is wonderful to use for simple text file modifications. However, if you need a more powerful text editor for creating programs or shell scripts, popular choices include the emacs and the vim editor.

 Real World Scenario

Dealing with Default Editors

Some utilities such as crontab (covered in Chapter 9) use a default editor (also called a *standard editor*) such as vim. If you are new to text editing, you may prefer to use a text editor that is fairly easy to use, so being forced to use an advanced editor is problematic.

You can change your account's standard editor via the EDITOR and VISUAL environment variables. The EDITOR variable was originally for line-based editors, such as the old ed utility. The VISUAL variable is for screen-based editors (text editors that take up the whole screen, such as nano, emacs, and vim).

Change your standard editor to your desired editor by typing, for example, **export EDITOR=nano** at the command line. Do the same for the VISUAL environment variable. Even better, add these lines to an environment file (covered in Chapter 9) so that they are set up automatically for you each time you log into the Linux system.

To start using the emacs text editor, type **emacs** followed by the file's name you wish to edit or create. Figure 1.2 shows an emacs text editor screen editing a newly created file named MyFile.txt.

FIGURE 1.2 Using the emacs text editor

Adding and modifying text, as well as moving around this editor, is fairly straightforward. However, to tap into the power of the emacs editor, you need to learn the various shortcut keystrokes. Here are a few examples:

▪ Press the Ctrl+X and then the Ctrl+S key combinations to save the editor buffer's contents to the file.

▪ Press the Ctrl+X and then the Ctrl+C key combinations to leave the editor.

▪ Press the Ctrl+H key combination and then the T key to reach the emacs tutorial.

Note that in the emacs editor documentation the Ctrl key is represented by a single C letter, and to add an additional key to it, the documentation uses a hyphen (-), instead of the traditional plus sign (+).

Though emacs commands are a little tricky as you begin using this editor, the benefits of learning the emacs editor include the following:

▪ Editing commands used in emacs can also be used to quickly edit your commands entered at the shell's command line.

▪ The emacs editor has a GUI counterpart with all the same editing features.

▪ You can focus on the editor's features you need most and learn its advanced capabilities later.

The emacs text editor is typically not installed by default. Installing software is covered in Chapter 2. Its software package name is also emacs.

Before we take a look at using the vim editor, we need to talk about vim versus vi. The vi editor was a Unix text editor, and when it was rewritten as an open source tool, it was improved. Thus, vim stands for "vi improved."

Often you'll find the vi command will start the vim editor. In other distributions, only the vim command will start the vim editor. Sometimes both commands work. Listing 1.26 demonstrates using the which utility to determine what command a CentOS distribution is using.

Listing 1.26: Using which to determine the editor command

```
$ which vim
/usr/bin/vim
$
$ which vi
alias vi='vim'
/usr/bin/vim
$
```

Listing 1.26 shows that this CentOS distribution has aliased the vi command to point to the vim command. Thus, for this distribution both the vi and vim commands will start the vim editor.

> Some distributions, such as Ubuntu, do not have the vim editor installed by default. Instead, they use an alternative, called vim.tiny, which will not allow you to try out all the various vim commands discussed here. You can check your distribution to see if vim is installed by obtaining the vim program filename. Type **type vi** and press Enter, and if you get an error or an alias, then enter **type vim**. After you receive the program's directory and filename, type the command **readlink -f** and follow it up with the directory and filename—for example, readlink -f /usr/bin/vi. If you see /usr/bin/vi.tiny, you need to either switch to a different distribution to practice the vim commands or install the vim package (see Chapter 2).

To start using the vim text editor, type **vim** or **vi**, depending on your distribution, followed by the name of the file you wish to edit or create. Figure 1.3 shows a vim text editor screen in action.

FIGURE 1.3   Using the vim text editor

In Figure 1.3 the file being edited is named numbers.txt. The vim editor works the file data in a memory buffer, and this buffer is displayed on the screen. If you open vim without a filename or the filename you entered doesn't yet exist, vim starts a new buffer area for editing.

The vim editor has a message area near the bottom line. If you have just opened an already created file, it will display the filename along with the number of lines and characters read into the buffer area. If you are creating a new file, you will see [New File] in the message area.

Understanding *vim* Modes

The vim editor has three standard modes as follows:

Command Mode   This is the mode vim uses when you first enter the buffer area; it is sometimes called normal mode. Here you enter keystrokes to enact commands. For example, pressing the J key will move your cursor down one line. Command is the best mode to use for quickly moving around the buffer area.

Insert Mode   Insert mode is also called edit or entry mode. This is the mode where you can perform simple editing. There are not many commands or special mode keystrokes. You enter this mode from command mode by pressing the I key. At this point, the message --Insert-- will display in the message area. You leave this mode by pressing the Esc key.

Ex Mode   This mode is sometimes also called colon commands because every command entered here is preceded with a colon (:). For example, to leave the vim editor and not save any changes you type **:q** and press the Enter key.

Exploring Basic Text-Editing Procedures

Since you start in command mode when entering the vim editor's buffer area, it's good to understand a few of the commonly used commands to move around in this mode. Table 1.2 contains several moving commands.

TABLE 1.2   Commonly used vim command mode moving commands

Keystroke(s)	Description
h	Move cursor left one character.
l	Move cursor right one character.
j	Move cursor down one line (the next line in the text).
k	Move cursor up one line (the previous line in the text).

Keystroke(s)	Description
w	Move cursor forward one word to front of next word.
e	Move cursor to end of current word.
b	Move cursor backward one word.
^	Move cursor to beginning of line.
$	Move cursor to end of line.
gg	Move cursor to the file's first line.
G	Move cursor to the file's last line.
nG	Move cursor to file line number n.
Ctrl+B	Scroll up almost one full screen.
Ctrl+F	Scroll down almost one full screen.
Ctrl+U	Scroll up half of a screen.
Ctrl+D	Scroll down half of a screen.
Ctrl+Y	Scroll up one line.
Ctrl+E	Scroll down one line.

If you have a large text file and need to search for something, there are keystrokes in command mode to do that as well. Type **?** to start a forward search or **/** to start a backward search. The keystroke will display at the vim editor's bottom and allow you to type the text to find. If the first item found is not what you need, press Enter, and then keep pressing the n key to move to the next matching text pattern.

Quickly moving around in the vim editor buffer is useful. However, there are also several editing commands that help to speed up your modification process. Table 1.3 lists the more commonly used command mode editing commands. Pay close attention to each letter's case, because lowercase keystrokes often perform different operations than uppercase keystrokes.

TABLE 1.3   Commonly used vim command mode editing commands

Keystroke(s)	Description
a	Insert text after cursor.
A	Insert text at end of text line.
dd	Delete current line.
dw	Delete current word.
i	Insert text before cursor.
I	Insert text before beginning of text line.
o	Open a new text line below cursor, and move to insert mode.
O	Open a new text line above cursor, and move to insert mode.
p	Paste copied text after cursor.
P	Paste copied (yanked) text before cursor.
yw	Yank (copy) current word.
yy	Yank (copy) current line.

In command mode, you can take the editing commands a step further by using their full syntax, which is as follows:

COMMAND [NUMBER-OF-TIMES] ITEM

For example, if you wanted to delete three words, you would press the D, 3, and W keys. If you wanted to copy (yank) the text from the cursor to the end of the text line, you would press the Y $ keys, move to the location you desired to paste the text, and press the P key.

 Keep in mind that some people stay in command mode to get where they need to be within a file and then press the I key to jump into insert mode for easier text editing. This is a convenient method to employ.

The third vim mode, Ex mode, has additional handy commands. You must be in command mode to enter into Ex mode. You cannot jump from insert mode to Ex mode. Therefore, if you're currently in insert mode, press the Esc key to go back to command mode first.

Table 1.4 shows a few Ex commands that can help you manage your text file. Notice that all the keystrokes include the necessary colon (:) to use Ex commands.

TABLE 1.4   Commonly used vim Ex mode commands

Keystrokes	Description
:! *command*	Execute shell *command* and display results, but don't quit editor.
:r! *command*	Execute shell *command* and include the results in editor buffer area.
:r *file*	Read *file* contents and include them in editor buffer area.

Saving Changes

After you have made any needed text changes in the vim buffer area, it's time to save your work. You can use one of many methods as shown in Table 1.5. Type **ZZ** in command mode to write the buffer to disk and exit your process from the vim editor.

TABLE 1.5   Saving changes in the vim text editor

Mode	Keystrokes	Description
Ex	:x	Write buffer to file and quit editor.
Ex	:wq	Write buffer to file and quit editor.
Ex	:wq!	Write buffer to file and quit editor (overrides protection).
Ex	:w	Write buffer to file and stay in editor.
Ex	:w!	Write buffer to file and stay in editor (overrides protection).
Ex	:q	Quit editor without writing buffer to file.
Ex	:q!	Quit editor without writing buffer to file (overrides protection).
Command	ZZ	Write buffer to file and quit editor.

After reading through the various mode commands, you may see why some people despise the vim editor. There are a lot of obscure commands to know. However, some people love the vim editor because it is so powerful.

> **TIP**
>
> Some distributions have a vim tutorial installed by default. This is a handy way to learn to use the vim editor. To get started, just type **vimtutor** at the command line. If you need to leave the tutorial before it is complete, just type the Ex mode command **:q** to quit.

It's tempting to learn only one text editor and ignore the others. Knowing at least two text editors is useful in your day-to-day Linux work. For simple modifications, the nano text editor shines. For more complex editing, the vim and emacs editors are preferred. All are worth your time to master.

Processing Text Using Filters

At the Linux command line, you often need to view files or portions of them. In addition, you may need to employ tools that allow you to gather data chunks or file statistics for troubleshooting or analysis purposes. The utilities in this section can assist in all these activities.

File-Combining Commands

Putting together short text files for viewing on your screen and comparing them is useful. The file-combining commands covered here will do just that.

The basic utility for viewing entire text files is the concatenate command. Though this tool's primary purpose in life is to join together text files and display them, it is often used just to display a single small text file. To view a small text file, use the cat command with the basic syntax that follows:

cat [*OPTION*]… [*FILE*]…

The cat command is simple to use. You just enter the command followed by any text file you want to read, such as shown in Listing 1.27.

Listing 1.27: Using the cat command to display a file

```
$ cat numbers.txt
42
2A
52
0010 1010
*
$
```

The cat command spits out the entire text file to your screen. When you get your prompt back, you know that the line above the prompt is the file's last line.

There is a handy new clone of the cat command called bat. Its developer calls it "cat with wings," because of the bat utility's many additional features. You can read about its features at github.com/sharkdp/bat.

In Listing 1.28 is an example of concatenating two files together to display their text contents one after the other using the cat command.

Listing 1.28: Using the cat command to concatenate files

```
$ cat numbers.txt random.txt
42
2A
52
0010 1010
*
42
Flat Land
Schrodinger's Cat
0010 1010
0000 0010
$
```

Both of the files displayed in Listing 1.28 have the number 42 as their first line. This is the only way you can tell where one file ends and the other begins, because the cat utility does not denote a file's beginning or end in its output.

Unfortunately, often the cat utility's useful formatting options go unexplored. Table 1.6 has a few of the more commonly used switches.

TABLE 1.6   The cat command's commonly used options

Short	Long	Description
-A	--show-all	Equivalent to using the option -vET combination.
-E	--show-ends	Display a $ when a newline linefeed is encountered.
-n	--number	Number all text file lines and display that number in the output.
-s	--squeeze-blank	Do not display repeated blank empty text file lines.
-T	--show-tabs	Display a ^I when a tab character is encountered.
-v	--show-nonprinting	Display nonprinting characters when encountered using either ^ and/or M- notation.

Being able to display nonprinting characters with the cat command is handy. If you have a text file that is causing some sort of odd problem when processing it, you can quickly see if there are any nonprintable characters embedded. In Listing 1.29 an example is shown of this method.

Listing 1.29: Using the cat command to display nonprintable characters

```
$ cat bell.txt

$ cat -v bell.txt
^G
$
```

In Listing 1.29, the first cat command displays the file, and it appears to simply contain a blank line. However, when the -v option is employed, you can see that a nonprintable character exists within the file. The ^G is in caret notation and indicates that the nonprintable Unicode character BEL is embedded in the file. This character causes a bell sound when the file is displayed.

> There are interesting variants of the cat command—bzcat, xzcat, and zcat. These utilities are used to display the contents of compressed files. (File compression is covered in Chapter 4.)

If you want to display two files side-by-side and you do not care how sloppy the output is, you can use the paste command. Just like school paste, it will glue them together, but the result will not necessarily be pretty. An example of using the paste command is shown in Listing 1.30.

Listing 1.30: Using the paste command to join together files side-by-side

```
$ cat random.txt
42
Flat Land
Schrodinger's Cat
0010 1010
0000 0010
$
$ cat numbers.txt
42
2A
52
0010 1010
*

$
```

```
$ paste random.txt numbers.txt
42        42
Flat Land          2A
Schrodinger's Cat          52
0010 1010          0010 1010
0000 0010          *
```

If you need a nicer display than paste can provide, consider using the pr command. If the files share the same data in a particular field, you can employ the join command as well.

File-Transforming Commands

Looking at a file's data in different ways is helpful not only in troubleshooting but in testing as well. We'll take a look at a few helpful file- transforming commands in this section.

Uncovering with *od*

Occasionally you may need to do a little detective work with files. These situations may include trying to review a graphics file or troubleshooting a text file that has been modified by a program. The od utility can help, because it allows you to display a file's contents in octal (base 8), hexadecimal (base 16), decimal (base 10), and ASCII. Its basic syntax is as follows:

od [*OPTION*]... [*FILE*]...

By default od displays a file's text in octal. An example is shown in Listing 1.31.

Listing 1.31: Using the od command to display a file's text in octal

```
$ cat fourtytwo.txt
42
fourty two
quarante deux
zweiundvierzig
forti to
$
$ od fourtytwo.txt
0000000 031064 063012 072557 072162 020171 073564 005157 072561
0000020 071141 067141 062564 062040 072545 005170 073572 064545
0000040 067165 073144 062551 075162 063551 063012 071157 064564
0000060 072040 005157
0000064
```

The first column of the od command's output is an index number for each displayed line. For example, in Listing 1.31, the line beginning with 0000040 indicates that the third line starts at octal 40 (decimal 32) bytes in the file.

You can use other options to improve the "readability" of the od command's display or to view different outputs (see the man pages for additional od utility options and their presentation). Listing 1.32 is an example of using the -cb options to display the characters in the file, along with each character's octal byte location in the text file.

Listing 1.32: Using the od -cb command to display additional information

```
$ od -cb fourtytwo.txt
0000000   4   2  \n   f   o   u   r   t   y       t   w   o  \n   q   u
        064 062 012 146 157 165 162 164 171 040 164 167 157 012 161 165
0000020   a   r   a   n   t   e       d   e   u   x  \n   z   w   e   i
        141 162 141 156 164 145 040 144 145 165 170 012 172 167 145 151
0000040   u   n   d   v   i   e   r   z   i   g  \n   f   o   r   t   i
        165 156 144 166 151 145 162 172 151 147 012 146 157 162 164 151
0000060       t   o  \n
        040 164 157 012
0000064
$
```

There is a proposal on the table to add a -u option to the od command. This option would allow the display of all Unicode characters, besides just the ASCII character subset now available. This would be a handy addition, so watch for this potential utility improvement.

Separating with *split*

One nice command to use is split. This utility allows you to divide a large file into smaller chunks, which is handy when you want to quickly create a smaller text file for testing purposes. The basic syntax for the split command is as follows:

```
split [OPTION]... [INPUT [PREFIX]]
```

You can divide up a file using size, bytes, lines, and so on. The original file (INPUT) remains unchanged, and additional new files are created, depending on the command options chosen. In Listing 1.33 an example shows using the option to split up a file by its line count.

Listing 1.33: Using the split -l command to split a file by line count

```
$ cat fourtytwo.txt
42
```

```
fourty two
quarante deux
zweiundvierzig
forti to
$
$ split -l 3 fourtytwo.txt split42
$
$ ls split42*
split42aa  split42ab
$
$ cat split42aa
42
fourty two
quarante deux
$
$ cat split42ab
zweiundvierzig
forti to
$
```

Notice that to split a file by its line count, you need to employ the -l (lowercase L) option and provide the number of text file lines to attempt to put into each new file. In the example, the original file has five text lines, so one new file (split42aa) gets the first three lines of the original file, and the second new file (split42ab) has the last two lines. Be aware that even though you specify the new files' name (*PREFIX*), the split utility tacks additional characters, such as aa and ab, onto the names, as shown in Listing 1.33.

 The tr command is another handy file-transforming command. It is covered later in this chapter.

File-Formatting Commands

Often to understand the data within text files, you need to reformat the data in some way. There are a couple of simple utilities you can use to do this.

Organizing with *sort*

The sort utility sorts a file's data. Keep in mind that it makes no changes to the original file; only the output is sorted. The basic syntax of this command is as follows:

sort [*OPTION*]... [*FILE*]...

If you want to order a file's content using the system's standard sort order, enter the sort command followed by the name of the file you wish to sort. Listing 1.34 shows an example of this.

Listing 1.34: Employing the sort command

```
$ cat alphabet.txt
Alpha
Tango
Bravo
Echo
Foxtrot
$
$ sort alphabet.txt
Alpha
Bravo
Echo
Foxtrot
Tango
$
```

If a file contains numbers, the data may not be in the order you desire using the sort utility. To obtain proper numeric order, add the -n option to the command, as shown in Listing 1.35.

Listing 1.35: Using the sort -n command

```
$ sort counts.txt
105
37
42
54
8
$ sort -n counts.txt
8
37
42
54
105
$
```

In Listing 1.35, notice that the first attempt to numerically order the file, using the sort command with no options, yields incorrect results. However, the second attempt uses the sort -n command, which properly orders the file numerically.

If you'd like to save the output from the sort command to a file, all it takes is adding the -o switch. For example, sort -o newfile.txt alphabet .txt will sort the alphabet.txt file and store its sorted contents in the newfile.txt file.

Numbering with *nl*

Another useful file-formatting command is the nl utility (number line utility). This little command allows you to number lines in a text file in powerful ways. It even allows you to use regular expressions (covered later in this chapter) to designate which lines to number. The nl command's syntax is fairly simple:

nl [*OPTION*]... [*FILE*]...

If you do not use any options with the nl utility, it will number only non-blank text lines. An example is shown in Listing 1.36.

Listing 1.36: Using the nl command to add numbers to non-blank lines

```
$ nl ContainsBlankLines.txt
     1  Alpha
     2  Tango

     3  Bravo
     4  Echo


     5  Foxtrot
$
```

If you would like all file's lines to be numbered, including blank ones, then you'll need to employ the -ba switch. An example is shown in Listing 1.37.

Listing 1.37: Using the nl -ba command to number all text file lines

```
$ nl -ba ContainsBlankLines.txt
     1  Alpha
     2  Tango
     3
     4  Bravo
     5  Echo
     6
     7
     8  Foxtrot
$
```

The sed command also allows you to format text files. However, because this utility uses regular expressions, it is covered after the regular expression section in this chapter.

File-Viewing Commands

When you operate at the command line, viewing files is a daily activity. For a short text file, using the cat command is sufficient. However, when you need to look at a large file or a portion of it, other commands are available that work better than cat, and they are covered in this section.

Using *more* or *less*

One way to read through a large text file is by using a *pager*. A pager utility allows you to view one text page at a time and move through the text at your own pace. The two most commonly used pagers are the more and less utilities.

Though rather simple, the more utility is a nice little pager utility. The command's syntax is as follows:

more [OPTION] FILE [...]

With more, you can move forward through a text file by pressing the spacebar (one page down) or the Enter key (one line down). However, you cannot move backward through a file. The utility displays at the screen's bottom how far along you are in the file. When you wish to exit from the more pager, you must press the Q key.

A more flexible pager is the less utility. Figure 1.4 shows using the less utility on the /etc/nsswitch.conf text file.

FIGURE 1.4   Using the less text pager

```
#
# /etc/nsswitch.conf
#
# An example Name Service Switch config file. This file should be
# sorted with the most-used services at the beginning.
#
# The entry '[NOTFOUND=return]' means that the search for an
# entry should stop if the search in the previous entry turned
# up nothing. Note that if the search failed due to some other reason
# (like no NIS server responding) then the search continues with the
# next entry.
#
# Valid entries include:
#
#       nisplus             Use NIS+ (NIS version 3)
#       nis                 Use NIS (NIS version 2), also called YP
#       dns                 Use DNS (Domain Name Service)
#       files               Use the local files
#       db                  Use the local database (.db) files
#       compat              Use NIS on compat mode
#       hesiod              Use Hesiod for user lookups
#       [NOTFOUND=return]   Stop searching if not found so far
#

# To use db, put the "db" in front of "files" for entries you want to be
# looked up first in the databases
#
# Example:
#passwd:    db files nisplus nis
#shadow:    db files nisplus nis
#group:     db files nisplus nis

passwd:     files sss
shadow:     files sss
/etc/nsswitch.conf
```

Though similar to the more utility in its syntax as well as the fact that you can move through a file a page (or line) at a time, this pager utility also allows you to move backward. Yet the less utility has far more capabilities than just that, which leads to the famous description of this pager, "less is more."

The less pager utility allows faster file traversal because it does not read the entire file prior to displaying the file's first page. You can also employ the up and down arrow keys to traverse the file as well as the spacebar to move forward a page and the Esc+V key combination to move back a page. You can search for a particular word within the file by pressing the ? key, typing in the word you want to find, and pressing Enter to search backward. Replace the ? key with the / key and you can search forward. Like the more pager, you do need to use the Q key to exit.

 By default, the Linux man page utility uses less as its pager. Learning the less utility's commands will allow you to search through various manual pages with ease.

The less utility has amazing capabilities. It would be well worth your time to peruse the less pager's man pages and play around using its various file search and traversal commands on a large text file.

Looking at files with *head*

Another handy tool for displaying portions of a text file is the head utility. The head command's syntax is shown as follows:

head [*OPTION*]... [*FILE*]...

By default, the head command displays the first 10 lines of a text file. An example is shown in Listing 1.38.

Listing 1.38: Employing the head command

```
$ head /etc/passwd
root:x:0:0:root:/root:/bin/bash
bin:x:1:1:bin:/bin:/sbin/nologin
daemon:x:2:2:daemon:/sbin:/sbin/nologin
adm:x:3:4:adm:/var/adm:/sbin/nologin
lp:x:4:7:lp:/var/spool/lpd:/sbin/nologin
sync:x:5:0:sync:/sbin:/bin/sync
shutdown:x:6:0:shutdown:/sbin:/sbin/shutdown
halt:x:7:0:halt:/sbin:/sbin/halt
mail:x:8:12:mail:/var/spool/mail:/sbin/nologin
operator:x:11:0:operator:/root:/sbin/nologin
$
```

A good command option to try allows you to override the default behavior of only displaying a file's first 10 lines. The switch to use is -n (or --lines=), followed by an argument. The argument determines the number of file lines to display, as shown in Listing 1.39.

Listing 1.39: Using the head command to display fewer lines

```
$ head -n 2 /etc/passwd
root:x:0:0:root:/root:/bin/bash
bin:x:1:1:bin:/bin:/sbin/nologin
$
$ head -2 /etc/passwd
root:x:0:0:root:/root:/bin/bash
bin:x:1:1:bin:/bin:/sbin/nologin
$
```

Notice in Listing 1.38 that the -n 2 switch and argument used with the head command display only the file's first two lines. However, the second command eliminates the n portion of the switch, and the command behaves just the same as the first command.

Viewing Files with *tail*

If you want to display a file's last lines instead of its first lines, employ the tail utility. Its general syntax is similar to the head command's syntax and is shown as follows:

```
tail [OPTION]... [FILE]...
```

By default, the tail command will show a file's last 10 text lines. However, you can override that behavior by using the -n (or --lines=) switch with an argument. The argument tells tail how many lines from the file's bottom to display. If you add a plus sign (+) in front of the argument, the tail utility will start displaying the file's text lines starting at the designated line number to the file's end. There are three examples of using tail in these ways in Listing 1.40.

Listing 1.40: Employing the tail command

```
$ tail /etc/passwd
saslauth:x:992:76:Saslauthd user:/run/saslauthd:/sbin/nologin
pulse:x:171:171:PulseAudio System Daemon:/var/run/pulse:/sbin/nologin
gdm:x:42:42::/var/lib/gdm:/sbin/nologin
setroubleshoot:x:991:985::/var/lib/setroubleshoot:/sbin/nologin
rpcuser:x:29:29:RPC Service User:/var/lib/nfs:/sbin/nologin
nfsnobody:x:65534:65534:Anonymous NFS User:/var/lib/nfs:/sbin/nologin
sssd:x:990:984:User for sssd:/:/sbin/nologin
gnome-initial-setup:x:989:983::/run/gnome-initial-setup/:/sbin/nologin
```

```
tcpdump:x:72:72::/:/sbin/nologin
avahi:x:70:70:Avahi mDNS/DNS-SD Stack:/var/run/avahi-daemon:/sbin/nologin
$
$ tail -n 2 /etc/passwd
tcpdump:x:72:72::/:/sbin/nologin
avahi:x:70:70:Avahi mDNS/DNS-SD Stack:/var/run/avahi-daemon:/sbin/nologin
$
$ tail -n +42 /etc/passwd
gnome-initial-setup:x:989:983::/run/gnome-initial-setup/:/sbin/nologin
tcpdump:x:72:72::/:/sbin/nologin
avahi:x:70:70:Avahi mDNS/DNS-SD Stack:/var/run/avahi-daemon:/sbin/nologin
$
```

One of the most useful `tail` utility features is its ability to watch log files. Log files typically have new messages appended to the file's bottom. Watching new messages as they are added is very handy. Use the `-f` (or `--follow`) switch on the `tail` command and provide the log filename to watch as the command's argument. You will see a few recent log file entries immediately. As you keep watching, additional messages will display as they are being added to the log file.

 Some log files have been replaced on various Linux distributions, and now the messages are kept in a journal file managed by `journald`. To watch messages being added to the journal file, use the `journalctl --follow` command.

To end your monitoring session using `tail`, you must use the Ctrl+C key combination. An example of watching a log file using the `tail` utility is shown snipped in Listing 1.41.

Listing 1.41: Watching a log file with the `tail` command

```
$ sudo tail -f /var/log/auth.log
[sudo] password for Christine:
Aug 27 10:15:14 Ubuntu1804 sshd[15662]: Accepted password […]
Aug 27 10:15:14 Ubuntu1804 sshd[15662]: pam_unix(sshd:sess[…]
Aug 27 10:15:14 Ubuntu1804 systemd-logind[588]: New sessio[…]
Aug 27 10:15:50 Ubuntu1804 sudo: Christine : TTY=pts/1 ; P[…]
Aug 27 10:15:50 Ubuntu1804 sudo: pam_unix(sudo:session): s[…]
Aug 27 10:16:21 Ubuntu1804 login[10703]: pam_unix(login:se[…]
Aug 27 10:16:21 Ubuntu1804 systemd-logind[588]: Removed se[…]
^C
$
```

If you are following along on your own system with the commands in this book, your Linux distribution may not have the /var/log/auth.log file. Try the /var/log/secure file instead.

File-Summarizing Commands

Summary information is handy to have when analyzing problems and understanding your files. Several utilities covered in this section will help you in summarizing activities.

Counting with *wc*

The easiest and most common utility for determining counts in a text file is the wc utility. The command's basic syntax is as follows:

```
wc [OPTION]... [FILE]...
```

When you issue the wc command with no options and pass it a filename, the utility will display the file's number of lines, words, and bytes in that order. Listing 1.42 shows an example.

Listing 1.42: Employing the wc command

```
$ wc random.txt
 5  9 52 random.txt
$
```

There a few useful and commonly used options for the wc command. These are shown in Table 1.7.

TABLE 1.7   The wc command's commonly used options

Short	Long	Description
-c	--bytes	Display the file's byte count.
-L	--max-line-length	Display the byte count of the file's longest line.
-l	--lines	Display the file's line count.
-m	--chars	Display the file's character count.
-w	--words	Display the file's word count.

An interesting wc option for troubleshooting configuration files is the -L switch. Generally speaking, line length for a configuration file will be under 150 bytes, though there are exceptions. Thus, if you have just edited a configuration file and that service is no longer working, check the file's longest line length. A longer than usual line length indicates you might have accidently merged two configuration file lines. An example is shown in Listing 1.43.

Listing 1.43: Using the wc command to check line length

```
$ wc -L /etc/nsswitch.conf
72 /etc/nsswitch.conf
$
```

In Listing 1.43, the file's line length shows a normal maximum line length of 72 bytes. This wc command switch can also be useful if you have other utilities that cannot process text files exceeding certain line lengths.

Pulling Out Portions with *cut*

To sift through the data in a large text file, it helps to quickly extract small data sections. The cut utility is a handy tool for doing this. It will allow you to view particular fields within a file's records. The command's basic syntax is as follows:

```
cut OPTION... [FILE]...
```

Before we delve into using this command, there are few basics to understand concerning the cut command. They are as follows:

Text File Records   A text file record is a single-file line that ends in a newline linefeed, which is the ASCII character LF. You can see if your text file uses this end-of-line character via the cat -E command. It will display every newline linefeed as a $. If your text file records end in the ASCII character NUL, you can also use cut on them, but you must use the -z option.

Text File Record Delimiter   For some of the cut command options to be properly used, fields must exist within each text file record. These fields are not database-style fields but instead data that is separated by some *delimiter*. A delimiter is one or more characters that create a boundary between different data items within a record. A single space can be a delimiter. The password file, /etc/passwd, uses colons (:) to separate data items within a record.

Text File Changes   Contrary to its name, the cut command does not change any data within the text file. It simply copies the data you wish to view and displays it to you. Rest assured that no modifications are made to the file.

The cut utility has a few options you will use on a regular basis. These options are listed in Table 1.8.

TABLE 1.8   The cut command's commonly used options

Short	Long	Description
-c *nlist*	--characters *nlist*	Display only the record characters in the *nlist* (e.g., 1–5).
-b *blist*	--bytes *blist*	Display only the record bytes in the *blist* (e.g., 1–2).
-d *d*	--delimiter *d*	Designate the record's field delimiter as *d*. This overrides the Tab default delimiter. Put *d* within quotation marks to avoid unexpected results.
-f *flist*	--fields *flist*	Display only the record's fields denoted by *flist* (e.g., 1,3).
-s	--only-delimited	Display only records that contain the designated delimiter.
-z	--zero-terminated	Designate the record end-of-line character as the ASCII character NUL.

A cut command in action is shown in Listing 1.44.

Listing 1.44: Employing the cut command

```
$ head -2 /etc/passwd
root:x:0:0:root:/root:/bin/bash
bin:x:1:1:bin:/bin:/sbin/nologin
$
$ cut -d ":" -f 1,7 /etc/passwd
root:/bin/bash
bin:/sbin/nologin
[…]
$
```

In Listing 1.44, the head command displays the password file's first two lines. This text file employs colons (:) to delimit the fields within each record. The first use of the cut command designates the colon delimiter using the -d option. Notice the colon is encased in quotation marks to avoid unexpected results. The -f option specifies that only fields 1 (username) and 7 (shell) should be displayed.

Occasionally it is worthwhile to save a cut command's output. You can do this by redirecting standard output, which is covered later in this chapter.

Discovering Repeated Lines with *uniq*

A quick way to find repeated lines in a text file is with the uniq utility. Just type **uniq** and follow it with the filename whose contents you want to check.

The uniq utility will find repeated text lines only if they come right after one another. Used without any options, the command will display only unique (non-repeated) lines. An example of using this command is shown in Listing 1.45.

Listing 1.45: Using the uniq command

```
$ cat NonUniqueLines.txt
A
C
C
A
$
$ uniq NonUniqueLines.txt
A
C
A
$
```

Notice that in the cat command's output there are actually two sets of repeated lines in this file. One set is the C lines, and the other set is the A lines. Because the uniq utility recognizes only repeated lines that are one after the other in a text file, only one of the C text lines is removed from the display. The two A lines are still both shown.

Digesting an MD5 Algorithm

The md5sum utility is based on the MD5 message-digest algorithm. It was originally created to be used in cryptography. It is no longer used in such capacities due to various known vulnerabilities. However, it is still excellent for checking a file's integrity. A simple example is shown in Listing 1.46.

Listing 1.46: Using md5sum to check the original file

```
$ md5sum fourtytwo.txt
0ddaa12f06a2b7dcd469ad779b7c2a33  fourtytwo.txt
$
```

The md5sum produces a 128-bit hash value. If you copy the file to another system on your network, run the md5sum on the copied file. If you find that the hash values of the original and copied file match, this indicates no file corruption occurred during its transfer.

WARNING   A malicious attacker can create two files that have the same MD5 hash value. However, at this point in time, a file that is not under the attacker's control cannot have its MD5 hash value modified. Therefore, it is imperative that you have checks in place to ensure that your file was not created by a third-party malicious user. An even better solution is to use a stronger hash algorithm.

Securing Hash Algorithms

The Secure Hash Algorithms (SHA) is a family of various hash functions. Though typically used for cryptography purposes, they can also be used to verify a file's integrity after it is copied or moved to another location.

Several utilities implement these various algorithms on Linux. The quickest way to find them is via the method shown in Listing 1.47. Keep in mind your particular distribution may store them in the /bin directory instead.

Listing 1.47: Looking at the SHA utility names

```
$ ls -1 /usr/bin/sha???sum
/usr/bin/sha224sum
/usr/bin/sha256sum
/usr/bin/sha384sum
/usr/bin/sha512sum
$
```

Each utility includes the SHA message digest it employs within its name. Therefore, sha256sum uses the SHA-256 algorithm. These utilities are used in a similar manner to the md5sum command. A few examples are shown in Listing 1.48.

Listing 1.48: Using sha256sum and sha512sum to check a file

```
$ sha256sum fourtytwo.txt
0b2b6e2d8eab41e73baf0961ec707ef98978bcd8c7
74ba8d32d3784aed4d286b  fourtytwo.txt
$
$ sha512sum fourtytwo.txt
ac72599025322643e0e56cff41bb6e22ca4fbb76b1d
7fac1b15a16085edad65ef55bbc733b8b68367723ced
3b080dbaedb7669197a51b3b6a31db814802e2f31  fourtytwo.txt
$
```

Notice in Listing 1.48 the different hash value lengths produced by the different commands. The sha512sum utility uses the SHA-512 algorithm, which is the best to use for security purposes and is typically employed to hash salted passwords in the /etc/shadow file on Linux.

You can use these SHA utilities, just like the md5sum program was used in Listing 1.46, to ensure a file's integrity when it is transferred. That way, file corruption is avoided as well as any malicious modifications to the file.

Using Regular Expressions

Many commands use *regular expressions*. A regular expression is a pattern template you define for a utility such as grep, which then uses the pattern to filter text. Employing regular expressions along with text-filtering commands expands your mastery of the Linux command line.

Using *grep*

A wonderful tool for sifting text is the grep command. The grep command is powerful in its use of regular expressions, which will help with filtering text files. But before we cover those, peruse Table 1.9 for commonly used grep utility options.

TABLE 1.9   The grep command's commonly used options

Short	Long	Description
-c	--count	Display a count of text file records that contain a *PATTERN* match.
-d action	--directories=action	When a file is a directory, if *action* is set to read, read the directory as if it were a regular text file; if *action* is set to skip, ignore the directory; and if *action* is set to recurse, act as if the - R, -r, or --recursive option was used.
-E	--extended-regexp	Designate the *PATTERN* as an extended regular expression.
-i	--ignore-case	Ignore the case in the *PATTERN* as well as in any text file records.
-R, -r	--recursive	Search a directory's contents, and for any subdirectory within the original directory tree, consecutively search its contents as well (recursively).
-v	--invert-match	Display only text files records that do *not* contain a *PATTERN* match.

The basic syntax for the grep utility is as follows:

```
grep [OPTION] PATTERN [FILE...]
```

A simple example is shown in Listing 1.49. No options are used, and the grep utility is used to search for the word root (*PATTERN*) within /etc/passwd (*FILE*).

Listing 1.49: Using a simple grep command to search a file

```
$ grep root /etc/passwd
root:x:0:0:root:/root:/bin/bash
operator:x:11:0:operator:/root:/sbin/nologin
$
```

Notice that the grep command returns each file record (line) that contains an instance of the *PATTERN*, which in this case was the word root.

You can also use a series of patterns stored in a file with a variation of the grep utility. An example of doing this is shown in Listing 1.50.

Listing 1.50: Using the grep command to search for patterns stored in a text file

```
$ cat accounts.txt
sshd
Christine
nfsnobody
$
$ fgrep -f accounts.txt /etc/passwd
sshd:x:74:74:Privilege-separated SSH:/var/empty/sshd:/sbin/nologin
Christine:x:1001:1001::/home/Christine:/bin/bash
nfsnobody:x:65534:65534:Anonymous NFS User:/var/lib/nfs:/sbin/nologin
$
$ grep -F -f accounts.txt /etc/passwd
sshd:x:74:74:Privilege-separated SSH:/var/empty/sshd:/sbin/nologin
Christine:x:1001:1001::/home/Christine:/bin/bash
nfsnobody:x:65534:65534:Anonymous NFS User:/var/lib/nfs:/sbin/nologin
$
```

The patterns are stored in the accounts.txt file, which is first displayed using the cat command. Next, the fgrep command is employed, along with the -f option to indicate the file that holds the patterns. The /etc/passwd file is searched for all the patterns stored within the accounts.txt file, and the results are displayed.

Also notice in Listing 1.49 that the third command is the grep -F command. The grep -F command is equivalent to using the fgrep command, which is why the two commands produce identical results.

Understanding Basic Regular Expressions

Basic regular expressions (BREs) include characters, such as a dot followed by an asterisk
(.*) to represent multiple characters and a single dot (.) to represent one character. They
also may use brackets to represent multiple characters, such as [a,e,i,o,u] (you do *not*
have to include the commas) or a range of characters, such as [A-z]. When brackets are
employed, it is called a *bracket expression.*

To find text file records that begin with particular characters, you can precede them
with a caret (^) symbol. For finding text file records where particular characters are at
the record's end, append them with a dollar sign ($) symbol. Both the caret and the dollar
sign symbols are called *anchor characters* for BREs, because they fasten the pattern to the
beginning or the end of a text line.

> You will see in documentation and technical descriptions different
> names for regular expressions. The name may be shortened to regex or
> regexp.

Using a BRE pattern is fairly straightforward with the grep utility. Listing 1.51 shows
some examples.

Listing 1.51: Using the grep command with a BRE pattern

```
$ grep daemon.*nologin /etc/passwd
daemon:x:2:2:daemon:/sbin:/sbin/nologin
[…]
daemon:/dev/null:/sbin/nologin
[…]
$
$ grep root /etc/passwd
root:x:0:0:root:/root:/bin/bash
operator:x:11:0:operator:/root:/sbin/nologin
$
$ grep ^root /etc/passwd
root:x:0:0:root:/root:/bin/bash
$
```

In the first snipped grep example within Listing 1.51, the grep command employs a pattern using the BRE .* characters. In this case, the grep utility will search the password file
for any instances of the word daemon within a record and display that record if it *also* contains the word nologin after the word daemon.

The next two grep examples in Listing 1.51 are searching for instances of the word root
within the password file. Notice that the one command displays two lines from the file. The
next command employs the BRE ^ character and places it before the word root. This regular
expression pattern causes grep to display only lines in the password file that *begin* with root.

If you would like to get a better handle on regular expressions, there are several good resources. Our favorite is Chapter 20 in the book *Linux Command Line and Shell Scripting Bible* by Blum and Bresnahan (Wiley, 2015).

You can also look at the man pages, section 7, on regular expressions (called *regex(7)* in the certification objectives). View this information by typing **man 7 regex** or **man -S 7 regex** at the command line.

The -v option is useful when auditing your configuration files with the grep utility. It produces a list of text file records that *do not* contain the pattern. Listing 1.52 shows an example of finding all the records in the password file that *do not* end in nologin. Notice that the BRE pattern puts the $ at the end of the word. If you were to place the $ before the word, it would be treated as a variable name instead of a BRE pattern.

Listing 1.52: Using the grep command to audit the password file

```
$ grep -v nologin$ /etc/passwd
root:x:0:0:root:/root:/bin/bash
sync:x:5:0:sync:/sbin:/bin/sync
[…]
Christine:x:1001:1001::/home/Christine:/bin/bash
$
```

If you need to filter out all the blank lines in a file (display only lines with text), use grep with the -v option to invert the matching pattern. Then employ the ^ and $ anchor characters like **grep -v ^$ *filename*** at the command line.

A special group of bracket expressions are *character classes*. These bracket expressions have predefined names and could be considered bracket expression shortcuts. Their interpretation is based on the LC_CTYPE locale environment variable (locales are covered in Chapter 6). Table 1.10 shows the more commonly used character classes.

TABLE 1.10   Commonly used character classes

Class	Description
[:alnum:]	Matches any alphanumeric characters (any case), and is equal to using the [0-9A-Za-z] bracket expression
[:alpha:]	Matches any alphabetic characters (any case), and is equal to using the [A-Za-z] bracket expression

Class	Description
`[:blank:]`	Matches any blank characters, such as tab and space
`[:digit:]`	Matches any numeric characters, and is equal to using the `[0-9]` bracket expression
`[:lower:]`	Matches any lowercase alphabetic characters, and is equal to using the `[a-z]` bracket expression
`[:punct:]`	Matches punctuation characters, such as !, #, $, and @
`[:space:]`	Matches space characters, such as tab, form feed, and space
`[:upper:]`	Matches any uppercase alphabetic characters, and is equal to using the `[A-Z]` bracket expression

For using character classes with the grep command, enclose the bracketed character class in another set of brackets. An example of using grep with the digit character class is shown in Listing 1.53.

Listing 1.53: Using the grep command and a character class

```
$ cat random.txt
42
Flat Land
Schrodinger's Cat
0010 1010
0000 0010
$
$ grep [[:digit:]] random.txt
42
0010 1010
0000 0010
$
```

Notice the extra brackets needed to properly use a character class. Thus, to use `[:digit:]`, you must type `[[:digit:]]` when employing this character class with the grep command.

> If you need to search for a character in a file that has special meaning in an expression or at the command line, such as the $ anchor character, precede it with a backslash (\). This lets the grep utility know you are searching for that character and not using it in an expression.

Understanding Extended Regular Expressions

Extended regular expressions (EREs) allow more complex patterns. For example, a vertical bar symbol (|) allows you to specify two possible words or character sets to match. You can also employ parentheses to designate additional subexpressions.

Using ERE patterns can be rather tricky. A few examples employing grep with EREs are helpful, such as the ones shown in Listing 1.54.

Listing 1.54: Using the grep command with an ERE pattern

```
$ grep -E "^root|^dbus" /etc/passwd
root:x:0:0:root:/root:/bin/bash
dbus:x:81:81:System message bus:/:/sbin/nologin
$
$ egrep "(daemon|s).*nologin" /etc/passwd
bin:x:1:1:bin:/bin:/sbin/nologin
daemon:x:2:2:daemon:/sbin:/sbin/nologin
[…]
$
```

In the first example, the grep command uses the -E option to indicate the pattern is an extended regular expression. If you did not employ the -E option, unpredictable results would occur. Quotation marks around the ERE pattern protect it from misinterpretation. The command searches for any password file records that start with either the word root or the word dbus. Thus, a caret (^) is placed prior to each word, and a vertical bar (|) separates the words to indicate that the record can start with either word.

In the second example in Listing 1.54, notice that the egrep command is employed. The egrep command is equivalent to using the grep -E command. The ERE pattern here also uses quotation marks to avoid misinterpretation and employs parentheses to issue a subexpression. The subexpression consists of a choice, indicated by the vertical bar (|), between the word daemon and the letter s. Also in the ERE pattern, the .* symbols are used to indicate there can be anything in between the subexpression choice and the word nologin in the text file record.

Take a deep breath. That was a lot to take in. However, as hard as BRE and ERE patterns are, they are worth using with the grep command to filter out data from your text files.

Using Streams, Redirection, and Pipes

One of the neat things about commands at the command line is that you can employ complex frameworks. These structures allow you to build commands from other commands, use a program's output as input to another program, put together utilities to perform custom operations, and so on.

Redirecting Input and Output

When processing and filtering text files, you may want to save the data produced. In addition, you may need to combine multiple refinement steps to obtain the information you need.

Handling Standard Output

It is important to know that Linux treats every object as a file. This includes the output process, such as displaying a text file on the screen. Each file object is identified using a *file descriptor*, an integer that classifies a process's open files. The file descriptor that identifies output from a command or script file is 1. It is also identified by the abbreviation STDOUT, which describes standard output.

By default, STDOUT directs output to your current terminal. Your process's current terminal is represented by the /dev/tty file.

A simple command to use when discussing standard output is the echo command. Issue the echo command along with a text string, and the text string will display to your process's STDOUT, which is typically the terminal screen. An example is shown in Listing 1.55.

Listing 1.55: Employing the echo command to display text to STDOUT

```
$ echo "Hello World"
Hello World
$
```

The neat thing about STDOUT is that you can redirect it via *redirection operators* on the command line. A redirection operator allows you to change the default behavior of where input and output are sent. For STDOUT, you redirect the output using the > redirection operator as shown in Listing 1.56.

Listing 1.56: Employing a STDOUT redirection operator

```
$ grep nologin$ /etc/passwd
bin:x:1:1:bin:/bin:/sbin/nologin
daemon:x:2:2:daemon:/sbin:/sbin/nologin
[…]
$ grep nologin$ /etc/passwd > NologinAccts.txt
$
$ less NologinAccts.txt
bin:x:1:1:bin:/bin:/sbin/nologin
daemon:x:2:2:daemon:/sbin:/sbin/nologin
[…]
$
```

In Listing 1.56, the password file is being audited for all accounts that use the /sbin/nologin shell via the grep command. The grep command's output is lengthy and was snipped in the listing. It would be so much easier to redirect STDOUT to a file.

This was done in Listing 1.56 by issuing the same grep command but tacking on a redirection operator, >, and a filename to the command's end. The effect was to send the command's output to the file NologinAccts.txt instead of the screen. Now the data file can be viewed using the less utility.

 WARNING If you use the > redirection operator and send the output to a file that already exists, that file's current data will be deleted. Use caution when employing this operator.

To append data to a preexisting file, you need to use a slightly different redirection operator. The >> operator will append data to a preexisting file. If the file does not exist, it is created, and the outputted data is added to it. Listing 1.57 shows an example of using this redirection operator.

Listing 1.57: Using a STDOUT redirection operator to append text

```
$ echo "Nov 16, 2019" > AccountAudit.txt
$
$ wc -l /etc/passwd >> AccountAudit.txt
$
$ cat AccountAudit.txt
Nov 16, 2019
44 /etc/passwd
$
```

The first command in Listing 1.57 puts a date stamp into the AccountAudit.txt file. Because that date stamp needs to be preserved, the next command appends STDOUT to the file using the >> redirection operator. The file can continue to be appended to using the >> operator for future commands.

Redirecting Standard Error

Another handy item to redirect is standard error. The file descriptor that identifies a command or script file error is 2. It is also identified by the abbreviation STDERR, which describes standard error. STDERR, like STDOUT, is by default sent to your terminal (/dev/tty).

The basic redirection operator to send STDERR to a file is the 2> operator. If you need to append the file, use the 2>> operator. Listing 1.58 shows a snipped example of redirecting standard error.

Listing 1.58: Employing a STDERR redirection operator

```
$ grep -d skip hosts: /etc/*
grep: /etc/anacrontab: Permission denied
grep: /etc/audisp: Permission denied
```

```
[…]
$
$ grep -d skip hosts: /etc/* 2> err.txt
/etc/nsswitch.conf:#hosts:       db files nisplus nis dns
/etc/nsswitch.conf:hosts:        files dns myhostname
[…]
$
$ cat err.txt
grep: /etc/anacrontab: Permission denied
grep: /etc/audisp: Permission denied
[…]
$
```

The first command in Listing 1.58 was issued to find any files with the /etc/ directory that contain the hosts: directive. Unfortunately, since the user does not have super user privileges, several permission denied error messages are generated. This clutters up the output and makes it difficult to see what files contain this directive.

To declutter the output, the second command in Listing 1.58 redirects STDERR to the err.txt file using the 2> redirection operator. This makes it much easier to see what files contain the hosts: directive. If needed, the error messages can be reviewed because they reside now in the err.txt file.

 Sometimes you want to send standard error and standard output to the same file. In these cases, use the &> redirection operator to accomplish your goal.

If you don't care to keep a copy of the error messages, you can always throw them away. This is done by redirecting STDERR to the /dev/null file as shown snipped in Listing 1.59.

Listing 1.59: Using a STDERR redirection operator to remove error messages

```
$ grep -d skip hosts: /etc/* 2> /dev/null
/etc/nsswitch.conf:#hosts:       db files nisplus nis dns
/etc/nsswitch.conf:hosts:        files dns myhostname
[…]
$
```

The /dev/null file is sometimes called the black hole. This name comes from the fact that anything you put into it, you cannot retrieve.

Regulating Standard Input

Standard input, by default, comes into your Linux system via the keyboard and/or other input devices. The file descriptor that identifies an input into a command or script file is 0. It is also identified by the abbreviation STDIN, which describes standard input.

As with STDOUT and STDERR, you can redirect STDIN. The basic redirection operator is the < symbol. The `tr` command is one of the few utilities that require you to redirect standard input. An example is shown in Listing 1.60.

Listing 1.60: Employing an STDIN redirection operator

```
$ cat Grades.txt
89 76 100 92 68 84 73
$
$ tr " " "," < Grades.txt
89,76,100,92,68,84,73
$
```

In Listing 1.60, the file `Grades.txt` contains various integers separated by a space. The second command utilizes the `tr` utility to change each space into a comma (,). Because the `tr` command requires the STDIN redirection symbol, it is also employed in the second command followed by the filename. Keep in mind that this command did not change the `Grades.txt` file. It only displayed to STDOUT what the file would look like with these changes.

It's nice to have a concise summary of the redirection operators. Therefore, we have provided one in Table 1.11.

TABLE 1.11 Commonly used redirection operators

Operator	Description
>	Redirect STDOUT to specified file. If file exists, overwrite it. If it does not exist, create it.
>>	Redirect STDOUT to specified file. If file exists, append to it. If it does not exist, create it.
2>	Redirect STDERR to specified file. If file exists, overwrite it. If it does not exist, create it.
2>>	Redirect STDERR to specified file. If file exists, append to it. If it does not exist, create it.
&>	Redirect STDOUT and STDERR to specified file. If file exists, overwrite it. If it does not exist, create it.
&>>	Redirect STDOUT and STDERR to specified file. If file exists, append to it. If it does not exist, create it.
<	Redirect STDIN from specified file into command.
<>	Redirect STDIN from specified file into command and redirect STDOUT to specified file.

Piping Data between Programs

If you really want to enact powerful and quick results at the Linux command line, you need to explore pipes. The pipe is a simple redirection operator represented by the ASCII character 124 (|), which is called the vertical bar, vertical slash, or vertical line.

 Be aware that some keyboards and text display the vertical bar not as a single vertical line. Instead, it looks like a vertical double dash.

With the pipe, you can redirect STDOUT, STDIN, and STDERR between multiple commands all on one command line. Now that is powerful redirection.

The basic syntax for redirection with the pipe symbol is as follows:

```
COMMAND1 | COMMAND2 [| COMMANDN]…
```

The syntax for pipe redirection shows that the first command, COMMAND1, is executed. Its STDOUT is redirected as STDIN into the second command, COMMAND2. Also, you can pipe more commands together than just two. Keep in mind that any command in the pipeline has its STDOUT redirected as STDIN to the next command in the pipeline. Listing 1.61 shows a simple use of pipe redirection.

Listing 1.61: Employing pipe redirection

```
$ grep /bin/bash$ /etc/passwd | wc -l
3
$
```

In Listing 1.61, the first command in the pipe searches the password file for any records that end in /bin/bash. This is essentially finding all user accounts that use the Bash shell as their default account shell. The output from the first command in the pipe is passed as input into the second command in the pipe. The wc -l command will count how many lines have been produced by the grep command. The results show that there are only three accounts on this Linux system that have the Bash shell set as their default shell.

You can get very creative using pipe redirection. Listing 1.62 shows a command employing four different utilities in a pipeline to audit accounts using the /sbin/nologin default shell.

Listing 1.62: Employing pipe redirection for several commands

```
$ grep /sbin/nologin$ /etc/passwd | cut -d ":" -f 1 | sort | less
abrt
adm
avahi
bin
chrony
[…]
:
```

In Listing 1.62, the output from the grep command is fed as input into the cut command. The cut utility removes only the first field from each password record, which is the account username. The output of the cut command is used as input into the sort command, which alphabetically sorts the usernames. Finally, the sort utility's output is piped as input into the less command for leisurely perusing through the account usernames.

In cases where you want to keep a copy of the command pipeline's output as well as view it, the tee command will help. Similar to a tee pipe fitting in plumbing, where the water flow is sent in multiple directions, the tee command allows you to both save the output to a file and display it to STDOUT. Listing 1.63 contains an example of this handy command.

Listing 1.63: Employing the tee command

```
$ grep /bin/bash$ /etc/passwd | tee BashUsers.txt
root:x:0:0:root:/root:/bin/bash
user1:x:1000:1000:Student User One:/home/user1:/bin/bash
Christine:x:1001:1001::/home/Christine:/bin/bash
$
$ cat BashUsers.txt
root:x:0:0:root:/root:/bin/bash
user1:x:1000:1000:Student User One:/home/user1:/bin/bash
Christine:x:1001:1001::/home/Christine:/bin/bash
$
```

The first command in Listing 1.63 searches the password file for any user account records that end in /bin/bash. That output is piped into the tee command, which displays the output as well as saves it to the BashUsers.txt file. The tee command is handy when you are installing software from the command line and want to see what is happening as well as keep a log file of the transaction for later review.

Using *sed*

Another interesting command-line program is a *stream editor*. There are times where you will want to edit text without having to pull out a full-fledged text editor. A stream editor modifies text that is passed to it via a file or output from a pipeline. This editor uses special commands to make text changes as the text "streams" through the editor utility.

The command to invoke the stream editor is sed. The sed utility edits a stream of text data based on a set of commands you supply ahead of time. It is a very quick editor because it makes only one pass through the text to apply the modifications.

The sed editor changes data based on commands either entered into the command line or stored in a text file. The process the editor goes through is as follows:

1. Reads one text line at a time from the input stream
2. Matches that text with the supplied editor commands
3. Modifies the text as specified in the commands
4. Displays the modified text

After the sed editor matches all the specified commands against a text line, it reads the next text line and repeats the editorial process. Once sed reaches the end of the text lines, it stops.

Before looking at some sed examples, it is important to understand the command's basic syntax. It is as follows:

```
sed  [OPTIONS] [SCRIPT]… [FILENAME]
```

By default, sed will use the text from STDIN to modify it according to the specified commands. An example is shown in Listing 1.64.

Listing 1.64: Using sed to modify STDIN text

```
$ echo "I like cake." | sed 's/cake/donuts/'
I like donuts.
$
```

Notice that the text output from the echo command is piped as input into the stream editor. The sed utility's s command (substitute) specifies that if the first text string, cake, is found, it is changed to donuts in the output. Note that the entire command after sed is considered to be the SCRIPT, and it is encased in single quotation marks. Also notice that the text words are delimited from the s command, the quotation marks, and each other via the forward slashes (/).

Keep in mind that just using the s command will not change all instances of a word within a text stream. Listing 1.65 shows an example of this.

Listing 1.65: Using sed to globally modify STDIN text

```
$ echo "I love cake and more cake." | sed 's/cake/donuts/'
I love donuts and more cake.
$
$ echo "I love cake and more cake." | sed 's/cake/donuts/g'
I love donuts and more donuts.
$
```

In the first command in Listing 1.65, only the first occurrence of the word cake was modified. However, in the second command a g, which stands for global, was added to the sed script's end. This caused all occurrences of cake to change to donuts.

You can also modify text stored in a file. Listing 1.66 shows an example of this.

Listing 1.66: Using sed to modify file text

```
$ cat cake.txt
Christine likes chocolate cake.
Rich likes lemon cake.
Tim only likes yellow cake.
```

```
Samantha does not like cake.
$
$ sed 's/cake/donuts/' cake.txt
Christine likes chocolate donuts.
Rich likes lemon donuts.
Tim only likes yellow donuts.
Samantha does not like donuts.
$
$ cat cake.txt
Christine likes chocolate cake.
Rich likes lemon cake.
Tim only likes yellow cake.
Samantha does not like cake.
$
```

In Listing 1.66, the file contains text lines that contain the word cake. When the cake.txt file is added as an argument to the sed command, its data is modified according to the script. Notice that the data in the file is not modified. The stream editor only displays the modified text to STDOUT. You could save the modified text to another file name via a STDOUT redirection operator, if desired.

 It may be tempting to think that the sed utility is operating on the text file as a whole, but it is not. The stream editor applies its commands to each text file line individually. Thus, in our previous example, if the word cake was found multiple times within a single text file line, you'd need to use the g global command to change all instances.

So far we've shown you only sed substitution commands, but you can also delete lines using the stream editor. To do so, you use the syntax of *'PATTERN/d'* for the sed command's *SCRIPT*. An example is shown in Listing 1.67. Notice the cake.txt file line that contains the word Christine is not displayed to STDOUT. It was "deleted" in the output, but it still exists within the text file.

Listing 1.67: Using sed to delete file text

```
$ sed '/Christine/d' cake.txt
Rich likes lemon cake.
Tim only likes yellow cake.
Samantha does not like cake.
$
```

You can also change an entire line of text. To accomplish this, you use the syntax of *'ADDRESScNEWTEXT'* for the sed command's *SCRIPT*. The *ADDRESS* refers to the file's line number, and the *NEWTEXT* is the different text line you want displayed. An example of this method is shown in Listing 1.68.

Listing 1.68: Using sed to change an entire file line

```
$ sed '4cI am a new line' cake.txt
Christine likes chocolate cake.
Rich likes lemon cake.
Tim only likes yellow cake.
I am a new line
$
```

The stream editor has some rather useful command options. The more commonly used ones are displayed in Table 1.12.

TABLE 1.12   The sed command's commonly used options

Short	Long	Description
-e *script*	--expression=script	Add commands in *script* to text processing. The *script* is written as part of the sed command.
-f *script*	--file=script	Add commands in *script* to text processing. The *script* is a file.
-r	--regexp-extended	Use extended regular expressions in script.

A handy option to use is the -e option. This allows you to employ multiple scripts in the sed command. An example is shown in Listing 1.69.

Listing 1.69: Using sed -e to use multiple scripts

```
$ sed -e 's/cake/donuts/ ; s/like/love/' cake.txt
Christine loves chocolate donuts.
Rich loves lemon donuts.
Tim only loves yellow donuts.
Samantha does not love donuts.
$
```

Pay close attention to the syntax change in Listing 1.69. Not only is the -e option employed, but the script is slightly different too. Now the script contains a semicolon (;) between the two script commands. This allows both commands to be processed on the text stream.

Generating Command Lines

Creating command-line commands is a useful skill. There are several different methods you can use. One such method employs the `xargs` utility. The best thing about this tool is that you sound like a pirate when you pronounce it, but it has other practical values as well.

By piping STDOUT from other commands into the `xargs` utility, you can build command-line commands on the fly. Listing 1.70 shows an example of doing this.

Listing 1.70: Employing the xargs command

```
$ touch EmptyFile1.txt EmptyFile2.txt EmptyFile3.txt
$
$ ls  EmptyFile?.txt
EmptyFile1.txt  EmptyFile2.txt  EmptyFile3.txt
$
$ ls -1 EmptyFile?.txt | xargs -p /usr/bin/rm
/usr/bin/rm EmptyFile1.txt EmptyFile2.txt EmptyFile3.txt ?...n
$
```

In Listing 1.70, three blank files are created using the `touch` command. The third command uses a pipeline. The first command in the pipeline lists any files that have the name EmptyFile*n*.txt. The output from the `ls` command is piped as STDIN into the `xargs` utility. The `xargs` command uses the `-p` option. This option causes the `xargs` utility to stop and ask permission before enacting the constructed command-line command. Notice that the absolute directory reference for the `rm` command is used (the `rm` command is covered in more detail in Chapter 4). This is sometimes needed when employing `xargs`, depending on your distribution.

The created command, in Listing 1.70, attempts to remove all three empty files with one `rm` command. We typed **n** and pressed the Enter key to preserve the three files instead of deleting them, because they are needed for the next example.

Another method to created command-line commands on the fly uses shell expansion. The technique here puts a command to execute within parentheses and precedes it with a dollar sign. An example of this method is shown in Listing 1.71.

Listing 1.71: Using the $() method to create commands

```
$ rm -i $(ls EmptyFile?.txt)
rm: remove regular empty file 'EmptyFile1.txt'? y
rm: remove regular empty file 'EmptyFile2.txt'? y
rm: remove regular empty file 'EmptyFile3.txt'? y
$
```

In Listing 1.71, the `ls` command is again used to list any files that have the name EmptyFile*n*.txt. Because the command is encased by the `$()` symbols, it does not display to STDOUT. Instead, the filenames are passed to the `rm -i` command, which inquires as whether or not to delete each found file. This method allows you to get very creative when building commands on the fly.

Summary

Understanding fundamental shell concepts and being able to effectively and swiftly use the right commands at the shell command line is important for your daily job. It allows you to gather information, peruse text files, filter data, and so on.

This chapter's purpose was to improve your Linux command-line tool belt. Not only will this help you in your day-to-day work life, but it will also help you successfully pass the LPI certification exam.

Exam Essentials

Express the different basic shell concepts.   The shell program provides the command-line prompt, which can be reached through a tty terminal or by employing a GUI terminal emulator. There are multiple shell programs, but the most popular is the Bash shell, which is typically located in the /bin/bash file. The /bin/sh file is often linked to the Bash shell program, but it may be linked to other shells, such as the Dash shell (/bin/dash). The shell in use can be checked via displaying the SHELL environment variable's contents with the echo utility. The current Linux kernel can be shown with the uname -a command.

Summarize the various utilities that can be employed to read text files.   To read entire small text files, you can use the cat and bat utilities. If you need to read only the first or last lines of a text file, employ either the head or tail command. For a single text line out of a file, the grep utility is useful. For reviewing a file a page at a time, you can use either the less or the more pager utility.

Describe the various methods used for editing text.   Editing text files is part of a system administrator's life. You can use full-screen editors such as the rather complicated vim text editor or the simple and easy-to-use nano editor. For fast and powerful text stream editing, employ the use of sed and its scripts.

Summarize the various utilities used in processing text files.   Filtering text file data can be made much easier with utilities such as grep, egrep, fgrep, and cut. Once that data is filtered, you may want to format it for viewing using sort, nl, or even the cat utility. If you need some statistical information on your text file, such as the number of lines it contains, the wc command is handy.

Explain both the structures and commands for redirection.   Employing STDOUT, STDERR, and STDIN redirection allows rather complex filtering and processing of text. The echo command can assist in this process. You can also use pipelines of commands to perform redirection and produce excellent data for review. In addition, pipelines can be used in creating commands on the fly with utilities, such as xargs.

Review Questions

You can find the answers in the appendix.

1. On Linux systems, which file typically now points to a shell program instead of holding a shell program?

   A. /bin/bash

   B. /bin/dash

   C. /bin/zsh

   D. /bin/sh

   E. /bin/tcsh

2. To see only the current Linux kernel version, which command should you use?

   A. uname

   B. echo $BASH_VERSION

   C. uname -r

   D. uname -a

   E. echo $SHELL

3. What will the echo \^New \^Style command display?

   A. \^New \^Style

   B. New Style

   C. Style New

   D. ^New ^Style

   E. \ew \tyle

4. You need to determine if the fortytwo.sh program is in a $PATH directory. Which of the following commands will assist you in this task? (Choose all that apply.)

   A. which fortytwo.sh

   B. cat fortytwo.sh

   C. echo $PATH

   D. fortytwo.sh

   E. /usr/bin/fortytwo.sh

5. You want to edit the file SpaceOpera.txt and decide to use the vim editor to complete this task. Which of the following are vim modes you might employ? (Choose all that apply.)

   A. Insert

   B. Change

   C. Command

   D. Ex

   E. Edit

6. You have a lengthy file named `FileA.txt`. What will the `head -15 FileA.txt` command do?

    A. Display all but the last 15 lines of the file

    B. Display all but the first 15 lines of the file

    C. Display the first 15 lines of the file

    D. Display the last 15 lines of the file

    E. Generate an error message

7. You are trying to peruse a rather large text file. A co-worker suggests you use a pager. Which of the following best describes what your co-worker is recommending?

    A. Use a utility that allows you to view the first few lines of the file.

    B. Use a utility that allows you to view one text page at time.

    C. Use a utility that allows you to search through the file.

    D. Use a utility that allows you to filter out text in the file.

    E. Use a utility that allows you to view the last few lines of the file.

8. Which of the following does not describe the `less` utility?

    A. It does not read the entire file prior to displaying the file's first page.

    B. You can use the up and down arrow keys to move through the file.

    C. You press the spacebar to move forward a page.

    D. You can use the Esc+V key combination to move backward a page.

    E. You can press the X key to exit from the utility.

9. The `cat -E MyFile.txt` command is entered and at the end of every line displayed is a $. What does this indicate?

    A. The text file has been corrupted somehow.

    B. The text file records end in the ASCII character NUL.

    C. The text file records end in the ASCII character LF.

    D. The text file records end in the ASCII character $.

    E. The text file records contain a $ at their end.

10. The cut utility often needs delimiters to process text records. Which of the following best describes a delimiter?

    A. One or more characters that designate the beginning of a line in a record

    B. One or more characters that designate the end of a line in a record

    C. One or more characters that designate the end of a text file to a command-line text processing utility

    D. A single space or a colon (:) that creates a boundary between different data items in a record

    E. One or more characters that create a boundary between different data items in a record

11. Which of the following utilities change text within a file? (Choose all that apply.)

   A. cut

   B. sort

   C. vim

   D. nano

   E. sed

12. A Unicode-encoded text file, MyUCode.txt, needs to be perused. Before you decide what utility to use in order to view the file's contents, you employ the wc command on it. This utility displays 2020 6786 11328 to STDOUT. What of the following is true? (Choose all that apply.)

   A. The file has 2,020 lines in it.

   B. The file has 2,020 characters in it.

   C. The file has 6,786 words in it.

   D. The file has 11,328 characters in it.

   E. The file has 11,328 lines in it.

13. The grep utility can employ regular expressions in its *PATTERN*. Which of the following best describes a regular expression?

   A. A series of characters you define for a utility, which uses the characters to match the same characters in text files

   B. ASCII characters, such as LF and NUL, that a utility uses to filter text

   C. Wildcard characters, such as * and ?, that a utility uses to filter text

   D. A pattern template you define for a utility, which uses the pattern to filter text

   E. Quotation marks (single or double) used around characters to prevent unexpected results

14. Which of the following is a BRE pattern that could be used with the grep command? (Choose all that apply.)

   A. Sp?ce

   B. "Space, the .*frontier"

   C. ^Space

   D. (lasting | final)

   E. frontier$

15. You need to search through a large text file and find any record that contains either Luke or Laura at the record's beginning. Also, the phrase "Father is" must be located somewhere in the record's middle. Which of the following is an ERE pattern that could be used with the egrep command to find this record?

   A. "Luke$|Laura$.*Father is"

   B. "^Luke|^Laura.Father is"

   C.   `"(^Luke|^Laura).Father is"`

   D.   `"(Luke$|Laura$).* Father is$"`

   E.   `"(^Luke|^Laura).*Father is.* "`

16. Which of the following best defines a file descriptor?

   A.   An environment variable, such as $PS1

   B.   A number that represents a process's open files

   C.   Another term for the file's name

   D.   A six character name that represents standard output

   E.   A symbol that indicates the file's classification

17. A file `data.txt` needs to be sorted numerically and its output saved to a new file `newdata.txt`. Which of the following commands can accomplish this task? (Choose all that apply.)

   A.   `sort -n -o newdata.txt data.txt`

   B.   `sort -n data.txt > newdata.txt`

   C.   `sort -n -o data.txt newdata.txt`

   D.   `sort -o newdata.txt data.txt`

   E.   `sort data.txt > newdata.txt`

18. By default, STDOUT goes to what item?

   A.   `/dev/tty`*n*, where *n* is a number

   B.   `/dev/null`

   C.   `>`

   D.   `/dev/tty`

   E.   `pwd`

19. Which of the following commands will display the file `SpaceOpera.txt` to output as well as a copy of it to the file `SciFi.txt`?

   A.   `cat SpaceOpera.txt | tee SciFi.txt`

   B.   `cat SpaceOpera.txt > SciFi.txt`

   C.   `cat SpaceOpera.txt 2> SciFi.txt`

   D.   `cat SpaceOpera.txt SciFi.txt`

   E.   `cat SpaceOpera.txt &> SciFi.txt`

20. Which of the following commands will put any generated error messages into the black hole?

   A.   `sort SpaceOpera.txt 2> BlackHole`

   B.   `sort SpaceOpera.txt &> BlackHole`

   C.   `sort SpaceOpera.txt > BlackHole`

   D.   `sort SpaceOpera.txt 2> /dev/null`

   E.   `sort SpaceOpera.txt > /dev/null`

Chapter

2

Managing Software and Processes

OBJECTIVES

- ✓ **102.3** Manage shared libraries
- ✓ **102.4** Use Debian package management
- ✓ **102.5** Use RPM and YUM package management
- ✓ **103.5** Create, monitor, and kill processes
- ✓ **103.6** Modify process execution priorities

A Linux system is only as good as the software you install on it. The Linux kernel by itself is pretty boring; you need applications such as web servers, database servers, browsers, and word processing tools to do anything useful with your Linux system. This chapter addresses the role of software on your Linux system and how you get and manage it.

We also discuss how Linux handles applications running on the system. Linux must keep track of lots of different programs, all running at the same time. Your goal as the Linux administrator is to make sure everything runs smoothly! This chapter shows just how Linux keeps track of all the active programs and how you can peek at that information. You'll also see how to use command-line tools to manage the programs running on your Linux system.

Looking at Package Concepts

Most Linux users want to download an application and use it. Thus, Linux distributions have created a system for bundling already compiled applications for distribution. This bundle is called a *package*, and it consists of most of the files required to run a single application. You can then install, remove, and manage the entire application as a single package rather than as a group of disjointed files.

Tracking software packages on a Linux system is called *package management*. Linux implements package management by using a database to track the installed packages on the system. The package management database keeps track of not only what packages are installed but also the exact files and file locations required for each application. Determining what applications are installed on your system is as easy as querying the package management database.

As you would expect, different Linux distributions have created different package management systems. However, over the years, two of these systems have risen to the top and become standards:

- Red Hat package management (RPM)
- Debian package management (Apt)

Each package management system uses a different method of tracking application packages and files, but they both track similar information:

- Application files: The package database tracks each individual file as well as the folder where it's located.

- Library dependencies: The package database tracks what library files are required for each application and can warn you if a dependent library file is not present when you install a package.

- Application version: The package database tracks version numbers of applications so that you know when an updated version of the application is available.

The sections that follow discuss the tools for using each of these package management systems.

Using RPM

Developed at Red Hat, the RPM Package Manager (RPM) utility lets you install, modify, and remove software packages. It also eases the process of updating software.

 Recursive acronyms use the acronym as part of the words that compose it. A famous example in the Linux world is GNU, which stands for "GNU's not Unix." RPM is a recursive acronym.

RPM Distributions and Conventions

The Red Hat Linux distribution, along with other Red Hat–based distros such as Fedora and CentOS, use RPM. In addition, there are other distributions that are not Red Hat based, such as openSUSE and OpenMandriva Lx, that employ RPM as well.

RPM package files have an .rpm file extension and follow this naming format:

PACKAGE-NAME-VERSION-RELEASE.ARCHITECTURE.rpm

PACKAGE-NAME   The *PACKAGE-NAME* is as you would expect—the name of the software package. For example, if you wanted to install the emacs text editor, most likely its RPM file would have a software package name of emacs. However, be aware that different distributions may have different *PACKAGE-NAME*s for the same program and that software package names may differ from program names.

VERSION   The *VERSION* is the program's version number and represents software modifications that are more recent than older version numbers. Traditionally a package's version number is formatted as two to three numbers and/or letters separated by dots (.). Examples include 1.13.1 and 7.4p1.

RELEASE   The RELEASE is also called the *build number*. It represents a smaller program modification than does the version number. In addition, due to the rise of continuous software delivery models, you often find version control system (VCS) numbers listed in the release number after a dot. Examples include 22 and 94.gitb2f74b2.

Some distros include the distribution version in the build number. For example, you find el7 (Red Hat Enterprise Linux v7) or fc29 (Fedora, formerly called Fedora Core, v29) after a dot.

ARCHITECTURE   This is a designation of the CPU architecture for which the software package was optimized. Typically you'll see x86_64 listed for 64-bit processors. Sometimes noarch is used, which indicates the package is architecturally neutral. Older CPU architecture designations include i386 (x86), ppc (PowerPC), and i586 and i686 (Pentium).

There are two types of RPM packages: source and binary. Most of the time, you'll want the binary package, because it contains the program bundle needed to successfully run the software. A source RPM contains the program's source code, which can be useful for analysis (or for incorporating your own package customizations). You can tell the difference between these two package file types because a source RPM has src as its *ARCHITECTURE* in the RPM filename.

It's helpful to look at some example RPM files. Listing 2.1 shows four different RPM files we downloaded on a CentOS distribution.

Listing 2.1: Viewing RPM package files on a CentOS distribution

```
# ls -1 *.rpm
docker-1.13.1-94.gitb2f74b2.el7.centos.x86_64.rpm
emacs-24.3-22.el7.x86_64.rpm
openssh-7.4p1-16.el7.x86_64.rpm
zsh-5.0.2-31.el7.x86_64.rpm
#
```

Notice the format naming variations between the version and release numbers. Although it can be difficult to determine where a version number ends and a release number begins, the trick is to look for the second dash (-) in the filename, which separates them.

If you want to obtain copies of RPM files on a Red Hat–based distro such as CentOS or Fedora, employ the yumdownloader utility. For example, use super user privileges and type **yumdownloader emacs** at the command line to download the emacs RPM file to your current working directory. On openSUSE, you'll need to employ the zypper install -d *package-name* command, using super user privileges. This will download the RPM package file(s) to a /var/cache/zypp/packages/ subdirectory.

The *rpm* Command Set

The main tool for working with RPM files is the *rpm* program. The rpm utility is a command-line program that installs, modifies, and removes RPM software packages. Its basic format is as follows:

rpm *ACTION* [*OPTION*] *PACKAGE-FILE*

Some common actions for the rpm command are described in Table 2.1.

TABLE 2.1   The rpm command actions

Short	Long	Description
-e	--erase	Removes the specified package
-F	--freshen	Upgrades a package only if an earlier version already exists
-i	--install	Installs the specified package
-q	--query	Queries whether the specified package is installed
-U	--upgrade	Installs or upgrades the specified package
-V	--verify	Verifies whether the package files are present and the package's integrity

Installing and Updating RPM Packages

To use the rpm command, you must have the .rpm package file downloaded onto your system. While you can use the -i action to install packages, it's more common to use the -U action, which installs the new package or upgrades the package if it's already installed.

You will always need to obtain super user privileges to install or update software packages. Many other package management commands need these privileges as well. You can typically gain the needed privileges by logging into the root account or by using the sudo utility, which requires your account be configured to be able to do so (see Chapter 10 for additional details).

Adding the -vh option is a popular combination that shows the progress of an update and what it's doing. An example of this is shown in Listing 2.2. Be aware that you need to employ super user privileges to install and/or update software packages.

Listing 2.2: Installing/upgrading an RPM package file

```
# rpm -Uvh zsh-5.0.2-31.el7.x86_64.rpm
Preparing...                    ################################ [100%]
Updating / installing...
  1:zsh-5.0.2-31.el7            ################################ [100%]
#
```

No one wants to type those hideously long package filenames. It is too easy to make typographical errors with all the dashes, dots, and numbers. Instead, employ the shell's command completion feature (also called *tab autocomplete*). Type in the *PACKAGE-NAME* portion of the package's file name and press the Tab key. As long as there are no other files with similar names, the shell will complete the rest of the package file's name for you. That's a nice feature!

Querying RPM Packages

Use the -q action to perform a simple query on the package management database for installed packages. An example is shown in Listing 2.3. Notice that for installed packages, such as zsh, the entire package filename, minus the .rpm file extension, displays.

Listing 2.3: Performing a simple query on an RPM package

```
# rpm -q zsh
zsh-5.0.2-31.el7.x86_64
#
# rpm -q docker
package docker is not installed
#
```

You can add several options to the query action to obtain more detailed information. Table 2.2 shows a few of the more commonly used query options.

TABLE 2.2 The rpm command query action options

Short option	Long option	Description
-c	--configfiles	Lists the names and absolute directory references of package configuration files
-i	--info	Provides detailed information, including version, installation date, and signatures

Short option	Long option	Description
N/A	--provides	Shows what facilities the package provides
-R	--requires	Displays various package requirements (dependencies)
-s	--state	Provides states of the different files in a package, such as normal (installed), not installed, or replaced
N/A	--what-provides	Shows to what package a file belongs

The -qi options provide a great deal of information on the package, as shown snipped in Listing 2.4.

Listing 2.4: Performing a detailed query on an RPM package

```
# rpm -qi zsh
Name        : zsh
Version     : 5.0.2
Release     : 31.el7
Architecture: x86_64
Install Date: Tue 09 Apr 2019 02:51:26 PM EDT
Group       : System Environment/Shells
Size        : 5854390
License     : MIT
Signature   : RSA/SHA256, Mon 12 Nov 2018 09:49:55 AM EST, Key ID 24c6a[…]
Source RPM  : zsh-5.0.2-31.el7.src.rpm
Build Date  : Tue 30 Oct 2018 12:48:17 PM EDT
Build Host  : x86-01.bsys.centos.org
Relocations : (not relocatable)
Packager    : CentOS BuildSystem <http://bugs.centos.org>
Vendor      : CentOS
URL         : http://zsh.sourceforge.net/
Summary     : Powerful interactive shell
Description :
The zsh shell is a command interpreter usable as an interactive login
[…]
#
```

Notice that from this detailed query, you can determine the package's version number, installation date, signature, and so on. However, there are a few missing data items, such as the package's dependencies.

To display a list of all the installed packages on your system that use RPM package management, type **rpm -qa** at the command line. Interestingly, you get the same detailed information on a specific package if you enter **rpm -qa PACKAGE-NAME** as you would using the -qi options.

Discovering an installed package's dependencies (requirements) is a handy troubleshooting tool. They are easily determined by employing the -qR options as shown snipped in Listing 2.5.

Listing 2.5: Determining an RPM package's dependencies

```
# rpm -qR zsh
[…]
libc.so.6()(64bit)
libc.so.6(GLIBC_2.11)(64bit)
[…]
libncursesw.so.5()(64bit)
librt.so.1()(64bit)
librt.so.1(GLIBC_2.2.5)(64bit)
libtinfo.so.5()(64bit)
[…]
#
```

An example of using the -qc options to determine what configuration files belong to a package is shown in Listing 2.6.

Listing 2.6: Determining configuration filenames that belong to an RPM package

```
# rpm -qc zsh
/etc/skel/.zshrc
/etc/zlogin
/etc/zlogout
/etc/zprofile
/etc/zshenv
/etc/zshrc
#
```

At some point in time, you may want to determine information such as an RPM package's signature or license from an uninstalled package file. It's fairly simple. Just add the -p option to your query, and use the package file name as an argument. For example, to query dependency information from the zsh package file we've been using in our examples, you would type **rpm -qRp zsh-5.0.2-31.el7.x86_64.rpm** at the command line.

Another handy RPM package database query uses the -q --whatprovides options and allows you to see to what package a file belongs. An example is shown in Listing 2.7. Notice you'll need to provide the file's absolute directory reference to the query.

Listing 2.7: Determining to what RPM package a file belongs

```
# rpm -q --whatprovides /usr/bin/zsh
zsh-5.0.2-31.el7.x86_64
#
```

Verifying RPM Packages

Keeping a watchful eye on your system's packages is an important security measure. For these operations, the rpm utility's verify action is helpful. If you receive nothing or a single dot (.) from the rpm -V command, that's a good thing. Table 2.3 shows the potential integrity response codes and what they mean.

TABLE 2.3   Verify action response codes for the rpm command

Code	Description
?	Unable to perform verification tests
5	Digest number has changed
c	File is a configuration file for the package
D	Device number (major or minor) has changed
G	Group ownership has changed
L	Link path has changed
missing	Missing file
M	Mode (permission or file type) has changed
P	Capabilities have changed
S	Size of file has changed
T	Time stamp (modification) has changed
U	User ownership has changed

An example of the verification process is shown in Listing 2.8.

Listing 2.8: Checking an RPM package's integrity

```
# rpm -V zsh
.....UGT.    /bin/zsh
.......T.  c /etc/zlogin
missing    c /etc/zprofile
#
```

In this example, response codes appear for the integrity check in Listing 2.8. Each file that has a discrepancy is listed. Using the code interpretations from Table 2.3, you can determine that the /bin/zsh file has had both its owner and group changed, and the modification time stamp differs from the one in the package database. The /etc/zlogin file is a zsh package configuration file, and its modification time stamp has also been changed. Notice too that the /etc/zprofile configuration file is missing.

If you are having problems with a program due to a missing library file, you can start the troubleshooting process by looking at the various libraries employed by the application using the ldd command. This utility is covered later in this chapter.

Removing RPM Packages

To remove an installed package, just use the -e action for the rpm command. An example is shown in Listing 2.9.

Listing 2.9: Removing an RPM package

```
# rpm -e zsh
warning: file /etc/zprofile: remove failed: No such file or directory
#
# rpm -q zsh
package zsh is not installed
#
```

The -e action doesn't show if it was successful, but it will display an error message if something goes wrong with the removal. Notice that in this case the /etc/zprofile file that we discovered was missing via the rpm -V command in Listing 2.8 is also noted by the removal process.

Extracting Data from RPMs

Occasionally you may need to extract files from an RPM package file without installing it. The *rpm2cpio* utility is helpful in these situations. It allows you to build a cpio archive (covered in detail in Chapter 4) from an RPM file as shown in Listing 2.10. This is the first step in extracting the files. Notice that you need to use the > redirection symbol (STDOUT redirection was covered in Chapter 1) in order to create the archive file.

Listing 2.10: Creating a cpio archive from an RPM package

```
$ rpm2cpio emacs-24.3-22.el7.x86_64.rpm > emacs.cpio
$
```

The next step is to move the files from the cpio archive into directories. This is accomplished via the cpio command using the -id options. The -i switch employs copy-in mode, which allows files to be copied in from an archive file. The -d switch creates subdirectories in the current working directory whose names match the directory names in the archive, with the exception of adding a preceding dot (.) to each name. A snipped example is shown in Listing 2.11. Notice we added the verbose option (-v) to display what the command was doing as it created the needed subdirectories and extracted the files.

Listing 2.11: Extracting the files from a cpio archive

```
$ cpio -idv < emacs.cpio
./usr/bin/emacs-24.3
./usr/share/applications/emacs.desktop
./usr/share/applications/emacsclient.desktop
./usr/share/icons/hicolor/128x128/apps/emacs.png
./usr/share/icons/hicolor/16x16/apps/emacs.png
./usr/share/icons/hicolor/24x24/apps/emacs.png
./usr/share/icons/hicolor/32x32/apps/emacs.png
./usr/share/icons/hicolor/48x48/apps/emacs.png
./usr/share/icons/hicolor/scalable/apps/emacs.svg
./usr/share/icons/hicolor/scalable/mimetypes/emacs-document.svg
28996 blocks
$
$ ls ./usr/bin/emacs-24.3
./usr/bin/emacs-24.3
```

After the files are finally extracted from the RPM package file and the subsequent cpio archive, you can explore them as needed.

Using YUM

The rpm commands are useful tools, but they have limitations. If you're looking for new software packages to install, it's up to you to find them. Also, if a package depends on other packages to be installed, it's up to you to install those packages first, and in the correct order. That can become somewhat of a pain to keep up with.

To solve that problem, each Linux distribution has its own central clearinghouse of packages, called a *repository*. The repository contains software packages that have been tested and known to install and work correctly in the distribution environment. By placing all known packages into a single repository, the Linux distribution can create a one-stop shopping location for installing all applications.

Most Linux distributions create and maintain their own repositories of packages. There are also additional tools for working with package repositories. These tools can interface directly with the package repository to find new software and even automatically find and install any dependent packages the application requires to operate.

Many third-party package repositories have also sprung up on the Internet that contain specialized or custom software packages not distributed as part of the official Linux distribution repository. The repository tools allow you to retrieve those packages as well.

The core tool used for working with Red Hat repositories is the *YUM* utility (short for YellowDog Update Manager, originally developed for the YellowDog Linux distribution). Its yum command allows you to query, install, and remove software packages on your system directly from an official Red Hat repository.

The yum command uses the /etc/yum.repos.d/ directory to hold files that list the different repositories it checks for packages. For a default CentOS system, that directory contains several repository files, as shown in Listing 2.12.

Listing 2.12: Viewing the /etc/yum.repos.d/ repository files on a CentOS distro

```
$ ls /etc/yum.repos.d/
CentOS-Base.repo        CentOS-CR.repo
CentOS-Debuginfo.repo   CentOS-fasttrack.repo
CentOS-Media.repo       CentOS-Sources.repo
CentOS-Vault.repo
$
```

Each file in the yum.repos.d folder contains information on a repository, such as its URL address and the location of additional package files within the repository. The yum program checks each of these defined repositories for the package requested on the command line.

The basic yum command syntax is

```
yum [OPTIONS] [COMMAND] [PACKAGE...]
```

The yum program is very versatile, and Table 2.4 shows the some of the commands you can use with it.

TABLE 2.4   The yum commands

Command	Description
check-update	Checks the repository for updates to installed packages
clean	Removes temporary files downloaded during installs
deplist	Displays dependencies for the specified package
groupinstall	Installs the specified package group
info	Displays information about the specified package
install	Installs the specified package
list	Displays information about installed packages
localinstall	Installs a package from a specified RPM file
localupdate	Updates the system from specified RPM files
provides	Shows to what package a file belongs
reinstall	Reinstalls the specified package
remove	Removes a package from the system
resolvedep	Displays packages matching the specified dependency
search	Searches repository package names and descriptions for specified keyword
shell	Enters yum command-line mode
update	Updates the specified package(s) to the latest version in the repository
upgrade	Updates specified package(s) but removes obsolete packages

Installing new applications is a breeze with yum as shown snipped in Listing 2.13.

Listing 2.13: Installing software with yum on a CentOS distro

```
# yum install emacs
[…]
Resolving Dependencies
--> Running transaction check
---> Package emacs.x86_64 1:24.3-22.el7 will be installed
--> Processing Dependency: emacs-common = 1:24.3-22.el7 for
package: 1:emacs-24.3-22.el7.x86_64
[…]
--> Running transaction check
---> Package ImageMagick.x86_64 0:6.7.8.9-16.el7_6 will be installed
[…]
--> Finished Dependency Resolution


Dependencies Resolved


================================================================================
 Package            Arch          Version            Repository       Size
================================================================================
Installing:
 emacs              x86_64        1:24.3-22.el7      base             2.9 M
Installing for dependencies:
 ImageMagick        x86_64        6.7.8.9-16.el7_6   updates          2.1 M
[…]
Transaction Summary
================================================================================
Install  1 Package (+8 Dependent packages)

Total download size: 26 M
Installed size: 92 M
Is this ok [y/d/N]: y
Downloading packages:
(1/9): OpenEXR-libs-1.7.1-7.el7.x86_64.rpm                    | 217 kB   00:01
[…]
(9/9): emacs-common-24.3-22.el7.x86_64.rpm                    |  20 MB   00:22
--------------------------------------------------------------------------------
Total                                              1.2 MB/s |  26 MB   00:22
```

```
Running transaction check
Running transaction test
Transaction test succeeded
Running transaction
[…]
  Installing : ImageMagick-6.7.8.9-16.el7_6.x86_64                      8/9
  Installing : 1:emacs-24.3-22.el7.x86_64                               9/9
[…]
  Verifying  : ImageMagick-6.7.8.9-16.el7_6.x86_64                      8/9
  Verifying  : 1:emacs-24.3-22.el7.x86_64                               9/9

Installed:
  emacs.x86_64 1:24.3-22.el7

Dependency Installed:
  ImageMagick.x86_64 0:6.7.8.9-16.el7_6    […]
  emacs-common.x86_64 1:24.3-22.el7        […]
  libXaw.x86_64 0:1.0.13-4.el7             […]
  libotf.x86_64 0:0.9.13-4.el7             […]

Complete!
#
```

One nice feature of yum is the ability to group packages together for distribution. Instead of having to download all of the packages needed for a specific environment (such as for a web server that uses the Apache, MySQL, and PHP servers), you can download the package group that bundles the packages together. Employ the yum grouplist command to see a list of the various package groups available, and use yum groupinstall *group-package-name* for an even easier way to get packages installed on your system.

 Recently, another RPM package management tool has been gaining in popularity. The *dnf* program (short for dandified yum) is included as part of the Fedora Linux distribution as a replacement for yum. As its name suggests, dnf provides some advanced features that yum is missing. One such feature is speeding up resolving dependency searches with library files.

Another nice feature of yum is the ability to reinstall software packages. If you find that a package file is missing or modified in some way, it can be easily fixed through a package reinstallation. A snipped example is shown in Listing 2.14.

Listing 2.14: Reinstalling software with the yum utility

```
# rpm -V emacs
missing      /usr/bin/emacs-24.3
#
# yum reinstall emacs
[…]
---> Package emacs.x86_64 1:24.3-22.el7 will be reinstalled
 […]
Total download size: 2.9 M
Installed size: 14 M
Is this ok [y/d/N]: y

[…]
Installed:
  emacs.x86_64 1:24.3-22.el7

Complete!
#
# rpm -V emacs

#
```

Notice in Listing 2.14 that the rpm -V emacs command discovers a missing file in the package. Using the yum reinstall feature quickly fixes the issue.

Removing a package with yum is just as easy as installing it. An example is shown snipped in Listing 2.15.

Listing 2.15: Removing software with the yum utility

```
# yum remove emacs
[…]
Remove  1 Package

Installed size: 14 M
Is this ok [y/N]: y
[…]
Removed:
  emacs.x86_64 1:24.3-22.el7

Complete!
#
```

Typically there is no need to modify the primary YUM configuration that is stored in the /etc/yum.conf file. This file contains settings (also called directives) that determine things such as where to record YUM log data. Although you can add third-party repositories by editing the primary configuration file or creating a /etc/yum.repos.d/ repository file manually, it is not recommended. The desired method is to install new repositories via RPM or YUM.

Using ZYpp

The openSUSE Linux distribution uses the RPM package management system and distributes software in .rpm files but doesn't use the yum or dnf tool. Instead, openSUSE has created its own package management tool called *ZYpp* (also called *libzypp*). Its zypper command allows you to query, install, and remove software packages on your system directly from an openSUSE repository. Table 2.5 lists the more commonly used zypper utility commands.

TABLE 2.5   The zypper commands

Command	Description
help	Displays overall general help information or help on a specified command
install	Installs the specified package
info	Displays information about the specified package
list-updates	Displays all available package updates for installed packages from the repository
lr	Displays repository information
packages	Lists all available packages or lists available packages from a specified repository
what-provides	Shows to what package a file belongs
refresh	Refreshes a repository's information
remove	Removes a package from the system
search	Searches for the specified package(s)
update	Updates the specified package(s) or if no package is specified, updates all currently installed packages to the latest version(s) in the repository
verify	Verifies that installed packages have their needed dependencies satisfied

For package installation, zypper operates in a similar manner to the yum utility. A snipped example is shown in Listing 2.16.

Listing 2.16: Installing software with the zypper utility

```
$ sudo zypper install emacs
[sudo] password for root:
[…]
Reading installed packages...
Resolving package dependencies...

The following 9 NEW packages are going to be installed:
  emacs emacs-info emacs-x11 etags libm17n0 libotf0 libXaw3d8 m17n-db
  m17n-db-lang

The following recommended package was automatically selected:
  m17n-db-lang

9 new packages to install.
Overall download size: 0 B. Already cached: 27.4 MiB. After the operation,
additional 111.6 MiB will be used.
Continue? [y/n/...? shows all options] (y): y

[…]
Checking for file conflicts: ...................................[done]
[…]
 (9/9) Installing: emacs-x11-25.3-lp150.2.3.1.x86_64 ..............[done]
$
```

The info command is helpful in that it displays information for the specified package as shown snipped in Listing 2.17.

Listing 2.17: Displaying package information with the zypper info command

```
$ zypper info emacs
[…]
Information for package emacs:
------------------------------
Repository     : openSUSE-Leap-15.0-Update
Name           : emacs
Version        : 25.3-lp150.2.3.1
Arch           : x86_64
```

```
Vendor          : openSUSE
Installed Size : 67.7 MiB
Installed       : Yes
Status          : up-to-date
Source package : emacs-25.3-lp150.2.3.1.src
Summary         : GNU Emacs Base Package
Description     :
    Basic package for the GNU Emacs editor. Requires emacs-x11 or
    emacs-nox.

$
```

The zypper utility is user-friendly and continually provides helpful messages to guide your package management process. For example, in Listing 2.18, the older method of determining what package a particular file belongs to is used (what-provides). In response, the zypper utility not only enacts the command but also provides information on the newer method to employ in the future.

Listing 2.18: Determining to which package a file belongs

```
$ which emacs
/usr/bin/emacs
$
$ zypper what-provides /usr/bin/emacs
Command 'what-provides' is replaced by 'search --provides --match-exact'.
See 'help search' for all available options.
Loading repository data...
Reading installed packages...

S  | Name  | Summary                 | Type
---+-------+-------------------------+--------
i+ | emacs | GNU Emacs Base Package | package
$
```

You can easily obtain help on the zypper tool through its man pages and interactively using the zypper help for general help or zypper help command for specific assistance.

In addition, the zypper utility allows you to shorten some of its commands. For example, you can shorten install to in, remove to re, and search to se, as shown in Listing 2.19.

Listing 2.19: Searching for a package with the zypper search command

```
$ zypper se nmap
Loading repository data...
```

```
Reading installed packages...

S | Name    | Summary                        | Type
--+---------+--------------------------------+--------
  | nmap    | Portscanner                    | package
  | nmapsi4 | A Graphical Front-End for Nmap | package
  | zenmap  | A Graphical Front-End for Nmap | package
$
```

Removing packages with zypper is simple as well. An example of the command, process, and utility's helpful messages is shown snipped in Listing 2.20.

Listing 2.20: Removing a package with the zypper remove command

```
$ sudo zypper remove emacs
[sudo] password for root:
[…]
The following application is going to be REMOVED:
  "GNU Emacs"

The following 2 packages are going to be REMOVED:
  emacs emacs-x11

2 packages to remove.
After the operation, 99.6 MiB will be freed.
Continue? [y/n/...? shows all options] (y): y
(1/2) Removing emacs-25.3-lp150.2.3.1.x86_64 ...........................[done]
(2/2) Removing emacs-x11-25.3-lp150.2.3.1.x86_64 ........................[done]
There are some running programs that might use files deleted by recent upgrade. You
may wish to check and restart some of them. Run 'zypper ps -s' to list these programs.
$
```

Managing software packages with RPM, YUM, and ZYpp is fairly easy once you understand when and how to use each utility. The same is true for Debian package management.

Using Debian Packages

As you can probably guess, the Debian package management system is mostly used on Debian-based Linux distros, such as Ubuntu. With this system you can install, modify, upgrade, and remove software packages. We'll explore this popular software package management system in this section.

Debian Package File Conventions

Debian bundles application files into a single .deb package file for distribution that uses the following filename format:

PACKAGE-NAME-VERSION-RELEASE_ARCHITECTURE.deb

This filenaming convention for .deb packages is very similar to the .rpm file format. However, in the *ARCHITECTURE*, you typically find amd64, denoting it was optimized for the AMD64/Intel64 CPU architecture. Sometimes all is used, indicating the package is architecturally neutral. A few .deb package files are shown in Listing 2.21.

Listing 2.21: Software packages with the .deb filenaming conventions

```
$ ls -1 *.deb
docker_1.5-1build1_amd64.deb
emacs_47.0_all.deb
openssh-client_1%3a7.6p1-4ubuntu0.3_amd64.deb
vim_2%3a8.0.1453-1ubuntu1_amd64.deb
zsh_5.4.2-3ubuntu3.1_amd64.deb
$
```

Keep in mind that packaging naming conventions are acceptable standards, but (within limits) do not have to be followed by the package developer. Thus, you may encounter variations.

If you want to obtain copies of Debian package files on a Debian-based distro, such as Ubuntu, employ the apt-get download command. For example, using super user privileges, type **sudo apt-get download vim** at the command line to download the vim Debian package file to your current working directory.

The *dpkg* Command Set

The core tool to use for handling .deb files is the *dpkg* program, which is a command-line utility that has options for installing, updating, and removing .deb package files on your Linux system. The basic format for the dpkg command is as follows:

dpkg [*OPTIONS*] *ACTION PACKAGE-FILE*

The *ACTION* parameter defines the action to be taken on the file. Table 2.6 lists the more common actions you'll need to use.

TABLE 2.6   The dpkg command actions

Short	Long	Description
-c	--contents	Displays the contents of a package file
-C	--audit	Searches for broken installed packages and suggests how to fix them
N/A	--configure	Reconfigures an installed package
N/A	--get-selections	Displays currently installed packages
-i	--install	Installs the package; if package is already installed, upgrades it
-I	--info	Displays information about an uninstalled package file
-l	--list	Lists all installed packages matching a specified pattern
-L	--listfiles	Lists the installed files associated with a package
-p	--print-avail	Displays information about an installed package
-P	--purge	Removes an installed package, including configuration files
-r	--remove	Removes an installed package but leaves the configuration files
-s	--status	Displays the status of the specified package
-S	--search	Locates the package that owns the specified files

Each action has a set of options that you can use to modify its basic behavior, such as forcing the overwrite of an already installed package or ignoring any dependency errors.

To use the dpkg program, you must have the .deb software package available on your system. Often you can find .deb versions of application packages ready for distribution on the application website. Also, most distributions maintain a central location for packages to download.

The Debian distribution also provides a central clearinghouse for Debian packages at www.debian.org/distrib/packages.

After you obtain the .deb package, you can look at the package's information stored in the file, including the version number and any dependencies, with the dpkg -I command. An example is shown snipped in Listing 2.22.

Listing 2.22: Looking at an uninstalled .deb package with the dpkg -I command

```
$ dpkg -I zsh_5.4.2-3ubuntu3.1_amd64.deb
 new Debian package, version 2.0.
 size 689912 bytes: control archive=2544 bytes.
    909 bytes,    20 lines        control
    3332 bytes,   42 lines        md5sums
[…]
Package: zsh
 Version: 5.4.2-3ubuntu3.1
 Architecture: amd64
 Maintainer: Ubuntu Developers <ubuntu-devel-discuss@lists.ubuntu.com>
 Installed-Size: 2070
 Depends: zsh-common (= 5.4.2-3ubuntu3.1), libc6 (>= 2.15),
libcap2 (>= 1:2.10), libtinfo5 (>= 6)
 Recommends: libc6 (>= 2.23), libncursesw5 (>= 6), libpcre3
 Suggests: zsh-doc
 Section: shells
 Priority: optional
 Homepage: https://www.zsh.org/
 Description: shell with lots of features
  Zsh is a UNIX command interpreter (shell) usable as an
[…]
 Original-Maintainer: Debian Zsh Maintainers <pkg-zsh-devel@li[…]
$
```

If you want to see the package file's contents, replace the -I option with the --contents switch. Be aware that you may need to pipe the output into a pager utility (see Chapter 1) for easier viewing.

When you determine you've got the right package, use dpkg with the -i action to install it, as shown in Listing 2.23. (Be aware that if the software is already installed, this process will upgrade it to the version in the package file.)

Listing 2.23: Installing a .deb package with the dpkg -i command

```
$ sudo dpkg -i zsh_5.4.2-3ubuntu3.1_amd64.deb
Selecting previously unselected package zsh.
(Reading database ... 171250 files and directories currently installed.)
```

```
Preparing to unpack zsh_5.4.2-3ubuntu3.1_amd64.deb ...
Unpacking zsh (5.4.2-3ubuntu3.1) ...
```
dpkg: dependency problems prevent configuration of zsh:
 zsh depends on zsh-common (= 5.4.2-3ubuntu3.1); however:
 Package zsh-common is not installed.

```
dpkg: error processing package zsh (--install):
 dependency problems - leaving unconfigured
Processing triggers for man-db (2.8.3-2ubuntu0.1) ...
Errors were encountered while processing:
 zsh
$
```

You can see in this example that the package management software checks to ensure that any required packages are installed and produces an error message if any are missing. This gives you a clue as to what other packages you need to install.

After installation you can view the package's status via the dpkg -s command. An example is shown snipped in Listing 2.24. Notice that the command's output shows the package is installed, as well as its version number and dependencies.

Listing 2.24: Displaying an installed package status with the dpkg -s command

```
$ dpkg -s zsh
Package: zsh
```
Status: install ok unpacked
```
Priority: optional
Section: shells
Installed-Size: 2070
Maintainer: Ubuntu Developers <ubuntu-devel-discuss@lists.ubuntu.com>
Architecture: amd64
Version: 5.4.2-3ubuntu3.1
Depends: zsh-common (= 5.4.2-3ubuntu3.1), libc6 (>= 2.15), libcap2 (>= 1:2.10),
libtinfo5 (>= 6)
Recommends: libc6 (>= 2.23), libncursesw5 (>= 6), libpcre3
Suggests: zsh-doc
Description: shell with lots of features
[…]
$
```

If you'd like to see all of the packages installed on your system, use the -l (lowercase L) option as shown snipped in Listing 2.25.

Listing 2.25: Displaying all installed packages with the dpkg -l command

```
$ dpkg -l
Desired=Unknown/Install/Remove/Purge/Hold
| Status=Not/Inst/Conf-files/Unpacked/halF-conf/Half-inst/trig-aWait/Trig
|/ Err?=(none)/Reinst-required (Status,Err: uppercase=bad)
||/ Name            Version        Architecture Description
+++-===============-=============-============-===============================
ii  accountsservic 0.6.45-1ubun amd64        query and manipulate accounts
ii  acl            2.2.52-3buil amd64        Access control list utilities
ii  acpi-support   0.142          amd64        scripts for handling ACPI
ii  acpid          1:2.0.28-1ub amd64        Advanced Config and Power
ii  adduser        3.116ubuntu1 all          add and remove users
[…]
iU  zsh            5.4.2-3ubunt amd64        shell with lots of features
$
```

Notice in Listing 2.25 that the installed packages have a status code before their name. The possible package status codes are shown in the first few lines as output by the dpkg command. For example, the last line that shows the zsh package displays the iU code. This means that while the package is installed (i), it is unpacked (U), but not configured, which is a problem. Earlier in Listing 2.23, we installed the packages, and the installation process denoted that a dependency, zsh-common, was missing.

> Imagine not having to deal with missing package dependencies! Well, a
> new trend in package management may do just that. It revolves around
> building software packages to include not only the primary application,
> but all its dependencies as well. One new package management system
> that employs this new and exciting method is Snappy for the Ubuntu dis-
> tribution. It uses the .snap file extension. The packages are called *snap
> packages*, and using Snappy requires installation of the snapd daemon.

For missing dependency problems, you can quickly check whether a particular package or library is installed via the dpkg -s action as shown snipped in Listing 2.26. Notice that as expected, the needed zsh-common package is not installed.

Listing 2.26: Displaying an uninstalled package status with the dpkg -s command

```
$ sudo dpkg -s zsh-common
dpkg-query: package 'zsh-common' is not installed and
no information is available
[…]
$
```

If you need to remove a package, you have two options. The -r action removes the package but keeps any configuration and data files associated with the package installed. This is useful if you're just trying to reinstall an existing package and don't want to have to reconfigure things.

If you really do want to remove the entire package, use the -P option, which purges the entire package, including configuration files and data files from the system. An example of this is shown in Listing 2.27.

Listing 2.27: Purging an installed package with the dpkg -P command

```
$ sudo dpkg -P zsh
(Reading database ... [...]
Removing zsh (5.4.2-3ubuntu3.1) ...
Purging configuration files for zsh (5.4.2-3ubuntu3.1) ...
Processing triggers for man-db (2.8.3-2ubuntu0.1) ...
$
```

Be very careful with the -p and -P options. They're easy to mix up. The -p option lists the packages, whereas the -P option purges the packages. Quite a difference!

The dpkg tool gives you direct access to the package management system, making it easier to install and manage applications on your Debian-based system.

Looking at the APT Suite

The *Advanced Package Tool (APT)* suite is used for working with Debian repositories. This includes the *apt-cache* program that provides information about the package database, and the *apt-get* program that does the work of installing, updating, and removing packages.

Just like dnf for RPM package management, Debian package management also has a new tool that is gaining in popularity — *apt*. (This utility should not be confused with the APT suite or the Python wrapper used on Linux Mint by the same name.) The new apt tool provides improved user interface features and simpler commands for managing Debian packages. In addition, apt uses easier-to-understand action names, such as full-upgrade. Its quick rise in popularity has gained it enough attention to land it on the LPIC-1 certification exam.

The APT suite of tools relies on the /etc/apt/sources.list file to identify the locations of where to look for repositories. By default, each Linux distribution enters its own repository location in that file. However, you can include additional repository locations if you install third-party applications not supported by the distribution.

Using *apt-cache*

Here are a few useful command options in the apt-cache program for displaying information about packages:

- depends: Displays the dependencies required for the package
- pkgnames: Shows all the packages installed on the system
- search: Displays the name of packages matching the specified item
- showpkg: Lists information about the specified package
- stats: Displays package statistics for the system
- unmet: Shows any unmet dependencies for all installed packages or the specified installed package

Typically you can issue the apt-cache commands without employing super user privileges. One handy command is apt-cache pkgnames, which displays all installed Debian packages on the system. An example is shown snipped in Listing 2.28. Notice that the pipe symbol (|) and the grep command (both covered in Chapter 1) are employed to quickly determine if any nano packages are currently installed.

Listing 2.28: Displaying all installed packages with the apt-cache pkgnames command

```
$ apt-cache pkgnames | grep ^nano
nano
[…]
nano-tiny
[…]
$
```

If you need to look for a particular package to install, the apt-cache search command is useful. A snipped example is shown in Listing 2.29.

Listing 2.29: Searching for a package with the apt-cache search command

```
$ apt-cache search zsh
zsh - shell with lots of features
zsh-common - architecture independent files for Zsh
zsh-dev - shell with lots of features (development files)
zsh-doc - zsh documentation - info/HTML format
[…]
$
```

When you have found the desired package, peruse its detailed information via the apt-cache showpkg command. The snipped example in Listing 2.30 provides data on the zsh package.

Listing 2.30: Displaying package information with the apt-cache showpkg command

```
$ apt-cache showpkg zsh
Package: zsh
Versions:
5.4.2-3ubuntu3.1 […]
[…]
Reverse Depends:
  usrmerge,zsh 5.2-4~
  zsh-static,zsh
  zsh:i386,zsh
  zsh-common,zsh 5.0.2-1
[…]
Dependencies:
5.4.2-3ubuntu3.1 - […]
5.4.2-3ubuntu3 - […]
Provides:
5.4.2-3ubuntu3.1 -
5.4.2-3ubuntu3 -
Reverse Provides:
$
```

The apt-cache utility provides several ways to discover package information. But you need another program to handle other package management functions.

Using *apt-get*

The workhorse of the APT suite of tools is the apt-get program. It's what you use to install, update, and remove packages from a Debian package repository. Table 2.7 lists the apt-get commands.

TABLE 2.7   The apt-get program action commands

Action	Description
autoclean	Removes information about packages that are no longer in the repository
check	Checks the package management database for inconsistencies
clean	Cleans up the database and any temporary download files
dist-upgrade	Upgrades all packages, but monitors for package dependencies

Action	Description
dselect-upgrade	Completes any package changes left undone
install	Installs or updates a package and updates the package management database
remove	Removes a package from the package management database
source	Retrieves the source code package for the specified package
update	Retrieves updated information about packages in the repository
upgrade	Upgrades all installed packages to newest versions

Installing a new package from the repository is as simple as specifying the package name with the install action. A snipped example of installing the zsh package with apt-get is shown in Listing 2.31.

Listing 2.31: Installing a package with the apt-get install command

```
$ sudo apt-get install zsh
Reading package lists... Done
Building dependency tree
Reading state information... Done
The following additional packages will be installed:
  zsh-common
Suggested packages:
  zsh-doc
The following NEW packages will be installed:
  zsh zsh-common
0 upgraded, 2 newly installed, 0 to remove and 0 not upgraded.
[...]
Unpacking zsh (5.4.2-3ubuntu3.1) ...
Setting up zsh-common (5.4.2-3ubuntu3.1) ...
Processing triggers for man-db (2.8.3-2ubuntu0.1) ...
Setting up zsh (5.4.2-3ubuntu3.1) ...
$
```

If any dependencies are required, the apt-get program retrieves those as well and installs them automatically. Notice in Listing 2.31 that the zsh-common package, which is a zsh dependency, is also installed.

The dist-upgrade action provides a great way to keep your entire Debian-based system up-to-date with the packages released to the distribution repository. Running that command will ensure that your packages have all the security and bug fixes installed and will not break packages due to unmet dependencies. However, that also means that you fully trust the distribution developers to put only tested packages in the repository. Occasionally a package may make its way into the repository before being fully tested and cause issues.

The install action does more than install packages. You can upgrade individual packages as well. An example of upgrading the emacs software is shown snipped in Listing 2.32.

Listing 2.32: Upgrading a package with the apt-get install command

```
$ sudo apt-get install emacs
Reading package lists... Done
Building dependency tree
Reading state information... Done
The following packages will be upgraded:
  emacs
1 upgraded, 0 newly installed, 0 to remove and 0 not upgraded.
1 not fully installed or removed.
Need to get 1,748 B of archives.
After this operation, 17.4 kB disk space will be freed.
[…]
Preparing to unpack .../archives/emacs_47.0_all.deb ...
Unpacking emacs (47.0) over (46.1) ...
Setting up emacs (47.0) ...
$
```

The APT suite is helpful in taking care of software package management. You just need to remember when to use apt-cache and when to use apt-get.

On modern Ubuntu distro versions, unattended upgrades are configured. This allows automatic security upgrades to software and requires no human intervention. If you want to turn this off, change the APT::Periodic::Update-Package-Lists directive in the /etc/apt/apt.conf.d/10periodic file from 1 to 0. Find out more about this feature by typing **man unattended-upgrade** at the command line.

Reconfiguring Packages

Typically everyone needs to modify configuration files to meet the needs of their system and users. However, if you make changes that cause serious unexpected problems, you may want to return to the package's initial installation state.

If the package required configuration when it was installed, you are in luck! Instead of purging the package and reinstalling it, you can employ the handy *dpkg-reconfigure* tool.

To use it, just type the command, followed by the name of the package you need to reconfigure. For example, if you needed to fix the cups (printing software covered in Chapter 6) utility, you would enter

```
sudo dpkg-reconfigure cups
```

This command will throw you into a text-based menu screen that will lead you through a series of simple configuration questions. An example of this screen is shown in Figure 2.1.

FIGURE 2.1   Using the dpkg-reconfigure utility

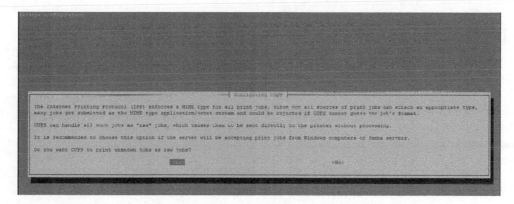

It's a good idea to employ the debconf-show utility, too. This tool allows you to view the package's configuration. An example is shown in Listing 2.33.

Listing 2.33: Displaying a package's configuration with the debconf-show utility

```
$ sudo debconf-show cups
* cupsys/backend: lpd, socket, usb, snmp, dnssd
* cupsys/raw-print: true
$
```

It would be worthwhile to run the debconf-show command and record the settings before and after running the dpkg-reconfigure utility. That way, you'll have documentation on the configuration before and after the package is reconfigured.

Another interesting trend in package management includes not only what is in the package but how the package's application is executed. Using virtualization concepts (covered in Chapter 5), Flatpak combines package management, software deployment, and application sandboxing (isolated in a separate environment) all together in one utility. It provides all the needed package dependencies as well as a sandbox for application execution. Thus, you can run the application in a confined virtualized environment, protecting the rest of your system from any application effects.

Managing Shared Libraries

In managing your system's applications, you need to understand libraries and, more specifically, shared libraries. In this section, we'll take a look at a few ways to oversee these resources.

Library Principles

A system *library* is a collection of items, such as program functions. *Functions* are self-contained code modules that perform a specific task within an application, such as opening and reading a data file.

The benefit of splitting functions into separate library files is that multiple applications that use the same functions can share the same library files. These files full of functions make it easier to distribute applications, but also make it more complicated to keep track of what library files are installed with which applications.

Linux supports two different flavors of libraries. One is static libraries (also called *statically linked libraries*) that are copied into an application when it is compiled. The other flavor is *shared libraries* (also called *dynamic libraries*) where the library functions are copied into memory and bound to the application when the program is launched. This is called *loading a library*.

If you have ever worked with Microsoft's Windows Server, you most likely have dealt with dynamic linked libraries (DLLs) files that have the .dll file extension. DLLs are similar to Linux shared libraries.

On Linux, like application packages, library files have naming conventions. A shared library file employs the following filename format:

lib*LIBRARYNAME*.so.*VERSION*

Keep in mind that just as with packages, these are naming guidelines (similar to pirate codes) and not laws.

Locating Library Files

When a program is using a shared function, the system will search for the function's library file in a specific order; looking in directories stored within the

1. LD_LIBRARY_PATH environment variable
2. Program's PATH environment variable
3. /etc/ld.so.conf.d/ folder
4. /etc/ld.so.conf file
5. /lib*/ and /usr/lib*/ folders

Be aware that the order of #3 and #4 may be flip-flopped on your system. This is because the /etc/ld.so.conf file loads configuration files from the /etc/ld.so.conf.d/ folder. An example of this file from a CentOS distro is shown (along with files residing in the /etc/ld.so.conf.d directory) in Listing 2.34.

Listing 2.34: Displaying the /etc/ld.so.conf file contents on CentOS

```
$ cat /etc/ld.so.conf
include ld.so.conf.d/*.conf
$
$ ls -1 /etc/ld.so.conf.d/
dyninst-x86_64.conf
kernel-3.10.0-862.9.1.el7.x86_64.conf
kernel-3.10.0-862.el7.x86_64.conf
kernel-3.10.0-957.10.1.el7.x86_64.conf
libiscsi-x86_64.conf
mariadb-x86_64.conf
$
```

If another library is located in the /etc/ld.so.conf file and it is listed above the include operation, then the system will search that library directory before the files in the /etc/ld.so.conf.d/ folder. This is something to keep in mind if you are troubleshooting library problems.

 It is important to know that the /lib*/ folders, such as /lib/ and /lib64/, are for libraries needed by system utilities that reside in the /bin/ and /sbin/ directories, whereas the /usr/lib*/ folders, such as /usr/lib/ and /usr/lib64/, are for libraries needed by additional software, such as database utilities like MariaDB.

If you peer inside one of the files within the /etc/ld.so.conf.d/ folder, you'll find that it contains a shared library directory name. Within that particular directory are the shared library files needed by an application. An example is shown in Listing 2.35.

Listing 2.35: Looking at the /etc/ld.so.conf.d/ file contents on CentOS

```
$ cat /etc/ld.so.conf.d/mariadb-x86_64.conf
/usr/lib64/mysql
$
$ ls /usr/lib64/mysql
libmysqlclient.so.18  libmysqlclient.so.18.0.0  plugin
$
```

Loading Dynamically

When a program is started, the *dynamic linker* (also called the *dynamic linker/loader*) is responsible for finding the program's needed library functions. After they are located, the dynamic linker will copy them into memory and bind them to the program.

Historically, the dynamic linker executable has a name like ld.so and ld-linux.so*, but its actual name and location on your Linux distribution may vary. You can employ the locate utility (covered in more detail in Chapter 4) to find its actual name and location, as shown snipped in Listing 2.36 on a CentOS distribution.

Listing 2.36: Locating the dynamic linker executable on CentOS

```
$ locate ld-linux
/usr/lib64/ld-linux-x86-64.so.2
/usr/share/man/man8/ld-linux.8.gz
/usr/share/man/man8/ld-linux.so.8.gz
$
```

When you've located the dynamic linker utility, you can try it out by using it to manually load a program and its libraries (it will run the program as well). An example of this on a CentOS distribution and employing the echo utility is shown in Listing 2.37.

Listing 2.37: Loading and running the echo command with the dynamic linker utility

```
$ /usr/lib64/ld-linux-x86-64.so.2 /usr/bin/echo "Hello World"
Hello World
$
```

Unfortunately in Listing 2.37, you cannot see all the shared libraries the dynamic linker loaded when it initiated the echo utility. However, if desired, you can use the ldd command to view a program's needed libraries, and it is covered later in this chapter.

Library Management Commands

Library directories are not the only resources for managing and troubleshooting application libraries. There are also a few useful tools you can employ. Along with those utilities are a few additional library concepts you should understand.

Managing the Library Cache

The *library cache* is a catalog of library directories and all the various libraries contained within them. The system reads this cache file to quickly find needed libraries when it is loading programs. This makes it much faster for loading libraries than searching through all the possible directory locations for a particular required library file.

When new libraries or library directories are added to the system, this library cache file must be updated. However, it is not a simple text file you can just edit. Instead, you have to employ the *ldconfig* command.

Fortunately, when you are installing software via one of the package managers, the ldconfig command is typically run automatically. Thus, the library cache is updated without any needed intervention from you. Unfortunately, you'll have to manually run the ldconfig command for any applications you are developing yourself.

 **Real World Scenario**

Developing New Libraries

Imagine you're on an open source development team that is creating a new dynamic function library for a Linux app, which will be offered in your favorite distribution's repository. The library file is stored in a development directory (/home/devops/library), and it is ready for testing.

To accommodate testing of the newly created program library, you'll need to modify the LD_LIBRARY_PATH environment variable by including the program in its definition as such:

export LD_LIBRARY_PATH=$LD_LIBRARY_PATH:/home/devops/library/

After testing and refinement of the new function library is completed, move the library file to its production folder (most likely somewhere in the /usr/lib*/ directory tree). And then create a library configuration file within the /etc/ld.so.conf.d/ directory that points to the library file's location.

When those items are completed, you'll need to manually update the library cache. Using super user privileges, issue the ldconfig command to load the new library into the catalog.

If you are troubleshooting the library cache, you can easily see what library files are cataloged by using the ldconfig -v command. An example of this is shown in Listing 2.38. The example command employs a pipe and the grep utility to search for a particular library, as well as redirects any errors into the black hole (these concepts were covered in Chapter 1).

Listing 2.38: Listing files in the library cache via the /ldconfig -v command

```
$ ldconfig -v 2> /dev/null | grep libmysqlclient
        libmysqlclient.so.18 -> libmysqlclient.so.18.0.0
$
```

Troubleshooting Shared Library Dependencies

The *ldd* utility can come in handy if you need to track down missing library files for an application. It displays a list of the library files required for the specified application. An example is shown using the echo command's file in Listing 2.39.

Listing 2.39: Using the ldd command to view an application's libraries

```
$ ldd /usr/bin/echo
        linux-vdso.so.1 =>  (0x00007ffd3bd64000)
        libc.so.6 => /lib64/libc.so.6 (0x00007f7c39eff000)
        /lib64/ld-linux-x86-64.so.2 (0x00007f7c3a2cc000)
$
```

The ldd utility output shows the echo program requires two external library files: the standard linux-vdso.so.1 and libc.so.6 files. The ldd utility also shows where those files are found on the Linux system, which can be helpful when troubleshooting issues with applications involving their library files.

> Sometimes a library is dependent on another library. So when you are troubleshooting a missing library file, you may need to use the ldd command on the libraries listed for the application in order to get to the root of the problem.

Managing Processes

Linux must keep track of lots of different programs, all running at the same time. This section covers how Linux keeps track of all the active applications, how you can peek at that information, as well as how to use command-line tools to manage the running programs.

Examining Process Lists

At any given time lots of active programs are running on the Linux system. Linux calls each running program a *process*. The Linux system assigns each process a *process ID (PID)* and manages how the process uses memory and CPU time based on that PID.

When a Linux system first boots, it starts a special process called the *init process*. The init process is the core of the Linux system; it runs scripts that start all of the other processes running on the system, including the processes that start the text consoles and graphical windows you use to log in (see Chapter 5).

Viewing Processes with *ps*

You can look at processes that are currently running on the Linux system by using the *ps* command. The default output of this command is shown in Listing 2.40.

Listing 2.40: Viewing your processes with the ps command

```
$ ps
  PID TTY          TIME CMD
 1615 pts/0    00:00:00 bash
 1765 pts/0    00:00:00 ps
$
```

By default, the ps program shows only the processes that are running in the current user shell. In this example, we only had the command prompt shell running (Bash) and, of course, the ps command.

The basic output of the ps command shows the PID assigned to each process, the terminal (TTY) that they were started from, and the CPU time that the process has used.

The tricky feature of the ps command (and the reason that makes it so complicated) is that at one time there were two versions of it in Linux. Each version had its own set of command-line options controlling the information it displayed. That made switching between systems somewhat complicated.

The GNU developers decided to merge the two versions into a single ps program, and of course, they added some additional switches of their own. Thus, the current ps program used in Linux supports three different styles of command-line options:

- Unix-style options, which are preceded by a dash

- Berkley Software Distribution (BSD)–style options, which are not preceded by a dash

- GNU long options, which are preceded by a double dash

This makes for lots of possible switches to use with the ps command. You can consult the ps manual page to see all possible options that are available. Most Linux administrators have their own set of commonly used switches that they remember for extracting pertinent information. For example, if you need to see every process running on the system, use the Unix-style -ef option combination, as shown snipped in Listing 2.41.

Listing 2.41: Viewing processes with the ps command and Unix-style options

```
$ ps -ef
UID        PID  PPID  C STIME TTY          TIME CMD
root         1     0  0 10:18 ?        00:00:03 /sbin/init splash
root         2     0  0 10:18 ?        00:00:00 [kthreadd]
root         4     2  0 10:18 ?        00:00:00 [kworker/0:0H]
```

Listing 2.41: Viewing processes with the ps command and Unix-style options *(continued)*

```
root         5     2  0 10:18 ?        00:00:00 [kworker/u2:0]
root         6     2  0 10:18 ?        00:00:00 [mm_percpu_wq]
root         7     2  0 10:18 ?        00:00:00 [ksoftirqd/0]
root         8     2  0 10:18 ?        00:00:00 [rcu_sched]
root         9     2  0 10:18 ?        00:00:00 [rcu_bh]
[…]
$
```

This format provides some useful information about the processes running:

- **UID:** The user responsible for running the process
- **PID:** The process ID of the process
- **PPID:** The process ID of the parent process (if the process was started by another process)
- **C:** The processor utilization over the lifetime of the process
- **STIME:** The system time when the process was started
- **TTY:** The terminal device from which the process was started
- **TIME:** The cumulative CPU time required to run the process
- **CMD:** The name of the program that was started in the process

Also notice in the -ef output that some process command names are shown in brackets. That indicates processes that are currently swapped out from physical memory into virtual memory on the hard drive.

Understanding Process States

Processes that are swapped into virtual memory are called *sleeping*. Often the Linux kernel places a process into sleep mode while the process is waiting for an event.

When the event triggers, the kernel sends the process a signal. If the process is in *interruptible sleep* mode, it will receive the signal immediately and wake up. If the process is in *uninterruptible sleep* mode, it only wakes up based on an external event, such as hardware becoming available. It will save any other signals sent while it was sleeping and act on them once it wakes up.

If a process has ended but its parent process hasn't acknowledged the termination signal because it's sleeping, the process is considered a *zombie*. It's stuck in a limbo state between running and terminating until the parent process acknowledges the termination signal.

Selecting Processes with *ps*

When troubleshooting or monitoring a system, it's helpful to narrow the ps utility's focus by viewing only a selected subset of processes. You may just want to view processes using a particular terminal or ones belonging to a specific group. Table 2.8 provides several ps command options you can employ to limit what is displayed. Keep in mind that these are not all the various selection switches available.

TABLE 2.8   Some ps program selection options

Option(s)	Description
a	Display every process on the system associated with a tty terminal
-A, -e	Display every process on the system
-C *CommandList*	Only display processes running a command in the *CommandList*
-g *GIDList*, or -group *GIDList*	Only display processes whose current effective group is in *GIDList*
-G *GIDList*, or -Group *GIDList*	Only display processes whose current real group is in *GIDList*
-N	Display every process except selected processes
p *PIDList*, -p *PIDList* or --pid *PIDList*	Only display *PIDList* processes
-r	Only display selected processes that are in a state of running
-t *ttyList*, or --tty *ttyList*	List every process associated with the *ttyList* terminals
-T	List every process associated with the current tty terminal
-u *UserList*, or --user *UserList*	Only display processes whose effective user (username or UID) is in *UserList*
-U *UserList*, or --User *UserList*	Only display processes whose real user (username or UID) is in *UserList*
x	Remove restriction of "associated with a tty terminal"; typically used with the a option

Notice that in Table 2.8 groups and users are designated as real or effective. Real indicates that this is the user or group the account is associated with when logging into the system and/or the primary account's group. Effective indicates that the user or group is using a temporary alternative user or group identification, as in the case of SUID and GUID permissions (covered in Chapter 10). Thus, if you want to make sure you see every process associated with a particular user or group, it's best to employ both the effective and real options. An example is shown in Listing 2.42.

Listing 2.42: Viewing effective and real username processes with the ps command

```
$ ps -u Christine -U Christine
  PID TTY          TIME CMD
 7802 ?        00:00:00 systemd
 7803 ?        00:00:00 (sd-pam)
 7876 ?        00:00:00 sshd
 7877 pts/0    00:00:00 bash
 7888 pts/0    00:00:00 ps
$
```

Viewing Processes with *top*

The ps command is a great way to get a snapshot of the processes running on the system, but sometimes you need to see more information. For example, if you're trying to find trends about processes that are frequently swapped in and out of memory, it's hard to do that with the ps command.

The *top* command can solve this problem. It displays process information similar to the ps command, but it does it in real-time mode. Figure 2.2 shows a snapshot of the top command in action.

FIGURE 2.2   The output of the top command

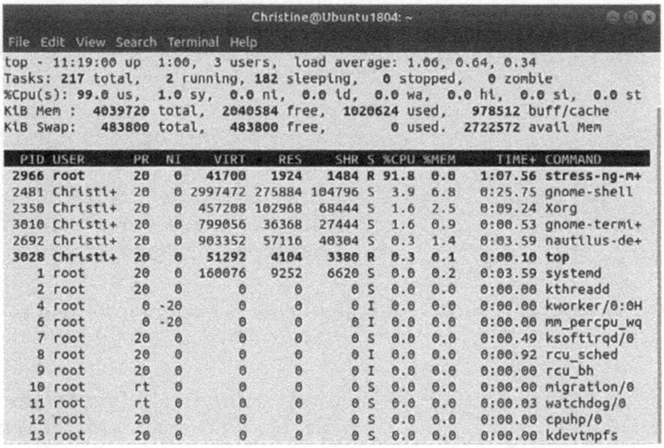

The first section of the top output shows general system information. The first line shows the current time, how long the system has been up, the number of users logged in, and the load average on the system.

The load average appears as three numbers: the 1-minute, 5-minute, and 15-minute load averages. The higher the values, the more load the system is experiencing. It's not uncommon for the 1-minute load value to be high for short bursts of activity. If the 15-minute load value is high, your system may be in trouble.

For a quick look at system load averages, employ the *uptime* command:

```
$ uptime
 11:19:43 up  1:01,  3 users,  load average: 1.03, 0.69, 0.37
$
```

It provides the exact same system load average information as does the top utility as well as data on how long the Linux system has been running.

The top utility's second line shows general process information (called tasks in top): how many processes are running, sleeping, stopped, or in a zombie state.

The next line shows general CPU information. The top display breaks down the CPU utilization into several categories depending on the owner of the process (user versus system processes) and the state of the processes (running, idle, or waiting).

Following that, in the top utility's output there are two lines that detail the status of the system memory. The first line shows the status of the physical memory in the system, how much total memory there is, how much is currently being used, and how much is free. The second memory line shows the status of the swap memory area in the system (if any is installed), with the same information.

For a quick look at memory usage, employ the *free* command:

```
$ free -h
              total        used        free      shared  buff/cache   available
Mem:           3.9G        1.0G        2.2G         30M        710M        2.6G
Swap:          472M          0B        472M
$
```

It provides similar memory information as does the top utility, but you have a wider choice of options. For example, the -h switch (human read-able), as shown in the proceeding example, adds unit labels for easier reading.

Finally, the next top utility section shows a detailed list of the currently running processes, with some information columns that should look familiar from the ps command output:

- **PID:** The process ID of the process
- **USER:** The username of the owner of the process
- **PR:** The priority of the process
- **NI:** The nice value of the process
- **VIRT:** The total amount of virtual memory used by the process
- **RES:** The amount of physical memory the process is using

- **SHR:** The amount of memory the process is sharing with other processes
- **S:** The process status (D = interruptible sleep, I = idle, R = running, S = sleeping, T = traced or stopped, and Z = zombie)
- **%CPU:** The share of CPU time that the process is using
- **%MEM:** The share of available physical memory the process is using
- **TIME+:** The total CPU time the process has used since starting
- **COMMAND:** The command-line name of the process (program started)

By default, when you start top, it sorts the processes based on the %CPU value. You can change the sort order by using one of several interactive commands. Each interactive command is a single character you can press while top is running and changes the behavior of the program. These commands are shown in Table 2.9.

TABLE 2.9   The top interactive commands

Command	Description
1	Toggles the single CPU and Symmetric Multiprocessor (SMP) state
b	Toggles the bolding of important numbers in the tables
I	Toggles Irix/Solaris mode
z	Configures color for the table
l	Toggles display of the load average information line
t	Toggles display of the CPU information line
m	Toggles display of the MEM and SWAP information lines
f	Adds or removes different information columns
o	Changes the display order of information columns
F or 0	Selects a field on which to sort the processes (%CPU by default)
< or >	Moves the sort field one column left (<) or right (>)
R	Toggles normal or reverse sort order
h	Toggles showing of threads
c	Toggles showing of the command name or the full command line (including parameters) of processes

Command	Description
i	Toggles showing of idle processes
S	Toggles showing of the cumulative CPU time or relative CPU time
x	Toggles highlighting of the sort field
y	Toggles highlighting of running tasks
z	Toggles color and mono mode
u	Shows processes for a specific user
n or #	Sets the number of processes to display
k	Kills a specific process (only if process owner or if root user)
r	Changes the priority (renice) of a specific process (only if process owner or if root user)
d or s	Changes the update interval (default three seconds)
W	Writes current settings to a configuration file
q	Exits the top command

You have lots of control over the output of the top command. Use the F or O command to toggle which field the sort order is based on. You can also use the r interactive command to reverse the current sorting. Using this tool, you can often find offending processes that have taken over your system.

A handy little utility for monitoring process information is the *watch* command. To use it, you enter **watch** and follow it by a command you'd like to enact over and over again. By default watch will reissue the command every two seconds. For example, you can type **watch uptime** to only monitor the system load. But you aren't limited to just process tracking commands. You can monitor a directory's changes in real time and more. See the watch utility's man pages for more information.

Employing Multiple Screens

If your Linux system has a GUI, it's simple to open multiple terminal emulators and arrange them side-by-side to monitor processes and enact commands, all while keeping an eye on additional items. However, if you are limited to using terminals in a nongraphical environment, you can still open window sessions side-by-side to perform multiple operations and monitor their displays. This is accomplished through a *terminal multiplexer*. Two popular multiplexers we'll cover in this section are screen and tmux.

Multiplexing with *screen*

The *screen* utility (also called *GNU Screen*) is often available in a distribution's repository, but typically it is not installed by default. After you install it, you can get started by typing **screen** at the command line to create your first window. A "welcome" display will ordinarily appear as shown in Figure 2.3.

FIGURE 2.3   The screen command's "welcome" display

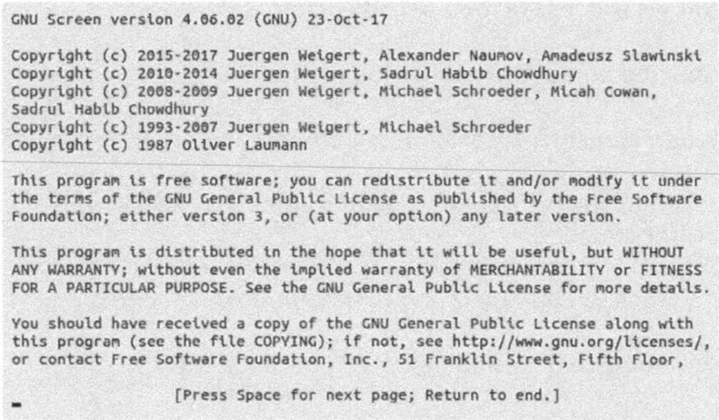

```
GNU Screen version 4.06.02 (GNU) 23-Oct-17

Copyright (c) 2015-2017 Juergen Weigert, Alexander Naumov, Amadeusz Slawinski
Copyright (c) 2010-2014 Juergen Weigert, Sadrul Habib Chowdhury
Copyright (c) 2008-2009 Juergen Weigert, Michael Schroeder, Micah Cowan,
Sadrul Habib Chowdhury
Copyright (c) 1993-2007 Juergen Weigert, Michael Schroeder
Copyright (c) 1987 Oliver Laumann

This program is free software; you can redistribute it and/or modify it under
the terms of the GNU General Public License as published by the Free Software
Foundation; either version 3, or (at your option) any later version.

This program is distributed in the hope that it will be useful, but WITHOUT
ANY WARRANTY; without even the implied warranty of MERCHANTABILITY or FITNESS
FOR A PARTICULAR PURPOSE. See the GNU General Public License for more details.

You should have received a copy of the GNU General Public License along with
this program (see the file COPYING); if not, see http://www.gnu.org/licenses/,
or contact Free Software Foundation, Inc., 51 Franklin Street, Fifth Floor,

               [Press Space for next page; Return to end.]
```

After you press the Enter key, a shell provides a command prompt. While it's a little hard to tell you are inside a screen window by using commands like ps, the screen -ls command and the w command can help, as shown in Listing 2.43.

Listing 2.43: Viewing your screen window with the screen -ls and w commands

```
$ ps
  PID TTY          TIME CMD
 9151 pts/5    00:00:00 bash
 9162 pts/5    00:00:00 ps
$
$ screen -ls
There is a screen on:
        9150.pts-0.Ubuntu1804   (04/16/2019 05:09:43 PM)         (Attached)
1 Socket in /run/screen/S-Christine.
$
$ w
 17:19:39 up  4:34,  2 users,  load average: 0.71, 0.54, 0.38
```

```
USER      TTY      FROM            LOGIN@   IDLE   JCPU   PCPU WHAT
Christin pts/0    192.168.0.101   16:14    2.00s  0.14s  0.00s screen
Christin pts/5    :pts/0:S.0      17:09    2.00s  0.07s  0.00s w
$
```

Notice the output from the screen -ls command displays an Attached window. The ID number in this case is 9150 (which also happens to be its PID). The w command's output shows two logged-in users; one is using the screen command, and the other is using the w command. The first user issued the screen command that created a second user process. The FROM column for the second user's process shows that this user was employing the pts/0 terminal and is now residing in screen window 0 (s.0) on the pts/5 terminal.

 A pts terminal is a pseudo-terminal. The /# after pts indicates which pseudo-terminal the user is employing. For example, pts/5 means that pseudo-terminal #5 is in use. You'll often see these terminal types when using a terminal emulator within a GUI, but they may also be used when using OpenSSH to reach and log into a Linux system, as is the case in this section.

The neat thing about the screen window is that you can issue a command within the window, detach from the window, and come back to it later, causing no ill effects on the command running in that window. To detach from a screen window, press Ctrl+A and then the D key. The screen -ls command will then display your detached window session. An example is shown in Listing 2.44.

Listing 2.44: Displaying a detached screen window with the screen -ls command

```
[detached from 9394.pts-0.Ubuntu1804]
$
$ screen -ls

There is a screen on:
        9394.pts-0.Ubuntu1804   (04/16/2019 05:42:45 PM)         (Detached)
1 Socket in /run/screen/S-Christine.
$
```

To reattach to the screen, you need to employ the screen -r screen-id command. Using the window screen in Listing 2.44, you would type **screen -r 9394** at the command line.

You can also split a window screen up into multiple windows, called *focuses*. To do this and to control the screen window(s), press the Ctrl+A key combination (called a *prefix shortcut*) and follow it with an additional key or key combination. A few of these additional key or key combinations are shown in Table 2.10.

TABLE 2.10   The screen utility prefix shortcut Ctrl+A commands

Key/Key Combination	Description
\	Kill all of a processes' windows and terminate screen
Shift+|	Split current screen window vertically into two focuses
Tab	Jump to next window focus
D	Detach from current screen window
K	Kill current window
N	Move to next screen window
P	Move to previous screen window
Shift+S	Split current screen window horizontally into two focuses

A handy setup to have is a screen window with three focuses, allowing you to monitor two items and issue commands from the third focus. To accomplish this, after logging into a terminal, do the following:

1. Type **screen** to create the first window screen.

2. Press the Enter key to exit the Welcome screen, if one is shown.

3. Issue your desired monitoring command, such as **top**.

4. Press the Ctrl+A prefix and then the Shift+S key combinations to split the window into two regions (focuses).

5. Press the Ctrl+A prefix and then the Tab key to jump to the bottom focus. You will not receive a shell prompt, because there is currently no window screen in this focus.

6. Press the Ctrl+A prefix and then the C key to create a window within the bottom focus. You should now have a command-line prompt.

7. Issue a monitoring command of your choice.

8. Press the Ctrl+A prefix and then the | key to split the current window vertically. Now the focus is in the lower-left window.

9. Press the Ctrl+A prefix and then the Tab key to jump to the lower-right focus. You will not receive a shell prompt, because there is currently no window screen in this focus.

10. Press the Ctrl+A prefix and then the C key to create a window within the lower-right focus. You should now have a command-line prompt.

11. Issue any commands of your choice in this third window focus.

12. After you are done using this three-way split window, press the Ctrl+A key combination and then the \ key. The screen command will ask if you want to quit and kill all your windows. Type **Y** and press Enter to enact the command.

In Figure 2.4, we created a three-focus monitoring window using the previous steps. In addition, we issued a stress test on the system's CPU and memory by installing and running the stress-ng utility.

FIGURE 2.4   A three-focus monitoring window using the screen utility

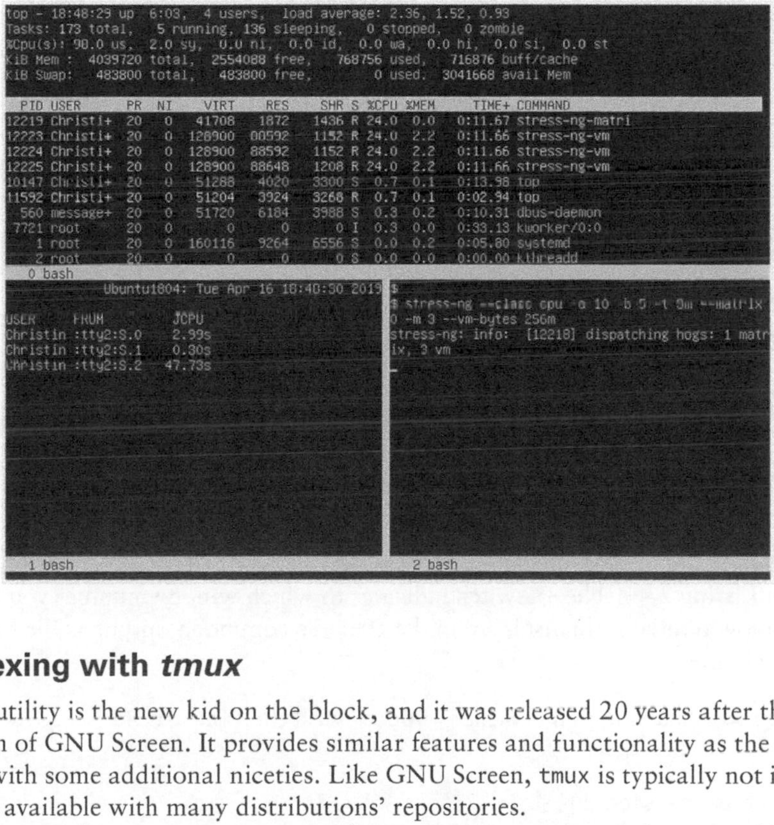

Multiplexing with *tmux*

The *tmux* utility is the new kid on the block, and it was released 20 years after the initial distribution of GNU Screen. It provides similar features and functionality as the screen program, with some additional niceties. Like GNU Screen, tmux is typically not installed by default but available with many distributions' repositories.

After you install it, you can get started by typing **tmux new** at the command line to create your first window. You immediately receive a shell prompt and can begin issuing commands, as shown in Figure 2.5.

FIGURE 2.5 The tmux new command's first window

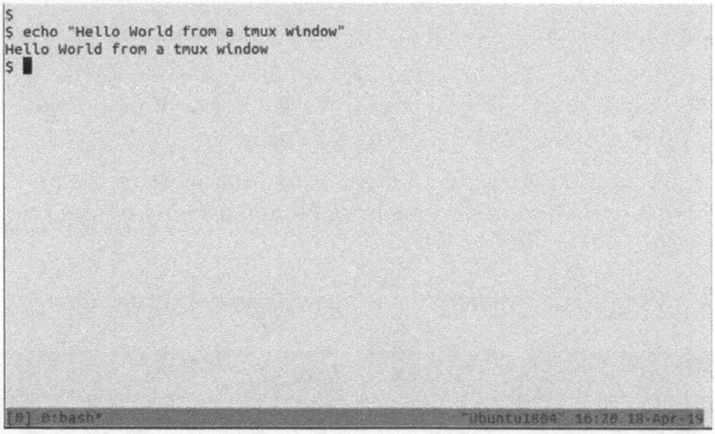

```
$
$ echo "Hello World from a tmux window"
Hello World from a tmux window
$ ▮



[0] 0:bash*                                          "ubuntu1804" 16:70 18-Apr-19
```

The tmux utility also employs a prefix shortcut. By default, it is the Ctrl+B key combination. To detach from a tmux window session, press the Ctrl+B prefix and then the D key. Similar to screen, you can employ tmux ls to see all your created and detached window sessions as shown in Listing 2.45.

Listing 2.45: Displaying a detached window with the tmux -ls command

```
$ tmux new
[detached (from session 0)]
$
$ tmux ls
0: 1 windows (created Thu Apr 18 16:28:13 2019) [80x23]
$
```

To reattach to a particular detached window session, use the attach-session argument as shown in Listing 2.46. The -t switch indicates to which window number you wish to attach. Window numbers are displayed in the tmux ls command output as the first number shown in each line.

Listing 2.46: Attaching to a detached window with the tmux attach-session command

```
$ tmux new
[detached (from session 1)]
$
$ tmux ls
0: 1 windows (created Thu Apr 18 16:28:13 2019) [80x23]
1: 1 windows (created Thu Apr 18 16:31:04 2019) [80x23]
$
$ tmux attach-session -t 0
```

You can also split a window screen up into multiple windows, called *panes*. There are several prefix shortcut commands (also called *key bindings*) that allow you to quickly create a pane and move between, destroy, or arrange windows. A few are shown in Table 2.11.

TABLE 2.11   The tmux utility prefix shortcut Ctrl+B commands

Key/Key Combination	Description
&	Kill the current window
%	Split current screen window vertically into two panes
"	Split current screen window horizontally into two panes
D	Detach from current window
L	Move to previous window
N	Move to next window
O	Move to next pane
Ctrl+O	Rotate panes forward in current window

If you are in a tmux window and cannot remember a particular needed key binding, there's a prefix shortcut command for that. Press the Ctrl+B key combination and then the ? key to view a complete list of all the various key bindings and more.

In Figure 2.6, we created another three-focus monitoring window, this time using the tmux utility.

FIGURE 2.6   A three-pane monitoring window using the tmux utility

```
top - 17:04:27 up  3:20,  9 users,  load average: 2.83, 1.48, 0.85
Tasks: 235 total,   5 running, 199 sleeping,   0 stopped,   0 zombie
%Cpu(s): 99.0 us,  1.0 sy,  0.0 ni,  0.0 id,  0.0 wa,  0.0 hi,  0.0 si,  0.0 st
KiB Mem :  4039720 total,  1984480 free,  1364348 used,   690892 buff/cache
KiB Swap:   483800 total,   483800 free,        0 used.  2386684 avail Mem

   PID USER      PR  NI    VIRT    RES    SHR S %CPU %MEM     TIME+ COMMAND
  3678 Christi+  20   0   41708   1820   1376 R 24.7  0.0   0:12.43 stress-ng-matri
  3682 Christi+  20   0  128900  88608   1168 R 24.3  2.2   0:12.43 stress-ng-vm
  3683 Christi+  20   0  128900  88608   1168 R 24.3  2.2   0:12.43 stress-ng-vm
  3684 Christi+  20   0  128900  88664   1224 R 24.3  2.2   0:12.42 stress-ng-vm

$
$ tmux ls                                       $ stress-ng --class cpu -a 10 -b 5 -t 3m
0: 1 windows (created Thu Apr 18 16:28:13 2019)   --matrix 0 -m 3 --vm-bytes 256m
[80x23]                                         stress-ng: info:  [3677] dispatching hog
1: 1 windows (created Thu Apr 18 16:31:04 2019) s: 1 matrix, 3 vm
[80x23]
2: 1 windows (created Thu Apr 18 16:53:24 2019)
[80x23] (attached)
$

[2] 0:stress-ng*                                "Ubuntu1804" 17:04 18-Apr-19
```

Understanding Foreground and Background Processes

Some programs can take a long time to run, and you may not want to tie up the command-line interface. Fortunately, there's a simple solution to that problem: run the program in background mode.

Sending a Job to the Background

Running a program in *background mode* is a fairly easy thing to do; just place an amper-sand symbol (&) after the command. A great program to use for background mode demonstration purposes is the sleep command. This utility is useful for adding pauses in shell scripts. You simply add an argument indicating the number of seconds you wish the script to freeze. Thus, sleep 3 would pause for three seconds. An example of sending this command to background mode is shown in Listing 2.47.

Listing 2.47: Sending a command to the background via the & symbol

```
$ sleep 3000 &
[1] 1539
$
$ jobs
[1]+  Running                 sleep 3000 &
$
$ jobs -l
[1]+  1539 Running            sleep 3000 &
$
```

When you send a command into the background, the system assigns it a job number as well as a PID. The job number is listed in brackets, [1], and in the Listing 2.47 example, the background process is assigned a PID of 1539. As soon as the system displays these items, a new command-line interface prompt appears. You are returned to the shell, and the command you executed runs safely in background mode.

Notice that in Listing 2.47 the *jobs* command is also employed. This utility allows you to see any processes that belong to you that are running in background mode. However, it displays only the job number. If you need the job's PID, you have to issue the jobs -l command.

When the background process finishes, it may display a message on the terminal similar to

```
[1]+  Done                    sleep 3000
```

This shows the job number and the status of the job (Done), along with the command that ran in the background.

Sending Multiple Jobs to the Background

You can start any number of background jobs from the command-line prompt. Each time you start a new job, the shell assigns it a new job number, and the Linux system assigns it a new PID, as shown in Listing 2.48.

Listing 2.48: Showing multiple background jobs with the jobs command

```
$ bash CriticalBackups.sh &
[2] 1540
$
$ jobs -l

[1]-  1539 Running                sleep 3000 &
[2]+  1540 Running                bash CriticalBackups.sh &
$
```

The second program sent to the background is a shell script (shell scripts are covered in Chapter 9) that performs important backups. This may take a while to run, so it is sent to the background and assigned the 2 job number.

In Listing 2.48, notice the plus sign (+) next to the new background job's number. It denotes the last job added to the background job stack. The minus sign (-) indicates that this particular job is the second-to-last process, which was added to the job stack.

Bringing Jobs to the Foreground

You don't have to leave your running programs in the background. If desired, you can return them to foreground mode. To accomplish this, use the *fg* command and the background job's number, preceded by a percent sign (%). An example is shown in Listing 2.49.

Listing 2.49: Bringing a background job to the foreground with the fg command

```
$ jobs -l
[1]-  1539 Running                sleep 3000 &
[2]+  1540 Running                bash CriticalBackups.sh &
$
$ fg %2
bash CriticalBackups.sh
```

The downside to moving a job back into foreground mode is you now have your terminal session tied up until the program completes.

 You don't have to run a program in foreground mode to see its output. By default, STDOUT (covered in Chapter 1) is sent to the terminal where a job was put into the background.

Sending a Running Program to the Background

If you have started a program in foreground mode and realize that it will take a while to run, you can still send it to background mode. First you must pause the process using the Ctrl+Z key combination; this will stop (pause) the program and assign it a job number.

After you have the paused program's job number, employ the bg command to send it to the background. An example is shown in Listing 2.50.

Listing 2.50: Sending a paused job to the background with the bg command

```
$ bash CriticalBackups.sh
^Z
[2]+  Stopped                 bash CriticalBackups.sh
$
$ bg %2
[2]+ bash CriticalBackups.sh &
$
$ jobs -l
[1]-  1539 Running            sleep 3000 &
[2]+  1540 Running            bash CriticalBackups.sh &
$
```

Thus, you can send programs to run in background mode before they are started or after they are initiated.

> **NOTE** When moving programs into the background or foreground, you are not required to add a percent sign (%) on the job number. However, it's a good habit to acquire, because when you stop programs using their job number, the percent sign *is* required. If you don't use it in this case, you may accidently stop the wrong process!

Stopping a Job

Stopping a background job before it has completed is fairly easy. It's accomplished with the *kill* command and the job's number. An example is shown in Listing 2.51.

Listing 2.51: Stopping a background job with the kill command

```
$ jobs -l
[1]-  1539 Running            sleep 3000 &
[2]+  1540 Running            bash CriticalBackups.sh &
$
$ kill %1
[1]-  Terminated          sleep 3000
```

```
$
$ jobs -l
```

```
[2]+  1540 Running                    bash CriticalBackups.sh &
$
```

Notice that with the kill command, the background job's number is preceded with a percentage sign (%). When the command is issued, a message indicating the job has been eradicated is displayed (terminated or killed). You should confirm this by reissuing the jobs command. Be aware that some background jobs need a stronger method to remove them. This topic is covered later in this chapter.

 WARNING   When stopping a program running in background mode with the kill command, it is critical to add a percent sign before the job's number. If you leave the sign off and have enough privileges, you could accidentally stop an important process on your Linux system, causing it to crash or hang.

Keeping a Job Running after Logout

Each background process is tied to your session's terminal. If the terminal session exits (for example, you log out of the system), the background process also exits. Some terminal emulators warn you if you have any running background processes associated with the terminal, but others don't.

If you want your script to continue running in background mode after you've logged off the terminal, you'll need to employ the *nohup* utility. This command will make your background jobs immune to hang-up signals, which are sent to the job when a terminal session exits. An example of using this command is shown in Listing 2.52.

Listing 2.52: Keeping a background job running after log out with the nohup command

```
$ nohup bash CriticalBackups.sh &
[1] 2090
$ nohup: ignoring input and appending output to 'nohup.out'

$
```

Notice that the nohup command will force the application to ignore any input from STDIN (covered in Chapter 1). By default STDOUT and STDERR are redirected to the $HOME/nohup.out file. If you want to change the output filename for the command to use, you'll need to employ the appropriate redirection operators on the nohup command string.

Managing Process Priorities

The scheduling priority for a process determines when it obtains CPU time and memory resources in comparison to other processes that operate at a different priority. However, you may run some applications that need either a higher or lower level of priority.

The *nice* and *renice* commands allow you to set and change a program's *niceness level*, which in turn modifies the priority level assigned by the system to an application. The nice command allows you to start an application with a nondefault niceness level setting. The format looks like this:

```
nice -n VALUE COMMAND
```

The VALUE parameter is a numeric value from –20 to 19. The lower the number, the higher priority the process receives. The default niceness level is zero.

The COMMAND argument indicates the program must start at the specified niceness level. An example is shown in Listing 2.53.

Listing 2.53: Modifying an program's niceness level with the nice command

```
$ nice -n 10 bash CriticalBackups.sh
```

When the program is running, you can open another terminal and view the application process via the ps command. An example is shown in Listing 2.54. Notice the value in the NI (nice) column is 10.

Listing 2.54: Displaying an program's non-default niceness level with the ps command

```
$ ps -l 1949
F S   UID   PID  PPID  C PRI  NI ADDR SZ WCHAN  TTY         TIME CMD
0 S  1001  1949  1527  0  90  10 - 4998 wait    pts/1       0:00 bash CriticalBac
$
```

To change the priority of a process that's already running, use the *renice* command:

```
renice PRIORITY [-p PIDS] [-u USERS] [-g GROUPS]
```

The renice command allows you to change the priority of multiple processes based on a list of PID values, all of the processes started by one or more users, or all of the processes started by one or more groups. An example of changing our already running CriticalBackup.sh program is shown in Listing 2.55.

Listing 2.55: Changing a running program's niceness level with the renice command

```
$ renice 15 -p 1949
1949 (process ID) old priority 10, new priority 15
$
```

Only if you have super user privileges can you set a nice value less than 0 (increase the priority) of a running process, as shown in Listing 2.56.

Listing 2.56: Increasing a running program's priority level with super user privileges

```
$ sudo renice -n -5 -p 1949
1949 (process ID) old priority 15, new priority -5
$
$ sudo renice -10 -p 1949
1949 (process ID) old priority -5, new priority -10
$
```

Notice that you can either employ the -n option or just leave it off. This works for both the nice and renice commands.

WARNING   For older Linux distributions, if you do not employ the -n option, you may need to use a dash in front of the niceness value. For example, to start a program with a nice value of 10, you would type **nice -10** followed by the application's name. To start a program with a nice value of negative 10, you would type **nice --10** followed by the application's name. That can be confusing!

Sending Signals to Processes

Sometimes a process gets hung up and just needs a gentle nudge to either get going again or stop. Other times, a process runs away with the CPU and refuses to give it up. In both cases, you need a command that will allow you to control a process. To do that, Linux follows the Unix method of interprocess communication.

In Linux, processes communicate with each other using process signals. A *process signal* is a predefined message that processes recognize and may choose to ignore or act on. The developers program how a process handles signals. Most well-written applications have the ability to receive and act on the standard Unix process signals. A few of these signals are shown in Table 2.12.

TABLE 2.12   Linux process signals

Number	Name	Description
1	HUP	Hangs up
2	INT	Interrupts
3	QUIT	Stops running

TABLE 2.12 Linux process signals *(continued)*

Number	Name	Description
9	KILL	Unconditionally terminates
11	SEGV	Segments violation
15	TERM	Terminates if possible
17	STOP	Stops unconditionally, but doesn't terminate
18	TSTP	Stops or pauses, but continues to run in background
19	CONT	Resumes execution after STOP or TSTP

Although a process can send a signal to another process, several commands are available in Linux that allow you to send signals to running processes.

 You'll often see the Linux process signals written with SIG attached to them. For example, TERM is also written as SIGTERM, and KILL is also SIGKILL.

Sending Signals with the *kill* Command

Besides stopping jobs, the kill command allows you to send signals to processes based on their process ID (PID). By default, the kill command sends a TERM signal to all the PIDs listed on the command line.

To send a process signal, you must either be the owner of the process or have super user privileges. The TERM signal only asks the process to kindly stop running. Most processes will comply as shown in Listing 2.57.

Listing 2.57: Stopping a process with the kill command and the default TERM signal

```
$ ps 2285
  PID TTY      STAT   TIME COMMAND
 2285 pts/0    S      0:00 bash SecurityAudit.sh
$
$ kill 2285
[1]+  Terminated              bash SecurityAudit.sh
$
$ ps 2285
  PID TTY      STAT   TIME COMMAND
$
```

WARNING

When you use the `kill` utility to stop a process, you use the process's PID. When you employ the `kill` command to terminate a background job, you use its job number preceded by a percent sign. It's easy to forget that percent sign when stopping background jobs. If you do, the system will attempt to stop the process whose PID you have specified—for example, typing **kill -9 1** when you meant to type **kill -9 %1**. With enough privileges, you can accidentally shut down or hang your system, so use caution!

Unfortunately, some processes will ignore the request. When you need to get forceful, the -s option allows you to specify other signals (using either their name or signal number). You can also leave off the -s switch and just precede the signal with a dash. An example of trying to kill off a stubborn process is shown in Listing 2.58.

Listing 2.58: Stopping a process with the `kill` command and a higher signal

```
$ ps 2305
  PID TTY       STAT    TIME COMMAND
 2305 pts/0     T       0:00 vi
$
$ kill 2305
$
$ ps 2305
  PID TTY       STAT    TIME COMMAND
 2305 pts/0     T       0:00 vi
$
$ kill -s HUP  2305
$
$ ps 2305
  PID TTY       STAT    TIME COMMAND
 2305 pts/0     T       0:00 vi
$
$ kill -9  2305
[1]+  Killed                  vi
$
$ ps 2305
  PID TTY       STAT    TIME COMMAND
$
```

Notice that the process was unaffected by the default TERM signal and the HUP signal. Thus, kill signal number 9 (KILL) had to be employed to stop the process.

The generally accepted procedure is to first try the TERM signal. If the process ignores that, try the INT or HUP signal. If the program recognizes these signals, it will try to gracefully stop doing what it was doing before shutting down. The most forceful signal is the KILL signal. When a process receives this signal, it immediately stops running. Use this as a last resort, as it can lead to corrupted files.

Sending Signals with the *killall* Command

Unfortunately, you can only use the process PID instead of its command name, making the kill utility difficult to use sometimes. The *killall* command is a nice solution, because it can select a process based on the command it is executing and send it a signal.

The killall utility operates similar to kill in that if no signal is specified, TERM is sent. Also, you can designate a signal using its name or number, and use the -s option or precede the signal with just a dash. An example of using killall to send the default TERM signal to a group of processes is shown snipped in Listing 2.59.

Listing 2.59: Stopping a group of processes with the killall command

```
$ ps
  PID TTY          TIME CMD
 1441 pts/0    00:00:00 bash
 1504 pts/0    00:00:00 stressor.sh
 1505 pts/0    00:00:00 stress-ng
 1506 pts/0    00:00:05 stress-ng-matri
 1507 pts/0    00:00:00 stressor.sh
 1508 pts/0    00:00:00 stress-ng
 1509 pts/0    00:00:02 stress-ng-matri
 1510 pts/0    00:00:00 stressor.sh
[…]
 1517 pts/0    00:00:00 ps
$
$ killall stress-ng
[…]
$
$ ps
  PID TTY          TIME CMD
 1441 pts/0    00:00:00 bash
 1519 pts/0    00:00:00 ps
$
```

In Listing 2.59, we accidentally (that's not true, we did it on purpose) started running a script multiple times. This script, stressor.sh, runs the stress-ng command to stress-test the system. Instead of taking the time to stop all these processes individually, we employed the killall command. By passing it the stress-ng command name, the killall utility searched the system, found any process we owned that was running the stress-ng program, and sent it the TERM signal, which stopped those processes.

Keep in mind that to send signals to processes you do not own via the killall command, you'll need super user privileges. This duplicates the kill utility's restrictions.

 Be careful of stopping processes that may have open files. Files can be damaged and unrepairable if the process is abruptly stopped. It's usually a good idea to run the lsof command first to see a list of the open files and their processes.

Sending Signals with the *pkill* Command

The *pkill* command is a powerful way to send processes' signals using selection criteria other than their PID numbers or commands they are running. You can choose by username, user ID (UID), terminal with which the process is associated, and so on. In addition, the pkill command allows you to use wildcard characters, making it a very useful tool when you've got a system that's gone awry.

Even better, the pkill utility works hand-in-hand with the *pgrep* utility. With pgrep, you can test out your selection criteria prior to sending signals to the selected processes via pkill.

In the example in Listing 2.60, the -t option is used on the pgrep utility to see all the PIDs attached to the tty3 terminal. The ps command is also used to inspect one of the processes a little further.

Listing 2.60: Stopping a group of processes with the pkill command

```
$ pgrep -t tty3
1716
1804
1828
1829
1831
1832
1836
1837
1838
1839
1840
$
```

```
$ ps 1840
  PID TTY       STAT    TIME COMMAND
 1840 tty3      R+      0:39 stress-ng --class cpu -a 10 -b 5 -t 5m --matrix 0
$
$ sudo pkill -t tty3
$
$ pgrep -t tty3
1846
$
$ ps 1846
  PID TTY       STAT    TIME COMMAND
 1846 tty3      Ss+     0:00 /sbin/agetty -o -p -- \u --noclear tty3 linux
$
```

Notice that, besides the preceding sudo, the pkill utility's syntax is identical to the pgrep command's syntax. Like the other signal-sending utilities, the pkill command by default sends a TERM signal, which requests that the group of processes all kindly stop running.

In Listing 2.60, after the TERM signal has been sent to the selected process group, the pgrep utility is used again and finds a process associated with the tty3 terminal. However, upon further investigation with ps, it is determined that the /sbin/aggetty program is running on tty3, which it is supposed to do, providing the login prompt at that terminal.

The pkill and pgrep commands have a variety of searches they can perform to locate the appropriate processes. Review their man page to find additional search criteria.

Summary

This chapter's purpose was to improve your knowledge of Linux command-line tools associated with software programs and their processes. Being able to install, update, and manage your Linux system's software applications is critical to maintaining your server. In addition, you need to know how to troubleshoot libraries that are required by systems' various packages.

When a program runs, it is called a process. Being able to execute programs in various modes, watch them, and use command-line tools to manage them is essential in managing processes. Troubleshooting problems may require you to use multiple windows as well as send signals to improperly acting processes.

Exam Essentials

Explain the different package concepts.   The software is bundled into packages that consist of most of the files required to run a single application. Tracking and maintaining these packages is accomplished by package management systems. A package management database tracks application files, library dependencies, application versions, and so on. Each distribution maintains its own central clearinghouse of software packages, which is called a repository and is accessible through the Internet.

Summarize the various RPM utilities.   RPM utilities provide the ability to install, modify, and remove software packages. RPM package files have an .rpm file extension, are downloaded to the local system, and are managed via the rpm tool. The YUM and ZYpp utilities also manage RPM software packages but obtain them from repositories.

Describe the various Debian package management utilities.   Debian bundles application files into a single .deb package file, which can be downloaded to the local system and managed via the dpkg program. The Advanced Package Tool (APT) suite is used for working with Debian repositories. This collection includes the apt-cache program that provides information about the package database, and the apt-get program that does the work of installing, updating, and removing packages. The new apt tool provides improved user interface features and simpler commands for managing Debian packages.

Explain shared library concepts and tools.   A system library is a collection of items, such as program functions, that are self-contained code modules that perform a specific task within an application. Shared libraries (also called dynamic libraries) are library functions that are copied into memory and bound to the application when the program is launched. This is called loading a library, and it can be done manually by using the modern versions of the ld.so and ld-linux.so* executables. When loading a library, the system searches the directories stored within the LD_LIBRARY_PATH environment variable and continues through additional directories if not found. To speed up this search, a library cache is employed, which is a catalog of library directories and all the various libraries contained within them. To update the cache, the ldconfig utility is used. To view libraries required by a particular program, use the ldd command.

Detail process management.   A process is a running program. The Linux system assigns each process a process ID (PID) and manages how the process uses memory and CPU time based on that PID and its priority. Process information can be viewed using the ps command. Real-time process data is provided by the top utility, which also provides system load information (that can also be obtained by uptime) and memory usage statistics (which is also displayed by the free command). Programs can be run in background mode to avoid tying up the terminal session by placing an ampersand symbol (&) after the command before you start it or by pausing the program with the Ctrl+Z key combination and using the bg utility to send it to the background. Programs running in the background can be viewed via the jobs command and, if desired, brought back to the foreground with the fg command. Processes can be set to run at a higher or lower priority with the nice or renice utilities.

Explain process troubleshooting principles.   When troubleshooting or monitoring a system, it's helpful to open window sessions side-by-side via a terminal multiplexer, such as screen or tmux, to perform multiple operations and monitor their displays. Also, it may be necessary to narrow the ps utility's focus by viewing only a selected subset of processes via certain command options. Signals can be sent to processes to control them or stop them if needed. The different utilities that are able to perform this service are the kill, killall, and pkill commands.

Review Questions

You can find the answers in the appendix.

1. On Linux, systems package manager databases typically contain what types of information? (Choose all that apply.)

   A. Application files

   B. Application file directory locations

   C. Installation by username

   D. Software version

   E. Library dependencies

2. What filename extension does the CentOS Linux distribution use for packages?

   A. .deb

   B. .zypp

   C. .dpkg

   D. .yum

   E. .rpm

3. Carol needs to install packages from a Red Hat–based repository. What programs can she use? (Choose all that apply.)

   A. dpkg

   B. zypper

   C. yum

   D. apt-get

   E. dnf

4. Scott wants to add a third-party repository to his Red Hat–based package management system. Where should he place a new configuration file to add it?

   A. /etc/yum.repos.d/

   B. /etc/apt/sources.list

   C. /usr/lib/

   D. /bin/

   E. /etc/

5. You need to extract files from an .rpm package file for review prior to installing them. What utilities should you employ to accomplish this task? (Choose all that apply.)

   A. cpio2rpm

   B. rpm

   C. rpm2cpio

   D. cpio

   E. yum

6. Natasha needs to install a new package on her Ubuntu Linux system. The package was distributed as a .deb file. What tool should she use?

   A. rpm

   B. yum

   C. dnf

   D. dpkg

   E. zypper

7. On his Debian-based package managed system, Tony wants to list all currently installed packages with missing dependencies. What command should he use?

   A. apt-cache unmet

   B. apt-cache stats

   C. apt-cache showpkg

   D. apt-cache search

   E. apt-cache depends

8. You've installed and configured a .deb package but did something incorrectly in the configuration process, and now the package will not run. What should you do next?

   A. Purge the package, and reinstall it.

   B. Uninstall the package, and then reinstall it.

   C. Reconfigure the package via the dpkg-reconfigure utility.

   D. Reconfigure the package via the debconf-show utility.

   E. Reconfigure the package via the dpkg or apt-get utilities.

9. Steve is working on an open source software development team to create a new application. He's completed a new shared library the program will be using and has moved it to the correct location. What command should Steve employ to update the system's library cache?

   A. ldd

   B. ldconfig

   C. ldcache

   D. ld.so

   E. ld-linux-x86-64.so.2

10. Library file locations may be stored where? (Choose all that apply.)

    A. The /usr/bin*/ directories

    B. The /ld.so.conf file

    C. The /etc/ld.so.conf.d/ directory

    D. The LD_LIBRARY_PATH environment variable

    E. The /lib* and /usr/lib*/ folders

11. What are the types of option styles available for the ps command? (Choose all that apply.)

    A. BSD style

    B. Linux style

    C. Unix style

    D. GNU style

    E. Numeric style

12. By default, if you specify no command-line options, what does the ps command display?

    A. All processes running on the terminal

    B. All active processes

    C. All sleeping processes

    D. All processes run by the current shell

    E. All processes run by the current user

13. Peter noticed that his Linux system is running slow and needs to find out what application is causing the problem. What tool should he use to show the current CPU utilization of all the processes running on his system?

    A. top

    B. ps

    C. lsof

    D. free

    E. uptime

14. What top command displays cumulative CPU time instead of relative CPU time?

    A. l

    B. F

    C. r

    D. y

    E. S

15. Natasha just created a new window using the GNU Screen utility and detached from it. She now wants to reattach to it. What command or keystroke sequence will allow Natasha to view her detached window's ID?

    A. screen

    B. screen -r

    C. tmux ls

    D. screen -ls

    E. Ctrl+A and D

16. Scott wants to run his large number crunching application in background mode in his terminal session. What symbol should he add to his command that runs the program in order to accomplish that?

    A. >

    B. &

    C. |

    D. >>

    E. %

17. How can you temporarily pause a program from running in foreground in a terminal session?

    A. Press the Ctrl+Z key combination

    B. Press the Ctrl+C key combination

    C. Start the command with the nohup command

    D. Start the command with the ampersand (&) command

    E. Start the command with the fg command

18. Scott has decided to run a program in the background due to its time to process. However, he realizes several hours later that the program is not operating correctly and may have been consuming large amounts of CPU time unnecessarily. He decides to stop the background job. What command should he first employ?

    A. Scott should issue the ps -ef command to see all his background jobs.

    B. Scott should issue the jobs -l command to see all his background jobs.

    C. Scott should issue the kill %1 command to stop his background job.

    D. Scott should issue the kill 1 command to stop his background job.

    E. Scott should issue the kill -9 1 command to stop his background job.

19. Hope has an application that crunches lots of numbers and uses a lot of system resources. She wants to run the application with a lower priority so it doesn't interfere with other applications on the system. What tool should she use to start the application program?

    A. renice

    B. bash

    C. nice

    D. nohup

    E. lower

20. Carol used the ps command to find the process ID of an application that she needs to stop. What command-line tool should she use to stop the application?

    A. killall

    B. pkill

    C. TERM

    D. kill

    E. pgrep

Chapter

3

Configuring Hardware

OBJECTIVES

✓ **101.1** Determine and configure hardware settings

✓ **102.1** Design hard disk layout

✓ **104.1** Create partitions and filesystems

✓ **104.2** Maintain the integrity of filesystems

✓ **104.3** Control mounting and unmounting of filesystems

Knowing how the Linux system interacts with the underlying hardware is a crucial job for every Linux system administrator. This chapter examines how your Linux system interacts with the hardware it's running on and how to make changes to that setup if necessary.

Configuring the Firmware and Core Hardware

Before we look at the individual hardware cards available, let's first look at how the core hardware operates. This section discusses what happens when you hit the power button on your Linux workstation or server.

Understanding the Role of Firmware

All IBM-compatible workstations and servers utilize some type of built-in firmware to control how the installed operating system starts. On older workstations and servers, this firmware was called the *Basic Input/Output System* (BIOS). On newer workstations and servers, a new method, called the *Unified Extensible Firmware Interface* (UEFI), is responsible for maintaining the system hardware status and launching an installed operating system.

Both methods eventually launch the main operating system program, but each method uses different ways of doing that. This section walks through the basics of both BIOS and UEFI methods, showing how they participate in the Linux boot process.

The BIOS Startup

The BIOS firmware found in older workstations and servers was somewhat limited. It had a simple menu interface that allowed you to change some settings to control how the system found hardware and define what device the BIOS should use to start the operating system.

One limitation of the original BIOS firmware was that it could read only one sector's worth of data from a hard drive into memory to run. As you can probably guess, that's not enough space to load an entire operating system. To get around that limitation, most operating systems (including Linux and Microsoft Windows) split the boot process into two parts.

First, the BIOS runs a *boot loader* program, a small program that initializes the necessary hardware to find and run the full operating system program. It is usually located at another place on the same hard drive but sometimes on a separate internal or external storage device.

The boot loader program usually has a configuration file so that you can tell it where to look to find the actual operating system file to run or even to produce a small menu allowing the user to boot between multiple operating systems.

To get things started, the BIOS must know where to find the boot loader program on an installed storage device. Most BIOS setups allow you to load the boot loader program from several locations:

- An internal hard drive
- An external hard drive
- A CD or DVD drive
- A USB memory stick
- An ISO file
- A network server using either NFS, HTTP, or FTP

When booting from a hard drive, you must designate which hard drive, and partition on the hard drive, the BIOS should load the boot loader program from. This is done by defining a *master boot record* (MBR).

The MBR is the first sector on the first hard drive partition on the system. There is only one MBR for the computer system. The BIOS looks for the MBR and reads the program stored there into memory. Since the boot loader program must fit in one sector, it must be very small, so it can't do too much. The boot loader program mainly points to the location of the actual operating system kernel file, stored in a boot sector of a separate partition installed on the system. There are no size limitations on the kernel boot file.

The boot loader program isn't required to point directly to an operating system kernel file; it can point to any type of program, including another boot loader program. You can create a primary boot loader program that points to a secondary boot loader program, which provides options to load multiple operating systems. This process is called *chainloading*.

The UEFI Startup

Although there were plenty of limitations with BIOS, computer manufacturers learned to live with them, and BIOS became the default standard for IBM-compatible systems for many years. However, as operating systems became more complicated, it eventually became clear that a new boot method needed to be developed.

Intel created the *Extensible Firmware Interface* (EFI) in 1998 to address some of the limitations of BIOS. It was somewhat of a slow process, but by 2005, the idea caught on with other vendors, and the Unified EFI (UEFI) specification was adopted as a standard.

These days just about all IBM-compatible desktop and server systems utilize the UEFI firmware standard.

Instead of relying on a single boot sector on a hard drive to hold the boot loader program, UEFI specifies a special disk partition, called the *EFI System Partition* (ESP), to store boot loader programs. This allows for any size of boot loader program, plus the ability to store multiple boot loader programs for multiple operating systems.

The ESP setup utilizes the old Microsoft File Allocation Table (FAT) filesystem to store the boot loader programs. On Linux systems, the ESP is typically mounted in the /boot/efi directory, and the boot loader files are typically stored using the .efi filename extension, such as linux.efi.

The UEFI firmware utilizes a built-in mini boot loader (sometimes referred to as a boot manager) that allows you to configure which boot loader program file to launch.

 WARNING   Not all Linux distributions support the UEFI firmware. If you're using a UEFI system, ensure that the Linux distribution you select supports it.

With UEFI you need to register each individual boot loader file you want to appear at boot time in the boot manager interface menu. You can then select the boot loader to run each time you boot the system.

After the firmware finds and runs the boot loader, its job is done. The boot loader step in the boot process can be somewhat complicated; the next section dives into covering that.

Device Interfaces

Each device you connect to your Linux system uses some type of standard protocol to communicate with the system hardware. The Linux kernel software must know how to send data to and receive data from the hardware device using those protocols. There are currently three popular standards used to connect devices.

PCI Boards

The *Peripheral Component Interconnect (PCI)* standard was developed in 1993 as a method for connecting hardware boards to PC motherboards. The standard has been updated a few times to accommodate faster interface speeds, as well as increasing data bus sizes on motherboards. The *PCI Express (PCIe)* standard is currently used on most server and desktop workstations to provide a common interface for external hardware devices.

Lots of different client devices use PCI boards to connect to a server or desktop workstation:

▪ **Internal hard drives:** Hard drives using the *Serial Advanced Technology Attachment (SATA)* and the *Small Computer System Interface (SCSI)* interface often use PCI boards to connect with workstations or servers. The Linux kernel automatically recognizes both SATA and SCSI hard drives connected to PCI boards.

- **External hard drives:** Network hard drives using the Fibre Channel standard provide a high-speed shared drive environment for server environments. To communicate on a fiber channel network, the server usually uses PCI boards that support the *host bus adapter (HBA)* standard.

- **Network interface cards:** Hard-wired network cards allow you to connect the workstation or server to a local area network (LAN) using the common RJ-45 cable standard. These types of connections are mostly found in high-speed network environments that require high throughput to the network.

- **Wireless cards:** PCI boards are available that support the IEEE 802.11 standard for wireless connections to LANs. Although they are not commonly used in server environments, they are very popular in workstation environments.

- **Bluetooth devices:** The Bluetooth technology allows for short-distance wireless communication with other Bluetooth devices in a peer-to-peer network setup. They are most commonly found in workstation environments.

- **Video accelerators:** Applications that require advanced graphics often use video accelerator cards, which offload the video processing requirements from the CPU to provide faster graphics. While these are popular in gaming environments, you'll also find video accelerator cards used in video processing applications for editing and processing movies.

- **Audio cards:** Similarly, applications that require high-quality sound often use specialty audio cards to provide advanced audio processing and play, such as handling Dolby surround sound to enhance the audio quality of movies.

 Most PCI boards utilize the Plug-and-Play (PnP) standard, which automatically determines the configuration settings for the boards so no two boards conflict with each other. If you do run into conflicts, you can use the `setpci` utility to view and manually change settings for an individual PCI board.

The USB Interface

The *Universal Serial Bus (USB)* interface has become increasingly popular due to its ease of use and its increasing support for high-speed data communication. Since the USB interface uses serial communications, it requires fewer connectors with the motherboard, allowing for smaller interface plugs.

The USB standard has evolved over the years. The original version, 1.0, supported data transfer speeds only up to 12 Mbps. The 2.0 standard increased the data transfer speed to 480 Mbps. The current USB standard, 3.2, allows for data transfer speeds up to 20 Gbps, making it useful for high-speed connections to external storage devices.

There are many different devices that can connect to systems using the USB interface. You can find hard drives, printers, digital cameras and camcorders, keyboards, mice, and network cards that have versions that connect using the USB interface.

There are two steps to get Linux to interact with USB devices. First, the Linux kernel must have the proper module installed to recognize the USB controller that is installed on your server, workstation, or laptops. The controller provides communication between the Linux kernel and the USB bus on the system. When the Linux kernel can communicate with the USB bus, any device you plug into a USB port on the system will be recognized by the kernel, but may not necessarily be useful. Second, the Linux system must then also have a kernel module installed for the individual device type plugged into the USB bus.

The GPIO Interface

The *General Purpose Input/Output (GPIO)* interface has become popular with small utility Linux systems, designed for controlling external devices for automation projects. This includes popular hobbyist Linux systems such as the Raspberry Pi and BeagleBone kits.

The GPIO interface provides multiple digital input and output lines that you can control individually, down to the single-bit level. The GPIO function is normally handled by a specialty integrated circuit (IC) chip, which is mapped into memory on the Linux system.

The GPIO interface is ideal for supporting communications to external devices such as relays, lights, sensors, and motors. Applications can read individual GPIO lines to determine the status of switches, turn relays on or off, or read digital values returned from any type of analog-to-digital sensors such as temperature or pressure sensors.

The GPIO interface provides a wealth of possibilities for using Linux to control objects and environments. You can write programs that control the temperature in a room, sense when doors or windows are opened or closed, sense motion in a room, or even control the operation of a robot.

The */dev* Directory

After the Linux kernel communicates with a device on an interface, it must be able to transfer data to and from the device. This is done using *device files*. Device files are files that the Linux kernel creates in the special /dev directory to interface with hardware devices.

To retrieve data from a specific device, a program just needs to read the Linux device file associated with that device. The Linux operating system handles all the unsightliness of interfacing with the actual hardware. Likewise, to send data to the device, the program just needs to write to the Linux device file.

As you add hardware devices such as USB drives, network cards, or hard drives to your system, Linux creates a file in the /dev directory representing that hardware device. Application programs can then interact directly with that file to store and retrieve data on the device. This is a lot easier than requiring each application to know how to directly interact with a device.

There are two types of device files in Linux, based on how Linux transfers data to the device:

- **Character device files:** Transfer data one character at a time. This method is often used for serial devices such as terminals and USB devices.
- **Block device files:** Transfer data in large blocks of data. This method is often used for high-speed data transfer devices such as hard drives and network cards.

The type of device file is denoted by the first letter in the permissions list, as shown in Listing 3.1.

Listing 3.1: Partial output from the /dev directory

```
$ ls -al sd* tty*
brw-rw---- 1 root disk    8,  0 Feb 16 17:49 sda
brw-rw---- 1 root disk    8,  1 Feb 16 17:49 sda1
crw-rw-rw- 1 root tty     5,  0 Feb 16 17:49 tty
crw--w---- 1 root tty     4,  0 Feb 16 17:49 tty0
crw--w---- 1 gdm  tty     4,  1 Feb 16 17:49 tty1
```

The hard drive devices, sda and sda1, show the letter b, indicating that they are block device files. The tty terminal files show the letter c, indicating that they are character device files.

Besides device files, Linux also provides a system called the *device mapper*. The device mapper function is performed by the Linux kernel. It maps physical block devices to virtual block devices. These virtual block devices allow the system to intercept the data written to or read from the physical device and perform some type of operation on them. Mapped devices are used by the Logical Volume Manager (LVM) for creating logical drives and by the Linux Unified Key Setup (LUKS) for encrypting data on hard drives when those features are installed on the Linux system.

 The device mapper creates virtual devices in the /dev/mapper directory. These files are links to the physical block device files in the /dev directory.

The */proc* Directory

The /proc directory is one of the most important tools you can use when troubleshooting hardware issues on a Linux system. It's not a physical directory on the filesystem, but instead a virtual directory that the kernel dynamically populates to provide access to information about the system hardware settings and status.

The Linux kernel changes the files and data in the /proc directory as it monitors the status of hardware on the system. To view the status of the hardware devices and settings, you just need to read the contents of the virtual files using standard Linux text commands.

Various /proc files are available for different system features, including the interrupt requests (IRQs), input/output (I/O) ports, and direct memory access (DMA) channels in use on the system by hardware devices. This section discusses the files used to monitor these features and how you can access them.

Interrupt Requests

Interrupt requests (IRQs) allow hardware devices to indicate when they have data to send to the CPU. The PnP system must assign each hardware device installed on the system a unique IRQ address. You can view the current IRQs in use on your Linux system by looking at the /proc/interrupts file using the Linux cat command, as shown in Listing 3.2.

Listing 3.2: Listing system interrupts from the /proc directory

```
$ cat /proc/interrupts
           CPU0
  0:        36   IO-APIC   2-edge       timer
  1:       297   IO-APIC   1-edge       i8042
  8:         0   IO-APIC   8-edge       rtc0
  9:         0   IO-APIC   9-fasteoi    acpi
 12:       396   IO-APIC   12-edge      i8042
 14:         0   IO-APIC   14-edge      ata_piix
 15:       914   IO-APIC   15-edge      ata_piix
 18:         2   IO-APIC   18-fasteoi   vboxvideo
 19:      4337   IO-APIC   19-fasteoi   enp0s3
 20:      1563   IO-APIC   20-fasteoi   vboxguest
 21:     29724   IO-APIC   21-fasteoi   ahci[0000:00:0d.0], snd_intel8x0
 22:        27   IO-APIC   22-fasteoi   ohci_hcd:usb1
NMI:         0   Non-maskable interrupts
LOC:     93356   Local timer interrupts
SPU:         0   Spurious interrupts
PMI:         0   Performance monitoring interrupts
IWI:         0   IRQ work interrupts
RTR:         0   APIC ICR read retries
RES:         0   Rescheduling interrupts
CAL:         0   Function call interrupts
TLB:         0   TLB shootdowns
TRM:         0   Thermal event interrupts
THR:         0   Threshold APIC interrupts
DFR:         0   Deferred Error APIC interrupts
MCE:         0   Machine check exceptions
MCP:         3   Machine check polls
HYP:         0   Hypervisor callback interrupts
```

```
ERR:           0
MIS:           0
PIN:           0    Posted-interrupt notification event
NPI:           0    Nested posted-interrupt event
PIW:           0    Posted-interrupt wakeup event
$
```

Some IRQs are reserved by the system for specific hardware devices, such as 0 for the system timer and 1 for the system keyboard. Other IRQs are assigned by the system as devices are detected at boot time.

I/O Ports

The system I/O ports are locations in memory where the CPU can send data to and receive data from the hardware device. As with IRQs, the system must assign each device a unique I/O port. This is yet another feature handled by the PnP system.

You can monitor the I/O ports assigned to the hardware devices on your system by looking at the /proc/ioports file, as shown in Listing 3.3.

Listing 3.3: Displaying the I/O ports on a system

```
$ sudo cat /proc/ioports
0000-0cf7 : PCI Bus 0000:00
  0000-001f : dma1
  0020-0021 : pic1
  0040-0043 : timer0
  0050-0053 : timer1
  0060-0060 : keyboard
  0064-0064 : keyboard
  0070-0071 : rtc_cmos
    0070-0071 : rtc0
  0080-008f : dma page reg
  00a0-00a1 : pic2
  00c0-00df : dma2
  00f0-00ff : fpu
  0170-0177 : 0000:00:01.1
    0170-0177 : ata_piix
  01f0-01f7 : 0000:00:01.1
    01f0-01f7 : ata_piix
  0376-0376 : 0000:00:01.1
    0376-0376 : ata_piix
  03c0-03df : vga+
  03f6-03f6 : 0000:00:01.1
    03f6-03f6 : ata_piix
```

Listing 3.3: Displaying the I/O ports on a system *(continued)*

```
0cf8-0cff : PCI conf1
0d00-ffff : PCI Bus 0000:00
  4000-403f : 0000:00:07.0
    4000-4003 : ACPI PM1a_EVT_BLK
    4004-4005 : ACPI PM1a_CNT_BLK
    4008-400b : ACPI PM_TMR
    4020-4021 : ACPI GPE0_BLK
  4100-410f : 0000:00:07.0
    4100-4108 : piix4_smbus
  d000-d00f : 0000:00:01.1
    d000-d00f : ata_piix
  d010-d017 : 0000:00:03.0
    d010-d017 : e1000
  d020-d03f : 0000:00:04.0
  d100-d1ff : 0000:00:05.0
    d100-d1ff : Intel 82801AA-ICH
  d200-d23f : 0000:00:05.0
    d200-d23f : Intel 82801AA-ICH
  d240-d247 : 0000:00:0d.0
    d240-d247 : ahci
  d248-d24b : 0000:00:0d.0
    d248-d24b : ahci
  d250-d257 : 0000:00:0d.0
    d250-d257 : ahci
  d258-d25b : 0000:00:0d.0
    d258-d25b : ahci
  d260-d26f : 0000:00:0d.0
    d260-d26f : ahci
$
```

There are lots of different I/O ports in use on the Linux system at any time, so your output will most likely differ from this example. With PnP, I/O port conflicts aren't very common, but it is possible that two devices are assigned the same I/O port. In that case, you can manually override the settings automatically assigned by using the `setpci` command.

Direct Memory Access

Using I/O ports to send data to the CPU can be somewhat slow. To speed things up, many devices use direct memory access (DMA) channels. DMA channels do what the name implies—they send data from a hardware device directly to memory on the system, without having to wait for the CPU. The CPU can then read those memory locations to access the data when it's ready.

As with I/O ports, each hardware device that uses DMA must be assigned a unique channel number. To view the DMA channels currently in use on the system, just display the /proc/dma file:

```
$ cat /proc/dma
 4: cascade
$
```

This output indicates that only DMA channel 4 is in use on the Linux system.

The /sys Directory

Yet another tool available for working with devices is the /sys directory. The /sys directory is another virtual directory, similar to the /proc directory. It is created by the kernel in the sysfs filesystem format, and it provides additional information about hardware devices that any user on the system can access.

Many different information files are available within the /sys directory. They are broken down into subdirectories based on the device and function in the system. You can take a look at the subdirectories and files available within the /sys directory on your system using the ls command-line command, as shown in Listing 3.4.

Listing 3.4: The contents of the /sys directory

```
$ sudo ls -al /sys
total 4
dr-xr-xr-x  13 root root    0 Feb 16 18:06 .
drwxr-xr-x  25 root root 4096 Feb  4 06:54 ..
drwxr-xr-x   2 root root    0 Feb 16 17:48 block
drwxr-xr-x  41 root root    0 Feb 16 17:48 bus
drwxr-xr-x  62 root root    0 Feb 16 17:48 class
drwxr-xr-x   4 root root    0 Feb 16 17:48 dev
drwxr-xr-x  14 root root    0 Feb 16 17:48 devices
drwxr-xr-x   5 root root    0 Feb 16 17:49 firmware
drwxr-xr-x   8 root root    0 Feb 16 17:48 fs
drwxr-xr-x   2 root root    0 Feb 16 18:06 hypervisor
drwxr-xr-x  13 root root    0 Feb 16 17:48 kernel
drwxr-xr-x 143 root root    0 Feb 16 17:48 module
drwxr-xr-x   2 root root    0 Feb 16 17:48 power
$
```

Notice the different categories of information that are available. You can obtain information about the system bus, devices, the kernel, and even the kernel modules installed.

Working with Devices

Linux provides a wealth of command-line tools to use the devices connected to your system, as well as to monitor and troubleshoot the devices if you experience problems. This section walks through some of the more popular tools you'll want to know about when working with Linux devices.

Finding Devices

One of the first tasks for a new Linux administrator is to find the different devices installed on the Linux system. Fortunately, there are a few command-line tools to help out with that.

The lsdev command-line command displays information about the hardware devices installed on the Linux system. It retrieves information from the /proc/interrupts, /proc/ioports, and /proc/dma virtual files and combines them together in one output, as shown in Listing 3.5.

Listing 3.5: Output from the lsdev command

```
$ sudo lsdev
Device          DMA    IRQ  I/O Ports
...
acpi                    9
ACPI                         4000-4003 4004-4005 4008-400b 4020-4021
ahci                         d240-d247 d248-d24b d250-d257 d258-d25b
ata_piix        14 15        0170-0177 01f0-01f7 0376-0376 03f6-03f6
cascade         4
dma                          0080-008f
dma1                         0000-001f
dma2                         00c0-00df
e1000                         d010-d017
enp0s3                  19
fpu                          00f0-00ff
i8042                   1 12
Intel                         d100-d1ff     d200-d23f
keyboard                     0060-0060   0064-0064
ohci_hcd:usb1           22
PCI                       0000-0cf7 0cf8-0cff 0d00-ffff
pic1                         0020-0021
pic2                         00a0-00a1
piix4_smbus                   4100-4108
rtc0                    8     0070-0071
rtc_cmos                     0070-0071
snd_intel8x0            21
timer                   0
timer0                        0040-0043
```

```
timer1                          0050-0053
vboxguest            20
vboxvideo            18
vga+                            03c0-03df
$
```

This gives you one place to view all the important information about the devices running on the system, making it easy to pick out any conflicts that can be causing problems.

The lsblk command displays information about the block devices installed on the Linux system. By default, the lsblk command displays all block devices, as shown in Listing 3.6.

Listing 3.6: The output from the lsblk command

```
$ lsblk
NAME          MAJ:MIN RM   SIZE RO TYPE MOUNTPOINT
loop0             7:0   0  34.6M  1 loop /snap/gtk-common-themes/818
loop1             7:1   0   2.2M  1 loop /snap/gnome-calculator/222
loop2             7:2   0  34.8M  1 loop /snap/gtk-common-themes/1122
loop3             7:3   0 169.4M  1 loop /snap/gimp/113
loop4             7:4   0   2.3M  1 loop /snap/gnome-calculator/238
loop5             7:5   0   13M   1 loop /snap/gnome-characters/117
loop6             7:6   0  34.2M  1 loop /snap/gtk-common-themes/808
loop7             7:7   0  89.5M  1 loop /snap/core/6130
loop8             7:8   0  14.5M  1 loop /snap/gnome-logs/45
loop9             7:9   0  53.7M  1 loop /snap/core18/719
loop10            7:10  0   91M   1 loop /snap/core/6350
loop11            7:11  0 140.7M  1 loop /snap/gnome-3-26-1604/74
loop12            7:12  0  53.7M  1 loop /snap/core18/594
loop13            7:13  0 169.4M  1 loop /snap/gimp/105
loop14            7:14  0  14.5M  1 loop /snap/gnome-logs/43
loop15            7:15  0   13M   1 loop /snap/gnome-characters/124
loop16            7:16  0   13M   1 loop /snap/gnome-characters/139
loop17            7:17  0  14.5M  1 loop /snap/gnome-logs/40
loop18            7:18  0 140.7M  1 loop /snap/gnome-3-26-1604/78
loop19            7:19  0   3.7M  1 loop /snap/gnome-system-monitor/57
loop20            7:20  0   2.3M  1 loop /snap/gnome-calculator/260
loop21            7:21  0   3.7M  1 loop /snap/gnome-system-monitor/54
loop22            7:22  0 169.4M  1 loop /snap/gimp/110
loop23            7:23  0  53.7M  1 loop /snap/core18/677
loop24            7:24  0   91M   1 loop /snap/core/6405
loop25            7:25  0 140.9M  1 loop /snap/gnome-3-26-1604/70
loop26            7:26  0   3.7M  1 loop /snap/gnome-system-monitor/51
```

Listing 3.6: The output from the lsblk command *(continued)*

```
sda                     8:0   0   10G  0 disk
└─sda1                  8:1   0   10G  0 part
  ├─ubuntu--vg-root   253:0   0    9G  0 lvm  /
  └─ubuntu--vg-swap_1 253:1   0  976M  0 lvm  [SWAP]
sr0                    11:0   1 1024M  0 rom
$
```

Notice that at the end of Listing 3.6, the lsblk command also indicates blocks that are related, as with the device-mapped LVM volumes and the associated physical hard drive. You can modify the lsblk output to see additional information or just display a subset of the information by adding command-line options. The -S option displays information only about SCSI block devices on the system:

```
$ lsblk -S
NAME HCTL       TYPE VENDOR  MODEL          REV TRAN
sda  2:0:0:0    disk ATA     VBOX HARDDISK  1.0 sata
sr0  1:0:0:0    rom  VBOX    CD-ROM         1.0 ata
$
```

This is a quick way to view the different SCSI drives installed on the system.

Working with PCI Cards

The lspci command allows you to view the currently installed and recognized PCI and PCIe cards on the Linux system. There are lots of command-line options you can include with the lspci command to display information about the PCI and PCIe cards installed on the system. Table 3.1 shows the most common ones.

TABLE 3.1   The lspci command-line options

Option	Description
-A	Define the method to access the PCI information
-b	Display connection information from the card point-of-view
-k	Display the kernel driver modules for each installed PCI card
-m	Display information in machine-readable format
-n	Display vendor and device information as numbers instead of text
-q	Query the centralized PCI database for information about the installed PCI cards
-t	Display a tree diagram that shows the connections between cards and buses

Option	Description
-v	Display additional information (verbose) about the cards
-x	Display a hexadecimal output dump of the card information

The output from the lspci command without any options shows all the devices connected to the system, as shown in Listing 3.7.

Listing 3.7: Using the lspci command

```
$ lspci
00:00.0 Host bridge: Intel Corporation 440FX - 82441FX PMC [Natoma] (rev 02)
00:01.0 ISA bridge: Intel Corporation 82371SB PIIX3 ISA [Natoma/Triton II]
00:01.1 IDE interface: Intel Corporation 82371AB/EB/MB PIIX4 IDE (rev 01)
00:02.0 VGA compatible controller: InnoTek Systemberatung GmbH VirtualBox Graphics Adapter
00:03.0 Ethernet controller: Intel Corporation 82540EM Gigabit Ethernet Controller (rev 02)
00:04.0 System peripheral: InnoTek Systemberatung GmbH VirtualBox Guest Service
00:05.0 Multimedia audio controller: Intel Corporation 82801AA AC'97 Audio Controller (rev 01)
00:06.0 USB controller: Apple Inc. KeyLargo/Intrepid USB
00:07.0 Bridge: Intel Corporation 82371AB/EB/MB PIIX4 ACPI (rev 08)
00:0d.0 SATA controller: Intel Corporation 82801HM/HEM (ICH8M/ICH8M-F) SATA Controller [AHCI mode] (rev 02)
$
```

You can use the output from the lspci command to troubleshoot PCI card issues, such as when a card isn't recognized by the Linux system.

Working with USB Devices

You can view the basic information about USB devices connected to your Linux system by using the lsusb command. Table 3.2 shows the options available with that command.

TABLE 3.2   The lsusb command options

Option	Description
-d	Display only devices from the specified vendor ID
-D	Display information only from devices with the specified device file
-s	Display information only from devices using the specified bus
-t	Display information in a tree format, showing related devices
-v	Display additional information about the devices (verbose mode)
-V	Display the version of the lsusb program

The basic lsusb program output is shown in Listing 3.8.

Listing 3.8: The lsusb output

```
$ lsusb
Bus 001 Device 003: ID abcd:1234 Unknown
Bus 001 Device 002: ID 80ee:0021 VirtualBox USB Tablet
Bus 001 Device 001: ID 1d6b:0001 Linux Foundation 1.1 root hub
$
```

Most systems incorporate a standard USB hub for connecting multiple USB devices to the USB controller. Fortunately, there are only a handful of USB hubs on the market, so all Linux distributions include the device drivers necessary to communicate with each of these USB hubs. That guarantees that your Linux system will at least detect when a USB device is connected.

Hardware Modules

The Linux kernel needs device drivers to communicate with the hardware devices installed on your Linux system. However, compiling device drivers for all known hardware devices into the kernel would make for an extremely large kernel binary file.

To avoid that situation, the Linux kernel uses kernel *modules*, which are individual hardware driver files that can be linked into the kernel at runtime. That way, the system can link only the modules needed for the hardware present on your system.

If the kernel is configured to load hardware device modules, the individual module files must be available on the system as well. If you're compiling a new Linux kernel, you'll also need to compile any hardware modules along with the new kernel.

Module files may be distributed either as source code that needs to be compiled or as binary object files on the Linux system that are ready to be dynamically linked to the main kernel binary program. If the module files are distributed as source code files, you must compile them to create the binary object file. The .ko file extension is used to identify the module object files.

The standard location for storing module object files is in the /lib/modules directory. This is where the Linux module utilities (such as insmod and modprobe) look for module object library files by default.

Some hardware vendors release module object files only for their hardware modules without releasing the source code. This helps them protect the proprietary features of their hardware, while still allowing their hardware products to be used in an open source environment. Although this arrangement violates the core idea of open source code, it has become a common ground between companies trying to protect their product secrets and Linux enthusiasts who want to use the latest hardware on their systems.

You should be familiar with a few different files when working with modules. You've already seen that the modules required to support a kernel are stored in the /lib/modules directory. Each kernel has its own directory for its own modules (such as /lib/modules/4.3.3), allowing you to create separate modules for each kernel version on the system if needed.

The modules the kernel will load at boot time are listed in the /etc/modules file, one per line. Most hardware modules can be loaded dynamically as the system automatically detects hardware devices, so this file may not contain very many modules.

If needed, you can customize a kernel module to define unique parameters required, such as hardware settings required for the device to operate. The kernel module configurations are stored in the /etc/modules.conf configuration file.

Finally, some modules may depend on other modules being loaded first to operate properly. These relationships are defined in the modules.dep file, stored in the /lib/modules/*version*/ directory, where *version* is the kernel version. The format for each entry is

```
modulefilename: dependencyfilename1 dependencyfilename2 ...
```

When you use the modules_install target to install the modules, it calls the depmod utility, which determines the module dependencies and generates the modules.dep file automatically. If you modify or add any modules after that, you must manually run the depmod command to update the modules.dep file.

Listing Installed Modules

A host of command-line commands can help you troubleshoot and fix kernel module issues. This section walks through the different module commands available to help with any module issues you might run into.

The first command is lsmod, which lists all modules installed on your system. Listing 3.9 shows an example of using the lsmod command on an Ubuntu system.

Listing 3.9: The lsmod command output

```
$ lsmod
Module                  Size  Used by
vboxsf                 39706  1
snd_intel8x0           38153  2
snd_ac97_codec        130285  1 snd_intel8x0
ac97_bus               12730  1 snd_ac97_codec
snd_pcm               102099  2 snd_ac97_codec,snd_intel8x0
snd_page_alloc         18710  2 snd_intel8x0,snd_pcm
snd_seq_midi           13324  0
snd_seq_midi_event     14899  1 snd_seq_midi
snd_rawmidi            30144  1 snd_seq_midi
snd_seq                61560  2 snd_seq_midi_event,snd_seq_midi
snd_seq_device         14497  3 snd_seq,snd_rawmidi,snd_seq_midi
snd_timer              29482  2 snd_pcm,snd_seq
```

Listing 3.9: The lsmod command output *(continued)*

```
rfcomm                 69160  0
hid_multitouch         17407  0
joydev                 17381  0
snd                    69322  12
snd_ac97_codec,snd_intel8x0,snd_timer,snd_pcm,snd_seq,snd_rawmidi,snd_seq_device,
snd_seq_midi
bnep                   19624  2
bluetooth             391136  10 bnep,rfcomm
serio_raw              13462  0
vboxvideo              12658  1
drm                   303102  2 vboxvideo
vboxguest             276728  7 vboxsf
i2c_piix4              22155  0
soundcore              12680  1 snd
video                  19476  0
mac_hid                13205  0
parport_pc             32701  0
ppdev                  17671  0
lp                     17759  0
parport                42348  3 lp,ppdev,parport_pc
hid_generic            12548  0
usbhid                 52659  0
hid                   106148  3 hid_multitouch,hid_generic,usbhid
psmouse               106692  0
ahci                   34091  3
libahci                32716  1 ahci
e1000                 145227  0
pata_acpi              13038  0
$
```

Notice that the lsmod command also shows which modules are used by other modules. This can be crucial information when you're trying to troubleshoot hardware issues.

Getting Module Information

If you need more information about a specific module, use the modinfo command, as shown in Listing 3.10.

Listing 3.10: The modinfo command output

```
$ modinfo bluetooth
filename:       /lib/modules/3.13.0-63-generic/kernel/net/bluetooth/bluetooth.ko
alias:          net-pf-31
```

```
license:        GPL
version:        2.17
description:    Bluetooth Core ver 2.17
author:         Marcel Holtmann <marcel@holtmann.org>
srcversion:     071210642A004CFE1860F30
depends:
intree:         Y
vermagic:       3.13.0-63-generic SMP mod_unload modversions
signer:         Magrathea: Glacier signing key
sig_key:        E2:53:28:1F:E2:65:EE:3C:EA:FC:AA:3F:29:2E:21:2B:95:F0:35:9A
sig_hashalgo:   sha512
parm:           disable_esco:Disable eSCO connection creation (bool)
parm:           disable_ertm:Disable enhanced retransmission mode (bool)
$
```

The modinfo command shows you exactly which module file is used to support the module, along with detailed information about where the module came from.

Installing New Modules

If you need to manually install a new module, there are two commands to help with that:

- insmod

- modprobe

The insmod command is the most basic, requiring you to specify the exact module file to load. As you've seen, the kernel module files are stored in the /lib/modules directory structure, with each kernel version having its own directory. If you look in that directory on your Linux system, you'll see a directory tree structure for the different types of hardware.

For example, Ubuntu Linux desktop systems have the following directory for Bluetooth hardware drivers:

/lib/modules/3.13.0-63-generic/kernel/drivers/bluetooth

This directory is for the currently installed Linux kernel on the system: 3.13.0-63. Inside that directory are different device driver module files for various types of Bluetooth systems:

```
$ ls -l
total 420
-rw-r--r-- 1 root root 23220 Aug 14 19:07 ath3k.ko
-rw-r--r-- 1 root root 14028 Aug 14 19:07 bcm203x.ko
-rw-r--r-- 1 root root 26332 Aug 14 19:07 bfusb.ko
-rw-r--r-- 1 root root 18404 Aug 14 19:07 bluecard_cs.ko
-rw-r--r-- 1 root root 19124 Aug 14 19:07 bpa10x.ko
```

```
-rw-r--r-- 1 root root 16964 Aug 14 19:07 bt3c_cs.ko
-rw-r--r-- 1 root root 38148 Aug 14 19:07 btmrvl.ko
-rw-r--r-- 1 root root 34204 Aug 14 19:07 btmrvl_sdio.ko
-rw-r--r-- 1 root root 17524 Aug 14 19:07 btsdio.ko
-rw-r--r-- 1 root root 14524 Aug 14 19:07 btuart_cs.ko
-rw-r--r-- 1 root root 53964 Aug 14 19:07 btusb.ko
-rw-r--r-- 1 root root 14188 Aug 14 19:07 btwilink.ko
-rw-r--r-- 1 root root 15572 Aug 14 19:07 dtl1_cs.ko
-rw-r--r-- 1 root root 74772 Aug 14 19:07 hci_uart.ko
-rw-r--r-- 1 root root 15156 Aug 14 19:07 hci_vhci.ko
$
```

Each file with the .ko extension is a separate module file for each device driver that you can install into the 3.13.0-63 kernel. To install the module, specify the filename on the insmod command line. Some modules also require parameters, which you must specify on the command line as well:

```
$ sudo insmod /lib/modules/3.13.0-49-generic/kernel/drivers/bluetooth/
btusb.ko
password:
$
```

The downside to using the insmod program is that you may run into modules that depend on other modules, and the insmod program will fail if those other modules aren't already installed. To make the process easier, the modprobe command helps resolve module dependencies for you.

Another nice feature of the modprobe command is that it understands module names, and it will search the module library for the module file that provides the driver for the module name.

Because of this versatility, there are many options available for the modprobe command. Table 3.3 shows the command-line options that you can use.

TABLE 3.3   The modprobe command options

Option	Description
-a	Insert all modules listed on the command line
-b	Apply any blacklist commands specified in the configuration file
-C	Specify a different configuration file other than the default

Option	Description
-c	Display the current configuration used.
-d	Specify the root directory to use for installing modules. The default is /.
-f	Force the module installation even if there are version issues.
-i	Ignore the install and remove commands specified in the configuration file for the module.
-n	Perform a dry run of the module install to see if it will work, without actually installing it.
-q	Quiet mode—doesn't display any error messages if the module installation or removal fails.
-r	Remove the module listed.
-s	Send any error messages to the syslog facility on the system.
-V	Display the program version and exit.
-v	Provide additional information (verbose) as the module is processed.

As you can see, the modprobe command is a full-featured tool all by itself. Perhaps the handiest feature is that it allows you to handle modules based on the module name and not have to list the full module filename:

```
$ sudo modprobe -iv btusb
insmod /lib/modules/3.13.0-63-generic/kernel/drivers/bluetooth/btusb.ko
$
```

Notice that by adding the -v option for verbose mode the output shows the insmod command automatically generated by the modprobe command. The insmod command shows the specific module file used to install the module.

Removing Modules

Normally it does no harm to install a module in the system if the hardware device is not present. The kernel just ignores unused modules. However, some Linux administrators prefer to keep the kernel as lightweight as possible, so the Linux developers created a method for removing unnecessary modules: the rmmod command. The rmmod command removes a module by specifying the module name.

However, our friend the modprobe command can also remove modules for us, so you don't need to memorize another command. Instead, just use the -r option with the modprobe command:

```
$ sudo modprobe -rv btusb
rmmod btusb
$
```

The modprobe -r command invokes the rmmod command automatically, removing the module by name. You can verify that the module has been removed by using the lsmod command.

Storage Basics

The most common way to persistently store data on computer systems is using a *hard disk drive (HDD)*. Hard disk drives are physical devices that store data using a set of disk platters that spin around, storing data magnetically on the platters with a movable read/write head that writes and retrieves magnetic images on the platters.

These days another popular type of persistent storage is called a *solid-state drive (SSD)*. These drives use integrated circuits to store data electronically. There are no moving parts contained in SSDs, making them faster and more resilient than HDDs. While currently SSDs are more expensive than HDDs, technology is quickly changing that, and it may not be long before HDDs are a thing of the past.

Linux handles both HDD and SSD storage devices the same way. It mostly depends on the connection method used to connect the drives to the Linux system. This section describes the different methods that Linux uses in connecting and using both HDD and SSD devices.

Types of Drives

While HDDs and SSDs differ in the way they store data, they both interface with the Linux system using the same methods. There are three main types of drive connections that you'll run into with Linux systems:

- *Parallel Advanced Technology Attachment (PATA)* connects drives using a parallel interface, which requires a wide cable. PATA supports two devices per adapter.

- *Serial Advanced Technology Attachment (SATA)* connects drives using a serial interface, but at a much faster speed than PATA. SATA supports up to four devices per adapter.

- *Small Computer System Interface (SCSI)* connects drives using a parallel interface, but with the speed of SATA. SCSI supports up to eight devices per adapter.

When you connect a drive to a Linux system, the Linux kernel assigns the drive device a file in the /dev directory. That file is called a *raw device*, as it provides a path directly to the drive from the Linux system. Any data written to the file is written to the drive, and reading the file reads data directly from the drive.

For PATA devices, this file is named /dev/hd*x*, where *x* is a letter representing the individual drive, starting with a. For SATA and SCSI devices, Linux uses /dev/sd*x*, where *x* is a letter representing the individual drive, again, starting with a. Thus, to reference the first SATA device on the system, you'd use /dev/sda, then for the second device /dev/sdb, and so on.

Drive Partitions

Most operating systems, including Linux, allow you to *partition* a drive into multiple sections. A partition is a self-contained section within the drive that the operating system treats as a separate storage space.

Partitioning drives can help you better organize your data, such as segmenting operating system data from user data. If a rogue user fills up the disk space with data, the operating system will still have room to operate on the separate partition.

Partitions must be tracked by some type of indexing system on the drive. Systems that use the old BIOS boot loader method use the *master boot record (MBR)* method for managing disk partitions. This method supports only up to four *primary partitions* on a drive. Each primary partition itself, however, can be split into multiple *extended partitions.*

Systems that use the UEFI boot loader method use the more advanced *GUID Partition Table (GPT)* method for managing partitions, which supports up to 128 partitions on a drive. Linux assigns the partition numbers in the order that the partition appears on the drive, starting with number 1.

Linux creates /dev files for each separate disk partition. It attaches the partition number to the end of the device name and numbers the primary partitions starting at 1, so the first primary partition on the first SATA drive would be /dev/sda1. MBR extended partitions are numbered starting at 5, so the first extended partition is assigned the file /dev/sda5.

Automatic Drive Detection

Linux systems detect drives and partitions at boot time and assign each one a unique device filename. However, with the invention of removable USB drives (such as memory sticks), which can be added and removed at will while the system is running, that method needed to be modified.

Most Linux systems now use the *udev* application. The udev program runs in the background at all times and automatically detects new hardware connected to the running Linux system. As you connect new drives, USB devices, or optical drives (such as CD and DVD devices), udev will detect them and assign each one a unique device filename in the /dev directory.

Another feature of the udev application is that it also creates *persistent device files* for storage devices. When you add or remove a removable storage device, the /dev name assigned to it may change, depending on what devices are connected at any given time. That can make it difficult for applications to find the same storage device each time.

To solve that problem, the udev application uses the /dev/disk directory to create links to the /dev storage device files based on unique attributes of the drive. udev creates four separate directories for storing links:

- */dev/disk/by-id*: Links storage devices by their manufacturer make, model, and serial number
- */dev/disk/by-label*: Links storage devices by the label assigned to them
- */dev/disk/by-path* Links storage devices by the physical hardware port they are connected to
- */dev/disk/by-uuid*: Links storage devices by the 128-bit universally unique identifier (UUID) assigned to the device

With the udev device links, you can specifically reference a storage device by a permanent identifier rather than where or when it was plugged into the Linux system.

Storage Alternatives

Standard partition layouts on storage devices do have their limitations. After you create and format a partition, it's not easy making it larger or smaller. Individual partitions are also susceptible to disk failures, in which case all data stored in the partition will be lost.

To accommodate more dynamic storage options, as well as fault-tolerance features, Linux has incorporated a few advanced storage management techniques. This section covers three of the more popular techniques you'll run into.

Multipath

The Linux kernel now supports Device Mapper (DM) multipathing, which allows you to configure multiple paths between the Linux system and network storage devices. Multipathing aggregates the paths providing for increased throughout while all paths are active, or fault tolerance if one of the paths becomes inactive.

The Linux DM multipathing tools include

- *dm-multipath*: The kernel module that provides multipath support
- *multipath*: A command-line command for viewing multipath devices
- *multipathd*: A background process for monitoring paths and activating/deactivating paths
- *kpartx*: A command-line tool for creating device entries for multipath storage devices

The DM multipathing feature uses the dynamic */dev/mapper* device file directory in Linux. Linux creates a /dev/mapper device file named mpath*N* for each new multipath storage device you add to the system, where *N* is the number of the multipath drive. That file acts as a normal device file to the Linux system, allowing you to create partitions and filesystems on the multipath device just as you would a normal drive partition.

Logical Volume Manager

The Linux *Logical Volume Manager (LVM)* also utilizes the /dev/mapper dynamic device directory to allow you to create virtual drive devices. You can aggregate multiple physical drive partitions into virtual volumes, which you then treat as a single partition on your system.

The benefit of LVM is that you can add and remove physical partitions as needed to a logical volume, expanding and shrinking the logical volume as needed.

Using LVM is somewhat complicated. Figure 3.1 demonstrates the layout for an LVM environment.

FIGURE 3.1   The Linux LVM layout

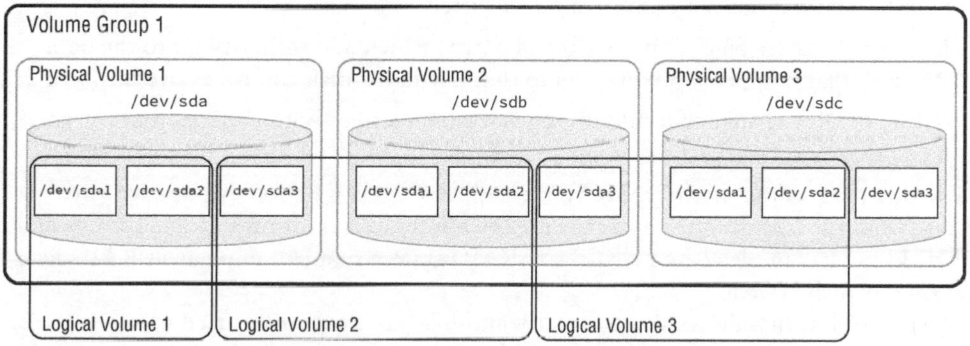

In the example shown in Figure 3.1, three physical drives each contain three partitions. The first logical volume consists of the first two partitions of the first drive. The second logical volume spans drives, combining the third partition of the first drive with the first and second partitions of the second drive to create one volume. The third logical volume consists of the third partition of the second drive, and the first two partitions of the third drive. The third partition of the third drive is left unassigned, and it can be added later to any of the logical volumes when needed.

For each physical partition, you must mark the partition type as the Linux LVM filesystem type in fdisk or gdisk. Then, you must use several LVM tools to create and manage the logical volumes:

- *pvcreate*: Creates a physical volume

- *vgcreate*: Groups physical volumes into a volume group

- *lvcreate*: Creates a logical volume from partitions in each physical volume

The logical volumes create entries in the /dev/mapper directory, which represent the LVM device you can format with a filesystem and use like a normal partition.

While the initial setup of an LVM is complicated, it does provide great benefits. If you run out of space in a logical volume, just add a new disk partition to the volume.

Using RAID Technology

Redundant Array of Inexpensive Disks (RAID) technology has changed the data storage environment for most data centers. RAID technology allows you to improve data access performance and reliability, as well as implement data redundancy for fault tolerance by combining multiple drives into one virtual drive. Several versions of RAID are commonly used:

- *RAID 0*: Disk striping, which spreads data across multiple disks for faster access
- *RAID 1*: Disk mirroring, which duplicates data across two drives
- *RAID 10*: Disk mirroring and striping, which provides striping for performance and mirroring for fault tolerance
- *RAID 4*: Disk striping with parity, which adds a parity bit stored on a separate disk so that data on a failed data disk can be recovered
- *RAID 5*: Disk striping with distributed parity, which adds a parity bit to the data stripe so that it appears on all disks so that any failed disk can be recovered
- *RAID 6*: Disk striping with double parity, which stripes both the data and the parity bit so that two failed drives can be recovered

The downside is that hardware RAID storage devices can be somewhat expensive (despite what the I stands for), and they are often impractical for most home uses. Because of that, Linux has implemented a software RAID system that can implement RAID features on any disk system.

The *mdadm* utility allows you to specify multiple partitions to be used in any type of RAID environment. The RAID device appears as a single device in the /dev/mapper directory, which you can then partition and format to a specific filesystem.

Partitioning Tools

After you connect a drive to your Linux system you'll need to create partitions on it (even if there's only one partition). Linux provides several tools for working with raw storage devices to create partitions. This section covers the most popular partitioning tools you'll run across in Linux.

Working with *fdisk*

The most common command-line partitioning tool is the *fdisk* utility. The fdisk program allows you to create, view, delete, and modify partitions on any drive that uses the MBR method of indexing partitions.

To use the fdisk program, you must specify the drive device name (not the partition name) of the device you want to work with:

```
$ sudo fdisk /dev/sda
[sudo] password for rich:
Welcome to fdisk (util-linux 2.23.2).

Changes will remain in memory only, until you decide to write them.
Be careful before using the write command.


Command (m for help):
```

The fdisk program uses its own command line that allows you to submit commands to work with the drive partitions. Table 3.4 shows the common commands you have available to work with.

TABLE 3.4 Common fdisk commands

Command	Description
a	Toggle a bootable flag
b	Edit BSD disk label
c	Toggle the DOS compatibility flag
d	Delete a partition
g	Create a new empty GPT partition table
G	Create an IRIX (SGI) partition table
l	List known partition types
m	Print this menu
n	Add a new partition
o	Create a new empty DOS partition table
p	Print the partition table
q	Quit without saving changes
s	Create a new empty Sun disk label

TABLE 3.4 Common fdisk commands *(continued)*

Command	Description
t	Change a partition's system ID
u	Change display/entry units
v	Verify the partition table
w	Write table to disk and exit
x	Extra functionality (experts only)

The p command displays the current partition scheme on the drive:

```
Command (m for help): p

Disk /dev/sda: 10.7 GB, 10737418240 bytes, 20971520 sectors
Units = sectors of 1 * 512 = 512 bytes
Sector size (logical/physical): 512 bytes / 512 bytes
I/O size (minimum/optimal): 512 bytes / 512 bytes
Disk label type: dos
Disk identifier: 0x000528e6

   Device Boot      Start         End      Blocks   Id  System
/dev/sda1   *        2048     2099199     1048576   83  Linux
/dev/sda2         2099200    20971519     9436160   83  Linux

Command (m for help):
```

In this example, the /dev/sda drive is sectioned into two partitions: sda1 and sda2. The Id and System columns refer to the type of filesystem the partition is formatted to handle. We cover that in the "Understanding Filesystems" section later. Both partitions are formatted to support a Linux filesystem. The first partition is allocated about 1 GB of space, whereas the second is allocated a little over 9 GB of space.

The fdisk command is somewhat rudimentary in that it doesn't allow you to alter the size of an existing partition; all you can do is delete the existing partition and rebuild it from scratch.

To be able to boot the system from a partition, you must set the boot flag for the partition. You do that with the a command. The bootable partitions are indicated in the output listing with an asterisk.

If you make any changes to the drive partitions, you must exit using the w command to write the changes to the drive.

Working with *gdisk*

If you're working with drives that use the GPT indexing method, you'll need to use the *gdisk* program:

```
$ sudo gdisk /dev/sda
[sudo] password for rich:
GPT fdisk (gdisk) version 1.0.3

Partition table scan:
  MBR: protective
  BSD: not present
  APM: not present
  GPT: present

Found valid GPT with protective MBR; using GPT.


Command (? for help):
```

The gdisk program identifies the type of formatting used on the drive. If the drive doesn't currently use the GPT method, gdisk offers you the option to convert it to a GPT drive.

 WARNING   Be careful with converting the drive method specified for your drive. The method you select must be compatible with the system firmware (BIOS or UEFI). If not, your drive will not be able to boot.

The gdisk program also uses its own command prompt, allowing you to enter commands to manipulate the drive layout, as shown in Table 3.5.

TABLE 3.5   Common gdisk commands

Command	Description
b	Back up GPT data to a file
c	Change a partition's name
d	Delete a partition
i	Show detailed information on a partition
l	List known partition types

TABLE 3.5   Common gdisk commands *(continued)*

Command	Description
n	Add a new partition
o	Create a new empty GUID partition table (GPT)
p	Print the partition table
q	Quit without saving changes
r	Recovery and transformation options (experts only)
s	Sort partitions
t	Change a partition's type code
v	Verify disk
w	Write table to disk and exit
x	Extra functionality (experts only)
?	Print this menu

You'll notice that many of the gdisk commands are similar to those in the fdisk program, making it easier to switch between the two programs.

The GNU *parted* Command

The GNU *parted* program provides yet another command-line interface for working with drive partitions:

```
$ sudo parted
GNU Parted 3.2
Using /dev/sda
Welcome to GNU Parted! Type 'help' to view a list of commands.
(parted) print
Model: ATA VBOX HARDDISK (scsi)
Disk /dev/sda: 15.6GB
Sector size (logical/physical): 512B/512B
Partition Table: gpt
```

```
Disk Flags:

Number  Start   End     Size    File system     Name  Flags
1       1049kB  1000MB  999MB   fat32                 boot, esp
2       1000MB  13.6GB  12.6GB  ext4
3       13.6GB  15.6GB  2000MB  linux-swap(v1)

(parted)
```

One of the selling features of the parted program is that it allows you to modify existing partition sizes, so you can easily shrink or grow partitions on the drive. The command prompt interface in GNU parted can be a bit cryptic at times, making it awkward for first-time users to get comfortable with. However, once you become familiar with the command structure there are lots of things you can do, making GNU parted a versatile tool.

Graphical Tools

Some graphical tools are also available to use if you're working from a graphical desktop environment. The most common of these is the GNOME Partition Editor, called *gparted*. Figure 3.2 shows an example of running gparted in an Ubuntu desktop environment.

FIGURE 3.2   The GParted interface

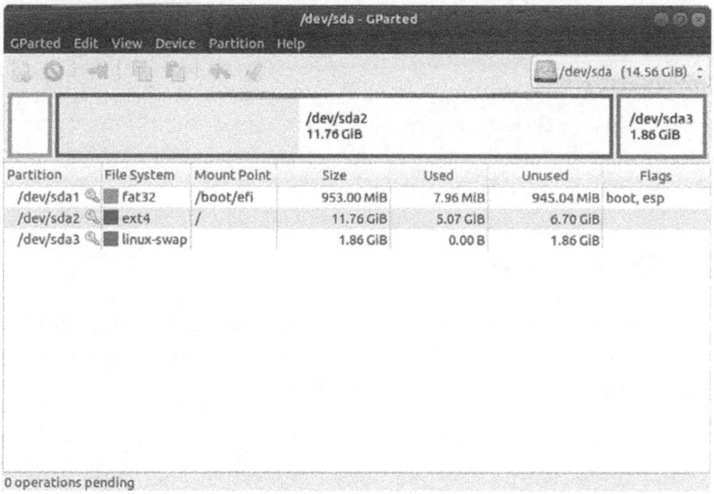

The gparted window displays each of the drives on a system one at a time, showing all partitions contained in the drive in a graphical layout. You right-click a partition to select options for mounting or unmounting, formatting, deleting, or resizing the partition.

While it's certainly possible to interact with a drive as a raw device, that's not usually how Linux applications work. A lot of work is involved in trying to read and write data to a raw device. Instead, Linux provides a method for handling the dirty work for us, which is covered in the next section.

Understanding Filesystems

Just like storing stuff in a closet, storing data in a Linux system requires some method of organization to be efficient. Linux utilizes *filesystems* to manage data stored on storage devices. A filesystem maintains a map to locate each file placed in the storage device. This section describes the Linux filesystem and shows how you can locate files and directories contained within it.

The Linux filesystem can be one of the most confusing aspects of working with Linux. Locating files on drives, CDs, and USB memory sticks can be a challenge at first.

If you're familiar with how Windows manages files and directories, you know that Windows assigns *drive letters* to each storage device you connect to the system. For example, Windows uses C: for the main drive on the system, or E: for a USB memory stick plugged into the system.

In Windows, you're used to seeing file paths such as

```
C:\Users\rich\Documents\test.docx
```

This path indicates the file is located in the Documents directory for the rich user account, which is stored on the disk partition assigned the letter C (usually the first drive on the system).

The Windows path tells you exactly what physical device the file is stored on. Linux, however, doesn't use this method to reference files. It uses a *virtual directory* structure. The virtual directory contains file paths from all the storage devices installed on the system, consolidated into a single directory structure.

The Virtual Directory

The Linux virtual directory structure contains a single base directory, called the *root directory*. The root directory lists files and directories beneath it based on the directory path used to get to them, similar to the way Windows does it.

Be careful with the terminology here. While the main admin user account in Linux is called root, that's not related to the root virtual directory folder. The two are separate, which can be confusing.

For example, a Linux file path could look like this:

/home/rich/Documents/test.doc

First, note that the Linux path uses forward slashes instead of the backward slashes that Windows uses. That's an important difference that trips up many novice Linux administrators. As for the path itself, also notice that there's no drive letter. The path indicates only that the file test.doc is stored in the Documents directory for the user rich; it doesn't give you any clues as to which physical device contains the file.

Linux places physical devices in the virtual directory using *mount points*. A mount point is a directory placeholder within the virtual directory that points to a specific physical device. Figure 3.3 demonstrates how this works.

FIGURE 3.3   The Linux virtual directory structure divided between two drives

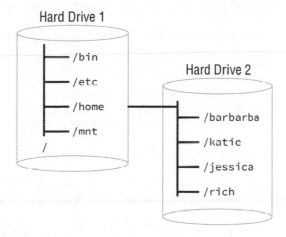

In Figure 3.3, there are two drives used on the Linux system. One drive is associated with the root of the virtual directory (indicated by the single forward slash). The second drive is mounted at the location /home, which is where the user directories are located. After the second drive is mounted to the virtual directory, files and directories stored on the drive are available under the /home directory.

Since Linux stores everything within the virtual directory, it can get somewhat complicated. Fortunately, a standard format has been defined for the Linux virtual directory called the Linux *filesystem hierarchy standard (FHS)*. The FHS defines core directory names and locations that should be present on every Linux system, as well as what type of data they should contain. Table 3.6 shows a few of the common directories defined in the FHS.

TABLE 3.6   Common Linux FHS directories

Directory	Description
/boot	Contains boot loader files used to boot the system
/etc	Contains system and application configuration files
/home	Contains user data files
/media	Used as a mount point for removable devices
/mnt	Also used as a mount point for removable devices
/opt	Contains data for optional third-party programs
/tmp	Contains temporary files created by system users
/usr	Contains data for standard Linux programs
/usr/bin	Contains local user programs and data
/usr/local	Contains data for programs unique to the local installation
/usr/sbin	Contains data for system programs and data
/var	Contains variable data files, including system and application logs

While the FHS helps standardize the Linux virtual filesystem, not all Linux distributions follow it completely. It's best to consult with your specific Linux distribution's documentation on how it manages files within the virtual directory structure.

Maneuvering Around the Filesystem

Using the virtual directory makes it a breeze to move files from one physical device to another. You don't need to worry about drive letters—just the locations within the virtual directory:

```
$ cp /home/rich/Documents/myfile.txt /media/usb
```

The full path to a file lists each directory within the virtual directory structure to walk your way down to find the file. This format is called an *absolute path*. The absolute path to a file always starts at the root directory (/) and includes every directory along the virtual directory tree to the file.

Alternatively, you can use a *relative path* to specify a file location. The relative path to a file denotes the location of a file relative to your current location within the virtual directory tree structure. If you were already in the Documents directory, you'd just need to type

```
$ cp myfile.txt /media/usb
```

When Linux sees that the path doesn't start with a forward slash, it assumes the path is relative to the current directory.

Formatting Filesystems

Before you can assign a drive partition to a mount point in the virtual directory, you must format it using a filesystem. There are numerous filesystem types that Linux supports, each with different features and capabilities. This section discusses those filesystems and how to format a drive partition for them.

Common Filesystem Types

Each operating system utilizes its own filesystem type for storing data on drives. Linux not only supports several of its own filesystem types, but also supports filesystems of other operating systems. This section covers the most common Linux and non-Linux filesystems that you can use in your Linux partitions.

Linux Filesystems

When you create a filesystem specifically for use on a Linux system, you can choose from four main filesystems:

- *btrfs*: A newer, high-performance filesystem that supports files up to 16 exbibytes (EiB) in size, and a total filesystem size of 16 EiB. It also can perform its own form of Redundant Array of Inexpensive Disks (RAID) as well as logical volume management (LVM) and subvolumes. It includes additional advanced features such as built-in snapshots for backup, improved fault tolerance, and data compression on the fly.

- *ecryptfs*: The Enterprise Cryptographic Filesystem (eCryptfs) applies a Portable Operating System Interface (POSIX)–compliant encryption protocol to data before storing it on the device. This provides a layer of protection for data stored on the device. Only the operating system that created the filesystem can read data from it.

- *ext3*: Also called ext3fs, this is a descendant of the original Linux ext filesystem. It supports files up to 2 tebibytes (TiB), with a total filesystem size of 16 TiB. It supports journaling, as well as faster startup and recovery.

- *ext4*: Also called ext4fs, it's the current version of the original Linux filesystem. It supports files up to 16 TiB, with a total filesystem size of 1 EiB. It also supports journaling and utilizes improved performance features.

- *reiserFS*: Created before the Linux ext3fs filesystem and commonly used on older Linux systems, it provides features now found in ext3fs and ext4fs. Linux has dropped support for the most recent version, reiser4fs.

- *swap*: The swap filesystem allows you to create virtual memory for your system using space on a physical drive. The system can then swap data out of normal memory into the swap space, providing a method of adding additional memory to your system. This is not intended for storing persistent data.

The default filesystem used by most Linux distributions these days is ext4fs. The ext4fs filesystem provides *journaling*, which is a method of tracking data not yet written to the drive in a log file, called the journal. If the system fails before the data can be written to the drive, the journal data can be recovered and stored upon the next system boot.

Many Linux administrators have taken a liking to the newer btrfs filesystem. The btrfs filesystem provides many advanced features, such as the ability to create a filesystem across multiple devices, automatic data compression, and the ability to create subvolumes.

Non-Linux Filesystems

One of the great features of Linux that makes it so versatile is its ability to read data stored on devices formatted for other operating systems, such as macOS and Windows. This feature makes it a breeze to share data between different systems running different operating systems.

Here's a list of the common non-Linux filesystems that Linux can handle:

- *CIFS*: The Common Internet Filesystem (CIFS) is a filesystem protocol created by Microsoft for reading and writing data across a network using a network storage device. It was released to the public for use on all operating systems.

- *exFAT*: The Extended File Allocation Table is a filesystem built on the original Microsoft FAT table architecture, and it's commonly used to format USB devices and SD cards.

- *HFS*: The Hierarchical Filesystem (HFS) was developed by Apple for its Mac systems. Linux can also interact with the more advanced HFS+ filesystem.

- *ISO-9660*: The ISO-9660 standard is used for creating filesystems on CD-ROM devices.

- *NFS*: The Network Filesystem (NFS) is an open source standard for reading and writing data across a network using a network storage device.

- *NTFS*: The New Technology Filesystem (NTFS) is the filesystem used by the Microsoft NT operating system and subsequent versions of Windows. Linux can read and write data on an NTFS partition as of kernel 2.6.x.

- *SMB*: The Server Message Block (SMB) filesystem was created by Microsoft as a proprietary filesystem used for network storage and interacting with other network devices (such as printers). Support for SMB allows Linux clients and servers to interact with Microsoft clients and servers on a network.

- *UDF*: The Universal Disk Format (UDF) is commonly used on DVD-ROM devices for storing data. Linux can both read data from a DVD and write data to a DVD using this filesystem.

- *VFAT*: The Virtual File Allocation Table (VFAT) is an extension of the original Microsoft File Allocation Table (FAT) filesystem. It's not commonly used on drives but is often used for removable storage devices such as USB memory sticks.

- *XFS*: The X Filesystem (XFS) was created by Silicon Graphics for their (now defunct) advanced graphical workstations. The filesystem provided advanced high-performance features that makes it still popular in Linux.

- *ZFS*: The Zettabyte Filesystem (ZFS) was created by Sun Microsystems (now part of Oracle) for its Unix workstations and servers. Another high-performance filesystem, it has features similar to the btrfs Linux filesystem.

It's generally not recommended to format a partition using a non-Linux filesystem if you plan on using the drive for only Linux systems. Linux supports these filesystems mainly as a method for sharing data with other operating systems.

Creating Filesystems

The Swiss army knife for creating filesystems in Linux is the mkfs program. The *mkfs* program is actually a front end to several individual tools for creating specific filesystems, such as the mkfs.ext4 program for creating ext4 filesystems.

The beauty of the mkfs program is that you need to remember only one program name to create any type of filesystem on your Linux system. Just use the -t option to specify the filesystem type:

```
$ sudo mkfs -t ext4 /dev/sdb1
mke2fs 1.44.1 (24-Mar-2018)
Creating filesystem with 2621440 4k blocks and 655360 inodes
Filesystem UUID: f9137b26-0caf-4a8a-afd0-392002424ee8
Superblock backups stored on blocks:
     32768, 98304, 163840, 229376, 294912, 819200, 884736, 1605632
Allocating group tables: done
Writing inode tables: done
Creating journal (16384 blocks): done
Writing superblocks and filesystem accounting information: done
$
```

Just specify the partition device filename for the partition you want to format on the command line. The mkfs program automatically calls the mke2fs program to create the ext4 partition. Notice that the mkfs program also does a lot of other things behind the scenes when formatting the filesystem. Each filesystem has its own method for indexing files and directories and tracking file access. The mkfs program creates all of the index files and tables necessary for the specific filesystem.

Be very careful when specifying the partition device filename. When you format a partition, any existing data on the partition is lost. If you specify the wrong partition name, you could lose important data or make your Linux system unable to boot.

It's usually a good idea to reserve some space on the hard drive for a swap area. The swap area acts as virtual memory to help expand the usable memory available to the CPU. You create a swap area using the mkswap command.

Mounting Filesystems

After you've formatted a drive partition with a filesystem, you can add it to the virtual directory on your Linux system. This process is called *mounting* the filesystem.

You can either manually mount the partition within the virtual directory structure from the command line or allow Linux to automatically mount the partition at boot time. This section walks through both of these methods.

Manually Mounting Devices

To temporarily mount a filesystem to the Linux virtual directory, use the *mount* command. The basic format for the mount command is

```
mount -f fstype device mountpoint
```

Use the -f command-line option to specify the filesystem type of the device:

```
$ sudo mount -t ext4 /dev/sdb1 /media/usb1
$
```

If you specify the mount command with no parameters, it displays all devices currently mounted on the Linux system. Be prepared for a long output, though, as most Linux distributions mount lots of virtual devices in the virtual directory to provide information about system resources. Listing 3.11 shows a partial output from a mount command.

Listing 3.11: Output from the mount command

```
$ mount
...
/dev/sda2 on / type ext4 (rw,relatime,errors=remount-ro,data=ordered)
/dev/sda1 on /boot/efi type vfat
 (rw,relatime,fmask=0077,dmask=0077,codepage=437,iocharset=iso8859
-1,shortname=mixed,errors=remount-ro)
...
/dev/sdb1 on /media/usb1 type ext4 (rw,relatime,data=ordered)
/dev/sdb2 on /media/usb2 type ext4 (rw,relatime,data=ordered)
rich@rich-TestBox2:~$
```

To save space, we trimmed down the output from the mount command to show only the physical devices on the system. Notice that the main hard drive device (/dev/sda) contains two partitions. You can also see that the USB memory stick device (/dev/sdb) contains two partitions.

The mount command uses the -o option to specify additional features of the filesystem, such as mounting it in read-only mode, user permissions assigned to the mount point, and how data is stored on the device. These options are shown in the output of the mount command. Usually you can omit the -o option to use the system defaults for the new mount point.

The downside to the mount command is that it only temporarily mounts the device in the virtual directory. When you reboot the system, you have to manually mount the devices again. This is usually fine for removable devices, such as USB memory sticks, but for more permanent devices it would be nice if Linux could mount them for us automatically. Fortunately for us, Linux can do just that.

To remove a mounted drive from the virtual directory, use the *umount* command (note the missing "n"). You can remove the mounted drive by specifying either the device filename or the mount point directory.

To mount a partition created as a swap area, you don't use the mount command but instead use the swapon command. The kernel will automatically flag the partition to be used as part of the virtual memory structure.

Automatically Mounting Devices

For permanent storage devices, Linux maintains the */etc/fstab* file to indicate which drive devices should be mounted to the virtual directory at boot time. The /etc/fstab file is a table that indicates the drive device file (either the raw file or one of its permanent udev file-names), the mount point location, the filesystem type, and any additional options required to mount the drive. Listing 3.12 shows the /etc/fstab file from an Ubuntu workstation.

Listing 3.12: The /etc/fstab file

```
$ cat /etc/fstab
# /etc/fstab: static file system information.
#
# Use 'blkid' to print the universally unique identifier for a
# device; this may be used with UUID= as a more robust way to name devices
# that works even if disks are added and removed. See fstab(5).
#
# <file system> <mount point>   <type> <options>         <dump>  <pass>
# / was on /dev/sda2 during installation
UUID=46a8473c-8437-4d5f-a6a1-6596c492c3ce /               ext4
 errors=remount-ro 0        1
# /boot/efi was on /dev/sda1 during installation
UUID=864B-62F5   /boot/efi       vfat      umask=0077      0       1
# swap was on /dev/sda3 during installation
UUID=8673447a-0227-47d7-a67a-e6b837bd7188 none             swap   sw
0       0
$
```

This /etc/fstab file references the devices by their Universally Unique Identifier (UUID) value, ensuring the correct drive partition is accessed no matter what order it appears in the raw device table. The first partition is mounted at the /boot/efi mount point in the virtual directory. The second partition is mounted at the root (/) of the virtual directory, and the third partition is mounted as a swap area for virtual memory.

You can manually add devices to the /etc/fstab file so that they are mounted automatically when the Linux system boots. However, if they don't exist at boot time, that will generate a boot error.

If you use the eCryptfs filesystem type on any partitions, they will appear in the */etc/crypttab* file and will be mounted automatically at boot time. While the system is running, you can also view all currently mounted devices, whether they were mounted automatically by the system or manually by users, by viewing the */etc/mtab* file.

Managing Filesystems

After you've created a filesystem and mounted it to the virtual directory, you may have to manage and maintain it to keep things running smoothly. This section walks through some of the Linux utilities available for managing the filesystems on your Linux system.

Retrieving Filesystem Stats

As you use your Linux system, there's no doubt that at some point you'll need to monitor disk performance and usage. A few different tools are available to help you do that:

- *df*: Displays disk usage by partition
- *du*: Displays disk usage by directory; good for finding users or applications that are taking up the most disk space
- *iostat*: Displays a real-time chart of disk statistics by partition
- *lsblk*: Displays current partition sizes and mount points

In addition to these tools, the /proc and /sys directories are special filesystems that the kernel uses for recording system statistics. Two files that can be useful when working with filesystems are the */proc/partitions* and */proc/mounts* files, which provide information on system partitions and mount points, respectively. Additionally, the */sys/block* directory contains separate directories for each mounted drive, showing partitions and kernel level stats.

WARNING   Some filesystems, such as ext3 and ext4, allocate a specific number of inodes when created. An inode is an entry in the index table that tracks files stored on the filesystem. If the filesystem runs out of inode entries in the table, you can't create any more files, even if space is available on the drive. Using the -i option with the df command will show you the percentage of inodes used on a filesystem and can be a lifesaver.

Filesystem Tools

Linux uses the e2fsprogs package of tools to provide utilities for working with ext filesystems (such as ext3 and ext4). The most popular tools in the e2fsprogs package are

- blkid: Display information about block devices, such as storage drives
- chattr: Change file attributes on the filesystem
- debugfs: Manually view and modify the filesystem structure, such as undeleting a file or extracting a corrupted file
- dumpe2fs: Display block and superblock group information
- e2label: Change the label on the filesystem
- resize2fs: Expand or shrink a filesystem
- tune2fs: Modify filesystem parameters

These tools help you fine-tune parameters on an ext filesystem, but if corruption occurs on the filesystem, you'll need the fsck program.

The XFS filesystem also has a set of tools available for tuning the filesystem. You'll most likely use the following:

- xfs_admin: Display or change filesystem parameters such as the label or UUID assigned

- xfs_db: Examine and debug an XFS filesystem

- xfs_fsr: Improve the organization of mounted filesystems

- xfs_info: Display information about a mounted filesystem, including the block sizes and sector sizes, as well as label and UUID information

- xfs_repair: Repair corrupted or damaged XFS filesystems

Although these ext and XFS tools are useful, they can't help fix things if the filesystem itself has errors. For that, the fsck program is the tool to use:

```
$ sudo fsck -f /dev/sdb1
fsck from util-linux 2.31.1
e2fsck 1.44.1 (24-Mar-2018)
Pass 1: Checking inodes, blocks, and sizes
Pass 2: Checking directory structure
Pass 3: Checking directory connectivity
Pass 4: Checking reference counts
Pass 5: Checking group summary information
/dev/sdb1: 11/655360 files (0.0% non-contiguous), 66753/2621440 blocks
$
```

The fsck program is a front end to several different programs that check the various filesystems to match the index against the actual files stored in the filesystem, such as the e2fsck program used in this example. If any discrepancies occur, run the fsck program in repair mode, and it will attempt to reconcile the discrepancies and fix the filesystem. If the fsck program is unable to repair the drive on the first run, try running it again a few times to fix any broken files and directory links. If running the fsck program multiple times doesn't repair the drive, you may have to resort to reformatting the drive and losing any data on it.

Summary

These days most Linux distributions do a great job of automatically detecting and installing hardware devices. However, it's a good idea to know how to find and change hardware device settings in case you ever need to modify things. The lsdev command displays the hardware settings for all devices connected to the Linux system. The lspci command displays hardware settings for PCI devices, and the lsusb command displays settings for USB devices. The kernel also populates the virtual /proc and /sys directories with real-time information about the system hardware status. The udev program monitors the system and automatically installs any kernel modules required to support hardware connected to a running system.

Most storage devices, such as hard disk drives and solid-state drives, allow you to partition them into subsections. Each partition works as a separate storage area that you can format with a Linux filesystem and mount in the Linux virtual directory at mount points. You can also utilize the Linux LVM technology to create virtual volumes consisting of one or more physical partitions and treat the virtual volume as a single partition. This allows you to dynamically add more disk space to an existing virtual volume to increase the storage area.

Linux provides a wealth of command-line tools for partitioning, formatting, and mounting partitions. The fdisk, gdisk, and parted tools provide a menu-driven method for creating, deleting, and modifying partitions on storage devices. After you've created a partition, you must format it using the mkfs tool. When you've formatted the partition with a Linux filesystem, you can mount it into the virtual directory using the mount command.

Linux also provides several tools for managing and repairing filesystems. The df and du commands are common tools for displaying available storage space on the system, and the fsck command is vital for repairing broken filesystems.

Exam Essentials

Describe how the BIOS and UEFI work on Linux systems.   The BIOS and UEFI are firmware embedded into computers to start the boot process. They check basic hardware components of the computer and launch the boot loader program to start the boot process.

Explain how to determine the hardware settings on a Linux system.   Linux provides several command-line tools for examining the hardware settings on the system, including lsdev, which displays information on all devices; lspci, which displays information on PCI devices; and lsusb, which displays information on USB devices. In addition to these tools, Linux provides the /proc and /sys virtual directories. The Linux kernel populates files in these directories in real time to display information and statistics on hardware devices.

Describe common disk types and their features.   Most legacy systems used hard disk drives (HDD) for data storage, but more modern computers use the solid-state drive (SSD) technology. Both types connect to the motherboard using three types of standard interfaces. The legacy PATA interface provides the basic slow-speed connection and is typically found in legacy systems. More modern computer systems now use the SATA interface, which is faster and more easily configured. The SCSI interface allows you to connect more disks together in a single interface and is often faster than SATA interfaces. However, it is more expensive and is usually only found on higher-end computers.

Explain the steps necessary to add a new hard drive to a Linux system.   First you must partition the hard drive to create one or more partitions. Each partition contains a single filesystem, which Linux uses to manage the files and directories stored on the storage device. The fdisk, gdisk, and parted utilities are available in Linux for partitioning a storage device. After you partition the storage device, you must format each partition using one type of filesystem. The most common filesystem currently used in Linux is ext4, but the btrfs filesystem is gaining in popularity due to some advanced features it implements. To create the filesystem, you must use the mkfs command. After creating the filesystem, you can mount the partition into the virtual directory using the mount command. If you want Linux to mount the partition automatically at boot time, add the partition to the /etc/fstab file.

Explain the tools available in Linux for managing and maintaining filesystems.   Linux provides several command-line tools for displaying the status of a filesystem. The df command displays disk usage by partition, and the du command displays disk usage by directory. If an error occurs on the partition, use the fsck utility to fix the partition.

Review Questions

You can find the answers in the appendix.

1. What program does the workstation firmware start at boot time?
    A. A boot loader
    B. The `fsck` program
    C. The Windows OS
    D. The `mount` command
    E. The `mkinitrd` program

2. Where does the firmware first look for a Linux boot loader program?
    A. The `/boot/grub` directory
    B. The master boot record (MBR)
    C. The `/var/log` directory
    D. A boot partition
    E. The `/etc` directory

3. Where does the workstation BIOS attempt to find a boot loader program? (Choose all that apply.)
    A. An internal hard drive
    B. An external hard drive
    C. A DVD drive
    D. A USB memory stick
    E. A network server

4. Where is the master boot record located? (Choose all that apply.)
    A. The first sector of the first hard drive on the system
    B. The boot partition of any hard drive on the system
    C. The last sector of the first hard drive on the system
    D. Any sector on any hard drive on the system
    E. The first sector of the second hard drive on the system

5. The EFI System Partition (ESP) is stored in the _____ directory on Linux systems.
    A. `/boot`
    B. `/etc`
    C. `/var`
    D. `/boot/efi`
    E. `/boot/grub`

6. The _____ firmware method has replaced BIOS on most modern IBM-compatible computers.
   A. FTP
   B. UEFI
   C. PXE
   D. NFS
   E. HTTPS

7. Which type of storage device uses integrated circuits to store data with no moving parts?
   A. SSD
   B. SATA
   C. SCSI
   D. HDD
   E. PATA

8. What raw device file would Linux create for the second SCSI drive connected to the system?
   A. /dev/hdb
   B. /dev/sdb
   C. /dev/sdb1
   D. /dev/hdb1
   E. /dev/sda

9. What tool creates a logical volume from multiple physical partitions?
   A. mkfs
   B. pvcreate
   C. lvcreate
   D. fdisk
   E. vgcreate

10. Which RAID levels can easily recover from a single failed hard drive? (Choose all that apply.)
    A. RAID 0
    B. RAID 4
    C. RAID 10
    D. RAID 5
    E. RAID 1

11. Which partitioning tool provides a graphical interface?
    A. gdisk
    B. gparted
    C. fdisk

D. parted

E. fsck

12. Which fdisk command displays the current partition table on the hard drive?

   A. v

   B. n

   C. m

   D. p

   E. d

13. Linux uses _____ to add the filesystem on a new storage device to the virtual directory.

   A. Mount points

   B. Drive letters

   C. /dev files

   D. /proc directory

   E. /sys directory

14. What filesystem is the latest version of the original Linux file system?

   A. reiserFS

   B. btrfs

   C. ext3

   D. ext4

   E. nfs

15. What tool do you use to create a new filesystem on a partition?

   A. fdisk

   B. mkfs

   C. fsck

   D. gdisk

   E. parted

16. Which filesystem type should you create to help extend the physical memory installed in a Linux workstation?

   A. ext3

   B. btrfs

   C. swap

   D. ext4

   E. NTFS

17. What tool do you use to manually add a filesystem to the virtual directory?

A. fsck

B. mount

C. umount

D. fdisk

E. mkfs

18. Which command allows you to remove a partition from the virtual directory on a running Linux system?

A. mount

B. umount

C. fsck

D. dmesg

E. mkinitramfs

19. The _____ program is a handy tool for repairing corrupted filesystems.

A. fsck

B. mount

C. umount

D. fdisk

E. mkfs

20. What tool should you use to determine the disk space used by a specific user account on the Linux system?

A. df

B. iostat

C. du

D. lsblk

E. blkid

Chapter

4

Managing Files

OBJECTIVES

✓ **103.3** Perform basic file management

✓ **104.5** Manage file permissions and ownership

✓ **104.6** Create and change hard and symbolic links

✓ **104.7** Find system files and place files in correct location

With Linux, the virtual filesystem is an interface provided by the kernel. Learning to deal with files within the directory structure is the next important step in understanding how to properly maintain your system.

Being able to list the files located in particular directories, find files, and use wildcard expansion rules to assist you in this maintenance task are critical skills. You also need to understand topics such as file archiving and compression, linking files, as well as basic file security principles employed by the Linux system. All these concepts and more are covered in this chapter to assist you in file management tasks.

Using File Management Commands

Files on a Linux system are stored within a single directory structure, called a virtual directory. The virtual directory contains files from all the computer's storage devices and merges them into a single directory structure. This structure has a single base directory called the *root directory* (/) that is often simply called *root*.

Viewing, creating, copying and moving, as well as deleting files in the virtual directory structure are important abilities. The following sections describe how to use command-line programs to accomplish these various tasks.

Naming and Listing Files

Before you go wandering around the virtual directory structure, it's a good idea to understand some basic concepts concerning looking at a directory's contents and employing features such as file globbing. In addition, you'll want to understand how to create files and a few tips on naming them.

Displaying Filenames with the *ls* Command

The most basic command for viewing a file's name and its various *metadata* is the list command. Metadata is information that describes and provides additional details about data.

To issue the list command, you use *ls* and any needed options or arguments. The basic syntax structure for the list command is as follows:

```
ls [OPTIONS]… [FILE]…
```

In the list command's syntax structure, there are various [OPTIONS] (also called switches) that you can add to display file metadata. Recall that the brackets indicate that switches are optional. The [*FILE*] argument shows you can add a directory or filename to the command's end to look at metadata for either specific files or files within other virtual directory structure locations.

Syntax structure is depicted for many command-line commands within the Linux system's manual pages, which are also called the man pages. To find a particular command's syntax structure, view its man page (e.g., man ls) and look in the Synopsis section.

When you issue the ls command with no additional arguments or options, it displays all the files' and subdirectories' names within the *present working directory* as shown in Listing 4.1.

Listing 4.1: Using the ls and pwd commands

```
$ ls
Desktop    Downloads  Pictures      Public      Videos
Documents  Music      Project47.txt Templates
$
$ pwd
/home/Christine
$
```

Your present working directory is the current location for your login process within the virtual directory structure. You can determine this location's directory name by issuing the *pwd* command, which is also shown in Listing 4.1.

To display more than file and directory name metadata, you need to add various options to the list command. Table 4.1 shows a few of the more commonly used options.

TABLE 4.1 The ls command's commonly used options

Short	Long	Description
-1	N/A	List one file or subdirectory name per line
-a	--all	Display all file and subdirectory names, including hidden files' names
-d	--directory	Show a directory's own metadata instead of its contents
-F	--classify	Classify each file's type using an indicator code (*,/,=,>,@, or |)
-i	--inode	Display all file and subdirectory names along with their associated index number

TABLE 4.1   The ls command's commonly used options *(continued)*

Short	Long	Description
-l	N/A	Display file and subdirectory metadata, which includes file type, file access permissions, hard link count, file owner, file's group, modification date and time, and filename
-R	N/A	Show a directory's contents, and for any subdirectory within the original directory tree, consecutively show its contents as well (recursively)

> Table 4.1 has the best ls command options to memorize, because you will use them often. However, it is worthwhile to try out all the various ls command options and option combinations. Take time to peruse the ls command's options in its man pages.

When you experiment with various command options, not only will you be better prepared for the LPIC-1 certification exam, you'll also find combinations that work well for your particular needs. The -lh option combination shown in Listing 4.2 makes the file size more human readable.

Listing 4.2: Exploring the ls -lh command

```
$ pwd
/home/Christine/Answers
$
$ ls -l
total 32
drwxrwxr-x. 2 Christine Christine     6 Aug 19 17:34 Everything
drwxrwxr-x. 2 Christine Christine     6 Aug 19 17:34 Life
-rw-r--r--. 1 Christine Christine 29900 Aug 19 17:37 Project42.txt
drwxrwxr-x. 2 Christine Christine     6 Aug 19 17:34 Universe
$
$ ls -lh
total 32K
drwxrwxr-x. 2 Christine Christine     6 Aug 19 17:34 Everything
drwxrwxr-x. 2 Christine Christine     6 Aug 19 17:34 Life
-rw-r--r--. 1 Christine Christine   30K Aug 19 17:37 Project42.txt
drwxrwxr-x. 2 Christine Christine     6 Aug 19 17:34 Universe
$
```

Be aware that some distributions include, by default, an *alias* (covered in Chapter 9) for the ls -l command. It is ll (two lowercase *L* characters) and is demonstrated on a CentOS distribution in Listing 4.3. An alias at the Linux command line is simply a short command that represents another, typically complicated, command. You can view all the current aliases your process has by typing **alias** at the command line.

Listing 4.3: Exploring the ll command

```
$ ls -l
total 32
drwxrwxr-x. 2 Christine Christine     6 Aug 19 17:34 Everything
drwxrwxr-x. 2 Christine Christine     6 Aug 19 17:34 Life
-rw-r--r--. 1 Christine Christine 29900 Aug 19 17:37 Project42.txt
drwxrwxr-x. 2 Christine Christine     6 Aug 19 17:34 Universe
$
$ ll
total 32
drwxrwxr-x. 2 Christine Christine     6 Aug 19 17:34 Everything
drwxrwxr-x. 2 Christine Christine     6 Aug 19 17:34 Life
-rw-r--r--. 1 Christine Christine 29900 Aug 19 17:37 Project42.txt
drwxrwxr-x. 2 Christine Christine     6 Aug 19 17:34 Universe
$
```

Creating and Naming Files

The *touch* command will allow you to create empty files on the fly. This command's primary purpose in life is to update a file's timestamps—access and modification. However, for studying purposes, touch is very useful in that you can quickly create files with which to experiment, as shown in Listing 4.4.

Listing 4.4: Using the touch command

```
$ touch Project43.txt
$
$ ls
Everything  Life  Project42.txt  Project43.txt  Universe
$
$ touch Project44.txt Project45.txt Project46.txt
$
$ ls
Everything  Project42.txt  Project44.txt  Project46.txt
Life         Project43.txt  Project45.txt  Universe
$
```

Notice in Listing 4.4 that with the touch command you can create a single file or multiple files at a time. To create multiple files, just list the files' names after the command separated by a space.

 Case matters for Linux file and directory names. For example, myfile.txt, MyFile.txt, and MYFILE.TXT are three distinct files on a Linux system.

Linux is very flexible when it comes to naming files. However, it is best to follow certain conventions to lessen confusion and difficulties surrounding nonconventional filenames. It's wise to avoid using the various shell metacharacters (first introduced in Chapter 1) within a file or directory's name:

* ? [ ] ' " \ $; & ( ) | ^ < >

If you do need to employ a metacharacter in the file's name, you'll most likely have to use shell quoting techniques (covered in Chapter 1) with the name on the command line. Spaces in file or directory names can be problematic as well and require shell quoting.

 A file's extension is another place you can get tripped up by being noncon-ventional. While you can make the file's extension anything you want, it's a bad idea. For example, the tar utility (covered later in this chapter) should have any archive files it produces end with a .tar file extension. If you make the extension .txt instead, you introduce unnecessary confusion.

The old saying goes, "On Linux, everything is a file." Well, if you aren't sure what type of file it is, that can be tricky. To quickly determine a file's type, use the file command as demonstrated in Listing 4.5.

Listing 4.5: Using the file command

```
$ file Project42.txt
Project42.txt: ASCII text
$
$ file Everything
Everything: directory
$
```

Notice that the Project42.txt file is indeed an ASCII text file, whereas the Everything file is a directory.

Exploring Wildcard Expansion Rules

When you use the ls command or many other command-line programs, specifying file and directory names can be a little difficult due to *file globbing*. File globbing occurs when you use wildcards, such as an asterisk (*) or a question mark (?), with a filename in a command. When wildcards are employed in this manner, file globbing causes the filename to expand into multiple names (also called *wildcard expansion*). For example, passw*d could be expanded into the filename password or passwrd.

When used as a wildcard, an asterisk represents any number of alphanumeric characters. An example of using an asterisk for file globbing with the ls command is shown in Listing 4.6.

Listing 4.6: Using an asterisk wildcard with the ls command

```
$ ls
cake.txt  carmelCake.sh  carmelPie.txt  carrotCake.txt
$
$ ls c*.txt
cake.txt  carmelPie.txt  carrotCake.txt
$
```

The question mark only represents a single character for file globbing, as shown in Listing 4.7.

Listing 4.7: Using a question mark wildcard with the ls command

```
$ ls
bard  bat  beat  bed  bet  bird  bit  bot  bunt
$
$ ls b?t
bat  bet  bit  bot
$
$ ls b??d
bard  bird
$
```

Notice that you can employ two question marks if you need to include two characters for your wildcard operation.

Both the question mark and the asterisk wildcards are case-insensitive. If you need case sensitivity, you'll need to use a different wildcard type.

Bracketed wildcards are handy, because you can select a whole range of characters for a specified location in a file or directory name. The brackets represent a single character location in the name, while the characters within the brackets are the ones that can be in that spot. An example is shown in Listing 4.8.

Listing 4.8: Using a bracketed wildcard with the ls command

```
$ ls
bard  bat  beat  bed  bet  bEt  bird  bit  bot  bunt
$
$ ls b[eio]t
bet  bit  bot
$
```

Notice that the bracketed wildcard is for the second character position within the filename. Thus, any file that begins with a b and ends with a t is selected, but only if it has an e, i, or o in its second character position. Bracketed wildcards also follow case sensitivity rules when used in this manner. Thus, the file bEt was not selected for display in Listing 4.8.

Just like the question mark, you can use multiple brackets for each character position in the filename you need to wildcard for file globbing. An example of this method is shown in Listing 4.9.

Listing 4.9: Using multiple bracketed wildcards with the ls command

```
$ ls
bard  bat  beat  bed  bet  bEt  bird  bit  bot  bunt
$
$ ls b[eu][an]t
beat  bunt
$
```

To use bracketed wildcards for a range of characters, instead of typing them all out, you can employ a dash. An example is shown in Listing 4.10.

Listing 4.10: Using a bracketed range wildcard with the ls command

```
$ ls b[a-z]t
bat  bet  bEt  bit  bot
$
```

Be careful here. Notice that using the range nullifies case sensitivity. Thus, in this case, the file bEt was selected for display.

You can negate the character selection by placing a caret symbol (^) in front of your bracketed characters. This causes the command-line program to select any file, *except* those that have matching characters at the bracketed spot. An example of this is shown in Listing 4.11.

Listing 4.11: Using a negated bracketed wildcard with the ls command

```
$ ls
bard  bat  beat  bed  bet  bEt  bird  bit  bot  bunt
$
$ ls b[^eio]t
bat  bEt
$
```

You can employ these various wildcards with more than just the `ls` command. However, use caution if the utility you are using is destructive. You'll want to make sure your wildcards are correct before doing something like deleting multiple files.

Understanding the File Commands

Now that you have a firm grasp on looking at a directory's contents and employing features, such as file globbing, you'll want to understand how to create directories, copy and move files, as well as delete them. We'll also make recommendations in this section that will help you avoid grievous mistakes, such as removing the wrong files.

Creating Directories

You can quickly create directories via the *mkdir* command. The `-F` option on the `ls` command will help you in this endeavor. It displays any directories, including newly created ones, with a / indicator code following each directory's name. Listing 4.12 provides a few examples.

Listing 4.12: Exploring the `mkdir` command

```
$ ls -F
Everything/  Project42.txt  Project44.txt  Project46.txt
Life/        Project43.txt  Project45.txt  Universe/
$
$ mkdir Galaxy
$
$ ls -F
Everything/  Life/          Project43.txt  Project45.txt  Universe/Galaxy/
Project42.txt  Project44.txt  Project46.txt
$
$ pwd
/home/Christine/Answers
$
$ mkdir /home/Christine/Answers/Galaxy/Saturn
$
$ ls -F Galaxy
Saturn/
$
```

To create a subdirectory in your present working directory, you simply enter the `mkdir` command followed by the subdirectory's name, as shown in Listing 4.12 for the `Galaxy` subdirectory. If you want to build a directory in a different location than your present working directory, you can use an absolute directory reference (covered in Chapter 1), as was done for creating the `Saturn` directory in Listing 4.12.

> If you are creating directories and moving into them from your present working directory, it is easy to become lost in the directory structure. Quickly move back to your previous present working directory using the cd – command or back to your home directory using just the cd command with no options.

Be aware when building directories that problems can happen when attempting to create a directory tree, as shown in Listing 4.13.

Listing 4.13: Avoiding problems with the mkdir command

```
$ ls -F
Everything/  Life/          Project43.txt  Project45.txt  Universe/
Galaxy/      Project42.txt  Project44.txt  Project46.txt
$
$ mkdir Projects/42/
mkdir: cannot create directory 'Projects/42/': No such file or directory
$
$ mkdir -p Projects/42/
$
$ ls -F
Everything/  Life/          Project43.txt  Project45.txt  Projects/
Galaxy/      Project42.txt  Project44.txt  Project46.txt  Universe/
$
$ ls -F Projects
42/
$
```

Notice an error occurs when you attempt to use the mkdir command to build the directory Projects and its 42 subdirectory. A subdirectory (42) cannot be created without its parent directory (Projects) preexisting. The mkdir command's -p option (or --parents) allows you to overwrite this behavior as shown in Listing 4.13 and successfully create directory trees.

> It is tedious to enter the ls –F command after each time you issue the mkdir command to ensure that the directory was built. Instead, use the –v option on the mkdir command to receive verification that the directory was successfully constructed.

Copying Files and Directories

To copy a file or directory locally, use the *cp* utility. To issue this command, you use cp along with any needed options or arguments. The basic syntax structure for the command is as follows:

cp [*OPTION*]… *SOURCE DEST*

The program's options, as shown in the structure, are not required. However, the source (*SOURCE*) and destination (*DEST*) are required, as shown in a basic cp command example within Listing 4.14.

Listing 4.14: Using the cp command

```
$ pwd
/home/Christine/SpaceOpera/Emphasis
$
$ ls
melodrama.txt
$
$ cp melodrama.txt space-warfare.txt
$
$ ls
melodrama.txt   space-warfare.txt
$
$ cp melodrama.txt
cp: missing destination file operand after 'melodrama.txt'
Try 'cp --help' for more information.
$
```

In Listing 4.14, the first time the cp command is used, both the source file and its destination are specified. Thus, no problems occur. However, the second time the cp command is used, the destination filename is missing. This causes the source file to not be copied and generates an error message.

There are several useful cp command options. Many will help protect you from making a grievous mistake, such as accidentally overwriting a file or its permissions. Table 4.2 shows a few of the more commonly used options.

TABLE 4.2 The cp command's commonly used options

Short	Long	Description
-a	--archive	Perform a recursive copy and keep all the files' original attributes, such as permissions, ownership, and timestamps.
-f	--force	Overwrite any preexisting destination files with same name as *DEST*.
-i	--interactive	Ask before overwriting any preexisting destination files with same name as *DEST*.
-n	--no-clobber	Do not overwrite any preexisting destination files with same name as *DEST*.

TABLE 4.2   The cp command's commonly used options *(continued)*

Short	Long	Description
-R, -r	--recursive	Copy a directory's contents, and also copy the contents of any subdirectory within the original directory tree (recursive).
-u	--update	Only overwrite preexisting destination files with the same name as *DEST*, if the source file is newer.
-v	--verbose	Provide detailed command action information as command executes.

When you're copying files over a network to a remote host, the file transfer process typically needs protection via encryption methods. OpenSSH can provide the needed data privacy for this type of copy using the scp command (see Chapter 10).

To copy a directory, you need to add the -R (or -r) option to the cp command. This option enacts a recursive copy. A recursive copy will create a new directory (*DEST*) and copy any files the source directory contains, source directory subdirectories, and their files as well. Listing 4.15 shows an example of how to do a recursive copy as well as how *not* to do one.

Listing 4.15: Performing a recursive copy with the cp command

```
$ pwd
/home/Christine/SpaceOpera
$
$ ls -F
Emphasis/
$
$ cp Emphasis Story-Line
cp: omitting directory 'Emphasis'
$
$ ls -F
Emphasis/
$
$ cp -R Emphasis Story-Line
$
$ ls -F
Emphasis/   Story-Line/
$
$ ls -R Emphasis
```

```
Emphasis:
chivalric-romance.txt        melodrama.txt
interplanatary-battles.txt   space-warfare.txt
$
$ ls -R Story-Line/
Story-Line/:
chivalric-romance.txt        melodrama.txt
interplanatary-battles.txt   space-warfare.txt
$
```

Notice that the first time the cp command is used in Listing 4.15, the -R option is not used, and thus the source directory is not copied. The error message generated, cp: omitting directory, can be a little confusing, but essentially it is telling you that the copy will not take place. When the cp -R command is used to copy the source directory in Listing 4.15, it is successful. The recursive copy option is one of the few command options that can be uppercase, -R, or lowercase, -r.

Moving/Renaming Files and Directories

To move or rename a file or directory locally, you use a single command: the *mv* command. The command's basic syntax is nearly the same as the cp command:

mv [*OPTION*]... *SOURCE DEST*

The commonly used mv command options are also similar to cp command options. However, you'll notice in Table 4.3 that there are fewer typical mv command options. As always, be sure to view the mv utility's man pages, using the man mv command, to review all the options for certification studying purposes and explore uncommon options, which may be useful to you.

TABLE 4.3   The mv command's commonly used options

Short	Long	Description
-f	--force	Overwrite any preexisting destination files with the same name as *DEST*.
-i	--interactive	Ask before overwriting any preexisting destination files with the same name as *DEST*.
-n	--no-clobber	Do not overwrite any preexisting destination files with the same name as *DEST*.
-u	--update	Only overwrite preexisting destination files with the same name as *DEST* if the source file is newer.
-v	--verbose	Provide detailed command action information as the command executes.

The move command is very simple to use. A few examples of renaming a file as well as employing the -i option to avoid renaming a file to a preexisting file are shown in Listing 4.16.

Listing 4.16: Using the mv command

```
$ ls
chivalric-romance.txt       melodrama.txt
interplanatary-battles.txt  space-warfare.txt
$
$ mv space-warfare.txt risk-taking.txt
$
$ ls
chivalric-romance.txt       melodrama.txt
interplanatary-battles.txt  risk-taking.txt
$
$ mv -i risk-taking.txt melodrama.txt
mv: overwrite 'melodrama.txt'? n
$
```

When renaming an entire directory, there are no additional required command options. Just issue the mv command as you would for renaming a file, as shown in Listing 4.17.

Listing 4.17: Renaming a directory using the mv command

```
$ pwd
/home/Christine/SpaceOpera
$
$ ls -F
Emphasis/  Story-Line/
$
$ mv -i Story-Line Story-Topics
$
$ ls -F
Emphasis/  Story-Topics/
$
```

You can move a file and rename it all in one simple mv command as shown in Listing 4.18. The *SOURCE* uses the file's current directory reference and current name. The *DEST* uses the file's new location as well as its new name.

Listing 4.18: Moving and renaming a file using the mv command

```
$ pwd
/home/Christine/SpaceOpera
$
$ ls
Emphasis   Story-Topics
$
$ ls Emphasis/
chivalric-romance.txt      melodrama.txt
interplanatary-battles.txt  risk-taking.txt
$
$ ls Story-Topics/
chivalric-romance.txt      melodrama.txt
interplanatary-battles.txt  space-warfare.txt
$
$ mv Emphasis/risk-taking.txt Story-Topics/risks.txt
$
$ ls Emphasis/
chivalric-romance.txt  interplanatary-battles.txt  melodrama.txt
$
$ ls Story-Topics/
chivalric-romance.txt       melodrama.txt  space-warfare.txt
interplanatary-battles.txt  risks.txt
$
```

In Listing 4.18, the file risk-taking.txt is located in the Emphasis directory. Employing a single mv command, it is moved to the Story-Topics directory and renamed to risks.txt at the same time.

Deleting Files and Directories

Tidying up an entire filesystem or simply your own directory space often starts with deleting unneeded files and directories. Understanding the commands and their switches is paramount to avoid mistakes in removing these items.

The most flexible and heavily used deletion utility is the remove tool. It is employed via the *rm* command, and the basic syntax is as follows:

```
rm [OPTION]… FILE
```

There are many very useful options for the rm utility, so be sure to view its man pages to see them all. The most commonly used options are listed in Table 4.4.

TABLE 4.4   The rm command's commonly used options

Short	Long	Description
-d	--dir	Delete any empty directories.
-f	--force	Continue on with the deletion process, even if some files designated by the command for removal do not exist, and do not ask prior to deleting any existing files.
-i	--interactive	Ask before deleting any existing files.
-I	N/A	Ask before deleting more than three files or when using the -r option.
-R, -r	--recursive	Delete a directory's contents, and also delete the contents of any subdirectory within the original directory tree (recursive).
-v	--verbose	Provide detailed command action information as command executes.

To delete a single file, you can use the rm command, designating the filename to remove and not using any switches. However, it is always a good idea to use the -i (or --interactive) option to ensure that you are not deleting the wrong file, as demonstrated in Listing 4.19.

Listing 4.19: Deleting a file using the rm command

```
$ ls Parrot-full-3.7_amd64.iso
Parrot-full-3.7_amd64.iso
$
$ rm -i Parrot-full-3.7_amd64.iso
rm: remove write-protected regular file 'Parrot-full-3.7_amd64.iso'? y
$
$ ls Parrot-full-3.7_amd64.iso
ls: cannot access Parrot-full-3.7_amd64.iso: No such file or directory
$
$ rm -i Parrot-full-3.7_amd64.iso
rm: cannot remove 'Parrot-full-3.7_amd64.iso': No such file or directory
$
$ rm -f Parrot-full-3.7_amd64.iso
$
```

Notice also in Listing 4.19 that when the file has been deleted, if you reissue the `rm -i` command, an error message is generated, but if you issue the `rm -f` command, it is silent concerning the missing file. The `-f` (or `--force`) switch is useful when you are deleting several files and you don't want to display any error messages.

Removing a directory tree or a directory full of files can be tricky. If you just issue the `rm -i` command, you will get an error message as shown in Listing 4.20. Instead, you need to add the `-R` or `-r` option in order for the directory and the files it is managing to be deleted.

Listing 4.20: Deleting a directory containing files using the `rm` command

```
$ cd SpaceOpera/
$
$ ls -F
Emphasis/  Story-Topics/
$
$ rm -i Emphasis/
rm: cannot remove 'Emphasis/': Is a directory
$
$ rm -ir Emphasis
rm: descend into directory 'Emphasis'? y
rm: remove regular empty file 'Emphasis/melodrama.txt'? y
rm: remove regular empty file 'Emphasis/interplanatary-battles.txt'? y
rm: remove regular empty file 'Emphasis/chivalric-romance.txt'? y
rm: remove directory 'Emphasis'? y
$
$ ls -F
Story-Topics/
$
```

If you have lots of files to delete, want to ensure that you are deleting the correct files, and don't want to have to answer **y** for every file to delete, employ the `-I` option instead of the `-i` switch. It will ask before deleting more than three files as well as when you are deleting a directory full of files and are using one of the recursive switches, as shown in Listing 4.21.

Listing 4.21: Employing the `rm` command's `-I` option

```
$ ls -F
Story-Topics/
$
$ rm -Ir Story-Topics/
rm: remove 1 argument recursively? y
$
$ ls -F
$
```

Deleting an empty directory (a directory containing no files) is very easy. Simply use the remove empty directories tool, using the *rmdir* command. You'll find that adding the -v (or --verbose) switch is helpful as well, as shown in Listing 4.22.

Listing 4.22: Using the `rmdir` command

```
$ mkdir -v EmptyDir
mkdir: created directory 'EmptyDir'
$
$ rmdir -v EmptyDir/
rmdir: removing directory, 'EmptyDir/'
$
```

If you want to remove a directory tree that is free of files but contains empty subdirectories, you can also employ the `rmdir` utility. The -p (or --parents) switch is required along with providing the entire directory tree name as an argument. An example is shown in Listing 4.23.

Listing 4.23: Using the `rmdir` command to delete an empty directory tree

```
$ mkdir -vp EmptyDir/EmptySubDir
mkdir: created directory 'EmptyDir'
mkdir: created directory 'EmptyDir/EmptySubDir'
$
$ rmdir -vp EmptyDir/EmptySubDir
rmdir: removing directory, 'EmptyDir/EmptySubDir'
rmdir: removing directory, 'EmptyDir'
$
```

You may have a situation where you need to remove only empty directories from a directory tree. In this case, you will need to use the `rm` command and add the -d (or --dir) switch, as shown in Listing 4.24.

Listing 4.24: Using the `rm` command to delete empty directories in a tree

```
$ mkdir -v EmptyDir
mkdir: created directory 'EmptyDir'
$
$ mkdir -v NotEmptyDir
mkdir: created directory 'NotEmptyDir'
$
$ touch NotEmptyDir/File42.txt
$
$ rm -id EmptyDir NotEmptyDir
rm: remove directory 'EmptyDir'? y
rm: cannot remove 'NotEmptyDir': Directory not empty
$
```

Understanding the commands used to create and remove directories along with the various commands to view, create, copy, move, rename, and delete files is important. Also, having a firm grasp on their commonly used command options is vital knowledge. This expertise is a valuable tool in your Linux command-line tool belt.

Compressing File Commands

Substantial files, such a backup files, can potentially deplete large amounts of disk or offline media space. You can reduce this consumption via data compression tools. The following popular utilities are available on Linux:

- gzip
- bzip2
- xz
- zip

The advantages and disadvantages of each of these data compression methods are explored in this section.

gzip   The *gzip* utility was developed in 1992 as a replacement for the old compress program. Using the Lempel-Ziv (LZ77) algorithm to achieve text-based file compression rates of 60–70 percent, gzip has long been a popular data compression utility. To compress a file, type **gzip** followed by the file's name. The original file is replaced by a compressed version with a .gz file extension. To reverse the operation, type **gunzip** followed by the compressed file's name.

bzip2   Developed in 1996, the *bzip2* utility offers higher compression rates than gzip but takes slightly longer to perform the data compression. The bzip2 utility employs multiple layers of compression techniques and algorithms. Until 2013, this data compression utility was used to compress the Linux kernel for distribution. To compress a file, type **bzip2** followed by the file's name. The original file is replaced by a compressed version with a .bz2 file extension. To reverse the operation, type **bunzip2** followed by the compressed file's name, which decompresses (deflates) the data.

Originally there was a bzip utility program. However, in its layered approach, a patented data compression algorithm was employed. Thus, bzip2 was created to replace it and uses the Huffman coding algorithm instead, which is patent free.

xz   Developed in 2009, the *xz* data compression utility quickly became very popular among Linux administrators. It boasts a higher default compression rate than bzip2 and gzip via the LZMA2 compression algorithm—though by using certain xz command options, you can employ the legacy LZMA compression algorithm, if needed or desired. The xz compression utility in 2013 replaced bzip2 for compressing the Linux kernel for distribution. To compress a file, type **xz** followed by the file's name. The original file is replaced by a compressed version with an .xz file extension. To reverse the operation, type **unxz** followed by the compressed file's name.

zip   The zip utility is different from the other data compression utilities in that it operates on multiple files. If you have ever created a zip file on a Windows operating system, then you've used this file format. Multiple files are packed together in a single file, often called a folder or an archive file, and then compressed. Another difference from the other Linux compression utilities is that zip does not replace the original file(s). Instead, it places a copy of the file(s) into an archive file.

To archive and compress files with zip, type **zip** followed by the final archive file's name, which traditionally ends in a .zip extension. After the archive file, type one or more names of files you desire to place into the compressed archive, separating them with a space. The original files remain intact, but a copy of them is placed into the compressed zip archive file. To reverse the operation, type **unzip** followed by the compressed archive file's name.

It's helpful to see a side-by-side comparison of the various compression utilities using their defaults. In Listing 4.25, an example on a CentOS Linux distribution is shown.

Listing 4.25: Comparing the various Linux compression utilities

```
# cp /var/log/wtmp wtmp
#
# cp wtmp wtmp1
# cp wtmp wtmp2
# cp wtmp wtmp3
# cp wtmp wtmp4
#
# ls -lh wtmp?
-rw-r--r--. 1 root root 210K Oct  9 19:54 wtmp1
-rw-r--r--. 1 root root 210K Oct  9 19:54 wtmp2
-rw-r--r--. 1 root root 210K Oct  9 19:54 wtmp3
-rw-r--r--. 1 root root 210K Oct  9 19:54 wtmp4
#
# gzip wtmp1
# bzip2 wtmp2
# xz wtmp3
# zip wtmp4.zip wtmp4
  adding: wtmp4 (deflated 96%)
#
# ls -lh wtmp?.*
-rw-r--r--. 1 root root 7.7K Oct  9 19:54 wtmp1.gz
-rw-r--r--. 1 root root 6.2K Oct  9 19:54 wtmp2.bz2
-rw-r--r--. 1 root root 5.2K Oct  9 19:54 wtmp3.xz
-rw-r--r--. 1 root root 7.9K Oct  9 19:55 wtmp4.zip
#
# ls wtmp?
wtmp4
#
```

In Listing 4.25, first the /var/log/wtmp file is copied to the local directory using super user privileges. Four copies of this file are then made. Using the ls -lh command, you can see in human-readable format that the wtmp files are 210K in size. Next, the various compression utilities are employed. Notice that when using the zip command, you must give it the name of the archive file, wtmp4.zip, and follow it with any filenames. In this case, only wtmp4 is put into the zip archive.

After the files are compressed with the various utilities, another ls -lh command is issued in Listing 4.25. Notice the various file extension names as well as the files' compressed sizes. You can see that the xz program produces the highest compression of this file, because its file is the smallest in size. The last command in the listing shows that all the compression programs but zip removed the original file.

 For the previous data compression utilities, you can specify the level of compression and control the speed via the -# option. The # is a number from 1 to 9, where 1 is the fastest but provides the lowest compression. A 9 is the slowest but the highest compression method. The zip utility does not yet support these levels for compression, but it does for decompression. Typically, the utilities use -6 as the default compression level. It is a good idea to review these level specifications in each utility's man page— there are useful but subtle differences.

If you need to view the contents of a compressed file, you can do so without switching the file back to an uncompressed format. Three variants of the cat command can help in this task: *bzcat*, *xzcat*, and *zcat*. These utilities temporarily decompress the file and show its contents to STDOUT. An example of creating an xz compressed file and using xcat to display its contents is shown in Listing 4.26.

Listing 4.26: Using the xcat command to view an xz compressed file's contents

```
$ xz alphabet.txt
$
$ ls alphabet*
alphabet.txt.xz
$
$ xzcat alphabet.txt.xz
Alpha
Tango
Bravo
Echo
Foxtrot
$
$ ls alphabet*
alphabet.txt.xz
$
```

Keep in mind that you need xzcat to display an xz compressed file. You cannot use it to display a bzip2 compressed file. To help keep things straight, as well as understand additional commands that mimic these various compressed file display commands, see Table 4.5.

TABLE 4.5   The compressed file display commands

Command	Equivalent	Description
bzcat	bzip2 -dc	Used to display bzip2 compressed files.
xzcat	xz --decompress --stdout	Displays the contents of xz compressed files.
zcat	gunzip -c	Used to display gzip compressed files. Some Unix-like systems have a gzcat command instead.

Notice that the zcat utility displays gzip compressed files and not zip files. That can be confusing.

If you have a data file that does not have the proper file extension, remember you can use the file command to uncover its type. For example, you could type **file *filename*** to determine whether it was a text file, an archive file, or something else. If it is a compressed data file, you'll even learn what compression method was used to create it. That's useful!

Archiving File Commands

There are several programs you can employ for managing backups. Some of the more popular products are Amanda, Bacula, Bareos, Duplicity, and BackupPC. Yet often these GUI and/or web-based programs have command-line utilities at their core. Our focus here is on some of those command-line utilities:

- cpio
- dd
- tar

Copying with *cpio*

The *cpio* utility's name stands for "copy in and out." It gathers together file copies and stores them in an archive file. The program has several nice options. The more commonly used ones are described in Table 4.6.

TABLE 4.6 The cpio command's commonly used options

Short	Long	Description
-I	N/A	Designates an archive file to use.
-i	--extract	Copies files from an archive or displays the files within the archive, depending upon the other options employed. Called copy-in mode.
N/A	--no-absolute-filenames	Designates that only relative path names are to be used. (The default is to use absolute path names.)
-o	--create	Creates an archive by copying files into it. Called copy-out mode.
-t	--list	Displays a list of files within the archive. This list is called a table of contents.
-v	--verbose	Displays each file's name as each file is processed.

To create an archive using the cpio utility, you have to generate a list of files and then pipe them into the command. Listing 4.27 shows an example of doing this task.

Listing 4.27: Employing cpio to create an archive

```
$ ls Project4?.txt
Project42.txt   Project43.txt   Project44.txt
Project45.txt   Project46.txt
$
$ ls Project4?.txt | cpio -ov > Project4x.cpio
Project42.txt
Project43.txt
Project44.txt
Project45.txt
Project46.txt
59 blocks
$
$ ls Project4?.*
Project42.txt   Project44.txt   Project46.txt
Project43.txt   Project45.txt   Project4x.cpio
$
```

Using the ? wildcard and the ls command, various text files within the present working directory are displayed first in Listing 4.27. This command is then used and its STDOUT is piped as STDIN to the cpio utility. (See Chapter 1 if you need a refresher on STDOUT and STDIN.) The options used with the cpio command are -ov, which create an archive containing copies of the listed files and display the file's name as they are copied. The archive file used is named Project4x.cpio. Though not necessary, it is considered good form to use the .cpio extension on cpio archive files.

You can back up data based on its metadata, and not its file location, via the cpio utility. For example, suppose you want to create a cpio archive for any files within the virtual directory system owned by the JKirk user account. You can use the find / -user JKirk command (covered later in this chapter) and pipe it into the cpio utility in order to create the archive file. This is a useful feature.

You can view the files stored within a cpio archive fairly easily. Just employ the cpio command again, and use its -itv options and the -I option to designate the archive file, as shown in Listing 4.28.

Listing 4.28: Using cpio to list an archive's contents

```
$ cpio -itvI Project4x.cpio
-rw-r--r--   1 Christin Christin 29900 Aug 19 17:37 Project42.txt
-rw-rw-r--   1 Christin Christin     0 Aug 19 18:07 Project43.txt
-rw-rw-r--   1 Christin Christin     0 Aug 19 18:07 Project44.txt
-rw-rw-r--   1 Christin Christin     0 Aug 19 18:07 Project45.txt
-rw-rw-r--   1 Christin Christin     0 Aug 19 18:07 Project46.txt
59 blocks
$
```

Though not displayed in Listing 4.28, the cpio utility maintains each file's absolute directory reference. Thus, it is often used to create system image and full backups.

To restore files from an archive, employ just the -ivI options. However, because cpio maintains the files' absolute paths, this can be difficult if you need to restore the files to another directory location. To do this, you need to use the --no-absolute-filenames option, as shown in Listing 4.29.

Listing 4.29: Using cpio to restore files to a different directory location

```
$ ls -dF Projects
Projects/
$
$ mv Project4x.cpio Projects/
$
$ cd Projects
```

```
$ pwd
/home/Christine/Answers/Projects
$
$ ls Project4?.*
Project4x.cpio
$
$ cpio -iv --no-absolute-filenames -I Project4x.cpio
Project42.txt
Project43.txt
Project44.txt
Project45.txt
Project46.txt
59 blocks
$
$ ls Project4?.*
Project42.txt   Project44.txt   Project46.txt
Project43.txt   Project45.txt   Project4x.cpio
$
```

In Listing 4.29 the `Project4x.cpio` archive file is moved into a preexisting subdirectory, `Projects`. By stripping the absolute path names from the archived files via the `--no-absolute filenames` option, you restore the files to a new directory location. If you wanted to restore the files to their original location, leave that option off and just use the other `cpio` switches shown in Listing 4.29.

Archiving with *tar*

The *tar* utility's name stands for tape archiver, and it is popular for creating data backups. As with `cpio`, with the tar command the selected files are copied and stored in a single file. This file is called a *tar archive file*. If this archive file is compressed using a data compression utility, the compressed archive file is called a *tarball*.

The `tar` program has several useful options. The more commonly used ones for creating data backups are described in Table 4.7.

TABLE 4.7   The tar command's commonly used tarball creation options

Short	Long	Description
-c	--create	Creates a tar archive file. The backup can be a full or incremental backup, depending on the other selected options.
-u	--update	Appends files to an existing tar archive file, but copies only those files that were modified since the original archive file was created.

TABLE 4.7   The tar command's commonly used tarball creation options *(continued)*

Short	Long	Description
-g	--listed-incremental	Creates an incremental or full archive based on metadata stored in the provided file.
-z	--gzip	Compresses tar archive file into a tarball using gzip.
-j	--bzip2	Compresses tar archive file into a tarball using bzip2.
-J	--xz	Compresses tar archive file into a tarball using xz.
-v	--verbose	Displays each file's name as each file is processed.

To create an archive using the tar utility, you have to add a few arguments to the options and the command. Listing 4.30 shows an example of creating a tar archive.

Listing 4.30: Using tar to create an archive file

```
$ ls Project4?.txt
Project42.txt   Project43.txt   Project44.txt
Project45.txt   Project46.txt
$
$ tar -cvf Project4x.tar Project4?.txt
Project42.txt
Project43.txt
Project44.txt
Project45.txt
Project46.txt
$
```

In Listing 4.30, three options are used. The -c option creates the tar archive. The -v option displays the filenames as they are placed into the archive file. Finally, the -f option designates the archive filename, which is Project42x.tar. Though not required, it is considered good form to use the .tar extension on tar archive files. The command's last argument designates the files to copy into this archive.

You can also use the old-style tar command options. For this style, you remove the single dash from the beginning of the tar option. For example, -c becomes c. Keep in mind that additional old-style tar command options must not have spaces between them. Thus tar cvf is valid, but tar c v f is not.

If you are backing up lots of files or large amounts of data, it is a good idea to employ a compression utility. This is easily accomplished by adding an additional switch to your tar command options. An example is shown in Listing 4.31, which uses gzip compression to create a tarball.

Listing 4.31: Using tar to create a tarball

```
$ tar -zcvf Project4x.tar.gz Project4?.txt
Project42.txt
Project43.txt
Project44.txt
Project45.txt
Project46.txt
$
$ ls Project4x.tar.gz
Project4x.tar.gz
$
```

Notice in Listing 4.31 that the tarball filename has the .tar.gz file extension. It is considered good form to use the .tar extension and tack on an indicator showing the compression method that was used. However, you can shorten it to .tgz if desired.

There are many compression methods. However, when you use a compression utility along with an archive and restore program for data backups, it is vital that you use a lossless compression method. A lossless compression is just as it sounds; no data is lost. The gzip, bzip2, xz, and zip utilities provide lossless compression. Obviously it is important not to lose data when doing backups.

There is a useful variation of this command to create both full and incremental backups. A simple example helps to explain this concept. The process for creating a full backup is shown in Listing 4.32.

Listing 4.32: Using tar to create a full backup

```
$ tar -g FullArchive.snar -Jcvf Project42.txz Project4?.txt
Project42.txt
Project43.txt
Project44.txt
Project45.txt
Project46.txt
$
$ ls FullArchive.snar Project42.txz
FullArchive.snar   Project42.txz
$
```

Notice the -g option in Listing 4.31. The -g option creates a file, called a snapshot file, FullArchive.snar. The .snar file extension indicates that the file is a tarball snapshot file. The snapshot file contains metadata used in association with tar commands for creating full and incremental backups. The snapshot file contains file timestamps, so the tar utility can determine whether a file has been modified since it was last backed up. The snapshot file is also used to identify any files that are new or to determine whether files have been deleted since the last backup.

The previous example created a full backup of the designated files along with the metadata snapshot file, FullArchive.snar. Now the same snapshot file will help determine whether any files have been modified, are new, or have been deleted to create an incremental backup, as shown in Listing 4.33.

Listing 4.33: Using tar to create an incremental backup

```
$ echo "Answer to everything" >> Project42.txt
$
$ tar -g FullArchive.snar -Jcvf Project42_Inc.txz Project4?.txt
Project42.txt
$
$ ls Project42_Inc.txz
Project42_Inc.txz
$
```

In Listing 4.33, the file Project42.txt is modified. Again, the tar command uses the -g option and points to the previously created FullArchive.snar snapshot file. This time, the metadata within FullArchive.snar shows the tar command that the Project42.txt file has been modified since the previous backup. Therefore, the new tarball only contains the Project42.txt file, and it is effectively an incremental backup. You can continue to create additional incremental backups using the same snapshot file as needed.

The tar command views full and incremental backups in levels. A full backup is one that includes all of the files indicated, and it is considered a level 0 backup. The first tar incremental backup after a full backup is considered a level 1 backup. The second tar incremental backup is considered a level 2 backup, and so on.

Whenever you create data backups, it is a good practice to verify them. Table 4.8 provides some tar command options for viewing and verifying data in a tar file.

TABLE 4.8   The tar command's commonly used archive verification options

Short	Long	Description
-d	--compare --diff	Compares a tar archive file's members with external files and lists the differences.
-t	--list	Displays a tar archive file's contents.
-W	--verify	Verifies each file as the file is processed. This option cannot be used with the compression options.

Verification can take several different forms. You might ensure that the desired files (sometimes called members) are included in the file by using the -v option on the tar command in order to watch the files being listed as they are included in the archive file.

You can also verify that desired files are included in your backup after the fact. Use the -t option to list tarball or archive file contents. An example is shown in Listing 4.34.

Listing 4.34: Using tar to list a tarball's contents

```
$ tar -tf Project4x.tar.gz
Project42.txt
Project43.txt
Project44.txt
Project45.txt
Project46.txt
$
```

You can verify files within an archive file by comparing them against the current files. The option to accomplish this task is the -d option. An example is shown in Listing 4.35.

Listing 4.35: Using tar to compare tarball members to external files

```
$ tar -df Project4x.tar.gz
Project42.txt: Mod time differs
Project42.txt: Size differs
$
```

Another good practice is to verify your files automatically immediately after the tar archive is created. This is easily accomplished by tacking on the -W option, as shown in Listing 4.36.

Listing 4.36: Using tar to verify backed-up files automatically

```
$ tar -Wcvf ProjectVerify.tar Project4?.txt
Project42.txt
Project43.txt
Project44.txt
Project45.txt
Project46.txt
Verify Project42.txt
Verify Project43.txt
Verify Project44.txt
Verify Project45.txt
Verify Project46.txt
$
```

You cannot use the -W option if you employ compression to create a tarball. However, you could create and verify the archive first and then compress it in a separate step. You can also use the -W option when you extract files from a tar archive. This is convenient for instantly verifying files restored from archives.

Table 4.9 lists some of the options that you can use with the tar utility to restore data from a tar archive file or tarball. Be aware that several options used to create a tar file, such as -g and -W, can also be used when restoring data.

TABLE 4.9   The tar command's commonly used file restore options

Short	Long	Description
-x	--extract --get	Extracts files from a tarball or archive file and places them in the current working directory
-z	--gunzip	Decompresses files in a tarball using gunzip
-j	--bunzip2	Decompresses files in a tarball using bunzip2
-J	--unxz	Decompresses files in a tarball using unxz

Extracting files from an archive or tarball is fairly simple using the tar utility. Listing 4.37 shows an example of extracting files from a previously created tarball.

Listing 4.37: Using tar to extract files from a tarball

```
$ mkdir Extract
$
$ mv Project4x.tar.gz Extract/
$
```

```
$ cd Extract
$
$ tar -zxvf Project4x.tar.gz
Project42.txt
Project43.txt
Project44.txt
Project45.txt
Project46.txt
$
$ ls
Project42.txt   Project44.txt   Project46.txt
Project43.txt   Project45.txt   Project4x.tar.gz
$
```

In Listing 4.37, a new subdirectory, Extract, is created. The tarball created back in Listing 4.31 is moved to the new subdirectory, and then the files are restored from the tarball. If you compare the tar command used in this listing to the one used in Listing 4.32, you'll notice that here the -x option was substituted for the -c option used in Listing 4.37. Also notice in Listing 4.37 that the tarball is not removed after a file extraction, so you can use it again and again, as needed.

> The tar command has many additional capabilities, such as using tar backup parameters and/or the ability to create backup and restore shell scripts. Take a look at GNU tar website, www.gnu.org/software/tar/manual, to learn more about this popular command-line backup utility.

Since the tar utility is the tape archiver, you can also place your tarballs or archive files on tape, if desired. After mounting and properly positioning your tape, substitute your SCSI tape device filename, such as /dev/st0 or /dev/nst0, in place of the archive or tarball filename within your tar command.

Duplicating with *dd*

The *dd* utility allows you to back up nearly everything on a disk, including the old Master Boot Record (MBR) partitions some older Linux distributions still employ. It's primarily used to create low-level copies of an entire hard drive or partition. It is often used in digital forensics for creating system images, copying damaged disks, and wiping partitions.

The command itself is fairly straightforward. The basic syntax structure for the dd utility is as follows:

```
dd  if=INPUT_DEVICE of=OUTPUT-DEVICE [OPERANDS]
```

The *OUTPUT-DEVICE* is either an entire drive or a partition. The *INPUT-DEVICE* is the same. Just make sure that you get the right device for out and the right one for in; otherwise, you may unintentionally wipe data.

Besides the of and if, there are a few other arguments (called operands) that can assist in dd operations. The more commonly used ones are described in Table 4.10.

TABLE 4.10   The dd command's commonly used operands

Operand	Description
bs=*BYTES*	Sets the maximum block size (number of *BYTES*) to read and write at a time. The default is 512 bytes.
count=*N*	Sets the number (*N*) of input blocks to copy.
status=*LEVEL*	Sets the amount (*LEVEL*) of information to display to STDERR.

The status=*LEVEL* operand needs a little more explanation. LEVEL can be set to one of the following:

▪ none only displays error messages.

▪ noxfer does not display final transfer statistics.

▪ progress displays periodic transfer statistics.

It is usually easier to understand the dd utility through examples. A snipped example of performing a bit-by-bit copy of one entire disk to another disk is shown in Listing 4.38.

Listing 4.38: Using dd to copy an entire disk

```
# lsblk
NAME            MAJ:MIN RM  SIZE RO TYPE MOUNTPOINT
[…]
sdb             8:16    0    4M  0 disk
└─sdb1          8:17    0    4M  0 part
sdc             8:32    0    1G  0 disk
└─sdc1          8:33    0 1023M  0 part
[…]
#
# dd if=/dev/sdb of=/dev/sdc status=progress
8192+0 records in
8192+0 records out
4194304 bytes (4.2 MB) copied, 0.232975 s, 18.0 MB/s
#
```

In Listing 4.38, the *lsblk* command is used first. When copying disks via the dd utility, it is prudent to make sure the drives are not mounted anywhere in the virtual directory structure. The two drives involved in this operation, /dev/sdb and /dev/sdc, are not mounted.

With the dd command, the if operand indicates the disk we wish to copy, which is the /dev/sdb drive. The of operand indicates that the /dev/sdc disk will hold the copied data. Also the status=progress will display periodic transfer statistics. You can see in Listing 4.38 from the transfer statistics that there is not much data on /dev/sdb, so the dd operation finished quickly.

You can also create a system image backup using a dd command similar to the one shown in Listing 4.38, with a few needed modifications. The basic steps are as follows:

1. Shut down your Linux system.

2. Attach the necessary spare drives. You'll need one drive the same size or larger for each system drive.

3. Boot the system using a live CD, DVD, or USB so that you can either keep the system's drives unmounted or unmount them prior to the backup operation.

4. For each system drive, issue a dd command, specifying the drive to back up with the if operand and the spare drive with the of operand.

5. Shut down the system, and remove the spare drives containing the system image.

6. Reboot your Linux system.

If you have a disk you are getting rid of, you can also use the dd command to zero out the disk. An example is shown in Listing 4.39.

Listing 4.39: Using dd to zero an entire disk

```
# dd if=/dev/zero of=/dev/sdc status=progress
1061724672 bytes (1.1 GB) copied, 33.196299 s, 32.0 MB/s
dd: writing to '/dev/sdc': No space left on device
2097153+0 records in
2097152+0 records out
1073741824 bytes (1.1 GB) copied, 34.6304 s, 31.0 MB/s
#
```

The if=/dev/zero uses the zero device file to write zeros to the disk. You need to perform this operation at least 10 times or more to thoroughly wipe the disk. You can also employ the /dev/random and/or the /dev/urandom device files to put random data onto the disk. This particular task can take a long time to run for large disks. It is still better to shred any disks that will no longer be used by your company.

Managing Links

Understanding file and directory links is a vital part of your Linux journey. While many quickly pick up how to link files, they do not necessarily understand the underlying link structure. And that can be a problem. In this section, we'll explore linking files as well as the implications of links.

There are two types of links. One is a symbolic link, which is also called a *soft link*. The other is a hard link, and we'll take a look at it first.

Establishing a Hard Link

A *hard link* is a file or directory that has one index (inode) number but at least two different filenames. Having a single inode number means that it is a single data file on the filesystem. Having two or more names means the file can be accessed in multiple ways. Figure 4.1 shows this relationship. In this diagram, a hard link has been created. The hard link has two filenames, one inode number, and therefore one filesystem location residing on a disk partition. Thus, the file has two names but is physically one file.

FIGURE 4.1   Hard link file relationship

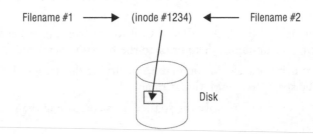

A hard link allows you to have a pseudo-copy of a file without truly copying its data. This is often used in file backups where not enough filesystem space exists to back up the file's data. If someone deletes one of the file's names, you still have another filename that links to its data.

To create a hard link, use the *ln* command. For hard links, the original file must exist prior to issuing the ln command. The linked file must not exist; it is created when the command is issued. Listing 4.40 shows this command in action.

Listing 4.40: Using the ln command to create a hard link

```
$ touch OriginalFile.txt
$
$ ls
OriginalFile.txt
$
$ ln OriginalFile.txt HardLinkFile.txt
$
$ ls
HardLinkFile.txt  OriginalFile.txt
$
$ ls -i
2101459 HardLinkFile.txt  2101459 OriginalFile.txt
$
$ touch NewFile.txt
$
```

```
$ ls -og
total 0
-rw-rw-r--. 2 0 Aug 24 18:09 HardLinkFile.txt
-rw-rw-r--. 1 0 Aug 24 18:17 NewFile.txt
-rw-rw-r--. 2 0 Aug 24 18:09 OriginalFile.txt
$
```

In Listing 4.40, a new blank and empty file, OriginalFile.txt, is created via the touch command. It is then hard-linked to the HardLinkFile.txt via the ln command. Notice that the OriginalFile.txt was created prior to issuing the ln command, and the HardLinkFile.txt file was created *by* issuing the ln command. The inode numbers for these files are checked using the ls -i command, and you can see the numbers are the same for both files.

Also in Listing 4.40, after the hard link is created and the inode numbers are checked, a new empty file is created called NewFile.txt. This was done to compare link counts. Using the ls -og command, the file's metadata is displayed, which includes file type, permissions, link counts, file size, creation dates, and filenames. This command is similar to ls -l but omits file owners and groups. You can quickly find the link counts in the command output. They are right next to the files' sizes, which are all 0 since the files are empty. Notice that both OriginalFile.txt and HardLinkFile.txt have a link count of 2. This is because they are both hard-linked to one other file. NewFile.txt has a link count of 1 because it is *not* hard-linked to another file.

 If you want to remove a linked file but not the original file, use the unlink command. Just type **unlink** at the command line and include the linked file name as an argument.

When you create and use hard links, there are a few important items to remember:

- The original file must exist before you issue the ln command.
- The second filename listed in the ln command must *not* exist prior to issuing the command.
- An original file and its hard links share the same inode number.
- An original file and its hard links share the same data.
- An original file and any of its hard links can exist in different directories.
- An original file and its hard links must exist on the same filesystem.

Constructing a Soft Link

Typically, a *soft link* file provides a pointer to a file that may reside on another filesystem. The two files do not share inode numbers because they do not point to the same data. Figure 4.2 illustrates the soft link relationship.

FIGURE 4.2   Soft link file relationship

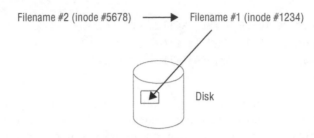

To create a *symbolic* link, the ln command is used with the -s or --symbolic option. An example is shown in Listing 4.41.

Listing 4.41: Using the ln command to create a soft link

```
$ touch OriginalSFile.txt
$
$ ls
OriginalSFile.txt
$
$ ln -s OriginalSFile.txt SoftLinkFile.txt
$
$ ls -i
2101456 OriginalSFile.txt  2101468 SoftLinkFile.txt
$
$ ls -og
total 0
-rw-rw-r--. 1  0 Aug 24 19:04 OriginalSFile.txt
lrwxrwxrwx. 1 17 Aug 24 19:04 SoftLinkFile.txt -> OriginalSFile.txt
$
```

Similar to a hard link, the original file must exist prior to issuing the ln -s command. The soft-linked file must not exist; it is created when the command is issued. In Listing 4.41, you can see via the ls -i command that soft-linked files do not share the same inode number, unlike hard-linked files. Also, soft-linked files do not experience a link count increase. The ls -og command shows this, and it also displays the soft-linked file's pointer to the original file.

Sometimes you have a soft-linked file that points to another soft-linked file. If you want to quickly find the final file, use the readlink -f command and pass one of the soft-linked filenames as an argument to it. The readlink utility will display the final file's name and directory location.

When creating and using soft links, keep in mind a few important items:

- The original file must exist before you issue the ln -s command.

- The second filename listed in the ln -s command must not exist prior to issuing the command.

- An original file and its soft links do not share the same inode number.

- An original file and its soft links do not share the same data.

- An original file and any of its soft links can exist in different directories.

- An original file and its soft links can exist in different filesystems.

 WARNING   Stale links can be a serious security problem. A stale link, sometimes called a dead link, is when a soft link points to a file that was deleted or moved. The soft-linked file itself is not removed or updated. If a file with the original file's name and location is created, the soft link now points to that new file. If a malicious file is put in the original file's place, your server's security could be compromised. Use symbolic links with caution and employ the unlink command if you need to remove a linked file.

File and directory links are easy to create. However it is important that you understand the underlying structure of these links in order to use them properly.

Looking at Practical Link Uses

When you're first introduced to hard and soft links on Linux, it's difficult to see their practical side. They actually have many uses when it comes to supporting your system. Here are a few:

Version Links   When you use a program launcher, such as python or java, it's convenient if you don't have to know the currently installed version. Soft links help with this, as shown here:

```
$ which java
/usr/bin/java
$
$ readlink -f /usr/bin/java
/usr/lib/jvm/java-1.8.0-openjdk-1.8.0.201.b09-2.el7_6.x86_64/jre/bin/java
```

This is true with libraries as well (libraries were covered in Chapter 2). The underlying library files can be updated without causing application disruption:

```
$ readlink -f /usr/lib64/mysql/libmysqlclient.so.18
/usr/lib64/mysql/libmysqlclient.so.18.0.0
```

Backups   Hard links are useful as a pseudo-backup. This is handy when you have a working shell script (covered in Chapter 9), program, or data file in your home directory. You can simply hard-link it to another filename in a subdirectory to protect you from yourself:

```
$ ln ImportantFile.txt SpaceOpera/ImportantFile.txt
$
$ ls -i ImportantFile.txt SpaceOpera/ImportantFile.txt
17671201 ImportantFile.txt  17671201 SpaceOpera/ImportantFile.txt
```

Now, if you accidentally delete ImportantFile.txt, you've got a backup copy filename that connects to the original data on the disk. That's convenient!

Command Substitution   As time goes on, program names change. To maintain backward compatibility to previous command names, often links are employed. In addition, a program may be called by multiple commands; thus links save the day here, too. One example is the make filesystem (mkfs) command for formatting ext2, 3, and 4 filesystems (covered in Chapter 3). These commands all share the same inode number. Thus, they are hard-linked, and though they have three names, are a single program, as shown here:

```
$ ls -i /sbin/mkfs.ext[234]
228513 /sbin/mkfs.ext2  228513 /sbin/mkfs.ext3  228513 /sbin/mkfs.ext4
```

In this case, the program determines which filesystem type to make based on the filename called. There's no need to waste disk space with three programs; one is enough. And for user simplicity, three filenames are provided.

Sometimes, for command substitution, you'll discover soft links are employed instead. This is the case for the /sbin/mkfs.msdos and mkfs.vfat filesystem formatting commands:

```
$ ls -l /sbin/mkfs.* | grep ^l
lrwxrwxrwx. 1 root root      8 Mar 19 17:10 /sbin/mkfs.msdos -> mkfs.fat
lrwxrwxrwx. 1 root root      8 Mar 19 17:10 /sbin/mkfs.vfat -> mkfs.fat
```

This is nice, because now a system admin doesn't have to remember that the command is actually mkfs.fat and can use mkfs.msdos or mkfs.vfat instead.

Now that you know how to create, copy, move, and delete files, as well as archive and link files, you can efficiently manage the files and directories in your charge. However, it is also critical to understand how file security is managed at the most basic level.

Managing File Ownership

The core security feature of Linux is file and directory permissions. Linux accomplishes that by assigning each file and directory an owner, and allowing that owner to set the basic security settings to control access to the file or directory. This section walks through how Linux handles ownership of files and directories.

Assessing File Ownership

Linux uses a three-tiered approach to protecting files and directories:

- **Owner:** Within the Linux system, each file and directory is assigned to a single owner.
- **Group:** The Linux system also assigns each file and directory to a single group of users. The administrator can assign that group specific privileges to the file or directory that differ from the owner privileges.
- **Others:** This category of permissions is assigned accounts that are neither the file owner nor in the assigned user group.

You can view the assigned owner and group for a file or directory by adding the -l option to the ls command, as shown in Listing 4.41.

Listing 4.42: Viewing file owner and group settings

```
$ ls -l
total 12
-rw-rw-r--  1 Rich sales 1521 Jan 19 15:38 customers.txt
-rw-r--r--  1 Christine sales  479 Jan 19 15:37 research.txt
-rw-r--r--  1 Christine sales  696 Jan 19 15:37 salesdata.txt
$
```

In Listing 4.42, the first column defines the access permissions assigned to the owner, group, and others. That will be discussed later in the "Controlling Access to Files" section of this chapter. The third column shows the user account assigned as the owner of the file (Rich or Christine). The fourth column shows the group assigned to the file (sales).

WARNING

Many Linux distributions (such as both Ubuntu and CentOS) assign each user account to a separate group with the exact same name as the user account. This helps prevent accidental sharing of files. However, this can also make things a little confusing when you're working with owner and group permissions and you see the same name appear in both columns. Be careful when working in this type of environment.

When a user creates a file or directory, by default the Linux system automatically assigns that user as the owner. It also uses the primary group of the user as the group designation for the file or directory.

Changing a File's Owner

Only the root user account or those with super user privileges can change the owner assigned to a file or directory by using the *chown* command. The chown command format looks like this:

```
chown [OPTIONS] NEWOWNER FILENAMES
```

The *NEWOWNER* parameter is the username of the new owner to assign to the file or directory, and *FILENAMES* is the name of the file or directory to change. You can specify more than one file or directory by placing a space between each file or directory name. An example of changing the owner of one file is shown in Listing 4.43.

Listing 4.43: Changing a file's owner with the chown command

```
$ sudo chown Christine customers.txt
$ ls -l
total 12
-rw-rw-r-- 1 Christine sales 1521 Jan 19 15:38 customers.txt
-rw-r--r-- 1 Christine sales  479 Jan 19 15:37 research.txt
-rw-r--r-- 1 Christine sales  696 Jan 19 15:37 salesdata.txt
$
```

A few command-line options are available for the chown command, but they are mostly obscure and not used much. One that may be helpful for you is the -R option, which recursively changes the owner of all files under the specified directory.

Changing a File's Group

The file or directory owner, the root user account, or an account with super user privileges can change the group assigned to the file or directory by using the *chgrp* command. The chgrp command uses this format:

chgrp [*OPTIONS*] *NEWGROUP FILENAMES*

The *NEWGROUP* parameter is the name of the new user group assigned to the file or directory, and the *FILENAMES* parameter is the name of the file or directory to change. If you're the owner of the file, you can only change the file's group to a group in which you have membership. The root user account and those with super user privileges can change the group to any group on the system. An example is shown in Listing 4.44.

Listing 4.44: Changing a file's group with the chgrp command

```
$ sudo chgrp marketing customers.txt
$ ls -l
total 12
-rw-rw-r-- 1 Christine marketing 1521 Jan 19 15:38 customers.txt
-rw-r--r-- 1 Christine sales       479 Jan 19 15:37 research.txt
-rw-r--r-- 1 Christine sales       696 Jan 19 15:37 salesdata.txt
$
```

The chgrp command also uses the -R option to recursively change the group assigned to all files and directories under the specified directory.

If you have super user privileges, the chown command allows you to change *both* the owner and group assigned to a file or directory at the same time using the format

chown NEWOWNER:NEWGROUP FILENAMES

This is often preferred over using the separate chgrp command. You can also avoid the chgrp command altogether by using

chown :NEWGROUP FILENAMES

Using chown this way can be done without any super user privileges, but you do have to own the file and be a member of the specified new group.

When you first log into the system, Linux sets your current group membership to the group listed in your user account record (covered in Chapter 7). You can check your current group's name by issuing the **id −gn** command.

If you have membership in another group and need to make that group your current group, type **newgrp *groupname*** at the command line. Keep in mind that after you log out, your current group will be set back to the group listed in your user account record.

Controlling Access to Files

When ownership and group membership for a file or directory are set, Linux allows certain accesses based on those settings. This section walks through how Linux handles the basic permissions settings that you can assign to any file or directory on your system.

Understanding Permissions

When you use the -l option, as shown in Listing 4.44, you'll find lots of information concerning a file, including its permission settings.

Listing 4.44: Viewing a file's long listing

```
$ ls -l cake.txt
-rw-rw-r--. 1 Christine Bakers 42 Apr 24 10:45 cake.txt
$
```

The data displayed in the long listing for a file or directory can be a little confusing. Here is a brief description of the different items along with their value in Listing 4.44:

- File type code (-)
- Permission string (rw-rw-r--)
- Hard link count (1)
- File owner (Christine)
- File group (Bakers)

- File size (42 bytes)
- Last modification date (April 24 10:45)
- Filename (cake.txt)

Before we cover permissions, you need to know a little more about the file type code. The different codes are described in Table 4.11.

TABLE 4.11 File type codes

Code	Description
–	The file is a binary file, a readable file (such as a text file), an image file, or a compressed file.
d	The file is a directory.
l	The file is a symbolic (soft) link to another file or directory.
p	The file is a named pipe or regular pipe used for communication between two or more processes.
s	The file is a socket file, which operates similar to a pipe but allows more styles of communication, such as bidirectional or over a network.
b	The file is a block device, such as a disk drive.
c	The file is a character device, such as a point-of-sale device.

Linux uses three types of permission controls. Note that the permissions have a slightly different meaning depending on whether they are set for a file or on a directory, as shown in Table 4.12.

TABLE 4.12 File vs. directory permissions

Permission	File	Directory
read	Provides the ability to read/view the data stored within the file	Allows a user to list files contained within directory
write	Allows a user to modify the data stored in the file	Lets the user create, move (rename), modify attributes of, and delete files within the directory
execute	Provides the ability to run the file as a script or binary on the system	Allows a user to change their present working directory to this location as long as this permission is set on all its parent directories as well

You can assign each tier of protection (owner, group, and other) different read, write, and execute permissions. This creates a set of nine different permissions that are assigned to each file and directory on the Linux system. Figure 4.3 shows the order in which the permissions are displayed in the ls -l output.

FIGURE 4.3   File permissions as displayed by the ls -l command

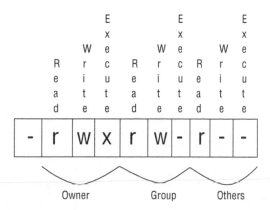

The first three characters denote the *owner* (sometimes called *user*) permissions in the order of read, write, and execute. A dash indicates the permission is not set, whereas the r, w, or x indicate the read, write, or execute permission is set. In Figure 4.3, the file has rw- for the owner permissions, which means the owner has permissions to read and write to the file but cannot execute, or run, the file. This is common with plain data files.

The second set of three characters denotes the *group* permissions for the file. Again, this uses the read, write, and execute order, with a dash indicating the permission is not set. A user who is not the file's owner but whose current group is equal to the file's group is granted these permissions to the file.

Finally, the third set of three characters denotes the permissions assigned to user accounts that are not the owner or a current member of the group assigned to the file or directory, called *other* (sometimes called *world*) permissions. The same order of read, write, and execute is used.

Changing a File's Mode

Either an account with super user privileges or the owner of the file/directory can change the assigned permissions by using the *chmod* command.

The format of the chmod command can be somewhat confusing. It uses two different modes for denoting the read, write, and execute permission settings for the owner, group, and other: symbol and octal mode.

Using *chmod* with Symbolic Mode

In *symbolic mode*, you denote permissions by using a letter code for the levels shown in Table 4.13 along with another letter code for the read (r), write (w), or execute (x) permission.

TABLE 4.13   Symbolic mode levels

Level	Description
u	owner
g	group
o	others
a	all tiers

The two codes are separated with a plus sign (+) if you want to add the permission, a minus sign (–) to remove the permission, or an equal sign (=) to set the permission as the only permission. Listing 4.45 shows an example of this.

Listing 4.45: Changing the file owner

```
$ chmod g-w customers.txt
$
$ ls -l
total 12
-rw-r--r--  1 Christine marketing 1521 Jan 19 15:38 customers.txt
-rw-r--r--  1 Christine sales       479 Jan 19 15:37 research.txt
-rw-r--r--  1 Christine sales       696 Jan 19 15:37 salesdata.txt
$
```

In Listing 4.45, the g-w code in the chmod command indicates to remove the write permission for the group from the customers.txt file.

You can combine letter codes for both to make multiple changes in a single chmod command, as shown in Listing 4.46.

Listing 4.46: Combining permission changes

```
$ chmod ug=rwx research.txt
$
$ ls -l
total 12
-rw-r--r-- 1 Christine marketing 1521 Jan 19 15:38 customers.txt
-rwxrwxr-- 1 Christine sales       479 Jan 19 15:37 research.txt
-rw-r--r-- 1 Christine sales       696 Jan 19 15:37 salesdata.txt
$
```

The ug code assigns the change to both the owner and the group, and the rwx code assigns the read, write, and execute permissions. The equal sign indicates to set those permissions.

WARNING If you choose to use symbolic mode for the chmod command, be aware that it's easy to get the codes confused. For example, don't use the o code thinking that it sets file owner permissions. Instead, it sets other (world) permissions. It would be a bad thing to provide the intended file owner's permissions to the world.

Using *chmod* with Octal Mode

The second mode available in chmod is called *octal mode*. With octal mode the nine permission bits are represented as three octal numbers, one each for the owner, group, and other permissions. Table 4.14 shows how the octal number matches the three symbolic mode permissions.

TABLE 4.14 Octal mode permissions

Octal value	Permission	Meaning
0	---	no permissions
1	--x	execute only
2	-w-	write only
3	-wx	write and execute
4	r--	read only
5	r-x	read and execute
6	rw-	read and write
7	rwx	read, write, and execute

You must specify the three octal values in the owner, group, and other in the correct order, as shown in Listing 4.47.

Listing 4.47: Using octal mode to assign permissions

```
$ chmod 664 research.txt
$
$ ls -l
total 12
-rw-r--r-- 1 Christine marketing 1521 Jan 19 15:38 customers.txt
-rw-rw-r-- 1 Christine sales       479 Jan 19 15:37 research.txt
-rw-r--r-- 1 Christine sales       696 Jan 19 15:37 salesdata.txt
$
```

The 664 octal mode set the owner and group permissions to read and write (6), but the others permission to read only (4). You can see the results from the ls output. This is a handy way to set all of the permissions for a file or directory in a single command.

Setting the Default Mode

When a user creates a new file or directory, the Linux system assigns it a default owner, group, and permissions. The default owner, as expected, is the user who created the file. The default group is the owner's primary group.

The user mask feature defines the default permissions Linux assigns to the file or directory. The user mask is an octal value that represents the bits to be removed from the default octal mode 666 permissions for files, or 777 permissions for directories.

The user mask value is set with the *umask* command. You can view your current umask setting by entering the command by itself on the command line as shown in Listing 4.48.

Listing 4.48: Viewing the current user mask setting via the umask command

```
$ umask
0022
$
```

The output of the umask command shows four octal values. The first octal value represents the mask for the SUID (4), SGID (2), and sticky (1) bits assigned to files and directories you create (covered later in this chapter). You'll notice, however, that in Listing 4.48, the value is set to 0, which means these bits are ignored. The next three octal values mask the owner, group, and other permission settings.

The mask is a bitwise (works with individual bits) operation applied to the permission bits on the file or directory. Any bit that's set in the mask is removed from the permissions for the file or directory. If a bit isn't set, the mask doesn't change the setting. Table 4.15 demonstrates how the umask values work in practice when creating files and directories on your Linux system. Note that we are ignoring the first octal value (which applies to SUID, SGID, and the sticky bit) for now and focusing on the last three.

TABLE 4.15   Results from common umask values for files and directories

umask	Created files	Created directories
000	666 (rw-rw-rw-)	777 (rwxrwxrwx)
002	664 (rw-rw-r--)	775 (rwxrwxr-x)
022	644 (rw-r--r--)	755 (rwxr-xr-x)
027	640 (rw-r-----)	750 (rwxr-x---)
077	600 (rw-------)	700 (rwx------)
277	400 (r--------)	500 (r-x------)

You can test this by determining your current user mask value, creating a new file and directory on your Linux system, and then reviewing the resulting permissions. An example is shown in Listing 4.49.

Listing 4.49: Viewing the effect of the current user mask setting on permissions

```
$ umask
0022
$
$ mkdir test1
$ touch test2
$ ls -l
[…]
drwxr-xr-x 2 rich rich 4096 Jan 19 17:08 test1
-rw-r--r-- 1 rich rich    0 Jan 19 17:08 test2
$
```

The umask value of 0022 created the default file permissions of rw-r--r-- , or octal 644, on the test2 file, and rwx-r-xr-x, or octal 755, on the test1 directory, as expected.

> It helps to think of the umask setting as the "undo" value, because it subtracts permissions from the default permissions for a newly created file or directory.

You can change the default umask setting for your user account by using the umask command from the command line. An example of doing this is shown in Listing 4.50.

Listing 4.50: Changing the user mask setting and viewing the change's effect

```
$ umask 027
$
$ touch test3
$ ls -l test3
-rw-r----- 1 rich rich 0 Jan 19 17:12 test3
$
```

The default permissions for the new file, test3, have changed to reflect the new umask setting.

> The umask value is normally set in a script that the Linux system runs at login time, such as in the /etc/profile file. If you override the setting from the command line, that will apply only for the duration of your session. You can override the system default umask setting by adding it to the appropriate environment file (covered in Chapter 9) in your $HOME directory.

Changing Special Access Modes

There are three special permission bits that Linux uses for controlling advanced behavior of files and directories: SUID, SGID, and the sticky bit.

Looking at SUID

The *Set User ID (SUID)* bit is used with executable files. It tells the Linux kernel to run the program with the permissions of the file owner and not the user account actually running the file. This feature is most commonly used in server applications that must run as the root user account to have access to all files on the system, but the Linux system starts them as a standard user account.

The SUID bit is indicated by an s in place of the execute permission letter for the file owner: rwsr-xr-x. The execute permission is assumed for the system to run the file. If the SUID bit is set on a file that doesn't have execute permission for the owner, it's indicated by a capital S.

A practical example of SUID on Linux is the passwd utility. The passwd utility allows you to change your password, which is stored in the /etc/shadow file (covered in Chapter 7). Because the shadow file only allows the root user (the file's owner) to write to it, you must temporarily gain the root user's permission status. This is done via the SUID permission set on the passwd program's file as shown in Listing 4.51.

Listing 4.51: Viewing the passwd utility's and /etc/shadow file's permissions

```
$ ls -l /etc/shadow
-rw-r----- 1 root shadow 1425 Mar 21 17:51 /etc/shadow
$
$ which passwd
/usr/bin/passwd
$
$ ls -l /usr/bin/passwd
-rwsr-xr-x 1 root root 59640 Jan 25  2018 /usr/bin/passwd
$
```

To set the SUID bit for a file, in symbolic mode add s to the owner permissions, or in octal mode include a 4 at the start of the octal mode setting.

```
# chmod u+s myapp
# chmod 4750 myapp
```

Looking at SGID

The *Set Group ID (SGID)* bit works differently in files and directories. For files, it tells Linux to run the program file with the file's group permissions. It's indicated by an s in the group execute position: rwxrwsr--. Like SUID, if the execute permission is not granted, the setting is benign and shown as a capital S in the group execute position.

For directories, the SGID bit helps us create an environment where multiple users can share files. When a directory has the SGID bit set, any files users create in the directory are assigned the group of the directory and not that of the user. That way, all users in that group can have the same permissions to all of the files in the shared directory.

To set the SGID bit, in symbolic mode add s to the group permissions, or in octal mode include a 2 at the start of the octal mode setting:

```
# chmod g+s /sales
# chmod 2660 /sales
```

Looking at the Sticky Bit

Finally, the *sticky bit* is used on directories to protect one of its files from being deleted by those who don't own the file, even if they belong to the group that has write permissions to the file. The sticky bit is denoted by a t in the execute bit position for others: rwxrw-r-t.

The sticky bit is often used on directories shared by groups. The group members have read and write access to the data files contained in the directory, but only the file owners can remove files from the shared directory. Typically the /tmp directory has the sticky bit set as shown in Listing 4.52.

Listing 4.52: Viewing the /tmp directory's sticky bit permission

```
$ ls -ld /tmp
drwxrwxrwt 12 root root 4096 Apr 25 13:50 /tmp
$
```

To set the sticky bit, in symbolic mode add t to the owner permissions, or in octal mode include a 1 at the start of the octal mode setting:

```
# chmod o+t /sales
# chmod 1777 /sales
```

Locating Files

There are many ways to find various files on your Linux system. The methods are important to know so that you can make good administrative decisions and/or solve problems quickly. They will save you time as you perform your administrative tasks, as well as help you pass the certification exam.

Getting to Know the FHS

Trying to locate files on your Linux system is sometimes tricky. Fortunately, there's a standard file location guide for the Linux called the Linux *filesystem hierarchy standard (FHS)* that can offer assistance.

WARNING   Although the FHS helps standardize where files are located on Linux, not all Linux distributions follow it completely. It's best to consult with your specific Linux distribution's documentation on how it manages files within the virtual directory structure.

The FHS defines core folder names and locations that should be present on every Linux system and what type of data they should contain. Table 4.16 shows just a few of the more common folders defined in the FHS.

TABLE 4.16   Common Linux FHS folders

Folder	Description
/	The root filesystem
/boot	Contains bootloader files used to boot the system
/dev	Holds device files
/home	Contains user data files
/lib	Holds shared libraries and kernel modules
/media	Traditionally used as a mount point for removable devices
/mnt	Used as the current mount point for removable devices
/opt	Contains data for optional third-party programs
/tmp	Contains temporary files created by system users
/usr	Contains data for standard Linux programs
/usr/bin	Contains local user programs and data
/usr/lib	Holds libraries for programming and software packages
/usr/local	Contains data for programs unique to the local installation
/usr/sbin	Contains data for system programs and data

NOTE   You can read the entire FHS standard at the Linux Foundation's reference specifications: refspecs.linuxfoundation.org.

Employing Tools to Locate Files

Besides using the FHS as a guide, there are many ways to find files on your Linux system. In this section, we'll explore several tools that assist in locating files.

Using the *which* Command

The *which* command shows you the full path name of a shell command passed as an argument. Examples of using this utility are shown in Listing 4.53.

Listing 4.53: Using the which command

```
$ which passwd
/usr/bin/passwd
$
$ which shutdown
/usr/sbin/shutdown
$
$ which line
/usr/bin/which: no line in (/usr/local/bin:/usr/bin:/usr/local/sbin:
/usr/sbin:/home/Christine/.local/bin:/home/Christine/bin)
$
$ echo $PATH
/usr/local/bin:/usr/bin:/usr/local/sbin:/usr/sbin:
/home/Christine/.local/bin:/home/Christine/bin
$
```

In the first example in Listing 4.53, the which command is used to find the program location of the passwd command. It displays the full path name of /usr/bin/passwd. The shutdown utility is located in an sbin directory. However, the line program is not installed on this system, and the which utility displays all the directories it searched to find the program. It uses the PATH environment variable, whose contents are also displayed in Listing 4.53, to determine which directories to search.

Environment variables are configuration settings that modify your process's environment. When you type a command (program) name, the PATH variable sets the directories Linux will search for the program binary. It is also used by other commands, such as the which utility. Note that directory names are separated by a colon (:) in the PATH list.

The which command is also handy for quickly determining if a command is using an alias. Listing 4.54 shows an example of this.

Listing 4.54: Using the which command to see a command alias

```
$ which ls
alias ls='ls --color=auto'
        /usr/bin/ls
$
$ unalias ls
$
$ which ls
/usr/bin/ls
$
```

When the which utility is used on the ls command in Listing 4.54, it shows that currently the ls command has an alias. Thus, when you type ls, it is as if you have typed the ls --color=auto command. After employing the unalias command on ls, the which utility shows only the ls program's location.

Using the *whereis* Command

Another command for locating files is the *whereis* utility. This utility allows you to locate any command's program binaries and locate source code files as well as any manual pages. Examples of using the whereis utility are shown in Listing 4.55.

Listing 4.55: Employing the whereis command

```
$ whereis diff
diff: /usr/bin/diff /usr/share/man/man1/diff.1.gz
/usr/share/man/man1p/diff.1p.gz
$
$ whereis line
line:
$
```

The first command issued in Listing 4.55 searches for program binaries, source code files, and manual pages for the diff utility. In this case, the whereis command finds a binary file as well as two manual page files. However, when whereis is used to locate files for the line utility, nothing is found on the system.

Using the *locate* Command

A very convenient and simple utility to use in finding files is the *locate* program. This utility searches a database, mlocate.db, which is located in the /var/lib/mlocate/ directory, to determine if a particular file exists on the local system. The basic syntax for the locate command is as follows:

```
locate [OPTION]... PATTERN...
```

Notice in the syntax that the locate utility uses a pattern list to find files. Thus, you can employ partial filenames and regular expressions and, with the command options, ignore case. Table 4.17 shows a few of the more commonly used locate command options.

TABLE 4.17   The locate command's commonly used options

Short	Long	Description
-A	--all	Display filenames that match all the patterns, instead of displaying files that match only one pattern in the pattern list.
-b	--basename	Display only filenames that match the pattern and do not include any directory names that match the pattern.
-c	--count	Display only the number of files whose name matches the pattern instead of displaying filenames.
-i	--ignore-case	Ignore case in the pattern for matching filenames.
-q	--quiet	Do not display any error messages, such as permission denied, when processing.
-r	--regexp R	Use the regular expression, R, instead of the pattern list to match filenames.
-w	--wholename	Display filenames that match the pattern and include any directory names that match the pattern. This is default behavior.

To find a file with the locate command, enter **locate** followed by the filename. If the file is on your system and you have permission to view it, the locate utility will display the file's directory path and name. An example of this is shown in Listing 4.56.

Listing 4.56: Using the locate command to find a file

```
$ locate Project42.txt
/home/Christine/Answers/Project42.txt
$
```

Using the locate command *PATTERN* can be a little tricky, due to default pattern file globbing. If you don't enter any wildcards into your pattern, the locate command, by default, adds wildcards to the pattern. So if you enter the pattern **passwd**, it is automatically turned into ***passwd***.

If you want to search for the base name passwd, with no file globbing, you must add quotation marks (single or double) around the pattern and precede the pattern with the \ character. A few examples of this are shown in Listing 4.57.

Listing 4.57: Using the locate command with no file globbing

```
$ locate -b passwd
/etc/passwd
/etc/passwd-
/etc/pam.d/passwd
/etc/security/opasswd
/usr/bin/gpasswd
[…]
/usr/share/vim/vim74/syntax/passwd.vim
$
$ locate -b '\passwd'
/etc/passwd
/etc/pam.d/passwd
/usr/bin/passwd
/usr/share/bash-completion/completions/passwd
$
```

The first example in Listing 4.57 shows what would happen if you allow the default file globbing to occur. Many more files are displayed than those named passwd. So many files are displayed that the listing had to be snipped to fit. However, in the second example, file globbing is turned off with the use of quotation marks and the \ character. Using this pattern with the locate utility provides the desired results of displaying files named passwd.

 If you do not have permission to view a directory's contents, the locate command cannot show files in that directory that match your *PATTERN*. Thus, some files may be missing from your display.

Keep in mind that the locate command's *PATTERN* is really a pattern list, so you can add additional patterns. Just be sure to separate them with a space as shown in Listing 4.58.

Listing 4.58: Using the locate command with a pattern list

```
$ locate -b '\passwd' '\group'
/etc/group
/etc/passwd
/etc/iproute2/group
/etc/pam.d/passwd
/usr/bin/passwd
/usr/share/X11/xkb/symbols/group
/usr/share/bash-completion/completions/passwd
$
```

Another problem you can run into deals with newly created or downloaded files. The locate utility is really searching the mlocate.db database as opposed to searching the virtual directory structure. This database is typically updated only one time per day via a cron job. Therefore, if the file is newly created, locate won't find it.

The mlocate.db database is updated via the *updatedb* utility. You can run it manually using super user privileges if you need to find a newly created or downloaded file. Be aware that it may take a while to run.

If you need to prevent some files from being found with the locate command, or quicken the nightly run of the mlocate.db database update, you can prevent certain directory locations from being scanned via the updatedb utility. Simply modify the */etc/updatedb.conf* configuration file, and modify one of the PRUNEFS, *PRUNENAMES*, or PRUNEPATHS directives in order to designate directories to skip during an updatedb scan. Type **man updatedb.conf** at the command line for more details.

Using the *find* Command

The *find* command is very flexible. It allows you to locate files based on data, such as who owns the file, when the file was last modified, permissions set on the file, and so on. The basic command syntax is as follows:

find   [*PATH*...] [*OPTION*] [*EXPRESSION*]

The *PATH* argument is a starting point directory, because you designate a starting point in a directory tree and find will search through that directory and all its subdirectories (recursively) for the file or files you seek. You can use a single period (.) to designate your present working directory as the starting point directory.

There are also options for the find command itself that handle such items as following or not following links and debugging. In addition, you can have a file deleted or a command executed if a particular file is located. See the file utility's man page for more information on these features.

The *EXPRESSION* command argument and its preceding *OPTION* control what type of metadata filters are applied to the search as well as any settings that may limit the search. Table 4.18 shows the more commonly used *OPTION* and *EXPRESSION* combinations.

TABLE 4.18   The find command's commonly used options and expressions

Option	Expression	Description
-cmin	*n*	Display names of files whose status changed *n* minutes ago.
-empty	N/A	Display names of files that are empty and are a regular text file or a directory.

TABLE 4.18 The find command's commonly used options and expressions *(continued)*

Option	Expression	Description
-gid	*n*	Display names of files whose group ID is equal to *n*.
-group	*name*	Display names of files whose group is *name*.
-inum	*n*	Display names of files whose inode number is equal to *n*.
-maxdepth	*n*	When searching for files, traverse down into the starting point directory's tree only *n* levels.
-mmin	*n*	Display names of files whose data changed *n* minutes ago.
-name	*pattern*	Display names of files whose name matches *pattern*. Many regular expression arguments may be used in the *pattern* and need to be enclosed in quotation marks to avoid unpredictable results. Replace –name with –iname to ignore case.
-nogroup	N/A	Display names of files where no group name exists for the file's group ID.
-nouser	N/A	Display names of files where no username exists for the file's user ID.
-perm	*mode*	Display names of files whose permissions matches *mode*. Either octal or symbolic modes may be used.
-size	*n*	Display names of files whose size matches *n*. Suffixes can be used to make the size more human readable, such as G for gigabytes.
-user	*name*	Display names of files whose owner is *name*.

The find utility has many features. Examples help clarify the use of this command. Listing 4.59 provides a few.

Listing 4.59: Employing the find command

```
$ find . -name "*.txt"
./Project47.txt
./Answers/Project42.txt
./Answers/Everything/numbers.txt
./Answers/Everything/random.txt
./Answers/Project43.txt
```

```
./Answers/Project44.txt
./Answers/Project45.txt
./Answers/Project46.txt
./SpaceOpera/OriginalSFile.txt
./SpaceOpera/SoftLinkFile.txt
$
$ find . -maxdepth 2 -name "*.txt"
./Project47.txt
./Answers/Project42.txt
./Answers/Project43.txt
./Answers/Project44.txt
./Answers/Project45.txt
./Answers/Project46.txt
./SpaceOpera/OriginalSFile.txt
./SpaceOpera/SoftLinkFile.txt
$
```

The first example in Listing 4.59 is looking for files in the present working directory's tree with a .txt file extension. Notice that the -name option's *pattern* uses quotation marks to avoid unpredictable results. In the second example, a -maxdepth option is added so that the find utility searches only two directories: the current directory and one subdirectory level down.

The find command is very handy for auditing your system on a regular basis as well as when you are concerned that your server has been hacked. The -perm option is useful for one of these audit types, and an example is shown in Listing 4.60.

Listing 4.60: Using the find command to audit a server

```
$ find /usr/bin -perm /4000
/usr/bin/newgrp
/usr/bin/chsh
/usr/bin/arping
/usr/bin/gpasswd
/usr/bin/chfn
/usr/bin/traceroute6.iputils
/usr/bin/pkexec
/usr/bin/passwd
/usr/bin/sudo
$
```

In Listing 4.60, the /usr/bin directory is being audited for the potentially dangerous SUID permission by using the find utility and its -perm option. The expression used is /4000, which will ask the find utility to search for SUID settings (octal code 4) and, due to the forward slash (/) in front of the number, ignore the other file permissions (octal codes 000). The resulting filenames all legitimately use SUID, and thus, nothing suspicious is going on here.

On older Linux systems, to enact a search as shown in Listing 4.60, you would enter **+4000** to designate the permission. The plus sign (+) is now deprecated for this use and has been replaced by the forward slash (/) symbol for the find command.

Quickly finding files as well as various types of information on your Linux server can help you be a more effective and efficient system administrator. It is a worthwhile investment to try out any of the commands or their options that are new to you.

Using the *type* Command

So you found the file, but you don't know what kind of file it is. You can employ the file command for some files, but another useful utility is the *type* program.

The type utility will display how a file is interpreted by the Bash shell if it is entered at the command line. Three categories it returns are alias, shell built-in, and external command (displaying its absolute directory reference). A few examples are shown in Listing 4.61.

Listing 4.61: Using the type command to determine a command's interpretation

```
$ type ls
ls is aliased to 'ls --color=auto'
$
$ type cd
cd is a shell builtin
$
$ type find
find is /usr/bin/find
$
```

Notice that the ls command on this system is an alias. The cd program is built into the Bash shell (covered in Chapter 1). The find command is an external command, because the type utility provides its absolute directory location within the Linux virtual directory structure.

You can get less information displayed by the type utility by employing the -t option, which just shows a brief name, such as builtin for the command type. You can get more information from the type utility by using the -a switch, such as the alias information and its binary's absolute directory location.

Summary

Being able to effectively and swiftly use the right file management utilities at the shell's command line is important for your daily job. It allows you to find files, generate backups, fix file permission problems, and so on. Not only will these skills help you in your day-to-day work life, but they will also help you successfully pass the LPIC-1 certification exam.

Exam Essentials

Explain basic commands for handling files and directories.   Typical basic file and directory management activities include viewing and creating files, copying and moving files, and deleting files. For viewing and creating files and directories, use the ls, touch, and mkdir commands. When you need to duplicate, rename, or move files, employ one of the mv and cp commands. You can quickly delete an empty directory using the rmdir utility, but for directories full of files, you will need to use the rm -r command. Also, if you need to ensure that you are removing the correct files, use the -i option on the rm utility.

Summarize compression methods.   The different utilities, gzip, bzip2, xz, and zip, provide different levels of lossless data compression. Each one's compression level is tied to how fast it operates. Reducing the size of archive data files is needed not only for backup storage but also for increasing transfer speeds across the network.

Compare the various archive/restore utilities.   The assorted command-line utilities each have their own strengths in creating data backups and restoring files. While cpio is one of the oldest, it allows for various files through the system to be gathered and put into an archive. The tar utility has long been used with tape media but provides rigorous and flexible archiving and restoring features, which make it still very useful in today's environment. The dd utility shines when it comes to making system images of an entire disk.

Describe both structures and commands involved in linking files.   Linking files is rather easy to do with the ln command. However, it is important for you to describe the underlying link structure. Hard-linked files share the same inode number, whereas soft-linked files do not. Soft or symbolic links can be broken if the file they link to is removed. It is also useful to understand the readlink utility to help you explore files that have multiple links.

Summarize the basic level of file and directory security available in Linux.   Linux provides basic file and directory security by utilizing three categories of read, write, and execute permissions. The file or directory owner is assigned one set of permissions, the primary group the file is assigned another set of permissions, and everyone else on the Linux system is assigned a third set of permissions. You can set the permissions in the three categories separately to control the amount of access the group members and others on the Linux system have.

Explain how to modify the permissions assigned to a file or directory.   Linux uses the chmod command to assign permissions to files and directories. The chmod command uses two separate modes to assign permissions: symbolic mode and octal mode. Symbolic mode uses a single letter to identify the category for the owner (u), group (g), everyone else (o), and all (a). Following that, a plus sign, minus sign, or equal sign is used to indicate to add, remove, or set the permissions. The permissions are also indicated by a single letter for read (r), write (w), or execute (x) permissions. In octal mode, an octal value represents the three permissions for each category. The three octal values define the full set of permissions assigned to the file or directory.

Describe how to find files on your Linux system.   To determine two text files' differences, the diff utility is helpful. With this utility, you can also employ redirection and modify the files to make them identical. When you need to quickly find files on your system and want to use simple tools, the which, whereis, and locate commands will serve you well. Keep in mind that the locate utility uses a database that is typically only updated one time per day, so you may need to manually update it via the updatedb command. When simple file location tools are not enough, there is a more complex searching utility: find. The type command is also helpful in that it provides information concerning how a program file will be interpreted in the shell.

Review Questions

You can find the answers in the appendix.

1. When choosing a filename to create on a Linux system, what characters should be avoided? (Choose all that apply.)

   A. Asterisk (*)

   B. Space

   C. Dash (-)

   D. Ampersand (&)

   E. Underscore (_)

2. You need to list all the filenames that contain the word `data` and have the `.txt` file extension in the present working directory. Which command should you use?

   A. `ls data*.txt`

   B. `ls data?.txt`

   C. `ls *data.txt`

   D. `ls ?data?.txt`

   E. `ls *data*.txt`

3. You need to list all the filenames that start with the word `File`, end with a single number, and have no file extension. Which command should you use?

   A. `ls File?`

   B. `ls File*`

   C. `ls File[0-9]`

   D. `ls File[^0-9]`

   E. `ls File[a-z]`

4. You are looking at a directory that you have not viewed in a long time and need to determine which files are actually directories. Which command is the best one to use?

   A. `mkdir -v`

   B. `ls`

   C. `ls -F`

   D. `ls -i`

   E. `ll`

5. You are using the `ls` command to look at a directory file's metadata but keep seeing metadata for the files within it instead. What command option will rectify this situation?

   A. `-a`

   B. `-d`

   C. `-F`

   D. `-l`

   E. `-R`

6. You have just created an empty directory called MyDir. Which command most likely did you use?

   A. mkdir -v MyDir

   B. touch MyDir

   C. cp -R TheDir MyDir

   D. mv -r TheDir MyDir

   E. rmdir MyDir

7. A long-time server administrator has left the company, and now you are in charge of her system. Her old user account directory tree, /home/Zoe/, has been backed up. Which command is the best one to use to quickly remove her files?

   A. cp -R /home/Zoe/ /dev/null/

   B. mv -R /home/zoe/ /dev/null/

   C. rm -Rf /home/Zoe/

   D. rm -ri /home/Zoe/

   E. rm -rI /home/Zoe

8. An administrator needs to create a full backup using the tar utility, compress it as much as possible, and view the files as they are being copied into the archive. What tar options should the admin employ?

   A. -xzvf

   B. -xJvf

   C. -czvf

   D. -cJf

   E. -cJvf

9. You need to create a low-level backup of all the data on the /dev/sdc drive and want to use the /dev/sde drive to store it on. Which dd command should you use?

   A. dd of=/dev/sde if=/dev/sdc

   B. dd of=/dev/sdc if=/dev/sde

   C. dd of=/dev/sde if=/dev/sdc count=5

   D. dd if=/dev/sde of=/dev/sdc count=5

   E. dd if=/dev/zero of=/dev/sdc

10. Which of the following can be used as backup utilities? (Choose all that apply.)

   A. The gzip utility

   B. The zip utility

   C. The tar utility

   D. The bzcat utility

   E. The dd utility

11. You are trying to decide whether to use a hard link or a symbolic link for a data file. The file is 5 GB, has mission-critical data, and is accessed via the command line by three other people. What should you do?

    A. Create a hard link so the file can reside on a different filesystem for data protection.

    B. Create three hard links and provide the links to the three other people for data protection.

    C. Create three symbolic links and protect the links from the three other people for data protection.

    D. Create a symbolic link so that the file can reside on a different filesystem.

    E. Create a symbolic link so that the links can share an inode number.

12. What command can you use to change the owner assigned to a file?

    A. chmod

    B. chown

    C. ln

    D. owner

    E. chgrp

13. Which of the following commands would change a file named endgame.txt with the current permission string of rwxrw-r-- to rw-rw-r--? (Choose all that apply.)

    A. umask 0100

    B. chmod o-x endgame.txt

    C. chmod u-x endgame.txt

    D. chmod 664 endgame.txt

    E. chmod o=rw endgame.txt

14. Which umask setting would cause created directories to have a permission of rwxrwxrw-?

    A. 0777

    B. 0001

    C. 0776

    D. 7770

    E. 1000

15. What special permissions bit allows standard users to run an application with root privileges?

    A. The sticky bit

    B. The SUID bit

    C. The SGID bit

    D. Execute

    E. Write

16. What special bit should you set to prevent users from deleting shared files created by some-one else?

    A. SUID

    B. SGID

    C. Sticky bit

    D. Read

    E. Write

17. You are trying to find a file on your Linux server whose name is conf. Employing the locate conf command for your search shows many directories that contain the letters conf. What is the best description for why this is happening?

    A. The locate utility searches for only for directory names.

    B. You did not employ the -d skip switch.

    C. It is most likely because the locate database is corrupted.

    D. You did not employ the appropriate regular expression.

    E. It is due to file globbing on the pattern name.

18. You want to search for a particular file, main.conf, using the find utility. This file most likely is located somewhere in the /etc/ directory tree. Which of the following commands is the best one to use in this situation?

    A. find -r /etc -name main.conf

    B. find / -name main.conf

    C. find /etc -maxdepth -name main.conf

    D. find /etc -name main.conf

    E. find main.conf /etc

19. Yesterday a co-worker, Michael, was fired for nefarious behavior. His account and home directory were immediately deleted. You need to audit the server to see if he left any files he owns out in the virtual directory system. Which of the following commands is the best one to use in this situation?

    A. find / -name Michael

    B. find / -user Michael

    C. find / -mmin 1440

    D. find ~ -user Michael

    E. find / -nouser

20. Due to an unusual emergency, Carol needs to quickly locate the stonetracker command's source code files. Which of the following is the best command to use in this case?

    A. which

    B. whereis

    C. locate

    D. find

    E. type

Chapter

5

Booting, Initializing, and Virtualizing Linux

OBJECTIVES

✓ **101.3** Change runlevels/boot targets and shutdown or reboot system

✓ **102.2** Install a boot manager

✓ **102.6** Linux as a virtualization guest

✓ **101.2** Boot the system

Like a beautiful ballet, a Linux system begins the boot process, appearing to easily perform the steps to a login screen and required services and applications. However, as a system administrator, you can't just enjoy the show. You must understand the entire underlying process to troubleshoot problems. In addition, the members of this ballet vary depending on your system's age and distribution. Each member has its own distinct configuration and operation, like dancers in a troupe.

Besides getting your system up and performing, you need to grasp the various ways to shut down your system or move it to a different state of operation, all the while keeping your users informed about what is going to happen. Methods here vary as well.

Finally, moving your Linux troupe to a new platform, such as a virtualized machine, is critical for you to comprehend. Many organizations are embracing these new stages to save money and time.

In this chapter, we'll look at all these concepts for both older and newer systems. With this knowledge, you can be the chief choreographer for your Linux system ensemble.

Understanding the Boot Process

When you turn on the power to your Linux system, it triggers a series of events that eventually leads to the login prompt. Normally, you don't worry about what happens behind the scenes of those events; you just log in and start using your applications. However, there may be times when your Linux system doesn't boot quite correctly. In this case, it helps to have a basic understanding of how Linux boots the operating system.

The Boot Process

The Linux boot process can be split into these main steps:

1. The server firmware starts, performing a quick check of the hardware, called a Power-On Self-Test (POST), and then it looks for a boot loader program to run from a bootable device.

2. The boot loader runs and determines what Linux kernel program to load.

3. The kernel program loads into memory; prepares the system, such as mounting the root partition; and then runs the initialization program.

4. The initialization process starts the necessary background programs required for the system to operate (such as a graphical desktop manager for desktops, or web and database applications for servers).

Although these steps may seem simple on the surface, there's a somewhat complicated ballet of operations that happens behind the scenes to keep the boot process working. Each step performs several actions as they prepare your system to run Linux.

Extracting Information about the Boot Process

You can monitor the Linux boot process by watching the system console screen as the system boots. You'll see lots of informative messages scroll by as the system detects hardware and loads the software.

 Some graphical desktop Linux distributions hide the boot messages on a separate console window when they start up. Often, you can hit either the ESC key or the Ctrl+Alt+F1 key combination to view those messages.

Usually the boot messages scroll by somewhat quickly and it's hard to see just what's happening. If you need to troubleshoot boot problems, you can review the boot-time messages using the *dmesg* command. Most Linux distributions copy the boot kernel messages into a special ring buffer in memory called the *kernel ring buffer*. The buffer is circular and set to a predetermined size. As new messages are logged into the buffer, older messages are rotated out.

The dmesg command displays the most recent boot messages that are currently stored in the kernel ring buffer, as shown snipped in Listing 5.1.

Listing 5.1: Using the dmesg command to display the kernel ring buffer's contents

```
$ dmesg
[    0.000000] Initializing cgroup subsys cpuset
[    0.000000] Initializing cgroup subsys cpu
[    0.000000] Initializing cgroup subsys cpuacct
[    0.000000] Linux version 3.10.0-957.10.1.el7.x86_64
(mockbuild@kbuilder.bsys.centos.org) (gcc version 4.8.5 20150623
(Red Hat 4.8.5-36) (GCC) ) #1 SMP Mon Mar 18 15:06:45 UTC 2019
[    0.000000] Command line: BOOT_IMAGE=/vmlinuz-3.10.0-957.10.1.el7.x86_64
root=/dev/mapper/centos-root ro crashkernel=auto rd.lvm.lv=centos/root
rd.lvm.lv=centos/swap rhgb quiet LANG=en_US.UTF-8
[    0.000000] e820: BIOS-provided physical RAM map:
[…]
[    0.000000] NX (Execute Disable) protection: active
[    0.000000] SMBIOS 2.5 present.
[…]
[    0.000000] Hypervisor detected: KVM
[    0.000000] e820: update [mem 0x00000000-0x00000fff] usable ==> reserved
[    0.000000] e820: remove [mem 0x000a0000-0x000fffff] usable
[    0.000000] e820: last_pfn = 0x120000 max_arch_pfn = 0x400000000
[…]
$
```

You can also view the kernel ring buffer using the journalctl utility (if available), as shown snipped in Listing 5.2. Keep in mind you'll need to use super user privileges, and the utility employs the less pager.

Listing 5.2: Using the journalctl utility to display the kernel ring buffer's contents

```
-- Logs begin at Tue 2019-04-30 11:21:34 EDT, end at Tue 2019-04-30 12:53:41 EDT
Apr 30 11:21:34 localhost.localdomain kernel: Initializing cgroup subsys cpuset
Apr 30 11:21:34 localhost.localdomain kernel: Initializing cgroup subsys cpu
Apr 30 11:21:34 localhost.localdomain kernel: Initializing cgroup subsys cpuacct
Apr 30 11:21:34 localhost.localdomain kernel: Linux version 3.10.0-957.10.1.el7.
Apr 30 11:21:34 localhost.localdomain kernel: Command line: BOOT_IMAGE=/vmlinuz-
Apr 30 11:21:34 localhost.localdomain kernel: e820: BIOS-provided physical RAM m
[…]
Apr 30 11:21:34 localhost.localdomain kernel: NX (Execute Disable) protection: a
Apr 30 11:21:34 localhost.localdomain kernel: SMBIOS 2.5 present.
[…]
Apr 30 11:21:34 localhost.localdomain kernel: Hypervisor detected: KVM
Apr 30 11:21:34 localhost.localdomain kernel: e820: update [mem 0x00000000-0x000
Apr 30 11:21:34 localhost.localdomain kernel: e820: remove [mem 0x000a0000-0x000
Apr 30 11:21:34 localhost.localdomain kernel: e820: last_pfn = 0x120000 max_arch
[…]
```

Some Linux distributions also store the boot messages in a log file, usually in the /var/log directory. For Debian-based systems, the file is usually /var/log/boot, and for Red Hat-based systems, the file is /var/log/boot.log. However, for those systems employing *systemd-journald* (covered in Chapter 7), the boot messages are stored in a journal file.

When troubleshooting boot problems, instead of slogging through the dmesg utility's output or one of the boot message log file's output, pipe their output into the grep command or the less utility (both covered in Chapter 1). That way, you can search for specific devices (such as /dev/sda), key phrases (such as disabled), and/or specific items (such as the loaded BOOT_IMAGE) easily.

While it helps to be able to see the different messages generated during boot time, it is also helpful to know just what generates those messages. These next sections discuss each of the boot steps and go through some examples showing how they work.

Looking at Firmware

All IBM-compatible workstations and servers utilize some type of built-in firmware to control just how the installed operating system starts. On older workstations and servers, this firmware was called the *Basic Input/Output System (BIOS)*. On newer workstations and servers, a new method called the *Unified Extensible Firmware Interface (UEFI)* maintains the system hardware status and launches an installed operating system.

The BIOS Startup

The BIOS firmware found in older workstations and servers was somewhat limited in what it could do. The BIOS firmware had a simple menu interface that allowed you to change some settings to control how the system found hardware and define what device the BIOS should use to start the operating system.

One limitation of the original BIOS firmware was that it could read only one sector's worth of data from a hard drive into memory in order to run. As you can probably guess, that's not enough space to load an entire operating system. To get around that limitation, most operating systems (including Linux and Microsoft Windows) split the boot process into two parts.

First, the BIOS runs a boot loader (sometimes written as bootloader) program. The *boot loader* is a small program that initializes the necessary hardware to find and run the full operating system, usually found at another location on the same hard drive but sometimes situated on a separate internal or external storage device.

The boot loader program usually has a configuration file, so you can tell it where to look to find the actual operating system file to run or even to produce a small menu allowing the user to choose between multiple operating systems.

To get things started, the BIOS must know where to find the boot loader program on an installed storage device. Most BIOS setups allow you to load the boot loader program from several locations:

- An internal hard drive
- An external hard drive
- A CD/DVD drive
- A USB flash drive
- A network server

When booting from a hard drive, you must designate which hard drive, and from which partition on the hard drive the BIOS should load the boot loader program. This is done by defining a *master boot record (MBR)*.

The MBR is the first sector on the first hard drive partition on the system. There is only one MBR for the computer system. The BIOS looks for the MBR and reads the program stored there into memory. Since the boot loader program must fit in one sector, it must be very small, so it can't do too much. The boot loader program mainly points to the location of the actual operating system kernel file, which is stored in a boot sector of a separate partition on the system. There are no size limitations on the kernel boot file.

> The boot loader program isn't required to point directly to an operating system kernel file—it can point to any type of program, including another boot loader program. You can create a primary boot loader program that points to a secondary boot loader program, which provides options to load multiple operating systems. This process is called *chainloading*.

The UEFI Startup

Although there were plenty of limitations with BIOS, computer manufacturers learned to live with them, and BIOS became the default standard for IBM-compatible systems for many years. However, as operating systems became more complicated, it eventually became clear that a new boot method needed to be developed.

Intel created the Extensible Firmware Interface (EFI) in 1998 to address some of the limitations of BIOS. The adoption of EFI was somewhat of a slow process, but by 2005, the idea caught on with other vendors, and the Universal EFI (UEFI) specification was adopted as a standard. These days, just about all IBM-compatible desktop and server systems utilize the UEFI firmware standard.

Instead of relying on a single boot sector on a hard drive to hold the boot loader program, UEFI specifies a special disk partition called the *EFI System Partition (ESP)* to store boot loader programs. This allows for any size of boot loader program, plus the ability to store multiple boot loader programs for multiple operating systems.

The ESP setup utilizes the old Microsoft File Allocation Table (FAT) filesystem to store the boot loader programs. On Linux systems, the ESP is typically mounted in the /boot/efi/ directory, and the boot loader files are commonly stored using the .efi filename extension.

The UEFI firmware utilizes a built-in mini boot loader (sometimes referred to as a *boot manager*), which allows you to configure the specific boot loader program file to launch.

> Not all Linux distributions support the UEFI firmware. If you're using a UEFI system, make sure that the Linux distribution you select supports it.

With UEFI, you need to register each individual boot loader file that you want to appear at boot time in the boot manager interface menu. You can then select the boot loader to run each time you boot the system.

Once the firmware finds and runs the boot loader, its job is done. The boot loader step in the boot process can be somewhat complicated. The next section dives into covering this step.

> If you're not sure whether your system is using UEFI, you can easily check. After the Linux system boots, issue the command `ls /sys/firmware/efi`. If you receive a `no such file or directory` message, then you're employing BIOS. On the other hand, if you see files, then your system booted using UEFI.

Looking at Boot Loaders

The boot loader program helps bridge the gap between the system firmware and the full Linux operating system kernel. In Linux, there are several choices of boot loaders to use, which are covered in this section.

Boot Loader Principles

The first version of the GRand Unified Bootloader (GRUB) boot loader (now called *GRUB Legacy*) was created in 1999 to provide a robust and configurable boot loader. GRUB quickly became the default boot loader for all Linux distributions, whether they were run on BIOS or UEFI systems.

GRUB2 was created in 2005 as a total rewrite of the GRUB Legacy system. It supports advanced features, such as the ability to load hardware driver modules and using logic statements to alter the boot menu options dynamically, depending on conditions detected on the system (such as if an external hard drive is connected).

Using GRUB Legacy as the Boot Loader

The GRUB Legacy boot loader was designed to simplify the process of creating boot menus and passing options to kernels. GRUB Legacy allows you to select multiple kernels and/or operating systems using both a menu interface as well as an interactive shell. With the menu interface, you configure options for each kernel or operating system you wish to boot up. With the interactive shell, you can customize boot commands on the fly.

Both the menu and the interactive shell utilize a set of commands that control features of the boot loader. This section walks you through how to configure the GRUB Legacy boot loader, how to install it, and how to interact with it at boot time.

Configuring GRUB Legacy

When you use the GRUB Legacy interactive menu, you need to tell it what options to show. You do that using special GRUB *menu commands*.

The GRUB Legacy system stores the menu commands in a standard text configuration file called *menu.lst*; it is stored in the /boot/grub/ directory. (Though not a requirement, some Linux distributions create a separate /boot partition on the hard drive.) Red Hat–derived Linux distributions (such as CentOS and Fedora) use *grub.conf* instead of menu.lst for the configuration file. Also, you may find that the menu.lst file is symbolically linked to the grub.conf file.

The GRUB Legacy configuration file consists of two sections:

- Global definitions
- Operating system boot definitions

The global definitions section defines commands that control the overall operation of the GRUB Legacy boot menu. The global definitions must appear first in the configuration file. There are only a handful of global settings that you can make. Table 5.1 shows these settings.

TABLE 5.1 GRUB Legacy global commands

Setting	Description
color	Specifies the foreground and background colors to use in the boot menu
default	Defines the default menu option to select
fallback	A secondary menu selection to use if the default menu option fails
hiddenmenu	Don't display the menu selection options
splashimage	Points to an image file to use as the background for the boot menu
timeout	Specifies the amount of time to wait for a menu selection before using the default

For GRUB Legacy, to define a value for a command, you just list the value as a command-line parameter:

```
default 0
timeout 10
color white/blue yellow/blue
```

The color command defines the color scheme for the menu. The first pair of colors defines the foreground/background for normal menu entries, and the second pair defines the foreground/background for the selected menu entry.

After the global definitions, you place definitions for the individual operating systems that are installed on the system. Each operating system should have its own definition section. There are a lot of boot definition settings that you can use to customize how the boot loader finds the operating system kernel file. Fortunately, only a few commands are required to define the operating system. The ones to remember are as follows:

- Title: The first line for each boot definition section, this is what appears in the boot menu.
- Root: Defines the disk and partition where the GRUB /boot folder partition is located on the system.

- **Kernel**: Defines the kernel image file stored in the /boot folder to load.
- **Initrd**: Defines the initial RAM disk file or filesystem, which contains drivers necessary for the kernel to interact with the system hardware.
- **Rootnoverify**: Defines non-Linux boot partitions, such as Windows.

The root command defines the hard drive and partition that contains the /boot folder for GRUB Legacy. Unfortunately, GRUB Legacy uses a somewhat odd way of referencing those values:

(hd*drive, partition*)

Also unfortunately, GRUB Legacy doesn't refer to hard drives the way Linux does; it uses a numbering system to reference both disks and partitions, starting at 0 instead of at 1. For example, to reference the first partition on the first hard drive of the system, you'd use (hd0,0). To reference the second partition on the first hard drive, you'd use (hd0,1).

The initrd command is another important feature in GRUB Legacy. It helps to solve a problem that arises when using specialized hardware or filesystems as the root drive. The initrd command defines a file that's mounted by the kernel at boot time as a RAM disk or filesystem. The kernel can then load modules from the RAM disk or filesystem, which then allows it to access hardware or filesystems not compiled into the kernel itself.

 Before Linux kernel v2.6, the initial RAM disk was used to hold kernel modules needed at boot time. Since that time, it has been replaced with the initial RAM filesystem (*initramfs*). It can be a little confusing, because the initrd command within the GRUB configuration file denotes either an initial RAM disk or an initial RAM filesystem. Which one used depends on your distribution and its age.

Listing 5.3 shows a sample GRUB configuration file that defines both a Windows and a Linux partition for booting.

Listing 5.3: Sample GRUB Legacy configuration file

```
default 0
timeout 10
color white/blue yellow/blue

title CentOS Linux
root (hd1,0)
kernel (hd1,0)/boot/vmlinuz
initrd /boot/initrd

title Windows
rootnoverify (hd0,0)
```

This example shows two boot options: one for a CentOS Linux system and one for a Windows system. The CentOS system is installed on the first partition of the second hard drive, and the Windows system is installed on the first partition of the first hard drive. The Linux boot selection specifies both the kernel file to load as well as the initrd image file to load into memory.

Installing GRUB Legacy

After you build the GRUB Legacy configuration file, you must install the GRUB Legacy program in the MBR. The command to do this is *grub-install*.

The grub-install command uses a single parameter that indicates the partition on which to install GRUB. You can specify the partition using either the Linux or the GRUB Legacy format. For example, to use the Linux format, you'd type

```
# grub-install /dev/sda
```

To install GRUB on the MBR of the first hard drive and use the GRUB Legacy format, you must enclose the hard drive format in quotes:

```
# grub-install '(hd0)'
```

If you're using the chainloading method and prefer to install a copy of GRUB Legacy on the boot sector of a partition instead of to the MBR of a hard drive, you must specify the partition, again using either the Linux or the GRUB format:

```
# grub-install /dev/sda1
# grub-install 'hd(0,0)'
```

 After making changes to the GRUB Legacy configuration file, you don't need to reinstall GRUB Legacy in the MBR. GRUB Legacy reads the configuration file each time it runs.

Interacting with GRUB Legacy

When you boot a system that uses the GRUB Legacy boot loader, you'll see a menu that shows the boot options that you defined in the configuration file. If you wait for the timeout to expire, the default boot option will process. Alternatively, you can use the arrow keys to select one of the boot options and then press the Enter key to select it.

You can also edit boot options on the fly from the GRUB menu:

1. Use the arrow key to move to the boot option you want to modify, and then press the E key.

2. Use the arrow key to move the cursor to the line that you need to modify, and then press the E key to edit it.

3. Press the B key to boot the system using the new values.

You can also press the C key at any time to enter an interactive shell mode (also called *GRUB command line*), allowing you to submit GRUB commands on the fly. You can leave the GRUB command line, and return to the menu, by pressing the ESC key.

Using GRUB 2 as the Boot Loader

Since the GRUB2 system was intended as an improvement over GRUB Legacy, many of the features are the same, with just a few twists. For example, the GRUB2 system changes the configuration file name to *grub.cfg*. Where the file is stored depends on your system's firmware:

- BIOS: The grub.cfg file is stored in the /boot/grub/ or /boot/grub2/ directory. (This allows you to have both GRUB Legacy and GRUB2 installed at the same time.)

- UEFI: The grub.cfg file is stored in the /boot/efi/EFI/*distro-name*/ directory.

An example of a grub.cfg file location on a UEFI system, which is a CentOS distribution, is shown in Listing 5.4.

Listing 5.4: GRUB2 configuration file location on a UEFI CentOS distro

```
# ls /boot/efi/EFI/centos/
BOOT.CSV      fonts      grubenv       mmx64.efi     shimx64-centos.efi
BOOTX64.CSV   grub.cfg   grubx64.efi   shim.efi      shimx64.efi
#
```

Configuring GRUB2

There are also a few changes to the commands used in GRUB2. A simplified snipped example of a GRUB2 configuration file is shown in Listing 5.5.

Listing 5.5: Simplified sample GRUB2 configuration file

```
[…]
menuentry "CentOS Linux" {
[…]
    set root=(hd1,1)
    linux16 /vmlinuz[…]
    initrd /initramfs[…]
}
menuentry "Windows" {
    set root=(hd0,1)
[…]
```

Notice that GRUB2 uses the set command to assign values to the root keyword, and it uses an equal sign to assign the device. GRUB2 utilizes environment variables to configure settings instead of commands.

To make things more confusing, GRUB2 changes the numbering system for partitions. Although it still uses 0 for the first hard drive, the first partition is set to 1. So to define the /boot directory on the first partition of the first hard drive, you now need to use

```
set root=(hd0,1)
```

Sometimes the format is slightly different, where msdos indicates a DOS partition's number or gpt indicates a GPT (covered in Chapter 3) partition's number:

```
set root ='hd0,msdos1'
```

For GRUB2, the commands to remember are as follows:

- Menuentry: The first line for each boot definition section; this is what appears in the boot menu.

- set root: Defines the disk and partition where the GRUB2 /boot directory partition is located on the system.

- linux, linux16: For BIOS systems, defines the kernel image file stored in the /boot directory to load.

- Linuxefi: For UEFI systems, defines the kernel image file stored in the /boot directory to load.

- Initrd: For BIOS systems, defines the initial RAM filesystem, which contains drivers necessary for the kernel to interact with the system hardware.

- Initrdefi: For UEFI systems, defines the initial RAM filesystem, which contains drivers necessary for the kernel to interact with the system hardware.

Notice in Listing 5.5 that you must enclose each individual boot section with braces immediately following the menuentry command. In addition, the rootnoverify command is not used in GRUB2. Non-Linux boot options are now defined the same as Linux boot options using the root environment variable.

 If you need some detailed GRUB guidance, the GNU organization has a nice manual at www.gnu.org/software/grub/manual/grub/grub.html. Be sure to peruse your distribution's GRUB documentation as well.

The configuration process for GRUB2 is also somewhat different. Although GRUB2 uses the /boot/grub/grub.cfg file as the configuration file, you should never modify that file. Instead, there are separate configuration files stored in the /etc/grub.d folder. This allows you (or the system) to create individual configuration files for each boot option installed on your system (for example, one configuration file for booting Linux and another for booting Windows).

For global commands, the /etc/default/grub configuration file is used. Typically, you should not modify this file either, but again use the configuration files in the /etc/grub.d/ directory. The format for some of the global commands has changed from the GRUB Legacy commands, such as GRUB_TIMEOUT instead of just timeout.

Most Linux distributions generate a new grub.cfg configuration file automatically after certain events, such as when upgrading the kernel. Usually, the distribution will keep a boot menu option pointing to the old kernel file, which is handy just in case the new one fails.

Installing GRUB2

Unlike with GRUB Legacy, you don't need to install GRUB2. All you need to do is to rebuild the main installation file. This is done by running either the *grub-mkconfig* or *grub2-mkconfig* program. They are essentially equivalent programs but may not both be installed on your system.

The grub2-mkconfig program reads configuration files stored in the /etc/grub.d folder and assembles the commands into the single grub.cfg configuration file.

You can update the configuration file manually by using super user privileges and running the grub2-mkconfig command:

```
# grub2-mkconfig > /boot/grub2/grub.cfg
```

Notice that you must either redirect the output of the grub2-mkconfig program to the grub.cfg configuration file or use the -o (or --output=) option to specify the output file. By default, the grub2-mkconfig program just outputs the new configuration file commands to standard output.

To further add to your GRUB installation choices, Ubuntu has the update-grub utility. This program issues the command grub-mkconfig -o /boot/grub/grub.cfg for you. It's always nice to save a few keystrokes.

Interacting with GRUB2

The GRUB2 boot loader produces a boot menu similar to the GRUB Legacy method. Figure 5.1 shows an Ubuntu GRUB2 menu interface. You can use arrow keys to switch between the various boot menu entries.

FIGURE 5.1   An Ubuntu GRUB2 menu

```
                         GNU GRUB  version 2.02

 ┌──────────────────────────────────────────────────────────────┐
 │ kubuntu                                                        │
 │ Advanced options for Ubuntu                                    │
 │ Memory test (memtest86+)                                       │
 │ Memory test (memtest86+, serial console 115200)                │
 │                                                                │
 │                                                                │
 │                                                                │
 │                                                                │
 │                                                                │
 │                                                                │
 │                                                                │
 │                                                                │
 └──────────────────────────────────────────────────────────────┘

      Use the ↑ and ↓ keys to select which entry is highlighted.
      Press enter to boot the selected OS, `e' to edit the commands
      before booting or `c' for a command-line.
```

> Some graphical desktops (such as Ubuntu) hide the GRUB boot menu behind a graphical interface. Usually, if you hold down the Shift key when the system first boots, this will display the GRUB boot menu.

If you want to edit a particular boot menu entry, when your cursor is on the appropriate boot option line, press the E key to edit the entry. Figure 5.2 illustrates the editing of an entry in the GRUB2 boot menu on an Ubuntu system.

FIGURE 5.2   Editing an Ubuntu GRUB2 menu entry

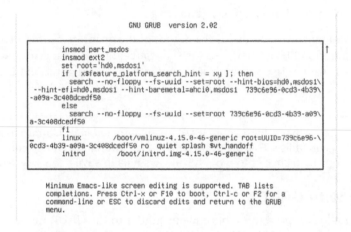

For understanding (and certification exam studying purposes) we've provided you two tables. One is for operating in the GRUB2 menu interface (Table 5.2), and the other displays the various basic GRUB2 entry editor keystrokes (Table 5.3).

TABLE 5.2   GRUB2 menu interface keystrokes

Key(s)	Description
Arrow	Select boot menu option
C	Starts the GRUB command-line interface
E	Enters editing mode for currently selected menu option
Enter	Boots currently selected menu option
P	Used to enter password, if required

The GRUB2 entry editor supports basic emacs editing keystrokes (covered in Chapter 1), which is handy. However, you should be familiar with a few additional items, listed in Table 5.3.

TABLE 5.3   GRUB2 entry editor keystrokes

Key(s)	Description
Arrow	Highlight the entry line to modify
Enter	Adds a new line (best to use at a line's end)
ESC	Discards any changes and return to menu interface
Ctrl+C	Starts the GRUB command-line interface
Ctrl+X	Boot system with edited entry

Adding Kernel Boot Parameters

Besides editing a GRUB configuration on the fly from its boot menu, you can provide options to the Linux kernel. This approach is especially useful in troubleshooting booting problems.

To accomplish this using the techniques outlined in the previous sections, edit the appropriate boot menu entry, find the line starting with kernel (GRUB Legacy) or linux* (GRUB2), go to the end of the line, add a space, and then tack on the kernel option(s). After you've completed that, boot the system using the appropriate keystroke.

A few of the more useful kernel parameters are listed in Table 5.4.

TABLE 5.4   Kernel parameters

Parameter	Description
console=	Set the console device
debug	Enable kernel debugging
init=	Execute the specified program, such as a Bash shell (/bin/bash) instead of /sbin/init
initrd=	Change the location of the initial RAM filesystem
mem	Set the total amount of available system memory
ro	Mount root filesystem as read-only
root=	Change the root filesystem

TABLE 5.4   Kernel parameters *(continued)*

Parameter	Description
rootflags=	Set root filesystem's mount options
rw	Mount root filesystem as read-write
selinux	Disable SELinux at boot time
single, Single, 1, or S	Boot a SysVinit system to single-user mode
systemd.unit=	Boot a systemd system to specified target

If you'd like to look at a complete list of kernel parameters, one is available at www.kernel.org/doc/Documentation/admin-guide/kernel-parameters.txt.

Using Alternative Boot Loaders

Although GRUB Legacy and GRUB2 are the most popular Linux boot loader programs, you may run into a few others, depending on which Linux distributions you are using.

> A legacy boot loader that predates GRUB Legacy is LILO. It's inability to handle UEFI systems as well as other difficulties brought its development to an end in December 2015.

The systemd-boot loader program is starting to gain popularity in Linux distributions that use the systemd initialization method (covered later in this chapter). This boot loader generates a menu of boot image options and can load any UEFI boot image.

The U-Boot boot loader (also called *Das U-Boot*) can boot from any type of disk. It can load any type of boot image.

The SYSLINUX project includes five separate boot loader programs that have special uses in Linux:

- SYSLINUX: A boot loader for systems that use the Microsoft FAT filesystem (popular for booting from USB flash drives)

- EXTLINUX: A mini-boot loader for booting from an ext2, ext3, ext4, or btrfs filesystem

- ISOLINUX: A boot loader for booting from a LiveCD or LiveDVD

- PXELINUX: A boot loader for booting from a network server

- MEMDISK: A utility for booting older DOS operating systems from the other SYSLINUX project boot loaders

Since UEFI can load any size of boot loader program, it's now possible to load a Linux operating system kernel directly without a special boot loader program. This feature was incorporated in the Linux kernel starting with version 3.3.0. However, this method isn't common, as boot loader programs can provide more versatility in booting, especially when working with multiple operating systems.

The Initialization Process

After your Linux system has traversed the boot process, it enters final system initialization, where it needs to start various services. A service, or daemon, is a program that performs a particular duty.

The initialization daemon (*init*) determines which services are started and in what order. This daemon also allows you to stop and manage the various system services. There are two initialization daemons with which you should be familiar:

SysVinit The SysVinit (SysV) was based on the Unix System V initialization daemon. Though it is not used by many major Linux distributions anymore, you still may find it lurking around that older Linux server at your company.

systemd The systemd initialization method is the new kid on the block. Started around 2010, it is now the most popular system service initialization and management mechanism. This daemon reduces initialization time by starting services in a parallel manner.

Before we start examining these system initialization daemons, it's a good idea to take a look at the `init` program itself. Classically, service startups are handled by the `init` program. This program can be located in the /etc/, the /bin/, or the /sbin/ directory. Also, it typically has a process ID (PID) of 1.

This information will assist you in determining which system initialization method your current Linux distribution is using—systemd or SysVinit. First find the `init` program's location using the `which` command. An example is shown in Listing 5.6.

Listing 5.6: Finding the `init` program file location

```
# which init
/sbin/init
#
```

Now that you know the `init` program's location, using super user privileges you can utilize the `readlink -f` command to see if the program is linked to another program, as shown in Listing 5.7.

Listing 5.7: Checking the `init` program for links

```
# readlink -f /sbin/init
/usr/lib/systemd/systemd
#
```

You can see in Listing 5.7 that this system is actually using systemd. You can verify this by taking a look at PID 1, as shown in Listing 5.8.

Listing 5.8: Checking PID 1

```
# ps -p 1
  PID TTY          TIME CMD
    1 ?        00:00:06 systemd
#
```

In Listing 5.8, the ps utility is used. This utility allows you to view processes. A process is a running program. The ps command shows you what program is running for a particular process in the CMD column. In this case, the systemd program is running. Thus, this Linux system is using systemd.

The init program or systemd is the parent process for every service on a Linux system. If your system has the pstree program installed, you can see a diagram depicting this relationship by typing **pstree -p 1** at the command line.

Keep in mind that these discovery methods are not foolproof. Also, there are other system initialization methods, such as the now-defunct *Upstart* that used the initctl utility as its daemon interface. The following brief list shows a few Linux distribution versions that used Upstart:

- Fedora v9–v14
- openSUSE v11.3–v12.2
- RHEL v6
- Ubuntu v6.10–v15.04

If you are using the distribution versions recommended in Chapter 1, know that those distributions are all systemd systems.

Using the systemd Initialization Process

The *systemd* approach introduced a major paradigm shift in how Linux systems manage services. Services can now be started when the system boots, when a particular hardware component is attached to the system, when certain other services are started, and so on. Some services can be started based upon a timer.

Exploring Unit Files

The easiest way to start exploring systemd is through the *systemd units*. A unit defines a service, a group of services, or an action. Each unit consists of a name, a type, and a configuration file. There are currently 12 different systemd unit types:

- automount
- device
- mount
- path
- scope
- service
- slice
- snapshot
- socket
- swap
- target
- timer

The *systemctl* utility is the main gateway to managing systemd and system services. Its basic syntax is as follows:

```
systemctl [OPTIONS...] COMMAND [NAME...]
```

You can use the systemctl utility to provide a list of the various units currently loaded in your Linux system. A snipped example is shown in Listing 5.9.

Listing 5.9: Looking at systemd units

```
$ systemctl list-units
UNIT                      LOAD    ACTIVE SUB      DESCRIPTION
[…]
smartd.service            loaded active running  Self Monitor[…]
sshd.service              loaded active running  OpenSSH serv[…]
sysstat.service           loaded active exited   Resets Syste[…]
[…]
graphical.target          loaded active active   Graphical I[…]
[…]
$
```

In Listing 5.9 you can see various units as well as additional information. Units are identified by their name and type using the format *name.type*. System services (daemons) have unit files with the .service extension. Thus, the Secure Shell (SSH) daemon, sshd, has a unit filename of sshd.service.

Many displays from the systemctl utility use the less pager by default. Thus, to exit the display, you must press the Q key. If you want to turn off the less pager for the systemctl utility, tack on the --no-pager option to the command.

Groups of services are started via *target unit* files. At system startup, the default.target unit ensures that all required and desired services are launched at system initialization. The systemctl get-default command displays the target file, as shown in Listing 5.10 on a CentOS distribution.

Listing 5.10: Looking at the default.target link

```
$ systemctl get-default
graphical.target
$
```

Table 5.5 shows the commonly used system boot target unit files.

TABLE 5.5   Commonly used system boot target unit files

Name	Description
graphical.target	Provides multiple users access to the system via local terminals and/or through the network. Graphical user interface (GUI) access is offered.
multi-user.target	Provides multiple users access to the system via local terminals and/or through the network. No GUI access is offered.
runlevel*n*.target	Provides backward compatibility to SysVinit systems, where n is set to 1–5 for the desired SysV runlevel equivalence.

In Table 5.5, you'll notice that systemd provides backward compatibility to the classic SysVinit systems. The SysV runlevels will be covered later in this chapter.

The master systemd configuration file is /etc/systemd/system.conf. In this file you will find all the default configuration settings commented out via a hash mark (#). Viewing this file is a quick way to see the current systemd configuration. If you need to modify the configuration, just edit the file. However, it would be wise to peruse the file's man page first by typing **man systemd-system.conf** at the command line.

Focusing on Service Unit Files

Service unit files contain information such as which environment file to use, when a service must be started, what targets want this service started, and so on. These configuration files are located in different directories.

Keep in mind that the directory location for a unit configuration file is critical, because if a file is found in two different directory locations, one will have precedence over the other. The following list shows the directory locations in ascending priority order:

1. */etc/systemd/system/*

2. */run/systemd/system/*

3. */usr/lib/systemd/system/*

To see the various service unit files available, you can again employ the `systemctl` utility. However, a slightly different command is needed than when viewing units, as shown in Listing 5.11.

Listing 5.11: Looking at systemd unit files

```
$ systemctl list-unit-files
UNIT FILE                               STATE
[…]
dev-hugepages.mount                     static
dev-mqueue.mount                        static
proc-fs-nfsd.mount                      static
[…]
nfs.service                             disabled
nfslock.service                         static
ntpd.service                            disabled
ntpdate.service                         disabled
[…]
ctrl-alt-del.target                     disabled
default.target                          static
emergency.target                        static
[…]
$
```

In addition to the unit file's base name, you can see a unit file's state in Listing 5.11. Their states are called *enablement states,* and they refer to when the service is started. There are at least 12 different enablement states, but you'll commonly see these 3:

- `enabled`: Service starts at system boot.

- `disabled`: Service does not start at system boot.

- `static`: Service starts if another unit depends on it. Can also be manually started.

To see what directory or directories store a particular systemd unit file(s), use the `systemctl` utility. An example on a CentOS distribution is shown in Listing 5.12.

Listing 5.12: Finding and displaying a systemd unit file

```
$ systemctl cat ntpd.service
# /usr/lib/systemd/system/ntpd.service
[Unit]
Description=Network Time Service
After=syslog.target ntpdate.service sntp.service

[Service]
Type=forking
EnvironmentFile=-/etc/sysconfig/ntpd
ExecStart=/usr/sbin/ntpd -u ntp:ntp $OPTIONS
PrivateTmp=true

[Install]
WantedBy=multi-user.target
$
```

Notice in Listing 5.12 that the first displayed line shows the ntpd.service base name and directory location of the unit file. The next several lines are the file's contents.

For service unit files, there are three primary configuration sections:

- [Unit]
- [Service]
- [Install]

Within the [Unit] section of the service unit configuration file, there are basic *directives*. A directive is a setting that modifies a configuration, such as the After setting shown in Listing 5.12. The more commonly used [Unit] section directives are described in Table 5.6.

TABLE 5.6 Commonly used service unit file [Unit] section directives

Directive	Description
After	Sets this unit to start after the designated units.
Before	Sets this unit to start before the designated units.
Description	Describes the unit.
Documentation	Sets a list of uniform resource identifiers (URIs) that point to documentation sources. The URIs can be web locations, system files, info pages, and man pages.
Conflicts	Sets this unit to *not* start with the designated units. If any of the designated units start, this unit is not started. (Opposite of Requires.)

Directive	Description
Requires	Sets this unit to start together with the designated units. If any of the designated units do not start, this unit is *not* started. (Opposite of Conflicts.)
Wants	Sets this unit to start together with the designated units. If any of the designated units do not start, this unit is *still* started.

There is a great deal of useful information in the man pages for systemd and unit configuration files. Just type **man -k systemd** to find several items you can explore. For example, explore the service type unit file directives and more via the man systemd.service command. You can find information on all the various directives by typing **man systemd .directives** at the command line.

The [Service] directives within a unit file set configuration items that are specific to that service. The commonly used [Service] section directives are described in Table 5.7.

TABLE 5.7   Commonly used service unit file [Service] section directives

Directive	Description
ExecReload	Indicates scripts or commands (and options) to run when unit is reloaded.
ExecStart	Indicates scripts or commands (and options) to run when unit is started.
ExecStop	Indicates scripts or commands (and options) to run when unit is stopped.
Environment	Sets environment variable substitutes, separated by a space.
EnvironmentFile	Indicates a file that contains environment variable substitutes.
RemainAfterExit	Set to either no (default) or yes. If set to yes, the service is left active even when the process started by ExecStart terminates. If set to no, then ExecStop is called when the process started by ExecStart terminates.
Restart	Service is restarted when the process started by ExecStart terminates. Ignored if a systemctl restart or systemctl stop command is issued. Set to no (default), on-success, on-failure, on-abnormal, on-watchdog, on-abort, or always.
Type	Sets the startup type.

You will only find a unit file [Service] section in a service unit file. This middle section is different for each unit type. For example, in auto-mount unit files, you would find an [Automount] section as the middle unit file section.

The [Install] directives within a unit file determine what happens to a service if it is enabled or disabled. An *enabled service* starts at system boot. A *disabled service* does *not* start at system boot. The commonly used [Install] section directives are described in Table 5.8.

TABLE 5.8   Commonly used service unit file [Install] section directives

Directive	Description
Alias	Sets additional names that can denote the service in systemctl commands.
Also	Sets additional units that must be enabled or disabled for this service. Often the additional units are socket type units.
RequiredBy	Designates other units that require this service.
WantedBy	Designates which target unit manages this service.

Focusing on Target Unit Files

For systemd, you need to understand the service unit files as well as the target unit files. The primary purpose of target unit files is to group together various services to start at system boot time. The default target unit file, default.target, is symbolically linked to the target unit file used at system boot. In Listing 5.13, the default target unit file is located and displayed using the systemctl command.

Listing 5.13: Finding and displaying the systemd target unit file

```
$ systemctl get-default
graphical.target
$
$ systemctl cat graphical.target
# /usr/lib/systemd/system/graphical.target
[…]
[Unit]
Description=Graphical Interface
Documentation=man:systemd.special(7)
Requires=multi-user.target
Wants=display-manager.service
```

```
Conflicts=rescue.service rescue.target
After=multi-user.target rescue.service rescue.target display-manager.service
AllowIsolate=yes
$
```

Notice in Listing 5.13 that the graphical.target unit file has many of the same directives as a service unit file. These directives were described back in Table 5.6. Of course, these directives apply to a target type unit file instead of a service type unit file. For example, the After directive in the graphical.target unit file sets this target unit to start after the designated units, such as multi-user.target. Target units, similar to service units, have various target dependency chains as well as conflicts.

In Listing 5.13, there is one directive we have not covered yet. The AllowIsolate directive, if set to yes, permits this target file to be used with the systemctl isolate command. This command is covered later in this chapter.

 Real World Scenario

Modifying systemd Configuration Files

Occasionally you may need to change a unit configuration file for your Linux system's requirements or add additional components. However, be careful when doing this task. You should not modify any unit files in the /lib/systemd/system/ or /usr/lib/systemd/system/ directory.

To modify a unit configuration file, copy the file to the /etc/systemd/system/ directory and modify it there. This modified file will take precedence over the original unit file left in the original directory. Also, it will protect the modified unit file from software updates.

If you just have a few additional components, you can extend the configuration. Using super user privileges, create a new subdirectory in the /etc/systemd/system/ directory named **service.service-name.d**, where **service-name** is the service's name. For example, for the openSSH daemon, you would create the /etc/systemd/system/ service.sshd.d directory. This newly created directory is called a drop-in file directory, because you can drop in additional configuration files. Create any configuration files with names like **description.conf**, where **description** describes the configuration file's purpose, such as local or script. Add your modified directives to this configuration file.

After you make these modifications, you must complete a few more steps. Find and compare any unit file that overrides another unit file by issuing the systemd-delta command. It will display any unit files that are duplicated, extended, redirected, and so on. Review this list. It will help you avoid any unintended consequences from modifying or extending a service unit file.

To have your changes take effect, issue the systemctl daemon-reload command for the service whose unit file you modified or extended. After you accomplish that task, issue the systemctl restart command to start or restart the service. These commands are explained in the next section.

Looking at *systemctl*

While there are various commands to manage systemd and system services, it is easier and faster to employ the systemctl utility.

Several basic systemctl commands are available for you to manage system services. One that is often used is the status command. It provides a wealth of information. A couple of snipped examples on a CentOS distro are shown in Listing 5.14.

Listing 5.14: Viewing a service unit's status via systemctl

```
$ systemctl status ntpd
● ntpd.service - Network Time Service
   Loaded: loaded (/usr/lib/systemd/system/ntpd.service;
 disabled; vendor preset: disabled)
   Active: inactive (dead)
$ systemctl status sshd
● sshd.service - OpenSSH server daemon
   Loaded: loaded (/usr/lib/systemd/system/sshd.service;
 enabled; vendor preset: enabled)
   Active: active (running) since Sat 2019-09-07 15:5[…]
     Docs: man:sshd(8)
           man:sshd_config(5)
 Main PID: 1130 (sshd)
    Tasks: 1
   CGroup: /system.slice/sshd.service
           └─1130 /usr/sbin/sshd -D
$
```

In Listing 5.14, the first systemctl command shows the status of the ntpd service. Notice the third line in the utility's output. It states that the service is disabled. The fourth line states that the service is inactive. In essence, this means that the ntpd service is not running (inactive) and is not configured to start at system boot time (disabled). Another item to look at within the ntpd service's status is the Loaded line. Notice that the unit file's complete filename and directory location is shown.

The status of the sshd service is also displayed, showing that sshd is running (active) and configured to start at system boot time (enabled).

There are several simple commands you can use with the systemctl utility to manage systemd services and view information regarding them. The more common commands are listed in Table 5.9. These systemctl commands generally use the following syntax:

```
systemctl COMMAND UNIT-NAME…
```

TABLE 5.9   Commonly used `systemctl` service management commands

Command	Description
daemon-reload	Load the unit configuration file of the running designated unit(s) to make unit file configuration changes without stopping the service. Note that this is different from the reload command.
disable	Mark the designated unit(s) to *not* be started automatically at system boot time.
enable	Mark the designated unit(s) to be started automatically at system boot time.
mask	Prevent the designated unit(s) from starting. The service cannot be started using the start command or at system boot. Use the --now option to immediately stop any running instances as well. Use the --running option to mask the service only until the next reboot or unmask is used.
restart	Stop and immediately restart the designated unit(s). If a designated unit is not already started, this will simply start it.
start	Start the designated unit(s).
status	Display the designated unit's current status.
stop	Stop the designated unit(s).
reload	Load the service configuration file of the running designated unit(s) to make service configuration changes without stopping the service. Note that this is different from the daemon-reload command.
unmask	Undo the effects of the mask command on the designated unit(s).

Notice the difference in Table 5.9 between the daemon-reload and the reload command. This is an important difference. Use the daemon-reload command if you need to load systemd unit file configuration changes for a running service. Use the reload command to load a service's modified configuration file. For example, if you modified the ntpd service's configuration file, /etc/ntp.conf, and wanted the new configuration to take immediate effect, you would issue the command **systemctl reload ntpd** at the command line.

Besides the commands in Table 5.9, there are some other handy systemctl commands you can use for managing system services. An example on a CentOS distro is shown in Listing 5.15.

Listing 5.15: Determining if a service is running via `systemctl`

```
# systemctl stop sshd
#
# systemctl is-active sshd
inactive
#
# systemctl start sshd
#
# systemctl is-active sshd
active
#
```

In Listing 5.15, the openSSH daemon (sshd) is stopped using `systemctl` and its `stop` command. Instead of the `status` command, the `is-active` command is used to quickly display that the service is stopped (`inactive`). The openSSH service is started back up and again the `is-active` command is employed showing that the service is now running, (`active`). Table 5.10 shows these useful service status–checking commands.

TABLE 5.10 Convenient `systemctl` service status commands

Command	Description
is-active	Displays active for running services and failed for any service that has reached a failed state.
is-enabled	Displays enabled for any service that is configured to start at system boot and disabled for any service that is *not* configured to start at system boot.
is-failed	Displays failed for any service that has reached a failed state and active for running services.

Services can fail for many reasons: for hardware issues, a missing dependency set in the unit configuration file, an incorrect permission setting, and so on. You can employ the `systemctl` utility's `is-failed` command to see whether a particular service has failed. An example is shown in Listing 5.16.

Listing 5.16: Determining if a service has failed via `systemctl`

```
$ systemctl is-failed NetworkManager-wait-online.service
failed
$
$ systemctl is-active NetworkManager-wait-online.service
failed
$
```

In Listing 5.16, you can see that this particular service has failed. Actually, it was a failure forced by disconnecting the network cable prior to boot, so you could see a service's failed status. If the service was not in failed state, the is-failed command would show an active status.

Examining Special systemd Commands

The systemctl utility has several commands that go beyond service management. You can manage what targets (groups of services) are started at system boot time, jump between various system states, and even analyze your system's boot time performance. We'll look at these various commands in this section.

One special command to explore is the systemctl is-system-running command. An example of this command is shown in Listing 5.17.

Listing 5.17: Determining a system's operational status

```
$ systemctl is-system-running
running
$
```

You may think the status returned above is obvious, but it means all is well with your Linux system currently. Table 5.11 shows other useful statuses.

TABLE 5.11   Operational statuses provided by systemctl is-system-running

Status	Description
running	System is fully in working order.
degraded	System has one or more failed units.
maintenance	System is in emergency or recovery mode.
initializing	System is starting to boot.
starting	System is still booting.
stopping	System is starting to shut down.

The maintenance operational status will be covered shortly in this chapter. If you receive degraded status, however, you should review your units to see which ones have failed and take appropriate action. Use the systemctl --failed command to find the failed unit(s) as shown snipped in Listing 5.18.

Listing 5.18: Finding failed units

```
$ systemctl is-system-running
degraded
$
$ systemctl --failed
  UNIT          LOAD    ACTIVE SUB     DESCRIPTION
● rngd.service loaded failed failed Hardware RNG Entropy Gatherer Daemon
[…]
$
```

Other useful systemctl utility commands deal with obtaining, setting, and jumping between the system's target. They are as follows:

- get-default
- set-default
- isolate

You've already seen the systemctl get-default command in action within Listing 5.13. This command displays the system's default target. As you may have guessed, you can set the system's default target with super user privileges via the systemctl set-target command.

The isolate command is handy for jumping between system targets. When this command is used along with a target name for an argument, all services and processes not enabled in the listed target are stopped. Any services and processes enabled and not running in the listed target are started. A snipped example is shown in Listing 5.19.

Listing 5.19: Jumping to a different target unit

```
# systemctl get-default
graphical.target
#
# systemctl isolate multi-user.target
#
# systemctl status graphical.target
[…]
   Active: inactive (dead) since Thu 2018-09-13 16:57:00 EDT; 4min 24s ago
     Docs: man:systemd.special(7)

Sep 13 16:54:41 localhost.localdomain systemd[1]: Reached target Graphical In...
Sep 13 16:54:41 localhost.localdomain systemd[1]: Starting Graphical Interface.
Sep 13 16:57:00 localhost.localdomain systemd[1]: Stopped target Graphical In...
Sep 13 16:57:00 localhost.localdomain systemd[1]: Stopping Graphical Interface.
[…]
#
```

In Listing 5.19, using super user privileges, the systemctl isolate command caused the system to jump from the default system target to the multi-user target. Unfortunately, there is no simple command to show your system's current target in this case. However, the systemctl status command is useful. If you employ the command and give it the previous target's name (graphical.target in this case), you should see that it is no longer active and thus not the current system target. Notice that a short history of the graphical target's starts and stops is also shown in the status display.

 The systemctl isolate command can be used only with certain targets. The target's unit file must have the AllowIsolate=yes directive set.

Two extra special targets are rescue and emergency. These targets, sometimes called modes, are described here:

Rescue Target   When you jump your system to the rescue target, the system mounts all the local filesystems, only the root user is allowed to log into the system, networking services are turned off, and only a few other services are started. The systemctl is-system-running command will return the maintenance status. Running disk utilities to fix corrupted disks is a useful task in this particular target. This target is similar to the SysVinit single-user mode, covered later in this chapter.

Emergency Target   When your system goes into emergency mode, the system mounts only the root filesystem, and it mounts it as read-only. Similar to rescue mode, it only allows the root user to log into the system, networking services are turned off, and only a few other services are started. The systemctl is-system-running command will return the maintenance status. If your system goes into emergency mode by itself, there are serious problems. This target is used for situations where even rescue mode cannot be reached.

Be aware that if you jump into either rescue or emergency mode, you'll only be able to log into the root account. Therefore, you need to have the root account password. Also, your screen may go blank for a minute, so don't panic. An example of jumping into emergency mode is shown in Listing 5.20.

Listing 5.20: Jumping to the emergency target unit

```
# systemctl isolate emergency
Welcome to emergency mode! After logging in, type "journalctl -xb" to view
system logs, "systemctl reboot" to reboot, "systemctl default" or ^D to
try again to boot into default mode.
Give root password for maintenance
(or type Control-D to continue):
#
# systemctl is-system-running
maintenance
#
```

Listing 5.20: Jumping to the emergency target unit (*continued*)

```
# systemctl list-units --type=target
UNIT             LOAD     ACTIVE  SUB     DESCRIPTION
emergency.target loaded   active  active  Emergency Mode
[…]
#
# systemctl default
#
```

In Listing 5.20, the systemctl command is employed to jump into emergency mode. Notice that you do not have to add the .target extension on the emergency target unit's filename. This is true with all systemd targets. When you reach emergency mode, you must enter the root password at the prompt. When you reach the command line, you can enter commands listed in the welcome display or try out some additional systemctl commands.

> Other targets you can jump to include reboot, poweroff, and halt. For example, just type in **systemctl isolate reboot** to reboot your system.

Notice in Listing 5.20 that when the systemctl is-system-running command is issued, the response is maintenance instead of running. Also, when the list-units command is employed, it shows that the emergency.target is active. The systemctl default command will cause the system to attempt to jump into the default target.

Using the SysV Initialization Process

Many server administrators have gone through the process of moving from a *SysVinit* system to a systemd system. Recall that systemd is backward compatible with SysVinit, so understanding SysVinit is important.

First, if you want to experiment with the original SysVinit commands without interference from systemd or the now defunct Upstart, find a Linux distribution that uses the SysVinit initialization method. One way to find one is to visit the DistroWatch website and use their search tool at distrowatch.com/search.php. Scroll down to the Search by Distribution Criteria section, and for Init software, select SysV. Any Linux distributions still using SysVinit will display in the search results.

To get clean SysVinit listings for this book, we used a blast from the Linux distribution past, Fedora 7. To grab an ISO copy of this old distribution, visit archives.fedoraproject .org/pub/archive/fedora/linux/releases/.

WARNING Using any older and no-longer-supported Linux distribution can open up your system to a whole host of problems. If you do choose to take this risk, minimize your exposure by putting the Linux distribution in a virtualized environment; do not install any network interface cards (NICs) for the virtual machine, and turn off access to the host machine's filesystem.

The next section should provide you with enough of a SysVinit understanding to manage a system using it or to help in a Linux server migration process to systemd.

Understanding Runlevels

At system boot time, instead of targets to determine what groups of services to start, SysVinit uses runlevels. These *runlevels* are defined in Table 5.12 and Table 5.13. Notice that different distributions use different runlevel definitions.

TABLE 5.12 Red Hat–based distribution SysVinit runlevels

Runlevel	Description
0	Shut down the system.
1, s, or S	Single-user mode used for system maintenance. (Similar to systemd rescue target.)
2	Multi-user mode without networking services enabled.
3	Multi-user mode with networking services enabled.
4	Custom.
5	Multi-user mode with GUI available.
6	Reboot the system.

Note that runlevels 0 and 6 are not true runlevels by definition. For example, a system in a powered-off state, which is runlevel 0, is not running.

TABLE 5.13 Debian-based distribution SysVinit runlevels

Runlevel	Description
0	Shut down the system.
1	Single-user mode used for system maintenance. (Similar to systemd rescue target.)

TABLE 5.13   Debian-based distribution SysVinit runlevels *(continued)*

Runlevel	Description
2	Multi-user mode with GUI available.
6	Reboot the system.

To determine your system's current and former runlevel, you employ the *runlevel* command. The first number or letter displayed indicates the previous runlevel (N indicates that the system is newly booted), and the second number indicates the current runlevel. An example is shown in Listing 5.21 of a newly booted Red Hat–based SysVinit system, which is running at runlevel 5.

Listing 5.21: Employing the runlevel command

```
# runlevel
N 5
#
```

Instead of using a default target like systemd, SysVinit systems employ a configuration file, */etc/inittab*. In the past, this file started many different services, but in later years it started only terminal services and defined the default runlevel for a system. The file line defining the default runlevel is shown in Listing 5.22.

Listing 5.22: The /etc/inittab file line that sets the default runlevel

```
# grep :initdefault: /etc/inittab
id:5:initdefault:
#
```

Within Listing 5.22, notice the number 5 between the id: and the :initdefault: in the /etc/inittab file record. This indicates that the system's default runlevel is 5. The initdefault is what specifies the runlevel to enter after the system boots.

> Look back at Table 5.5 in this chapter. You'll see that systemd provides backward compatibility to SysVinit via runlevel targets, which can be used as the default target and/or in switching targets via the systemctl isolate command.

Setting the default runlevel is the first step in configuring certain services to start at system initialization. Next, each service must have an initialization script located typically in the /etc/init.d/ directory. Listing 5.23 shows a snipped example of the various scripts in this directory. Note that the -1F options are used on the ls command to display the scripts in a single column and to tack on a file indicator code. The * file indicator code denotes that these files are executable programs (Bash shell scripts in this case).

Listing 5.23: Listing script files in the /etc/init.d/ directory

```
# ls -1F  /etc/init.d/
anacron*
atd*
[…]
crond*
cups*
[…]
ntpd*
[…]
ypbind*
yum-updatesd*
#
```

These initialization scripts are responsible for starting, stopping, restarting, reloading, and displaying the status of various system services. The program that calls these initialization scripts is the rc script, and it can reside in either the /etc/init.d/ or the /etc/rc.d/ directory. The rc script runs the scripts in a particular directory. The directory picked depends on the desired runlevel. Each runlevel has its own subdirectory in the /etc/rc.d/ directory, as shown in Listing 5.24.

Listing 5.24: Runlevel subdirectories in the /etc/rc.d/ directory

```
# ls /etc/rc.d/
init.d  rc0.d  rc2.d  rc4.d  rc6.d    rc.sysinit
rc      rc1.d  rc3.d  rc5.d  rc.local
#
```

Notice in Listing 5.24 that there are seven subdirectories named rcn.d, where n is a number from 0 to 6. The rc script runs the scripts in the rcn.d subdirectory for the desired runlevel. For example, if the desired runlevel is 3, all the scripts in the /etc/rc.d/rc3.d/ directory are run. Listing 5.25 shows a snippet of the scripts in this directory.

Listing 5.25: Files in the /etc/rc.d/rc3.d directory

```
# ls -1F /etc/rc.d/rc3.d/
K01smolt@
K02avahi-dnsconfd@
K02NetworkManager@
[…]
K99readahead_later@
```

Listing 5.25: Files in the /etc/rc.d/rc3.d directory *(continued)*

```
S00microcode_ctl@
S04readahead_early@
[…]
S55cups@
S99local@
S99smartd@
#
```

Notice in Listing 5.25 that the script names start with either a K or an S, are followed by a number, and then their service name. The K stands for kill (stop), and the S stands for start. The number indicates the order in which this service should be stopped or started for that runlevel. This is somewhat similar to the After and Before directives in the systemd service type unit files.

The files in the /etc/rc.d/rc*n*.d/ directories are all symbolic links to the scripts in the /etc/init.d/ directory. Listing 5.26 shows an example of this.

Listing 5.26: Displaying the /etc/rc.d/rc3.d/S55cups link

```
# readlink -f /etc/rc.d/rc3.d/S55cups
/etc/rc.d/init.d/cups
#
```

The rc script goes through and runs all the K scripts first, passing a stop argument to each script. It then runs all the S scripts, passing a start argument to each script. This not only ensures that the proper services are started for a particular runlevel but also allows jumping between runlevels after system initialization and thus stopping and starting certain services for that new runlevel.

 If you need to enact certain commands or run any scripts as soon as system initialization is completed, there is a file for that purpose. The /etc/rc.local script allows you to add additional scripts and or commands. Just keep in mind that this script is not run until all the other SysVinit scripts have been executed.

Scripts are central to the SysVinit process. To understand SysVinit scripts, be sure to read through Chapter 9 first. That chapter will help you understand Bash shell script basics, which in turn will help you to understand the SysVinit script contents.

Investigating SysVinit Commands

The various SysVinit commands help in starting and stopping services, managing what services are deployed at various runlevels, and jumping between runlevels on an already running Linux system. We cover the various SysVinit commands in this section.

Jumping between runlevels is a little different than jumping between systemd targets. It uses the *init* or *telinit* utility to do so. These two utilities are essentially twins and can be interchanged for each other. To jump between runlevels on a SysVinit system, the basic syntax is as follows:

```
init Destination-Runlevel
telinit Destination-Runlevel
```

Listing 5.27 shows an example of jumping on a SysVinit system from the current runlevel 5 to the destination runlevel 3. Note that the runlevel command is employed to show the previous and current runlevels.

Listing 5.27: Jumping from runlevel 5 to runlevel 3

```
# runlevel
N 5
#
# init 3
#
# runlevel
5 3
#
```

Keep in mind you can shut down a SysVinit system by entering **init 0** or **telinit 0** at the command line as long as you have the proper privileges. You can also reboot a SysVinit system by typing **init 6** or **telinit 6** at the command line.

To view a SysVinit managed service's status and control whether it is currently running, use the *service* utility. This utility has the following basic syntax:

```
service SCRIPT COMMAND [OPTIONS]
```

The SCRIPT in the service utility refers to a particular service script within the /etc/init.d/ directory. The service utility executes the script, passing it the designated COMMAND. Service scripts typically have the same name as the service. Also, you only have to provide a script's base name and not the directory location. As an example, for the NTP service script, /etc/init.d/ntpd, you only need to use the ntpd base name.

Table 5.14 describes commonly used items you can employ for the COMMAND portion of the service utility. Keep in mind that if the COMMAND is not handled by the script or handled differently than it's commonly handled, you'll get an unexpected result.

TABLE 5.14   Commonly used service utility commands

Command	Description
restart	Stop and immediately restart the designated service. Note that if a designated service is not already started, a FAILED status will be generated on the stop attempt, and then the service will be started.

TABLE 5.14   Commonly used service utility commands *(continued)*

Command	Description
start	Start the designated service.
status	Display the designated service's current status.
stop	Stop the designated service. Note if a designated service is already stopped, a FAILED status will be generated on the stop attempt.
reload	Load the service configuration file of the running designated service. This allows you to make service configuration changes without stopping the service. Note that if you attempt the reload command on a stopped service, a FAILED status will be generated.

It helps to see examples of the service utility in action. Listing 5.28 provides a few for your review.

Listing 5.28: Employing the service utility

```
# service httpd status
httpd is stopped
#
# service httpd start
Starting httpd:                        [  OK  ]
#
# service httpd status
httpd (pid 14124 14123 […]) is running...
#
# service httpd stop
Stopping httpd:                        [  OK  ]
#
# service httpd status
httpd is stopped
#
# service --status-all
anacron is stopped
atd (pid 2024) is running...
[…]
ypbind is stopped
yum-updatesd (pid 2057) is running...
#
```

The last `service` utility example in Listing 5.28 is worth pointing out. This command allows you to view all the services on your system along with their current status. Keep in mind that this list will scroll by quickly, so it's a good idea to redirect its STDOUT to the `less` pager utility so that you can view the display more comfortably.

Although some SysVinit commands have been modified to work with systemd utilities, others, such as `service --status-all`, might produce unpredictable or confusing results. As tempting as it is to hang on to past commands, those habits may cause you problems in the future. It is best to learn native systemd commands and employ them instead.

As you can see, managing the SysVinit scripts and their associated runlevels can be tricky. However, if you have to take care of one of these systems, you now understand the tools that can help you.

Stopping the System

Besides the various SysVinit and systemd commands you can use to shut down or reboot a system, there are a few additional utilities you can employ to enact these tasks no matter what system initialization your system uses:

- *halt*: Stops all processes and shuts down the CPU.
- *poweroff*: Stops all processes, shuts down the CPU, and sends signals to the hardware to power down.
- *reboot*: Stops all processes, shuts down the CPU, and then restarts the system.
- *shutdown*: Stops all processes, shuts down the CPU, and sends signals to the hardware to power down.

On most modern systemd initialization systems, the `halt`, `poweroff`, and `reboot` commands are symbolically linked to the `systemctl` utility.

The interesting thing about the `halt`, `poweroff`, and `reboot` commands is that they can each do the other's job. They all have the following options available to accomplish this:

- `--halt`: Makes the command behave like `halt`.
- `-p, --poweroff`: Makes the command behave like `poweroff`.
- `--reboot`: Makes the command behave like `reboot`.

When powering off a system, after the processes are stopped and the CPU is shut down, signals are sent to the hardware telling the various components to power down. For operating systems using Advanced Configuration and Power Interface (ACPI)–compliant chipsets, these are ACPI signals. These special communications are handled by the ACPI daemon, *acpid*. This daemon manages signals sent to various hardware devices via predefined settings for particular events, such as pressing the system's power button or closing a laptop system's lid.

The utility with the most flexibility in rebooting or powering off your system is the shutdown command. Its basic syntax is as follows:

shutdown [*OPTIONS...*] *TIME* [*WALL-MESSAGE*]

The [*OPTIONS*] include switches to halt the system (-H), power off the system (-P), and reboot the system (-r), as well as several other useful selections. After you've started a shutdown process, you can typically cancel it using the shutdown -c command. See the man pages for additional shutdown options you may desire to use.

If no [*OPTIONS*] are used, the shutdown command performs differently depending on the distribution you are using.

The *TIME* parameter allows you to specify a time to enact the shutdown options. It takes many formats, such as a military time layout specified as *hh*:*mm*. You can indicate the number of minutes from the current system time using a +n or n format. The shutdown command allows the now time parameter to indicate 0 minutes from now (immediately). On some distributions, if *TIME* is not specified, a +1 is assumed. See the man pages for all the *TIME* specifications available on your distribution.

The [*WALL-MESSAGE*] parameter lets you modify the shutdown command message sent to any logged-in users. Wall messaging is covered in the next section.

For any utility used to shut down the system, the processes are sent a SIGTERM signal (covered in Chapter 2). This allows the various running programs to close their files properly and gracefully terminate. However, in unusual cases, you may have a situation where a process refuses to shut down. You can use the lsof -p *PID* command to see if the running program has any files open. If not, then you can attempt to use the kill -9 *PID* command. However, always tread cautiously in these cases.

Notifying the Users

When you perform any function that changes the system's state for logged-in users, it's a good idea to let them know ahead of time so that they can wrap up any work before being kicked out. Besides the old standbys of email, automated text messaging, and company intranet web pages, a Linux system offers the following additional utilities and files to help with communication:

- `/etc/issue`: Contains text to be displayed on the tty terminal login screens (prior to logging into the system).
- `/etc/issue.net`: Contains logon screen messages for remote logins.
- `/etc/motd`: Called the Message of the Day file, contains text that is displayed after a user has logged into a tty terminal.
- `/bin/notify-send` (or `/usr/bin/notify-send`): Sends messages to a user employing the GUI but who is not logged into a tty terminal or does not have a GUI terminal emulator open.
- `/bin/wall` (or `/usr/bin/wall`): Sends messages (called *wall messages*) to users logged into a tty terminal or who have a GUI terminal emulator open and have their message status set to "yes."

The method(s) you choose depend on which one(s) best meet your company's communication policies and needs.

> By default, the `systemctl` utility (covered earlier in this chapter) will send a `wall` message when any of its following commands are issued: emergency, halt, power-off, reboot, or rescue. To prevent a `wall` message from being sent while using `systemctl`, include the `--no-wall` option in its command line.

The *wall* command sends simple messages to certain system users—those who are currently logged into a terminal (tty#) or a terminal-emulator (pts/#) and have their message status set to "yes." To check your own message status, you can employ the `mesg` command as shown in Listing 5.29.

Listing 5.29: Viewing your message status with the `mesg` command

```
$ mesg
is y
$
```

Notice from the previous example, the `mesg` command shows the current message status. You can issue the **mesg y** command to turn on messaging and **mesg n** to turn it off.

> To see who is currently logged into the system and whether or not they have their message status set to "yes," use the `who -T` command. All users who can receive `wall` messages will have a plus (+) following their username.

Figure 5.3 and Figure 5.4 show the `wall` command in action. Notice in Figure 5.3 that the message is written *after* the `wall` command is issued. You enter the message and then press the Ctrl+d key combination to send the communication.

FIGURE 5.3   Issuing the wall command

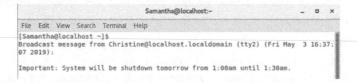

```
$
$ who -T
Christine  + tty2         2019-05-03 16:34
Timothy    - tty3         2019-05-03 16:25
Rich       + tty4         2019-05-03 16:27
Samantha ? :0             2019-05-03 16:28 (:0)
Samantha + pts/0          2019-05-03 16:29 (:0)
$
$ wall
Important: System will be shutdown tomorrow from 1:00am until 1:30am.
$
Broadcast message from Christine@localhost.localdomain (tty2) (Fri May  3 16:37:
07 2019):

Important: System will be shutdown tomorrow from 1:00am until 1:30am.
```

The wall message is disruptive, as shown in Figure 5.4. However, the user receiving the message can simply press the Enter key to receive their prompt back.

FIGURE 5.4   Receiving wall command output

```
                       Samantha@localhost:~              _  □  ×

 File  Edit  View  Search  Terminal  Help

[Samantha@localhost ~]$
Broadcast message from Christine@localhost.localdomain (tty2) (Fri May  3 16:37:
07 2019):

Important: System will be shutdown tomorrow from 1:00am until 1:30am.
```

> The shutdown command's [wall message] parameter operates similar to the wall command with one major difference: it ignores the mesg setting on a terminal. Therefore, the message can be written on any terminal whether a user's message status is set to "yes" or not. Some distributions offer the --no-wall option. It allows a shutdown to proceed with no wall messages sent to users, except for the super user issuing the shutdown command.

Booting and initializing a Linux system is quite the complicated dance. Shutting it down, changing the system's current state, and keeping users informed while doing so adds demanding steps to this system administration ballet. In the next section, we'll take the dance to a new level by looking at virtualizing the systems.

Virtualizing Linux

When something is virtual, it does not physically exist but instead is simulated. In the information technology world, this simulation can apply to computer systems, which is accomplished through special software. In this section, we'll take a look at the various types of simulations available, the terminology associated with them, as well as some of the various tools involved.

Looking at Virtual Machines

Virtual machines (VMs) are simulated computer systems that appear and act as physical machines to their users. The process of creating these virtual machines is called *virtualization*.

Managing VMs

The primary software tool used to create and manage VMs is a *hypervisor*, which has been historically called either a *virtual machine monitor* or a *virtual machine manager* (VMM). Hypervisors come in two basic flavors: Type 1 and Type 2. (However, you'll find that some hypervisor software doesn't neatly fit into either category.)

The easier to understand is the Type 2 hypervisor, so we'll start there. A Type 2 hypervisor is a software application that operates between its created virtual machine (*guest*) and the physical system (*host*) on which the hypervisor is running. A diagrammed example of a Type 2 hypervisors is shown in Figure 5.5.

FIGURE 5.5   A Type 2 hypervisor example

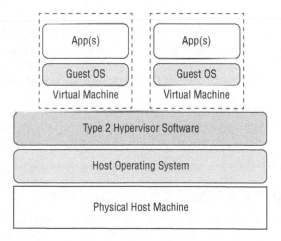

A Type 2 hypervisor acts as a typical software application in that it interacts with the host's operating system. However, its distinction lies in the fact that it provides one or more virtualized environments or virtual machines. These VMs each have their own operating system (guest OS) and can have various applications running on them. The host OS on the physical system can be completely different than the VM's guest OS.

There are several Type 2 hypervisors from which to choose. A few options that run on Linux include Oracle VirtualBox and VMware Workstation Player.

> When creating VMs with a Type 2 hypervisor, it is important to determine if you have enough resources, such as RAM, on your physical host machine. Keep in mind that you will need to accommodate the host OS, Type 2 hypervisor software, as well as the guest OS and applications on each VM.

A Type 1 hypervisor eliminates the need for the physical host's OS. This software runs directly on the physical system and due to this is sometimes called a *bare-metal* hypervisor. A diagrammed example of a Type 1 hypervisor is shown in Figure 5.6.

FIGURE 5.6   A Type 1 hypervisor example

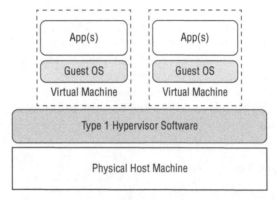

There are also several Type 1 hypervisors from which to choose. A few options include KVM, Xen, and Hyper-V. An interesting feature with KVM and Hyper-V is that they can both be started while the host OS is running. These hypervisors then take over for the host OS and run as a Type 1 hypervisor. This is a case where the VMMs don't neatly fit into the Type 1 category.

 For Linux, KVM is built in. KVM's kernel component has been included in the Linux kernel since v2.6.20.

Creating a Virtual Machine

There are many ways to create a virtual machine. When first starting out, most people will create a Linux virtual machine from the ground up; they set up the VM specifications within the hypervisor software of their choice and use an ISO file (live or otherwise) to install the guest operating system.

 A virtual machine is made up of either one file or a series of files that reside on the host machine. Whether it is a single file or multiple files depends on the hypervisor used. The file (or files) contains configuration information, such as how much RAM is needed, as well as the VM's data, such as the guest OS and any installed application binaries.

Lots of choices exist for creating VMs. Which methods you use depend on your organization's needs as well as the number of VMs you must deploy. The following describes some common options:

Clone   A *clone* is essentially a copy of another guest VM. Just like in science fiction, a VM clone is identical to its original. The files that make up the original VM are copied to a new filesystem location, and the VM is given a new name.

Hypervisors typically have easy methods for creating clones. However, before you start up a cloned VM, it is important to check the VM's settings. For example, some hypervisors do not issue a new NIC MAC address (covered in Chapter 8) when creating a VM clone. This could cause network issues should you have two running VMs that have identical NIC MAC addresses. The following is a brief list of items that may need to be modified for a Linux clone:

- Host name
- NIC MAC address
- NIC IP address, if using a static IP
- Machine ID
- Any items employing a universally unique identifier (UUID)
- Configuration settings on the clone that employ any item in this list

WARNING   Your system's machine ID is a unique hexadecimal 32-character identifier. The ID is stored in the /etc/machine-id file. D-Bus (covered in Chapter 3) will use this ID, if its own machine ID file, /var/lib/dbus/machine-id, does not exist. Typically on modern distributions, the *D-Bus machine ID* file will not exist or will be symbolically linked to the /etc/machine-id file. Problems can ensue if you clone a machine and boot it so that the two machines share the same ID. These problems may include not being able to get an IP address if your network manager is configured to use the machine's ID instead of a NIC's MAC address for DHCP services. To prevent this problem, after you clone a VM, you'll need to address the duplicate machine ID. Typically, you can do this on the clone by performing the following steps:

1. Delete the machine ID file: **rm /etc/machine-id**

2. Delete the D-Bus ID file: **rm /var/lib/dbus/machine-id**

3. Regenerate the ID: **dbus-uuidgen --ensure**

Keep in mind that your distribution may require additional steps, such as linking the /var/lib/dbus/machine-id file to /etc/machine-id (soft links were covered in Chapter 4). Be sure to peruse your distro's documentation prior to changing a machine's identity.

Open Virtualization Format   Another handy method employs the Open Virtualization Format (OVF). The OVF is a standard administered by the Distributed Management Task Force (DMTF) organization. This standard allows the hypervisor to export a VM's files into the OVF file format for use in other hypervisors. After you export the files, you can import them into any other hypervisor that honors the standard. It's like cloning a machine between two different VMM software applications. Be sure to change the appropriate settings on the new VMs, such as host name, if the VMs will be running on the same local network.

While the OVF file standard creates multiple files, some hypervisors recognize a single compressed archive file of OVF files, called an Open Virtualization Archive (OVA). This is useful if you need to transfer a VM's files across a network to a different host system.

Template   Outside of computing, a template is a pattern or mold that is used to guide the process of creating an item. In word processing, a template is often employed to provide formatting models, such as when creating a business letter.

In virtualization, a VM *template* is a master copy. It is similar to a VM clone, except you cannot boot it. Virtual machines are created using these templates as their base.

To create a template, you need a *system image* (sometimes called a *VM image*). This image contains the guest OS, any installed applications, as well as configuration and data files. The system image is created from a VM you have configured as your base system. You direct the hypervisor software to generate a template, which is often a file or set of files. Now, you can employ this system image to create several virtual machines based on that template.

Keep in mind that for a template-created VM you may need to modify items prior to booting it. The same list covered in the "Clone" section applies here.

There are additional choices for creating virtual machines besides the ones listed here. For example, some companies offer software that will scan your current system and create a VM of it. The term used for these software offerings is *physical-to-virtual* (P2V).

> If you have hypervisor software installed, most likely you can employ the `virsh` shell utility (not typically installed by default) to manage your VMs using shell scripts, which is convenient. You'll need the `libvirt` library installed as well to support this utility.

Integrating via Linux Extensions

Before you jump into creating virtual machines, it's important to check that your Linux host system will support virtualization and the hypervisor product you have chosen. This support is accomplished via various *extensions* and modules.

A hardware extension is based within the system's CPU. It grants the hypervisor the ability to access the CPU directly, instead of going through the host OS, which improves performance.

> While your server may have everything it needs to run VMs, if the virtualization is disabled in the BIOS, it won't work. Check your system's BIOS documentation and ensure that virtualization is enabled. Also be aware that many hypervisors require a 64-bit CPU to operate, which you check via the `lscpu` utility.

First, you should determine if your system's CPU has these hardware extensions available. You can research this via the /proc/cpuinfo file's flag information. Type **grep ^flags /proc/cpuinfo** to view the various enabled features of your server's CPU. If enabled, you should see one of the following:

- For Intel CPUs: vmx
- For AMD CPUs: svm

> If you see the hypervisor flag (instead of vmx or svm), this means your Linux OS is not running on a physical machine, but a virtual one. You can check to see which hypervisor is being employed via the virt-what utility, which may or may not be installed on your Linux distro by default.

To use these CPU extensions and support the chosen hypervisor software, the appropriate Linux modules (covered in Chapter 3) must be loaded. You'll need to review your hypervisor's documentation to determine what modules are needed.

To check if a needed module is already loaded, use the lsmod command. An example is shown here, checking for support of the KVM hypervisor:

```
lsmod | grep -i kvm
```

If you find that the needed hypervisor modules are not loaded, employ the modprobe command to insert them. An example of loading up a needed KVM hypervisor module is shown here:

```
sudo modprobe kvm-amd
```

> When your Linux VM is up and running, you may want to install guest utilities and drivers provided by the hypervisor (if available). These tools are typically installed inside the VM from the guest OS and provide nice features such as folders shared between the guest and the host machine. Some hypervisors offer diagnostic data utilities for managing your guest's apps. For VM guests with GUIs, hypervisor-provided drivers can improve graphics and deliver additional mouse handling features.

Understanding Containers

Containers are virtual entities, but they are different from virtual machines and serve distinct purposes. Whereas a VM provides an entire guest operating system, a container's focus is typically on a single app, application stack, or environment. Instead of a hypervisor, a container is managed by a container engine. A diagrammed example of a container is shown in Figure 5.7.

FIGURE 5.7 A container example

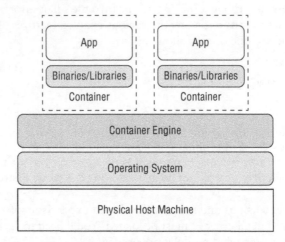

Notice in Figure 5.7 that the physical machine's operating system is shared among the containers. However, each container has its own set of binaries and needed libraries to support its app, application stack, or environment.

A container's focus depends on its purpose in life. Two container focal points are

Application Containers   These containers focus on a single application, or an application stack, such as a web server. Application containers are heavily used in development and operations (DevOps). Software developers can modify their company's app in a newly created container. This same container, with the modified app, is then tested and eventually moved into production on the host machine. The old production container is destroyed. Using containers in this way eliminates production and development environment differences and provides little to no downtime for app users. Thus, containers are very popular in continuous software deployment environments. The example back in Figure 5.7 shows two application containers.

Operating System Containers   While containers are useful for developers, system admins can love them too. You can use a container that provides a fully functioning Linux OS space and is isolated from your host machine. Some in TechOps use containers to test their applications and needed libraries on various Linux distributions. Other system admins, prior to upgrading their host system distro, try out their environment on an upgraded Linux distribution. You can also employ VMs for these different evaluations, but containers provide a faster-to-deploy and more lightweight test area.

Docker is a very popular container engine for applications. In this particular software as well as other container engine programs (such as LXC, which is useful for testing workloads), you can employ system images to deploy several containers based on that image.

Virtualizing an application typically does not make it perform faster and should not be the primary motivation for moving it to a virtualized environment. Although containers allow you to quickly deploy applications, they will not cause an app to run more swiftly. Some hypervisors are termed *efficient hypervisors*, but that is only when there is a small performance difference between the physical environment and its virtualized self.

Looking at Infrastructure as a Service

With the high expenses of maintaining hardware and providing the electricity to run servers as well as cool them, many companies are looking to cloud-based data centers. For virtualization, companies turn to *Infrastructure as a Service (IaaS)* providers.

With IaaS, the provider furnishes not only the hypervisor but the data center(s) as well—servers, disks, and networking infrastructure. Your virtualized environment is reached over the Internet.

Many of these IaaS providers also offer various data center locations around the world, allowing you to pick the one closest to your customers. Often you can select additional data centers to run your VMs or containers if needed for performance or to act as backup locations should your chosen primary data center experience a disaster.

A few of the more popular IaaS providers are Amazon Web Services (AWS), Google Cloud Platform's Google Compute Engine, Digital Ocean, Rackspace, and Microsoft's Azure. Each not only grants IaaS but also offers additional utilities allowing you to monitor, manage, and protect your virtualized environment.

Often IaaS providers furnish more than just virtualization infrastructure services; they may also offer Platform as a Service (PaaS) and/or Software as a Service (SaaS). The name for providers that offer one or more of these services is typically cloud service provider (CSP).

When using a cloud-based virtualized environment, you should know a few additional terms that will assist in selecting a CSP. They are as follows:

Computing Instance   A *computing instance*, sometimes called a *cloud instance*, is a single virtual machine or container running on a cloud platform. When an instance is started, this is called *provisioning* an instance.

Cloud Type   A CSP will offer public, private, and hybrid clouds. Public clouds are just as they sound—open to the public via the Internet or application programming interfaces (APIs). Access to their instances is controlled via virtual firewalls, gateways, and network routers. These clouds reside solely on the CSP's infrastructure.

Private cloud instances are only accessible to those who own and manage the cloud instances. Access to these private cloud instances is often controlled via the same methods as public clouds. They too reside solely on the CSP's infrastructure.

Hybrid clouds are interesting in that they are typically a combination of instances on the CSP's infrastructure as well as instances or physical computers at a company's local data center. Hybrid clouds are popular with organizations who do not need all the features (or the price) of a CSP's cloud infrastructure.

Elasticity   Elasticity allows an instance to automatically scale up or scale down, depending on current demand. This may mean that additional instances are created to meet bursts of traffic (called *horizontal scaling*), and when traffic wanes, then the instances are deprovisioned. It can also mean that additional resources are provided (or removed from) an instance to meet demand (called *vertical scaling*).

Load Balancing   Load balancing occurs when a virtualized environment has multiple instances. The current demand is spread across the multiple instances to provide balanced loads to each instance, instead of hitting one instance with a majority of the traffic.

Management Console or Portal   To set up your instances and choose the various CSP features, many providers offer a web browser–based graphical utility called a management console or portal. Through these consoles, you can modify access to private and public clouds, choose storage types, start or stop instances, and perform monitoring of your running VMs or containers.

Block and Object Storage   *Block storage* is familiar to most system admins. Typically the underlying hardware is configured as disk drives in RAID configurations. Fixed-size storage volumes can be permanently or temporarily attached as physical devices to instances. From there, they can be mounted and used as needed. However, if block storage is not mounted, it cannot be accessed.

Object storage is different in that it can be accessed through the management console or through the web. Typically, the CSP provides data protection services for object storage, and you can store any kinds of data you desire.

Remote Instance Access   While the console or portal gives you the high-level view of your various cloud instances, there are times you need to log directly into an instance. A preferred method employs using OpenSSH to access your instance's IP address. But instead of using a username and password, many CSPs provide an *SSH host key* (covered in Chapter 10). This method furnishes a secured encrypted connection and access method to log directly into your remote cloud instances.

Keep in mind that not all CSPs offer all these features. It's up to you to review various CSPs and determine what your organization needs and can afford to purchase.

Cloud-init is a Canonical product (the same people who produce the Ubuntu distributions). On their website, cloud-init.io, Canonical describes *cloud-init* best: "Cloud images are operating system templates and every instance starts out as an identical clone of every other instance. It is the user data that gives every cloud instance its personality and cloud-init is the tool that applies user data to your instances automatically."

The cloud-init service is available for CSPs, such as Amazon Web Services (AWS), Microsoft Azure, and Digital Ocean. And your virtual machines don't have to be in a cloud to use cloud-init. It can also bootstrap local virtual machines using hypervisor software like VMware and KVM. In addition, it is supported by most major Linux distributions. (It is called an industry standard for a reason.) If you would like to take a look at the cloud-init utility, you can install it via the *cloud-init* package.

Summary

From the POST to being able to log in and access needed applications, your Linux system performs a seemingly easy process. However, the techniques are more complicated under-neath the surface. Starting with the firmware or firmware interface and proceeding to the boot loader and onward through the system initialization mechanism, a Linux system finally becomes available and ready for use.

You can employ various techniques for shutting down a system. The method you use depends on the initialization method and business requirements of your Linux machine. However, before moving your system into a different state, such as shutdown or single-user mode, it's a good idea to inform your users.

Moving your system from running directly on a physical system to a virtualized envi-ronment, such as a virtual machine or a container, is becoming very popular among businesses. You will need to understand the basic concepts of providing a virtualized environment within your company's data center, and/or using IaaS is critical for modern TechOps.

In this chapter, we looked at all these concepts for both older and newer systems. This will not only help you pass the certification exam, but also assist in migration projects for Linux systems in order to get their environment current.

Exam Essentials

Summarize the boot process and key components.   After the firmware starts, it performs a POST and then looks for a boot loader program to load. This firmware can be the older BIOS that looks for the boot loader in the MBR or the newer UEFI that looks for boot loaders files, typically with an .efi file extension name in the ESP mounted at the /boot/ efi/ directory. The boot loader finds the Linux kernel and puts it into RAM. The kernel performs various tasks that include launching the system's initialization process, which in turn starts up the appropriate applications and services. Boot kernel messages are stored in the kernel ring buffer, and if needed, you can view these messages shortly after boot time via the dmesg or, if available, the journalctl utility. Depending on your Linux system's distribution, you can typically view the boot messages at any time in a log file, such as /var/log/boot or /var/log/boot.log.

Describe the different boot loaders and their use.   The certification focuses on two boot loaders: the GRand Unified Bootloader (GRUB) boot loader (now called *GRUB Legacy*) and its rewrite, GRUB2. The GRUB Legacy configuration file is /boot/grub/menu.lst and/or /boot/grub/grub.conf. The GRUB2 configuration file is stored in either the / boot/grub/ or /boot/grub2/ directory, and it is named grub.cfg for BIOS systems. For UEFI systems, the GRUB2 configuration file is /boot/efi/EFI/*distro-name*/grub.cfg. You do not modify the GRUB2 configuration file but instead add configuration files with global directives in the /etc/grub.d/ directory and individual configuration files with boot options, also in the /boot/grub.d/ folder. For GRUB Legacy, you initially install the program in the MBR using the grub-install command with no further action needed for configuration file updates. For GRUB2, to rebuild the configuration file after you make changes, run the grub-mkconfig, grub2-mkconfig, or update-grub utility. Each boot loader has various menu commands you can use to edit the options during boot and doing things such as passing various kernel parameters.

Compare the various system initialization methods.   The older SysVinit and the new systemd initialization methods can enable or disable various services to start at system boot time as well as additional service management items. systemd employs unit files to manage services and target files to manage groups of services. The systemctl utility is the primary interface for controlling systemd-managed services. It can enable or disable services at system boot, start or stop services during normal operation, and set or show the current system target.

The SysVinit initialization method uses the service utility to start and stop various services via scripts stored in the /etc/init.d/ directory. These scripts are also used at system initialization, and the runlevel set in the /etc/inittab file determines which ones are used. The rc script runs the scripts in the appropriate /etc/rc.d/rc*n*.d/directory, when *n* is equal to the runlevel. These scripts are symbolic links to the scripts in the /etc/init.d/ directory, and start or stop the services as directed. The init and telinit commands also accept a runlevel number allowing you to jump between runlevels on the fly.

Outline the various methods for stopping the system.   Besides using the systemctl and init (or telinit) commands to shut down a system, you can also use the halt, poweroff, reboot, and/or shutdown utilities. Whether you use systemctl or init (or telinit) depends on which system initialization method your server employs. The other commands are available on all systems and can do each other's jobs via various switches. The shutdown command is the most flexible and provides additional options.

Summarize various ways to notify users of events. Users can be notified of various events through information placed in the /etc/issue, /etc/issue.net, and/or /etc/motd files. In addition, messages can be sent on the fly via the notify-send or wall utility. The wall command will send messages only to those users who are currently logged into a terminal (tty#) or a terminal-emulator (pts/#) and have their message status set to "yes." You can view the message status for all those users with the who -T command, and an individual user can view/set their status via the mesg utility. The shutdown command and some of the systemctl utility's options also send wall messages, but the mesg setting on a terminal is ignored.

Describe guest virtualization concepts. A virtual machine is a simulated computer system that appears and acts like a physical machine to its user. VMs are managed via hypervisors, which come in two flavors: type 1, which runs as the physical system's (host) OS (also called *bare-metal hypervisor*), and type 2, which runs on top of the host's OS. VMs can be built by cloning, using templates, or employing OVF files or an OVA file. When using these methods, it is important to ensure the VM's host name, NIC MAC address, NIC IP address (if static), machine ID, UUIDs, and configuration files employing these items are reviewed and modified, if needed.

Containers are different from VMs in that they do not necessarily have a full-blown guest OS, but instead just employ the binaries and libraries they need to support the application or application stack. They are managed by a container engine instead of a hypervisor and come in two flavors: application container or operating system container.

Many companies are now moving their virtualized infrastructure to a cloud service provider (CSP) who offers IaaS. A single virtual machine (called a *computing* or *cloud instance*) is managed via a management console (or portal). Multiple VMs can be provisioned through products like cloud-init and services such as elasticity. If needed, system admins can log into an instance using an SSH host key.

Review Questions

You can find the answers in the appendix.

1. What memory area does Linux use to store boot messages?
    A. BIOS
    B. GRUB boot loader
    C. MBR
    D. Initrd RAM disk
    E. Kernel ring buffer

2. Which of the following commands may allow you to examine the most recent boot messages? (Choose all that apply.)
    A. `less /var/log/kernel.log`
    B. `less /var/log/boot`
    C. `less /var/log/boot.log`
    D. `dmesg`
    E. `journalctl`

3. What program does a system's firmware start at boot time?
    A. A boot loader
    B. The BIOS program
    C. The UEFI program
    D. The POST command
    E. The `init` program

4. Where does the BIOS firmware first look for a Linux boot loader program?
    A. The `/boot/grub/` directory
    B. Master boot record (MBR)
    C. The `/var/log/` directory
    D. A boot partition
    E. The `/etc/` directory

5. The EFI System Partition (ESP) is stored in which directory on a Linux system?
    A. `/boot/`
    B. `/boot/grub/`
    C. `/boot/grub2/`
    D. `/boot/efi/`
    E. `/boot/esp/`

6. What file extension does UEFI bootloader files use?

   A. .cfg

   B. .uefi

   C. .lst

   D. .conf

   E. .efi

7. A system admin needs to view her GRUB Legacy configuration files. Where should she look?

   A. /boot/grub

   B. /boot/grub2

   C. /boot/efi

   D. /etc/grub

   E. /etc/grub2

8. An administrator wants to change one of his GRUB Legacy boot menu options displayed from Windows 10 to That Other OS. What word should start the line he should change in his GRUB Legacy configuration file ?

   A. hiddenmenu

   B. kernel

   C. title

   D. menuentry

   E. rootnoverify

9. What command must you run to install GRUB Legacy to the MBR?

   A. grub-mkconfig

   B. grub2-mkconfig

   C. update-grub

   D. grub-install

   E. No need to install

10. You need to specify the root partition in your GRUB2 configuration file. The /boot directory is on /dev/sdb2. What line would you include?

    A. root(hd1,2)

    B. set root=(hd1,2)

    C. set root= \

    D. root(hd1,1)

    E. set root=(hd1,1)

11. Rey is troubleshooting a startup problem on her Linux system that employs GRUB2. She would like to enable kernel debugging. What should she do when she reaches the GRUB2 boot menu?

    A. Edit the appropriate boot menu entry, find the line starting with linux*, go to the end of the line, add a space, and then type **debug** and press Ctrl+C.

    B. Select the appropriate GRUB 2 menu option, and then use the Force while GRUB2 is loading the correct Linux kernel.

    C. Edit the appropriate boot menu entry, find the line starting with linux*, go to the end of the line, add a space, and then type **debug** and press Ctrl+X.

    D. Edit the appropriate boot menu entry, find the line starting with kernel, go to the end of the line, add a space, and then type **debug** and press Ctrl+C.

    E. Edit the appropriate boot menu entry, find the line starting with kernel, go to the end of the line, add a space, and then type **debug** and press Ctrl+X.

12. Which of the following is true concerning systemd service units? (Choose all that apply.)

    A. Services can be started at system boot time.

    B. Services can be started in parallel.

    C. Backward compatibility to SysVinit runlevels is offered.

    D. A service can be started after all other services are started.

    E. A service can be prevented from starting at system boot time.

13. Which of the following is *not* a systemd target unit?

    A. runlevel7.target

    B. emergency.target

    C. graphical.target

    D. multi-user.target

    E. rescue.target

14. You need to modify a systemd service unit configuration. Where should the modified file be located?

    A. /etc/system/systemd/

    B. /usr/lib/system/systemd/

    C. /etc/systemd/system/

    D. /usr/lib/systemd/system/

    E. /run/system/systemd/

15. You have modified an openSSH service's configuration file, /etc/ssh/ssh_config. The service is already running. What is the best command to use with systemctl to make this modified file take immediate effect?

    A. reload

    B. daemon-reload

    C. restart

D. mask

E. unmask

16. You need to change the system's default target. What systemctl command should you use to accomplish this task?

A. get-default

B. set-default

C. isolate

D. is-enabled

E. is-active

17. Your older Debian-based Linux distribution system uses SysVinit. It soon is going to be upgraded to a Debian-based distro that uses systemd. To start some analysis, you enter the runlevel command. Which of the following are results you may see? (Choose all that apply.)

A. N 5

B. 3 5

C. N 2

D. 2 3

E. 1 2

18. You've recently become the system administrator for an older Linux server, which still uses SysVinit. You determine that its default runlevel is 3. What file did you find that information in?

A. /etc/inittab

B. /etc/rc.d

C. /etc/init.d/rc

D. /etc/rc.d/rc

E. /etc/rc.local

19. System administrator Luke is training an intern, Rey. Luke manages a systemd system whose users are primarily software developers and project leaders. He has planned a system reboot and informed the various system users via many methods several days in advance. However, before the system reboot, Luke wants to demonstrate to Rey how the wall command will notify some users, but not others. What command should he employ to show her which users will receive the wall messages?

A. systemctl reboot

B. shutdown -r now "System rebooting…"

C. reboot

D. who -T

E. mesg

20. Kilo has just cloned 10 VMs from a clone system image. He needs to ensure that the clones can all run together on the same local network segment. What items should he check and modify if needed? (Choose all that apply.)

    A. NIC MAC address

    B. VM template

    C. Host name

    D. CPU extensions

    E. Machine ID

Exam 102-500

Chapter

6

Configuring the GUI, Localization, and Printing

OBJECTIVES

A *graphical user interface* (GUI) is a set of programs that allow a user to interact with the computer system via icons, windows, and various other visual elements. While some believe that you should administer a system via the text-based command line only, it is still important to understand the Linux GUI (pronounced "gooey"). You may need to use certain GUI utilities to administer the system and its security.

Many end users prefer a graphical-based user interface (UI). Therefore, making sure your Linux systems meet their wants and needs is important. Different Linux distributions come with various default desktop environments, which you may need to install and manage for those users. Administering the underlying software that supports these interfaces is necessary too. In addition, because nowadays users rarely connect directly to the physical server, you need to understand remote desktops and their client/server model. Remote desktop interactions that travel over the network are prone to privacy problems, so it is crucial to secure these GUI transmissions. The various desktop environments, their supporting frameworks, and how to securely provide a remote desktop GUI are all topics covered in this chapter.

Another important feature in Linux is how it customizes things based on your location in the world. Linux must display dates and times, monetary values, and language characters, based on where in the world you are located. This chapter also covers how to set and customize your Linux system to handle and display values based on your location.

Finally, another method of retrieving data from your Linux system is printing. This chapter covers how to set up printing in your Linux system to interact with whatever printers are available in your environment.

Understanding the GUI

Many players are involved in providing a Linux system user interface. The desktop environment that you see on your monitor display is only a piece of this puzzle. Figure 6.1 is a rudimentary depiction of serving a GUI to a user.

As seen in Figure 6.1, the windows manager is an intermediary in this scenario. A *windows manager* is a program that communicates with the display server (sometimes called a windows server) on behalf of the UI. Each particular desktop environment has its own default window manager, such as Mutter, Kwin, Muffin, Marco, and Metacity.

FIGURE 6.1   Serving the GUI components

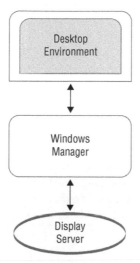

In this section, we will focus on the *display server*. The display server is a program that uses a communication protocol to transmit the desires of the UI to the operating system, and vice versa. The communication protocol, called the display server protocol, can operate over a network.

Another member in the display server team is the *compositor*. A compositor program arranges various display elements within a window to create a screen image to be passed back to the client.

> To understand a compositor program, it helps to look at history. In a time before computers were printing documents, compositors were people. Physical frames (called chases) were used to hold wooden blocks. These blocks had letters or images carved on them. A compositor would arrange the wooden blocks into the frames to make words and/or images. The compositor would hand the frames to the printer, who was also a person. The printer would put ink on the blocks and then press the frames onto paper. Thus, a printed document would result. A compositor program operates in a similar manner, except it is using multiple elements that are composed into a single screen image and handed off to the client.

Understanding the X11 Architecture

The *X Window System* (X for short) is the display server used for Linux systems. It was developed in the 1980s, so it has been around for a long time. This display server has endured the test of time.

Originally in Linux there was only one software package that supported X, called XFree86. However, in 2004 the XFree86 project changed their licensing requirements, which caused many Linux distributions to switch to the X.Org foundation's implementation of X, simply called *X.Org*.

The X.Org's display server fully implements the X Window System version 11 standards, including using the same configuration file format as the original XFree86 package. However, many distributions created their own customizations of the X.Org server; thus, you will see a wide variety of names concerning the Linux X display server, such as X.org-X11, X, X11, and X.Org Server. We'll use either X or X11 in this chapter.

Within the past few years, a new X display server package called *Wayland* has made headway in the Linux world. The Wayland package provides more advanced features that support newer display hardware and security, and supports additional types of input devices. Wayland is quickly gaining followers in the Linux world and may soon become the default display server used in most Linux distributions.

This section walks through the basics of both the X.Org and Wayland display servers.

Examining X.Org

The X.Org package keeps track of display card, monitor, and input device information in a configuration file, using the original XFree86 format. The primary configuration file is /etc/X11/xorg.conf, though the file is sometimes stored in the /etc/ directory. Typically, however, this file is no longer used. Instead, individual applications or devices store their own X11 settings in separate files stored in the /etc/X11/xorg.conf.d directory. When the X11 server boots, it reads the configuration settings stored in those files to customize how it interacts with different display cards, monitors, keyboards, mice, and other input or output devices.

Don't be surprised, though, if you go looking on your Linux system for either the xorg.conf file or the xorg.conf.d directory and don't find either of them. The X.Org software can create the session configuration on the fly using runtime auto-detection of the hardware involved with each GUI's session. These days, the X.Org software can detect most common hardware devices, so no manual configuration is required.

However, in some cases, auto-detection might not work properly, and you need to make X11 configuration changes. In this case, you can manually create the configuration file. To do this, shut down the X Server by going to a command prompt, using the command sudo telinit 3 (this usually works on both SysVinit and systemd systems), and using super user privileges to generate the file via the Xorg -configure command. The file, named xorg.conf.new, will be in your local directory. Make any necessary tweaks, rename the file, move the file to its proper location, and restart the X server.

The xorg.conf file has several sections. Each section contains important configuration information:

- Input Device: Configures the session's keyboard and mouse
- Monitor: Sets the session's monitor configuration
- Modes: Defines video modes

- `Device`: Configures the session's video card(s)
- `Screen`: Sets the session's screen resolution and color depth
- `Module`: Denotes any modules that need to be loaded
- `Files`: Sets file path names, if needed, for fonts, modules, and keyboard layout files
- `Server Flags`: Configures global X server options
- `Server Layout`: Links together all the session's input and output devices

Keep in mind that many desktop environments also provide dialog boxes in their UI, which allow you to configure your GUI X sessions. Most likely you will have no need to create or tweak the X11 configuration file. However, if you really want to dig into the X11 configuration file's details, view its man page via the `man 5 xorg.conf` command.

If you need to troubleshoot X problems, the X.Org package provides some help. If something goes wrong with the display process, the X.Org server generates the `.xsession-errors` file in your Home directory (often referred to as `~/.xsession-errors`). This is a standard text log file that indicates what went wrong with the X.Org server.

In addition, two utilities are available that can help: `xdpyinfo` and `xwininfo`. The `xdpyinfo` command provides information about the X.Org server, including the different screen types available, the default communicate parameter values, protocol extension information, and so on.

The `xwininfo` utility provides window information. If no options are given, an interactive utility asks you to click on the window for which you desire statistics. The displayed stats include location information, the window's dimensions (width and height), color map ID, and so on.

Be aware that the `xwininfo` command will hang if you are running a Wayland session instead of an X.Org session. Press Ctrl+C to exit out of the hung command.

If your X.Org session hangs for any reason, you can reset it by pressing the Ctrl+Alt+Backspace key combination. This restarts the X server, which will attempt to auto-detect the hardware again and generate the configuration file.

Figuring Out Wayland

Wayland is a replacement for the X.Org display server. It is designed to be simpler, more secure, and easier to develop and maintain than the X.Org software. Wayland specifically defines the communication protocol between a display server and its various clients. However, Wayland is also an umbrella term that covers the compositor, the window server, and the display server.

The Wayland protocol was initially released back in 2009, and it is now used by many current Linux desktop environments such as GNOME Shell and KDE Plasma. If you really want to dig down into Wayland, visit its website at https://wayland.freedesktop.org/.

Checking Your Display Server

If you are not sure what display server your desktop environment is currently using, X11 or Wayland, you can quickly determine the answer. The following steps will guide your discovery.

1. Log in to your system's GUI. This will start a GUI session for you.

2. Open a terminal emulator application.

3. Type **echo $WAYLAND_DISPLAY** at the command line and press the Enter key. If you get no response and just a command-line prompt back, most likely your system is using X11. If you receive a response, then your desktop environment is probably using Wayland. An additional test will help you ensure what is in use.

4. You need to get the GUI session number, so type **loginctl** and press Enter. Note the session number.

5. Type the command **loginctl show-session** *session-number* **-p Type** at the command line, where *session-number* is the number you obtained in the previous step. If you receive Type=Wayland, then your desktop environment is using Wayland. If instead you receive Type=X11, then your system is using the X11 display server.

The Wayland compositor is Weston. However, Weston provides a rather basic desktop experience. It was created as a Wayland compositor reference implementation. For those of you who are unfamiliar with the term *reference implementation*, it means that Weston was created to be a compositor requirements example for those developers who want to create their own Wayland compositor. Thus, Weston's core focus is correctness and reliability.

Wayland's compositor is swappable. In other words, you can use a different compositor if you need a more full-featured desktop experience. Several compositors are available for use with Wayland, including Arcan, Sway, Lipstick, and Clayland, to name a few. However, you may not need to go out and get a Wayland compositor. Many desktop environments create their own Wayland compositors, which is typically embedded within their windows manager. For example, Kwin and Mutter both fully handle Wayland compositor tasks.

If you have any legacy X11 applications that will not support Wayland, do not despair. There is the XWayland software, which is available in the Weston package. XWayland allows X-dependent applications to run on the X server and display via a Wayland session.

If your UI is using Wayland but you are having GUI issues, you can try a few trouble-shooting techniques. The following steps through some basic approaches.

Try the GUI without Wayland.   If your Linux distribution has multiple flavors of the desktop environment (with Wayland or with X11), log out of your GUI session and pick the desktop environment without Wayland. If your UI problems are resolved, then you know it has most likely something to do with Wayland.

If you do not have multiple flavors of the desktop environment and you are using the GNOME shell user interface, turn off Wayland by following these steps:

1. Using super user privileges, edit the /etc/gdm3/custom.conf file.

2. Remove the # from the #WaylandEnable=false line and save the file.

3. Reboot the system and log in to a GUI session and see if the problems are gone.

Check your system's graphics card.   If your system seems to be running fine under X11 but gets problematic when running under Wayland, check your graphics card. The easiest method is to go to the graphic card vendor's website and see if their drivers support Wayland. Many do, but there are a few famous holdouts that shall go unnamed here.

Use a different compositor.   If you are using a desktop environment's built-in compositor or one of the other compositors, try installing and using the Weston compositor package instead. Remember that Weston was built for reliability. If Weston is not in your distribution's software repository, you can get it from https://github.com/wayland-project/ Weston. This site also contains helpful documentation. If using Weston solves your GUI problem, then you have narrowed down the culprit.

 Be aware that some desktop environment commands won't work when you have a Wayland session. For example, if you are using GNOME Shell, the gnome-shell --replace command will do nothing but generate the message Window manager warning: Unsupported session type.

Managing the GUI

With some operating systems, your GUI is fairly rigid. You may be able to move or add a few icons, change a background picture, or tweak a few settings. However, with Linux, the GUI choices are almost overwhelming and the flexibility is immense.

This flexibility comes from lots of different components working together, with each one customizable in its own way. This section walks through the different components in the standard GUI environment.

Standard GUI Features

On Linux a GUI is a series of components that work together to provide the graphical setting for the UI. One of these components is the *desktop environment*. A desktop environment provides a pre-determined look and feel to the GUI. It is typically broken up into the following graphical sections and functions:

Desktop Settings   Desktop settings consist of programs that allow you to make configuration changes to the desktop environment. For example, you may want desktop windows to activate when the mouse hovers over them instead of when clicking on them.

Display Manager   The desktop environment's login screen is where you choose a username and enter a password to gain system access. If multiple desktop environments are installed on the system, the display manager allows you to choose between them prior to logging in. These login screens are often modified by corporations to contain a legal statement concerning appropriate use of the system and/or a company logo.

File Manager   This program allows you to perform file maintenance activities graphically. Often a folder icon is shown for directories within the manager program. You can perform such tasks as moving a file, viewing directory contents, copying files, and so on.

Icons   An icon is a picture representation of a file or program. It is activated via mouse clicks, finger touches (if the screen is a touchscreen), voice commands, and so on.

Favorites Bar   This window area contains popular icons, which are typically used more frequently. These icons can be removed or added as desired. Some desktop environments update the bar automatically as you use the system to reflect your regularly used icons.

Launch   This program allows you to search for applications and files. It can also allow certain actions, such as start or open, to be performed on the search results.

Menus   These window areas are typically accessed via an icon. They contain lists of files and/or programs, as well as sublists of additional file and/or program selections.

Panels   Panels are slim and typically rectangular areas located at the very top or bottom of a desktop environment's main window. They can also be at the desktop's far left or right. They often contain notifications, system date and/or time, program icons, and so on.

System Tray   A system tray is a special menu, commonly attached to a panel. It provides access to programs that allow users to log out, lock their screen, manage audio settings, view notifications, shut down or reboot the system, and so on.

Widgets   Widgets are divided into applets, screenlets, desklets, and so on. They are programs that provide the user information or functionality on the desktop. For example, current sports news may be displayed continually to a screenlet. Another example is a sticky note applet that allows users to put graphical windows on their desktop that look like sticky notes and add content to them.

Windows Manager   These client programs determine how the windows (also called frames) are presented on the desktop. These programs control items such as the size and appearance of the windows. They also manage how additional windows can be placed, such as either next to each other or overlapping.

Many Linux users are very passionate about the desktop environment they use—and for good reason. There are several excellent ones from which you can choose. We'll cover a few of these desktop environments in this chapter and look at universal accessibility to them as well.

The X GUI Login System

By default, when a Linux system boots, it presents a text login console. This works just fine for server environments but is somewhat lacking in today's desktop world. Most desktop users prefer some type of graphical login screen to appear, allowing them to select a graphical desktop environment (if more than one is available on the system), and log in using their user ID and password.

The display manager component is responsible for controlling the graphical login feature. Just about every desktop Linux distribution installs a display manager package that starts at boot time to present a graphical login environment. Every Linux display manager package uses the *X Display Manager Control Protocol (XDMCP)* to handle the graphical login process. Figure 6.2 shows the display manager used in Ubuntu.

FIGURE 6.2   The Ubuntu display manager login screen

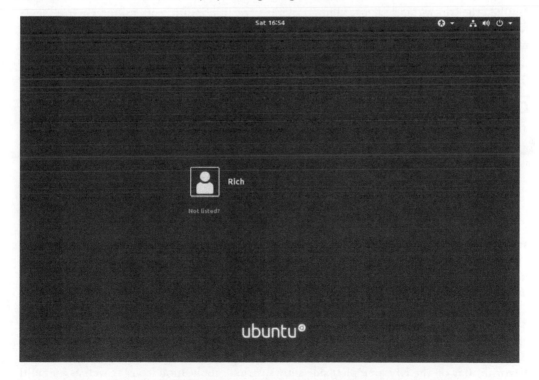

The *X Display Manager (XDM)* package is the basic display manager software available for Linux. It presents a generic user ID and password login screen, passing the login attempt off to the Linux system for verification. If the system authenticates the login attempt, XDM starts up the appropriate X server environment and Windows desktop environment.

Although the XDM display manager is somewhat generic, there are some configuration features you can modify to change things a bit. The main configuration file is /etc/X11/xdm/xdm-config. In most situations, you'll never need to modify any of these settings.

Most window managers create their own display manager and expand the capabilities of the XDM display manager. Here are a few of the more popular display managers you'll see:

- KDM: The default display manager used by the KDE desktop environment

- GDM: The default display manager used by the GNOME desktop environment

- LightDM: A bare-bones display manager used in lightweight desktop environments such as Xfce

Common Linux Desktop Environments

Unlike other operating systems, Linux provides a wealth of different desktop environments for you to choose from. While most Linux distributions focus on a single desktop environment, you're still free to install a different desktop environment yourself.

This section covers the most common desktop environments you'll encounter in the various Linux distributions.

Getting to Know GNOME

The GNOME desktop environment was created around the late 1990s. It is very popular and is found by default on Linux distributions such as CentOS and Ubuntu. Currently it is maintained by a large group of volunteers who belong to the GNOME Foundation. You can find out more about the GNOME project at www.gnome.org.

The year 2011 was a pivotal time in GNOME's history. GNOME 2 was a more traditional desktop user interface, and when GNOME 3 (now formally called GNOME Shell) was released in 2011, with its nontraditional interface, many users reacted strongly. This spurred a few GNOME project forks. However, over time and with a few changes, GNOME Shell gained ground. For those who still prefer the traditional desktop user interface that GNOME 2 provided, the GNOME Classic desktop environment is available.

Figure 6.3 shows a GNOME Shell desktop environment on an Ubuntu distribution.

Notice in Figure 6.3 that a panel is located at the GNOME Shell frame's top. The panel contains a clock as well as a system tray on the far right. The Activities button on the panel's far left allows you to switch between windows and provides the Search bar. The Favorites Bar on the UI frame's left side shows various application icons as well as an multi-dot icon, which is the Apps button. The Apps button displays various application icons that allow you to quickly access a desired program.

FIGURE 6.3   The GNOME Shell desktop environment

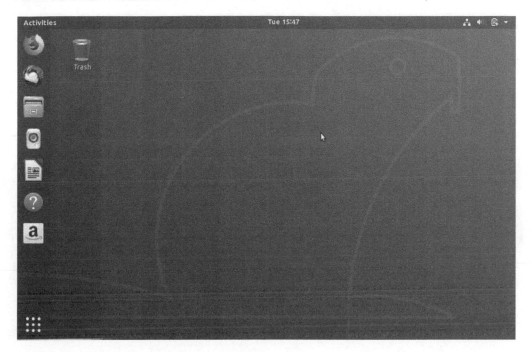

 Keep in mind that a default desktop environment may be modified slightly for each Linux distribution. For example, GNOME Shell on CentOS does not have a Favorites Bar displaying unless you click Activities in the panel, whereas GNOME Shell on Ubuntu automatically displays the Favorites Bar.

To better understand a particular graphical interface, try out a desktop environment for yourself. However, to help you with memorizing the assorted components making up these different desktops, we are providing tables where you can compare and contrast the distinct graphical environments. Some of the GNOME Shell's various components are briefly described in Table 6.1.

TABLE 6.1   GNOME Shell desktop environment default components

Name	Program name and/or description
Display Manager	GNOME Display Manager (GDM).
File Manager	GNOME Files (sometimes just called Files). Formerly called Nautilus.
Favorites Bar	GNOME Shell Dash (sometimes called the Dock).

TABLE 6.1 GNOME Shell desktop environment default components *(continued)*

Name	Program name and/or description
Panels	A single panel located at GNOME Shell frame's top.
System Tray	Located on the right-hand side of the single panel.
Windows Manager	Mutter.

An interesting feature of the GNOME Shell is that the panel, which contains the system tray, is available on the Display Manager as well as within the GNOME Shell.

Probing KDE Plasma

The Kool Desktop Environment (KDE) got its start in 1996, with its first version released in 1998. Through time, the name KDE was no longer just referring to a desktop environment, but instead it specified the project's organization and the strong community that supported it. KDE had many additional software projects besides its famous desktop environment. Thus, in 2009 KDE's desktop environment was rebranded as KDE Plasma. You can find out about the KDE group as well as its various products at www.kde.org.

Figure 6.4 shows a KDE Plasma desktop environment on an openSUSE Leap distribution.

FIGURE 6.4 The KDE Plasma desktop environment

In Figure 6.4, notice that the panel is located at the primary UI frame's bottom. This is a more traditional panel location used on older systems and one of the reasons KDE Plasma is known for being a good desktop environment for those who are new to Linux. On this panel, the system tray, which contains notifications, the time, and various other plasmoids (widgets), is located on the panel's right side. The Application menu, a launcher for various programs as well as containing the Favorites Bar, is on the panel's far-left side. Table 6.2 briefly describes some of the KDE Plasma components.

TABLE 6.2 KDE Plasma desktop environment default components

Name	Program name and/or description
Display Manager	SDDM (Simple Desktop Display Manager)
File Manager	Dolphin
Favorites Bar	Displayed inside Application menu
Panels	A single panel located at the Plasma frame's bottom
System Tray	Located on the right side of the single panel
Widgets	Called Plasmoids
Windows Manager	Kwin

To help those users who are familiar with accessing their files via folder icons, KDE Plasma offers a folder view. You can see folders depicted in the default UI on the openSUSE Leap distribution in Figure 6.4. These icons on the primary desktop window allow you to launch the Dolphin file manager and jump straight to the directory named on the folder icon.

Many desktop environments have multiple UIs available for each user called *workspaces*. Workspaces are individual desktops. For example, you can have two GUI apps open on one workspace and just a terminal emulator open on the other workspace. Switching between the workspaces can be done via mouse clicks or keystroke combinations, such as Ctrl+Alt+Up arrow or Down arrow on Fedora 28's Wayland desktop environment. Using multiple workspaces can be very handy, especially if you need to quickly look productive at work when your boss walks by.

Considering Cinnamon

The Cinnamon desktop environment got its start in 2011, when many users reacted strongly to the release of GNOME 3 (now GNOME Shell). Developers of the Mint Linux distribution began creating Cinnamon as a fork of GNOME 3. It was officially "GNOME-free" as of late 2013. Cinnamon is still managed by the Mint development team, and you can find out more at their website: www.linuxmint.com.

Cinnamon, like KDE Plasma, is known for being a good UI for those who are new to Linux. Figure 6.5 shows a Cinnamon desktop environment on a Fedora Workstation distribution.

FIGURE 6.5 The Cinnamon desktop environment

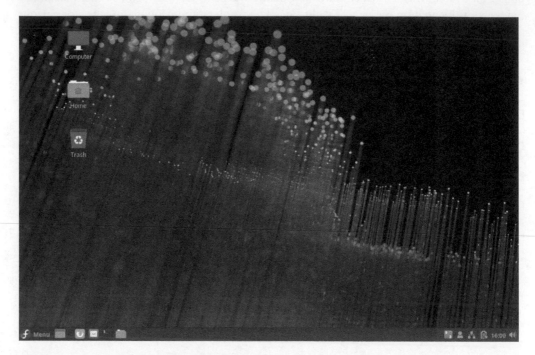

Notice in Figure 6.5 the bottom panel of the primary UI frame. On this panel, the system tray, which contains audio controls, the time, and various other widgets, is located on the panel's right side. The Menu, a launcher for various programs as well as containing the Favorites Bar, is on the panel's far-left side. Note that the Cinnamon panel also contains icons for quick launching.

If you want to install a Cinnamon desktop environment on one of the distributions you installed, we recommend you try it on Fedora 28 Workstation. Just follow these steps:

1. Use an account that has super user privileges. This is typically the account you set up during the system installation.

2. Access a terminal and enter the command **sudo dnf groupinstall -y "Cinnamon Desktop"** at the command line. Be sure to include the command's quotation marks.

3. When the installation is complete, reboot your system.

4. Access the Cinnamon desktop environment via a menu provided by the system's display manager's gear icon.

The Cinnamon desktop environment layout should be somewhat familiar, because it is very similar to the KDE Plasma default layout. They both have folder icons on the main UI windows. Table 6.3 briefly describes some of the Cinnamon components.

TABLE 6.3   Cinnamon desktop environment default components

Name	Program name and/or description
Display Manager	LightDM
File Manager	Nemo (a fork of Nautilus)
Favorites Bar	Displayed inside Application menu
Panels	A single panel (called the Cinnamon panel) located at the Cinnamon frame's bottom
System Tray	Located on the right side of the single panel
Widgets	Cinnamon Spices
Windows Manager	Muffin (a fork of GNOME Shell's Mutter)

The Cinnamon Spices go beyond just applets and desklets for modifying your desktop environment. They also include themes and extensions that you can download and install to make your Cinnamon UI experience truly unique. The official Cinnamon Spices repository is at https://cinnamon-spices.linuxmint.com/.

Making Acquaintance with MATE

The MATE desktop environment also got its start in 2011, when GNOME 3 (now GNOME Shell) was released. It was started by an Arch Linux distribution user who resides in Argentina. Pronounced Ma-Tay, this desktop environment was officially released only two months after it was announced and was derived from GNOME 2. The desktop environment is available on a wide variety of Linux distributions, such as Arch Linux, Debian, Fedora, Ubuntu, Linux Mint, and so on.

 MATE is named after a tea made from a plant's dried leaves. The plant (Ilex paraguariensis) is native to South America. Mate tea is the national drink of Argentina. It is purported to have the health benefits of tea as well as provide mental alertness similar to drinking coffee.

If you've ever used the old GNOME 2 desktop environment, MATE will feel very familiar. Figure 6.6 shows a MATE desktop environment on an Ubuntu Desktop distribution.

FIGURE 6.6 The MATE desktop environment

In Figure 6.6 there are two panels in the MATE desktop environment. One is at the primary UI frame's top, and the other is at its bottom. The system tray, which contains audio controls, the time, and various other widgets, is located on the top panel's right side. Applications, a menu-driven launcher for various programs, is on the top panel's far-left side. Note that this top panel also contains icons for quick launching.

If you want to install a MATE desktop environment on one of the distributions you installed in Chapter 1, we recommend you try it on Ubuntu Desktop 18-04. Use an account that has super user privileges. This is typically the account you set up during the system installation. Access a terminal and enter the command **sudo apt-get update** at the command line to update your system's repositories. When you get a prompt back, install the tasksel program. The tasksel program is a graphical utility that installs multiple related packages as a harmonized process. In other words, it makes installing certain packages with lots of dependencies easy. To install it, follow these steps:

1. Type **sudo apt-get install tasksel** at the command line.

2. Enter **sudo tasksel install ubuntu-mate-desktop** to install the MATE desktop environment.

3. When the installation is complete, reboot your system.

4. You can access the MATE desktop environment via a menu provided by the system's display manager's gear icon.

On the MATE desktop environment's bottom panel, in the lower-left corner you'll see the Show Desktop Button icon. This is handy if you have several windows open in the main UI frame. Just click the Show Desktop Button icon and all the windows currently open will be hidden to the lower panel. You can restore all the windows on the lower panel simply by clicking the Show Desktop Button icon again. Table 6.4 briefly describes some of the MATE components.

TABLE 6.4 MATE desktop environment default components

Name	Program name and/or description
Display Manager	LightDM.
File Manager	Caja (a fork of Nautilus).
Favorites Bar	A Favorites Menu is used instead and is accessed via the Applications menu–driven launcher.
Panels	One panel at the bottom of the MATE frame and the other panel at the top of the MATE UI.
System Tray	Located on the right side of the top panel.
Windows Manager	Marco (a fork of Metacity).

You can add additional widgets to your MATE UI's top panel. Just right-click the panel, and from the drop-down menu, select Add To Panel. This will open a window of applets you can install.

Going Bare-Bones with Xfce

One drawback to the fancier Linux graphical desktops is that they require a fair amount of CPU and memory resources to operate. In the past, Linux was known to give new life to old hardware, often running on systems that Windows or macOS couldn't. However, with the fancier graphical desktops in Linux, that is no longer the case.

However, as with all things Linux, you have more choices. There are several low-end graphical desktops that run perfectly fine with minimal resources. Of these, the most popular is the Xfce graphical desktop.

The Xfce desktop was developed in 1996 as an extension of the UNIX Common Desktop Environment (CDE) using the XForms graphical toolkit (that's where the "Xf" part of the name comes from). Over the years, Xfce has been rewritten and no longer uses code from XForms or CDE, but it has remained a solid lightweight graphical desktop for the Linux world. Figure 6.7 shows the standard Xfce desktop as used in the XUbuntu Linux distribution.

FIGURE 6.7   The Xfce desktop used in the XUbuntu Linux distribution

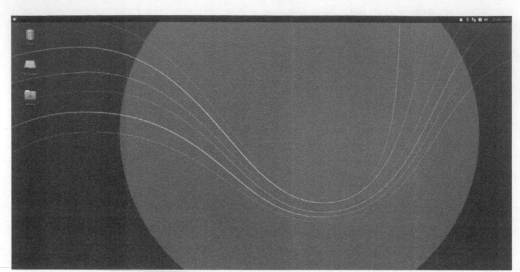

For the XUbuntu distribution, the Xfce desktop has been designed to mimic the basic features of the standard Ubuntu GNOME desktop but with some limited functionality. Table 6.5 lists the features available in the XUbuntu Xfce desktop.

TABLE 6.5   Xfce desktop environment default components

Name	Program name and/or description
Display Manager	LightDM
File Manager	Thunar
Favorites Bar	A single icon at the left side of the panel; displays favorites, recent applications, and the application menu
Panels	A single panel located at the top of the window
System Tray	A set of icons on the right side of the panel
Windows Manager	The specialized Xfwm, which utilizes its own compositor manager

Although you won't find a lot of fancy features in Xfce, if you need to run a Linux distribution on older hardware, the Xfce desktop environment will most likely work just fine and give new life to your old hardware.

Providing Accessibility

In a GUI environment, accessibility deals with a user's ability to use the desktop environment. While the default desktop environment provided by a Linux distribution works for many people, accessibility settings allow the accommodation of all potential users. This includes individuals who may have vision impairment, who have concerns with using the mouse, who deal with finger movement issues, and so on. It's important to know the desktop environment configurations for these accommodations so that you can help to provide access for all.

Each desktop environment will provide slightly different methods for configuring accessibility. But most settings can be accomplished through desktop environment control panels, such as the Universal Access panel in GNOME Shell settings.

Even though most desktop environments provide differently named accessibility control panels, you can usually quickly find the panels using the environment's search facilities. Good search terms include **universal access, accessibility**, and **assistive technologies**.

Figure 6.8 shows the Universal Access menu opened from the UI top panel. You can find more accessibility settings in the access control panel by searching for **universal access** in the GNOME Shell's search feature.

FIGURE 6.8   Universal access top panel menu in GNOME Shell

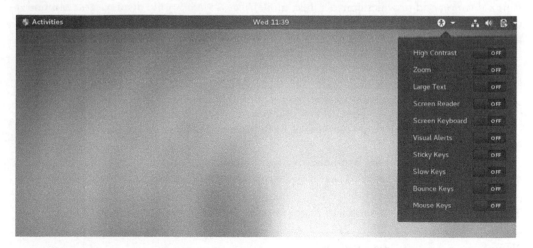

For users who are seriously visually impaired or who just have poor eyesight, several accessibility settings are available that may help. Table 6.6 describes common visual impairment settings.

TABLE 6.6 Common visual impairment accessibility settings

Name	Description
Cursor Blinking	Modifies the cursor blink rate to make it easier to locate the cursor on the screen.
Cursor Size	Modifies the cursor size.
High Contrast	Increases the windows' and buttons' brightness and darkens window edges as well as text and the cursor.
Large Text	Modifies the font size, often called a screen magnifier.
Screen Reader	Uses a screen reader to read the UI aloud. Popular choices include Orca screen reader and Emacspeak.
Sound Keys	Beeps when Caps Lock or Num Lock is turned on (off). Also called toggle keys.
Zoom	Amplifies the screen or a screen portion to different magnification levels.

If a blind user has access to a braille display, you can install the `brltty` package, which is available in most Linux distributions' repositories. The `brltty` package operates as a Linux daemon and provides console (text mode) access via a braille display. You can find out more about this software at its official headquarters, `http://mielke.cc/brltty/`. Be aware that you can also use the Orca screen reader with a refreshable braille display.

 If you are not able to hear sound alerts on your Linux system, you can enable visual alerts. Then, if something occurs that normally produces a sound, a visual flash is performed instead. You can set the visual alert to flash a single window or flash the entire display.

For those users who have hand and/or finger impairments, there are several accessibility settings to allow full functional use of the system. Common settings are listed in Table 6.7.

TABLE 6.7 Common hand and finger impairment accessibility settings

Name	Description
Bounce Keys	Keyboard option that helps to compensate for single keys accidentally pressed multiple times.
Double-Click Delay	Mouse option that modifies the amount of time allowed between double mouse clicks.

Name	Description
Gestures	Mouse option that activates programs and/or options by combining both mouse clicks and keyboard presses.
Hover Click	Mouse option that triggers a mouse click when the pointer is hovered over an item.
Mouse Keys	Mouse option that allows you to use keyboard keys to emulate the mouse functions.
Repeat Keys	Keyboard option that modifies how long a key must be pressed down as well as a delay to acknowledge the key repeat. Also called keyboard repeat rate.
Screen Keyboard	Keyboard option that displays a visual keyboard on the UI that can be manipulated by a mouse or other pointing device to emulate keystrokes.
Simulated Secondary Click	Mouse option that sets a primary key to be pressed along with a mouse click to emulate secondary mouse clicks.
Slow Keys	Keyboard option that modifies how long a key must be pressed down to acknowledge the key.
Sticky Keys	Keyboard option that sets keyboard modifier keys, such as Ctrl and Shift, to maintain their pressed status until a subsequent key is pressed.

AccessX was a program that provided many of the options in Table 8.6. Thus, you will often see it referred to in the accessibility control panels, such as in the Typing Assist (AccessX) option. One interesting AccessX setting is Enable By Keyboard, which allows you to turn on or off accessibility settings via keystrokes on the keyboard.

Using X11 for Remote Access

The X11 system utilizes a classic client/server model for serving up graphical desktops. In most situations, the client and server both run on the same physical device, but that doesn't need to be the case. You can have a remote X11 client connect to the X11 server to display the graphical desktop on a remote system.

There are several different techniques for implementing remote connections of X11 desktop environments. This section walks through the most popular ones.

Remote X11 Connections

The simplest way to run an X11 desktop remotely is to just forward the standard X11 desktop protocol stream across the network to the remote client. For example, assume the host workstation1 is located in a remote area but you need to run a graphical program from it using your local host, called workstation2. Follow these steps to accomplish that:

1. Log in to the workstation2 host using the standard graphical desktop environment.

2. Open a terminal session to obtain a command prompt.

3. Type **xhost +*workstation1***, where ***workstation1*** is either the hostname of the remote workstation1 host or its IP address. The xhost command allows the client workstation to receive data from the sending remote workstation.

4. Log in to the remote host workstation2 using a secure shell (SSH) connection. This will provide a standard text command prompt interface.

5. At the command prompt, type **export DISPLAY=*workstation2*:0.0**, where **workstation2** is the hostname or IP address of your local workstation. This command redirects any graphical output generated on the remote workstation1 to the local workstation2 X server.

6. Launch a graphical application from the command prompt on workstation1. The graphical desktop will appear as a new window in your local workstation2 desktop.

7. When you're done, close the launched program and type **xhost -workstation1** on your local workstation2 host to remove the permissions to receive data from the remote host.

> Besides the xhost command, you may need to allow connections through any firewall software running on your Linux system. The X11 desktop uses TCP ports in the range of 6000 to 6063. Also, the xhost command allows X connections from remote hosts to your local workstation only for the current session. If you regularly send graphical windows from a specific remote host to your local workstation, you can add the entry to the X11 server configuration files. The xauth command allows you to add, remove, and list remote hosts in the X11 configuration file.

Tunneling Your X11 Connection

Another method that provides remote GUI interactions within a secure tunnel is *X11 forwarding*. X11 forwarding allows you to interact with various X11-based graphical utilities on a remote system through an encrypted network connection. This method is enacted using the openSSH service.

First you need to check to see if X11 forwarding is permitted. This setting is in the openSSH configuration file, /etc/ssh/sshd_config. The directive X11Forwarding should be set to yes in the remote system's configuration file. If the directive is set to no, then you must modify it to employ X11 forwarding. In Listing 6.1 a check is performed on the configuration file for this directive on a CentOS distribution.

Listing 6.1: Checking the `AllowTCPForwarding` directive

```
# grep "X11Forwarding yes" /etc/ssh/sshd_config
X11Forwarding yes
#
```

After you have made any necessary configuration file modifications, the command to use is ssh -X *user@remote-host*. Similar to earlier ssh command uses, the *user* is the user account that resides on the *remote-host* system. The *remote-host* has the GUI utilities you wish to employ and can be designated via an IP address or a hostname. Figure 6.9 shows connecting from a remote Fedora client to a CentOS server and using a graphical utility on that server.

FIGURE 6.9   Forwarding X11

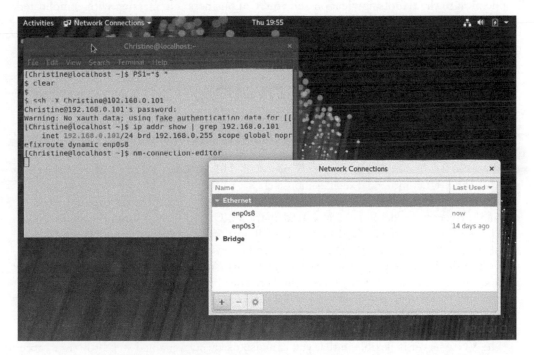

It's always a good idea to check your IP address to ensure you have successfully reached the remote system. In Figure 6.9, the ip addr show command is employed for this purpose. After you have completed your work, just type **exit** to log out of the X11 forwarding session.

You may read about using X11 forwarding via the ssh -Y command, which is called trusted X11. This does not mean the connection is more secure. In fact, it is quite the opposite. When employing this command, you are treating the remote server as a trusted system. This approach can cause many security issues and should be avoided.

Using Remote Desktop Software

While using the built-in client/server feature of X11 is nice, it can be a bit cumbersome. Fortunately, there's a whole crop of remote desktop applications available in Linux that do the hard work for us.

Remote desktop software uses a client/server model to provide a server application on a remote host and a client application on a local host. All you need to do is point the client application to the remote application and you're in business. No messing with complicated forwarding or tunneling schemes.

In this section we will take a look at some of common remote desktop implementations for Linux. They include VNC, Xrdp, NX, and SPICE.

Viewing VNC

Virtual network computing (VNC) was developed by the Olivetti & Oracle Research Lab, which has since closed down. Many of the original developers now continue work on the VNC software from a company called RealVNC. The VNC software is multiplatform and employs the Remote Frame Buffer (RFB) protocol. This protocol allows a user on the client side to send GUI commands, such as mouse clicks, to the server. The server sends desktop frames back to the client's monitor. RealVNC Ltd., which consists of the original VNC original project team developers, now trademark VNC.

The VNC server offers a GUI service at TCP port $5900 + n$, where n equals the display number, usually 1 (port 5901). On the command line you point the VNC client (called a viewer) to the VNC server's hostname and TCP port. Alternatively, you can use the display number instead of the whole TCP port number. The client user is required to enter a predetermined password, which is for the VNC server and not Linux system authentication. After the client user has authenticated with VNC, the user is served up the desktop environment's display manager output so that system authentication can take place.

The VNC server is flexible in that you can also use a Java-enabled web browser to access it. It provides that service at TCP port $5800 + n$. HTML5 client web browsers are supported as well.

Two types of desktop UIs are available for VNC clients: persistent and static. Persistent desktops are UIs that do not change when presented. This is similar to a local desktop experience: the user has certain windows open, the user locks the screen and engages in an activity away from the local system, the user comes back and unlocks the screen, and the user finds the GUI in the exact same state it was left in. Persistent desktops are available only via web browser access. Static desktops do not provide a saved-state GUI. When you come back to the desktop, you won't see any of your open windows but instead the default desktop environment.

The following are positive benefits when using VNC:

- It has lots of flexibility in providing remote desktops.
- Desktops are available for multiple users.
- Both persistent and static desktops are available.
- It can provide desktops on an on-demand basis.
- An SSH tunnel can be employed via ssh or a client viewer command-line option to encrypt traffic.

The following are potential difficulties or concerns with VNC:

- The VNC server handles only mouse movements and keystrokes. It does not deal with file and audio transfer or printing services for the client.
- VNC, by default, does not provide traffic encryption, so you must employ another means of protection, such as tunneling through openSSH.
- The VNC server password is stored as plaintext in a server file.

Besides VNC, there are alternatives that implement the VNC technology. A popular implementation of VNC for Linux is TigerVNC. The TigerVNC website is at https:// tigervnc.org/. It also works on Windows, so you can connect to either a remote Linux or Windows system. For installing the server on a Linux system, use the tigervnc-server package name. You'll need to perform some setup to prepare for clients and configure the server to provide the proper client requirements. You can find several excellent tutorials on the web. If you want to install the VNC client, just use the tigervnc package name.

When accessing a remote desktop via commands at the command line, be sure to use a terminal emulator in the GUI environment. If you attempt to use a text-mode terminal outside the GUI to issue these commands, you will not be successful.

When you have the TigerVNC server installed, you control it with the vncserver and vncconfig commands. After making the appropriate server firewall modifications, the client can use the vncviewer command to connect to the server system and get a remote desktop. For example, a server (example.com) has been configured properly to serve a remote desktop to you at display number 1. You would access the desktop from another system via the vncviewer example.com:1 command. Figure 6.10 shows a TigerVNC connection from a Fedora system into a CentOS server, which is providing the user a GNOME Shell desktop environment.

FIGURE 6.10   Using TigerVNC

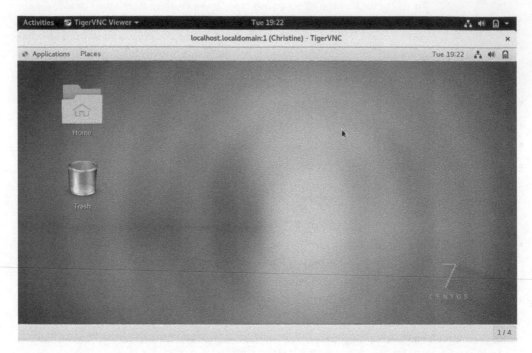

When configuring your VNC server, be sure to employ openSSH port forwarding for the VNC server ports (covered later in this chapter). Also configure your firewalls to allow traffic through port 22 (or whatever port number you are using for SSH traffic).

Grasping Xrdp

Xrdp is an alternative to VNC. It supports the Remote Desktop Protocol (RDP) and uses X11rdp or Xvnc to manage the GUI session.

Xrdp provides only the server side of an RDP connection. It allows access from several RDP client implementations, such as rdesktop, FreeFDP, and Microsoft Remote Desktop Connection.

Xrdp comes systemd-ready, so you can simply install, enable, and start the server using the systemctl commands. The package name on Linux is xrdp. Note that it may not be in your Linux distribution's standard repositories.

After installing and starting the Xrdp server, adjust the firewall so that traffic can access the standard RDP port (TCP 3389). Now direct your RDP client choice to the server via its hostname or IP address, and if necessary, provide the client the RDP port number.

Depending on your RDP client, you may be presented with a screen that denotes that the server is not trusted. If this is the server you just set up, you are fine to continue. You will need to enter the Linux system's user authentication information, but the login screen depends on the Xrdp client software you are using. An example of Xrdp in action is shown in Figure 6.11.

FIGURE 6.11   Using Xrdp

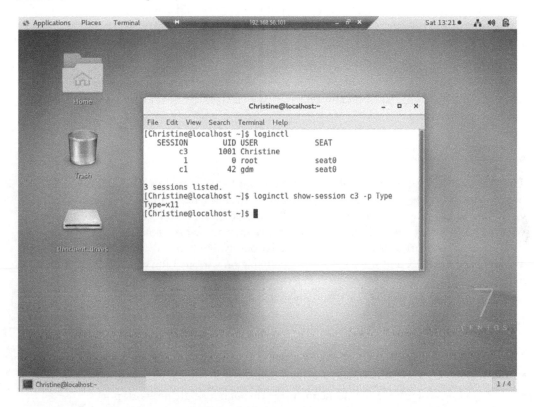

Figure 6.11 shows a connection from a Windows 10 system to a CentOS 7 Linux server, which is running the Xrdp server. Notice the output from the commands run in the terminal emulator. You can see that an X11 session is being deployed.

The following are positive benefits of using Xrdp:

- Xrdp uses RDP, which encrypts its traffic using Transport Layer Security (TLS).

- A wide variety of open source RDP client software is available.

- You can connect to an already existing connection to provide a persistent desktop.

- The Xrdp server handles mouse movements and keystrokes as well as with audio transfers and mounting of local client drives on the remote system.

You can determine the various Xrdp configuration settings in the /etc/xrdp/xrdp.ini file. An important setting in this file is the security_layer directive. If set to negotiate, the default, the Xrdp server will negotiate with the client for the security method to use. Three methods are available:

- tls: Provides SSL (TLS 1.0) encryption for server authentication and data transfer. Be aware that this falls short of the encryption level needed for compliance with the Payment Card Industry (PCI) standards.

- negotiate: Sets the security method to be the highest the client can use. This is problematic if the connection is over a public network and the client must use the standard RDP security method.

- Rdp: Sets the security method to standard RDP security. This method is not safe from man-in-the-middle attacks.

Xrdp is fairly simple to use. Also, because so many Windows-oriented users are already familiar with Remote Desktop Connection, it typically does not take long to employ it in the office environment.

Exploring NX

The NX protocol, sometimes called NX technology, was created by NoMachine (www.nomachine.com) around 2001. NX is another remote desktop sharing protocol. Its v3.5's core technology was open source and available under the GNU GPL2 license. Yet, when version 4 was released, NX became proprietary and closed source.

However, there are several open source variations available based on the NX3 technology. They include FreeNX and X2Go. Both are available on various Linux distributions but not necessarily in their default software repositories.

The following are positive benefits of using NX products:

- They provide excellent response times even over low-bandwidth connections that have high-latency issues.

- They are faster than VNC-based products.

- They use openSSH tunneling by default, so traffic is encrypted.

- They support multiple simultaneous users through a single network port.

NX technology compresses the X11 data so that there is less data to send over the network, which improves response times. It also heavily employs caching data to provide an improved remote desktop experience.

Studying SPICE

Another interesting remote connection protocol is Simple Protocol for Independent Computing Environments (SPICE). Originally it was a closed source product developed by Qumranet in 2007. However, Red Hat purchased Qumranet in 2008 and made SPICE open source. Its website is here: www.spice-space.org.

SPICE (sometimes written as Spice, as we will from this point on) was developed to provide a good remote desktop product that would allow connections to your various virtual machines. Now, typically Spice is used for providing connections with KVM virtual machines, moving into VNC's territory.

 Both VNC and Spice provide remote desktop connections to KVM virtual machines, commonly used in cloud environments.

Spice is platform independent and has some very nice additional features as well. They include:

- Spice's client side uses multiple data socket connections, and you can have multiple clients.

- Spice delivers desktop experience speeds similar to a local connection.

- Spice consumes low amounts of CPU, so you can use it with various servers that have multiple virtual machines and not adversely affect their performance.

- Spice allows high-quality video streaming.

- Spice provides live migration features, which means there are no connection interruptions if the virtual machine is being migrated to a new host.

While Spice has a single server implementation, it has several client implementations. These include remote-viewer and GNOME Boxes.

Another benefit of employing Spice is its strong security features. Transmitted data can be sent plaintext or traffic can be encrypted using TLS. Authentication between the Spice client and remote Spice server is implemented using Simple Authentication and Security Layer (SASL). This framework allows various authentication methods, as long as they are supported by SASL. Kerberos is a supported method.

If you are still dealing with X11, you can use X.Org-created Xspice to act as a stand-alone Spice server as well as an X server.

Understanding Localization

The world is full of different languages. Not only does each country have its own language (or sometimes, sets of languages), but each country also has its own way in which people write numerical values, monetary values, and the time and date. For a Linux system to be useful in any specific location, it must adapt to the local way of doing all those things.

Localization is the ability to adapt a Linux system to a specific locale. To accomplish this, the Linux system must have a way to identify how to handle the characters contained in the local language. This section discusses just how Linux does that.

Character Sets

At their core, computers work with ones and zeros, and Linux is no different. However, for a computer to interact with humans, it needs to know how to speak our language. This is where character sets come in.

A *character set* defines a standard code used to interpret and display characters in a language. Quite a few different character sets are used in the world for representing characters. The most common ones you'll run into (and the ones you'll see on the LPIC-1 exam) are as follows:

- *ASCII*: The American Standard Code for Information Interchange (ASCII) uses 7 bits to store characters found in the English language.

- *ISO-8859*: The International Organization for Standardization (ISO) worked with the International Electrotechnical Commission (IEC) to produce a series of standard codes for handling international characters. There are 15 separate standards (ISO-8859-1 through ISO-8859-15) for defining different character sets.

- *Unicode*: The Unicode Consortium, composed of many computing industry companies, created an international standard that uses a 3-byte code and can represent every character known to be in use in all countries of the world.

- *UTF*: The Unicode Transformation Format (UTF) transforms the long Unicode values into either 1-byte (*UTF-8*) or 2-byte (*UTF-16*) simplified codes. For work in English-speaking countries, the UTF-8 character set is replacing ASCII as the standard.

When you've decided on a character set for your Linux system, you'll need to know how to configure your Linux system to use it, which is shown in the following section.

Environment Variables

Linux stores locale information in a special set of environment variables (see Chapter 9). Programs that need to determine the locale of the Linux system just need to retrieve the appropriate environment variable to see what character set to use.

Linux provides the *locale* command to help you easily display these environment variables. Listing 6.2 shows the locale environment variables as set on a CentOS system installed in the United States.

Listing 6.2: The Linux `locale` environment variables

```
$ locale
LANG=en_US.UTF-8
LC_CTYPE="en_US.UTF-8"
LC_NUMERIC="en_US.UTF-8"
LC_TIME="en_US.UTF-8"
LC_COLLATE="en_US.UTF-8"
LC_MONETARY="en_US.UTF-8"
LC_MESSAGES="en_US.UTF-8"
LC_PAPER="en_US.UTF-8"
LC_NAME="en_US.UTF-8"
LC_ADDRESS="en_US.UTF-8"
LC_TELEPHONE="en_US.UTF-8"
LC_MEASUREMENT="en_US.UTF-8"
LC_IDENTIFICATION="en_US.UTF-8"
LC_ALL=
$
```

The output of the `locale` command defines the localization information in the format

language_country.character set

In the example shown in Listing 6.2, the Linux system is configured for United States English, using the UTF-8 character set to store characters.

The *LC_* environment variables themselves each represent a category of more environment variables that relate to the locale settings. You can explore the environment variables contained within a category by using the -ck option, along with the category name, as shown in Listing 6.3.

Listing 6.3: The detailed settings for the LC_MONETARY localization category

```
$ locale -ck LC_MONETARY
LC_MONETARY
int_curr_symbol="USD "
currency_symbol="$"
mon_decimal_point="."
mon_thousands_sep=","
mon_grouping=3;3
positive_sign=""
negative_sign="-"
...
monetary-decimal-point-wc=46
monetary-thousands-sep-wc=44
monetary-codeset="UTF-8"
$
```

The environment variables shown in Listing 6.3 control what characters and formats are used for representing monetary values. Programmers can fine-tune each of the individual environment variables to customize exactly how their programs behave within the locale.

Setting Your Locale

There are three components to how Linux handles localization. A locale defines the language, the country, and the character set the system uses. Linux provides a few different ways for you to change each of these localization settings. This section shows how to do that.

Installation Locale Decisions

When you first install the Linux operating system, one of the prompts available during the install process is for the default system language. Figure 6.12 shows the prompt from a CentOS 7 installation.

FIGURE 6.12   The language option in a CentOS installation

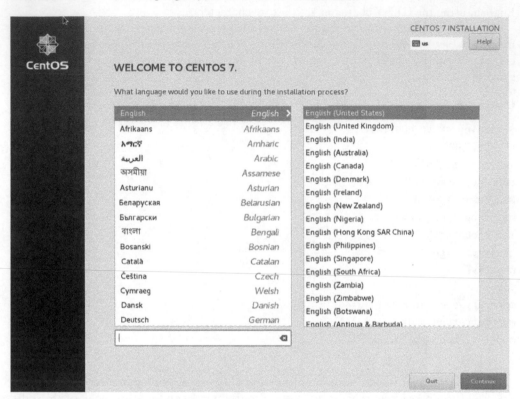

When you select a language from the menu, the Linux installation script automatically sets the localization environment variables appropriately for that country and language to include the character set required to represent the required characters. Often that's all you need to do to set up your Linux system to operate correctly in your locale.

Changing Your Locale

After you've already installed the Linux operating system, you can still change the localization values that the system uses. Two methods are available that let you do that. You can manually set the LC_ environment variables, or you can use the localectl command.

Manually Changing the Environment Variables

For the manual method, change the individual LC_ localization environment variables just as you would any other environment variable by using the export command:

```
$ export LC_MONETARY=en_GB.UTF-8
```

That works well for changing individual settings, but doing so would be tedious if you wanted to change the entire localization for the system.

Instead of having to change all of the LC_ environment variables individually, the LANG environment variable controls all of them at one place:

```
$ export LANG=en_GB.UTF-8
$ locale
LANG=en_GB.UTF-8
LC_CTYPE="en_GB.UTF-8"
LC_NUMERIC="en_GB.UTF-8"
LC_TIME="en_GB.UTF-8"
LC_COLLATE="en_GB.UTF-8"
LC_MONETARY="en_GB.UTF-8"
LC_MESSAGES="en_GB.UTF-8"
LC_PAPER="en_GB.UTF-8"
LC_NAME="en_GB.UTF-8"
LC_ADDRESS="en_GB.UTF-8"
LC_TELEPHONE="en_GB.UTF-8"
LC_MEASUREMENT="en_GB.UTF-8"
LC_IDENTIFICATION="en_GB.UTF-8"
LC_ALL=
$
```

Some Linux systems require that you also set the LC_ALL environment variable, so it's usually a good idea to set that along with the LANG environment variable.

> This method changes the localization for your current login session. If you need to permanently change the localization, you'll need to add the export command to the .bashrc file in your $HOME folder so that it runs each time you log in.

The *localectl* Command

If you're using a Linux distribution that utilizes the systemd set of utilities, you have the localectl command available. By default, the *localectl* command just displays the current localization settings:

```
$ localectl
   System Locale: LANG=en_US.UTF-8
       VC Keymap: us
      X11 Layout: us
$
```

Not only does it show the LANG environment variable setting, but it also shows the keyboard layout mapping, as well as the X11 graphical environment layout.

The localectl command supports many options, but the most common are to list all of the locales installed on your system with the list-locales option and to change the localization by using the set-locale option:

```
$ localectl set-locale LANG=en_GB.utf8
```

That makes for an easy way to change the localization settings for your entire Linux system.

If you just need to convert a file stored using one character set to another character set, use the handy iconv command-line tool.

Looking at Time

The date and time associated with a Linux system are crucial to the proper operation of the system. Linux uses the date and time to keep track of running processes, to know when to start or stop jobs, and to log important events that occur. Having your Linux system coordinated with the correct time and date for your location is a must.

Linux handles the time as two parts: the time zone associated with the location of the system and the actual time and date within that time zone. This section walks through how to change both values.

Working with Time Zones

One of the most important aspects of time is the *time zone*. Each country selects one or more time zones, or offsets from the standard Coordinated Universal Time (UTC) time, to determine time within the country. If your Linux environment includes having servers located in different time zones, knowing how to set the proper time zone is critical.

Most Debian-based Linux systems define the local time zone in the */etc/timezone* file, whereas most Red Hat–based Linux systems use */etc/localtime*. These files are not in a text format, so you can't simply edit the /etc/timezone or /etc/localtime file to view or change your time zone. Instead, you must copy a template file stored in the */usr/share/zoneinfo* folder.

To determine the current time zone setting for your Linux system, use the date command, with no options:

```
$ date
Fri Aug  2 05:52:29 EDT 2019
$
```

The time zone appears as the standard three-letter code at the end of the date and time display, before the year.

To change the time zone for a Linux system, copy or link the appropriate time zone template file from the /usr/share/zoneinfo folder to the /etc/timezone or /etc/localtime location. The /usr/share/zoneinfo folder is divided into subfolders based on location. Each location folder may also be subdivided into more detailed location folders. Eventually, you'll see a time zone template file associated with your specific time zone, such as /usr/share/zoneinfo/US/Eastern.

> If you don't know the formal name of your time zone, run the tzselect command from the command prompt. It determines your timezone value based on answers to several location questions.

Before you can copy the new time zone file, you'll need to remove the original timezone or localtime file:

```
$ sudo mv /etc/localtime /etc/localtime.bak
$ sudo ln -s /usr/share/zoneinfo/US/Pacific /etc/localtime

$ date
Fri Aug  2 02:55:28 PDT 2019
$
```

The new time zone appears in the output from the date command.

> If you just need to change the time zone for a single session or program, instead of changing the system time zone you can set the time zone using the TZ environment variable. That overrides the system time zone for the current session.

Setting the Time and Date

After you have the correct time zone for your Linux system, you can work on setting the correct time and date values. A few different commands are available to do that.

Legacy Commands

There are two legacy commands that you should be able to find in all Linux distributions for working with time and date values:

- *hwclock*: Displays or sets the time as kept on the internal BIOS or UEFI clock on the workstation or server
- *date*: Displays or sets the date as kept by the Linux system

The hwclock command provides access to the hardware clock built into the physical workstation or server that the Linux system runs on. You can use the hwclock command to set the system time and date to the hardware clock on the physical workstation or server. It also allows you to change the hardware clock to match the time and date on the Linux system.

The date command is the Swiss army knife of time and date commands. It allows you to display the time and date in a multitude of formats, and it lets you set the time and/or date. The + option allows you to specify the format used to display the time or date value by defining command sequences:

```
$ date +"%A, %B %d %Y"
Friday, August 02 2019
$
```

Table 6.8 shows the various command sequences available in the date command.

TABLE 6.8   The date format command sequences

Sequence	Description
%a	The abbreviated weekday name
%A	The full weekday name
%b	The abbreviated month name
%B	The full month name
%c	The date and time
%C	The century (e.g., 20)
%d	The numeric day of month
%D	The full numeric date
%e	The day of month, space padded
%F	The full date in SQL format (YYYY-MM-dd)
%g	The last two digits of year of the ISO week number
%G	The year of the ISO week number
%h	An alias for %b
%H	The hour in 24-hour format
%I	The hour in 12-hour format

Sequence	Description
%j	The numeric day of year
%k	The hour in 24-hour format, space padded
%l	The hour in 12-hour format, space padded
%m	The numeric month
%M	The minute
%n	A newline character
%N	The nanoseconds
%p	AM or PM
%P	Lowercase am or pm
%r	The full 12-hour clock time
%R	The full 24-hour hour and minute
%s	The seconds since 1970-01-01 00:00.00 UTC
%S	The second
%t	A tab character
%T	The full time in hour:minute:second format
%u	The numeric day of week; 1 is Monday
%U	The numeric week number of year, starting on Sunday
%V	The ISO week number
%w	The numeric day of week; 0 is Sunday
%W	The week number of year, starting on Monday
%x	The locale's date representation as month/day/year or day/month/year
%X	The locale's full time representation
%y	The last two digits of the year

TABLE 6.8   The date format command sequences *(continued)*

Sequence	Description
%Y	The full year
%z	The time zone in +hhmm format
%:z	The time zone in +hh:mm format
%::z	The time zone in +hh:mm:ss fotmat
%:::z	The numeric time zone with: to necessary precision
%Z	The alphabetic time zone abbreviation

As you can see in Table 6.8, the date command provides numerous ways for you to display the time and date in your programs and shell scripts.

You can also set the time and date using the date command by specifying the value in the format

date *MMDDhhmm*[[*CC*]*YY*][.*ss*]

The month, date, hour, and minute values are required, with the year and seconds assumed, or you can include the year and seconds as well if you prefer.

The *timedatectl* Command

If your Linux distribution uses the systemd set of utilities (see Chapter 6), you can use the *timedatectl* command to manage the time and date settings on your system:

```
$ timedatectl
                  Local time: Fri 2019-08-02 06:00:20 EDT
              Universal time: Fri 2019-08-02 10:00:20 UTC
                    RTC time: Fri 2019-08-02 10:00:19
                   Time zone: US/Eastern (EDT, -0400)
   System clock synchronized: no
systemd-timesyncd.service active: yes
              RTC in local TZ: no
$
```

The timedatectl command provides one-stop shopping for all of the time information, including the hardware clock, called RTC; the date information; and the time zone information.

You can also use the `timedatectl` command to modify any of those settings as well by using the `set-time` option:

```
$ sudo timedatectl set-time "2019-08-02 06:15:00"
```

You can also use the `timedatectl` command to synchronize the workstation or server hardware clock and the Linux system time.

WARNING   Most Linux systems connected to the Internet use the Network Time Protocol (NTP) to keep the time and date synchronized with a centralized time server. If your Linux system does this, you won't be able to alter the time or date by using either the `date` or `timedatectl` command.

Configuring Printing

Just like the video environment in Linux, printing in Linux can be somewhat complex. With a myriad of different types of printers available, trying to install the correct printer drivers as well as using the correct printer protocol to communicate with them can be a nightmare.

Fortunately, the *Common Unix Printing System (CUPS)* solves many of those problems for us. CUPS provides a common interface for working with any type of printer on your Linux system. It accepts print jobs using the PostScript document format and sends them to printers using a *print queue* system.

The print queue is a holding area for files sent to be printed. The print queue is normally configured to support not only a specific printer but also a specific printing format, such as landscape or portrait mode, single-sided or double-sided printing, or even color or black-and-white printing. There can be multiple print queues assigned to a single printer, or multiple printers that can accept jobs assigned to a single print queue.

The CUPS software uses the Ghostscript program to convert the PostScript document into a format understood by the different printers. The Ghostscript program requires different drivers for the different printer types to know how to convert the document to make it printable on that type of printer. This is done using configuration files and drivers. Fortunately, CUPS installs many different drivers for common printers on the market and automatically sets the configuration requirements to use them. The configuration files are stored in the /etc/cups directory.

To define a new printer on your Linux system, you can use the CUPS web interface. Open your browser and navigate to `http://localhost:631/`. Figure 6.13 shows the web interface used by CUPS.

The CUPS web interface allows you to define new printers, modify existing printers, and check on the status of print jobs sent to each printer. Not only does CUPS recognize directly connected printers, but you can also configure network printers using several standard network printing protocols, such as the Internet Printing Protocol (IPP) or the Microsoft Server Message Block (SMB) protocol.

FIGURE 6.13 The CUPS main web page

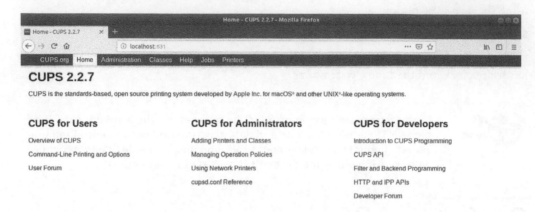

Aside from the CUPS web interface, a few command-line tools are available that you can use for interacting with the printers and print queues:

- cancel: Cancels a print request
- cupsaccept: Enables queuing of print requests
- cupsdisable: Disables the specified printer
- cupsenable: Enables the specified printer
- cupsreject: Rejects queuing of print requests

Besides the standard CUPS command-line commands, CUPS also accepts commands from the legacy BSD command-line printing utility:

- lpc: Start, stop, or pause the print queue
- lpq: Display the print queue status, along with any print jobs waiting in the queue
- lpr: Submit a new print job to a print queue
- lprm: Remove a specific print job from the print queue

If you're working from the command line, you can check the status of any print queue, as well as submit print jobs, as shown in Listing 6.4.

Listing 6.4: Printing from the command line in Linux

```
$ lpq -P EPSON_ET_3750_Series
EPSON_ET_3750_Series is ready
no entries
$ lpr -P EPSON_ET_3750_Series test.txt
$ lpq -P EPSON_ET_3750_Series
EPSON_ET_3750_Series is ready and printing
Rank    Owner   Job    File(s)                    Total Size
active  rich    1      test.txt                   1024 bytes
$
```

The first line in Listing 6.4 uses the lpq command to check the status of the print queue, which shows the printer is ready to accept new jobs and doesn't currently have any jobs in the print queue. The lpr command submits a new print job to print a file. After submitting the new print job, the lpq command shows the printer is currently printing and shows the print job that's being printed.

Summary

Creating, managing, and troubleshooting a GUI environment for yourself and the system's users involves an important skill set. You need to understand the distinct desktop environments, their supporting frameworks, and how to transmit them safely and securely across the network.

The various desktop environments, such as GNOME Shell, KDE Plasma, MATE, Cinnamon, and Xfce, provide many environments to meet different needs and tastes. The currently evolving world of display servers, which includes primarily Wayland and the older X.Org, supports these GUI desktops.

Linux provides GUI desktop environments with many accessibility features, which allow most UI needs to be met. The various keyboard and mouse settings help those with hand or finger difficulties. There are also many utilities for the vision impaired, including screen readers and zoom features.

Accessing a GUI across the network is accomplished through the use of remote desktop software. VNC, Xrdp, and NX are a few examples. Spice is unique in that its primary focus is providing remote desktop access to virtual machines.

Linux systems support many different languages by incorporating different character sets. A character set defines how the Linux system displays and uses the characters contained in the language. While Linux supports many different character sets, the most common ones are ASCII, ISO-8859, Unicode, UTF-8, and UTF-16. The ASCII character set is useful only for English language characters, whereas the UTF-8 and UTF-16 character sets are commonly used to support other languages.

The Linux system maintains the character set configuration as a group of environment variables that begin with LC_. The locale command displays all of the localization environment variables. Each individual LC_ environment variable represents a category of other environment variables that fine-tune the localization settings even further. You can display those environment variable settings by including the -ck option to the locale command.

You must define a time zone for your Linux system. Debian-based Linux distributions use the /etc/timezone file to determine the system time zone, whereas Red Hat–based Linux distributions use the /etc/localtime file. Both files utilize a binary format, so you can't edit them directly. Linux maintains a library of time zone files in the /usr/share/zoneinfo folder. Just copy or link the appropriate time zone file from the /usr/share/zoneinfo folder to the time zone file for your Linux system.

The CUPS software provides a standard method for applications to send documents to both local and network printers. CUPS provides a web-based interface for easily adding, removing, and modifying printers, including both local and network printers. It also provides a few command-line utilities and supports some legacy command-line utilities for working with printers.

Exam Essentials

Outline the various GUI sections and functions.   A desktop environment provides a predetermined look and feel to the GUI. It has graphical sections such as a favorites bar, launch areas, menus, panels, and a system tray. The GUI also has typical functions like desktop settings, a display manager, a file manager, icons to access programs, widgets, and a windows manager.

Describe the various GUI desktop environments.   The primary desktop environments used for current Linux distributions include GNOME Shell, KDE Plasma, MATE, and Xfce.

Summarize available universal access utilities.   The distinct accessibility tools are located in menus or panels. These panels have various locations around the desktop environments and have names like Universal Access, Accessibility, and Assistive Technologies. It is best to use a desktop environment's search feature to locate them. The various access tools for vision-impaired users include cursor blinking, cursor size, contrast modifications, text size enlargement, sound keys, zoom functions, and screen readers. For those individuals who need access to braille technologies, the brltty software is available. Displayed windows can be set to flash instead of providing a sound alert for those who are hearing impaired. When someone has trouble using the keyboard, there are many settings available such as bounce keys, repeat keys, screen keyboard, slow keys, and sticky keys. For mouse use difficulties, the tools to explore are double-click delays, gestures, hover clicks, mouse keys, and simulated secondary clicks.

Explain the display server's role.   A display server is a program or program group that uses a communication protocol to convey information between the GUI and the operating system. The communication protocol is called the display server protocol and can operate over a network. One critical program used with the display server is the compositor. The compositor arranges display elements within a window to create a screen image. Two important display servers are Wayland and X.Org. X.Org is an older display server that has been around for a while. Wayland is a newer display server that adds many needed security features and is easier to maintain.

Describe the available remote desktop software.   Remote desktop software provides a fully functional desktop environment over the network from a remote server. It uses a client/server model, and there are several packages from which to choose. They include VNC, Xrdp, NX, and Spice.

Describe how Linux works with different languages.   Linux stores and displays language characters by using character sets. ASCII, Unicode, and UTF-8 are the most commonly used character sets for Linux.

Explain how to change the current character set on a Linux system.   You can use the export command to change the LANG or LC_ALL environment variables to define a new characters set. If your Linux distribution uses the systemd utilities, you can also use the localectl command to display or change the system character set.

Describe how the time zone is set on a Linux system.   Time zones are defined in Linux by individual files in the /usr/share/zoneinfo folder. Debian-based Linux distributions copy the appropriate time zone file to the /etc/timezone file, whereas Red Hat–based Linux distributions use the /etc/localtime file. To change the time zone for an individual script or program, use the TZ environment variable.

Summarize the tools you have available to work with the time and date on a Linux system. The hwclock command allows you to sync the Linux system time with the hardware clock on the system, or vice versa. The date command allows you to display the time and date in a multitude of formats or set the current time and date. The timedatectl command is from the systemd utilities, and it allows you to display lots of different information about the system and hardware time and date, and lets you set them.

Explain how Linux handles printers and how you can configure your Linux system to access network printers.   Linux uses the CUPS package for handling all printing tasks. CUPS provides a web-based interface allowing administrators to add, remove, and modify both local and network printers on the Linux system. CUPS also provides several utilities for working with printers from the command line if needed.

Review Questions

You can find the answers in the appendix.

1. Which of the following best describes a desktop environment?
   A. A set of programs that allow a user to interact with the system via icons, windows, and various other visual elements
   B. A screen where you choose a username and enter a password to gain system access
   C. A series of components that work together to provide the graphical setting for the user interface
   D. A program that allows you to perform file maintenance activities graphically
   E. A set of programs that determine how the windows are presented on the desktop

2. Which of the following are GUI components? (Choose all that apply.)
   A. Favorites bar
   B. File manager
   C. Icons
   D. Command line
   E. System tray

3. Which of the following is not used by default within GNOME Shell?
   A. KDM
   B. Files
   C. Mutter
   D. GDM
   E. Doc

4. Which of the following is the KDE Plasma files manager?
   A. Nautilus
   B. Plasmoid
   C. Dolphin
   D. Kwin
   E. Nemo

5. Which of the following describes the sound keys accessibility setting?
   A. Sounds are made when Caps Lock or Num Lock key is turned on or off.
   B. A program that reads the GUI aloud, such as Orca.
   C. A cursor blink rate modification to make it easier to locate the cursor on the screen.
   D. Output to a refreshable braille display that is provided by the Orca screen reader.
   E. The screen or a screen portion is amplified to different magnification levels.

6. A blind co-worker who is programming on the Linux server is suddenly having odd problems with his braille display device. You determine that you need to restart the braille service. Assuming the appropriate systemd unit file is available, which command would you use?

   A. `systemctl restart braille`

   B. `systemctl reload braille`

   C. `systemctl restart brailled`

   D. `systemctl restart brltty`

   E. `systemctl reload brltty`

7. Which of the following best describes the slow keys accessibility setting?

   A. A keyboard option that modifies how long a key must be pressed down to acknowledge the key

   B. A keyboard option that sets keyboard modifier keys, such as Ctrl and Shift, to maintain their pressed status until a subsequent key is pressed

   C. A keyboard option that modifies how long a key must be pressed down as well as a delay to acknowledge the key repeat

   D. A keyboard option that sets a primary key to be pressed along with a mouse click to emulate secondary mouse clicks

   E. A keyboard option that displays a visual keyboard on the UI that can be manipulated by a mouse or other pointing device to emulate keystrokes

8. Which of the following communicates with the Linux operating system to transmit the UI wants and needs?

   A. Window manager

   B. Display manager

   C. Desktop environment

   D. Windows server

   E. Display server

9. Which of the following is true concerning Wayland? (Choose all that apply.)

   A. Currently, X11 is more secure than Wayland.

   B. Wayland uses the `$WAYLAND_DISPLAY` environment variable.

   C. Wayland's only compositor is Weston.

   D. X11Wayland supports legacy X11 programs.

   E. Set `WaylandDisable` to `true` to disable Wayland in GNOME Shell.

10. Which of the following commands will help you determine whether your display server is Wayland or X11?

   A. `$WAYLAND_DISPLAY`

   B. `echo $AccessX`

   C. `loginctl`

   D. `echo $X11`

   E. `runlevel`

11. Which of the following is true concerning X11? (Choose all that apply.)

    A. XFree86 is the dominant X server.

    B. The X.Org Foundation develops an X server.

    C. The X server is being replaced by Wayland.

    D. X11 means a user can have 11 sessions.

    E. X is short for X Window System.

12. Your system is running an X display server and a user's graphical user interface is not acting properly. Which of the following commands can you use first to diagnose potential problems? (Choose all that apply.)

    A. xwininfo

    B. Xorg -configure

    C. xcpyinfo

    D. xdpyinfo

    E. loginctl

13. Which of the following are remote desktops? (Choose all that apply.)

    A. Spice

    B. NX

    C. Xrdp

    D. VNC

    E. Caja

14. Which of the following are remote desktops that are typically used with virtual machines? (Choose all that apply.)

    A. Spice

    B. NX

    C. Xrdp

    D. VNC

    E. All of the above

15. Which of the following protocols does Xrdp employ?

    A. Remote frame buffer protocol

    B. Wayland protocol

    C. NX technology protocol

    D. Simple Protocol for ICEs

    E. Remote desktop protocol

16. You (username Samantha) are logged in to a laptop (IP address 192.168.0.42) running a Linux GNOME Classic desktop environment at your company desk in Building A. A problem has occurred on a rack-mounted Linux system (IP address 192.168.0.7), in Building C. You need to securely access a GUI application on the remote system that uses X11. What command should you use?

    A. `ssh -Y Samantha@192.168.0.7`

    B. `ssh -X Samantha@192.168.0.7`

    C. `ssh -Y Samantha@192.168.0.42`

    D. `ssh -X Samantha@192.168.0.42`

    E. `ssh -L Samantha@192.168.0.42`

17. Which character set uses a 3-byte code and can represent characters from most languages used in the world?

    A. ASCII

    B. LC_ALL

    C. UTF-8

    D. UTF-16

    E. Unicode

18. What Linux command displays all of the localization environment variables and their values?

    A. `date`

    B. `time`

    C. `hwclock`

    D. `LANG`

    E. `locale`

19. What two environment variables control all of the localization settings?

    A. `LC_MONETARY`

    B. `LC_NUMERIC`

    C. `LANG`

    D. `LC_CTYPE`

    E. `LC_ALL`

20. What CUPS command-line command allows you to halt sending print jobs to a queue?

    A. `cancel`

    B. `cupsaccept`

    C. `cupsenable`

    D. `cupsreject`

    E. `lpq`

Chapter

7

Administering the System

OBJECTIVES

✓ **107.1 Manage user and group accounts and related system files**

✓ **108.1 Maintain system time**

✓ **108.2 System logging**

✓ **108.3 Mail Transfer Agent (MTA) basics**

One of the goals in systems administration is to ensure that all the servers in your care are running efficiently. Managing user accounts, email, log files, and system time are all tasks involved in this process.

In this chapter we'll dig down into the nitty-gritty of creating, modifying, and deleting user accounts and groups. We'll also explore email utilities and concepts that are helpful in troubleshooting as well as using system email. Log files that are critical for troubleshooting problems and keeping a watchful eye on security are covered as well. Finally, we'll take a look at properly maintaining a system's time and the various services you can employ to do so.

Managing Users and Groups

If you want to buy a famous and expensive piece of art, you should make sure it isn't a fake. In other words, you want to make sure it is authentic. The same is true for allowing users access to a computer system. You want to make sure they are authentic users who have received prior authorization to access the system. This process is called *authentication* and is formerly defined as determining if a person or program is who they claim to be.

Besides user authentication, you need to know how to check a user's access to files, manage group memberships, and change passwords. These functions are intertwined. This section covers administering the access controls Linux uses to check a user's credentials and permit or deny access to the system as well as to its files.

Understanding Users and Groups

User accounts and their underlying framework are at the center of credential management and access controls. These accounts are a part of Linux's discretionary access control (DAC). DAC is the traditional Linux security control, where access to a file, or any object, is based on the user's identity and current group membership.

Groups are an organizational structure that are also part of DAC. When a user account is created, it is given membership to a particular group, called the account's default group. Though a user account can have lots of group memberships, its process can have only one designated current group at a time. The default group is an account's current group, when the user first logs into the system.

Configuring User Accounts

Adding and modifying user account credentials, which includes usernames, account information, and passwords, is an important (but tedious) part of system administration. In addition, you need to know how to delete these credentials, when warranted.

To add a new user account on the system, the *useradd* utility is typically used. However, the process involves players besides the useradd command. A depiction of the process is illustrated in Figure 7.1.

FIGURE 7.1   The process of adding a user account

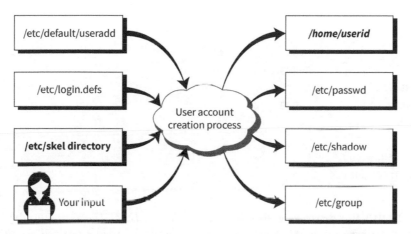

You can see in Figure 7.1 that several team players are involved in the account creation process. Notice that the /etc/skel directory is bolded. This is because, depending on the other configuration files, it may not be used in the process. The same goes for the */home/userid* directory. It may not be created or it may have an alternative name, depending on the system's account creation configuration. You'll learn more about these directories shortly.

Before we jump into the useradd utility details, let's look at the two files and the directory involved in the creation side of the process.

The */etc/login.defs* File

The *etc/login.defs* configuration file is typically installed by default on most Linux distributions. It contains directives for use in various shadow password suite commands. *Shadow password suite* is an umbrella term for commands dealing with account credentials, such as the useradd, userdel, and passwd commands.

The directives in this configuration file control password length, how long until the user is required to change the account's password, whether or not a home directory is created by default, and so on. The file is typically filled with comments and commented-out directives (which make the directives inactive). Listing 7.1 shows only the active directives within the /etc/login.defs file, after stripping out blank and comment lines on a CentOS distribution.

Listing 7.1: Active directives in the /etc/login.defs configuration file

```
$ grep -v ^$ /etc/login.defs | grep -v ^\#
MAIL_DIR          /var/spool/mail
PASS_MAX_DAYS    99999
PASS_MIN_DAYS    0
PASS_MIN_LEN     5
PASS_WARN_AGE    7
UID_MIN                    1000
UID_MAX                   60000
SYS_UID_MIN                 201
SYS_UID_MAX                 999
GID_MIN                    1000
GID_MAX                   60000
SYS_GID_MIN                 201
SYS_GID_MAX                 999
CREATE_HOME      yes
UMASK            077
USERGROUPS_ENAB  yes
ENCRYPT_METHOD   SHA512
$
```

Notice the UID_MIN directive within Listing 7.1. A *user ID (UID)* is the number used by Linux to identify user accounts. A *user account,* sometimes called a *normal account,* is any account an authorized human with the appropriate credentials has been given to access the system and perform daily tasks. While humans use account names, Linux uses UIDs. The UID_MIN indicates the lowest UID allowed for user accounts. On the system in Listing 7.1, UID_MIN is set to 1000. This is typical, though some systems set it at 500.

System accounts are accounts that provide services (daemons) or perform special tasks, such as the root user account. A system account's minimum UID is set by the SYS_UID_MIN, and its maximum is set by the SYS_UID_MAX directive. The settings in this file are typical, but keep in mind that these settings are for accounts created *after* the initial Linux distribution installation.

Some additional directives critical to common user account creation are covered in Table 7.1.

TABLE 7.1 A few vital /etc/login.defs directives

Name	Description
PASS_MAX_DAYS	Number of days until a password change is required. This is the password's expiration date.
PASS_MIN_DAYS	Number of days after a password is changed until the password may be changed again.

Name	Description
PASS_MIN_LENGTH	Minimum number of characters required in password.
PASS_WARN_AGE	Number of days a warning is issued to the user prior to a password's expiration.
CREATE_HOME	Default is no. If set to yes, a user account home directory is created.
ENCRYPT_METHOD	The method used to hash account passwords.

The /etc/login.defs file is only one of the configuration files used for the user account process's creation side. The other file is covered next.

The */etc/default/useradd* File

The */etc/default/useradd* file is another configuration file that directs the process of creating accounts. It typically is a much shorter file than the /etc/login.defs file. An example from a CentOS distribution is shown in Listing 7.2.

Listing 7.2: The /etc/default/useradd configuration file

```
$ cat /etc/default/useradd
# useradd defaults file
GROUP=100
HOME=/home
INACTIVE=-1
EXPIRE=
SHELL=/bin/bash
SKEL=/etc/skel
CREATE_MAIL_SPOOL=yes
$
$ sudo useradd -D
GROUP=100
HOME=/home
INACTIVE=-1
EXPIRE=
SHELL=/bin/bash
SKEL=/etc/skel
CREATE_MAIL_SPOOL=yes
$
```

Notice in Listing 7.2 that there are two different ways to display the active directives in this file. You can use the cat command or invoke the *useradd -D* command with super user privileges. Both are equally simple to use. One cool fact about the useradd -D command is that you can use it to modify the directives within the /etc/default/useradd file.

In Listing 7.2, notice the HOME directive. It is currently set to /home, which means that any newly created user accounts will have their account directories located within the /home directory. Keep in mind that if CREATE_HOME is not set or is set to no within the /etc/login.defs file, a home directory is *not* created by default.

Some additional directives critical to common user account creation are covered in Table 7.2.

TABLE 7.2 A few vital /etc/default/useradd directives

Name	Description
HOME	Base directory for user account directories.
INACTIVE	Number of days after a password has expired and has not been changed until the account will be deactivated. See PASS_MAX_DAYS in Table 7.1.
SKEL	The skeleton directory.
SHELL	User account default shell program.

The SHELL directive needs a little more explanation. Typically it is set to /bin/bash, which means when you access the command line, your user process is running the /bin/bash shell program. This program provides you with the prompt at the command line and handles any commands you enter there.

> Be aware that some distributions, such as Ubuntu, set the SHELL directive by default to /bin/sh, which is a symbolic link to another shell. On Ubuntu this links to the Dash shell instead of the Bash shell.

The */etc/skel/* Directory

The */etc/skel* directory, or the *skeleton* directory (see Table 7.2) as it is commonly called, holds files. If a home directory is created for a user, these files are to be copied to the user account's home directory, when the account is created. Listing 7.3 shows the files within the /etc/skel directory on a CentOS distribution.

Listing 7.3: Files in the /etc/skel directory

```
$ ls -a /etc/skel
.  ..  .bash_logout  .bash_profile  .bashrc  .mozilla
$
```

In Listing 7.3, the ls command was employed with the -a option so that hidden files (files starting with a dot) are displayed. Recall that hidden files do not normally display without the -a option on the ls command. These files are account environment files as well as a configuration file directory for the Mozilla Firefox web browser. We'll cover environment files later in Chapter 9. You can modify any of these files or add new files and directories, if needed.

 The /etc/skel files are copied to user account home directories only when the account is created. Therefore, if you make changes to the files later, you'll have to migrate those changed files to current user accounts either by hand or by shell scripts.

Now that we've covered the files on the creation side of the user account creation process, let's look at the files and directories that are built or modified as part of the process. Go back and look at Figure 7.1, if necessary, to refresh your memory of the various file and directory names.

The */etc/passwd* File

Account information is stored in the */etc/passwd* file. Each account's data occupies a single line in the file. When an account is created, a new record for that account is added to the /etc/passwd file. A snipped example is shown in Listing 7.4.

Listing 7.4: Account records in the /etc/passwd file

```
$ cat /etc/passwd
root:x:0:0:root:/root:/bin/bash
bin:x:1:1:bin:/bin:/sbin/nologin
daemon:x:2:2:daemon:/sbin:/sbin/nologin
[…]
tcpdump:x:72:72::/:/sbin/nologin
user1:x:1000:1000:User One:/home/user1:/bin/bash
Christine:x:1001:1001:Christine B:/home/Christine:/bin/bash
[…]
$
```

The /etc/passwd file records contain several fields. Each field in a record is delimited by a colon (:). There are seven fields in total, described in Table 7.3.

TABLE 7.3   The /etc/passwd file's record fields

Field No.	Description
1	User account's username.
2	Password field. Typically this file is no longer used to store passwords. An x in this field indicates passwords are stored in the /etc/shadow file.

TABLE 7.3   The /etc/passwd file's record fields *(continued)*

Field No.	Description
3	User account's user identification number (UID).
4	User account's group identification number (GID).
5	Comment field. This field is optional. Traditionally it contains the user's full name.
6	User account's home directory.
7	User account's default shell. If set to /sbin/nologin or /bin/false, then the user cannot interactively log into the system.

You would think that the password file would hold passwords, but due to its file permissions, the password file can be compromised. Therefore, passwords are stored in the more locked-down /etc/shadow file.

 You may find yourself working for an organization that has passwords stored in the /etc/passwd file. If so, politely suggest that the passwords be migrated to the /etc/shadow file via the pwconv command. If the organization refuses, walk, or even better run, to the door and go find a job at a different company.

You may have noticed that in an /etc/password record, field #7 may contain either the /sbin/nologin or the /bin/false default shell. This is to prevent an account from interactively logging into the system. /sbin/nologin is typically set for system service account records. System services (daemons) do need to have system accounts, but they do *not* interactively log in. Instead, they run in the background under their own account name. If a malicious person attempted to interactively log in using the account (and they made it past other blockades, which you'll learn about shortly), they are politely kicked off the system. Basically, /sbin/nologin displays a brief message and logs you off before you reach a command prompt. If desired, you can modify the message shown by creating the file /etc/nologin.txt and adding the desired text.

The /bin/false shell is a little more brutal. If this is set as a user account's default shell, no messages are shown, and the user is just logged out of the system.

The */etc/shadow* File

Another file that is updated when an account is created is the *letc/shadow* file. It contains information regarding the account's password, even if you have not yet provided a password for the account. Like the /etc/passwd file, each account's data occupies a single file line. A snipped example is shown in Listing 7.5.

Listing 7.5: Account records in the /etc/shadow file

```
$ sudo cat /etc/shadow
root:!::0:99999:7:::
bin:*:17589:0:99999:7:::
daemon:*:17589:0:99999:7:::
[…]
user1: $6$bvqdqU[…]:17738:0:99999:7:::
Christine: Wb8I8Iw$6[…]:17751:0:99999:7:::
[…]
$
```

The /etc/shadow records contain several fields. Each field in a record is delimited by a colon (:). There are nine fields in total, described in Table 7.4.

TABLE 7.4   The /etc/shadow file's record fields

Field No.	Description
1	User account's username.
2	Password field. The password is a salted and hashed password. A !! or ! indicates a password has not been set for the account. A ! or an * indicates the account cannot use a password to log in. A ! in front of a password indicates the account has been locked.
3	Date of last password change in Unix Epoch time (days) format.
4	Number of days after a password is changed until the password may be changed again.
5	Number of days until a password change is required. This is the password's expiration date.
6	Number of days a warning is issued to the user prior to a password's expiration (see field #5).
7	Number of days after a password has expired (see field #5) and has not been changed until the account will be deactivated.
8	Date of account's expiration in Unix Epoch time (days) format.
9	Called the special flag. It is a field for a special future use, is currently not used, and is blank.

Notice that field #1 is the account's username. This is the only field shared with the /etc/passwd file.

> Unix Epoch time, which is also called POSIX time, is the number of sec-
> onds since January 1, 1970, although the /etc/shadow file expresses it in
> days. It has a long history with Unix and Linux systems and will potentially
> cause problems in the year 2038. You don't have to drag out your calcula-
> tor to determine what a field's date is using the Epoch. Instead, the chage
> utility, covered later in this chapter, does that for you.

It's vital to understand the different possible expirations. When password expiration has occurred, there is a grace period. The user will have a certain number of days (designated in field #7) to log into the account using the old password but must change the password immediately. However, if password expiration has occurred and the user does *not* log into the system in time, the user is effectively locked out of the system.

With account expiration, there is no grace period. After the account expires, the user cannot log into the account with its password.

> If you have temporary workers, such as interns or external contractors,
> who use your Linux system, be sure to set up their accounts to expire. That
> way, if you forget to remove the account after they are no longer working
> at your company, they cannot access the account after the expiration date.

You may have noticed that we have not yet covered the /etc/group file. It does get modified as part of the account creation process. However, that discussion is saved for the section "Configuring Groups" later in this chapter.

The Account Creation Process

Distributions tend to vary greatly in their configuration when it comes to user accounts. Therefore, before you launch into creating accounts with the useradd utility, it's wise to review some directives within each distro's user account configuration files (see Tables 7.1 and 7.2). In Listing 7.6, the CREATE_HOME and SHELL directives are checked on a CentOS distribution.

Listing 7.6: Checking user account directives on CentOS

```
$ grep CREATE_HOME /etc/login.defs
CREATE_HOME       yes
$
$ sudo useradd -D | grep SHELL
SHELL=/bin/bash
$
```

You can see on this distribution that the home directory will be created by default, because CREATE_HOME is set to yes. The SHELL directive is pointing to the Bash shell, /bin/bash, which is the typical shell for most interactive user accounts.

The useradd command, as mentioned earlier, is the primary tool for creating user accounts on most distributions. Creating an account on CentOS distribution with the useradd utility is shown in Listing 7.7.

Listing 7.7: Creating a user account on CentOS

```
$ sudo useradd DAdams
[sudo] password for Christine:
$
$ grep ^DAdams /etc/passwd
DAdams:x:1002:1002::/home/DAdams:/bin/bash
$
$ sudo grep ^DAdams /etc/shadow
DAdams:!!:17806:0:99999:7:::
$
$ sudo ls -a /home/DAdams/
.  ..  .bash_logout  .bash_profile  .bashrc  .mozilla
$
```

Because the CentOS distribution we are using in Listing 7.7 has the CREATE_HOME directive set to yes and SHELL set to /bin/bash, there is no need to employ any useradd command options. The only argument needed is the user account name, which is DAdams. After the utility is used to create the account in Listing 7.7, notice that records now exist for the new user account in both the /etc/passwd and /etc/shadow files. Also, a new directory was created, /home/DAdams, which contains files from the /etc/skel/ directory. Keep in mind that at this point no password has been added to the DAdams account yet, and thus its record in the /etc/shadow file shows !! in the password field.

Now let's take a look at creating an account on a different Linux distribution. The Ubuntu Desktop distro does things a little differently. In Listing 7.8, you can see that CREATE_HOME is *not* set, so it will default to no.

Listing 7.8: Checking user account directives on Ubuntu Desktop

```
$ grep CREATE_HOME /etc/login.defs
$
$ useradd -D | grep SHELL
SHELL=/bin/sh
$
```

Also in Listing 7.8, notice that the SHELL directive is set to /bin/sh instead of the Bash shell. This means that when you create an interactive user account, you will need to specify the Bash shell, if desired.

Therefore, when creating a user account on this Ubuntu distribution, if you want the account to have a home directory and use the Bash shell, you will need to employ additional useradd command switches. The useradd utility has many useful options for various needs; the most typical ones are listed in Table 7.5.

TABLE 7.5   The useradd command's commonly used options

Short	Long	Description
-c	--comment	Comment field contents. Traditionally it contains the user's full name. Optional.
-d	--home or --home-dir	User's home directory specification. Default action is set by the HOME and CREATE_HOME directives.
-D	--defaults	Display /etc/default/useradd directives.
-e	--expiredate	Date of account's expiration in *YYYY-MM-DD* format. Default action is set by the EXPIRE directive.
-f	--inactive	Number of days after a password has expired and has not been changed until the account will be deactivated. A -1 indicates account will never be deactivated. Default action is set by the INACTIVE directive.
-g	--gid	Account's group membership, which is active when user logs into system (default group).
-G	--groups	Account's additional group memberships.
-m	--create-home	If it does not exist, create the user account's home directory. Default action is set by the CREATE_HOME directive.
-M	N/A or --no-create-home	Do *not* create the user account's home directory. Default action is set by the CREATE_HOME directive.
-s	--shell	Account's shell. Default action is set by the SHELL directive.
-u	--uid	Account's user identification (UID) number.
-r	--system	Create a system account instead of a user account.

We need to employ a few of the switches in Table 7.5 to create a user account on the Ubuntu Desktop distribution. An example is shown in Listing 7.9.

Listing 7.9: Creating a user account on Ubuntu Desktop

```
$ sudo useradd -md /home/JKirk -s /bin/bash JKirk
[sudo] password for Christine:
$
$ grep ^JKirk /etc/passwd
JKirk:x:1002:1002::/home/JKirk:/bin/bash
$
$ sudo grep ^JKirk /etc/shadow
JKirk:!:17806:0:99999:7:::
$
$ sudo ls -a /home/JKirk/
.  ..  .bash_logout  .bashrc  examples.desktop  .profile
$
$ sudo ls -a /etc/skel
.  ..  .bash_logout  .bashrc  examples.desktop  .profile
$
```

Notice in Listing 7.9 that three options are used along with the useradd command. Because this system does not have the CREATE_HOME directive set, the -m option is needed to force useradd to make a home directory for the account. The -d switch designates that the directory name should be /home/JKirk. Because the SHELL directive is set to /bin/sh on this system, the -s option is needed to set the account's default shell to /bin/bash.

After the utility is used to create the account in Listing 7.9, notice that records now exist for the new user account in the /etc/passwd and /etc/shadow files. Also, a new directory was created, /home/JKirk, which contains files from this distro's /etc/skel/ directory. Keep in mind at this point that no password has been added to the JKirk account yet, and thus its record in the /etc/shadow file shows ! in the password field.

 The Ubuntu and Debian distributions promote the use of the adduser program instead of the useradd utility. Their man pages refer to the useradd command as a "low-level utility." Some other distros include a symbolic link to useradd named adduser, which may help (or not). The adduser configuration information is typically stored in the /etc/adduser.conf file.

Another way to view account records in the /etc/passwd and /etc/shadow files is via the *getent* utility. For this program you pass only the filename followed by the account name whose record you wish to view. The command is employed in Listing 7.10 to view the account that was created in Listing 7.9.

Listing 7.10: Using getent to view a user account on Ubuntu Desktop

```
$ getent passwd JKirk
JKirk:x:1002:1002::/home/JKirk:/bin/bash
$
$ getent shadow JKirk
$
$ sudo getent shadow JKirk
JKirk:!:17806:0:99999:7:::
$
```

Notice in Listing 7.10 that when super user privileges are not used with getent for the shadow file, nothing is returned. This is because getent honors the security settings on the /etc/shadow file.

> If you need to modify the /etc/default/useradd file's directive settings, instead of using a text editor you can employ the useradd -D command. Just tack on the needed arguments. For example, to modify the SHELL directive to point to the Bash shell, use super user privileges and issue the useradd -D -s /bin/bash command.

When creating an account, you can create a password via the crypt utility and then add it when the account is created via the -p option on the useradd utility. However, not only is that cumbersome, but it's also considered a bad practice. In the next section, we'll cover creating and managing account passwords properly.

Maintaining Passwords

When you first create an interactive account, you should immediately afterward create a password for that account using the *passwd* utility. In Listing 7.11, a password is created for the new DAdams account on a CentOS system.

Listing 7.11: Using passwd for a new account on CentOS

```
$ sudo passwd DAdams
Changing password for user DAdams.
New password:
Retype new password:
passwd: all authentication tokens updated successfully.
$
```

You can also update a password for a particular user using the passwd utility and pass the user's account name as an argument, similar to what is shown in Listing 7.11. If you need to update your own account's password, just enter **passwd** with no additional command arguments.

You can do more than set and modify passwords with the passwd utility. You can also lock or unlock accounts, set an account's password to expired, delete an account's password, and so on. Table 7.6 shows commonly used passwd switches; all of these options require super user privileges.

TABLE 7.6   The passwd command's commonly used options

Short	Long	Description
-d	--delete	Removes the account's password.
-e	--expire	Sets an account's password as expired. User is required to change account password at next login.
-i	--inactive	Sets the number of days after a password has expired and has not been changed until the account will be deactivated.
-l	--lock	Places an exclamation point (!) in front of the account's password within the /etc/shadow file, effectively preventing the user from logging into the system using the account's password.
-n	--minimum	Sets the number of days after a password is changed until the password may be changed again.
-S	--status	Displays the account's password status.
-u	--unlock	Removes a placed exclamation point (!) from the account's password within the /etc/shadow file.
-w	-warning or --warndays	Sets the number of days a warning is issued to the user prior to a password's expiration.
-x	--maximum or -maxdays	Sets the number of days until a password change is required. This is the password's expiration date.

One option in Table 7.6 needs a little more explanation, and that is the -S option. An example is shown in Listing 7.12.

Listing 7.12: Using passwd -S to view an account's password status

```
$ sudo passwd -S DAdams
DAdams PS 2018-10-01 0 99999 7 -1 (Password set, SHA512 crypt.)
$
```

In Listing 7.12, the DAdams account's password status is displayed. The status contains the account password's state, which is either a usable password (P), no password (NP), or a locked password (L). After the password state, the last password change date is shown, followed by the password's minimum, maximum, warning, and inactive settings. Additional status is shown within the parentheses, which includes whether or not the password is set as well as the hash algorithm used to protect it.

You can also use the *chage* utility to display similar password information but in a more human-readable format, as shown in Listing 7.13.

Listing 7.13: Using chage -l to view an account's password status

```
$ sudo chage -l DAdams
Last password change                                    : Oct 02, 2018
Password expires                                        : never
Password inactive                                       : never
Account expires                                         : never
Minimum number of days between password change          : 0
Maximum number of days between password change          : 99999
Number of days of warning before password expires       : 7
$
```

The chage program can modify password settings as well. You can either employ various command options (see its man pages for details) or use the chage utility interactively, as shown in Listing 7.14.

Listing 7.14: Using chage to change an account password's settings

```
$ sudo chage DAdams
Changing the aging information for DAdams
Enter the new value, or press ENTER for the default

        Minimum Password Age [0]: 5
        Maximum Password Age [99999]: 30
        Last Password Change (YYYY-MM-DD) [2018-10-02]:
        Password Expiration Warning [7]: 15
        Password Inactive [-1]: 3
        Account Expiration Date (YYYY-MM-DD) [-1]:
$
```

Notice in Listing 7.14 that the password expiration warning is set to 15 days. This is a good setting if your company allows two-week vacations.

Modifying Accounts

The utility employed to modify accounts is the *usermod* program. Similar to the passwd command, you can lock and unlock accounts, as shown in Listing 7.15.

Listing 7.15: Using usermod to lock an account

```
$ sudo usermod -L  DAdams
$
$ sudo passwd -S DAdams
DAdams LK 2018-10-01 5 30 15 3 (Password locked.)
$
$ sudo getent shadow DAdams
DAdams:!$6$B/zCaNx[…]:17806:5:30:15:3::
$
$ sudo usermod -U  DAdams
$
$ sudo passwd -S DAdams
DAdams PS 2018-10-01 5 30 15 3 (Password set, SHA512 crypt.)
$
```

Notice in Listing 7.15 that the usermod -L command is used to lock the DAdams account. The passwd -S command shows the password status is LK, indicating it is locked. In Listing 7.15, the snipped getent utility output shows that an exclamation point (!) was placed in front of the DAdams account's password, which is what is causing the account to be locked. The lock is then removed via the usermod -U command and the status is rechecked.

You can make many modifications to user accounts via the usermod utility's switches. The commonly used switches are shown in Table 7.7.

TABLE 7.7   The usermod command's commonly used options

Short	Long	Description
-c	--comment	Modify the comment field contents.
-d	--home	Set a new user home directory specification. Use with the -m option to move the current directory's files to the new location.
-e	--expiredate	Modify the account's expiration date. Use *YYYY-MM-DD* format.
-f	--inactive	Modify the number of days after a password has expired and has not been changed that the account will be deactivated. A -1 indicates account will never be deactivated.
-g	--gid	Change the account's default group membership.
-G	--groups	Update the account's additional group memberships. If only specifying new group membership, use the -a option to avoid removing the other group memberships.

TABLE 7.7   The usermod command's commonly used options *(continued)*

Short	Long	Description
-l	--login	Modify the account's username to the specified one. Does not modify the home directory.
-L	--lock	Lock the account by placing an exclamation point in front of the password within the account's /etc/shadow file record.
-s	--shell	Change the account's shell.
-u	--uid	Modify the account's user identification (UID) number.
-U	--unlock	Unlock the account by removing the exclamation point from the front of the password within the account's /etc/shadow file record.

Notice that you can change an account's default group and provide memberships to additional groups. Account groups are covered in detail later in this chapter.

Where usermod comes in handy is in a situation where you've created an account but forgot to check the distribution's account creation configuration settings. Listing 7.16 shows an example of this on an Ubuntu Desktop distribution.

Listing 7.16: Using usermod to modify an account

```
$ sudo useradd -md /home/DBowman DBowman
$
$ sudo getent passwd DBowman
DBowman:x:1003:1003::/home/DBowman:/bin/sh
$
$ sudo usermod -s /bin/bash DBowman
$
$ sudo getent passwd DBowman
DBowman:x:1003:1003::/home/DBowman:/bin/bash
$
```

In Listing 7.16, the user account DBowman is created, but when the account record is checked using the getent utility, it shows that the /bin/sh shell is being used instead of the Bash shell. To fix this problem, the usermod command is employed with the -s option, and the account's shell is modified to the /bin/bash shell instead.

Deleting Accounts

Deleting an account on Linux is fairly simple. The *userdel* utility is the key tool in this task. The most common option to use is the -r switch. This option will delete the account's home directory tree and any files within it. Listing 7.17 shows an example of deleting an account.

Listing 7.17: Using userdel to delete an account

```
$ sudo ls -a /home/DBowman
.  ..  .bash_logout  .bashrc  examples.desktop  .profile
$
$ sudo getent passwd DBowman
DBowman:x:1003:1003::/home/DBowman:/bin/bash
$
$ sudo userdel -r DBowman
userdel: DBowman mail spool (/var/mail/DBowman) not found
$
$ sudo ls -a /home/DBowman
ls: cannot access '/home/DBowman': No such file or directory
$
$ sudo getent passwd DBowman
$
```

The first two commands in Listing 7.17 show that the /home/DBowman directory exists and has files within it and that the account does have a record within the /etc/passwd file. The third command includes the userdel -r command to delete the account as well as the home directory. Notice that an error message is generated stating that the /var/mail/ DBowman file could not be found. This is not a problem. It just means that this file was not created when the account was created. Finally, the last two commands show that both the /home/DBowman directory and its files were removed and that the /etc/passwd file no longer contains a record for the DBowman account.

 Real World Scenario

Account Deletion Policies

Prior to deleting any accounts on a system, check with your employer's human resources staff and/or legal department or counsel. There may be policies in place concerning file retention for terminated or retired employees as well as those individuals who have left the company to change jobs. You may be required to back up files prior to deleting them from the system and/or perform some other types of documentation. If your employer has no such policy, it is a good idea to suggest that one be developed.

Configuring Groups

Groups are identified by their name as well as their *group ID (GID)*. This is similar to how users are identified by UIDs in that the GID is used by Linux to identify a particular group, whereas humans use group names.

If a default group is not designated when a user account is created, then a new group is created. This new group has the same name as the user account's name and it is assigned a new GID. To see an account's default group, you can use the getent command to view the /etc/passwd record for that account. Recall that the fourth field in the record is the account's GID, which is the default group. Review Table 7.3 earlier in the chapter if you need a refresher on the various /etc/passwd record fields. Listing 7.18 shows an example of viewing an account's default group information for the DAdams account, which was created on a CentOS distribution.

Listing 7.18: Viewing an account's group memberships

```
$ getent passwd DAdams
DAdams:x:1002:1002::/home/DAdams:/bin/bash
$
$ sudo groups DAdams
DAdams : DAdams
$
$ getent group DAdams
DAdams:x:1002:
$
$ grep 1002 /etc/group
DAdams:x:1002:
$
```

The first command in Listing 7.18 shows that the DAdams account's default group has a GID of 1002, but it does not provide a group name. The *groups* command does show the group name, which is the same as the user account name, DAdams. This is typical when no default group was designated at account creation time. The third command, another getent command, shows that the group DAdams does indeed map to the 1002 GID. The fourth command confirms this information.

To add a user to a new group or change the account's default group, the group must pre-exist. This task is accomplished via the *groupadd* utility. The group's GID will be automatically set by the system, but you can override this default behavior with the -g command option. An example of creating a new group is shown in Listing 7.19.

Listing 7.19: Using the groupadd utility to create a new group

```
$ sudo groupadd -g 1042 Project42
$
$ getent group Project42
Project42:x:1042:
$
$ grep Project42 /etc/group
Project42:x:1042:
$
```

Notice in Listing 7.19 that super user privileges are required to create a new group. The getent utility, as well as the grep command, is used to show the new group record in the */etc/group* file. The fields in the /etc/group file are delimited by a colon (:) and are as follows:

- Group name
- Group password: An x indicates that, if a group password exists, it is stored in the /etc/gshadow file.
- GID
- Group members: User accounts that belong to the group, separated by a comma.

The Ubuntu and Debian distributions promote the use of the addgroup program instead of the groupadd program. They consider the groupadd command to be a low-level utility.

The new group created did not have a group password created for it. However, the x in the Project42 group record within the /etc/group file does not prove this. To make sure there is no group password, the /etc/gshadow file, where group passwords are stored, is checked in Listing 7.20.

Listing 7.20: Checking for a group password

```
$ sudo getent gshadow Project42
Project42:!::
$
```

The command in Listing 7.20 shows the Project42 group's record within the /etc/gshadow file. The second field contains an explanation point (!), which indicates that no password has been set for this group.

Group passwords, if set, allow user accounts access to groups to whom they do not belong. If a group password is used, this password is typically shared among the various users who need access to the group. This is a bad security practice. Passwords should never be shared. Each account needs to have its own password, and access to groups should be allowed only via group membership, not group passwords.

After a new group is created, you can set group membership by simply adding user accounts to the group. Listing 7.21 shows an example of doing this with the usermod command.

Listing 7.21: Employing usermod to add an account to a group

```
$ sudo groups DAdams
DAdams : DAdams
$
$ sudo usermod -aG Project42 DAdams
$
$ sudo groups DAdams
DAdams : DAdams Project42
$
$ getent group Project42
Project42:x:1042:DAdams
$
```

Notice that the usermod command in Listing 7.21 uses two options, -aG. The -G adds the DAdams account as a member of the Project42 group, but the -a switch is important because it preservers any previous DAdams account group memberships. After the DAdams account is added as a Project42 group member, you can see in the last two command results that the /etc/group file record for Project42 was updated.

If you need to modify a particular group, the *groupmod* command is helpful. A group's GID is modified with the -g option, whereas a group's name is modified with the -n switch. In Listing 7.22, the Project42 group's GID is modified.

Listing 7.22: Using groupmod to modify a group

```
$ getent group Project42
Project42:x:1042:DAdams
$
$ sudo groupmod -g 1138 Project42
$
$ getent group Project42
Project42:x:1138:DAdams
$
```

Notice in Listing 7.22 that the Project42 group's GID is modified to 1138. The getent command confirms the /etc/group file was updated. If the 1138 GID was already in use by another group, the groupmod command would have displayed an error message and not changed the group's GID.

To remove a group, the *groupdel* utility is employed. An example is shown in Listing 7.23.

Listing 7.23: Using groupdel to delete a group

```
$ sudo groupdel Project42
$
```

```
$ getent group Project42
$
$ sudo groups DAdams
DAdams : DAdams
$
$ sudo find / -gid 1138 2>/dev/null
$
```

Notice in Listing 7.23 that once the Project42 group is deleted, the getent command shows that the Project42 group record has been removed from the /etc/group file. What is really nice is that any member of that deleted group has also had their group information updated, as shown in the third command.

When you have removed a group, it is important to search through the directory system for any files that may have access settings for that group. You can do this audit by using the find command and the deleted group's GID. An example of this task is shown as the fourth command. If you need help remembering how to use the find utility, go back to Chapter 4, where the command was originally covered.

Adding, modifying, and deleting user accounts and groups are basic but important skills. Keeping these tasks running smoothly makes the Linux system experience better for your users and makes your system more secure.

Managing Email

Email is one of the most-used features of the Internet. Whether it's creating a small, intraoffice email system or creating a Linux email server to support thousands of users, understanding email services on a Linux system has become a necessity.

Understanding Email

Before we take a look at email servers in Linux, let's first examine how Linux handles email in general. Linux follows the Unix method of handling email. One of the main innovations of the Unix operating system was to make email processing software modular.

Instead of having one monolithic program that handles all of the pieces required for sending and receiving mail, Linux uses multiple small programs that work together to process messages. Email functions are broken into separate pieces and then assigned to separate programs running on the system. Figure 7.2 shows you how most open source email software modularizes email functions in a Linux environment.

FIGURE 7.2   The Linux modular email environment

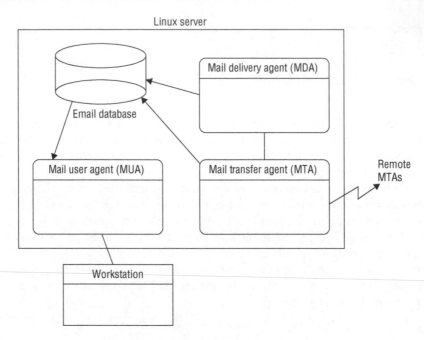

As you can see, the Linux email server is normally divided into three separate functions:

- The *mail transfer agent (MTA)* sends incoming emails (and outgoing emails being delivered locally) to a mail delivery agent (MDA) or local user's inbox. For outbound messages being transferred to a remote system, the agent establishes a communication link with another MTA program on the remote host to transfer the email.

- The mail delivery agent (MDA) is a program that delivers messages to a local user's inbox.

- The mail user agent (MUA) is an interface for users to read messages stored in their mailboxes. MUAs do not receive messages; they only display messages that are already in the user's mailbox.

The lines between these three functions are often fuzzy. Some Linux email packages combine functionality for the MTA and MDA functions, whereas others combine the MDA and MUA functions.

Choosing Email Software

Three popular MTA packages are in wide use in the Linux world:

Sendmail   The *Sendmail* MTA program was originally one of the most popular Linux MTA programs mainly due to its extreme versatility. Several standard features in Sendmail have become synonymous with email systems—message forwarding, user aliases, and mail lists.

Unfortunately, with versatility comes complexity. The Sendmail program's large configuration file often becomes overwhelming for novice mail administrators to handle. Around 2005, several security vulnerabilities plagued Sendmail, which also contributed to its drop in popularity.

Postfix   Wietse Venema, a security expert and programmer at IBM, wrote the *Postfix* program to be a complete MTA package replacement. Postfix is written as a modular program; it uses several different programs to implement the MTA functionality.

One of Postfix's best features is its simplicity. In addition, it enhances security over MTA products like Sendmail. Though not as flexible as Exim, Postfix is still highly popular. You can find out more at www.postfix.org.

Exim   Philip Hazel developed the *Exim* MTA program for the University of Cambridge in 1995. Although essentially it is a drop-in replacement for Sendmail, the configuration is quite different.

One of Exim's best features is its flexibility. It is available in most Linux distribution repositories and comes with a reasonable default configuration. Details on Exim are at www.exim.org.

Working with Email

Besides knowing the names of a few popular MTA programs, it is important to know how to use an MDA app. Additional email administration tasks, such as viewing an email queue and forwarding email messages, are also necessary for those managing Linux systems.

Sending and Receiving Email

Historically, the binmail program has been the most popular MDA program used on Linux systems. You might not recognize it by its official name, but you may have used it by its system name: *mail*. The name binmail comes from its typical location on the system, /bin/mail (or /usr/bin/mail).

The binmail program became popular because of its simplicity. By default, it can read email messages stored in the /var/spool/mail/ directory, or you can provide command-line options to point to the user's $HOME/mail file. No configuration is required for binmail to do its job.

Unfortunately, its simplicity means that binmail is limited in its functions. Because of that, some mail administrators have sought alternative MDA programs, and it is no longer installed by default on all Linux distributions.

 If you'd like to follow along with using the binmail program, you may need to install it on your Linux distribution. For Ubuntu, the package name is bsd-mailx, and for CentOS, though it is typically installed by default, the package name is mailx. Software package installation is covered in Chapter 2.

For sending email messages, the binmail program has the following basic syntax:

```
mail [OPTIONS] recipient…
```

The recipient can be either a username on the same system or a fully qualified email address, such as jdoe@example.com. You also can designate multiple addresses as the recipient. A few of the more commonly used *OPTIONS* include:

-s *subject*: Adds a subject line to the email. If your *subject* contains spaces, you will need to encase it in quotation marks.

-cc *recipient*: Designates an email address or addresses to receive a copy of the message. All email *recipient*s can see this address or addresses.

-bc *recipient*: Designates an email address or addresses to receive a copy of the message. Only the sender can see this address or addresses.

-v: Displays delivery details for the email message

An example of sending an email to a local user on the same Linux system is shown in Listing 7.24.

Listing 7.24: Using mail to send an email message

```
$ mail -s "LPIC-1 Book Progress" rich
Hi Rich,
I'm working on Chapter 7 right now.
How's Chapter 8 coming along?
Best regards,
Christine
EOT
$
```

Notice in Listing 7.24 that the subject matter is enclosed in quotation marks. This is important if your email subject line has spaces within it. Because the email is being sent to a user, rich, on the same system, only the username is needed.

When you press the Enter key after typing the mail command syntax, the program waits for you to enter your message without any prompts. When you have finished typing your message, you'll need to signal the mail utility to send the message. To do this, press the Enter key and then the Ctrl+D key combination. You'll see an EOT, which stands for "end of transmission," and be returned to the shell command-line prompt.

WARNING If your system is using Postfix as its MTA and you have usernames that are *not* lowercase, be aware that email may not be delivered. You'll have to either make the usernames all lowercase or dig into the various fixes for allowing multiple-case usernames with Postfix. You can check the /var/log/maillog or /var/log/mail.log file to find messages concerning undeliverable emails.

To read your emails, simply type the `mail` command and press Enter. You'll see a list of email messages (if you have any) and their associated index number, and you'll receive a & prompt. At the prompt, type the number of the email you wish to read. An example is shown snipped in Listing 7.25.

Listing 7.25: Using `mail` to read an email message

```
$ whoami
rich
$
$ mail
Heirloom Mail version 12.5 7/5/10.  Type ? for help.
"/var/spool/mail/rich": 1 message 1 new
>N  1 christine@localhost.  Wed May 22 13:04  23/721   "LPIC-1 Book Progress"
& 1
Message  1:
[…]
From: christine@localhost.localdomain
Status: R

Hi Rich,
I'm working on Chapter 7 right now.
How's Chapter 8 coming along?
Best regards,
Christine

& q
Held 1 message in /var/spool/mail/rich
You have mail in /var/spool/mail/rich
$
```

If you wish to delete email messages, type **d #**, where # is the number of the email message you wish to delete. When you are done reading and/or deleting your email messages, type **q** at the `mail` prompt to quit the utility.

If you don't have any email messages and you use the mail program to attempt to read a message, you'll receive the No email for *username* response.

If you have your email file stored in a nondefault location, you can tell the `mail` utility where to find it. Just tack on the `-f` *DirectoryName/FileName* option to the `mail` command.

If you have the correct permissions and need to read another user's email messages, you can also use the -f option along with the appropriate argument to designate the user's email file location. If the other user has their email file in a default location, you can use the -u *username* option and argument instead.

Checking the Email Queue

Occasionally problems occur and your outbound mail cannot be sent. You can quickly see this problem arising by viewing the local mail queue. There are two commands to accomplish this task: *mailq* and *sendmail -bp*.

To see these commands in action, we created an email that cannot be sent out due to a phony recipient email address. This bad email address causes the message to get stuck in the local mail queue long enough for us to view it. The event is shown in Listing 7.26.

Listing 7.26: Using mailq and sendmail -bp to view the local email queue

```
$ mail -s "Test of Mail Queue" bogususer@example.com
Testing mail queue
EOT
$
$ mailq
-Queue ID- --Size-- ----Arrival Time---- -Sender/Recipient-------
62D301CE55*     474 Wed May 22 14:03:20  christine@localhost.localdomain
                                          bogususer@example.com

-- 0 Kbytes in 1 Request.
$
$ sendmail -bp
-Queue ID- --Size-- ----Arrival Time---- -Sender/Recipient-------
62D301CE55*     474 Wed May 22 14:03:20  christine@localhost.localdomain
                                          bogususer@example.com

-- 0 Kbytes in 1 Request.
$
```

If there is nothing in the mail queue, when you enter the mailq or sendmail -bp command, you will receive the following response:

```
Mail queue is empty
```

The mail queue location(s) varies depending on which MTA you employ. It is typically located somewhere in the /var/spool/ directory tree. A quick way to locate the queue directory(ies) with the stuck mail files is to use super user privileges and the find command. Enter **find /var/**

spool -name *QueueID* at the command line, where *QueueID* is the identification number listed under the Queue ID column in the mailq or sendmail -bp command output. After you have the directory location(s), you can employ the rm utility to delete it.

Redirecting Email

An email alias allows you to redirect email messages to a different recipient. For example, on a corporate web server, instead of listing your email address (and at the same time letting every hacker in the world know your username) you can employ an alias, such as hostmaster. Via aliases, you configure email messages sent to hostmaster to go to your account instead.

Aliases are useful not only for security purposes but for common misspellings as well. If you have a difficult username, such as bresnahan, you can set up aliases for the prevalent incorrect spellings, such as breshan or brenanan. That way, you'll never miss an email.

While you do need to use super user privileges, there are only two steps to setting up an email alias:

1. Add the alias to the */etc/aliases* file.

2. Run the *newaliases* command to update the aliases database, */etc/aliases.db*.

The /etc/aliases.db is a binary file. Thus, you want to edit the text-based /etc/aliases file with your new aliases and run the newaliases command to update the binary file.

The format of the alias records in the /etc/aliases file is

ALIAS-NAME: RECIPIENT1[,RECIPIENT2[,…]]

An example of setting up an alias for the hostmaster is shown snipped in Listing 7.27. Prior to the modification, email for hostmaster was sent to the root account. After the /etc/aliases file modification and the newaliases command is run, email for hostmaster is now sent to two different accounts, christine and rich.

Listing 7.27: Using /etc/aliases and -newaliases to set up email aliases

```
# grep ^hostmaster /etc/aliases
hostmaster:     root
#
# nano /etc/aliases
#
# grep ^hostmaster /etc/aliases
hostmaster:     christine,rich
#
# newaliases
#
```

Listing 7.27: Using /etc/aliases and -newaliases to set up email aliases *(continued)*

```
# mail -s "Test of Aliases" hostmaster
Testing the new hostmaster alias
EOT
#
# exit
[…]
$ whoami
christine
$
$ mail
[…]
>N  1 root                    Wed May 22 15:10  18/656   "Test of Aliases"
& 1
Message  1:
[…]
To: hostmaster@localhost.localdomain
Subject: Test of Aliases
[…]
From: root@localhost.localdomain (root)
Status: R

Testing the new hostmaster alias

&
```

As shown in Listing 7.27, it's always a good idea to test out an alias modification. This is because many administrators forget to run the newaliases command after their modification to the /etc/aliases file.

Although aliases are useful for security and common misspellings, when a fellow team member is going to be gone on vacation for a few weeks, forwarding email is handy.

Setting up a forwarding email is done at the user level. It also involves only two steps:

1. The user creates the *.forward* file in their $HOME directory and puts in the username who should be receiving the forwarded emails.

2. The chmod command is used on the .forward file to set the permissions to 644 (octal). File permissions were covered in Chapter 4.

It's helpful to see an example of setting up a .forward file in order to forward email. One is provided in Listing 7.28.

Listing 7.28: Using .forward to forward email messages

```
$ whoami
christine
$
$ pwd
/home/christine
$
$ echo rich > .forward
$
$ chmod 644 .forward
$
$ mail -s "Testing of Forward" christine
Testing my .forward file
EOT
$
$ mail
[…]
>   1 root              Wed May 22 15:10   19/667   "Test of Aliases"
& q
Held 1 message in /var/spool/mail/christine
$
$ su - rich
Password:
[…]
$ mail
Heirloom Mail version 12.5 7/5/10.   Type ? for help.
"/var/spool/mail/rich": 3 messages 1 new 2 unread
    1 christine@localhost.  Wed May 22 13:04   24/732   "LPIC-1 Book Progress"
 U  2 root              Wed May 22 15:10   19/666   "Test of Aliases"
>N  3 christine@localhost.  Wed May 22 15:39   21/799   "Testing of Forward"
& 3
Message  3:
[…]
Subject: Testing of Forward
[…]
Status: R

Testing my .forward file

& q
Held 3 messages in /var/spool/mail/rich
$
```

Notice that after the .forward file was created and the proper permissions set on it, when an email was sent to christine, it was forwarded to rich instead. To stop the forwarding, all christine needs to do is delete the .forward file in her $HOME directory:

```
$ pwd
/home/christine
$ rm -i .forward
rm: remove regular file '.forward'? y
$
```

 When referring to files in a user's home directory, such as the .forward file, it can be written multiple ways. You may see $HOME/.forward, ~/.forward, or /home/*username*/.forward.

Emulating Commands

Because Sendmail was a popular MTA for so long, the Postfix MTA program wanted to maintain compatibility with it. To accomplish this, Postfix implemented a *sendmail emulation layer*. This allows certain Sendmail commands to work with the Postfix program. These commands include

- mailq
- sendmail -bp
- newaliases
- sendmail -I

We've covered all the commands in the preceding list except for sendmail -I. It operates just like the newaliases command.

You can find out more about the Sendmail emulation layer at www.postfix.org/sendmail.1.html.

Although we've only just touched on managing email, the concepts we've covered here are a good step in the right direction. You can use these various tools to assist in troubleshooting Linux email problems.

Using Log and Journal Files

Lots of things happen on a Linux system while it's running. Part of your job as a Linux administrator is to know everything that is happening and to watch for when things go wrong. The primary tool for accomplishing that task is the logging service.

All Linux distributions implement some method of *logging*. Logging directs short messages that indicate what events happen, and when they happen, to users, files, or even remote hosts for storage. If something goes wrong, the Linux administrator can review the log entries to help determine the cause of the problem.

Examining the syslog Protocol

In the early days of Unix, a range of different logging methods tracked system and application events. Applications used different logging methods, making it difficult for system administrators to troubleshoot issues.

In the mid-1980s Eric Allman defined a protocol for logging events from his Sendmail mail application called *syslog*. The syslog protocol quickly became a de facto standard for logging both system and application events in Unix, and it made its way to the Linux world.

What made the syslog protocol so popular is that it defines a standard message format that specifies the time stamp, type, severity, and details of an event. That standard can be used by the operating system, applications, and even devices that generate errors.

The type of event is defined as a *facility* value. The facility defines what is generating the event message, such as a system resource or an application. Table 7.8 lists the facility values defined in the syslog protocol.

TABLE 7.8   The syslog protocol facility values

Code	Keyword	Description
0	kern	Messages generated by the system kernel
1	user	Messages generated by user events
2	mail	Messages from a mail application
3	daemon	Messages from system applications running in background
4	auth	Security or authentication messages
5	syslog	Messages generated by the logging application itself
6	lpr	Printer messages
7	news	Messages from the news application
8	uucp	Messages from the Unix-to-Unix copy program
9	cron	Messages generated from the cron job scheduler
10	authpriv	Security or authentication messages

TABLE 7.8   The syslog protocol facility values *(continued)*

Code	Keyword	Description
11	ftp	File Transfer Protocol application messages
12	ntp	Network Time Protocol application messages
13	security	Log audit messages
14	console	Log alert messages
15	solaris-cron	Another scheduling daemon message type
16-23	local0-local7	Locally defined messages

As you can tell from Table 7.8, the syslog protocol covers many different types of events that can appear on a Linux system.

Each event is also marked with a *severity*. The severity value defines how important the message is to the health of the system. Table 7.9 shows the severity values as defined in the syslog protocol.

TABLE 7.9   The syslog protocol severity values

Code	Keyword	Description
0	emerg	The event causes the system to be unusable
1	alert	An event that requires immediate attention
2	crit	An event that is critical but doesn't require immediate attention
3	err	An error condition that allows the system or application to continue
4	warning	A non-normal warning condition in the system or application
5	notice	A normal but significant condition message
6	info	An informational message from the system
7	debug	Debugging messages for developers

Combining the facility and severity codes with a short informational message provides enough logging information to troubleshoot most problems in Linux.

Viewing the History of Linux Logging

Over the years there have been many open source logging projects for Linux systems. The ones that have been the most prominent are as follows:

- *sysklogd*: The original syslog application, it includes two programs: the `syslogd` program to monitor the system and applications for events, and the `klogd` program to monitor the Linux kernel for events.

- *syslogd-ng*: Added advanced features, such as message filtering and the ability to send messages to remote hosts.

- *rsyslog*: The project claims the "r" stands for "rocket fast." Speed is the focus of the rsyslog project, and the `rsyslogd` application has quickly become the standard logging package for many Linux distributions.

- *systemd-journald*: Part of the systemd application for system startup and initialization (see Chapter 5), many Linux distributions are now using this for logging. It does not follow the syslog protocol but instead uses a completely different way of reporting and storing system and application events.

The following sections dive into the details of the two most popular logging applications: `rsyslogd` and `systemd-journald`.

Logging Basics Using *rsyslogd*

The *rsyslogd* application utilizes all of the features of the original syslog protocol, including the configuration format and logging actions. This section walks through how to configure the `rsyslogd` logging application and where to find the common log files it generates.

Configuring *rsyslogd*

The `rsyslogd` program uses the `/etc/rsyslogd.conf` configuration file and, on some distributions, `*.conf` files in the `/etc/rsyslog.d/` directory to define what events to listen for and how to handle them. The configuration file(s) contains rules that define how the program handles syslog events received from the system, kernel, or applications. The format of an `rsyslogd` rule is

```
facility.priority action
```

The `facility` entry uses one of the standard syslog protocol facility keywords. The `priority` entry uses the severity keyword as defined in the syslog protocol, but with a twist. When you define a severity, `syslogd` will log all events with that severity or higher (lower severity code). Thus, the entry

```
kern.crit
```

logs all kernel event messages with a severity of critical, alert, or emergency. To log only messages with a specific severity, use an equal sign before the priority keyword:

kern.=crit

You can also use wildcard characters for either the facility or priority. The following entry logs all events with an emergency severity level:

*.emerg

The *action* entry defines what rsyslogd should do with the received syslog message. Six action options are available:

- Forward to a regular file
- Pipe the message to an application
- Display the message on a terminal or the system console
- Send the message to a remote host
- Send the message to a list of users
- Send the message to all logged-in users

Listing 7.29 shows the entries in the configuration file for an Ubuntu 18.04 system.

Listing 7.29: The rsyslogd.conf configuration entries for Ubuntu 18.04

```
auth,authpriv.*          /var/log/auth.log
*.*;auth,authpriv.none   -/var/log/syslog
kern.*                   -/var/log/kern.log
mail.*                   -/var/log/mail.log
mail.err                 /var/log/mail.err
*.emerg                  :omusrmsg:*
```

The first entry shown in Listing 7.29 defines a rule to handle all auth and authpriv facility type messages. This shows that you can specify multiple facility types by separating them with commas. The rule also uses a wildcard character for the priority, so all severity levels will be logged. This rule indicates that all security event messages will be logged to the /var/log/auth.log file.

The second entry defines a rule to handle all events (*.*), except security events (the .none priority). The event messages are sent to the /var/log/syslog file. The minus sign in front of the filename tells rsyslogd to not sync the file after each write, increasing the performance. The downside to this is if the system crashes before the next normal system sync, you may lose the event message.

The last entry defines a rule to handle all emergency events. The omusrmsg command indicates that you want to send the event message to a user account on the system. When you specify the wildcard character, this rule sends all emergency event messages to all users on the system.

For comparison, Listing 7.30 shows the entries in the rsyslogd configuration file for a CentOS 7 system.

Listing 7.30: The rsyslog.conf configuration file for CentOS 7

```
*.info;mail.none;authpriv.none;cron.none    /var/log/messages
authpriv.*                                   /var/log/secure
mail.*                                       -/var/log/maillog
cron.*                                       /var/log/cron
*.emerg                                      :omusrmsg:*
uucp,news.crit                               /var/log/spooler
local7.*                                     /var/log/boot.log
```

Notice that Red Hat–based systems use the /var/log/messages file for informational messages and the /var/log/secure file for security messages.

Sending Log Messages to a Log Server

A common server these days in many data centers is a *central logging host* that receives and stores logs for all its various log client systems. Configuring your system to act as a *logging client* is fairly easy using the rsyslog application's configuration file(s).

To send all your log messages to a central logging host server, edit the /etc/rsyslogd .conf configuration file and go to the file's bottom. You'll need to add a line to the file with syntax that follows the standard *facility.priority action* of the syslog protocol. Typically, most administrators send everything to the remote logging server, so the *.* is used to designate the *facility.priority*. However, the action for sending log messages to a remote server has the following special syntax:

TCP|UDP[(z#)]HOST:[PORT#]

This action syntax is rather confusing, so let's step through it:

- *TCP|UDP*: You can select either the TCP or UDP protocols (covered in Chapter 8) to transport your log messages to the central log server. UDP can lose data, so you should select TCP if your log messages are important. Use a single at sign (@) to select UDP and double at signs (@@) to choose TCP.

- [(z#)]: The brackets indicate this syntax is optional. The z selects zlib to compress the data prior to traversing the network, and the # picks the compression level, which can be any number between 1 (lowest compression) and 9 (highest compression). Note that you must enclose the z and the number between parentheses, such as (z5).

- HOST: This syntax designates the central logging server either by a fully qualified domain name (FQDN), such as example.com, or an IP address. If you use an IPv6 address, it must be encased in brackets.

- [*PORT#*]: The brackets indicate that this syntax is optional. This designates the port on the remote central logging host where the log service is listening for incoming traffic.

An example is helpful here. Let's say you want to send all your log messages to a remote logging host that is located at loghost.ivytech.edu and listen for incoming log message TCP traffic on port 6514. To minimize network use, you'd like to compress log messages with the highest compression. On each client system, you'll need to add the following line to the bottom of the /etc/rsyslog.conf file:

```
*.*   @@(z9)loghost.ivytech.edu:6514
```

After you make this modification, you'll need to reload the configuration file or restart the rsyslogd service to begin transmitting log messages to the active central logging server.

Rotating Log Files

As you can guess, for busy Linux systems it doesn't take long to generate large log files. To help combat that, many Linux distributions install the *logrotate* utility. It automatically splits rsyslogd log files into archive files based on a time or the size of the file. You can usually identify archived log files by a numerical extension added to the log filename. An example is shown in Listing 7.31 of the /var/log/btmp file (this file contains bad attempts to log into the system and is displayed using the lastb command).

Listing 7.31: The /var/log/btmp file and a rotated version of itself

```
$ ls /var/log/btmp*
/var/log/btmp   /var/log/btmp-20190501
$
```

The logrotate utility does more than rotate log files. It can also compress, delete, and if desired, mail a log file to a designated account.

To ensure the files are handled in a timely manner, the logrotate utility is typically run every day as a cron job (cron is covered in Chapter 9). It employs the /etc/logrotate.conf configuration file to determine how each log file is managed. A logrotate configuration file on a CentOS system is shown in Listing 7.32.

Listing 7.32: Viewing the /etc/logrotate.conf file on a CentOS distribution

```
$ cat /etc/logrotate.conf
# see "man logrotate" for details
# rotate log files weekly
weekly

# keep 4 weeks worth of backlogs
rotate 4

# create new (empty) log files after rotating old ones
create

# use date as a suffix of the rotated file
dateext
```

```
# uncomment this if you want your log files compressed
#compress

# RPM packages drop log rotation information into this directory
include /etc/logrotate.d

# no packages own wtmp and btmp -- we'll rotate them here
/var/log/wtmp {
    monthly
    create 0664 root utmp
        minsize 1M
    rotate 1
}

/var/log/btmp {
    missingok
    monthly
    create 0600 root utmp
    rotate 1
}

# system-specific logs may be also be configured here.
$
```

One nice feature about the /etc/logrotate.conf file is that it is well commented (nearly every item following a # is a comment) and fairly easy to understand. The first half of this file contains global directives (settings). For example, notice the dateext option. This option directs logrotate to use the current date in an archived (rotated) log file's name, as was shown in Listing 7.31. If the dateext option is *not* employed, the rotated log files will have a number as their file extension, with the biggest number indicating the oldest log file:

```
mail.log
mail.log.1
mail.log.2
```

In the second half of the /etc/logrotate.conf file in Listing 7.32 are specific rotation settings for the /var/log/wtmp and /var/log/btmp log files. These options apply to only these particular log files and override any global settings.

Notice in Listing 7.32 that right before the nonglobal settings is the line

```
include /etc/logrotate.d
```

This line tells logrotate to use any configuration files stored in the /etc/logrotate.d/ directory for *additional* specific log file rotation options. The configuration files here are given the same name as the log files they managed, as shown in Listing 7.33.

Listing 7.33: Looking at the /etc/logrotate.d/ files on a CentOS distribution

```
$ ls /etc/logrotate.d/
bootlog   glusterfs    libvirtd.qemu   psacct   syslog
chrony    iscsiuiolog  numad           samba    wpa_supplicant
cups      libvirtd     ppp             sssd     yum
$
$ cat /etc/logrotate.d/bootlog
/var/log/boot.log
{
    missingok
    daily
    copytruncate
    rotate 7
    notifempty
}
$
```

Notice that the /etc/logrotate.d/boot.log contents are similar to the settings for the /var/log/wtmp and /var/log/btmp log files within the /etc/logrotate.conf file. A few of the more common specific logrotate directives for the various log files are shown in Table 7.10.

TABLE 7.10 The more common logrotate directives for specific log files

Directive	Description
hourly	Log file is rotated hourly. If this setting is employed, the schedule for the logrotate cron job typically needs modification.
daily	Log file is rotated daily.
weekly n	Log file is rotated weekly on the n day of the week, where 0 is equal to Sunday, 1 is equal to Monday, 2 is equal to Tuesday, and so on to 6 for Saturday. 7 is a special number that indicates the log file is rotated every 7 days, regardless of the current day of the week.
monthly	Log file is rotated the first time logrotate is run within the current month.
size n	Rotates log file based on size and not time, where n indicates the file's size that triggers a rotation (n followed by nothing or k assumes kilobytes, M indicates megabytes, and G denotes gigabytes).
rotate n	Log files rotated more than n times are either deleted or mailed, depending on other directives. If n equals 0, rotated files are deleted, instead of rotated.

Directive	Description
dateformat *format-string*	Modify the dateext setting's date string using the *format-string* specification.
missingok	If log file is missing, do not issue an error message and continue on to the next log file.
notifempty	If the log file is empty, do not rotate this log file, and continue on to the next log file.

There are many more directives you can set to fine-tune your log files' rotation. To view all the various settings, type **man logrotate** at the command line.

 Many distributions maintain a logrotate status file located in the /var/lib/logrotate/ directory, which is helpful for troubleshooting or viewing the latest log rotation. On CentOS, the filename is logrotate .status, and on Ubuntu, it is the status file.

Making Log Entries

If you create and run scripts on your Linux system (see Chapter 9), you may want to log your own application events. You can do that with the *logger* command-line tool:

```
logger [-isd] [-f file] [-p priority] [-t tag] [-u socket] [message]
```

The -i option specifies the process ID (PID) of the program that created the log entry as part of the event message. The -p option allows you to specify the event priority. The -t option lets you specify a tag to add to the event message to help make finding the message in the log file easier. You can either specify the message as text in the command line or specify it as a file using the -f option. The -d and -u switches are advanced options for sending the event message to the network. The -s option sends the event message to the standard error output.

An example of using logger in a script would look like this:

$ **logger This is a test message from rich**

On an Ubuntu system, you can look at the end of the /var/log/syslog file to see the log entry:

$ **tail /var/log/syslog**

...

Feb 8 20:21:02 myhost rich: This is a test message from rich

Notice that rsyslogd added the time stamp, host, and user account for the message. This is a great troubleshooting tool!

Finding Event Messages

Generally, most Linux distributions create log files in the /var/log directory. Depending on the security of the Linux system, many log files are readable by everyone, but some may not be.

As seen earlier in Listing 7.29 and Listing 7.30, most Linux distributions create separate log files for different event message types, although they don't always agree on the log filenames.

It's also common for individual applications to have a separate directory under the /var/log directory for their own application event messages, such as /var/log/apache2 for the Apache web server.

Since rsyslogd log files are text files, you can use any of the standard text tools available in Linux, such as cat, head, tail, as well as filtering tools, such as grep, to view the files and search them.

One common trick for administrators is to watch a log file by using the -f option with the tail command. That displays the last few lines in the log file but then monitors the file for any new entries and displays those too.

Journaling with *systemd-journald*

The systemd system services package includes the *systemd-journald* journal utility for logging. Notice that we called it a *journal utility* instead of a logging utility. The systemd-journald program uses a completely different method of storing event messages from the syslog protocol. However, it does store syslog messages as well as notes from the kernel, boot events, service messages, and so on.

This section discusses how to use the systemd-journald program to track event messages on your Linux system.

Configuring *systemd-journald*

The systemd-journald service reads its configuration from the /etc/systemd/journald. conf configuration file. When you examine this file, you'll notice settings that control how the application works and controls items, such as the journal file's size. Table 7.11 describes commonly modified directives.

TABLE 7.11   The journald.conf file commonly modified directives

Directive	Description
Storage=	Set to auto, persistent, volatile, or none. Determines how systemd-journald stores event messages. (Default is auto.)
Compress=	Set to yes or no. If yes, journal files are compressed. (Default is yes.)
ForwardToSyslog=	Set to yes or no. If yes, any received messages are forwarded to a separate syslog program, such as rsyslogd, running on the system. (Default is yes.)

Directive	Description
ForwardToWall=	Set to yes or no. If yes, any received messages are forwarded as wall messages to all users currently logged into the system. (Default is yes.)
MaxFileSec=	Set to a number followed by a time unit (such as month, week, or day) that sets the amount of time before a journal file is rotated (archived). Typically this is not needed if a size limitation is employed. To turn this feature off, set the number to 0 with no time unit. (Default is 1month.)
RuntimeKeepFree=	Set to a number followed by a unit (such as K, M, or G) that sets the amount of disk space systemd-journald must keep free for other disk usages when employing volatile storage. (Default is 15% of current space.)
RuntimeMaxFileSize=	Set to a number followed by a unit (such as K, M, or G) that sets the amount of disk space systemd-journald journal files can consume if it is volatile.
RuntimeMaxUse=	Set to a number followed by a unit (such as K, M, or G) that sets the amount of disk space systemd-journald can consume when employing volatile storage. (Default is 10% of current space.)
SystemKeepFree=	Set to a number followed by a unit (such as K, M, or G) that sets the amount of disk space systemd-journald must keep free for other disk usages when employing persistent storage. (Default is 15% of current space.
SystemMaxFileSize=	Set to a number followed by a unit (such as K, M, or G) that sets the amount of disk space systemd-journald journal files can consume if it is persistent.
SystemMaxUse=	Set to a number followed by a unit (such as K, M, or G) that sets the amount of disk space systemd-journald can consume when employing persistent storage. (Default is 10% of current space.)

Changing a journal file from being volatile to persistent is covered later in this chapter. Thus, the Storage directive settings in Table 7.11 need a little more explanation, because they are involved in this activity:

- auto: Causes systemd-journald to look for the /var/log/journal directory and store event messages there. If that directory doesn't exist, it stores the event messages in the temporary /run/log/journal directory, which is deleted when the system shuts down.

- persistent: Causes systemd-journald to automatically create the /var/log/journal directory if it doesn't currently exist and store event messages there.

- volatile: Forces systemd-journald to store only event messages in the temporary /run/log/journal directory.

- none: Event messages are discarded.

 Quite a few settings allow you to customize exactly how systemd-journald works in your system. For a full list and explanation of all the settings, type man journald.conf at the command prompt.

Looking at Journal Files

You may have one or more active journal files on your system, depending on how systemd-journald is configured. For example, if you have Storage set to persistent, you can employ the SplitMode directive to divide up the journal file into multiple active files— one per user as well as a system journal file.

The file(s) directory location is contingent on whether or not the journal is persistent. In either case, the system's active journal file is named system.journal, with user active journal files (if used) named *user-UID*.journal.

These journal files are rotated automatically when a certain size or time is reached, depending on the directives set in the journal.conf file. After the files are rotated, they are renamed and considered archived. The archived journal filenames start with either system or *user-UID*, contain an @ followed by several letters and numbers, and end in a .journal file extension.

Listing 7.34 is snipped and shows active and archived journal files on an Ubuntu distribution.

Listing 7.34: Viewing the active and archived journal files on an Ubuntu distro

```
$ ls /var/log/journal/e9af6ca5a8fb4a70b2ddec4b1894014d/
system@220262350f2a468c87bb85484e9ad813-0000000000000001-0005897bfdead50c.journal
system@220262350f2a468c87bb85484e9ad813-00000000000197b0-000589f47e451cdc.journal
system@80103f1d22df49c7beee5c818e58f96f-0000000000000001-000587c56d17a0fd.journal
[…]
system.journal
user-1000@be988ab4869e43239d9cfdebd38c7e72-0000000000000451-000571ee64814f08.journal
user-1000@be988ab4869e43239d9cfdebd38c7e72-0000000000004e25-000584a03f80097a.journal
[…]
user-1000.journal
user-1001@e19748f488ce450b94e17fed79ee9669-00000000000028c7-000572dfa721935c.journal
[…]
user-1001.journal
[…]
$
```

Notice that this system employs both system and user journal files and that several of the files have been archived. The `systemd-journald` configuration dictates when the archived journal files are removed from the system based on size directives, such as `SystemMaxFileSize`, or time directives, such as `MaxFileSec`.

 On some systems, you can manually rotate (archive) active journal files. If this feature is available on your system, you can do this via the `journalctl --rotate` command.

Layering Your Logging

If desired (or required), you can have both `systemd-journald` and a syslog protocol application, such as `rsyslog`, running and working together. There are two primary ways to accomplish this:

Journal Client Method This method allows a syslog protocol program to act as a *journal client*, reading entries stored in the journal file(s). It is typically the preferred way, because it avoids losing any important messages that may occur during the system boot, before the syslog service starts. Also for `rsyslog`, this is commonly already configured, which is handy.

For `rsyslog`, if this method is not already configured or you'd like to check your system, look in the /etc/rsyslog.conf file. It needs to have the `imuxsock` and/or `imjournal` module being loaded via `ModLoad` without a preceding pound sign (#), as shown here:

```
$ grep ModLoad /etc/rsyslog.conf | grep -E "imjournal | imuxsock"
$ModLoad imuxsock # provides support for local system logging […]
$ModLoad imjournal # provides access to the systemd journal
$
```

Forward to Syslog Method This method employs the file /run/systemd/journal/syslog. Messages are forwarded to the file (called a socket) where a syslog protocol program can read them.

To use this method, you need to modify the journal configuration file, /etc/systemd/journald.conf, and set the `ForwardToSyslog` directive to yes. Keep in mind that you'll need to load the modified journald.conf file into `systemd-journald` in order for it to take effect. Unfortunately, you cannot employ the `systemctl reload` option to load the new configuration for `systemd-journald`. Instead, using super user privileges, you must restart the service:

```
systemctl restart systemd-journald
```

Making the Journal Persistent

On some distributions, the journal entries are stored in the /run/log/journal directory, which is *volatile*, meaning it is removed, and the journal entries are lost whenever the system is shut down. Therefore, typically system admins set the `Storage` directive within the journald.conf file, changing it to `persistent`.

When this configuration is loaded (via a systemctl restart, which was covered earlier), systemd-journald automatically creates the /var/log/journal directory, moves the journal file to its new location, and starts storing journal entries in it. Also, since this file is *persistent*, the file survives system shut downs and reboots, and its entries are not removed.

While you can set the Storage directory to auto and create the /var/log/journal directory yourself, it's a little tricky getting the directory permissions set correctly. Thus, it's best to let systemd-journald do the work for you.

Viewing Journal Entries

The systemd-journald program doesn't store journal entries in text files. Instead it uses its own binary file format that works similar to a database. Although this makes it a little harder to view journal entries, it does provide for quick searching for specific event entries.

The *journalctl* program is our interface to the journal files. The basic format for the journalctl command is

journalctl [*OPTIONS...*] [*MATCHES...*]

The *OPTIONS* control how data returned by the *MATCHES* is displayed and/or additionally filtered. Table 7.12 lists commonly used switches. To view all of the various available options, type **man journalctl** at the command line.

TABLE 7.12   The journalctl utility's commonly used options

Short option	Long option	Description
-a	--all	Display all data fields, including unprintable characters.
-e	--pager-end	Jump to the end of the journal and display the entries.
-k	--dmesg	Display only kernel entries.
-n *number*	--lines=*number*	Show the most recent *number* journal entries.
-r	--reverse	Reverse the order of the journal entries in the output.
-S *date*	--since=*date*	Show journal entries starting at *date*, where date is formatted as YYYY-MM-DD:HH:MM:SS. If time specification is left off of date, then 00:00:00 is assumed. Keywords such as yesterday, today, tomorrow, and now can all replace date.
-U *date*	--until=*date*	Show journal entries until *date* is reached in the entries. *date* formatting is the same as it is for the -S option.
-u *unit* or *pattern*	--unit=*unit* or *pattern*	Show only journal entries for the systemd *unit* or systemd units that match *pattern*.

By default the journalctl utility employs the less pager to display its entries. If you desire this to be turned off, use the --no-pager option.

A simple example of using journalctl without *MATCHES* and showing the last 10 messages on an Ubuntu system is shown snipped in Listing 7.35.

Listing 7.35: Viewing output from the journalctl command using only options

```
$ sudo journalctl -n 10 --no-pager
-- Logs begin at Wed 2018-07-25 12:02:39 EDT, end at Wed 2019-[…]
May 29 16:22:59 Ubuntu1804 systemd[2114]: Listening on GnuPG c[…]
May 29 16:22:59 Ubuntu1804 systemd[2114]: Reached target Paths[…]
May 29 16:22:59 Ubuntu1804 systemd[2114]: Listening on D-Bus U[…]
May 29 16:22:59 Ubuntu1804 systemd[2114]: Reached target Socke[…]
May 29 16:22:59 Ubuntu1804 systemd[2114]: Reached target Basic[…]
May 29 16:22:59 Ubuntu1804 systemd[1]: Started User Manager fo[…]
May 29 16:22:59 Ubuntu1804 systemd[2114]: Reached target Defau[…]
May 29 16:22:59 Ubuntu1804 systemd[2114]: Startup finished in […]
May 29 16:24:01 Ubuntu1804 sudo[2225]: Christine : TTY=pts/0 ;[…]
May 29 16:24:01 Ubuntu1804 sudo[2225]: pam_unix(sudo:session):[…]
$
```

The *MATCHES* for the journalctl utility filter what type of journal entries to display. Table 7.13 lists the various commonly used filters that are available.

TABLE 7.13   The common journalctl *MATCHES* parameter used for filtering

Match	Description
field	Match the specific *field* in the journal. Can enter multiple occurrences of *field* on same line but must be separated with a space. You can separate multiple *field* specifications with a plus sign (+) to use a *logical or* between them.
OBJECT_PID=*pid*	Match only entries made by the specified application *pid*.
PRIORITY=*value*	Match only entries with the specified priority value. The value can be set to one of the following numbers or keywords: emerg (0), alert (1), crit (2), err (3), warning (4), notice (5), info (6), debug (7).
_HOSTNAME=*host*	Match only entries from the specified *host*.
_SYSTEMD_UNIT=*unit.type*	Match only entries made by the specified systemd *unit.type*.

TABLE 7.13   The common journalctl *MATCHES* parameter used for filtering *(continued)*

Match	Description
_TRANSPORT=*transport*	Match only entries received by the specified *transport* method.
_UDEV_SYSNAME=*dev*	Match only entries received from the specified device.
_UID=*userid*	Match only entries made by the specified user ID.

Keep in mind that Table 7.13 lists only a few of the commonly used *MATCHES*. To view all the various available *MATCHES*, type **man systemd-journal-fields** at the command line.

> To use journalctl to view all the various journal entries, you'll need to be logged in as the root user, use super user privileges, or typically belong to the systemd-journal group. Recognize that your distribution may use a different group for this task.

When you are looking for specific event entries in the journal, use the desired filters and options to target specific items. In snipped Listing 7.36, only today's entries for the ssh.service systemd service unit are displayed.

Listing 7.36: Using filters with the journalctl command

```
$ sudo journalctl --since=today _SYSTEMD_UNIT=ssh.service
-- Logs begin at Wed 2018-07-25 12:02:39 EDT, end at Wed 2019-05-29 [...]
May 29 14:10:50 Ubuntu1804 sshd[772]: Server listening on 0.0.0.0 port 22.
May 29 14:10:50 Ubuntu1804 sshd[772]: Server listening on :: port 22.
May 29 14:10:55 Ubuntu1804 sshd[772]: Received SIGHUP; restarting.
[...]
May 29 16:09:38 Ubuntu1804 sshd[2047]: Connection closed by 127.0.0.1 [...]
May 29 16:22:58 Ubuntu1804 sshd[2112]: Accepted password for Christine [...]
May 29 16:22:58 Ubuntu1804 sshd[2112]: pam_unix(sshd:session): session [...]
$
```

Employing various journalctl filters makes digging through journal files much easier.

> The journalctl utility has a feature similar to using tail -f on a log file. Just employ the journalctl -f or --follow switch, and you will see the last few entries and additional entries as they are added to the journal. When you are done watching, press the Ctrl+C key combination to quit.

Maintaining the Journal

Besides configuring a persistent journal and keeping the journal disk usage in check, you have a few manual management activities you can employ for maintaining your journal file(s).

You can check the current disk usage of the journal file(s) by employing the `journalctl --disk-usage` command. An example on an Ubuntu distro is shown in Listing 7.37.

Listing 7.37: Checking journal file disk usage

```
$ journalctl --disk-usage
Archived and active journals take up 344.0M in the file system.
$
```

The output from the command in Listing 7.37 shows how much current disk space all the journal files, active and archived, are taking up on the partition.

While `systemd-journald` can automatically clean up disk space via settings in the `journald.conf` file, you can do so manually as well. In this case, you employ a vacuum... well, actually it's vacuum options available on the `journalctl` command:

```
--vacuum-size
--vacuum-time
```

As you would expect, `--vacuum-size` removes journal files until the disk space consumed by journal files reaches the designated size. You follow the option with a number and tack on a unit (K, M, G, or T) to set the size. Be aware that this removes only *archived* journal files and has no effect on any active journal files.

For the `--vacuum-time` option, you designate the oldest journal entries allowed, and the rest are deleted. The time is denoted with a number as well as a time unit (s, min, h, days, months, weeks, or years), such as 10months. Like the `size` option, the `time` option affects only archived journal files. The active files are left untouched.

While you can combine the two different switches if needed, the snipped example in Listing 7.38 uses only the `size` option to pare down on disk usage.

Listing 7.38: Cleaning up journal file disk usage

```
$ journalctl --disk-usage
Archived and active journals take up 344.0M in the file system.
$
$ sudo journalctl --vacuum-size=300M
Deleted archived journal
[…]
Vacuuming done, freed 24.0M of archived journals from /var/log/journal/
e9af6ca5a8fb4a70b2ddec4b1894014d.
$
$ journalctl --disk-usage
Archived and active journals take up 320.0M in the file system.
$
```

Notice that after the vacuuming was completed, another journalctl --disk-usage command was issued, but it shows 320.0M instead of the 300M size set on the vacuum option. This is because though the disk-usage switch shows both active and archived journal files, the vacuum options work *only* on archived journal files.

 If you'd like to back up your active journal file(s), you should be fine simply copying them first. However, right before you make a copy, run the journalctl --sync command to ensure all the entries are moved from their queue into the file.

Viewing Different Journal Files

If you need to retrieve a journal file from a rescued system but view it first or look at the entries in an archived or copied journal file, a few journalctl switches are available that can help.

Because journalctl looks for the active journal files in either the /run/log/journal or the /var/log/journal directory, you can point it to a different directory location where a copied or another system's journal file is located by using the -D *directory-name* or --directory=*directory-name* option.

If the file you are trying to view has a different name than system.journal or user-*UID*.journal, use the --file=*pattern* option on the journalctl command. Set the *pattern* to be the exact name of the file you wish to view. However, if there are several files, you can employ file globbing within the *pattern* (file globbing was covered in Chapter 4) to match several files.

If you have recently rescued your system and now have two or more journal files with entries to view, you can merge them. To do this, use the -m or --merge switches on the journalctl utility. Keep in mind this does not *physically* merge the journal files but instead merges their entries in the output for your perusal.

 The systemd-journald journal utility allows you to send your system's journals to a centralized journal host system via systemd-journal-remote. To view all the various journal files' entries on the central host, you'll need to employ the -m or --merge option when using the journalctl command.

Making Journal Entries

Similar to using logger for syslog protocol programs, you can add journal entries from the command line or scripts using the *systemd-cat* tool. In order to do so, you must pipe your command's STDOUT into the utility:

```
command | systemd-cat
```

An example of employing the systemd-cat command is shown in Listing 7.39. Notice that the test message was successfully added to the active journal file.

Listing 7.39: Adding a journal entry with the systemd-cat utility

```
$ echo "Test of systemd-cat" | systemd-cat
$
$ journalctl --no-pager | grep systemd-cat
May 30 17:43:46 Ubuntu1804 cat[2599]: Test of systemd-cat
$
```

If your system allows an installed syslog protocol program to act as a journal client by loading the imuxsock module, you can use the logger utility as well to make journal entries. An example of this is shown snipped in Listing 7.40.

Listing 7.40: Adding a journal entry with the logger utility

```
$ logger "Test of logger"
$
$ journalctl -r
-- Logs begin at Thu 2018-07-26 18:19:45 EDT, end at Thu 2019-05-30 […]
[…]
May 30 17:45:29 Ubuntu1804 Christine[2606]: Test of logger
[…]
May 30 17:43:46 Ubuntu1804 cat[2599]: Test of systemd-cat
 […]
$
```

By employing the -r option (reverse) on the journalctl command, you can see recent entries, which in this case includes both the systemd-cat and the logger utilities' entries. Notice that logger adds the username to the entry.

Properly controlling your logs and journals is helpful in troubleshooting problems as well as tracking down potential security issues. Next, we'll look at a concept that goes hand in hand with managing logs and journals.

Maintaining the System Time

Keeping the correct times on all servers is crucial. Many elements depend on accurate time, such as programs designed to run at particular moments, remote services that expect accurate client times (and will reject the client if their times are inaccurate), and maintaining accurate log message time stamps in order to properly investigate client/server issues.

Understanding Linux Time Concepts

Local time is also called *wall clock time*. Historically, people glanced at a clock on the wall (or their analog watches) to determine when to go to scheduled meetings, take lunch breaks, and leave work to go home. The official standard name for this is *localtime*.

If you are dealing with people around the world, it's often easier to use a different standard called *Coordinated Universal Time (UTC)*, and yes, that abbreviation is correct. UTC is a time that does not change according to an individual's time zone (time zones were covered in Chapter 6). Thus, the UTC time in Indianapolis, Indiana, is equal to the UTC time in Helsinki, Finland. You can say, "I'll contact you at 9:44 UTC tomorrow from Algiers, New Orleans" to your business partner in New York City, and they will know the exact time without using any special calculations. (You can see the current UTC time on several websites, including `time.is/UTC`.)

Linux systems commonly maintain two types of time clocks. One is software based, and the other is hardware based. The *hardware clock*, in this case, is also called the *real-time clock*. This clock attempts to maintain the correct time, even when the system is powered down by using power from the system battery (traditionally called the *CMOS battery*).

When the system boots, the Linux OS gets the time from the hardware clock and updates its *software clock*. This clock runs only while the system is up and is used by many utilities on Linux, which is why it is sometimes called *system time*. Unfortunately the Linux software clock has a tendency to become inaccurate, especially if it is a busy system.

Viewing and Setting Time

You can view (and change) the time on both the hardware and software clocks as well as switch them between using UTC and localtime. The various utilities to do so have their own special syntax and benefits.

Using the *hwclock* Utility

The command that is primarily used for the hardware clocks is *hwclock*, and its syntax is as follows:

hwclock [*OPTIONS...*]

The commonly used *OPTIONS* for the *hwclock* utility are described in Table 7.14.

TABLE 7.14 Common hwclock utility options

Short option	Long option	Description
N/A	--localtime	Sets the hardware clock to use the localtime standard
-r	--show	Displays the current hardware clock time
-s	--hctosys	Reads the current hardware clock time, and sets the software clock to that time
-u	--utc	Sets the hardware clock to use the UTC standard
-w	--systohc	Reads the current software clock time, and sets the hardware clock to that time

An example of reading the hardware clock and displaying its time is shown in Listing 7.41.

Listing 7.41: Reading the hardware clock time using the hwclock -r command

```
$ hwclock -r
hwclock: Cannot access the Hardware Clock via any known method.
hwclock: Use the --debug option to see the details of our search
 for an access method.
$
$ sudo hwclock -r
2019-05-31 14:01:17.622439-0400
$
```

Notice that the hwclock utility requires super user privileges, even to read the time. Also note that the date is shown, and the time is displayed in military format. On some distributions, you see time displayed using an a.m./p.m. format instead.

> It's best to keep your hardware clock using the UTC standard. If you switch it to the localtime standard, problems may ensue. They can include problems with daylight saving changes and time zone shifts.

Using the *date* Utility

The software clock primarily uses the *date* command and/or the timedatectl utility (covered in the next section) to view/set the system time. The date command's syntax is

```
date [-u|--utc|--universal] [MMDDhhmm[[CC]YY][.ss]]
```

To view the current system time, you enter **date** at the command line. No special privileges or options are needed:

```
$ date
Fri May 31 14:11:23 EDT 2019
```

Setting the system time with the *date* utility takes a little more work. If you are specifying localtime, then no switches are needed, but if you are setting UTC, then use one of the following options: -u, --utc, or --universal.

> You may not be able to set the time on the software clock with the date command if your system is already using Network Time Protocol (NTP) or Simple Network Time Protocol (SNTP), covered later in this chapter. You can check for these active services by issuing **systemctl status ntpd**, **systemctl status chronyd**, and **systemctl status systemd-timesyncd**. If any of those commands show an active service, you may be unable to set the system time with the date command.

An example of modifying the system time on a CentOS distribution using super user privileges is shown in Listing 7.42.

Listing 7.42: Changing the software clock time using the date command

```
# date
Fri May 31 14:26:48 EDT 2019
#
# date 05301430
Thu May 30 14:30:00 EDT 2019
#
# date
Thu May 30 14:30:02 EDT 2019
#
```

To set the system time using date, you must first specify the current month, in this case May (05), the current date, the 31st (31), and then the time using military format. We change the time from 14:26 to 14:30 (1430). If desired, you can also optionally specify the century (*CC*), the year (*YY*), and the desired seconds (.*ss*), as shown earlier in the date command's syntax.

> If you need to modify your server's time zone, the concepts for this task are covered in Chapter 6.

Using the *timedatectl* Utility

The *timedatectl* utility is the preferred method for manually managing the Linux software clock. The command alone without any options provides a great deal of information. (You can get the same information by tacking on the status option, but there is no need to do so.) An example of this on a CentOS distribution is shown in Listing 7.43.

Listing 7.43: Using the timedatectl command on a CentOS distribution

```
$ timedatectl
      Local time: Fri 2019-05-31 15:41:27 EDT
  Universal time: Fri 2019-05-31 19:41:27 UTC
        RTC time: Fri 2019-05-31 19:21:20
       Time zone: America/New_York (EDT, -0400)
     NTP enabled: yes
NTP synchronized: yes
 RTC in local TZ: no
      DST active: yes
 Last DST change: DST began at
                  Sun 2019-03-10 01:59:59 EST
                  Sun 2019-03-10 03:00:00 EDT
```

```
Next DST change: DST ends (the clock jumps one hour backwards) at
                 Sun 2019-11-03 01:59:59 EDT
                 Sun 2019-11-03 01:00:00 EST
$
```

The command's output may be different depending on your distribution. Listing 7.44 provides an example of using the timedatectl utility to show the current time information on an Ubuntu distro.

Listing 7.44: Using the timedatectl command on an Ubuntu distribution

```
$ timedatectl
                      Local time: Fri 2019-05-31 15:25:13 EDT
                  Universal time: Fri 2019-05-31 19:25:13 UTC
                        RTC time: Fri 2019-05-31 19:25:14
                       Time zone: America/Indiana/Indianapolis (EDT, -0400)
       System clock synchronized: yes
systemd-timesyncd.service active: yes
                 RTC in local TZ: no
$
```

Notice from the two previous listings that the system clock manages a lot of information, including the system time in localtime and UTC standards, the time zone, as well as daylight saving time.

To change the system time, you need to employ the timedatectl command and use super user privileges. In addition, add the set-time option and date/time with the following syntax:

```
timedatectl set-time "YYYY-MM-DD HH:MM:SS"
```

An example of doing this is shown on a CentOS distribution in Listing 7.45.

Listing 7.45: Using the timedatectl command to set the system time

```
# date
Fri May 31 15:59:13 EDT 2019
#
# timedatectl set-time "2019-05-31 16:15:00"
Failed to set time: Automatic time synchronization is enabled
#
# timedatectl set-ntp 0
#
# timedatectl set-time "2019-05-31 16:15:00"
#
# date
Fri May 31 16:15:04 EDT 2019
#
```

Notice in Listing 7.45 that the first attempt to change the system time failed, because automatic time synchronization is enabled. To turn this off, use the `timedatectl set-ntp 0` command. You can reenable it later by issuing the same command, but change the 0 to a 1.

> If you are following along with the commands in the book and cause yourself problems by changing the software clock on your system, you can typically make things right again by rebooting. Just type **reboot**, and press Enter at the command line.

You can also manage a few items on the hardware clock with the `timedatectl` utility. For example, you can flip-flop the clock between using the localtime and UTC standard. The syntax to accomplish this is

`timedatectl set-local-rtc` *Boolean-value*

To force the hardware clock to use the localtime standard, set *Boolean-value* to 1. To change it to the UTC standard, switch *Boolean-value* to 0.

Understanding the Network Time Protocol

The *Network Time Protocol (NTP)* is a network protocol used to synchronize clocks over a network in order to provide accurate time. The clocks can be on personal computer systems, network routers, servers, and so on. Programs implementing NTP can typically operate as both a client and a server, and they can perform peer-to-peer as well.

To provide accurate time, NTP uses what is called a *clock stratum* scheme, which provides a layered approach to accessing correct time sources. The stratums are numbered from 0 to 15. The devices at stratum 0 are highly accurate time-keeping hardware devices, such as atomic clocks. The next level down is stratum 1, which consists of computers that are directly connected to the stratum 0 devices. Continuing down the stratum configuration, the stratum 2 servers use network time protocol client software that allows them to request time data served up by the stratum 1 computers.

Every stratum has potentially thousands of NTP clients, each receiving time updates from NTP servers in the higher stratum or each other (called *NTP peers*). Figure 7.3 provides a sample illustration of this concept.

Stratum 0 devices have the most accurate time, with the directly connected Stratum 1 computers being the next most precise. After those two stratum levels, requested time updates travel as data in packets across the network. Because network travel time for the packets may take milliseconds (or more), the time becomes less accurate for the servers lower in the stratum configuration.

FIGURE 7.3   The NTP protocol clock stratum

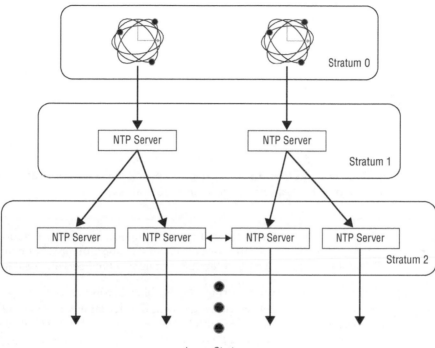

Lower Stratums

However, the NTP protocol attempts to minimize travel time using special rules that allow packets carrying time data to traverse more quickly between the NTP server and client. Programs that implement the NTP client/server protocol also typically have a mechanism for appropriately adjusting the time in order to offset NTP packet travel time.

The Simple Network Time Protocol (SNTP) mentioned earlier in the chapter is a simplified version of NTP. Although NTP can achieve high levels of time accuracy, SNTP is more for applications or systems not dependent on accurate clocks.

If you have never selected an NTP time source, looking at the clock stratum can make it seem rather difficult. But don't fret, it's not. You do have several good choices that are free and open to the public.

pool.ntp.org   One of the most popular NTP servers is actually a cluster of servers that work together in what is called a *pool*. Each time server that participates in the pool is a volunteer. To use the NTP server pool, when you configure your NTP client application, enter *pool.ntp.org* as your NTP server (note that the syntax is a little different than shown here for the configuration and will be covered later in this chapter). Each time a clock update request goes to pool.ntp.org, a different pool member provides a response. The official website is ntppool.org, and this site provides some nice explanations on how to use these pool servers on Linux systems.

A lovely feature of the NTP server pool is that you can dig down into the pool to find clusters of servers that meet special requirements. For example, most distributions come with their own subgrouping in the pool, such as centos.pool.ntp.org and Ubuntu.pool.ntp.org. These distro groupings allow you to set up an NTP client application and test it prior to picking another time server.

Other subgroupings in the pool let you use physically closer NTP servers, which may assist in providing more accurate time. For example, if your NTP client application resides in Canada, you can use pooled servers from either north-america.pool.ntp.org or ca.pool.ntp.org. Keep in mind that if you use pool.ntp.org the NTP pool software does its best to provide time from a server that is close to your system.

If you have a need for more accurate time and lower network resource usage, do not use pool.ntp.org or one of its subgroupings. For example, if your Internet service provider (ISP) provides a time server, use it instead.

Google Time Servers and Smear An interesting time problem revolves around leap seconds. Because the earth's rotation has been slowing down, our actual day is about 0.001 seconds less than 24 hours. To compensate for this on our computers, leap seconds were introduced. About every 19 months or so, NTP passes a leap second announcement. This is typically handled without any problems and the clocks are set backward by one second. However, some applications have problems, especially those on other systems that are not handling leap seconds.

To combat this problem, Google introduced free public time servers that use NTP and smear the leap second over the course of time so that there is no need to issue a leap second announcement. This is called *leap-smearing*. The Google leap-smearing NTP servers are time$n$.google.com, where n is set to 1 through 4. If you choose to use a leap-smearing time server on your system, you should not mix in time servers on your NTP client program that do not employ this technique.

Server Lists If leap-smearing and pools of NTP servers don't meet your system's needs, you have other choices. For example, there is a list of time servers you can peruse at support.ntp.org/bin/view/Servers/WebHome. Be sure to read the site's Rules of Engagement prior to selecting and using the NTP servers on this list.

If your applications need highly accurate time, do not use an NTP-client program with an Internet-based time source. Instead, investigate clock hardware that can be integrated with your server or act as a local time server.

If you need to implement an NTP client program, you have choices. You can either employ the NTP daemon (ntpd) or use the newer chrony daemon (chronyd).

Using the NTP Daemon

For years the NTP program was synonymous with the network time protocol, and on Linux they were often spoken of interchangeably. But it does have some limitations, such as keeping time accurate when the network has high traffic volumes, which is why alternatives such as chrony were developed.

The NTP program is installed by default on some distributions and not on others. The package name is ntp, so you can check to see if it is installed (or if you need to do so) by using the appropriate package management tool (covered in Chapter 2).

Configuring the NTP daemon

The NTP daemon is *ntpd* and its primary configuration file is /etc/ntp.conf. It contains, among other directives, the NTP time servers you wish to use. The directive name for setting these is server. The server lines from an /etc/ntp.conf file on a CentOS distribution are shown in Listing 7.46.

Listing 7.46: Looking at the tserver directives in the /etc/ntp.conf file

```
$ grep ^server /etc/ntp.conf
server 0.centos.pool.ntp.org iburst
server 1.centos.pool.ntp.org iburst
server 2.centos.pool.ntp.org iburst
server 3.centos.pool.ntp.org iburst
$
```

Notice that by default the NTP servers chosen are from the CentOS pool. When designating servers from the pool.ntp.org or a subgroup, to make the syntax correct you need to place a 0 before the first one, 0.centos.pool.ntp.org, a 1 before the second one, and so on. Notice also the iburst at the end of each line. This directive helps to speed up the initial time synchronization.

When ntpd starts, it sends packets to every time server configured within the /etc/ntp.conf file. From the servers' replies, it chooses the fastest responder as the one to use as its NTP server.

 Port 123 is used by ntpd, so prior to starting up the NTP daemon make sure that port is accessible through the firewall.

On older Linux systems, you had to deal with something called *insane time*, which occurred when your system's time was more than 17 minutes different than real time, and the NTP servers would not talk to your system because of it. Therefore, it was a common practice to manually update your software clock before starting ntpd.

While on modern distributions insane time is no longer a problem, it's still handy to know how to manually update your system time via NTP utilities. The command to use is *ntpdate*. You'll need super user privileges and one of your time servers listed in the /etc/ntpd.conf file to pass to it as an argument:

```
ntpdate 0.pool.ntp.org
```

When you are ready to start up ntpd, use super user privileges and the systemctl command:

```
systemctl start ntpd
```

(If your system does not use systemd, see Chapter 2 for alternative methods to start services.) Be sure to enable it as well so that the ntpd service will start at system boot via the systemctl enable ntpd command.

Immediately after starting, ntpd will begin the processes of synchronizing your software clock. Be sure to wait at least 10 to 15 minutes before checking its status. You can do this via the ntpstat command, as shown in Listing 7.47.

Listing 7.47: Viewing the software time synchronization via the ntpstat command

```
$ ntpstat
synchronised to NTP server (74.6.168.73) at stratum 3
   time correct to within 70 ms
   polling server every 128 s
$
```

Notice that not only does the *ntpstat* command show you how accurate your software clock is currently and how often polling for the correct time is taking place, but you also get to see the IP address of the NTP server and what stratum level it operates on.

Managing the NTP Service

Besides employing the ntpstat command to periodically check on the accuracy of your software clock, you can view a table showing what time servers your ntpd is polling and when the last synchronization took place. The command that provides this information is *ntpq –p*. An example is shown in Listing 7.48.

Listing 7.48: Viewing time server and polling information via the ntpq command

```
$ ntpq -p
     remote           refid      st t when poll reach   delay   offset  jitter
==============================================================================
+vps5.ctyme.com  216.218.254.202  2 u   260  128  376   70.606   17.175  14.527
*t2.time.gq1.yah 208.71.46.33     2 u    40  128  377   74.892   17.062   7.880
 dfw1.ntp5.mattn .STEP.          16 u     - 1024    0    0.000    0.000   0.000
+helium.constant 128.59.0.245     2 u    10  128  377   42.163   18.043   9.173
$
```

If desired, once your software clock is fairly accurate via NTP, you can manually set the hardware clock to its time. Just use the `hwclock -systohc` command covered earlier in this chapter.

Using the chrony Daemon

The chrony daemon (*chronyd*) has many improvements over ntpd. It can keep accurate time even on systems that have busy networks or that are down for periods of time, and even on virtualized systems. In addition, it synchronizes the system clock faster than does ntpd, and it can easily be configured to act as a local time server itself. With few exceptions, most distributions recommend that you employ the chrony service for software clock synchronization.

You'll find on CentOS and other Red Hat–based distros that the chrony program is installed by default, but not enabled on boot (by default). The package name is chrony, and it is available in most distribution repositories. So if you need to install it, you can do so by using the appropriate package management tool (covered in Chapter 2).

You'll find that on Ubuntu, when chrony is installed it is automatically started and enabled on boot. To start it on CentOS, user super user privileges and type **systemctl start chronyd** at the command line. Use the same command again, but replace start with enable to have chrony start at system boot time.

Configuring the chrony Daemon

The primary configuration file for chrony is the chrony.conf file, and it may be stored in the /etc/ or the /etc/chrony/ directory. Typically, there is no need to modify anything in this configuration file, but you might want to look at a few items.

The configuration file contains, among other directives, the NTP time servers to use. The directive name for setting these is either server or pool. For chrony, the server directive is typically used for a single time server designation, whereas pool indicates a server pool. The /etc/chrony/chrony.conf file pool lines from an Ubuntu distribution are shown in Listing 7.49.

Listing 7.49: Looking at the pool directives in the /etc/chrony/chrony.conf file

```
$ grep ^pool /etc/chrony/chrony.conf
pool ntp.ubuntu.com          iburst maxsources 4
pool 0.ubuntu.pool.ntp.org iburst maxsources 1
pool 1.ubuntu.pool.ntp.org iburst maxsources 1
pool 2.ubuntu.pool.ntp.org iburst maxsources 2
$
```

Notice that the pool settings are similar to the ntpd server settings in the /etc/ntp.conf file. The maxsources parameter is one exception to this similarity. It designates the maximum number of time servers from the designated source. If one of those servers goes down, chrony finds another one to take its place.

Port 123 is used by chronyd, so before starting up the chrony daemon, make sure that port is accessible through the firewall.

Another directive you should check in the chrony.conf file is the rtcsync directive. This handy setting directs chrony to periodically update the hardware time (real-time clock). If you find it on its own configuration file line with nothing else, then it is set for chrony:

rtcsync

With this directive set and chrony running, you'll no longer have to employ that hard-to-remember hwclock command (hwclock --systohc) to update the real-time clock with the software clock's time. Now that's an improvement.

If you modify the configuration and chronyd is not already started, to start it use super user privileges and the systemctl command:

systemctl start chronyd

If chronyd is already started and you have to modify the configuration file, you'll need to restart it instead:

systemctl restart chronyd

(If your system does not use systemd, see Chapter 2 for alternative methods to start services.) If necessary, be sure to enable it as well so that the chronyd service will start at system boot via the systemctl enable chronyd command.

Managing the chrony Service

The chrony service provides the chronyc command-line utility for managing it. Several commands are available that are similar to or that surpass the ntpd commands.

If you are familiar with employing ntpq -p for viewing your system's time sources, you can use *chronyc* sources -v instead. An example of this command is shown in Listing 7.50 on an Ubuntu distribution using chrony.

Listing 7.50: Looking at source time servers via the chronyc sources -v command

```
$ chronyc sources -v
210 Number of sources = 8

  .-- Source mode  '^' = server, '=' = peer, '#' = local clock.
 / .- Source state '*' = current synced, '+' = combined , '-' = not combined,
| /   '?' = unreachable, 'x' = time may be in error, '~' = time too variable.
||                                                 .- xxxx [ yyyy ] +/- zzzz
||      Reachability register (octal) -.          |  xxxx = adjusted offset,
||      Log2(Polling interval) --.      |         |  yyyy = measured offset,
||                                \      |         |  zzzz = estimated error.
||                                 |     |          \
```

```
MS Name/IP address          Stratum Poll Reach LastRx Last sample
===============================================================================
^+ alphyn.canonical.com          2  10   377    413   -461us[ -418us] +/-   101ms
^+ golem.canonical.com           2  10   337    142   +30us[  +30us] +/-    95ms
^+ chilipepper.canonical.com     2  10   377    918   -797us[ -760us] +/-    81ms
^+ pugot.canonical.com           2  10   377     21  -2184us[-2184us] +/-    87ms
^* 4.53.160.75                   2  10   377    229   -327us[ -281us] +/-    50ms
^+ vps3.cobryce.com              2  10   377    416  +4806us[+4850us] +/-    70ms
^+ B1-66ER.matrix.gs             2  10   377    21m   -315us[ -363us] +/-    60ms
^+ 2.time.dbsinet.com            2   9   175    601  -3138us[-3097us] +/-    93ms
$
```

There is a lot of useful information in that display. Notice that at the top it tells you the current number of time server sources (8) that chronyd is employed.

Along the same lines but providing more statistical information on the time server sources is chronyc sourcestats. An example is shown in Listing 7.51.

Listing 7.51: Viewing time server stats via the chronyc sourcestats command

```
$ chronyc sourcestats
210 Number of sources = 8
Name/IP Address            NP  NR  Span  Frequency  Freq Skew  Offset   Std Dev
===============================================================================
alphyn.canonical.com       31  15   87m    +0.322     0.287    -180us    677us
golem.canonical.com        31  18   91m    -0.006     0.137    -470us    275us
chilipepper.canonical.com  31  14   96m    -0.044     0.163    -661us    383us
pugot.canonical.com        28  16   87m    -0.029     0.350    -637us    575us
4.53.160.75                31  20   90m    +0.003     0.166    -553us    370us
vps3.cobryce.com           30  14   87m    -0.195     0.531   +4453us    936us
B1-66ER.matrix.gs          30  13   72m    -0.095     0.351    +523us    635us
2.time.dbsinet.com         27  16   71m    +0.073     0.327   -2801us    431us
$
```

If you want something that lets you see whether your software clock is being synchronized like the netstat command shows, along with a lot more information concerning the software clock's performance, try out the chronyc tracking command. An example is shown in Listing 7.52.

Listing 7.52: Viewing software clock information via the chronyc tracking command

```
$ chronyc tracking
Reference ID    : 0435A04B (4.53.160.75)
Stratum         : 3
Ref time (UTC)  : Sat Jun 01 19:22:01 2019
```

Listing 7.52: Viewing software clock information via the chronyc tracking command *(continued)*

```
System time     : 0.000197749 seconds slow of NTP time
Last offset     : -0.000001978 seconds
RMS offset      : 0.001266906 seconds
Frequency       : 31.578 ppm fast
Residual freq   : +0.000 ppm
Skew            : 0.077 ppm
Root delay      : 0.034032539 seconds
Root dispersion : 0.022529230 seconds
Update interval : 1027.0 seconds
Leap status     : Normal
$
```

There are several other useful chronyc commands you can use to manage and monitor chrony. To peruse them all, enter **man chronyc** at the command line.

Summary

In this chapter, we took a close look at creating, modifying, and deleting user accounts and groups. We explored email utilities and concepts that are helpful in troubleshooting as well as using system email. In addition, we studied log files that are critical for troubleshooting problems and keeping a watchful eye on security. Finally, we looked at how to properly maintain a system's time.

These skills will assist you in ensuring that all the servers in your care are running efficiently. In addition, your systems will have fewer problems, the troubles you encounter can be solved sooner, and with these skills, you can spend more time away from work.

Exam Essentials

Describe the players in managing user accounts.   The /etc/login.defs and /etc/default/useradd files configure various settings for the useradd command's default behavior. Because the directive settings within these files vary from distribution to distribution, it is wise to peruse them prior to employing the useradd utility to create accounts. When an account is created, the /etc/passwd, /etc/shadow, and /etc/group files are all modified. Depending on the user account creation configuration, a user home directory may be created and files copied to it from the /etc/skel/ directory. To modify user accounts, you employ the usermod command and to delete them the userdel utility. Account information can be viewed using the getent utility. Employ the chage command to view an account's /etc/shadow record information as well as modify it.

Summarize managing groups.   The commands involved in creating, modifying, and deleting groups are the groupadd, groupmod, and groupdel commands. These commands cause modifications to the /etc/group file. If you need to add a user to a group, you need to employ the usermod utility. A user can easily switch from the account's default group to another group in which the account is a member by using the newgrp program. Account group membership can be audited via the groups and getent commands as well as by viewing the /etc/group file.

Explain how to use various email utilities.   Managing and troubleshooting the three MTAs (Sendmail, Postfix, Exim) can be accomplished using various available email utilities. To view an account's mail on the system, use the binmail utility, mail. For messages that may be stuck on the system, look at the mail queue using either the mailq or sendmail -bp command. You can set up email aliases by editing the /etc/aliases file and then running the newaliases command, which will update the aliases database, /etc/aliases.db. To temporarily forward emails, a user can create the .forward file in their home directory, put in the username to whom the emails should be sent, and then set the proper permissions on the file. Because the Sendmail MTA was so popular, Postfix provides a Sendmail emulation layer, which allows Sendmail commands to be used on their system.

Clarify how rsyslogd logging operates.   The rsyslogd service implements the syslog protocol. It uses the /etc/rsyslogd.conf configuration file, and on some distributions includes the /etc/rsyslog.d/*.conf files. Within the configuration files, rules determine what to log and where to log it via the *facility.priority action* format. Log messages can be sent to a remote logging server (with or without compression) using the *TCP|UDP[(z#)]HOST:[PORT#]* format. Log files are rotated with the logrotate cron job, which is configured in the /etc/logrotate.conf file. Log messages can be generated manually using the logger command.

Summarize how to review and manage journal entries.   The systemd-journald service is responsible for journal message data. The daemon is controlled via the /etc/systemd/journal.conf configuration file. By default the journal files are stored in the /run/system/journal/ directory tree, which makes them volatile. To make the files persistent and store them in the /var/log/journal/ directory tree, the Storage directive within the configuration file is changed to persistent and the systemd-journald service restarted. The rsyslog utility can act as a journal client as long as certain criteria are met. For example, the imuxsock and/or imjournal modules are loaded in the /etc/rsyslog.conf file.

Journal entries can only be viewed using the journalctl utility. To view system journal data, you must either use super user privileges or be a member of the systemd-journal group. To view the entire current journal data file, simply use the journalctl command with no parameters. To screen journal data, use the various filters available with the journalctl utility. Journal files are automatically rotated based on size or time settings in the journal.conf file. Active journal files are moved to archived journal files, their names are modified, and in some cases older archived journal files are deleted. Administrators can also manually clean up archived journal files by employing the journalctl command along with the vacuum options. Manual journal entries are created using the systemd-cat utility, and if the configuration for rsyslog meets certain criteria, the logger command as well.

Describe the various NTP daemons.   The older ntpd provides NTP client/server services and uses the /etc/ntp.conf as its configuration file. The server lines within the file designate time servers or time server clusters, such as 0.pool.ntp.org, from which to poll for the correct time. You can manually set the system time (software clock) using a server designation in the configuration file via the ntpdate command. You can view time synchronization status using the ntpstat utility, and you can view polling activity and statistic through the ntpq -p command.

The newer chronyd provides NTP client server services and uses the /etc/chrony.conf or /etc/chrony/chrony.conf configuration file. The server lines within the file typically designate a single time server, whereas pool lines designate time server clusters, such as 0.ubuntu.pool.ntp.org, from which to poll for the correct time. The rtcsync directive tells chrony to periodically update the hardware time (real-time clock). Utilities that assist in viewing the chrony time sources include the chronyc sources and chronyc sourcestats commands. Additional information can be gleaned from the chronyc tracking utility.

Review Questions

You can find the answers in the appendix.

1. Which of the following are fields within a /etc/passwd file record? (Choose all that apply.)

   A. User account's username

   B. Password

   C. Password change date

   D. Special flag

   E. UID

2. Which of the following are fields within an /etc/shadow file record? (Choose all that apply.)

   A. Maximum password age

   B. Account expiration date

   C. Password

   D. Comment

   E. Default shell

3. Which of the following commands will allow you to view the NUhura account's record data in the /etc/passwd file? (Choose all that apply.)

   A. getent NUhura passwd

   B. cat /etc/passwd

   C. passwd NUhura

   D. grep NUhura /etc/passwd

   E. getent passwd NUhura

4. You create an account using the useradd utility, except for some reason the account's home directory was not created. Which of the following most likely caused this to occur?

   A. The HOME directive is set to no.

   B. You did not employ super user privileges.

   C. The CREATE_HOME directive is not set.

   D. The INACTIVE directive is set to -1.

   E. The EXPIRE date is set and it is before today.

5. Which of the following commands will allow you to switch temporarily from your account's default group to another group with whom you have membership?

   A. The usermod command

   B. The newgrp command

   C. The groups command

   D. The groupadd command

   E. The groupmod command

6. Which of the following commands is the best one to add JKirk as a member to a new group called the NCC-1701 group and not remove any of the account's previous group memberships?

    A. usermod -g NCC-1701 JKirk

    B. usermod -G NCC-1701 JKirk

    C. usermod -aG NCC-1701 JKirk

    D. groupadd NCC-1701

    E. groupmod NCC-1701 JKirk

7. Which of the following could be used to view the members of the NCC-1701 group? (Choose all that apply.)

    A. groups NCC-1701

    B. getent group NCC-1701

    C. getent groups NCC-1701

    D. grep NCC-1701 /etc/group

    E. grep NCC-1701 /etc/groups

8. What command can you use to check if there is a long list of messages in the email queue? (Choose all that apply.)

    A. systemctl sendmail status

    B. sendmail -bp

    C. sendmail -bq

    D. mailq

    E. ls /var/spool

9. Your email server receives a message addressed to support. The support address has an alias of wesley on this computer. Assuming the system is properly configured, what account will receive the email message?

    A. support

    B. None

    C. Account in ~/.forward

    D. root

    E. wesley

10. Which syslog facility keyword represents event messages received from the system job scheduler?

    A. cron

    B. user

    C. kern

    D. console

    E. auth

11. What syslog severity level has the highest priority ranking in `rsyslogd`?

   A. `crit`

   B. `alert`

   C. `emerg`

   D. `notice`

   E. `err`

12. What configuration file does `rsyslogd` use by default?

   A. `rsyslog.conf`

   B. `journald.conf`

   C. `syslogd.conf`

   D. `rsyslog.d`

   E. `syslog.d`

13. What `journalctl` option displays the most recent journal entry first?

   A. `-a`

   B. `-l`

   C. `-r`

   D. `-e`

   E. `-n`

14. You want to manually add an entry to the system's active journal. What command can you use to do this?

   A. `journalctl`

   B. `journalctl-cat`

   C. `systemd-cat`

   D. `systemdd-journal`

   E. `journalctl -logger`

15. Which of the following are clocks or time that can be typically viewed or modified on a Linux system? (Choose all that apply.)

   A. Hardware clock

   B. System time

   C. Software clock

   D. Atomic clock

   E. Real-time clock

16. Which of the following utilities will allow you to change the time on a Linux system's hardware clock?

    A. hwclock

    B. date

    C. timedatectl

    D. ntpdate

    E. rtcsync

17. What command will allow you to see the system time in both its current time zone as well as in UTC?

    A. hwclock -r

    B. date

    C. timedatectl

    D. ntpq -p

    E. chronyc sources

18. Which of the following is a correct configuration lines in the /etc/ntp.conf file for the ntpd service, assuming you will be using the pool.ntp.org time servers? (Choose all that apply.)

    A. server pool.ntp.org iburst

    B. pool pool.ntp.org iburst maxsources 2

    C. service pool.ntp.org iburst

    D. server 0.pool.ntp.org iburst

    E. service 0.pool.ntp.org iburst

19. A system administrator, Geordi, has recently configured and started the ntpd service to obtain accurate time for his system's software clock. He'd like to update the hardware clock, but wants to quickly check if the software clock is now synchronized. What is the best command he should use?

    A. ntpdate

    B. ntpstat

    C. ntpq -p

    D. date

    E. hwclock -w

20. Miles wants to configure his newly installed chrony. Which of the following might be a configuration file he needs to view/modify? (Choose all that apply.)

    A. /etc/ntp.conf

    B. /etc/ntp/chrony.conf

    C. /etc/chrony.d/chrony.conf

    D. /etc/chrony.conf

    E. /etc/chrony/chrony.conf

Chapter

8

Configuring Basic Networking

OBJECTIVES

✓ **109.1** Fundamentals of internet protocols

✓ **109.2** Persistent network configuration

✓ **109.3** Basic network troubleshooting

✓ **109.4** Configure client side DNS

These days it's almost a necessity to have your Linux system connected to some type of network. Whether it's the need to share files and printers on a local network, or the need to connect to the Internet to download updates and security patches, most Linux systems have some type of network connection.

This chapter looks at how to configure your Linux system to connect to a network, as well as how to troubleshoot network connections if things go wrong. Unfortunately, there are a few different methods for configuring network settings in Linux, and you'll need to know them all for the LPIC-1 exam. First, we'll cover the common locations for the configuration files in Linux distributions. Next, we'll examine the different tools you have at your disposal that help make configuring the network settings easier. After that, you'll learn some simple network troubleshooting techniques.

Networking Basics

Before we take a look at how Linux handles network connectivity, let's go through the basics of *computer networking*. Computer networking is how we get data from one computer system to another. To help simplify things, computer networks are often described as layered systems. Different layers play different roles in the process of getting the data from one network device to another.

There's lots of debate, though, on just how best to split up the networking layers. While the standard Open Systems Interconnection (OSI) network model uses seven layers, we'll use a simplified four-layer approach to describing the network functions:

- The physical layer
- The network layer
- The transport layer
- The application layer

The following sections detail the parts contained in each of these four layers.

The Physical Layer

The physical layer consists of the hardware required to connect your Linux system to the network. If you've ever connected a computer to either a home or office network, we're sure you're already familiar with the two main methods used to connect network devices: wired and wireless network connections.

Wired network connections use a series of network switches to connect network devices using special Ethernet cables. The network switch accepts data packets from the network device and then sends the data packets to the correct destination device on the network. For large office network installations, switches are usually connected in a cascade design to help reduce traffic load on the network. Switches can be interconnected with one another to help segment the network traffic into smaller areas. Figure 8.1 demonstrates a common layout for a wired network.

FIGURE 8.1   A wired office network infrastructure

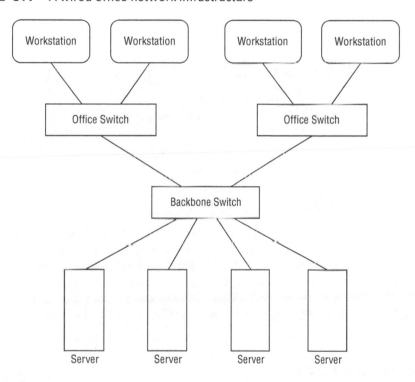

While the term "wired" may make you think of copper cables, it can also apply to network connections that use *fiber-optic cables*. Fiber-optic cables use light to transmit data down a thin glass strand, achieving faster speeds and covering longer distances than conventional copper connections. Although wired networking can be cumbersome, it does provide the fastest network speeds (currently up to 100 gigabits per second). For that reason, wired networking is still popular in Linux server environments where high throughput is a must.

Nowadays, though, most small office and home networks utilize *wireless networking*. Instead of using physical wires or fiber cables to connect devices, wireless networking uses radio signals to transmit the data between the network device and a *network access point*. The access point works in a similar way to the switch in that it controls how data is sent to each network device communicating with it.

Each access point uses a unique *service set identifier* (SSID) to identify it from other access points, which can be a text name or a number. You just tell your Linux system which access point to connect to by specifying the correct SSID value. Figure 8.2 demonstrates a common wireless network layout.

FIGURE 8.2   A wireless network infrastructure

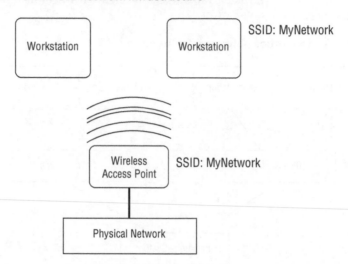

The downside to wireless networking is that you can't control where the radio signals travel. It's possible that someone outside of your home will see your access point signals and try to connect to them. Because of that, it's important to implement some type of encryption security on your access point. Only devices using the correct encryption key can connect to the wireless access point. Common wireless encryption techniques are Wired Equivalent Privacy (WEP), Wi-Fi Protected Access (WPA), and Wi-Fi Protected Access version 2 (WPA2).

The Network Layer

The *network layer* controls how data is sent between connected network devices, both in your local network and across the Internet. For data to get to the correct destination device, some type of network addressing scheme must be used to uniquely identify each network device. The most common method for doing that is the *Internet Protocol* (IP).

While the IP network protocol is by far the most popular in use, it's not the only network protocol available. Apple uses a proprietary protocol called AppleTalk to allow Apple computers to communicate with one another on a local network, and Novell used the IPX/SPX protocol for communication between Novell network servers and clients. These network protocols, however, have faded from standard use and aren't covered on the LPIC-1 exam.

To connect your Linux system to an IP network you'll need four pieces of information:

- An IP address
- A hostname
- A default router
- A netmask value

The following sections walk through what each of these values represent.

The IP Address

In an IP network, each network device is assigned a unique 32-bit address. Networking layer software embeds the source and destination IP addresses into the data packet so that networking devices know how to handle the data packet and the Linux system knows which packets to read and which to ignore.

To make it easier for humans to recognize the address, IP addresses are split into four 8-bit values, represented by decimal numbers, with a period between each value. This format is called *dotted-decimal notation*. For example, a standard IP address in dotted-decimal notation looks like 192.168.1.10.

IP addresses are split into two sections. One part of the IP address represents the *network address*. All devices on the same physical network have the same network address portion of their IP addresses. For example, if your home network is assigned the network address 192.168.1.0, all of the network devices must start with the IP address 192.168.1.

The second part represents the *host address*. Each device on the same network must have a unique host address. Figure 8.3 demonstrates assigning unique IP addresses to devices on a local network.

FIGURE 8.3 Network addressing on a local network

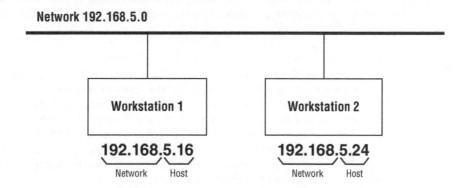

To complicate things even further, an updated IP network protocol has been introduced called *IP Version 6* (IPv6). The IPv6 networking scheme uses 128-bit addresses instead of the 32-bit addresses used by IP, which allows for lots more network devices to be uniquely identified on the Internet.

The IPv6 method uses hexadecimal numbers to identify addresses. The 128-bit address is split into eight groups of four hexadecimal digits separated by colons, such as

`fed1:0000:0000:08d3:1319:8a2e:0370:7334`

If one or more groups of four digits is 0000, that group or those groups may be omitted, leaving two colons:

`fed1::08d3:1319:8a2e:0370:7334`

However, only one group of zeroes can be compressed this way.

The IPv6 protocol also provides for two different types of host addresses:

▪ Link local addresses

▪ Global addresses

The IPv6 software on a host device automatically assigns the *link local address*. The link local address uses a default network address of `fe80::` and then derives the host part of the address from the media access control (MAC) address built into the network card. This ensures that any IPv6 device can automatically communicate with any other IPv6 device on a local network without any configuration.

The IPv6 global address works similarly to the original IP version: each network is assigned a unique network address, and each host on the network must have a unique host address.

Netmask Address

The *netmask* address distinguishes between the network and host address portions in the IP address by using 1 bit to show which bits of the 32-bit IP address are used by the network and 0 bits to show which bits represent the host address. Since most people don't like working with binary numbers, the netmask address is usually shown in dotted-decimal format. For example, the netmask address 255.255.255.0 indicates the first three decimal numbers in the IP address represent the network address, and the last decimal number represents the host address.

> There is another way to represent netmask addresses called Classless Inter-Domain Routing (CIDR) notation. CIDR notation represents the netmask as just the number of masked bits in the IP address. CIDR notation is usually shown with a slash between the network address and the CIDR value. Thus, the network 192.168.1.0 and netmask 255.255.255.0 would have the CIDR notation of 192.168.1.0/24. Although CIDR notation is becoming popular in the networking world, Linux configuration files still use the netmask value to define the network.

When working on the Internet, it's crucial that no two physical Internet connections have the same IP address. To accomplish that, the Internet Assigned Numbers Authority (IANA) maintains strict control over the assignment of IP network addresses. However, not all networks need to be connected to the Internet, so to differentiate those networks, IANA has made the distinction between public and private IP networks.

Specific subnetwork ranges are reserved for private IP networks:

- 10.0.0.0 to 10.255.255.255
- 172.16.0.0 to 172.31.255.255
- 192.168.0.0 to 192.168.255.255

These private IP addresses can't be used for Internet traffic; they work only on local networks.

As you can imagine, with the popularity of the Internet, it didn't take long for IANA to run out of available public IP address networks. However, in a brilliant move, the idea of network address translation (NAT) saved the day. A NAT server can take an entire private IP network and assign it a single public IP address on the Internet. This is how you can connect your entire home network to a single ISP Internet connection and everything works.

Default Router

With IP and IPv6, devices can communicate directly only with other devices on the same physical network. To connect different physical networks together, you use a *router*. A router passes data from one network to another. Devices that need to send packets to hosts on remote networks must use the router as a go-between. Usually a network will contain a single router to forward packets to an upper-level network. This is called a *default router* (or sometimes, a *default gateway*). Network devices must know the local default gateway for the network to be able to forward packets to remote hosts.

Thus, for a device to communicate in an IP network, it must know three separate pieces of information:

- Its own host address on the network
- The netmask address for the local physical network
- The address of a local router used to send packets to remote networks

Here's an example of what you would need:

- Host address: 192.168.20.5
- Netmask address: 255.255.255.0
- Default gateway: 192.168.20.1

With these three values in hand you're almost ready to configure your Linux system for working on the Internet. There's just one more piece of the puzzle you'll need to worry about, and we'll look at that in the next section.

Host Names

With all of these IP addresses, it can be impossible trying to remember just what servers have what addresses. Fortunately for us, yet another network standard is available that can help out. The *Domain Name System* (DNS) assigns a name to hosts on the network.

With DNS, each network address is assigned a *domain name* (such as linux.org) that uniquely identifies the network, and each host in that network is assigned a unique *host name*, which is added to the domain name to uniquely identify the host on the network.

Thus, to find the host shadrach on the domain example.org, you'd use the DNS name shadrach.example.org. The DNS system uses servers to map host and domain names to the specific network addresses required to communicate with that server. Servers responsible for defining the network and host names for a local network interoperate with upper-level DNS servers to resolve remote host names.

To use DNS in your network applications, all you need to configure is the address of the DNS server that services your local network. From there, your local DNS server can find the address of any host name anywhere on the Internet.

Dynamic Host Configuration Protocol

There's one more network layer feature that we need to discuss before we move on to configuring the Linux system. Trying to keep track of host addresses for all of the devices on a large network can become cumbersome. Keeping individual IP address assignments straight can be a challenge, and often you'll run into the situation where two or more devices accidentally are assigned the same IP address.

The *Dynamic Host Configuration Protocol* (DHCP) was created to make it easier to configure client workstations, which don't necessarily need to use the same IP address all the time. With DHCP, the client communicates with a DHCP server on the network using a temporary address. The DHCP server then tells the client exactly which IP address, netmask address, default gateway, and even DNS server to use. Each time the client reboots, it may receive a different IP address, but that doesn't matter as long as it's unique on the network.

These days, most home network routers include a DHCP server function, so all you need to do is set your Linux client to use DHCP and you're done. You don't need to know any of the "behind the scenes" details of the network addresses.

WARNING   Although DHCP is great for clients, it's not a good idea to use for servers. Servers need to have a fixed IP address so that clients can always find them. While it's possible to configure static IP addresses in DHCP, usually it's safest to manually configure the network information for servers. This is called a *static host address*.

The Transport Layer

The *transport layer* can often be the most confusing part of the network. Whereas the network layer helps get data to a specific host on the network, the transport layer helps get the data to the correct application contained on the host. It does that by using *ports*.

Ports are sort of like apartment numbers. Each application that's running on a network server is assigned its own port number, just like different apartments in the same apartment building are assigned separate apartment numbers. To send data to a specific application on a server, the client software needs to know both the server IP address (just like the apartment building address) and the transport layer port number (just like the apartment number).

Two common transport protocols are used in the IP networking world:

- Transmission Control Protocol (TCP)

- User Datagram Protocol (UDP)

The *Transmission Control Protocol (TCP)* transport protocol sends data using a guaranteed delivery method. It ensures that the server receives each portion of data that the client computer sends, and vice versa. The downside is that a lot of overhead is required to track and verify all of the data sent, which can slow down the data transfer speed.

For data that's sensitive to transfer speed (such as real-time data like voice and video), that can cause unwanted delays. The alternative to this is the *User Datagram Protocol (UDP)* transport protocol. UDP doesn't bother to ensure delivery of each portion of the data—it just sends the data out on the network and hopes it gets to the server!

Though losing data may sound like a bad thing, for some applications (such as voice and video) it's perfectly acceptable. Missing audio or video packets just show up as blips and breaks in the final audio or video result. As long as most of the data packets arrive, the audio and video is understandable.

 Though not used for sending application data, there is one more transport layer protocol that you'll need to know about. There's a need for network devices to communicate "behind the scenes" with each other, passing network management information around the network. The *Internet Control Message Protocol (ICMP)* provides a simple way for network devices to pass information such as error messages and network routing information to make it easy for each client to find the required resource on the network.

The Application Layer

The application layer is where all the action happens. This is where the network programs process the data sent across the network and then return a result. Most network applications behave using the *client/server paradigm*. With the client/server paradigm, one network device acts as the server, offering some type of service to multiple network clients (such as a web server offering content via web pages). The server listens for incoming connections on a specific transport layer port assigned to the application. The clients must know what transport layer port to use to send requests to the server application.

To simplify that process, both TCP and UDP use *well-known ports* to represent common applications. These port numbers are reserved so that network clients know to use them when looking for specific application hosts on the network. Table 8.1 shows some of the more common well-known application ports.

TABLE 8.1   TCP and UDP well-known ports

Port	Protocol	Application
20	TCP	File Transfer Protocol (FTP) data
21	TCP	File Transfer Protocol (FTP) control messages
22	TCP	Secure Shell (SSH)
23	TCP	Telnet interactive protocol
25	TCP	Simple Mail Transfer Protocol (SMTP)
53	TCP&UDP	Domain Name System (DNS)
80	TCP	Hypertext Transfer Protocol (HTTP)
110	TCP	Post Office Protocol version 3 (POP3)
123	UDP	Network Time Protocol (NTP)
139	TCP	NetBIOS Session Service
143	TCP	Internet Message Access Protocol (IMAP)
161	UDP	Simple Network Management Protocol (SNMP)
162	UDP	Simple Network Management Protocol trap
389	TCP	Lightweight Directory Access Protocol (LDAP)
443	TCP	Hypertext Transfer Protocol (HTTPS) over TLS/SSL
465	TCP	Authenticated SMTP (SMTPS)
514	TCP&UDP	Remote Shell (TCP) or Syslog (UDP)
636	TCP	Lightweight Directory Access Protocol over TLS/SSL (LDAPS)
993	TCP	Internet Message Access Protocol over TLS/SSL (IMAPS)
995	TCP	Post Office Protocol 3 over TLS/SSL (POP3S)

If you think trying to remember all of those port numbers is a hassle, you're not alone. In an attempt to simplify ports, there's somewhat of an ad hoc standard for assigning names each of the well-known port numbers. Each Linux system maintains a list of its network port names in the /etc/services file. Network applications can read this file when working with network ports and use the name instead of the port number. This approach of displaying port names instead of numbers is commonly used in network troubleshooting tools.

Now that you've seen the basics of how Linux uses networking to transfer data between systems, our next section dives into the details of how to configure these features in your Linux system.

Configuring Network Features

There are five main pieces of information you need to configure in your Linux system to interact on a network:

- The host address
- The network subnet address
- The default router (sometimes called the gateway)
- The system host name
- A DNS server address for resolving host names

We have three ways to configure this information in Linux systems:

- Manually editing network configuration files
- Using a graphical tool included with your Linux distribution
- Using command-line tools

The following sections walk through each of these methods.

Network Configuration Files

Linux systems that utilize the systemd initialization method normally use the *systemd-networkd* daemon to detect network interfaces and automatically create entries for them in the network configuration files. You can modify those files manually to tweak or change network settings if necessary.

Unfortunately, though, no single standard configuration file exists that all distributions use. Instead, different distributions use different configuration files to define the network settings. Table 8.2 shows the most common network configuration files that you'll run into.

TABLE 8.2   Linux network configuration files

Distribution	Network configuration location
Debian-based	`/etc/network/interfaces` file
Red Hat–based	`/etc/sysconfig/network-scripts` directory
OpenSUSE	`/etc/sysconfig/network` file

Although each of the Linux distributions uses a different method of defining the network settings, they all have similar features. Most configuration files define each of the required network settings as separate values in the configuration file. Listing 8.1 shows an example from a Debian-based Linux system.

Listing 8.1: Sample Debian network static configuration settings

```
auto eth0
iface eth0 inet static
    address 192.168.1.77
    netmask 255.255.255.0
    gateway 192.168.1.254
iface eth0 inet6 static
    address 2003:aef0::23d1::0a10:00a1
    netmask 64
    gateway 2003:aef0::23d1::0a10:0001
```

The example shown in Listing 8.1 assigns both an IP and an IPv6 address to the wired network interface designated as eth0.

Listing 8.2 shows how to define the IP network settings automatically using a DHCP server on the network.

Listing 8.2: Sample Debian network DHCP configuration settings

```
auto eth0
iface eth0 inet dhcp
iface eth0 inet6 dhcp
```

If you just want to assign an IPv6 *link local address*, which uniquely identifies the device on the local network, but not retrieve an IPv6 address from a DHCP server, replace the inet6 line with this:

```
iface eth0 inet6 auto
```

The auto attribute tells Linux to assign the link local address, which allows the Linux system to communicate with any other IPv6 device on the local network but not a global address.

 Since version 17.04, the Ubuntu distribution has deviated from the standard Debian method and utilizes the Netplan tool to manage network settings. Netplan uses simple YAML text files in the /etc/netplan folder to define the network settings for each network interface installed on the system. By default, Netplan passes the network settings off to the Network Manager tool, so you don't need to worry about how the Netplan configuration files are set.

For Red Hat–based systems, you'll need to define the network settings in two separate files. The first file defines the network and netmask addresses in a file named after the network interface name (such as ifcfg-enp0s3). Listing 8.3 shows an example from a CentOS Linux system.

Listing 8.3: Sample CentOS network interface configuration settings

```
TYPE=Ethernet
PROXY_METHOD=none
BROWSER_ONLY=no
BOOTPROTO=dhcp
DEFROUTE=yes
IPV4_FAILURE_FATAL=no
IPV6INIT=yes
IPV6_AUTOCONF=yes
IPV6_DEFROUTE=yes
IPV6_FAILURE_FATAL=no
IPV6_ADDR_GEN_MODE=stable-privacy
NAME=enp0s3
UUID=c8752366-3e1e-47e3-8162-c0435ec6d451
DEVICE=enp0s3
ONBOOT=yes
IPV6_PRIVACY=no
```

The second file required on Red Hat–based systems is the network file, which defines the host name and default gateway, as shown in Listing 8.4.

Listing 8.4: Sample CentOS network file configuration settings

```
NETWORKING=yes
HOSTNAME=mysystem
GATEWAY=192.168.1.254
```

Listing 8.4: Sample CentOS network file configuration settings (*continued*)

```
IPV6FORWARDING=yes
IPV6_AUTOCONF=no
IPV6_AUTOTUNNEL=no
IPV6_DEFAULTGW=2003:aef0::23d1::0a10:0001
IPV6_DEFAULTDEV=eth0
```

Notice that the Red Hat network configuration file also defines the host name assigned to the Linux system. For other types of Linux systems, storing the host name in the /etc/hostname file has become somewhat of a de facto standard. However, some Linux distributions use /etc/HOSTNAME instead.

If you're working with a Linux system that uses the systemd initialization method, use the hostnamectl program to set the host name value. The hostnamectl program also allows you to set what's called a "pretty" name for the system, which is used by some utilities on the local system to provide a more detailed description of the device, such as "Rich's laptop."

You will also need to define a DNS server so that the system can use DNS host names. For systemd systems, the DNS server is generated by the systemd-resolved program. For legacy SysVinit systems, that's handled in the /etc/resolv.conf configuration file:

```
domain mydomain.com
search mytest.com
nameserver 192.168.1.1
```

The domain entry defines the domain name assigned to the network. By default, the system will append this domain name to any host names you specify. The search entry defines any additional domains used to search for host names. The nameserver entry is where you specify the DNS server assigned to your network. Some networks can have more than one DNS server; just add multiple nameserver entries in the file.

To help speed up connections to commonly used hosts, you can manually enter their host names and IP addresses into the /etc/hosts file on your Linux system. The /etc/nsswitch.conf file defines whether the Linux system checks this file before or after using DNS to look up the host name.

Graphical Tools

The *Network Manager* tool is a popular program used by many Linux distributions to provide a graphical interface for defining network connections. The Network Manager tool starts automatically at boot time and appears in the system tray area of the desktop as an icon.

If your system detects a wired network connection, the icon appears as a mini-network with blocks connected together. If your system detects a wireless network connection, the icon appears as an empty radio signal. When you click the icon, you'll see a list of the available wireless networks detected by the network card (as shown in Figure 8.4).

FIGURE 8.4   Network Manager showing a wireless network connection

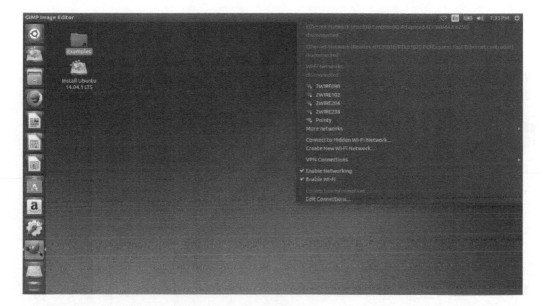

Click your access point to select it from the list. If your access point is encrypted, you'll be prompted to enter the password to gain access to the network.

When your system is connected to a wireless access point, the icon appears as a radio signal. Click the icon, and then select Edit Connections to edit the network connection settings for the system, shown in Figure 8.5.

FIGURE 8.5   The Network Manager edit configurations window

You can select the network connection to configure (either wireless or wired), and then click the Edit button to change the current configuration.

The Network Manager tool allows you to specify all four of the network configuration values by using the manual configuration option or to set the configuration to use DHCP to determine the settings. Network Manager automatically updates the appropriate network configuration files with the updated settings.

Command-Line Tools

If you're not working with a graphical desktop client environment, you'll need to use the Linux command-line tools to set the network configuration information. You have quite a few different command-line tools at your disposal. This section covers the ones you're most likely to run into (and the ones you'll most likely see on the LPIC-1 exam).

Network Manager Command-Line Tools

The Network Manager tool also provides two different types of command-line tools:

- nmtui: Provides a simple text-based menu tool
- nmcli: Provides a text-only command-line tool

Both of these tools help guide you through the process of setting the required network information for your Linux system. The *nmtui* tool displays a stripped-down version of the graphical tool, where you can select a network interface and assign network properties to it, as shown in Figure 8.6.

FIGURE 8.6   The Network Manager nmtui command-line tool

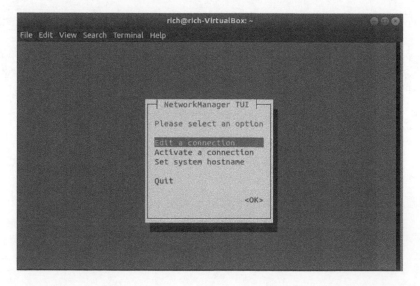

The *nmcli* tool doesn't attempt to use any type of graphics capabilities—it just provides a command-line interface where you can view and change the network settings. By default, the command displays the current network devices and their settings, as shown in Listing 8.5.

Listing 8.5: The default output of the nmcli command

```
$ nmcli
enp0s3: connected to Wired connection 1
        "Intel 82540EM Gigabit Ethernet Controller (PRO/1000 MT Desktop Adapter)
        ethernet (e1000), 08:00:27:2C:35:D2, hw, mtu 1500
        ip4 default, ip6 default
        inet4 192.168.1.77/24
        route4 0.0.0.0/0
        inet6 2600:1702:1ce0:eeb0::6d0/128
        inet6 fe80::16d2:b8f:7f78:f3ed/64
        route6 2600:1702:1ce0:eeb0::/60
        route6 2600:1702:1ce0:eeb0::/64
        route6 ::/0
        route6 ff00::/8
        route6 fe80::/64
        route6 fe80::/64

        ...
```

The nmcli command uses command-line options to allow you to set the network settings:

```
# nmcli con add type ethernet con-name eth1 ifname enp0s3 ip4
10.0.2.10/24 gw4 192.168.1.254
```

Legacy Tools

If your Linux distribution doesn't support one of the Network Manager tools, there are usually legacy tools, including utilities from the *net-tools* package, available in most Linux distributions. Here are a few of the basic command-line tools that you can use:

- ethtool: Displays Ethernet settings for a network interface
- ifconfig: Displays or sets the IP address and netmask values for a network interface
- iwconfig: Sets the SSID and encryption key for a wireless interface
- route: Sets the default router address

The *ethtool* command allows you to peek inside the network interface card Ethernet settings and change any properties that you may need to communicate with a network device, such as a switch.

By default, the ethtool command displays the current configuration settings for the network interface, as shown in Listing 8.6.

Listing 8.6: Output from the ethtool command

```
$ ethtool enp0s3
Settings for enp0s3:
        Supported ports: [ TP ]
        Supported link modes:   10baseT/Half 10baseT/Full
                                100baseT/Half 100baseT/Full
                                1000baseT/Full
        Supported pause frame use: No
        Supports auto-negotiation: Yes
        Supported FEC modes: Not reported
        Advertised link modes:  10baseT/Half 10baseT/Full
                                100baseT/Half 100baseT/Full
                                1000baseT/Full
        Advertised pause frame use: No
        Advertised auto-negotiation: Yes
        Advertised FEC modes: Not reported
        Speed: 1000Mb/s
        Duplex: Full
        Port: Twisted Pair
        PHYAD: 0
        Transceiver: internal
        Auto-negotiation: on
        MDI-X: off (auto)
Cannot get wake-on-lan settings: Operation not permitted
        Current message level: 0x00000007 (7)
                               drv probe link
        Link detected: yes
$
```

You can change features such as speed, duplex, and whether or not the network interface attempts to auto-negotiate features with the switch.

The *ifconfig* command is a legacy command for configuring network device settings. It allows you to set the network address and subnet mask for a network interface:

```
$ sudo ifconfig enp0s3 down 10.0.2.10 netmask 255.255.255.0
```

You can list all of the network interface settings on your system using the ifconfig command with no command-line options, as shown in Listing 8.7.

Listing 8.7: Displaying network interface information

```
$ ifconfig
enp0s3: flags=4163<UP,BROADCAST,RUNNING,MULTICAST>  mtu 1500
        inet 192.168.1.77  netmask 255.255.255.0  broadcast 192.168.1.255
        inet6 2600:1702:1ce0:eeb0:66dc:cedc:10ff:9ee6  prefixlen 64  scopeid 0x0<global>
        inet6 fe80::16d2:b8f:7f78:f3ed  prefixlen 64  scopeid 0x20<link>
        inet6 2600:1702:1ce0:eeb0:48e3:1865:5544:8200  prefixlen 64  scopeid 0x0<global>
        ether 08:00:27:2c:35:d2  txqueuelen 1000  (Ethernet)
        RX packets 293593  bytes 431675620 (431.6 MB)
        RX errors 0  dropped 0  overruns 0  frame 0
        TX packets 119754  bytes 9135701 (9.1 MB)
        TX errors 0  dropped 0 overruns 0  carrier 0  collisions 0

lo: flags=73<UP,LOOPBACK,RUNNING>  mtu 65536
        inet 127.0.0.1  netmask 255.0.0.0
        inet6 ::1  prefixlen 128  scopeid 0x10<host>
        loop  txqueuelen 1000  (Local Loopback)
        RX packets 1206  bytes 125586 (125.5 KB)
        RX errors 0  dropped 0  overruns 0  frame 0
        TX packets 1206  bytes 125586 (125.5 KB)
        TX errors 0  dropped 0 overruns 0  carrier 0  collisions 0

$
```

Instead of using the long ifconfig command format to activate or deactivate a network interface, you can use the simpler ifup or ifdown command. Just add the interface name with the command to easily activate or deactivate the interface.

Before you can use the ifconfig command to assign an address to a wireless interface, you must assign the wireless SSID and encryption key values using the iwconfig command:

```
# iwconfig wlan0 essid "MyNetwork" key s:mypassword
```

The essid parameter specifies the access point SSID name, and the key parameter specifies the encryption key required to connect to it. Notice that the encryption key is preceded by an s:. That allows you to specify the encryption key in ASCII text characters; otherwise, you'll need to specify the key using hexadecimal values.

If you don't know the name of a local wireless connection, you can use the iwlist command to display all of the wireless signals your wireless card detects. Just specify the name of the wireless device, and use the scan option:

```
$ iwlist wlan0 scan
```

To set the default gateway, use the route command:

```
# route add default gw 192.168.1.254
```

You can also use the route command by itself to view the current default router config-ured for the system:

```
$ route
Kernel IP routing table
Destination     Gateway         Genmask          Flags Metric Ref Use Iface
default         192.168.1.254   0.0.0.0          UG    0      0   0   enp0s3
192.168.1.0     *               255.255.255.0    U     1      0   0   enp0s3
$
```

In this example, the default router defined for the Linux system is 192.168.1.254 and is available from the enp0s3 network interface. The output also shows that to get to the 192.168.1.0 network you don't need a gateway, because that's the local network the Linux system is connected to.

If your network is connected to multiple networks via multiple routers, you can manu-ally create the routing table in the system by using the add or del command-line option for the route command. The format for that is

```
route [add] [del] target gw gateway
```

where *target* is the target host or network and *gateway* is the router address.

The *iproute2* Package

Most of the legacy command-line network tools have been replaced with the newer *iproute2* package. The main utility in the iproute2 package is the ip command.

The ip command is more robust than the old ifconfig command, and it is becoming the more popular method for defining network settings from the command line. The ip utility uses several command options to display the current network settings or define new network settings. Table 8.3 shows these command options.

TABLE 8.3 The ip utility command options

Parameter	Description
address	Display or set the IPv4 or IPv6 address on the device
addrlabel	Define configuration labels
l2tp	Tunnel Ethernet over IP
link	Define a network device
maddress	Define a multicast address for the system to listen to

Parameter	Description
monitor	Watch for netlink messages
mroute	Define an entry in the multicast routing cache
mrule	Define a rule in the multicast routing policy database
neighbor	Manage ARP or NDISC cache entries
netns	Manage network namespaces
ntable	Manage the neighbor cache operation
route	Manage the routing table
rule	Manage entries in the routing policy database
tcpmetrics	Manage TCP metrics on the interface
token	Manage tokenized interface identifiers
tunnel	Tunnel over IP
tuntap	Manage TUN/TAP devices
xfrm	Manage IPSec policies for secure connections

Each command option has parameters that define what to do, such as display network settings, or that modify existing network settings. Listing 8.8 demonstrates how to display the current network settings using the show parameter.

Listing 8.8: The ip address output

```
$ ip address show
rich@rich-VirtualBox:~$ ip address show
1: lo: <LOOPBACK,UP,LOWER_UP> mtu 65536 qdisc noqueue state UNKNOWN group default qlen 1000
    link/loopback 00:00:00:00:00:00 brd 00:00:00:00:00:00
    inet 127.0.0.1/8 scope host lo
       valid_lft forever preferred_lft forever
    inet6 ::1/128 scope host
       valid_lft forever preferred_lft forever
2: enp0s3: <BROADCAST,MULTICAST,UP,LOWER_UP> mtu 1500 qdisc fq_codel state UP group default qlen 1000
    link/ether 08:00:27:2c:35:d2 brd ff:ff:ff:ff:ff:ff
```

Listing 8.8: The ip address output (*continued*)

```
    inet 192.168.1.77/24 brd 192.168.1.255 scope global dynamic noprefixroute enp0s3
       valid_lft 84487sec preferred_lft 84487sec
    inet6 2600:1702:1ce0:eeb0::6d0/128 scope global dynamic noprefixroute
       valid_lft 5606sec preferred_lft 5306sec
    inet6 2600:1702:1ce0:eeb0:48e3:1865:5544:8200/64 scope global temporary dynamic
       valid_lft 3305sec preferred_lft 3305sec
    inet6 2600:1702:1ce0:eeb0:66dc:cedc:10ff:9ee6/64 scope global dynamic mngtmpaddr noprefixroute
       valid_lft 3305sec preferred_lft 3305sec
    inet6 fe80::16d2:b8f:7f78:f3ed/64 scope link noprefixroute
       valid_lft forever preferred_lft forever
$
```

This example shows two network interfaces on the Linux system:

- lo: The local loopback interface
- enp0s3: A wired network interface

The *local loopback interface* is a special virtual network interface. Any local program can use it to communicate with other programs just as if they were across a network. That can simplify transferring data between programs.

The enp0s3 network interface is the wired network connection for the Linux system. The ip command shows the IP address assigned to the interface (there's both an IP and an IPv6 link local address assigned), the netmask value, and some basic statistics about the packets on the interface.

If the output doesn't show a network address assigned to the interface, you can use the ip command to specify the host address and netmask values for the interface:

```
# ip address add 192.168.1.77/24 dev enp0s3
```

Then use the ip command to set the default router for the network interface:

```
# ip route add default via 192.168.1.254 dev enp0s3
```

Finally, make the network interface active by using the link option:

```
# ip link set enp0s3 up
```

Being able to set the IP address, netmask, and default router values all from a single command is what's made the iproute2 package so popular.

 You can fine-tune networking parameters for a network interface using the /etc/sysctl.conf configuration file. This file defines kernel parameters that the Linux system uses when interacting with the network interface. This has become a popular method to use for setting advanced security features, such as to disable responding to ICMP messages by setting the icmp_echo_ignore_broadcasts value to 1, or if your system has multiple network interface cards, to disable packet forwarding by setting the ip_forward value to 0.

Getting Network Settings Automatically

If your network uses DHCP, you'll need to ensure that a proper DHCP client program is running on your Linux system. The DHCP client program communicates with the network DHCP server in the background and assigns the necessary IP address settings as directed by the DHCP server. Three common DHCP programs are available for Linux systems:

- dhcpcd
- dhclient
- pump

The dhcpcd program is becoming the most popular of the three, but you'll still see the other two used in some Linux distributions.

When you use your Linux system's software package manager utility to install the DHCP client program, it sets the program to automatically launch at boot time and handle the IP address configuration needed to interact on the network.

If you're working with a Linux server that acts as a DHCP server, the /etc/dhcpd.conf file contains the IP address settings that the server offers to DHCP clients. The file contains a section for each subnet the DHCP server services:

```
subnet 10.0.2.0 netmask 255.255.255.0 {
        option routers                  192.168.1.254;
        option subnet-mask              255.255.255.0;

        option domain-name              "mynetwork.com";
        option domain-name-servers      192.168.1.254;

        option time-offset              -18000;     # Eastern Standard Time

    range 10.0.2.1 10.0.2.100;
}
```

Bonding Network Cards

One final network configuration setting you may run into in Linux distributions has to do with network interface *bonding*. Bonding allows you to aggregate multiple interfaces into one virtual network device.

You can then tell the Linux system how to treat the virtual network device using three different basic types:

- *Load balancing*: Network traffic is shared between two or more network interfaces.
- *Aggregation*: Two or more network interfaces are combined to create one larger network pipe.
- *Active/passive*: One network interface is live, and the other is used as a backup for fault tolerance.

You can choose from seven different bonding modes, as shown in Table 8.4.

TABLE 8.4 Network interface bonding modes

Mode	Name	Description
0	balance-rr	Provides load balancing and fault tolerance using interfaces in a round-robin approach
1	active-backup	Provides fault tolerance using one interface as the primary and the other as a backup
2	balance-xor	Provides load balancing and fault tolerance by transmitting on one interface and receiving on the second
3	broadcast	Transmits all packets on all interfaces
4	802.3ad	Aggregates the interfaces to create one connection combining the interface bandwidths
5	balance-tlb	Provides load balancing and fault tolerance based on the current transmit load on each interface
6	balance-alb	Provides load balancing and fault tolerance based on the current receive load on each interface

To initialize network interface bonding, you must first load the bonding module in the Linux kernel:

```
$ sudo modprobe bonding
```

This creates a bond0 network interface, which you can then define using the ip utility:

```
$ sudo ip link add bond0 type bond mode 4
```

Once you've defined the bond type, you can add the appropriate network interfaces to the bond using the ip utility:

```
$ sudo ip link set eth0 master bond0
$ sudo ip link set eth1 master bond0
```

The Linux system will then treat the bond0 device as a single network interface utilizing the load balancing or aggregation method you defined.

If you have multiple network interface cards on your Linux system and choose to connect them to separate networks, you can configure your Linux system to act as a bridge between the two networks. The brctl command allows you to control how the bridging behaves. To do this, though, you must set the ip_forward kernel parameter in the /etc/sysctl.conf file to 1 to enable bridging.

Basic Network Troubleshooting

Once you have a Linux system running, there are a few things you can do to check that things are operating properly. This section walks through the commands you should know to monitor the network activity, including watching what processes are listening on the network and what connections are active from your system.

Sending Test Packets

One way to test network connectivity is to send test packets to known hosts. Linux provides the ping and ping6 commands to do that. The ping and ping6 commands send *Internet Control Message Protocol* (ICMP) packets to remote hosts using either the IP (*ping*) or IPv6 (*ping6*) protocols. ICMP packets work behind the scenes to track connectivity and provide control messages between systems. If the remote host supports ICMP, it will send a reply packet back when it receives a ping packet.

The basic format for the ping command is to just specify the IP address of the remote host:

```
$ ping 10.0.2.2
PING 10.0.2.2 (10.0.2.2) 56(84) bytes of data.
64 bytes from 10.0.2.2: icmp_seq=1 ttl=63 time=14.6 ms
64 bytes from 10.0.2.2: icmp_seq=2 ttl=63 time=3.82 ms
64 bytes from 10.0.2.2: icmp_seq=3 ttl=63 time=2.05 ms
64 bytes from 10.0.2.2: icmp_seq=4 ttl=63 time=0.088 ms
64 bytes from 10.0.2.2: icmp_seq=5 ttl=63 time=3.54 ms
64 bytes from 10.0.2.2: icmp_seq=6 ttl=63 time=3.97 ms
64 bytes from 10.0.2.2: icmp_seq=7 ttl=63 time=0.040 ms
^C
--- 10.0.2.2 ping statistics ---
7 packets transmitted, 7 received, 0% packet loss, time 6020ms
rtt min/avg/max/mdev = 0.040/4.030/14.696/4.620 ms
$
```

The ping command continues sending packets until you press Ctrl+C. You can also use the -c command-line option to specify a set number of packets to send, then stop.

For the ping6 command, things get a little more complicated. If you're using an IPv6 link local address, you also need to tell the command which interface to send the packets out on:

```
$ ping6 -c 4 fe80::c418:2ed0:aead:cbce%enp0s3
PING fe80::c418:2ed0:aead:cbce%enp0s3(fe80::c418:2ed0:aead:cbce) 56 data
bytes
64 bytes from fe80::c418:2ed0:aead:cbce: icmp_seq=1 ttl=128 time=1.47 ms
64 bytes from fe80::c418:2ed0:aead:cbce: icmp_seq=2 ttl=128 time=0.478 ms
64 bytes from fe80::c418:2ed0:aead:cbce: icmp_seq=3 ttl=128 time=0.777 ms
```

```
64 bytes from fe80::c418:2ed0:aead:cbce: icmp_seq=4 ttl=128 time=0.659 ms

--- fe80::c418:2ed0:aead:cbce%enp0s3 ping statistics ---
4 packets transmitted, 4 received, 0% packet loss, time 3003ms
rtt min/avg/max/mdev = 0.478/0.847/1.475/0.378 ms
$
```

The %enp0s3 part tells the system to send the ping packets out the enp0s3 network interface for the link local address.

 Unfortunately, these days many hosts don't support ICMP packets because they can be used to create a denial-of-service (DOS) attack against the host. Don't be surprised if you try to ping a remote host and don't get any responses.

Tracing Routes

Sending ping packets can be a useful tool, but there's not much you learn if the ping test packet doesn't come back. You have no way of knowing where in the path between your client and the remote server the network failed. That's where the traceroute and tracepath commands come in.

The traceroute command, and its IPv6 version traceroute6, shows the steps (called hops in network terms) taken to get from your local network to the remote host. It finds each router hop along the path by sending ICMP packets with short time-to-live (TTL) values so that each test packet can survive only one hop further than the previous packet. This can map all of the routers the test packets traverse getting to the final destination.

The tracepath command, and its IPv6 version tracepath6, also show the steps taken to get to a remote host but use UDP packets instead of ICMP packets. These have a better chance of being allowed to pass through routers in the Internet, so the tracepath command is often successful when the traceroute command fails:

```
$ tracepath 192.168.1.254
 1?: [LOCALHOST]                        pmtu 1500
 1:  _gateway                                          6.218ms reached
 1:  homeportal                                        4.366ms reached
     Resume: pmtu 1500 hops 1 back 1
$
```

Another benefit of using UDP packets is that you don't need to be the root super user to send UDP packets, so any user account on the Linux system can use the tracepath command.

A common use for the tracepath command by networking professionals is in finding MTU mismatches between network hops in a path. The maximum transmission unit (MTU) is the size of the largest data packet allowed by a network device. If one device in the path can accept only smaller-sized packets, other devices in the network path need to break longer packets into shorter ones, slowing down the transmission.

Finding Host Information

Sometimes the problem isn't with network connectivity but with the DNS host name system. You can test a host name using the *host* command:

```
$ host www.linux.org
www.linux.org is an alias for linux.org.
linux.org has address 107.170.40.56
linux.org mail is handled by 20 mx.iqemail.net.
$
```

The host command queries the DNS server to determine the IP addresses assigned to the specified host name. By default, it returns all IP addresses associated with the host name. Some hosts are supported by multiple servers in a load balancing configuration. The host command will show all of the IP addresses associated with those servers:

```
$ host www.google.com
www.google.com has address 74.125.138.104
www.google.com has address 74.125.138.105
www.google.com has address 74.125.138.147
www.google.com has address 74.125.138.99
www.google.com has address 74.125.138.103
www.google.com has address 74.125.138.106
www.google.com has IPv6 address 2607:f8b0:4002:c0c::67
$
```

You can also specify an IP address for the host command and it will attempt to find the host name associated with it:

```
$ host 107.170.40.56
56.40.170.107.in-addr.arpa domain name pointer iqdig11.iqnection.com.
$
```

Notice, though, that often an IP address will resolve to a generic server host name that hosts the website and not the website alias, as is the case here with the www.linux.org IP address.

Another great tool to use is the *dig* command. The dig command displays all DNS data records associated with a specific host or network. For example, you can look up the information for a specific host name:

$ **dig www.linux.org**

```
; <<>> DiG 9.9.4-RedHat-9.9.4-18.el7_1.5 <<>> www.linux.org
;; global options: +cmd
;; Got answer:
;; ->>HEADER<<- opcode: QUERY, status: NOERROR, id: 45314
;; flags: qr rd ra; QUERY: 1, ANSWER: 2, AUTHORITY: 0, ADDITIONAL: 1

;; OPT PSEUDOSECTION:
; EDNS: version: 0, flags:; udp: 4096
;; QUESTION SECTION:
;www.linux.org.                 IN      A

;; ANSWER SECTION:
www.linux.org.          14400   IN      CNAME   linux.org.
linux.org.              3600    IN      A       107.170.40.56

;; Query time: 75 msec
;; SERVER: 192.168.1.254#53(192.168.1.254)
;; WHEN: Sat Feb 06 17:44:29 EST 2016
;; MSG SIZE  rcvd: 72

$
```

Or you can look up DNS data records associated with a specific network service, such as a mail server:

$ **dig linux.org MX**

```
; <<>> DiG 9.9.5-3ubuntu0.5-Ubuntu <<>> linux.org MX
;; global options: +cmd
;; Got answer:
;; ->>HEADER<<- opcode: QUERY, status: NOERROR, id: 16202
;; flags: qr rd ra; QUERY: 1, ANSWER: 1, AUTHORITY: 0, ADDITIONAL: 1

;; OPT PSEUDOSECTION:
; EDNS: version: 0, flags:; udp: 4096
;; QUESTION SECTION:
;linux.org.                     IN      MX
```

```
;; ANSWER SECTION:
linux.org.              3600    IN      MX      20 mx.iqemail.net.

;; Query time: 75 msec
;; SERVER: 127.0.1.1#53(127.0.1.1)
;; WHEN: Tue Feb 09 12:35:43 EST 2016
;; MSG SIZE  rcvd: 68

$
```

If you need to look up DNS information for multiple servers or domains, the *nslookup* command provides an interactive interface where you can enter commands:

```
$ nslookup
> www.google.com
Server:         192.168.1.254
Address:        192.168.1.254#53

Non-authoritative answer:
Name:   www.google.com
Address: 172.217.2.228
> www.wikipedia.org
Server:         192.168.1.254
Address:        192.168.1.254#53

Non-authoritative answer:
Name:   www.wikipedia.org
Address: 208.80.153.224
> exit

$
```

You can also dynamically specify the address of another DNS server to use for the name lookups, which is a handy way to determine whether your default DNS server is at fault if a name resolution fails.

One final DNS tool available is the *getent* command. The getent command is a generic tool used to look for entries in any type of text database on the Linux system. It's commonly used to look up user entries in the /etc/passwd file:

```
$ getent passwd rich
rich:x:1000:1000:Rich,,,:/home/rich:/bin/bash
$
```

but it can also come in handy when looking up hosts.

When using getent to look up a host name, it parses through the host databases as defined in the /etc/nsswitch.conf configuration file to include the local /etc/hosts file. Thus, if you have a lot of local network hosts defined in the /etc/hosts file, it'll return those host names quicker than using the standard host or dig command. If you use the command without specifying a host name, it returns all hosts stored in the local /etc/hosts file:

```
$ getent hosts
127.0.0.1       localhost
127.0.1.1       rich-VirtualBox
192.168.1.200   mydatabase
192.18.1.201    myserver
127.0.0.1       ip6-localhost ip6-loopback
$
```

Or you can query for a specific host:

```
$ getent hosts mydatabase
192.168.1.200   mydatabase
$
```

That can come in handy when you're trying to troubleshoot a host connection.

Advanced Network Troubleshooting

Besides the simple network tests shown in the previous section, Linux has some more advanced programs that can provide more advanced information about the network environment. Sometimes it helps to be able to see what network connections are active on a Linux system. There are two ways to troubleshoot that issue: the netstat command and the ss command.

The *netstat* Command

The *netstat* command can provide a wealth of network information for you. By default, it lists all open network connections on the system:

```
# netstat
Active Internet connections (w/o servers)
Proto Recv-Q Send-Q Local Address           Foreign Address         State
Active UNIX domain sockets (w/o servers)
Proto RefCnt Flags       Type       State         I-Node   Path
unix  2      [ ]         DGRAM                    10825    @/org/freedesktop/systemd1/notify
unix  2      [ ]         DGRAM                    10933    /run/systemd/shutdownd
```

```
unix  6      [ ]        DGRAM                     6609      /run/systemd/journal/socket
unix  25     [ ]        DGRAM                     6611      /dev/log
unix  3      [ ]        STREAM     CONNECTED      25693
unix  3      [ ]        STREAM     CONNECTED      20770     /var/run/dbus/system_bus_socket
unix  3      [ ]        STREAM     CONNECTED      19556
unix  3      [ ]        STREAM     CONNECTED      19511
unix  2      [ ]        DGRAM                     24125
unix  3      [ ]        STREAM     CONNECTED      19535
unix  3      [ ]        STREAM     CONNECTED      18067     /var/run/dbus/system_bus_socket
unix  3      [ ]        STREAM     CONNECTED      32358
unix  3      [ ]        STREAM     CONNECTED      24818     /var/run/dbus/system_bus_socket
...
```

The netstat command produces lots of output, since normally lots of programs use network services on Linux systems. You can limit the output to just TCP or UDP connections by using the -t command-line option for TCP connections or –u for UDP connections:

```
$ netstat -t
Active Internet connections (w/o servers)
Proto Recv-Q Send-Q Local Address          Foreign Address        State
tcp    1      0 10.0.2.15:58630            productsearch.ubu:https CLOSE_WAIT
tcp6   1      0 ip6-localhost:57782        ip6-localhost:ipp       CLOSE_WAIT
$
```

You can also get a list of what applications are listening on which network ports by using the -l option:

```
$ netstat -l
Active Internet connections (only servers)
Proto Recv-Q Send-Q Local Address          Foreign Address     State
tcp     0      0 ubuntu02:domain          *:*                 LISTEN
tcp     0      0 localhost:ipp            *:*                 LISTEN
tcp6    0      0 ip6-localhost:ipp        [::]:*              LISTEN
udp     0      0 *:ipp                    *:*
udp     0      0 *:mdns                   *:*
udp     0      0 *:36355                  *:*
udp     0      0 ubuntu02:domain          *:*
udp     0      0 *:bootpc                 *:*
udp     0      0 *:12461                  *:*
udp6    0      0 [::]:64294               [::]:*
udp6    0      0 [::]:60259               [::]:*
udp6    0      0 [::]:mdns                [::]:*
...
```

As you can see, just a standard Linux workstation still has lots of things happening in the background, waiting for connections.

Yet another great feature of the netstat command is that the –s option displays statistics for the different types of packets the system has used on the network:

```
# netstat -s
Ip:
    240762 total packets received
    0 forwarded
    0 incoming packets discarded
    240747 incoming packets delivered
    206940 requests sent out
    32 dropped because of missing route
Icmp:
    57 ICMP messages received
    0 input ICMP message failed.
    ICMP input histogram:
        destination unreachable: 12
        timeout in transit: 38
        echo replies: 7
    7 ICMP messages sent
    0 ICMP messages failed
    ICMP output histogram:
        echo request: 7
IcmpMsg:
        InType0: 7
        InType3: 12
        InType11: 38
        OutType8: 7
Tcp:
    286 active connections openings
    0 passive connection openings
    0 failed connection attempts
    0 connection resets received
    0 connections established
    239933 segments received
    206091 segments send out
    0 segments retransmited
    0 bad segments received.
    0 resets sent
```

```
Udp:
    757 packets received
    0 packets to unknown port received.
    0 packet receive errors
    840 packets sent
    0 receive buffer errors
    0 send buffer errors
UdpLite:
TcpExt:
    219 TCP sockets finished time wait in fast timer
    15 delayed acks sent
    26 delayed acks further delayed because of locked socket
    Quick ack mode was activated 1 times
    229343 packet headers predicted
    289 acknowledgments not containing data payload received
    301 predicted acknowledgments
    TCPRcvCoalesce: 72755
IpExt:
    InNoRoutes: 2
    InMcastPkts: 13
    OutMcastPkts: 15
    InOctets: 410722578
    OutOctets: 8363083
    InMcastOctets: 2746
    OutMcastOctets: 2826
#
```

The netstat statistics output can give you a rough idea of how busy your Linux system is on the network, or if a specific issue exists with one of the protocols installed.

Examining Sockets

The netstat tool provides a wealth of network information, but it can often be hard to determine which program is listening on which open port. The *ss* command can come to your rescue for that.

A program connection to a port is called a *socket*. The ss command can link which system processes are using which network sockets that are active:

```
$ ss -anpt
State      Recv-Q Send-Q Local Address:Port          Peer Address:Port
LISTEN     0      100      127.0.0.1:25                  *:*
LISTEN     0      128          *:111                     *:*
```

```
LISTEN      0      5      192.168.122.1:53                         *:*
LISTEN      0      128         *:22                         *:*
LISTEN      0      128    127.0.0.1:631                       *:*
LISTEN      0      100        ::1:25                        :::*
LISTEN      0      128        :::111                        :::*
LISTEN      0      128        :::22                         :::*
LISTEN      0      128       ::1:631                        :::*
ESTAB       0      0         ::1:22                      ::1:40490
ESTAB       0      0        ::1:40490                     ::1:22
users:(("ssh",pid=15176,fd=3))
$
```

The -anpt option displays both listening and established TCP connections, as well as the process they're associated with. This output shows that the SSH port (port 22) has an established connection and is controlled by process ID 15176, the ssh program.

The *netcat* Utility

One final tool that can come in handy for troubleshooting network issues is the netcat (nc) utility. The netcat utility can read from and write to any network port, making it a virtual Swiss army knife for the networking world. You can use netcat to test just about any type of network situation, including building your very own client/server test tool.

For example, to have netcat listen for incoming client connections on TCP port 2000, use the -l command option:

```
$ nc -l 2000
```

Then, from another Linux system you can use netcat to connect to the listening server:

```
$ nc 192.168.1.77 2000
```

When the connection is established, anything you type in either the client or the server side is sent to the other end of the connection and displayed. For example, when you type text at the client, like so:

```
$ nc 192.168.1.77 2000
This is a test
```

it appears in the output back on the server:

```
$ nc -l 2000
This is a test
```

What makes netcat even more versatile is that it accepts input from redirection and piping, so you can easily use it in scripts to create simple ad hoc servers and clients for just about any network testing you need to do.

EXERCISE 8.1

Determining the Network Environment

This exercise will demonstrate how to quickly assess the network configuration and programs for your Linux system without having to dig through lots of configuration files. To document your system network information, follow these steps:

1. Log in as root, or acquire root privileges by using su or sudo with each of the commands that follow.

2. Type **ip address show** to display the current network interfaces on your system. You will most likely see a loopback interface (named l0) and one or more network interfaces. Write down the IP (called inet) and IPv6 (called inet6) addresses assigned to each network interface, along with the hardware address and the network mask address.

3. If your system has a wireless network card, type **iwlist wlan0 scan** to view the wireless access points in your area.

4. If your system has a wireless network card, type **iwconfig** to display the current wireless settings for your network interface.

5. Type **route** to display the routes defined on your system. Note the default gateway address assigned to your system. It should be on the same network as the IP address assigned to the system.

6. Type **cat /etc/resolv.conf** to display the DNS settings for your system.

7. Type **netstat -l** to display the programs listening for incoming network connections. The entries marked as unix are using the loopback address to communicate with other programs internally on your system.

8. Type **ss -anpt** to display the processes that have active network ports open on your system.

Summary

Connecting Linux systems to networks can be painless if you have the correct tools. To connect the Linux system you'll need an IP address, a netmask address, a default router, a host name, and a DNS server. If you don't care what IP address is assigned to your Linux system, you can obtain those values automatically using DHCP. However, if you are running a Linux server that requires a static IP address, you may need to configure these values manually.

Linux stores network connection information in configuration files. You can manually modify the files to store the appropriate network information, or you can use a graphical or command-line tool to do that. The Network Manager tool is the most popular graphical tool used by Linux distributions. It allows you to configure both wired and wireless network settings from a graphical window. The Network Manager icon in the desktop panel area shows network connectivity, as well as basic wireless information for wireless network cards.

If you must configure your network settings from the command line, there are a few different tools you'll need to use. For wireless connections you'll need to use the iwconfig command to set the wireless access point and SSID key. For both wireless and wired connections, you need to use the ifconfig or ip command to set the IP address and netmask values for the interface. You may also need to use the route command to define the default router for the local network.

To use host names instead of IP addresses, you must define a DNS server for your network. You do that in the /etc/resolv.conf configuration file. You will also need to define the host name for your Linux system in either the /etc/hostname or the /etc/HOSTNAME file.

When your network configuration is complete, you may have to do some additional troubleshooting for network problems. The ping and ping6 commands allow you to send ICMP packets to remote hosts to test basic connectivity. If you suspect issues with host names, you can use the host and dig commands to query the DNS server for host names.

For more advanced network troubleshooting, you can use the netstat and ss commands to display what applications are using which network ports on the system.

Exam Essentials

Describe the command-line utilities required to configure and manipulate Ethernet network interfaces. To set the IP and netmask addresses on an Ethernet interface, you use the ifconfig or ip command. To set the default router (or gateway) for a network, you use the route command or the ip route command. Some Linux distributions that have Network Manager installed can use the nmtui or nmcli command to configure all three values.

Explain how to configure basic access to a wireless network. Linux uses the iwlist command to list all wireless access points detected by the wireless network card. You can configure the settings required to connect to a specific wireless network using the iwconfig command. At a minimum, you'll need to configure the access point SSID value and most likely specify the encryption key value to connect to the access point.

Describe how to manipulate the routing table on a Linux system. The route command displays the existing router table used by the Linux system. You can add a new router by using the add option or remove an existing router by using the del option. You can specify the default router (gateway) used by the network by adding the default keyword to the command.

Summarize the tools you would need to analyze the status of network devices. The ifconfig and ip commands display the current status of all network interfaces on the system. You can also use the netstat or ss command to display statistics for all listening network ports.

Describe how Linux initializes the network interfaces. Debian-based Linux systems use the /etc/network/interfaces file to configure the IP address, netmask, and default router. Red Hat–based Linux systems use files in the /etc/sysconfig/network-scripts folder. The ifcfg-emp0s3 file contains the IP address and netmask settings, and the network file contains the default router settings. These files are examined at boot-up to determine the network interface configuration. Newer versions of Ubuntu use the Netplan tool, which stores the network configuration in the /etc/netplan folder.

Explain how to test network connectivity. The ping and ping6 commands allow you to send ICMP messages to remote hosts and display the response received.

Describe one graphical tool used to configure network settings in Linux. The Network Manager tool provides a graphical interface for changing settings on the network interfaces. The Network Manager appears as an icon in the desktop panel area. If your Linux system uses a wireless network card, the icon appears as a radio signal, whereas for wired network connections it appears as a mini-network. When you click the icon, it shows the current network status and, for wireless interfaces, a list of the access points detected. When you open the Network Manager interface, it allows you to either set static IP address information or configure the network to use a DHCP server to dynamically set the network configuration.

Review Questions

You can find the answers in the appendix.

1. What network layer feature defines the network the system is connected to?
   A. IP address
   B. Default router
   C. Host name
   D. Netmask
   E. DNS server

2. Newer versions of Ubuntu use which tool to set network address information?
   A. netstat
   B. Netplan
   C. iwconfig
   D. route
   E. ifconfig

3. Which command displays the duplex settings for an Ethernet card?
   A. ethtool
   B. netstat
   C. iwconfig
   D. iwlist
   E. route

4. Which command displays what processes are using which ports on a Linux systems?
   A. iwconfig
   B. ip
   C. ping
   D. nmtui
   E. ss

5. If your Linux server doesn't have a graphical desktop installed, what two tools could you use to configure network settings from the command line?
   A. nmcli
   B. iwconfig
   C. ip
   D. netstat
   E. ping

6. What network setting defines the network device that routes packets intended for hosts on remote networks?

   A. Default router

   B. Netmask

   C. Host name

   D. IP address

   E. DNS server

7. What device setting defines a host that maps a host name to an IP address?

   A. Default router

   B. Netmask

   C. Host name

   D. IP address

   E. DNS server

8. What is used to automatically assign an IP address to a client?

   A. Default router

   B. DHCP

   C. ARP table

   D. netmask

   E. `ifconfig`

9. What type of network address is used so that all devices on a local network don't need an Internet IP address but can communicate with one another?

   A. Dynamic address

   B. Private address

   C. Static address

   D. Host name

   E. MAC address

10. Which command would you use to find the mail server for a domain?

   A. `dig`

   B. `netstat`

   C. `ping6`

   D. `host`

   E. `ss`

11. What command would you use to find out what application was using a specific TCP port on the system?

   A. ip

   B. ss

   C. host

   D. dig

   E. ifconfig

12. What folder does Red Hat–based systems use to store network configuration files?

   A. /etc/sysconfig/network-scripts

   B. /etc/network

   C. /etc/ifcfg-eth0

   D. /etc/ifconfig

   E. /etc/iwconfig

13. Which configuration line sets a dynamic IP address for a Debian system?

   A. iface eth0 inet static

   B. iface eth0 inet dhcp

   C. auto eth0

   D. iface eth0 inet6 auto

   E. BOOTPROTO=dynamic

14. Which file contains a list of DNS servers the Linux system can use to resolve host names?

   A. /etc/dhcpd.conf

   B. /etc/resolv.conf

   C. /etc/nsswitch.conf

   D. /etc/network/interfaces

   E. /etc/sysctl.conf

15. Which ifconfig format correctly assigns an IP address and netmask to the eth0 interface?

   A. ifconfig eth0 up 192.168.1.50 netmask 255.255.255.0

   B. ifconfig eth0 255.255.255.0 192.168.1.50

   C. ifconfig up 192.168.1.50 netmask 255.255.255.0

   D. ifconfig up

   E. ifconfig down

16. What command displays all of the available wireless networks in your area?
    - **A.** iwlist
    - **B.** iwconfig
    - **C.** ifconfig
    - **D.** ip
    - **E.** arp

17. What option sets the wireless access point name in the iwconfig command?
    - **A.** key
    - **B.** netmask
    - **C.** address
    - **D.** essid
    - **E.** channel

18. What command can you use to both display and set the IP address, netmask, and default router values?
    - **A.** ifconfig
    - **B.** iwconfig
    - **C.** router
    - **D.** ifup
    - **E.** ip

19. Which of the following is a correct netmask value?
    - **A.** 255.255.255.0
    - **B.** 255.255.0.255
    - **C.** 192.168.1.0
    - **D.** 192.168.0.1
    - **E.** 0.255.255.255

20. Which bonding mode would you use to combine two network interfaces to create a single network interface with double the amount of bandwidth to your Linux server?
    - **A.** balance-rr: mode 0
    - **B.** aggregation: mode 4
    - **C.** active/backup: mode 1
    - **D.** balance-tlb: mode 5
    - **E.** balance-arb: mode 6

Chapter

9

Writing Scripts

OBJECTIVES

✓ **105.2** Customize or write simple scripts

✓ **107.2** Automate system administration tasks by scheduling jobs

Linux system administrators often need to perform the same tasks over and over, such as checking available disk space on the system or creating user accounts. Instead of entering multiple commands every time, you can write scripts that run in the shell to do these tasks automatically for you. This chapter explores how Bash shell scripts work and demonstrates how you can write your own scripts to automate everyday activities on your Linux system.

Shell Variables

Before talking about writing scripts, it's a good idea to see how the Bash shell stores data for us to use in our scripts. The Bash shell uses a feature called *environment variables* to store information about the shell session and the working environment (thus the name environment variables). This feature stores the data in memory so that any program or script running from the shell can easily access it. This is a handy way to store persistent data that identifies features of the user account, system, shell, or anything else you need to store.

There are two types of environment variables in the Bash shell:

- Global variables
- Local variables

This section describes each type of environment variable and shows how to use them.

Even though the Bash shell uses specific environment variables that are consistent, different Linux distributions often add their own environment variables. The environment variable examples you see in this chapter may differ slightly from what's available in your specific Linux distribution. If you run into an environment variable not covered here, check the documentation for your Linux distribution.

Global Environment Variables

Global environment variables are visible from the shell session and from any child processes that the shell spawns. Local variables are available only in the shell that creates them. This makes global environment variables useful in applications that spawn child processes requiring information from the parent process.

The Linux system sets several global environment variables when you start your Bash session (for more details about what variables are started at that time, see the "Locating System Environment Variables" section later in this chapter). The system environment variables always use all capital letters to differentiate them from normal user environment variables.

To view the global environment variables, use the printenv command, as shown in Listing 9.1.

Listing 9.1: Output from the printenv command

```
$ printenv
HOSTNAME=testbox.localdomain
TERM=xterm
SHELL=/bin/bash
HISTSIZE=1000
SSH_CLIENT=192.168.1.2 1358 22
OLDPWD=/home/rich/test/test1
SSH_TTY=/dev/pts/0
USER=rich
LS_COLORS=no=00:fi=00:di=00;34:ln=00;36:pi=40;33:so=00;35:
bd=40;33;01:cd=40;33;01:or=01;05;37;41:mi=01;05;37;41:ex=00;32:
*.cmd=00;32:*.exe=00;32:*.com=00;32:*.btm=00;32:*.bat=00;32:
*.sh=00;32:*.csh=00;32:*.tar=00;31:*.tgz=00;31:*.arj=00;31:
*.taz=00;31:*.lzh=00;31:*.zip=00;31:*.z=00;31:*.Z=00;31:
*.gz=00;31:*.bz2=00;31:*.bz=00;31:*.tz=00;31:*.rpm=00;31:
*.cpio=00;31:*.jpg=00;35:*.gif=00;35:*.bmp=00;35:*.xbm=00;35:
*.xpm=00;35:*.png=00;35:*.tif=00;35:
MAIL=/var/spool/mail/rich
PATH=/usr/kerberos/bin:/usr/lib/ccache:/usr/local/bin:/bin:/usr/bin:
/home/rich/bin
INPUTRC=/etc/inputrc
PWD=/home/rich
LANG=en_US.UTF-8
SSH_ASKPASS=/usr/libexec/openssh/gnome-ssh-askpass
SHLVL=1
HOME=/home/rich
LOGNAME=rich
CVS_RSH=ssh
SSH_CONNECTION=192.168.1.2 1358 192.168.1.4 22
LESSOPEN=|/usr/bin/lesspipe.sh %s G_BROKEN_FILENAMES=1
_=/usr/bin/printenv
$
```

As you can see, lots of global environment variables get set for the Bash shell. Most of them are set by the system during the login process.

To display the value of an individual environment variable, use the echo command. When referencing an environment variable, you must place a dollar sign before the environment variable name:

```
$ echo $HOME
/home/rich
$
```

As mentioned, global environment variables are also available to child processes running under the current shell session:

```
$ bash
$ echo $HOME
/home/rich
$
```

In this example, after starting a new shell using the bash command, we displayed the current value of the HOME environment variable, which the system sets when you log into the main shell. Sure enough, the value is also available from the child shell process.

Local Environment Variables

Local environment variables, as their name implies, can be seen only in the local process in which they are defined. Don't get confused, though, about local environment variables; they are just as important as global environment variables. In fact, the Linux system also defines standard local environment variables for you by default.

Trying to see the list of local environment variables is a little tricky. Unfortunately, there isn't a command that displays only local environment variables. The *set* command displays all environment variables set for a specific process. However, this also includes the global environment variables.

Listing 9.2 shows the output from a sample set command.

Listing 9.2: Output from the set command

```
$ set
BASH=/bin/bash
BASH_ARGC=()
BASH_ARGV=()
BASH_LINENO=()
BASH_SOURCE=()
BASH_VERSINFO=([0]="3" [1]="2" [2]="9" [3]="1" [4]="release"
[5]="i686-redhat-linux-gnu")
BASH_VERSION='3.2.9(1)-release'
COLORS=/etc/DIR_COLORS.xterm
```

```
COLUMNS=80
CVS_RSH=ssh
DIRSTACK=()
EUID=500
GROUPS=()
G_BROKEN_FILENAMES=1
HISTFILE=/home/rich/.bash_history
HISTFILESIZE=1000
HISTSIZE=1000
HOME=/home/rich
HOSTNAME=testbox.localdomain
HOSTTYPE=i686
IFS=$' \t\n'
INPUTRC=/etc/inputrc
LANG=en_US.UTF-8
LESSOPEN='|/usr/bin/lesspipe.sh %s'
LINES=24
LOGNAME=rich
LS_COLORS='no=00:fi=00:di=00;34:ln=00;36:pi=40;33:so=00;35:bd=40;33;
01:cd=40;33;01:or=01;05;37;41:mi=01;05;37;41:ex=00;32:*.cmd=00;32:
*.exe=00;32:*.com=00;32:*.btm=00;32:*.bat=00;32:*.sh=00;32:
*.csh=00;32:*.tar=00;31:*.tgz=00;31:*.arj=00;31:*.taz=00;31:
*.lzh=00;31:*.zip=00;31:*.z=00;31:*.Z=00;31:*.gz=00;31:*.bz2=00;31:
*.bz=00;31:*.tz=00;31:*.rpm=00;31:*.cpio=00;31:*.jpg=00;35:
*.gif=00;35:*.bmp=00;35:*.xbm=00;35:*.xpm=00;35:*.png=00;35:
*.tif=00;35:'
MACHTYPE=i686-redhat-linux-gnu
MAIL=/var/spool/mail/rich
MAILCHECK=60
OPTERR=1
OPTIND=1
OSTYPE=linux-gnu
PATH=/usr/kerberos/bin:/usr/lib/ccache:/usr/local/bin:/bin:/usr/bin:
/home/rich/bin
PIPESTATUS=([0]="0")
PPID=3702
PROMPT_COMMAND='echo -ne
"\033]0;${USER}@${HOSTNAME%%.*}:${PWD/#$HOME/~}"; echo -ne "\007"'
PS1='[\u@\h \W]\$ '
PS2='> '
PS4='+ '
```

Listing 9.2: Output from the set command *(continued)*

```
PWD=/home/rich
SHELL=/bin/bash
SHELLOPTS=braceexpand:emacs:hashall:histexpand:history:
interactive-comments:monitor
SHLVL=2
SSH_ASKPASS=/usr/libexec/openssh/gnome-ssh-askpass
SSH_CLIENT='192.168.1.2 1358 22'
SSH_CONNECTION='192.168.1.2 1358 192.168.1.4 22'
SSH_TTY=/dev/pts/0
TERM=xterm
UID=500
USER=rich
_=-H
consoletype=pty
$
```

You'll notice that all of the global environment variables seen from the printenv command appear in the output from the set command. However, quite a few additional environment variables now appear—these are the local environment variables.

Setting Local Environment Variables

When you start a Bash shell (or spawn a shell script), you're allowed to create local variables that are visible within your shell process. You can assign either a numeric or a string value to an environment variable by assigning the variable to a value using the equal sign:

```
$ test=testing
$ echo $test
testing
$
```

Any time you need to reference the value of the test environment variable, just reference it by the name $test.

If you need to assign a string value that contains spaces, you'll need to use a quotation mark to delineate the beginning and the end of the string:

```
$ test=testing a long string
-bash: a: command not found
$ test='testing a long string'
$ echo $test
testing a long string
$
```

Without the single quotation marks, the Bash shell assumes that the next character is another command to process. Notice that for the local environment variable we defined, we used lowercase letters, whereas the system environment variables we've seen so far have all used uppercase letters.

This is a standard convention in the Bash shell. If you create new environment variables, it is recommended (but not required) that you use lowercase letters. This helps distinguish your personal environment variables from the scores of system environment variables.

WARNING It's extremely important that there are no spaces between the environment variable name, the equal sign, and the value. If you put any spaces in the assignment, the Bash shell interprets the value as a separate command:

```
$ test2 = test
-bash: test2: command not found
$
```

After you set a local environment variable, it's available for use anywhere within your shell process. However, if you spawn another shell, it's not available in the child shell:

```
$ bash
$ echo $test

$ exit
exit
$ echo $test
testing a long string
$
```

In this example we started a child shell and, as you can see, the test environment variable is not available in the child shell (it contains a blank value). After we exited the child shell and returned to the original shell, the test local environment variable was still available.

Similarly, if you set a local environment variable in a child process, when you leave the child process, the local environment variable is no longer available:

```
$ bash
$ test=testing
$ echo $test
testing
$ exit
exit
$ echo $test

$
```

The `test` environment variable set in the child shell doesn't exist when we go back to the parent shell.

Setting Global Environment Variables

Global environment variables are visible from any child processes created by the process that sets the global environment variable. The method used to create a global environment variable is to create a local environment variable and then export it to the global environment. This is done by using the export command:

```
$ echo $test
testing a long string
$ export test
$ bash
$ echo $test
testing a long string
$
```

After exporting the local environment variable `test`, we started a new shell process and viewed the value of the `test` environment variable. This time, the environment variable kept its value, as the export command made it global.

WARNING   Notice that when exporting a local environment variable, you don't use the dollar sign to reference the variable's name.

Locating System Environment Variables

The Linux system uses environment variables to identify itself in programs and scripts. This provides a convenient way to obtain system information for your programs. The trick is in how these environment variables are set.

When you start a Bash shell by logging into the Linux system, by default Bash checks several files for commands. These files are called startup files. The startup files Bash processes depend on the method you use to start the Bash shell. There are three ways of starting a Bash shell:

▪   As a default login shell at login time

▪   As an interactive shell that is not the login shell

▪   As a noninteractive shell to run a script

The following sections describe the startup files the Bash shell executes in each of these startup methods.

Login Shell

When you log into the Linux system, the Bash shell starts as a login shell. The login shell looks for four different startup files to process commands from. The order in which the Bash shell processes the files is

1. `/etc/profile`

2. `$HOME/.bash_profile`

3. `$HOME/.bash_login`

4. `$HOME/.profile`

The `/etc/profile` file is the main default startup file for the Bash shell. Whenever you log into the Linux system, Bash executes the commands in the `/etc/profile` startup file. Different Linux distributions place different commands in this file.

Most Linux distributions also check for files in the `/etc/profile.d` directory to run at startup. This makes it easier for individual applications to set environment variables without having to modify the main `/etc/profile` file.

The remaining three startup files are all used for the same function—to provide a user-specific startup file for defining user-specific environment variables. Most Linux distributions use only one of these three startup files:

*   `$HOME/.bash_profile`
*   `$HOME/.bash_login`
*   `$HOME/.profile`

Notice that all three files start with a dot, making them hidden files (they don't appear in a normal `ls` command listing). Since they are in the user's HOME directory, each user can edit the files and add their own environment variables that are active for every Bash shell session they start.

Though not commonly done, you can also use the `$HOME/.bash_logout` file to run scripts when you log out from your Linux session.

Interactive Shell

If you start a Bash shell without logging into a system (such as if you just type **bash** at a CLI prompt or open a GUI terminal), you start what's called an interactive shell. The interactive shell doesn't act like the login shell, but it still provides a CLI prompt for you to enter commands.

If Bash is started as an interactive shell, it doesn't process the /etc/profile file. Instead, it checks for the .bashrc file in the user's HOME directory (often referred to as ~/.bashrc).

The .bashrc file does two things. First, it checks for a common /etc/bash.bashrc file. The common bash.babshrc file provides a way for you to set scripts and variables used by all users who start an interactive shell. Second, it provides a place for the user to enter personal aliases and private script functions.

Noninteractive Shell

Finally, the last type of shell is a noninteractive shell. This is the shell that the system starts to execute a shell script. This is different in that there isn't a CLI prompt to worry about. However, there may still be specific startup commands you want to run each time you start a script on your system.

To accommodate that situation, the Bash shell provides the BASH_ENV environment variable. When the shell starts a noninteractive shell process, it checks this environment variable for the name of a startup file to execute. If one is present, the shell executes the commands in the file. On most Linux distributions, this environment value is not set by default.

Using Command Aliases

Though not environment variables per se, shell command aliases behave in much the same manner. A *command alias* allows you to create an alias name for common commands (along with their parameters) to help keep your typing to a minimum.

Most likely your Linux distribution has already set some common command aliases for you. To see a list of the active aliases, use the alias command with the -p parameter:

```
$ alias -p
alias l.='ls -d .* --color=tty'
alias ll='ls -l --color=tty'
alias ls='ls --color=tty'
alias vi='vim'
alias which='alias | /usr/bin/which --tty-only --read-
alias--show-dot --show-tilde'
$
```

Notice that in this example, the Linux distribution uses an alias to override the standard ls command. It automatically provides the --color parameter, using color to indicate file and directory objects in the listings.

You can create your own aliases by using the alias command:

```
$ alias li='ls -il'
$ li
total 52
  4508 drwxr-xr-x 2 rich rich 4096 Jun 12 11:21 Desktop
  4512 drwxr-xr-x 2 rich rich 4096 Jun 12 11:21 Documents
  4509 drwxr-xr-x 2 rich rich 4096 Jun 12 11:21 Downloads
```

```
401354 -rw-r--r-- 1 rich rich 8980 Jun 12 11:06 examples.desktop
388616 -rw-r--r-- 1 rich rich   10 Jul  5 11:41 file1
389657 -rw-r--r-- 1 rich rich   12 Jul  5 11:41 file2
  4513 drwxr-xr-x 2 rich rich 4096 Jun 12 11:21 Music
389659 -rwxr--r-- 1 rich rich  200 Jul  5 11:41 myscript.sh
388895 -rw-r--r-- 1 rich rich   36 Jun 27 14:23 nc
  4514 drwxr-xr-x 2 rich rich 4096 Jun 28 08:47 Pictures
  4511 drwxr-xr-x 2 rich rich 4096 Jun 12 11:21 Public
417850 drwxr-xr-x 3 rich rich 4096 Jun 28 08:46 snap
  4510 drwxr-xr-x 2 rich rich 4096 Jun 12 11:21 Templates
  4515 drwxr-xr-x 2 rich rich 4096 Jun 12 11:21 Videos
$
```

After you define an alias value, you can use it at any time in your shell, including in shell scripts.

Command aliases act like local environment variables. They're valid only for the shell process in which they're defined:

```
$ alias li='ls -il'
$ bash
$ li
bash: li: command not found
$
```

Of course, now you know a way to solve that problem. Since the Bash shell always reads the $HOME/.bashrc startup file when starting a new interactive shell, just put command alias statements there, and they will be valid for all shells you start.

The Basics of Shell Scripting

Shell scripting allows you to write small programs that automate activities on your Linux system. Shell scripts can save you time by giving you the flexibility to quickly process data and generate reports that would be cumbersome to do by manually entering multiple commands at the command prompt. You can automate just about anything you do at the command prompt using shell scripts.

This section walks through the basics of what shell scripts are and how to get started writing them.

Running Multiple Commands

So far in this book we've been entering a single command at the command prompt and viewing the results. One exciting feature of the Linux command line is that you can enter multiple commands on the same command line and Linux will process them all. Just place a semicolon between each command you enter:

```
$ date ; who
Thu Feb 20 19:20:06 EST 2019
rich     :0          2019-02-20 19:15 (:0)
$
```

The Linux Bash shell runs the first command (date) and displays the output; then it runs the second command (who) and displays the output from that command, immediately following the output from the first command. Though this may seem trivial, it is the basis of how shell scripts work.

Redirecting Output

Another building block of shell scripting is the ability to store command output. Often when you run a command, you'd like to save the output for future reference. To help with this, the Bash shell provides output redirection.

Output redirection allows us to redirect the output of a command from the monitor to another device, such as a file. This feature comes in handy when you need to log data from a shell script that runs after business hours, so you can see what the shell script did when it ran.

To redirect the output from a command, you use the greater-than symbol (>) after the command and then specify the name of the file that you want to use to capture the redirected output. This is demonstrated in Listing 9.3.

Liting 9.3: Redirecting output to a file

```
$ date > today.txt
$ cat today.txt
Thu Feb 20 19:21:12 EST 2019
$
```

The example shown in Listing 9.3 redirects the output of the date command to the file named today.txt. Notice that when you redirect the output of a command, nothing displays on the monitor output. All of the text from the output is now in the file, as shown by using the cat command to display the file contents.

The greater-than output redirection operator automatically creates a new file for the output, even if the file already exists. If you prefer, you can append the output to an existing file by using the double greater-than symbol (>>), as shown in Listing 9.4.

Listing 9.4: Appending command output to a file

```
$ who >> today.txt
$ cat today.txt
Thu Feb 20 19:21:12 EST 2019
rich     :0          2019-02-20 19:15 (:0)
$
```

The today.txt file now contains the output from the original date command in Listing 9.3, and the output from the who command run in Listing 9.4.

In Linux, everything is a file, including the input and output processes of a command. Linux identifies files with a file descriptor, which is a non-negative integer. The Bash shell reserves the first three file descriptors for input and output. File descriptor 0 is called STDIN and points to the standard input for the shell, which is normally the keyboard. File descriptor 1 is called STDOUT, which points to the standard output for the shell, typically the monitor. This is where the standard output messages go. File descriptor 2 is called STDERR, which is where the shell sends messages identified as errors. By default, this points to the same device as the STDOUT file descriptor, the monitor. You can redirect only the errors from your shell script to a separate file from the normal output by using 2> instead of the standard > output redirection character. This allows you to specify a separate file for monitoring error messages from commands.

Output redirection is a crucial feature in shell scripts. With it, we can generate log files from our scripts, giving us a chance to keep track of things as the script runs in background mode on the Linux system.

Piping Data

Whereas output redirection allows us to redirect command output to a file, *piping* allows us to redirect the output to another command. The second command uses the redirected output from the first command as input data. This feature comes in handy when using commands that process data, such as the sort command.

The piping symbol is the bar (|) symbol, which usually appears above the backslash key on U.S. keyboards. Listing 9.5 shows an example of using piping.

Listing 9.5: Piping command output to another command

```
$ ls | sort
Desktop
Documents
Downloads
Music
Pictures
Public
Templates
test.txt
today.txt
Videos
$
```

The output from the ls command is sent directly to the sort command as input but behind the scenes. You don't see the output from the ls command displayed on the monitor; you see only the output from the last command in the pipe line, which in this case is the sort command. There's no limit to how many commands you can link together with piping.

> The >, >>, and | symbols are part of a group of characters often referred to as metacharacters. Metacharacters are characters that have special meaning when used in the Linux shell. If you need to use a metacharacter as a standard character (such as using the > character as a greater-than symbol in your output instead of as a redirect symbol), you must identify the metacharacter by either placing a backslash (\) in front of it or enclosing the metacharacter in single (') or double quotes ("). This method is called *escaping*.

The Shell Script Format

Placing multiple commands on a single line, either by using the semicolon or piping, is a great way to process data, but it can still get rather tedious. Each time you want to run the set of commands, you need to type them all at the command prompt.

However, Linux allows us to place multiple commands in a text file and then run the text file as a program from the command line. This is called a shell script because we're scripting out commands for the Linux shell to run.

Shell script files are plain text files. To create a shell script file, you just need to use any text editor that you're comfortable with. If you're working from a KDE-based graphical desktop, you can use the KWrite program, or if you're working from a GNOME-based graphical desktop, you can use the GEdit program.

> Shell script files must be text files. If you use a word processing program to create the file (or even copy and paste text from a word processing document into a file), the script will not run correctly in the shell.

If you're working directly in a command-line environment, you still have some options. Many Linux distributions include either the pico or nano editor to provide a graphical editor environment by using ASCII control characters to create a full-screen editing window.

If your Linux distribution doesn't include either the pico or nano editor, there is still one last resort: the vi editor. The vi editor is a text-based editor that uses simple single-letter commands. It's the oldest text editor in the Linux environment, dating back to the early days of Unix, which may be one reason why it's not overly elegant or user-friendly.

When you've chosen your text editor, you're ready to create your shell scripts. First, for your shell script to work you'll need to follow a specific format for the shell script file. The first line in the file must specify the Linux shell required to run the script. This is written in somewhat of an odd format:

```
#!/bin/bash
```

The Linux world calls the combination of the pound sign and the exclamation symbol (#!) the *shebang*. It signals to the operating system which shell to use to run the shell script. Most Linux distributions support multiple Linux shells, but the most common is the Bash shell. You can run shell scripts written for other shells, as long as that shell is installed on the Linux distribution.

After you specify the shell, you're ready to start listing the commands in your script. You don't need to enter all of the commands on a single line; Linux allows you to place them on separate lines. Also, the Linux shell assumes each line is a new command in the shell script, so you don't need to use semicolons to separate the commands. Listing 9.6 shows an example of a simple shell script file.

Listing 9.6: A simple shell script file

```
$ cat test1.sh
#!/bin/bash
# This script displays the date and who's logged in
date
who
$
```

The test1.sh script file shown in Listing 9.6 starts out with the shebang line identifying the Bash shell, the standard shell in Linux. The second line in the code shown in Listing 9.6 demonstrates another feature in shell scripts. Lines that start with a pound sign are called *comment lines*. They allow you to embed comments into the shell script program to help you remember what the code is doing. The shell skips comment lines when processing the shell script. You can place comment lines anywhere in your shell script file after the opening shebang line.

 Notice in Listing 9.6 we used the .sh filename extension on the shell script file. Although this is not required in Linux, it's become somewhat of a de facto standard among programmers. It helps identify that the text file is a shell script that can be run at the command line.

Running the Shell Script

If you just enter a shell script file at the command prompt to run it, you may be a bit disappointed:

```
$ test1.sh
test1.sh: command not found
$
```

Unfortunately, the shell doesn't know where to find the `test1.sh` command in the virtual directory. The reason for this is the shell uses a special environment variable called `PATH` to list directories where it looks for commands. If your local `HOME` folder is not included in the `PATH` environment variable list of directories, you can't run the shell script file directly. Instead, you must use either a relative or an absolute path name to point to the shell script file. The easiest way to do that is by adding the `./` relative path shortcut to the file:

```
$ ./test1.sh
bash: ./test1.sh: Permission denied
$
```

Now the shell can find the program file, but there's still an error message. This time the error is telling us that we don't have permissions to run the shell script file. A quick look at the shell script file using the `ls` command with the `-l` option shows the permissions set for the file:

```
$ ls -l test1.sh
-rw-r--r-- 1 rich rich 73 Feb 20 19:37 test1.sh
$
```

By default, the Linux system didn't give anyone execute permissions to run the file. You can use the chmod command to add that permission for the file owner:

```
$ chmod u+x test1.sh
$ ls -l test1.sh
-rwxr--r-- 1 rich rich 73 Feb 20 19:37 test1.sh
$
```

The u+x option adds execute privileges to the owner of the file. You should now be able to run the shell script file and see the output:

```
$ ./test1.sh
Thu Feb 20 19:48:27 EST 2019
rich      :0              2019-02-20 19:15 (:0)
$
```

Running the script directly from the command prompt spawns a new subshell for the script, making any local environment variables in the shell not available to the script. If you want to make any local environment variables available for use in the shell script, launch the script using the exec command:

```
$ exec ./test1.sh
Thu Feb 20 19:51:27 EST 2019
rich      :0              2019-02-20 19:15 (:0)
$
```

The exec command runs the script in the current shell.

Now that you've seen the basics for creating and running shell scripts, the next section dives into some more advanced features you can add to make fancier shell scripts.

Advanced Shell Scripting

The previous section walked through the basics of how to group normal command-line commands together in a shell script file to run in the Linux shell. This section adds to that by showing more features available in shell scripts to make them look and act more like real programs.

Displaying Messages

When you string commands together in a shell script file, the output may be somewhat confusing to look at. It would help to be able to customize the output by separating the output and adding our own text between the output from the listed commands.

The *echo* command allows you to display text messages from the command line. When used at the command line, it's not too exciting:

```
$ echo This is a test
This is a test
$
```

But with echo, you can now insert messages anywhere in the output from the shell script file. Listing 9.7 demonstrates how this is done.

Listing 9.7: Displaying messages from shell scripts

```
$ cat test1.sh
#!/bin/bash
# This script displays the date and who's logged in
echo The current date and time is:
date
echo
echo "Let's see who's logged into the system:"
who
$ ./test1.sh
The current date and time is:
Thu Feb 20 19:55:44 EST 2019

Let's see who's logged into the system:
rich     :0            2019-02-20 19:15 (:0)
$
```

The shell script shown in Listing 9.7 adds three echo commands to the test1.sh script. Notice that the first echo command doesn't use any quotes, but the third one does. The reason for that is the text output from the third echo command contains single quotes. The single quote is also a metacharacter in the shell, which will confuse the echo command, so you need to place double quotes around the text. Also notice that the second echo command doesn't have any text on the line. That outputs a blank line, which is useful when you want to separate output from multiple commands.

Using Variables in Scripts

Part of programming is the ability to temporarily store data to use later on in the program. As mentioned earlier in the "Shell Variables" section, you do that in the Bash shell by using either global or local variables. This method also works when working with shell scripts.

Using Global Environment Variables

As discussed earlier in the "Using Variables" section, global environment variables are often used to track specific system information, such as the name of the system, the name of the user logged into the shell, the user's user ID (UID), the default home directory for the user, and the search path the shell uses to find executable programs. You can tap into these environment variables from within your scripts by using the environment variable name, preceded by a dollar sign, as shown in Listing 9.8.

Listing 9.8: The test2.sh shell script file to display environment variables

```
$ cat test2.sh
#!/bin/bash
# display user information from the system.
echo User info for userid: $USER
echo UID: $UID
echo HOME: $HOME
$
```

The $USER, $UID, and $HOME environment variables are commonly used to display information about the logged-in user. If you run the test2.sh shell script shown in Listing 9.8, the output should look like this:

```
$ chmod u+x test2.sh
$ ./test2.sh
User info for userid: rich
UID: 1000
HOME: /home/rich
$
```

The values you see should be related to your user account. This allows you to dynamically retrieve information about the user account running your shell script to customize the output.

Defining Local Variables

Most variables used in shell scripts are local variables used for storing your own data within your shell scripts. You assign values to local variables using the equal sign. Spaces must not appear between the variable name, the equal sign, and the value. Here are a few examples:

```
var1=10
var2=23.45
var3=testing
var4="Still more testing"
```

The shell script automatically determines the data type used for the variable value. Listing 9.9 shows an example of writing a shell script that uses local variables.

Listing 9.9: Using local variables in a shell script

```
$ cat test3.sh
#!/bin/bash
# testing variables
days=10
guest=Katie
echo $guest checked in $days days ago
$
```

Running the test3.sh script from Listing 9.9 produces the following output:

```
$ chmod u+x test3.sh
$ ./test3.sh
Katie checked in 10 days ago
$
```

After you store the data in a local variable, you can reference it anywhere in your shell script. However, remember that local variables defined within the shell script are accessible only from within the shell script by default. If you want the variables within a shell script to be visible from the parent shell that launched the shell script, use the export command.

WARNING

Be careful when using variables within the echo statement. Since variable names are just text values, if you try to append text to a variable name, the shell will then consider the text as part of the variable name and you won't get the results you expected. If you need to do that, you can enclose the variable name in braces, such as ${guest}. This ensures any text appended to the end of the variable will be separate from the variable name.

Command-Line Arguments

One of the most versatile features of shell scripts is the ability to pass data into the script when you run it. This allows you to customize the script with new data each time you run it.

One method of passing data into a shell script is to use *command-line arguments*. Command-line arguments are data you include on the command line when you run the command. Just start listing them after the command, separating each data value with a space, in this format:

```
command argument1 argument2 ...
```

You retrieve the values in your shell script code using special numeric *positional variables*. Use the variable $1 to retrieve the first command-line argument, $2 the second argument, and so on. Listing 9.10 shows how to use positional variables in your shell script.

Listing 9.10: Using command-line arguments in a shell script

```
$ cat test4.sh
#!/bin/bash
# Testing command line arguments
echo $1 checked in $2 days ago
$ chmod u+x test4.sh
$ ./test4.sh Barbara 4
Barbara checked in 4 days ago
$ ./test4.sh Jessica 5
Jessica checked in 5 days ago
$
```

The test4.sh shell script uses two command-line arguments. The $1 variable holds the name of the person, and the $2 variable holds the number of days ago they checked in. When you run the test4.sh shell script, be sure to include both data values in the command line. The shell won't produce an error message if a positional variable doesn't exist; you just won't get the results you expected:

```
$ ./test4.sh rich
rich checked in days ago
$
```

It's up to you to check if the positional variable exists within your program code. We'll explore how to do that later when we discuss logic statements.

Getting User Input

Providing command-line options and parameters is a great way to get data from your script users, but sometimes your script needs to be more interactive. There are times when you have to ask a question while the script is running and wait for a response from the person running your script. The Bash shell provides the read command just for this purpose.

Basic Reading

The read command accepts input from the standard input (the keyboard) or from another file descriptor. After receiving the input, the read command places the data into a standard variable. Listing 9.11 shows the read command at its simplest.

Listing 9.11: Accepting user input in your scripts

```
$ cat test5.sh
#!/bin/bash
# testing the read command

echo -n "Enter your name: "
read name
echo "Hello $name, welcome to my program."
$ ./test5.sh
Enter your name: Rich Blum
Hello Rich Blum, welcome to my program.
$
```

Notice that the echo command that produced the prompt uses the -n option. This suppresses the newline character at the end of the string, allowing the script user to enter data immediately after the string instead of on the next line. This gives your scripts a more form-like appearance.

In fact, the read command includes the -p option, which allows you to specify a prompt directly in the read command line. Listing 9.12 demonstrates this feature.

Listing 9.12: Using the read command with the -p option

```
$ cat test6.sh
#!/bin/bash
# testing the read -p option

read -p "Please enter your age:" age
days=$[ $age * 365 ]
echo "That makes you over $days days old!"
$ ./test6.sh
Please enter your age:10
That makes you over 3650 days old!
$
```

You'll notice in the Listing 9.11 example, when I typed my name the read command assigned both my first name and last name to the same variable. The read command will assign all data entered at the prompt to a single variable, or you can specify multiple variables. Each data value entered is assigned to the next variable in the list. If the list of variables runs out before the data does, the remaining data is assigned to the last variable:

```
$ cat test7.sh
#!/bin/bash
# entering multiple variables

read -p "Enter your name: " first last
echo "Checking data for $last, $first…"
$ ./test7.sh
Enter your name: Rich Blum
Checking data for Blum, Rich…
$
```

You can also specify no variables on the read command line. If you do that, the read command places any data it receives in the special environment variable REPLY:

```
$ cat test8.sh
#!/bin/bash
# testing the REPLY environment variable

read -p "Enter a number: "
factorial=1
for (( count=1; count <= $REPLY; count++ ))
do
    factorial=$[ $factorial * $count ]
done
echo "The factorial of $REPLY is $factorial"
$ ./test8.sh
Enter a number: 5
The factorial of 5 is 120
$
```

This example uses the for loop, which is explained later on in "Logic Statements," to iterate through the numbers from 1 to the entered number. The REPLY environment variable will contain all of the data entered in the input, and it can be used in the shell script like any other variable.

Timing Out

There's a danger when using the read command. It's quite possible that your script will get stuck waiting for the script user to enter data. If the script must go on regardless of whether any data was entered, you can use the -t option specify a timer. The -t option specifies the number of seconds for the read command to wait for input. When the timer expires, the read command returns a non-zero exit status:

```
$ cat test9.sh
#!/bin/bash
# timing the data entry

if read -t 5 -p "Please enter your name: " name
then
    echo "Hello $name, welcome to my script"
else
    echo
    echo "Sorry, too slow!"
fi
$ ./test9.sh
Please enter your name: Rich
Hello Rich, welcome to my script
$ ./test9.sh
Please enter your name:
Sorry, too slow!
$
```

Since the read command exits with a non-zero exit status if the timer expires, it's easy to use the standard structured statements, such as an if statement or a while loop, to track what happened. In this example, when the timer expires the if statement fails, and the shell executes the commands in the else section.

Instead of timing the input, you can also set the read command to count the input characters. When a preset number of characters has been entered, it automatically exits, assigning the entered data to the variable. This is shown in Listing 9.13.

Listing 9.13: Counting input characters

```
$ cat test10.sh
#!/bin/bash
# getting just one character of input

read -n1 -p "Do you want to continue [Y/N]? " answer
case $answer in
Y | y) echo
      echo "fine, continue on…";;
N | n) echo
      echo OK, goodbye
      exit;;
```

Listing 9.13: Counting input characters (*continued*)

```
esac
echo "This is the end of the script"
$ ./test10.sh
Do you want to continue [Y/N]? Y
fine, continue on…
This is the end of the script
$ ./test10.sh
Do you want to continue [Y/N]? n
OK, goodbye
$
```

In Listing 9.13 the read command uses the -n option with the value of 1, instructing it to accept only a single character before exiting. As soon as you press the single character to answer, the read command accepts the input and passes it to the variable. There's no need to press the Enter key.

Silent Reading

There are times when you need input from the script user but you don't want that input to display on the monitor. The classic example of this is when entering passwords, but there are plenty of other types of data that you will need to hide.

The -s option prevents the data entered in the read command from being displayed on the monitor (actually, the data is displayed, but the read command sets the text color to the same as the background color). Here's an example of using the -s option in a script:

```
$ cat test11.sh
#!/bin/bash
# hiding input data from the monitor

read -s -p "Enter your password: " pass
echo
echo "Is your password really $pass?"
$ ./test11.sh
Enter your password:
Is your password really T3st1ng?
$
```

The data typed at the input prompt doesn't appear on the monitor but is assigned to the variable just fine for use in the script.

The Exit Status

When a shell script ends, it returns an *exit status* back to the parent shell that launched it. The exit status tells us whether the shell script completed successfully.

Linux provides us with the special $? variable, which holds the exit status value from the last command that executed. To check the exit status of a command, you must view the $? variable immediately after the command ends. It changes values according to the exit status of the last command executed by the shell:

```
$ who
rich      :0              2019-02-20 23:16 (:0)
$ echo $?
0
$
```

By convention, the exit status of a command that successfully completes is 0. If a command completes with an error, then a positive integer value appears as the exit status.

You can change the exit status of your shell scripts by using the exit command. Just specify the exit status value you want in the exit command:

```
$ /bin/bash
$ exit 120
exit
$ echo $?
120
$
```

In this example we started a new child shell with the /bin/bash command and then used the exit command to exit the child shell with an exit status code of 120. Back in the parent shell, we then displayed the $? variable value to see if it matched what we had set in the exit command. As you write more complicated scripts, you can indicate errors by changing the exit status value. That way, by checking the exit status you can easily debug your shell scripts.

Writing Script Programs

So far we've explored how to combine regular command-line commands within a shell script to automate common tasks that you may perform as the system administrator. But shell scripts allow us to do much more than just that. The Bash shell provides more programming-like commands that allow us to write full-fledged programs within our shell scripts, such as capturing command output, performing mathematical operations, checking variable and file conditions, and looping through commands. This section walks through some of the advanced programming features available to us from the Bash shell.

Command Substitution

Quite possibly one of the most useful features of shell scripts is the ability to store and process data. So far we've discussed how to use output redirection to store output from a command to a file and piping to redirect the output of a command to another command. There's another technique, however, that can give you more flexibility in storing and using data in your scripts.

Command substitution allows you to assign the output of a command to a user variable in the shell script. After the output is stored in a variable, you can use standard Linux string manipulation commands (such as sort or grep) to manipulate the data before displaying it.

To redirect the output of a command to a variable, you need to use one of two command substitution formats:

- Placing backticks (`) around the command
- Using the command within the $() function

Both methods produce the same result: redirecting the output from the command into a user variable. Listing 9.14 demonstrates using both methods.

Listing 9.14: Demonstrating command substitution

```
$ var1=`date`
$ echo $var1
Fri Feb 21 18:05:38 EST 2019
$ var2=$(who)
$ echo $var2
rich :0 2019-02-21 17:56 (:0)
$
```

The output from the command substitutions is stored in the appropriate variables. You can then use those variables anywhere in your script program as a standard string value.

WARNING The backtick character is not the same as a single quote. It's the character usually found on the same key as the tilde character (~) on U.S. keyboards. Because of the confusion between backticks and single quotes, it's become more popular in the Linux world to use the $() function format.

Performing Math

Eventually you'll want to do more than just manipulate text strings in your shell scripts. The world revolves around numbers, and at some point you'll probably need to do some mathematical operations with your data. Unfortunately, this is one place where the Bash shell shows its age. The mathematical features in the Bash shell aren't quite as fancy as the features found in newer shells, such as the Z shell. However, there are a couple of ways to use simple mathematical functions in Bash shell scripts.

To include mathematical expressions in your shell scripts, you use a special format. This format places the equation within the brackets:

```
result=$[ 25 * 5 ]
```

You can perform lots of different mathematical operations on data using this method, but there is a limitation. The $[] format allows you to use integers only; it doesn't support floating-point values.

If you need to do floating-point calculations, things get considerably more complicated in the Bash shell. One solution is to use the bc command-line calculator program. The bc calculator is a tool in Linux that can perform floating-point arithmetic:

```
$ bc
bc 1.07.1
Copyright 1991-1994, 1997, 1998, 2000, 2004, 2006, 2008, 2012-2017 Free Software
Foundation, Inc.
This is free software with ABSOLUTELY NO WARRANTY.
For details type 'warranty'.
12 * 5.4
64.8
3.156 * (3 + 5)
25.248
quit
$
```

Unfortunately, the bc calculator has some limitations of its own. The floating-point arithmetic is controlled by a built-in variable called scale. You must set this variable to the desired number of decimal places you want in your answers, or you won't get what you were looking for:

```
$ bc -q
3.44 / 5
0
scale=4
3.44 / 5
.6880
quit
$
```

To embed a bc calculation into your script, things get a bit complicated. You must use command substitution to capture the output of the calculation into a variable, but there's a twist. The basic format you need to use is

```
variable=$(echo "options; expression" | bc)
```

The first parameter, *options*, allows us to set the bc variables, such as the scale variable. The *expression* parameter defines the mathematical expression to evaluate using bc. Though this looks pretty odd, it works:

```
$ var1=$(echo "scale=4; 3.44 / 5" | bc)
$ echo $var1
.6880
$
```

This is not ideal, but it works for small projects. If you have a larger programming project that requires lots of calculations, we suggest looking into the Z shell. It supports lots of advanced mathematical functions and features. For more information on the Z shell, see our *Linux Command Line and Shell Scripting Bible, Edition 3* book from Wiley Publishing (2015).

Logic Statements

So far all of the shell scripts presented process commands in a linear fashion, one command after another. However, not all programming is linear. There are times when you'd like your program to test for certain conditions—such as whether a file exists or if a mathematical expression is 0—and perform different commands based on the results of the test. For that, the Bash shell provides *logic statements*.

Logic statements allow us to test for a specific condition and then branch to different sections of code based on whether the condition evaluates to a True or False logical value. There are a couple of different ways to implement logic statements in Bash scripts.

The *if* Statement

The most basic logic statement is the *if condition statement*. The format for the if condition statement is

```
if [ condition ]
then
    commands
fi
```

The square brackets used in the if statement are a shorthand way of using the test command. The test command evaluates a condition and returns a True logical value if the test passes or a False logical value if the test fails. If the condition passes, the shell runs the commands in the then section of code, or if the *condition* evaluates to a False logical value, the shell script skips the commands in the then section of code.

The condition test expression has quite a few different formats in the Bash shell programming. There are built-in tests for numerical values, string values, and even files and directories. Table 9.1 lists the different built-in tests that are available.

TABLE 9.1   Condition tests

Test	Type	Description
n1 -eq *n2*	Numeric	Checks if *n1* is equal to *n2*
n1 -ge *n2*	Numeric	Checks if *n1* is greater than or equal to *n2*
n1 -gt *n2*	Numeric	Checks if *n1* is greater than *n2*

Test	Type	Description
n1 -le *n2*	Numeric	Checks if *n1* is less than or equal to *n2*
n1 -lt *n2*	Numeric	Checks if *n1* is less than *n2*
n1 -ne *n2*	Numeric	Checks if *n1* is not equal to *n2*
str1 = *str2*	String	Checks if *str1* is the same as *str2*
str1 != *str2*	String	Checks if *str1* is not the same as *str2*
str1 < *str2*	String	Checks if *str1* is less than *str2*
str1 > *str2*	String	Checks if *str1* is greater than *str2*
-n *str1*	String	Checks if *str1* has a length greater than zero
-z *str1*	String	Checks if *str1* has a length of zero
-d *file*	File	Check if *file* exists and is a directory
-e *file*	File	Checks if *file* exists
-f *file*	File	Checks if *file* exists and is a file
-r *file*	File	Checks if *file* exists and is readable
-s *file*	File	Checks if *file* exists and is not empty
-w *file*	File	Checks if *file* exists and is writable
-x *file*	File	Checks if *file* exists and is executable
-O *file*	File	Checks if *file* exists and is owned by the current user
-G *file*	File	Checks if *file* exists and the default group is the same as the current user
file1 -nt *file2*	File	Checks if *file1* is newer than *file2*
file1 -ot *file2*	File	Checks if *file1* is older than *file2*

Listing 9.15 shows an example of using if condition statements in a shell script.

Listing 9.15: Using if condition statements

```
$ cat test12.sh
#!/bin/bash
# testing the if condition
if [ $1 -eq $2 ]
then
   echo "Both values are equal!"
   exit
fi

if [ $1 -gt $2 ]
then
   echo "The first value is greater than the second"
   exit
fi

if [ $1 -lt $2 ]
then
   echo "The first value is less than the second"
   exit
fi
$
```

The test12.sh script shown in Listing 9.15 evaluates two values entered as parameters on the command line:

```
$ chmod u+x test12.sh
$ ./test12.sh 10 5
The first value is greater than the second
$
```

Only the command from the if statement that evaluated to a True logical value was processed by the shell script.

 NOTE You can combine tests by using the Boolean AND (&&) and OR (||) symbols.

The *case* Statement

Often you'll find yourself trying to evaluate the value of a variable, looking for a specific value within a set of possible values, similar to what we demonstrated in Listing 9.15. Instead of having to write multiple if statements testing for all of the possible conditions, you can use a *case* statement.

The case statement allows you to check multiple values of a single variable in a list-oriented format:

```
case variable in
pattern1) commands1;;
pattern2 | pattern3) commands2;;
*) default commands;;
esac
```

The case statement compares the variable specified against the different patterns. If the variable matches the pattern, the shell executes the commands specified for the pattern. You can list more than one pattern on a line, using the bar operator to separate each pattern. The asterisk symbol is the catchall for values that don't match any of the listed patterns. Listing 9.16 shows an example of using the case statement.

Listing 9.16: Using the case statement

```
$ cat test13.sh
#!/bin/bash
# using the case statement

case $USER in
rich | barbara)
    echo "Welcome, $USER"
    echo "Please enjoy your visit";;
testing)
    echo "Special testing account";;
jessica)
    echo "Don't forget to log off when you're done";;
*)
    echo "Sorry, you're not allowed here";;
esac
$ chmod u+x test6.sh
$ ./test13.sh

Welcome, rich
Please enjoy your visit
$
```

The case statement provides a much cleaner way of specifying the various options for each possible variable value.

Loops

When you're writing scripts, you'll often find yourself in a situation where it would come in handy to repeat the same commands multiple times, such as applying a command against all of the files in a directory. The Bash shell provides some basic looping commands to accommodate that.

The *for* Loop

The for statement iterates through every element in a series, such as files in a directory or lines in a text document. The format of the for command is

```
for variable in series ; do
    commands
done
```

The *variable* becomes a placeholder, taking on the value of each element in the series in each iteration. The commands can use the variable just like any other variable that you define in the script. Listing 9.17 shows how to use a for loop to iterate through all of the files in a directory.

Listing 9.17: Using the for loop

```
$ cat test14.sh
#!/bin/bash
# iterate through the files in the Home folder
for file in $(ls | sort) ; do
   if [ -d $file ]
   then
      echo "$file is a directory"
   fi
   if [ -f $file ]
   then
      echo "$file is a file"
   fi
done
$
```

If you run the test14.sh shell script, you should see a listing of the files and directories in your Home directory:

```
$ ./test14.sh
Desktop is a directory
Documents is a directory
Downloads is a directory
Music is a directory
Pictures is a directory
```

```
Public is a directory
Templates is a directory
test1.sh is a file
test2.sh is a file
test3.sh is a file
test4.sh is a file
test5.sh is a file
test6.sh is a file
test7.sh is a file
today.txt is a file
Videos is a directory
$
```

That saves a lot of coding from having to check each file manually in a bunch of if or case statements.

A common use of the for statement is to iterate through a series of numbers. Instead of having to list all of the numbers individually, you can use the seq command. The seq command outputs a series of numbers. Just specify the start, end, and interval values needed for the series.

The *while* Loop

Another useful loop statement is the while command. This is its format:

```
while [ condition ] ; do
    commands
done
```

The while loop keeps looping as long as the condition specified evaluates to a True logical value. When the condition evaluates to a False logical value, the looping stops. The condition used in the while loop is the same as that for the if-then statement, so you can test numbers, strings, and files. Listing 9.18 demonstrates using the while loop to calculate the factorial of a number.

Listing 9.18: Calculating the factorial of a number

```
$ cat test15.sh
#!/bin/bash
number=$1
factorial=1
while [ $number -gt 0 ] ; do
    factorial=$[ $factorial * $number ]
    number=$[ $number - 1 ]
done
echo The factorial of $1 is $factorial
```

The shell script retrieves the first parameter passed to the script and uses it in the while loop. The while loop continues looping as long as the value stored in the $number variable is greater than 0. In each loop iteration, that value is decreased by 1, so at some point the while condition becomes False. When that occurs, the $factorial variable contains the final calculation. When you run the test15.sh program, you should get the following results:

```
$ ./test15.sh 5
The factorial of 5 is 120
$ ./test15.sh 6
The factorial of 6 is 720
$
```

The while loop took all of the hard work of iterating through the series of numbers. Now you can plug in any number as the command-line parameter and calculate the factorial value!

 The opposite of the while command is the until command. It iterates through a block of commands until the test condition evaluates to a True logical value.

Functions

As you start writing more complex shell scripts, you'll find yourself reusing parts of code that perform specific tasks. Sometimes it's something simple, such as displaying a text message and retrieving an answer from the script users. Other times it's a complicated calculation that's used multiple times in your script as part of a larger process.

In each of these situations, it can get tiresome writing the same blocks of code over and over again in your script. It would be nice to write the block of code just once and then be able to refer to that block of code anywhere in your script without having to rewrite it.

The Bash shell provides a feature allowing you to do just that. *Functions* are blocks of script code that you assign a name to and then reuse anywhere in your code. Any time you need to use that block of code in your script, all you need to do is use the function name you assigned it (referred to as *calling* the function). This section describes how to create and use functions in your shell scripts.

There are two formats you can use to create functions in Bash shell scripts. The first format uses the keyword function, along with the function name you assign to the block of code:

```
function name {
    commands
}
```

The *name* attribute defines a unique name assigned to the function. Each function you define in your script must be assigned a unique name.

The *commands* are one or more Bash shell commands that make up your function. When you call the function, the Bash shell executes each of the commands in the order they appear in the function, just as in a normal script.

The second format for defining a function in a Bash shell script more closely follows how functions are defined in other programming languages:

```
name() {
commands

}
```

The empty parentheses after the function name indicate that you're defining a function. The same naming rules apply in this format as in the original shell script function format.

To use a function in your script, specify the function name on a line, just as you would any other shell command. Listing 9.19 demonstrates how to do this.

Listing 9.19: Using a function in a shell script

```
$ cat test16.sh
#!/bin/bash
# using a function in a script

function func1 {
    echo "This is an example of a function"
}

count=1
while [ $count -le 5 ]
do
    func1
    count=$[ $count + 1 ]
done

echo "This is the end of the loop"
func1
echo "Now this is the end of the script"
$ ./test16.sh
This is an example of a function
This is an example of a function
This is an example of a function
This is an example of a function
This is an example of a function
This is the end of the loop
This is an example of a function
Now this is the end of the script
$
```

In Listing 9.19, each time the func1 function name is referenced in the code, the Bash shell returns to the func1 function definition and executes the commands defined there.

The Bash shell uses the return command to exit a function with a specific exit status. The return command allows you to specify a single integer value to define the function exit status, providing an easy way for you to programmatically set the exit status of your function:

```
$ cat test17.sh
#!/bin/bash
# using the return command in a function

function dbl {
    read -p "Enter a value: " value
    echo "doubling the value"
    return $[ $value * 2 ]
}

dbl
echo "The new value is $?"
$
```

The dbl function doubles the value contained in the $value variable provided by the user input. It then returns the result using the return command, which the script displays using the $? variable.

Just as you can capture the output of a command to a shell variable, you can also capture the output of a function to a shell variable. You can use this technique to retrieve any type of output from a function to assign to a variable:

```
result=$(dbl)
```

Running Scripts in Background Mode

There are times when running a shell script directly from the command-line interface is inconvenient. Some scripts can take a long time to process, and you may not want to tie up the command-line interface waiting. While the script is running, you can't do anything else in your terminal session. Fortunately, there's a simple solution to that problem. The following sections describe how to run your scripts in background mode on your Linux system.

Running in the Background

Running a shell script in background mode is a fairly easy thing to do. To run a shell script in background mode from the command-line interface, just place an ampersand symbol after the command:

```
$ ./test18.sh &
[1] 19555
$ This is test program
Loop #1
Loop #2

$ ls -l
total 8
-rwxr--r--    1 rich    rich            219 Feb  26 19:27 test18.sh
* $ Loop #3
```

When you place the ampersand symbol after a command, it separates the command from the Bash shell and runs it as a separate background process on the system. The first thing that displays is the line

```
[1] 19555
```

The number in the square brackets is the *job number* the shell assigns to the background process. The shell assigns each process started a unique job number. The next number is the process ID (PID) the Linux system itself assigns to the process. So every process running in a shell has a unique job number, and every process running on the Linux system has a unique PID.

As soon as the system displays these items, a new command-line interface prompt appears. You are returned to the shell, and the command you executed runs safely in background mode.

At this point, you can enter new commands at the prompt (as shown in the example). However, while the background process is still running, it still uses your terminal monitor for output messages. You'll notice from the example that the output from the test1.sh script appears in the output intermixed with any other commands that are run from the shell.

When the background process finishes, it displays a message on the terminal:

```
[1]+  Done                    ./test18.sh
```

This shows the job number and the status of the job (Done), along with the command used to start the job.

Running Multiple Background Jobs

You can start any number of background jobs at the same time from the command-line prompt:

```
$ ./test18.sh &
[1] 19582
$ This is test program
Loop #1
$ ./test18.sh &
[2] 19597
$ This is test program
Loop #1
$ ./test18.sh &
[3] 19612
$ This is test program
Loop #1
Loop #2
Loop #2
Loop #2
```

Each time you start a new job, the shell assigns it a new job number, and the Linux system assigns it a new PID. You can see that all of the scripts are running by using the ps command:

```
$ ps au
USER       PID %CPU %MEM   VSZ  RSS TTY       STAT START   TIME COMMAND
rich 19498 0.0 1.2 2688 1628 pts/0 S 11:38 0:00 -bash
rich 19582 0.0 0.9 2276 1180 pts/0 S 11:55 0:00 /bin/bash ./test18.sh
rich 9597  0.1 0.9 2276 1180 pts/0 S 11:55 0:00 /bin/bash ./test18.sh
rich 19612 0.1 0.9 2276 1180 pts/0 S 11:55 0:00 /bin/bash ./test18.sh
rich 19639 0.0 0.4 1564 552  pts/0 S 11:56 0:00 sleep 10
rich 19640 0.0 0.4 1564 552  pts/0 S 11:56 0:00 sleep 10
rich 19641 0.0 0.4 1564 552  pts/0 S 11:56 0:00 sleep 10
rich 19642 0.0 0.5 2588 744  pts/0 R 11:56 0:00 ps au
$
```

Each of the background processes you start appears in the ps command output listing of running processes. If all of the processes display output in your terminal session, things can get pretty messy pretty quickly. Fortunately, there's a simple way to solve that problem, which we'll discuss in the next section.

You need to be careful when using background processes from a terminal session. Notice in the output from the ps command that each of the background processes is tied to the terminal session (pts/0) terminal. If the terminal session exits, the background process also exits. Some terminal emulators warn you if you have any running background processes associated with the terminal, while others don't. If you want your script to continue running in background mode after you've logged off the console, there's something else you need to do. The next section discusses that process.

Running Scripts Without a Console

There will be times when you want to start a shell script from a terminal session and then let the script run in background mode until it finishes, even if you exit the terminal session. You can do this by using the *nohup* command.

The nohup command runs another command blocking any SIGHUP signals that are sent to the process. This prevents the process from exiting when you exit your terminal session.

You can combine the nohup command with the ampersand to run a script in background and not allow it to be interrupted:

```
$ nohup ./test18.sh &
[1] 19831
$ nohup: appending output to  'nohup.out'
$
```

Just as with a normal background process, the shell assigns the command a job number, and the Linux system assigns a PID number. The difference is that when you use the nohup command, the script ignores any SIGHUP signals sent by the terminal session if you close the session.

Because the nohup command disassociates the process from the terminal, the process loses the output link to your monitor. To accommodate any output generated by the command, the nohup command automatically redirects output messages to a file, called nohup.out.

The nohup.out file contains all of the output that would normally be sent to the terminal monitor. After the process finishes running, you can view the nohup.out file for the output results:

```
$ cat nohup.out
This is a test program
Loop #1
Loop #2
Loop #3
```

```
Loop #4
Loop #5
Loop #6
Loop #7
Loop #8
Loop #9
Loop #10
This is the end of the test program
$
```

The output appears in the nohup.out file just as if the process ran on the command line!

WARNING If you run another command using nohup, the output is appended to the existing nohup.out file. Be careful when running multiple commands from the same directory, as all of the output will be sent to the same nohup.out file, which can get confusing.

Sending Signals

The Bash shell can send control signals to processes running on the system. This allows you to stop or interrupt a runaway application process if necessary. There are two basic Linux signals you can generate using key combinations on the keyboard to interrupt or stop a foreground process.

Interrupting a Process

The Ctrl+C key combination generates a SIGINT signal and sends it to any processes currently running in the shell. The SIGINT signal interrupts the running process, which for most processes causes them to stop (it is possible to code a script to ignore interrupt signals, but this is not common). You can test this by running a command that normally takes a long time to finish and pressing the Ctrl+C key combination:

```
$ sleep 100

$
```

The Ctrl+C key combination doesn't produce any output on the monitor; it just stops the current process running in the shell.

Pausing a Process

Instead of terminating a process, you can pause it in the middle of whatever it's doing. Sometimes this can be a dangerous thing (for example, if a script has a file lock open on a crucial system file), but often it allows you to peek inside what a script is doing without actually terminating the process.

The Ctrl+Z key combination generates a SIGTSTP signal, stopping any processes running in the shell. Stopping a process is different than terminating the process, as stopping the process leaves the program still in memory and able to continue running from where it left off. In the next section, "Job Control," you'll learn how to restart a process that's been stopped.

When you use the Ctrl+Z key combination, the shell informs you that the process has been stopped:

```
$ sleep 100

[1]+  Stopped                 sleep 100
$
```

The number in the square brackets indicates the job number for the process in the shell. If you have a stopped job assigned to your shell session, Bash will warn you if you try to exit the shell:

```
$ exit
logout
There are stopped jobs.
$
```

You can view the stopped job by using the ps command:

```
$ ps au
USER PID   %CPU %MEM  VSZ  RSS TTY    STAT  START   TIME COMMAND
rich 20560  0.0  1.2  2688 1624 pts/0  S     05:15   0:00 -bash
rich 20605  0.2  0.4  1564  552 pts/0  T     05:22   0:00 sleep 100
rich 20606  0.0  0.5  2584  740 pts/0  R     05:22   0:00 ps au
$
```

The ps command shows the status of the stopped job as T, which indicates the command is either being traced or is stopped.

If you really want to exit the shell with the stopped job still active, just type the exit command again. The shell will exit, terminating the stopped job. Alternately, now that you know the PID of the stopped job, you can use the kill command to send a SIGKILL signal to terminate it:

```
$ kill -9 20605
$
[1]+  Killed                  sleep 100
$
```

When you kill the job, initially you won't get any response. However, the next time you do something that produces a shell prompt, you'll see a message indicating that the job was killed. Each time the shell produces a prompt, it also displays the status of any jobs that have changed states in the shell.

Job Control

In the previous section, you saw how to use the Ctrl+Z key combination to stop a job running in the shell. After you stop a job, the Linux system lets you either kill or restart it. Restarting a stopped process requires sending it a SIGCONT signal.

The function of starting, stopping, killing, and resuming jobs is called *job control*. With job control, you have full control over how processes run in your shell environment.

This section describes the commands used to view and control jobs running in your shell.

Viewing Jobs

The key command for job control is the *jobs* command. The jobs command allows you to view the current jobs being handled by the shell. Listing 9.20 uses a shell script to demonstrate viewing a stopped job.

Listing 9.20: Stopping a running job

```
$ cat test19.sh
#!/bin/bash
# testing job control

echo "This is a test program $$"
count=1
while [ $count -le 10 ] ; do
    echo "Loop #$count"
    sleep 10
    count=$[ $count + 1 ]
done
echo "This is the end of the test program"
$ ./test19.sh
This is a test program 29011
Loop #1

[1]+  Stopped                 ./test19.sh
$ ./test19.sh > test19.sh.out &
[2] 28861
$
$ jobs
[1]+  Stopped                 ./test19.sh
[2]-  Running                 ./test19.sh >test19.shout &
$
```

The script shown in Listing 9.20 uses the $$ variable to display the PID that the Linux system assigns to the script; then it goes into a loop, sleeping for 10 seconds at a time for each iteration. In the example, we start the first script from the command-line interface and then stop it using the Ctrl+Z key combination. Next, another job is started as a background process, using the ampersand symbol. To make life a little easier, we redirected the output of that script to a file so that it wouldn't appear on the monitor.

After the two jobs were started, we used the jobs command to view the jobs assigned to the shell. The jobs command shows both the stopped and the running jobs, along with their job numbers and the commands used in the jobs.

The jobs command uses a few different command-line parameters, shown in Table 9.2.

TABLE 9.2   The jobs command parameters

Parameter	Description
-l	List the PID of the process along with the job number.
-n	List only jobs that have changed their status since the last notification from the shell.
-p	List only the PIDs of the jobs.
-r	List only the running jobs.
-s	List only stopped jobs.

You probably noticed the plus and minus signs in the output in Listing 9.20. The job with the plus sign is considered the *default job*. It would be the job referenced by any job control commands if a job number wasn't specified in the command line. The job with the minus sign is the job that would become the default job when the current default job finishes processing. There will only be one job with the plus sign and one job with the minus sign at any time, no matter how many jobs are running in the shell.

Listing 9.21 shows an example of how the next job in line takes over the default status when the default job is removed.

Listing 9.21: Demonstrating job control

```
$ ./test19.sh
This is a test program 29075
Loop #1

[1]+  Stopped                 ./test19.sh
$ ./test19.sh
```

Listing 9.21: Demonstrating job control *(continued)*

```
This is a test program 29090
Loop #1


[2]+  Stopped                 ./test19.sh
$ ./test19.sh

This is a test program 29105
Loop #1


[3]+  Stopped                 ./test19.sh
$ jobs -l
[1]  29075 Stopped            ./test19.sh
[2]- 29090 Stopped            ./test19.sh
[3]+ 29105 Stopped            ./test19.sh
$ kill -9 29105
$ jobs -l
[1]- 29075 Stopped            ./test19.sh
[2]+ 29090 Stopped            ./test19.sh
$
```

In Listing 9.21 we started, then stopped, three separate processes. The jobs command listing shows the three processes and their status. Note by the PID numbers that the default process (the one listed with the plus sign) is 29105, the last process started.

We then used the kill command to send a SIGHUP signal to the default process. In the next jobs listing, the job that previously had the minus sign, 29090, is now the default job.

Restarting Stopped Jobs

Under Bash job control, you can restart any stopped job as either a background process or a foreground process. A foreground process takes over control of the terminal you're working on, so be careful about using that feature.

To restart a job in background mode, use the bg command, along with the job number:

```
$ bg 2
[2]+ ./test20.sh &
Loop #2
$ Loop #3
Loop #4

$ jobs
[1]+  Stopped                 ./test20.sh
[2]-  Running                 ./test20.sh &
```

```
$ Loop #6
Loop #7
Loop #8
Loop #9
Loop #10
This is the end of the test program

[2]-  Done                    ./test20.sh
$
```

Since we restarted the job in background mode, the command-line interface prompt appears, allowing us to continue with other commands. The output from the jobs command now shows that the job is indeed running (as you can tell from the output now appearing on the monitor).

To restart a job in foreground mode, use the fg command, along with the job number:

```
$ jobs
[1]+  Stopped                 ./test20.sh
$ fg 1
./test20
Loop #2
Loop #3
```

Since the job is running in foreground mode, we don't get a new command-line interface prompt until the jobs finishes.

Running Like Clockwork

I'm sure that, as you start working with scripts, there'll be a situation in which you'll want to run a script at a preset time, usually at a time when you're not there. There are two common ways of running a script at a preselected time:

- The at command
- The cron table

Each method uses a different technique for scheduling when and how often to run scripts. The following sections describe each of these methods.

Scheduling a Job Using the *at* Command

The *at* command allows you to specify a time when the Linux system will run a script. It submits a job to a queue with directions on when the shell should run the job. Another command, atd, runs in the background and checks the job queue for jobs to run. Most Linux distributions start this automatically at boot time.

The atd command checks a special directory on the system (usually /var/spool/at) for jobs submitted using the at command. By default, the atd command checks this directory every 60 seconds. When a job is present, the atd command checks the time the job is set to be run. If the time matches the current time, the atd command runs the job.

The following sections describe how to use the at command to submit jobs to run and how to manage jobs.

The *at* Command Format

The basic at command format is pretty simple:

```
 at [-f filename] time
```

By default, the at command submits input from STDIN to the queue. You can specify a filename used to read commands (your script file) using the -f parameter.

The *time* parameter specifies when you want the Linux system to run the job. You can get pretty creative with how you specify the time. The at command recognizes lots of different time formats:

- A standard hour and minute, such as 10:15

- An AM/PM indicator, such as 10:15PM

- A specific named time, such as now, noon, midnight, or teatime (4PM)

If you specify a time that's already past, the at command runs the job at that time on the next day.

Besides specifying the time to run the job, you can also include a specific date, using a few different date formats:

- A standard date format, such as MMDDYY, MM/DD/YY, or DD.MM.YY

- A text date, such as Jul 4 or Dec 25, with or without the year

- You can also specify a time increment:
  - Now + 25 minutes
  - 10:15PM tomorrow
  - 10:15 + 7 days

When you use the at command, the job is submitted into a *job queue*. The job queue holds the jobs submitted by the at command for processing. There are 26 different job queues available for different priority levels. Job queues are referenced using lowercase letters, a through z. By default, all at jobs are submitted to job queue a, the highest-priority queue. If you want to run a job at a lower priority, you can specify the letter using the -q parameter.

Retrieving Job Output

When the job runs on the Linux system, there's no monitor associated with the job. Instead, the Linux system uses the email address of the user who submitted the job. Any output destined to STDOUT or STDERR is mailed to the user via the mail system.

Listing 9.22 shows a simple example of using the at command to schedule a job to run.

Listing 9.22: Using the at command to start a job

```
$ date
Thu Feb 28 18:48:20 EST 2019
$ at -f test3.sh 18:49
job 2 at Thu Feb 28 18:49:00 2019
$ mail
Heirloom Mail version 12.5 7/5/10.  Type ? for help.
"/var/spool/mail/rich": 1 message 1 new
>N  1 Rich                 Thu Feb 28 18:49  15/568   "Output from your job "
&
Message  1:
From rich@localhost.localdomain  Thu Feb 28 18:49:00 2019
Return-Path: <rich@localhost.localdomain>

X-Original-To: rich
Delivered-To: rich@localhost.localdomain
Subject: Output from your job          2
To: rich@localhost.localdomain
Date: Thu, 28 Feb 2019 18:49:00 -0500 (EST)
From: rich@localhost.localdomain (Rich)
Status: R

"This script ran at 18:49:00"
"This is the end of the script"

&
```

As seen in Listing 9.22, when we ran the at command, it produced a warning message, indicating what shell the system uses to run the script (the default shell assigned to /bin/sh, which for Linux is the Bash shell), along with the job number assigned to the job and the time the job is scheduled to run.

When the job completes, nothing appears on the monitor, but the system generates an email message. The email message shows the output generated by the script. If the script doesn't produce any output, it won't generate an email message, by default. You can change that by using the -m option in the at command. This generates an email message, indicating the job completed, even if the script doesn't generate any output.

Listing Pending Jobs

The atq command allows you to view what jobs are pending on the system:

```
$ at -f test21.sh 19:15
warning: commands will be executed using /bin/sh
job 7 at 2007-11-04 10:15
$ at -f test21.sh 4PM
warning: commands will be executed using /bin/sh
job 8 at 2007-11-03 16:00
$ at -f test21.sh 1PM tomorrow
warning: commands will be executed using /bin/sh
job 9 at 2007-11-04 13:00
$ atq
7       2007-11-04 10:15 a
8       2007-11-03 16:00 a
9       2007-11-04 13:00 a
$
```

The job listing shows the job number, the date and time the system will run the job, and the job queue the job is stored in.

Removing Jobs

When you know the information about what jobs are pending in the job queues, you can use the atrm command to remove a pending job:

```
$ atrm 8
$ atq
7       2007-11-04 10:15 a
9       2007-11-04 13:00 a
$
```

Just specify the job number you want to remove. You can only remove jobs that you submit for execution. You can't remove jobs submitted by others.

If you're using a Linux distribution that uses the systemd startup method, you can also use the systemd-run command to schedule a job to run at a specific time. The systemd-run command uses a somewhat complicated format, but it allows you to fine-tune exactly when a job should run (down to the millisecond of time), providing a wealth of options for you. To list jobs scheduled using the systemd-run command, you'll need to use the systemctl command. Consult your Linux system documentation if you'd like to learn more about the systemd-run statement.

Scheduling Regular Scripts

Using the at command to schedule a script to run at a preset time is great, but what if you need that script to run at the same time every day or once a week or once a month? Instead of having to continually submit at jobs, you can use another feature of the Linux system.

The Linux system uses the *cron* program to allow you to schedule jobs that need to run on a regular basis. The cron program runs in the background and checks special tables, called *cron tables* (also called crontab for short), for jobs that are scheduled to run.

The *cron* Table

The cron table uses a special format for allowing you to specify when a job should be run. The format for the cron table is

min hour dayofmonth month dayofweek command

The cron table allows you to specify entries as specific values, ranges of values (such as 1–5), or as a wildcard character (the asterisk). For example, if you want to run a command at 10:15 a.m. every day, you would use the cron table entry of

15 10 * * * *command*

The wildcard character used in the *dayofmonth*, *month*, and *dayofweek* fields indicates that cron will execute the command every day of every month at 10:15 a.m. To specify a command to run at 4:15 p.m. every Monday, you would use

15 16 * * 1 *command*

You can specify the *dayofweek* entry either as a three-character text value (mon, tue, wed, thu, fri, sat, sun) or as a numeric value, with 0 being Sunday and 6 being Saturday.

Here's another example: to execute a command at 12 noon on the first day of every month, you'd use the format

00 12 1 * * *command*

The *dayofmonth* entry specifies a date value (1–31) for the month.

When specifying the command or shell to run, you must use its full path name. You can add any command-line parameters or redirection symbols you like, as a regular command line:

15 10 * * * /home/rich/test21.sh > test21out

The cron program runs the script using the user account that submitted the job. Thus, you must have the proper permissions to access the command and output files specified in the command listing.

Building the *cron* Table

All system users can have their own cron table (including the root user) for running scheduled jobs. Linux provides the crontab command for handling the cron table. To list an existing cron table, use the -l parameter:

```
$ crontab -l
no crontab for rich
$
```

By default, each user's cron table file doesn't exist. To add entries to your cron table, use the -e parameter. When you do that, the crontab command automatically starts the vi editor with the existing cron table, or an empty file if it doesn't yet exist.

EXERCISE 9.1

Writing a Bash Script to View the Password Information for System Users

This exercise walks through how to write a Bash script to view the password information for all user accounts configured on the Linux system.

1. Log into your Linux graphical desktop and open a command prompt window.

2. At the command prompt, open a text editor of your choice and create the text file pwinfo.sh by typing *nano pwinfo.sh*, *pico pwinfo.sh*, or *vi pwinfo.sh*.

3. Enter the following code into the new text file:

```
#!/bin/bash
# pwinfo.sh - display password information for all users
list=$(cut -d : -f 1 /etc/passwd)
for user in $list ; do
    echo Password information for $user
    sudo chage -l $user
    echo "----------"
done
```

4. Save the file using the appropriate save command for your editor.

5. Give yourself execute permissions to the file by typing *chmod u+x pwinfo.sh*.

6. Run the shell script by typing *./pwinfo.sh*.

7. Enter your password at the sudo prompt.

   You should see the chage password information listed for all of the user accounts configured on the system.

Summary

The Bash shell provides both local and global environment variables that you can access from within your shell scripts. Global environment variables allow you to retrieve information about the shell environment your script is running in, such as what user account started the shell, and information about that user account. Local environment variables allow you to store and retrieve data from within your script, making it act like a real program.

With basic shell scripting, you can combine multiple commands together to run them as a single command. You can use output redirection to redirect the output of a command to a file that you can read later on, or you can use piping to redirect the output of one command to use as input data for another command.

When you add multiple commands to a text file to run, you must start the text file with the shebang (#!) line, which identifies the Linux shell to use. You'll also need to give yourself execute permissions to run the file by using the chmod command with the u+x option. You may also need to either specify the full path to the file when you run it from the command prompt, or modify the PATH environment variable on your system so that the shell can find your shell script files.

The Bash shell provides additional features that you can add to your shell script files to make them look more like real programs. The echo statement allows you to interject text output between the command outputs in the script to help modify the output your script produces.

The Bash shell also provides advanced programming features that you can use in your shell scripts. Command substitution allows you to capture the output from a command into a variable so that you can extract information from the command output within your shell script. The Bash shell supports rudimentary integer math operations, but it is not overly adept at handling floating-point numbers. You'll need help from other programs such as the bc calculator to do that.

The Bash shell also supports some standard programming features such as if and case logic statements, allowing you to test numbers, strings, and files for specific conditions, and run commands based on the outcome of those conditions. It also supports both for and while loops, which allow you to iterate through groups of data, processing each element within a set of commands. These features can help make your Bash shell scripts perform just like a real program.

By default, when you run a script in a terminal session shell, the interactive shell is suspended until the script completes. You can cause a script or command to run in background mode by adding an ampersand sign (&) after the command name. When you run a script or command in background mode, the interactive shell returns, allowing you to continue entering more commands. Any background processes run using this method are still tied to the terminal session. If you exit the terminal session, the background processes also exit.

In addition to controlling processes while they're running, you can determine when a process starts on the system. Instead of running a script directly from the command-line interface prompt, you can schedule the process to run at an alternative time. There are several different ways to accomplish this. The at command allows you to run a script once at a preset time. The cron program provides an interface that can run scripts at a regularly scheduled interval.

Exam Essentials

Explain environment variables and how Linux uses them.   Environment variables store data in memory for shell sessions. Environment variables set within a shell are considered local variables, accessible by the local shell only. Using the export command allows an environment variable to be accessed globally by other shell sessions. The system administrator can set standard environment variables for all users by placing them in the /etc/profile file, and individual users can set their own environment variables in the .bash_profile, .profile, or .bashrc file in their HOME directory.

Describe how to link multiple command-line commands together in a shell script.   The Bash shell allows us to place multiple commands sequentially in a file and will then process each command when you run the file from the command line. The output from each command will appear in the command-line output.

Explain how you can handle data within a Bash shell script.   The Bash shell provides two ways to handle data within commands. Output redirection allows you to redirect the output of a command to a text file, which you, or another command, can read later. Piping allows you to redirect the output of one command to use as the input data for another command. The output never displays on the monitor when you run the shell script; the data transfer happens behind the scenes.

Explain the type of data you can access from within a shell script.   The Bash shell provides access to environment variables, which contain information about the shell environment the script is running in. You can obtain information about the system as well as the user account that's running the shell script. The shell script also has access to positional variables, which allow you to pass data to the shell script from the command line when you run the shell script.

Describe how you can manipulate output data from a command before you use it in another command within a shell script.   Command substitution allows you to redirect the output of a command to a user variable in your shell script. You can then use standard Linux text processing commands to manipulate the data, such as sort it or extract data records from it, before redirecting the variable data to another command.

Describe how the Bash shell performs mathematical operations.   The Bash shell uses the $[] symbol to define mathematical equations to process. The Bash shell can perform only integer math, so this capability is somewhat limited.

Explain the different methods for implementing logic within a Bash shell script. The Bash shell supports if statements and the case statement. They both allow you to perform a test on a numerical value, string value, or a file, and then run a block of commands based on the outcome of the test.

Describe how to run a shell script in background mode from your console or terminal session. To run a shell script in background mode, include the ampersand sign (&) after the shell script command on the command line. The shell will run the script in background mode and produce another command prompt for you to continue within the shell.

Explain how you can disconnect a shell script from the console or terminal session so that it can continue running if the session closes. The nohup command disconnects the shell script from the shell session and runs it as a separate process. If the console or terminal session exits, the shell script will continue running.

Explain how you can stop or pause a shell script running in the foreground on a console or terminal session. To stop a shell script running in the foreground of a console or terminal session, press the Ctrl+C key combination. To pause a running shell script, press the Ctrl+Z key combination.

Describe how to list shell scripts running in background mode within a console or terminal session. The jobs command allows you to list the commands that are running within the console or terminal session. The output from the jobs command displays both the job number assigned by the shell and the process ID assigned by the Linux system.

Describe how to run a shell script at a specific time. The at command allows you to schedule a job to run at a specific time. You can specify the time by using an exact value, such as 10:00PM, or by using common date and time references, such as 10:00AM tomorrow.

Explain how to run a shell script automatically at a set time every day. The cron process runs every minute and checks for jobs that are scheduled to run. You must define the jobs to run in the cron table by using the crontab command.

Review Questions

You can find the answers in the appendix.

1. What character or characters make up the shebang used in Linux to define the shell used for a shell script?

    A. >>

    B. #!

    C. |

    D. >

    E. 2>

2. What character or characters do you use to redirect all output from a command to a new file?

    A. >>

    B. #!

    C. |

    D. >

    E. 2>

3. What chmod permissions should you assign to a file to run it as a shell script?

    A. 644

    B. u+r

    C. u+x

    D. u+w

    E. u=wr

4. What environment variable contains the username of the user who started the shell?

    A. $USER

    B. $UID

    C. $HOME

    D. $BASH

    E. $1

5. How do you assign the numeric value 10 to the variable var1?

    A. var1=$(10)

    B. var1 = 10

    C. var1=10

    D. var1="10"

    E. var1=`10`

6. What if condition test should you use to determine whether an object exists and is a file?

   A. -e

   B. -f

   C. -d

   D. -x

   E. -w

7. What character or combination of characters do you use to redirect the output of one command to another command?

   A. >>

   B. #!

   C. |

   D. >

   E. 2>

8. What command do you use to change the exit status returned by the shell script?

   A. #!

   B. $?

   C. $1

   D. exit

   E. while

9. What command should you use to perform a command substitution to assign the output of a command to a variable in your shell script?

   A. >

   B. >>

   C. $[]

   D. |

   E. $()

10. What command should you use to perform a mathematical operation in your shell script?

   A. >

   B. >>

   C. $[]

   D. |

   E. $()

11. What command do you use to start a shell script in background mode from your console session?

    A. >

    B. &

    C. |

    D. >>

    E. nohup

12. What command do you use to disconnect a shell script from the current console so that it can continue to run after the console exits?

    A. >

    B. &

    C. |

    D. >>

    E. nohup

13. How can you get a runaway shell script to stop running in your console session?

    A. Start it with the nohup command.

    B. Start it with the ampersand (&) command.

    C. Press Ctrl+C while the script is running.

    D. Redirect the output using the pipe symbol.

    E. Use the kill command to stop it.

14. How can you temporarily pause a shell script from running in foreground in a console session?

    A. Press the Ctrl+Z key combination.

    B. Press the Ctrl+C key combination.

    C. Start the command with the nohup command.

    D. Start the command with the ampersand (&) command.

    E. Start the command with the fg command.

15. How do you determine the default job running in a console session?

    A. By the PID number

    B. By the job number

    C. By a plus sign next to the job number in the jobs output

    D. By a minus sign next to the job number in the jobs output

    E. By using the ps command

16. What command do you use to retrieve a shell script running in background mode and run it in foreground mode on the console session?

    A. bg

    B. fg

    C. nohup

    D. &

    E. at

17. What command allows you to run a shell script at a specific time?

    A. nohup

    B. &

    C. at

    D. |

    E. >

18. What program runs shell scripts at multiple preset times automatically?

    A. at

    B. nohup

    C. &

    D. cron

    E. atq

19. When will the cron table entry 10 5 * * * myscript run the specified shell script?

    A. At 10:05 a.m. every day

    B. On May 10 every year

    C. On October 5 every year

    D. At 5:10 p.m. every day

    E. At 5:10 a.m. every day

20. What command do you use to list the cron table entries for your user account?

    A. cron

    B. at

    C. crontab

    D. jobs

    E. nohup

Chapter

10

Securing Your System

OBJECTIVES

✓ **110.1** Perform security administration tasks

✓ **110.2** Set up host security

✓ **110.3** Securing data with encryption

Securing your systems is a crucial task. The variety of computer attacks and security breaches escalates every day. Thus, the need to improve your servers' security grows as well.

System administrators must know how to set at least a basic level of host security. This includes auditing the network services their systems offer, reviewing system configurations to ensure that local security policies are properly enforced, and employing appropriate techniques to secure both data and communications. We'll cover those topics and more in this chapter on system security.

Administering Network Security

Imagine a home with a door to the outside from every room in the house. That would be a lot of locks to check before leaving the house or going to bed. In the world of network security, having services on your system that are not used is similar to having unnecessary doors to the outside. A term used in cybersecurity that applies to this scenario is *attack surface*. An attack surface is all the various points where a malicious person may try to gain access to something for nefarious reasons.

Continuing the analogy, envision that the multidoor home has a few doors with old locks that no longer properly work and need to be replaced or repaired. This situation is similar to older security software on your system that needs to be updated, reconfigured, or even ousted so that more modern and secure applications can take its place.

In this section, we'll take a look at auditing your system for unused services in order to minimize its attack surface. We'll also look at some older network security technology and how it should be handled.

Disabling Unused Services

One method for minimizing your system's attack surface is by disabling unused services (daemons) on your system. Having less software running lessens the various targets a malicious actor (another name for an attacker) can leverage.

While it is tempting to think you know every service running on your Linux system, to be sure, it's always a good idea to run a thorough audit. In this section, we'll look at various examinations you can conduct to see what services your system is offering.

Discovering Open Ports with *nmap*

The Network Mapper (*nmap*) utility is often used for penetration testing (the practice of testing a system, its network, and its apps to find computer security weaknesses that a malicious attacker could exploit). However, it is also very useful for network service auditing.

Though it's typically not installed by default, except on pen testing distributions such as Kali Linux, most distros have the nmap package in their standard repositories. See Chapter 2, "Managing Software and Processes," for how to install packages.

The nmap command was specifically developed as a network port scanning application. It can scan multiple remote network servers, documenting all of the ports and protocols that they support.

Typically, when a network service starts, it opens a network port and listens for incoming connections. The nmap utility performs standard TCP and UDP connection examinations that meet our needs here.

The snipped example in Listing 10.1 shows using nmap inside the system's firewall by designating 127.0.0.1 (the local loopback address) as the server to scan. In order to see which TCP protocol services the IPv4 ports are offering, the -sT options (scan TCP) are used. You can also add the -p option to specify the port range, if desired.

Listing 10.1: Viewing TCP ports and services inside the firewall using the nmap utility

```
$ nmap -sT 127.0.0.1
[…]
Nmap scan report for localhost (127.0.0.1)
Host is up (0.0017s latency).
Not shown: 996 closed ports
PORT     STATE SERVICE
22/tcp   open  ssh
25/tcp   open  smtp
111/tcp open  rpcbind
631/tcp open  ipp

Nmap done: 1 IP address (1 host up) scanned in 0.23 seconds
$
```

Notice that after the first few lines of output from the nmap utility, three columns of data are displayed: PORT, STATE, SERVICE. The first line of this information in Listing 10.1 is

```
22/tcp   open  ssh
```

This information lets us know that port 22 is open and listening for TCP connections for the OpenSSH (ssh) service. If you don't recognize a service's name, you can employ the /etc/services file to assist you (this file was covered in Chapter 8, "Configuring Basic Networking").

If you are following along with the commands in the book, be aware that the services your system offers may not be the same ones offered by our systems. Thus, some of the command outputs, such as those from the nmap utility, may show different results than what you will see on your system(s).

It's a good idea to see what ports are offering services outside the system's firewall util-ity. To do this, use the server's IP address (as the designated server to scan) with the nmap utility and the same options. An example is shown snipped in Listing 10.2. This is handy, because not only can you find out what ports and TCP protocol services are being offered, you can tell what ports/services the firewall utility is blocking as well.

Listing 10.2: Viewing TCP ports and services outside the firewall using the nmap utility

```
$ nmap -sT 192.168.0.103
[…]
Nmap scan report for 192.168.0.103
Host is up (0.0015s latency).
Not shown: 998 closed ports
PORT    STATE SERVICE
22/tcp  open  ssh
111/tcp open  rpcbind


Nmap done: 1 IP address (1 host up) scanned in 0.21 seconds
$
```

For a proper audit, also scan the ports offering UDP protocol services inside and outside the system's firewall. To do this, you'll need to employ super user privileges and repeat the same two previous nmap commands but change the -sT option to a -sU:

```
nmap -sU 127.0.0.1
nmap -sU 192.168.0.103
```

If your network is running IPv6, to do the nmap scans you'll need to tack on the -6 option and provide the appropriate IPv6 system address. A snipped example of scanning inside the firewall for UDP protocol services on a system attached to an IPv6 network is shown in Listing 10.3.

Listing 10.3: Viewing UDP ports and services inside the firewall using the nmap utility

```
# nmap -sU -6 ::1
[…]
Nmap scan report for localhost (::1)
Host is up (0.000049s latency).
Not shown: 999 closed ports
PORT    STATE SERVICE
111/udp open  rpcbind


Nmap done: 1 IP address (1 host up) scanned in 0.21 seconds
#
```

WARNING   Do not run the network mapper utility outside your home network without permission. For more information, read the nmap utility's legal issue guide at nmap.org/book/legal-issues.html.

Identifying Open Ports with *netstat*

Another tool that is useful for network service auditing is the *netstat* utility. Be aware that this program is now deprecated. The term *deprecated* means that at some time in the future, this utility will no longer be installed by default or offered in the various distributions' repositories. So, though you need to know it for older systems, don't count on it being around.

NOTE   The primary replacement for the netstat utility is the ss command.

The netstat command is very versatile, but with versatility comes complexity. Lots of command-line options are available in netstat that allow you to customize just what information it returns. For auditing purposes, display only ports that are listening for incoming TCP packets by using the -t (or --tcp) option along with the -l (or --listening) switch as shown in Listing 10.4.

Listing 10.4: Viewing TCP ports and services using the netstat utility

```
$ netstat --tcp --listening
Active Internet connections (only servers)
Proto Recv-Q Send-Q Local Address           Foreign Address        State
tcp        0      0 0.0.0.0:sunrpc          0.0.0.0:*              LISTEN
tcp        0      0 localhost.locald:domain 0.0.0.0:*              LISTEN
tcp        0      0 0.0.0.0:ssh             0.0.0.0:*              LISTEN
tcp        0      0 localhost:ipp           0.0.0.0:*              LISTEN
tcp        0      0 localhost:smtp          0.0.0.0:*              LISTEN
tcp6       0      0 [::]:sunrpc             [::]:*                LISTEN
tcp6       0      0 [::]:ssh                [::]:*                LISTEN
tcp6       0      0 localhost:ipp           [::]:*                LISTEN
tcp6       0      0 localhost:smtp          [::]:*                LISTEN
$
```

Notice that it displays information for both IPv4 and IPv6 by default. For auditing UDP ports and services, replace the -t (or --tcp) option with a -u (or --udp) switch.

In Listing 10.4, the name after the local address and the colon (:) is the port name as defined in the /etc/services file. If the port number isn't defined in the /etc/services file, it appears as a number.

Ports and sockets are important structures in Linux networking. Understanding the difference between them will help in the auditing process.

A port is a number used by protocols, such as TCP and UDP, to identify which service or application is transmitting data. For example, port 22 is a well-known port designated for OpenSSH, and DNS listens on port 53. TCP and UDP packets contain both the packet's source and destination ports in their headers.

A network socket is a single endpoint of a network connection's two endpoints. That single endpoint is on the local system and bound to a particular port. Thus, a network socket uses a combination of an IP address (the local system) and a port number.

Surveying Network Sockets via *ss* and *systemd.socket*

The *ss* command can come to your rescue for replacing the obsolete netstat tool's network service auditing functionality. The -ltu option displays only listening (-l) TCP (-t) and UDP (-u) network sockets for both IPv4 and IPv6. A snipped example is shown in Listing 10.5.

Listing 10.5: Viewing listening TCP/UDP network sockets using the ss utility

```
$ ss -ltu
Netid  State     Recv-Q Send-Q Local Address:Port          Peer Address:Port
[…]
udp    UNCONN    0      0      :::sunrpc             :::*
udp    UNCONN    0      0      :::822               :::*
[…]
tcp    LISTEN    0      128    *:ssh                *:*
tcp    LISTEN    0      128    127.0.0.1:ipp               *:*
tcp    LISTEN    0      100    127.0.0.1:smtp              *:*
[…]
tcp    LISTEN    0      128    :::ssh               :::*
tcp    LISTEN    0      128     ::1:ipp                :::*
tcp    LISTEN    0      100     ::1:smtp               :::*
$
```

A relatively newer method for creating network sockets (as well as other socket types) is via systemd. It uses an activation method that makes it possible to start listening sockets in parallel outside of their attached services, which speeds up the entire process (called *systemd.sockets* in the certification exam objectives). Thus, this provides an additional arena for network service auditing.

There are a few methods you can use while auditing systemd managed network sockets, and the best place to start is via the `systemctl` utility (first covered in Chapter 5, "Booting, Initializing, and Virtualizing Linux"). In snipped Listing 10.6, the command is used along with the `list-sockets` argument and several options to make the display a little easier to read.

Listing 10.6: Viewing systemd managed sockets using the `systemctl` utility

```
$ systemctl list-sockets --all --no-pager --full
LISTEN                              UNIT             ACTIVATES
[…]
/var/run/cups/cups.sock             cups.socket      cups.service
[…]
0.0.0.0:111                         rpcbind.socket   rpcbind.service
0.0.0.0:111                         rpcbind.socket   rpcbind.service
[…]
[::]:111                            rpcbind.socket   rpcbind.service
[::]:111                            rpcbind.socket   rpcbind.service
[::]:22                             sshd.socket
[…]
28 sockets listed.
$
```

You've probably already noticed that you will see many more types of sockets besides just network sockets in this command's output. The trick is to look for familiar network service names (example: sshd) and/or port numbers (example: 22) in the output.

To find the potential network socket systemd configuration (unit) files, employ a different `systemctl` command, as shown snipped in Listing 10.7.

Listing 10.7: Viewing systemd managed socket unit files using the `systemctl` utility

```
$ systemctl list-unit-files --type=socket --no-pager
UNIT FILE               STATE
[…]
cups.socket             enabled
[…]
rpcbind.socket          enabled
[…]
sshd.socket             disabled
[…]

32 unit files listed.
$
```

One handy fact about this systemctl command's output is that you can quickly determine whether the network socket is enabled or disabled for systemd. A disabled value only means systemd does not manage that particular network socket; it does *not* mean the service is disabled. In Listing 10.7, the rpcbind socket is enabled, whereas the sshd socket shows as disabled.

For the enabled sockets, you need to do a little more research before you can call this part of the audit complete. Take a look at the contents of each enabled network socket's unit file. An example of viewing the rpcbind socket unit file is shown in Listing 10.8.

Listing 10.8: Viewing contents of a systemd socket unit file using the systemctl utility

```
$ systemctl cat rpcbind.socket
# /usr/lib/systemd/system/rpcbind.socket
[Unit]
Description=RPCbind Server Activation Socket

[Socket]
ListenStream=/var/run/rpcbind.sock

# RPC netconfig can't handle ipv6/ipv4 dual sockets
BindIPv6Only=ipv6-only
ListenStream=0.0.0.0:111
ListenDatagram=0.0.0.0:111
ListenStream=[::]:111
ListenDatagram=[::]:111

[Install]
WantedBy=sockets.target
$
```

The unit file's contents will give you more clues as to what port this socket is using (111 in this case), as well as additional network socket configuration information. If desired, you can view the various potential settings of these socket unit files by typing **man systemd.socket** at the command line.

Auditing Open Files with *lsof* and *fuser*

Besides viewing ports and network sockets, you can use open files to trace down offered network services on your system. The *lsof* command lists currently open files. Since Linux treats network connections and sockets as files, they will appear in the lsof output list.

The lsof command produces lots of output, so it's best to filter it. For example, if you're interested in auditing only UDP protocol sockets and connections, use the -iUDP option as shown snipped in Listing 10.9. Notice you can see both IPv4 and IPv6 along with additional helpful auditing information.

Listing 10.9: Displaying UDP open files via the lsof utility

```
# lsof -iUDP
COMMAND     PID   USER    FD    TYPE DEVICE SIZE/OFF NODE NAME
systemd     1     root    50u   IPv4 22181      0t0  UDP *:sunrpc
systemd     1     root    52u   IPv6 22183      0t0  UDP *:sunrpc
rpcbind     2773  rpc     5u    IPv4 22181      0t0  UDP *:sunrpc
rpcbind     2773  rpc     7u    IPv6 22183      0t0  UDP *:sunrpc
rpcbind     2773  rpc     10u   IPv4 22798      0t0  UDP *:822
rpcbind     2773  rpc     11u   IPv6 22799      0t0  UDP *:822
[…]
#
```

 You will need to employ super user privileges to have the lsof utility work correctly. If you receive no output from the lsof program, most likely you are issuing the command as a standard user.

In snipped Listing 10.10, the lsof utility's output is filtered to display network sockets in a state of listening (-sTCP:LISTEN) for only TCP packets (-iTCP).

Listing 10.10: Displaying TCP listening open files via the lsof utility

```
# lsof -iTCP -sTCP:LISTEN
COMMAND   PID   USER    FD    TYPE DEVICE SIZE/OFF NODE NAME
systemd   1     root    49u   IPv4 22180      0t0  TCP *:sunrpc (LISTEN)
systemd   1     root    51u   IPv6 22182      0t0  TCP *:sunrpc (LISTEN)
rpcbind   2773  rpc     4u    IPv4 22180      0t0  TCP *:sunrpc (LISTEN)
rpcbind   2773  rpc     6u    IPv6 22182      0t0  TCP *:sunrpc (LISTEN)
sshd      3404  root    3u    IPv4 29484      0t0  TCP *:ssh (LISTEN)
sshd      3404  root    4u    IPv6 29486      0t0  TCP *:ssh (LISTEN)
cupsd     3406  root    11u   IPv6 30292      0t0  TCP localhost:ipp (LISTEN)
cupsd     3406  root    12u   IPv4 30293      0t0  TCP localhost:ipp (LISTEN)
master    3653  root    13u   IPv4 30584      0t0  TCP localhost:smtp (LISTEN)
master    3653  root    14u   IPv6 30585      0t0  TCP localhost:smtp (LISTEN)
[…]
#
```

You can dig down deeper and see not only more information concerning a particular port for TCP protocol traffic, but established connections to that port as well. Just employ a variation of the -i option that uses an argument of *PROTOCOL:PORT* as shown in Listing 10.11.

Listing 10.11: Displaying open files for a particular protocol and port via the lsof utility

```
# lsof -i tcp:22
COMMAND   PID        USER    FD    TYPE DEVICE SIZE/OFF NODE NAME
sshd      3404       root    3u    IPv4 29484       0t0 TCP *:ssh (LISTEN)
sshd      3404       root    4u    IPv6 29486       0t0 TCP *:ssh (LISTEN)
sshd      4501       root    3u    IPv4 39036       0t0 TCP localhost.localdomain:
ssh->192.168.0.101:61500 (ESTABLISHED)
sshd      4507 Christine    3u    IPv4 39036       0t0 TCP localhost.localdomain:
ssh->192.168.0.101:61500 (ESTABLISHED)
#
```

Another utility that allows further auditing is the *fuser* command. It will display a program or user's process ID (PID) that is employing the protocol and port. An example of this is shown in Listing 10.12, where the -v option is used to provide additional details and the -n switch is used to specify the protocol followed by the port number.

Listing 10.12: Displaying the PIDs using TCP and a particular port via the fuser utility

```
# fuser -vn tcp 22
                   USER        PID ACCESS COMMAND
22/tcp:            root       3404 F.... sshd
                   root       4501 F.... sshd
                   Christine  4507 F.... sshd
#
```

Listing 10.13 shows the same thing, except it pinpoints the UDP protocol. Note that you must specify both the protocol and the port with the fuser command.

Listing 10.13: Displaying the PIDs using UDP and a particular port via the fuser utility

```
# fuser -vn udp 822
                   USER        PID ACCESS COMMAND
822/udp:           rpc        2773 F.... rpcbind
#
```

Notice that as with the lsof command, you must employ super user privileges with the fuser utility.

Don't forget to use your system initialization utilities as part of your service audit. For systemd systems, type **systemctl list-unit-files -t service | grep enabled** to view all the services started (enabled) at system boot.

On all SysVinit systems, you can start your auditing process by looking at the initialization scripts stored in the */etc/init.d/* directory. Each script's name is the name of a service SysVinit manages.

To continue the audit process on SysVinit systems, for Red Hat–based distros use super user privileges and type `chkconfig --list` at the command line to audit the various services started at the different run levels. For SysVinit Debian-based distributions, employ the `service --status-all` command.

On rather old SysVinit distribution versions, you may want to review the */etc/inittab* file as well. There may be services started in this file.

Disabling the Services

When you have determined via the auditing process what network daemons are running/ enabled on your system, use (or create one) a required network services list. Then methodi-cally go through and disable the daemons that are not required. The method you employ depends on the system's initialization method.

For systemd systems, it just takes a few steps. First, stop the service, if it is running, and check that it is stopped via the following commands using super user privileges:

```
systemctl stop SERVICE-NAME
systemctl status SERVICE-NAME
```

Of course, you'll want to substitute the name of the service you want to stop for the *SERVICE-NAME* portion of the commands.

When the service is stopped, be sure to disable it, employing super user privileges, so that when the system reboots, it won't start.

```
systemctl disable SERVICE-NAME
```

After you've issued the preceding command, check to ensure that it is truly disabled. You should receive a `disabled` message from this command:

```
systemctl is-enabled SERVICE-NAME
```

 If you are using a distribution that employs the now-defunct Upstart system initialization daemon, you'll need to use different methods for disabling the unneeded services than described here. Review your distro's Upstart documentation. Start by entering **man initctl** at the command line.

For SysVinit systems, you'll need to first stop the service, if it is running, and check that it is stopped via the following commands using super user privileges:

```
service SERVICE-NAME stop
service SERVICE-NAME status
```

To disable the service on a Red Hat–based distribution, use super user privileges and the following command (substituting the name of the service for *SERVICE-NAME*):

```
chkconfig SERVICE-NAME off
```

Then check that it is disabled (off) at every runlevel displayed by this command:

```
chkconfig --list SERVICE-NAME
```

 If the network service is not needed, consider going beyond disabling and uninstall it as well. Removing software packages was covered in Chapter 2.

To disable a network service on a Debian-based distro, use super user privileges and the following command:

```
update-rc.d -f SERVICE-NAME remove
```

The -f option on the preceding command is needed only if a script exists for the service (*SERVICE-NAME*) in the /etc/init.d/ directory.

Unneeded network services are but one vector in your systems' attack surfaces. But with these unnecessary services disabled (or uninstalled), you have one less item to worry about.

Using Super Server Restrictions

Typically, when a network service (daemon) starts, such as chronyd (covered in Chapter 7), it opens a port. You can think of a port number as an identification number assigned to a network service. Incoming network packets that contain the network service's port number trigger that service into action. While the network service is waiting for packets containing its port number, it is in a wait state, which is called *listening*. Often a daemon is said to be "directly listening on the port" when it is in this state.

Instead of listening directly on a port, some network services can employ a *super server* (also called a *super daemon*) to act as a guard for them. Instead of the network service, the super server directly listens for packets containing the designated port number. When such a packet comes into the system, after initial processing the super server starts the network service and hands the packet off to it. When concurrent requests come in, the super server can start additional network service processes as required.

Using this method systems boot faster, because network services are not started until needed. Also, you can put additional controls into place. For example, you can set limits on network service use, and you can fine-tune connection logging.

Configuring *xinetd*

The original super server on Linux systems was inetd. It was supplanted by *xinetd*, which is called the *extended super daemon* due to its additional security features.

The primary configuration file for xinetd is */etc/xinetd.conf*. This file typically contains only global default options. A snipped example of this file on a CentOS distribution is shown in Listing 10.14.

Listing 10.14: Looking at the /etc/xinetd.conf file

```
$ cat /etc/xinetd.conf
#
[…]
defaults
{
# The next two items are intended to be a quick access place to
# temporarily enable or disable services.
#
#       enabled         =
#       disabled        =

# Define general logging characteristics.
        log_type        = SYSLOG daemon info
        log_on_failure  = HOST
        log_on_success  = PID HOST DURATION EXIT

# Define access restriction defaults
#
#       no_access       =
#       only_from       =
#       max_load        = 0
        cps             = 50 10
        instances       = 50
        per_source      = 10

# Address and networking defaults
#
#       bind            =
#       mdns            = yes
        v6only          = no

# setup environmental attributes
#
#       passenv         =
        groups          = yes
        umask           = 002

[…]
}


includedir /etc/xinetd.d

$
```

In the /etc/xinetd.conf file, any line with a preceding pound sign (#) is a comment line and thus inactive. Notice at the bottom of the file the includedir directive:

```
includedir /etc/xinetd.d
```

This setting causes individual service configuration files stored in the */etc/xinetd.d/* directory to be included in the super server's structure.

> If you cannot find the /etc/xinetd.conf file on your system, most likely the xinetd package is not installed. See Chapter 2 for how to install this package on your system if desired.

The more commonly used xinetd directives are described in Table 10.1. If you want to peruse them all, enter **man xinetd.conf** at the command line.

TABLE 10.1   Commonly used /etc/xinetd.conf directives

Name	Description
cps	Specifies the maximum rate of incoming connections to the network service. The first number sets the maximum rate before the service pauses, and the second number establishes the number of seconds to pause.
instances	Sets the maximum number of service processes that can be active at the same time. Set to UNLIMITED to allow no limits.
logtype	Determines where log messages are sent. If set to SYSLOG, log messages are sent to the syslog protocol application, and the syslog *facility* and *severity* must be set as well (see Chapter 7). If set to FILE, log messages are appended to the filename listed.
log_on_failure	Establishes what additional information, besides the service ID, is logged when a server process cannot be started. The data that can be included is HOST, USERID, and ATTEMPT.
log_on_success	Sets what information is logged when a server process is started and when it exits. The data that can be included is PID, HOST, USERID, EXIT, DURATION, and TRAFFIC.
max_load	Determines the one-minute load average that when reached, the network service stops accepting connections, until the load level drops.
no_access	Establishes remote hosts banned from this network service.
only_from	Sets the remote hosts or subnets which may use this network service.
per_source	Specifies the maximum number of network server processes that can be started per IP address.

Configuring *xinetd* Services

The default options in the /etc/xinetd.conf file can be overridden by settings in a network service's configuration file stored in the /etc/xinetd.d/ directory. An example of this type of configuration file is shown snipped in Listing 10.15. The echo-stream service sends back any data sent to it, and it is used for measuring packet round-trip times between two systems.

Notice in the file that there are mandatory settings for each service, such as id. Also, directives are available to override the global settings in the /etc/xinetd.conf file. Inactive directives are set as inactive via the # mark.

Listing 10.15: Looking at the echo stream's /etc/xinetd.d/ configuration file

```
$ cat /etc/xinetd.d/echo-stream
# This is the configuration for the tcp/stream echo service.

service echo
{
# This is for quick on or off of the service
        disable         = yes

# The next attributes are mandatory for all services
        id              = echo-stream
        type            = INTERNAL
        wait            = no
        socket_type     = stream
#       protocol        =  socket type is usually enough
[…]
# Logging options
#       log_type        =
#       log_on_success  =
#       log_on_failure  =

[…]
# Access restrictions
#       only_from       =
#       no_access       =
#       access_times    =
#       cps             = 50 10
#       instances       = UNLIMITED
#       per_source      = UNLIMITED
#       max_load        = 0
[…]
}

$
```

An important directive in the individual network service configuration files is the disable setting. If set to yes, the service is disabled. However, if disable is set to no, the service is active. It would be wise to peruse the various configuration files to ensure that the network services your system needs to run are set to disable = no, and vice versa for those that shouldn't be running.

When the xinetd configuration files are properly set, you'll need to start or restart xinetd. Use the appropriate method, which depends on your system's initialization method (covered in Chapter 5).

 If you've done any investigation into systemd.sockets, you may believe that it makes super servers like xinetd obsolete. At this point in time, that is not true. The xinetd super server offers more functionality than systemd.sockets can currently deliver. The website 0pointer.de/blog/projects/inetd.html provides more insight into this topic, if you are interested.

Restricting via TCP Wrappers

TCP Wrappers are an older method for controlling access to network services. If a service can employ TCP Wrappers, it will have the *libwrap* library compiled with it. You can check for support by using the ldd command as shown snipped in Listing 10.16. Notice that TCP Wrappers can be used by the openSSH service on an Ubuntu system.

Listing 10.16: Using the ldd command to check for TCP Wrappers support

```
$ which sshd
/usr/sbin/sshd
$
$ ldd /usr/sbin/sshd | grep libwrap
        libwrap.so.0 […]
$
```

TCP Wrappers employ two files to determine who can access a particular service. These files are */etc/hosts.allow* and */etc/hosts.deny*. As you can tell by their names, the hosts.allow file typically allows access to the designated service in the form of a whitelist, whereas the hosts.deny file commonly blocks access to all addresses included in a black-list. These files have simple record syntax:

SERVICE: *IPADDRESS…*

The search order of these files is critical. For an incoming service request, the following takes place:

- The hosts.allow file is checked for the remote IP address or hostname.
  - If found, access is allowed, and no further checks are made.

- The hosts.deny file is checked for the remote address.
  - If found, access is denied.
  - If not found, access is allowed.

Because access is allowed if the remote system's address is not found in either file, it is best to employ the ALL wildcard in the /etc/hosts.deny file:

```
ALL: ALL
```

This disables all access to all services for any IP address not listed in the /etc/hosts.allow file. Be aware that some distributions use PARANOID instead of ALL for the address wildcard.

The record's *IPADDRESS* can be either IPv4 or IPv6. To list individual IP addresses in the hosts.allow file, you specify them separated by commas:

```
sshd: 172.243.24.15, 172.243.24.16, 172.243.24.17
```

Typing in every single IP address that is allowed to access the OpenSSH service is not necessary. You can specify entire subnets. For example, if you needed to allow all the IPv4 addresses in a Class C network access on a server, you specify only the first three address octets followed by a trailing dot:

```
sshd: 172.243.24.
```

 TCP Wrappers were created prior to the time administrators used firewalls. While they are still used by some, their usefulness is limited, and they are considered deprecated by many distributions. It is best to move this protection to your firewall.

Administering Local Security

Part of securing your system is dealing with local security. This includes understanding password protections and making sure they are properly enforced. A rather important security measure, which sometimes goes unmanaged, is correctly enforcing secure root account access. These topics, along with setting limits and locating potentially dangerous files on your system, are covered in this section.

Securing Passwords

While passwords and their files were originally covered in Chapter 7, there are a few additional items that you need to know in order to properly manage accounts and keep your servers secure. Understanding the underlying principles in securing passwords will help.

Looking at Password Storage

Early Linux systems stored their passwords in the /etc/passwd file. The passwords were hashed. A hashed password is created using a one-way cryptographic mathematical algorithm that takes plaintext (text humans can read and understand) and turns it into secure ciphertext, which is unintelligible to humans and machines. Hashing is one-way, because you cannot take the ciphertext and use the algorithm to turn it back into plaintext. Linux adds salt to the password hashing process, which adds additional data to make the hashed password even more secure.

However, some clever malicious actors created something called *rainbow tables*. A rainbow table is a dictionary of potential plaintext passwords that have been hashed into ciphertext. Programs that use these rainbow tables allow you to enter a password's hash and it displays the password as plaintext:

Password Hash: **$6$6XL3hyx7$NxhJjoLGWSx0KLS/xcbxjADlgIJqXAJoggtCNzFM.1LuWLH**
pfOYBInGQYW3P717wtyQjsXhMpcbxJ0pmTDw.I
Password: 1234

With attacker tools like rainbow tables, the /etc/passwd file permissions make any passwords stored in it vulnerable:

```
$ ls -l /etc/passwd
-rw-r--r--. 1 root root 2631 Jun 12 18:04 /etc/passwd
```

With these permission settings, everyone who has access to the system can read this file (file permissions were covered in Chapter 4, "Managing Files"). Thus, everyone would have access to the hashed passwords and be able to potentially employ rainbow tables or other attacker tools to discover the account's plaintext passwords.

In order to protect the account passwords, they were moved from the /etc/passwd file to the more locked down /etc/shadow file:

```
$ ls -l /etc/shadow
----------. 1 root root 2143 Jun 12 18:04 /etc/shadow
```

These file permission settings prevent the world from viewing the password hashes. (Some distributions have slightly different file permissions on the /etc/shadow file, but in essence the effect is the same.)

Though mentioned in Chapter 7, it's worthwhile to mention it again. If your Linux system is still storing passwords in the /etc/passwd file, you need to move them to the /etc/shadow file. The pwconv utility can perform this operation for you.

When you log into your account, the password prompt accepts the plaintext password you type into the field. To check the password's correctness, the system runs the entered plaintext through the hashing algorithm, adding the salt as it goes, which produces a ciphertext. If the produced ciphertext matches the password hash stored in the /etc/shadow file, the system acknowledges the entered password is correct.

Because the /etc/shadow file only allows the root user (the file's owner) to write to it, for a regular user to change their account's password, they have to temporarily gain the root user's permission status. This is done via the SUID permission set on the passwd program's file as shown in Listing 10.17.

Listing 10.17: Viewing the passwd utility's and /etc/shadow file's permissions

```
$ ls -l /etc/shadow
-rw-r----- 1 root shadow 1425 Mar 21 17:51 /etc/shadow
$
$ which passwd
/usr/bin/passwd
$
$ ls -l /usr/bin/passwd
-rwsr-xr-x 1 root root 59640 Jan 25  2018 /usr/bin/passwd
$
```

Thus, while running the passwd program, you temporarily become the root user. After you are done with the program, you return to your normal self. However, you cannot start the process of changing another account's password without employing super user privileges as shown in Listing 10.18.

Listing 10.18: Using the passwd utility's and super user privileges to change another account's password

```
$ passwd BCrusher
passwd: You may not view or modify password information for BCrusher.
$
$ sudo passwd BCrusher
[sudo] password for Christine:
Enter new UNIX password:
Retype new UNIX password:
passwd: password updated successfully
$
```

When typing in the new password for the account, it will not display to the screen. If you are used to seeing at least asterisks or some other representative characters, having nothing displayed as you type may seem odd.

Dealing with Password Problems

With proper security, access problems will occur. Being able to quickly resolve password problems will keep your users happy and more willing to go along with proper security measures. If a user can reach the system but cannot access their account after entering their username and password, there are a few troubleshooting items you can explore.

If the account is a newly created account, confirm that it was properly built. New system administrators often create user accounts with the useradd command (see Chapter 7) but forget to add its password with the passwd utility. Use either the grep or getent command to check the /etc/passwd and /etc/shadow file records. An example is shown in Listing 10.19 for a new user account, JKirk, on an Ubuntu Desktop distribution.

Listing 10.19: Viewing a user account records with the getent command

```
$ sudo getent passwd JKirk
JKirk:x:1002:1002::/home/JKirk:/bin/bash
$
$ sudo getent shadow JKirk
JKirk:!:17806:0:99999:7:::
$
```

Notice that in the password field for the JKirk shadow record, there is an exclamation mark (!). This indicates a password was not created for the account.

Make sure your system users know that usernames are *case sensitive* on Linux. Other operating systems, such as Windows, have usernames that are case insensitive, and this can cause confusion.

Determine if the account is locked. You can employ the passwd -S or the getent command to check this, as shown snipped in Listing 10.20.

Listing 10.20: Checking if an account is locked with the passwd and getent commands

```
$ sudo passwd -S KJaneway
KJaneway L 01/02/2019 0 99999 7 -1
$
$ sudo getent shadow KJaneway
KJaneway:!$6$[…]0:17898:0:99999:7:::
$
```

The L after the user KJaneway account's name indicates the account is locked. However, that code is also shown for accounts that have no password set. Thus, the getent command is also employed. The exclamation point (!) at the front of the account password's field verifies that the account is indeed locked. To unlock the account, if desired, use super user privileges and the usermod -U or the passwd -u command.

Check the user's keyboard. Sometimes incorrect keyboard mappings or corrupt hardware can cause wrong characters to be sent to authentication programs.

The account may have expired. Account expiration dates are typically set up for temporary account users, such as contractors or interns. You can view this information using the chage command, as shown snipped in Listing 10.21.

Listing 10.21: Checking if an account is expired with the chage command

```
$ date
Wed Jan  2 16:17:48 EST 2019
$
$ sudo chage -l JArcher
[…]
Account expires             : Jan 01, 2019
[…]
```

Notice that this account's expiration date has passed. Therefore, the JArcher account is now expired and the user cannot log into it. If this was a mistake or you need to modify it, use super user privileges and the chage -E command to set a new expiration date for the account.

Confirm the user is using the correct password, and check if the account's password is expired. Employ the chage -l command to view this as well.

 It is important to stay up-to-date on current guidelines concerning length and complexity of passwords. The National Institute of Standards and Technology (NIST) has a nice guideline at pages.nist.gov/800-63-3/ sp800-63b.html that can help. To implement these recommendations, you may need to employ pluggable authentication modules (PAM), such as pam_unix.so, pam_pwhistory.so, and pam_pwquality.so. You can find more information about PAM at linux-pam.org.

Limiting *root* Access

Appropriate account management enhances a system's security. The following is a basic list of what to do in order to properly manage accounts:

- Do not permit logins to the root user account.
- Allow only one user per user account.
- Set expiration dates on temporary user accounts.
- Remove unused user accounts.

The focus in this section is on the root user account. Overall, it is not a good idea to log into the root user account even if you are the only one who uses it. There are alternatives that accommodate various system administrator needs.

Switching the User with *su*

With the *su* utility, you can quickly log into the other account or just issue a few commands. To log into the root user account, enter **su** followed by a dash (-). You will need to enter the root user's password to gain access:

```
$ su -
Password:
# whoami
root
```

> You will not be able to use the su - method to log into the root account on any distribution that blocks the root logins by default, such as Ubuntu. While you could just enter **su** and then the correct password to log into the root user account, this is not wise, because not everything may be set up correctly to perform tasks that require super user privileges. The dash (-) after the su command starts a new shell environment and executes the root's profile.

To enter another user's account, you employ su - again, but follow it with the account's username:

```
$ su - rich
Password:
$ whoami
rich
```

After you have switched to the desired account, you can issue several commands using that user account's privileges. When you have completed your tasks, type **exit** or **logout** to leave the account.

If you need to issue only a single command using super user privileges, you can employ the su -c command. For example, to change another account's password you need super user privileges. As long as you have the root account's password, you can accomplish this, as shown snipped in Listing 10.22.

Listing 10.22: Issuing a single command as another user via the su -c command

```
$ whoami
Christine
$
$ su -c "passwd rich"
[…]
passwd: all authentication tokens updated successfully.
$
$ whoami
Christine
$
```

The first password prompt in the previous listing is asking for the root user account password. After that, the passwd rich command is being executed using the root user account's privileges. Notice that passwd rich is encapsulated by quotation marks. Whenever you have a space within the command you are passing to another account, you'll need to quote it.

Doing the Job as a Super User with *sudo*

While the su command is helpful, it still does not fully meet the security requirement of not permitting logins to the root user account. Fortunately, the *sudo* utility can help with this.

Logging in as the root user can set up what is called a *repudiation environment*. A repudiation environment means that a person can deny actions. Therefore, if a system administrator uses the root account to perform some illegal or trouble making activity, the admin can legally deny being responsible for that activity. Systems where every user has an account and password and no one can log into the root user's account sets up a *nonrepudiation environment*. This means actions are logged and responsibility for them cannot be easily denied. A nonrepudiation environment can be created using sudo.

The sudo utility allows a user to issue a single command with super user privileges. All use of the sudo command is documented in a log file or journal that includes tracking data, such as who did what and when.

The primary configuration file for the sudo utility is the */etc/sudoers* file. A snipped example of a /etc/sudoers file on an Ubuntu distribution system is shown in Listing 10.23.

Listing 10.23: Viewing the /etc/sudoers configuration file

```
$ sudo cat /etc/sudoers
[sudo] password for Christine:
#
# This file MUST be edited with the 'visudo' command as root.
#
[…]
# User privilege specification
root    ALL=(ALL:ALL) ALL

# Members of the admin group may gain root privileges
%admin ALL=(ALL) ALL

# Allow members of group sudo to execute any command
%sudo    ALL=(ALL:ALL) ALL

# See sudoers(5) for more information on "#include" directives:

#includedir /etc/sudoers.d
$
```

In Listing 10.23, the line starting with root is a typical configuration that provides full access to a user. Access for a particular user in the /etc/sudoers is designated using this format:

```
USERNAME   HOSTNAME-OF-SYSTEM=(USER:GROUP)  COMMANDS
```

So for the root user record in the /etc/sudoers file, the root account can use super user privileges on the system no matter what its host name (ALL=), run the commands as any user (ALL:) or as any group member (:ALL), and execute any commands (ALL).

WARNING   Never open the sudoers file using a standard editor. If multiple users open the sudoers file at the same time, odd things can happen and corrupt the file. The visudo command securely opens the file in an editor so you can make changes. It operates in the same manner as the vi editor (covered in Chapter 1).

To make things easier, many distributions add groups in the /etc/sudoers file that provide full super user privileges, such as sudo or wheel. Group records in the sudoers file are preceded with a percent sign (%). When you need to provide sudo access to a new account, you add the user account to the group (usermod -aG was covered in Chapter 7), instead of modifying the /etc/sudoers file. Some distributions, such as Ubuntu, automatically add the primary user account as a sudo group member during installation, as shown snipped here in Listing 10.24.

Listing 10.24: Viewing a sudo user's groups on an Ubuntu distribution

```
$ whoami
Christine
$ groups
Christine […]sudo […]
$
```

It's a good idea to include additional users or groups in a configuration file within the /etc/sudoers.d/ directory, instead of modifying the /etc/sudoers file. The #includedir /etc/sudoers.d line within the primary sudoers file will cause the system to read all the files within the /etc/sudoers.d/ directory as part of the sudo configuration.

When everything is properly configured, a user who has sudo privileges adds the sudo command prior to every command needing super user privileges and provides the account password, if asked. A few examples are shown snipped in Listing 10.25.

Listing 10.25: Using sudo to gain super user privileges

```
$ sudo getent shadow BCrusher
[sudo] password for Christine:
BCrusher:$6$[…]Uy.:18060:0:99999:7:::
$
```

```
$ sudo chage -l BCrusher
Last password change                                 : Jun 13, 2019
[…]
Maximum number of days between password change       : 99999
Number of days of warning before password expires    : 7
$
$ journalctl -r -n 10 | grep sudo
[…]
Jun 13 15:56:40 Ubuntu1804 sudo[3609]: Christine : TTY=pts/0 ;
PWD=/home/Christine ; USER=root ; COMMAND=/usr/bin/chage -l BCrusher
[…]
Jun 13 15:56:27 Ubuntu1804 sudo[3607]: Christine : TTY=pts/0 ;
PWD=/home/Christine ; USER=root ; COMMAND=/usr/bin/getent shadow BCrusher
$
```

Notice that the sudo command usage was properly tracked by events issued to the journal file. Thus, the desired nonrepudiation environment exists, enhancing the system's security.

Auditing User Access

Several utilities allow you to audit which users are currently accessing the system as well as users who have accessed it in the past. You can also review various information concerning user accounts.

Understanding the *who* and *w* Utilities

With the *who* command, you can view information concerning your own account or look at every current user on the system. Examples are shown in Listing 10.26.

Listing 10.26: Using the who command

```
$ who
rich    tty2          2019-10-03 13:12
Christine pts/0         2019-10-03 14:10 (192.168.0.102)
$
$ who am i
Christine pts/0         2019-10-03 14:10 (192.168.0.102)
$
$ who mom likes
Christine pts/0         2019-10-03 14:10 (192.168.0.102)
$
```

Notice in Listing 10.26 that when the who command is used by itself, it shows all the current system users, the terminal they are using, the date and time they entered the system, and in cases of remote users, their remote IP address. If you add the arguments am i to the who utility, it will display information concerning only the current process's account. The last command is useful if you need to prove a few things to your siblings.

Though it is a very short command, the *w* utility provides a great deal of useful information. An example is shown in Listing 10.27.

Listing 10.27: Employing the w command

```
$ w
 09:58:31 up 49 min,  5 users,  load average: 0.81, 0.37, 0.27
USER      TTY      LOGIN@   IDLE   JCPU   PCPU WHAT
Christin pts/1    09:14    2.00s  0.04s  0.01s w
Rich     tty3     09:56    1:35   0.85s  0.81s top
Kevin    tty4     09:57    1:03  16.17s 16.14s ls --color=[…]
Tim      tty5     09:57   38.00s  0.08s  0.03s nano data42[…]
$
```

Notice the w command's verbose output in Listing 10.27. The first displayed line shows the following information:

▪ The current time

▪ How long the system has been up

▪ How many users are currently accessing the system

▪ The CPU load averages for the last 1, 5, and 15 minutes

The next several lines concern current system user information. The columns are as follows:

▪ USER: The account's name

▪ TTY: The account's currently used terminal

▪ LOGIN@: When the user logged into the account

▪ IDLE: How long it has been since the user interacted with the system

▪ JCPU: How much total CPU time the account has used

▪ PCPU: How much CPU time the account's current command (process) has used

▪ WHAT: What command the account is currently running

The w utility pulls user information from the /var/run/utmp file. It also gathers additional data for display from the /proc/ directory files.

> If you have identified a nefarious user currently on your system, you can lock their account (covered in Chapter 7) and then kill their process ID (PID) in order to boot them off the system. If you'd like to keep any additional users from logging into the system, until you get the issue resolved create the nologin file. Do this by using super user privileges and issuing **touch /etc/nologin** at the command line. When this file exists, users will not be able to log into the system. If desired, you can add a message within the file to let users attempting to access the system know what's going on.

Displaying Access History with the *last* Utility

The *last* command pulls information from the */var/log/wtmp* file and displays a list of accounts showing the last time they logged in or out of the system or if they are still logged on. A snipped example is shown in Listing 10.28.

Listing 10.28: Using the last command

```
$ last
Tim       tty5                          Thu Oct  4 09:57   still logged in
Kevin     tty4                          Thu Oct  4 09:57   still logged in
Rich      tty3                          Thu Oct  4 09:56   still logged in
Christin  pts/1       192.168.0.102     Thu Oct  4 09:14   still logged in
Christin  pts/0       192.168.0.102     Wed Oct  3 14:10 - 15:32  (01:22)
[…]
wtmp begins Thu Jul 26 16:30:32 2019
$
```

Be aware that the /var/log/wtmp file typically gets automatically rotated via the cron utility, which is covered in Chapter 9. If you need to gather information from old wtmp files, you can employ the -f switch. For example, you could type in **last -f /var/log/wtmp.1** to view data from the /var/log/wtmp.1 file.

The last command and the various other utilities covered in these sections are rather helpful for auditing current users and discovering when they last logged into the system. In addition, they are helpful commands even when you are troubleshooting non-security-related problems.

Setting Login, Process, and Memory Limits

The *ulimit* command allows you to restrict access to system resources for each user account. This is very helpful to prevent a runaway program from accidentally causing an outage on your system.

Listing 10.29 shows the output from running the ulimit command with the -a option, which displays the settings for the current user account.

Listing 10.29: Looking at account limits via the `ulimit` command

```
$ ulimit -a
core file size          (blocks, -c) 0
data seg size           (kbytes, -d) unlimited
scheduling priority             (-e) 0
file size               (blocks, -f) unlimited
pending signals                 (-i) 19567
max locked memory       (kbytes, -l) 16384
max memory size         (kbytes, -m) unlimited
open files                      (-n) 1024
pipe size            (512 bytes, -p) 8
POSIX message queues     (bytes, -q) 819200
real-time priority              (-r) 0
stack size              (kbytes, -s) 8192
cpu time               (seconds, -t) unlimited
max user processes              (-u) 19567
virtual memory          (kbytes, -v) unlimited
file locks                      (-x) unlimited
$
```

As a user account consumes system resources, it places a load on the system, but in CPU time and memory. If you're working in a multiuser Linux environment, you may need to place restrictions on how many resources each user account can consume. This includes the number of logins, processes, and memory usage per user account.

That's where the `ulimit` command comes in. Table 10.2 shows the command-line options you can use to restrict specific resources for the user account.

TABLE 10.2   The `ulimit` command options

Option	Description
-a	List the limits for the current user account
-c	Set the maximum core file size
-d	Set the maximum data segment size for processes
-e	Set the maximum allowed scheduling priority
-f	Set the maximum file size allowed to be written
-i	Set the maximum number of pending signals

Option	Description
-k	Set the maximum number of kqueues that can be allocated
-l	Set the maximum size of memory that can be locked
-m	Set the maximum resident set size
-n	Set the maximum number of open file descriptors
-p	Set the maximum pipe size in 512k blocks
-r	Set the maximum real-time scheduling priority value
-s	Set the maximum stack size
-t	Set the maximum amount of CPU time the user account is allowed
-u	Set the maximum number of processes the user can run simultaneously
-v	Set the maximum amount of virtual memory available to the user
-x	Set the maximum number of file locks

As you can tell from Table 10.2, with the ulimit command the Linux administrator can place some pretty severe restrictions on just what an individual user account can do on the system.

The ulimit command is typically placed in the system's environment files (covered in Chapter 9) so that the limits are set when a user logs into the system.

Locating SUID/SGID Files

While the special permissions, SUID and SGID (covered in Chapter 4), are needed by many utilities on a Linux system, it can also be a way for malicious actors to cause problems. Recall that the SUID permission causes the user executing the script to obtain the permissions of the file's owner. Thus, if the file is owned by the root account, the user essentially becomes root while they are running the script.

It's a good idea to periodically audit your system to ensure the files that have these two special permissions are supposed to have them. The utility that helps here is the find command (covered in Chapter 4).

The exact command to employ with super user privileges is

```
find / -perm /6000 -type f
```

The command can be broken down as follows:

- The / after the find command indicates we want to search through the entire virtual directory system, starting at the root directory (/).

- The -perm option lets the find utility know we want to locate files based only on their permissions.

- The -perm option argument used is /6000, which will ask the find utility to search for both SUID (octal code 4) plus SGID (octal code 2), which provides the 6 in 6000.

- The forward slash (/) in front of the octal code (6000) tells the find utility to ignore the other file permissions (octal codes 000).

- The -type f option asks find to look at file permissions only and ignore any directories.

On older Linux systems, to enact this search, you would enter **+6000** to designate the permission. The plus sign (+) is now deprecated for this use and has been replaced by the forward slash (/) symbol for the find command.

Thus, this command issued at the command line will find every file on your system that has either SUID or SGID permissions. Because there are a reasonable number of files that validly have these settings, it would be wise to save the output to a text file by redirecting standard output (STDOUT):

```
find / -perm /6000 -type f > SUID-SGID_Audit.txt
```

After you have this report, review it to ensure that all the files listed should have those permissions. Then you can lock down the audit file's permissions and use the file as a baseline report for later audits. This would be a great shell script (covered in Chapter 9) that you run periodically as a cron job, alerting you to any changes. An example of the commands is shown snipped in Listing 10.30.

Listing 10.30: Using find to audit the system for SUID and SGID file permissions

```
$ sudo find / -perm /6000 -type f > SUID-SGID_Audit_June-13.txt
[…]
$
$ diff SUID-SGID_Audit.txt SUID-SGID_Audit_June-13.txt
164a165
> /usr/bin/threat-actor
$
$ ls -l /usr/bin/threat-actor
-rwsrwsrwx 1 root root 0 Jun 13 17:25 /usr/bin/threat-actor
$
```

Notice in Listing 10.30 that a new audit file was created. When it was compared against the baseline file (`SUID-SGID_Audit.txt`) with the `diff` utility, a difference was found. In other words, a new file on the system has SUID, SGID, or both permissions. Thus, the `ls -l` command was employed on the new filename, and sure enough, the new file has both SUID and SGID permissions set on it.

Implementing a nonrepudiation environment via the `sudo` utility, auditing file permissions, as well as limiting process resource usage are a few things you can do to strengthen your system's local security. While understanding how passwords are secured on a Linux system also aids in this process, it's helpful to know some additional cryptographic concepts that we'll cover next.

Exploring Cryptography Concepts

The primary purpose of cryptography is to encode data in order to hide it or keep it private. In cryptography, *plaintext* (text that can be read by humans or machines) is turned into *ciphertext* (text that cannot be read by humans or machines) via cryptographic algorithms. Turning plaintext into ciphertext is called *encryption*. Converting text from ciphertext back into plaintext is called *decryption*.

Cryptographic algorithms use special data called *keys* for encrypting and decrypting; they are also called *cipher keys*. When encrypted data is shared with others, some of these keys must also be shared.

Discovering Key Concepts

It is critical to understand cipher keys and their role in the encryption/decryption process. Cipher keys come in two flavors—private and public/private.

Private Keys   *Symmetric keys*, also called *private* or *secret* keys, encrypt data using a cryptographic algorithm and a *single* key. Plaintext is both encrypted and decrypted using the same key, and it is typically protected by a password called a passphrase. Symmetric key cryptography is very fast. Unfortunately, if you need others to decrypt the data, you have to share the private key, which is its primary disadvantage.

Public/Private Key Pairs   *Asymmetric keys*, also called public/private key pairs, encrypt data using a cryptographic algorithm and *two* keys. Typically the public key is used to encrypt the data and the private key decrypts the data. The private key can be protected with a passphrase and is kept secret. The public key of the pair is meant to be shared.

Asymmetric keys are used by system users as well as many applications, such as SSH. Figure 10.1 provides a scenario of using a public/private key pair between two people.

FIGURE 10.1 Asymmetric encryption example

Notice in Figure 10.1 that in order for Bob to encrypt data (a message in this case) for Helen, he must use her public key. Helen in turn uses her private key to decrypt the data. However, problems occur if Helen is not sure that she is really getting Bob's unmodified encrypted file. She may be getting an encrypted file from a nefarious user named Evelyn and accidentally decrypt her encrypted message. This is a *man-in-the-middle* attack. Digital signatures, which are covered later, help in this situation.

Securing Data

An important concept in cryptography, covered briefly earlier, is hashing. *Hashing* uses a one-way mathematical algorithm that turns plaintext into a fixed-length ciphertext. Because it is one way, you cannot "de-hash" a hashed ciphertext. The ciphertext created by hashing is called a *message digest*, hash, hash value, fingerprint, or signature.

The beauty of a cryptographic message digest is that it can be used in data comparison. For example, if hashing produces the same message digest for plaintext `FileA` and for plaintext `FileB`, then both files contain the same data. This type of hash is often used in cyberforensics.

Hashing is useful for things like making sure a large downloaded file was not corrupted when it was being transferred. However, cryptographic hashing must use an algorithm that is collision free. In other words, the hashing algorithm cannot create the same message digest for two different inputs. Some older hash algorithms, such as MD5, are not collision free.

A *keyed message digest* is created using the plaintext file along with a private key. This cryptographic hash type is strong against multiple malicious attacks and often employed in Linux applications, such as OpenSSH.

Signing Transmissions

Another practical implementation of hashing is in *digital signatures*. A digital signature is a cryptographic token that provides authentication and data verification. It is simply a message digest of the original plaintext data, which is then encrypted with a user's private key and sent along with the ciphertext.

The ciphertext receiver decrypts the digital signature with the sender's public key so that the original message digest is available. The receiver also decrypts the ciphertext and then hashes its plaintext data. When the new message digest is created, the data receiver can compare the new message digest to the sent message digest. If they match, the digital signature is authenticated, which means the encrypted data did come from the sender. Also, it indicates the data was not modified in transmission.

Looking at SSH

When you connect over a network to a remote server, if it is not via an encrypted method, network sniffers can view the data being sent and received. Secure Shell (SSH) has resolved this problem by providing an encrypted means for communication. It is the de facto standard software used by those wishing to send data securely to/from remote systems.

SSH employs public/private key pairs (asymmetric) for its encryption. When an SSH connection is being established between two systems, each sends its public key to the other.

Exploring Basic SSH Concepts

You'll typically find *OpenSSH* (www.openSSH.com) installed by default on most distributions. However, if for some reason you are unable to use basic SSH services, you may want to check if the needed OpenSSH packages are installed (managing packages was covered in Chapter 2). The following shows the distributions used by this book and their basic OpenSSH service package names:

- CentOS: openssh, openssh-clients, openssh-server
- Ubuntu: openssh-server, openssh-client

To create a secure OpenSSH connection between two systems, use the *ssh* command. The basic syntax is as follows:

```
ssh [OPTIONS] USERNAME@HOSTNAME
```

If you attempt to use the ssh command and get a no route to host message, first check whether the sshd daemon is running. On a systemd system, the command to use with super user privileges is **systemctl status sshd**. If the daemon is running, check your firewall settings.

For a successful encrypted connection, both systems (client and remote) must have the OpenSSH software installed and the sshd daemon running. A snipped example is shown in Listing 10.31 connecting from a CentOS system to a remote openSUSE Linux server.

Listing 10.31: Using ssh to connect to a remote system

```
$ ssh Christine@192.168.0.105
The authenticity of host '192.168.0.105 (192.168.0.105)' can't be established.
ECDSA key fingerprint is SHA256:BnaCbm+ensyrkflKk1rRSVwxHi4NrBWOOSOdU+14m7w.
ECDSA key fingerprint is MD5:25:36:60:b7:99:44:d7:74:1c:95:d5:84:55:6a:62:3c.
Are you sure you want to continue connecting (yes/no)? yes
Warning: Permanently added '192.168.0.105' (ECDSA) to the list of known hosts.
Password:
[…]
Have a lot of fun...
Christine@linux-1yd3:~> ip addr show | grep 192.168.0.105
    inet 192.168.0.105/24 […] dynamic eth1
Christine@linux-1yd3:~>
Christine@linux-1yd3:~> exit
logout
Connection to 192.168.0.105 closed.
$
$ ls .ssh
known_hosts
$
```

In Listing 10.31, the ssh command uses no options, includes the remote system account username, and uses the remote system's IPv4 address instead of its hostname. Note that you do *not* have to use the remote system account username if the local account name is identical. However, in this case, you do have to enter the remote account's password to gain access to the remote system.

The OpenSSH application keeps track of any previously connected hosts in the ~/.ssh/known_hosts file. This data contains the remote servers' public keys.

The ~/ symbol combination represents a user's home directory. You may also see in documentation $HOME as the representation. Therefore, to generically represent any user's home directory that contains a hidden subdirectory .ssh/ and the known_hosts file, it is written as ~/.ssh/known_hosts or $HOME/.ssh/known_hosts.

If you have not used ssh to log into a particular remote host in the past, you'll get a scary-looking message like the one shown in Listing 10.31. The message just lets you know that this particular remote host is not in the known_hosts file. When you type **yes** at the message's prompt, the host is added to the collective.

 If you have previously connected to the remote server and you get a warning message that says WARNING: REMOTE HOST IDENTIFICATION HAS CHANGED, pay attention. It's possible that the remote server's public key has changed. However, it may also indicate that the remote system is being spoofed or has been compromised by a malicious user.

The cp utility, which was covered back in Chapter 4, allows you to copy files on the same system. Similar to the cp utility, scp lets you copy files, but it employs SSH to copy the files to a remote system over an encrypted tunnel. To use the scp command, add the *username@hostname* before the destination file's location. An example is shown in Listing 10.32.

Listing 10.32: Using scp to securely transfer a file over SSH

```
$ ls Project42.txt
Project42.txt
$
$ scp Project42.txt Christine@192.168.0.104:~
Christine@192.168.0.104's password:
Project42.txt                                100%    0     0.0KB/s    00:00
$
```

In Listing 10.32, the Project42.txt file is sent to a remote system using the scp command. Notice that the remote system's username and IP address has an added colon (:). This is to designate that the file is being transferred to a remote system. If you did not add the colon, the scp command would not transfer the file. It would simply rename the file to a filename with Christine@ and tack on the IP address too.

After the colon, the file's directory destination is designated. The ~ symbol indicates that you want to place the file in the user's home directory. You could also give the file a new name, if desired.

Besides copying files, you can use OpenSSH to send commands to a remote system. Just add the command, between quotation marks, to the ssh command's end. An example is shown in Listing 10.33.

Listing 10.33: Using ssh to send a command to a remote system

```
$ ssh Christine@192.168.0.104 "ls Project42.txt"
Christine@192.168.0.104's password:
Project42.txt
$
```

In Listing 10.33, the command checks if our file was properly copied to the remote system. The Project42.txt file was successfully transferred.

> Over time users tend to ignore the WARNING: REMOTE HOST IDENTIFICATION HAS CHANGED message. Thus, it's a good idea to help a user avoid experiencing this warning when first connecting to a system. To do that, you'll need to configure a known_hosts file for all the users on the system. However, you don't have to do it for each individual user. Instead, the ssh_known_hosts file is used by all users on the system and can contain the remote server's public keys for all the systems they will connect to. You will have to manually create the file, and it typically resides in the /etc/ssh/ directory. With the *etc/ssh/ssh_know_hosts* file in place, users will receive the warning message only when something has changed and should be investigated. This will help in keeping your system more secure.

Configuring SSH

It's a good idea to review the various OpenSSH configuration files and their directives. Ensuring that your encrypted connection is properly configured is critical for securing remote system communications. Table 10.3 lists the primary OpenSSH configuration files.

TABLE 10.3   Primary OpenSSH configuration files

Configuration File	Description
~/.ssh/config	Contains OpenSSH client configurations. May be overridden by ssh command options.
/etc/ssh/ssh_config	Contains OpenSSH client configurations. May be overridden by ssh command options or settings in the ~/.ssh/config file.
/etc/ssh/sshd_config	Contains the OpenSSH daemon (sshd) configurations.

If you need to make SSH configuration changes, it is essential to know which configuration file(s) to modify. The following guidelines can help:

- For an individual user's connections to a remote system, create and/or modify the client side's ~/.ssh/config file.
- For every user's connection to a remote system, create and modify the client side's /etc/ssh/ssh_config file.
- For incoming SSH connection requests, modify the /etc/ssh/sshd_config file on the server side.

Keep in mind that in order for an SSH client connection to be successful, besides proper authentication, the client and remote server's SSH configuration must be compatible.

There are several OpenSSH configuration directives. You can peruse them all via the man pages for the ssh_config and sshd_config files. However, there are a few vital directives for the sshd_config file:

- AllowTcpForwarding: Permits SSH port forwarding.

- ForwardX11: Permits X11 forwarding.

- PermitRootLogin: Permits the root user to log in through an SSH connection. (Default is yes.) Typically, should be set to no.

- Port: Sets the port number the OpenSSH daemon (sshd) listens on for incoming connection requests. (Default is 22.)

An example of why you might change the client's ssh_config or ~/.ssh/config file is when the remote system's SSH port is modified in the sshd_config file. In this case, if the client-side configuration files were not changed to match this new port, the remote user would have to modify their ssh command's options. An example of this is shown snipped in Listing 10.34. In this listing, the remote Ubuntu server has OpenSSH listening on port 1138, instead of the default port 22, and the user must use the -p option with the ssh command to reach the remote server.

Listing 10.34: Using ssh to connect to a nondefault port on a remote system

```
$ ssh -p 1138 192.168.0.104
[…]
Christine@192.168.0.104's password:
Welcome to Ubuntu 18.04.1 LTS (GNU/Linux 4.15.0-36-generic x86_64)
[…]
Christine@Ubuntu1804:~$
Christine@Ubuntu1804:~$ ip addr show | grep 192.168.0.104
    inet 192.168.0.104/24 […]
Christine@Ubuntu1804:~$
Christine@Ubuntu1804:~$ exit
logout
Connection to 192.168.0.104 closed.
$
```

To relieve the OpenSSH client users of this trouble, create or modify the ~/.ssh/config file for individual users, or for all client users, modify the /etc/ssh/ssh_config file. Set Port to 1138 within the configuration file. This makes it easier on both the remote users and the system administrator.

Generating SSH Keys

Typically, OpenSSH will search for its system's public/private key pairs. If they are not found, OpenSSH automatically generates them. These key pairs, also called *host keys*, are stored in the /etc/ssh/ directory within files. In Listing 10.35, key files' names are displayed.

Listing 10.35: Looking at OpenSSH key files

```
$ ls -1 /etc/ssh/*key*
/etc/ssh/ssh_host_ecdsa_key
/etc/ssh/ssh_host_ecdsa_key.pub
/etc/ssh/ssh_host_ed25519_key
/etc/ssh/ssh_host_ed25519_key.pub
/etc/ssh/ssh_host_rsa_key
/etc/ssh/ssh_host_rsa_key.pub
$
```

In Listing 10.35, both private and public key files are shown. The public key files end in the .pub filename extension, whereas the private keys have no filename extension. The filenames follow this standard:

ssh_host_*KeyType*_key

The key filename's *KeyType* corresponds to the digital signature algorithm used in the key's creation. The different algorithm types you may see on your system are as follows:

- rsa (Rivest–Shamir–Adleman) is the oldest type, widely used, and highly supported.
- dsa (Digital Signature Algorithm) is a Federal Information Processing Standard for digital signatures. Deprecated.
- ecdsa (Elliptical Curve Digital Signature Algorithm) is an Elliptic Curve implementation of DSA.
- ed25519 is a variation of the Edwards-curve Digital Signature Algorithm (EdDSA) that offers better security than dsa and ecdsa.

 It is critical that the private key files are properly protected. Private key files should have a 0640 or 0600 (octal) permission setting and be root owned. However, public key files need to be world readable. File permissions were covered in Chapter 4.

There may be times you need to manually generate these keys or create new ones. To do so, use the *ssh-keygen* utility. In Listing 10.36, a snipped example of using ssh-keygen is shown.

Listing 10.36: Using ssh-keygen to create new public/private key pair

```
$ sudo ssh-keygen -t rsa -f /etc/ssh/ssh_host_rsa_key
Generating public/private rsa key pair.
/etc/ssh/ssh_host_rsa_key already exists.
Overwrite (y/n)? y
Enter passphrase (empty for no passphrase):
Enter same passphrase again:
Your identification has been saved in /etc/ssh/ssh_host_rsa_key.
Your public key has been saved in /etc/ssh/ssh_host_rsa_key.pub.
The key fingerprint is:
[…]
$
```

The ssh-keygen command has several options. For the commands in Listing 10.36, only two are employed. The -t option sets the *KeyType*, which is rsa in this example. The -f switch designates the private key file to store the key. The public key is stored in a file with the same name, but the .pub file extension is added. Notice that this command asks for a passphrase, which is associated with the private key.

Authenticating with SSH Keys

Entering the password for every command employing SSH can be tiresome. However, you can use keys instead of a password to authenticate. A few steps are needed to set up this authentication method:

1. Log into the SSH client system.
2. Generate an SSH ID key pair.
3. Securely transfer the public SSH ID key to the SSH server computer.
4. Log into the SSH server system.
5. Add the public SSH ID key to the *~/.ssh/authorized_keys* file on the server system.

Let's look at these steps in a little more detail. First, you should log into the client system via the account you will be using as the SSH client. On that system, generate the SSH ID key pair via the ssh-keygen utility. You must designate the correct key pair filename, which is id_*TYPE*, where TYPE is dsa, rsa, or ecdsa. An example of creating an SSH ID key pair on a client system is shown snipped in Listing 10.37.

Listing 10.37: Using ssh-keygen to create an SSH ID key pair

```
$ ssh-keygen -t rsa -f ~/.ssh/id_rsa
Generating public/private rsa key pair.
Enter passphrase (empty for no passphrase):
```

Listing 10.37: Using ssh-keygen to create an SSH ID key pair *(continued)*

```
Enter same passphrase again:
Your identification has been saved in /home/Christine/.ssh/id_rsa.
Your public key has been saved in /home/Christine/.ssh/id_rsa.pub.
[…]
$
$ ls .ssh/
id_rsa   id_rsa.pub   known_hosts
$
```

Notice in Listing 10.37 the key file's name. The ssh-keygen command in this case generates a private key, stored in the ~/.ssh/id_rsa file, and a public key, stored in the ~/.ssh/id_rsa.pub file. You may enter a passphrase if desired. In this case, no passphrase was entered.

> The public and private key filenames depend on the type (-t) that you choose. If you choose rsa, the files generated are id_rsa and id_rsa .pub. If you select dsa, the filenames are id_dsa and id_dsa.pub. And if you choose ecdsa, the files generated are id_ecdsa and id_ecdsa.pub. However, whatever you select, the files are stored in the ~/.ssh/ directory.

After these keys are generated on the client system, the public key must be copied to the server system. Using a secure method is best, and the *ssh-copy-id* utility allows you to do this. Not only does it copy over your public key, it also stores it in the server system's ~/.ssh/authorized_keys file for you. In essence, it completes steps 3 through 5 in a single command. A snipped example of using this utility is shown in Listing 10.38.

Listing 10.38: Using ssh-copy-id to copy the SSH public ID key

```
$ ssh-copy-id -n Christine@192.168.0.104
[…]
Would have added the following key(s):

ssh-rsa AAAAB3NzaC1yc2EAAAADAQABAAABAQCsP[…]
8WJVE5RWAXN[…]
=-=-=-=-=-=-=
$ ssh-copy-id  Christine@192.168.0.104
[…]Source of key(s) to be installed: "/home/Christine/.ssh/id_rsa.pub"
[…]
Christine@192.168.0.104's password:

Number of key(s) added: 1
[…]
$
```

Notice in Listing 10.38 that the ssh-copy-id -n command is employed first. The -n option allows you to see what keys would be copied and installed on the remote system without actually doing the work (a dry run).

The next time the command is issued in Listing 10.38, the -n switch is removed. Thus, the id_rsa.pub key file is securely copied to the server system, and the key is installed in the ~/.ssh/authorized_keys file. Notice that when using the ssh-copy-id command, the user must enter their password to allow the public ID key to be copied over to the server.

Now that the public ID key has been copied over to the SSH server system, the ssh command can be used to connect from the client system to the server system with no need to enter a password. This is shown along with using the scp command in Listing 10.39. Note that at the IP address's end, you must add a colon (:) when using the scp command to copy over files.

Listing 10.39: Testing out password-less SSH connections

```
$ ssh Christine@192.168.0.104
Welcome to Ubuntu 18.04.1 LTS (GNU/Linux 4.15.0-36-generic x86_64)
[…]
Christine@Ubuntu1804:~$ ls .ssh
authorized_keys  known_hosts
Christine@Ubuntu1804:~$
Christine@Ubuntu1804:~$ exit
logout
Connection to 192.168.0.104 closed.
$
$ scp Project4x.tar Christine@192.168.0.104:~
Project4x.tar      100%   40KB   6.3MB/s   00:00
$
$ ssh Christine@192.168.0.104
Welcome to Ubuntu 18.04.1 LTS (GNU/Linux 4.15.0-36-generic x86_64)
[…]
Christine@Ubuntu1804:~$ ls
Desktop    Downloads        Music     Project4x.tar  Templates
Documents  examples.desktop Pictures  Public         Videos
Christine@Ubuntu1804:~$ exit
logout
Connection to 192.168.0.104 closed.
$
```

If your Linux distribution does not have the ssh-copy-id command, you can employ the scp command to copy over the public ID key. In this case you would have to manually add the key to the bottom of the ~/.ssh/authorized_keys file. To do this, you can use the cat command and the >> symbols to redirect and append the public ID key's standard output to the authorized keys file.

Authenticating with the Authentication Agent

Another method to connect to a remote system with SSH is via the authentication agent. Using the agent, you only need to enter your password to initiate the connection. After that, the agent remembers the password during the agent session. A few steps are needed to set up this authentication method:

1. Log into the SSH client system.
2. Generate an SSH ID key pair and set up a passphrase.
3. Securely transfer the public SSH ID key to the SSH server computer.
4. Log into the SSH server system.
5. Add the public SSH ID key to the ~/.ssh/authorized_keys file on the server system.
6. Start an agent session.
7. Add the SSH ID key to the agent session.

Steps 1 through 5 are nearly the same steps performed for setting up authenticating with SSH ID keys instead of a password. One exception to note is that a passphrase *must* be created when generating the SSH ID key pair for use with an agent. An example of setting up an ECDSA key to use with an SSH agent is shown snipped in Listing 10.40.

Listing 10.40: Generating and setting up an ID key to use with the SSH agent

```
$ ssh-keygen -t ecdsa -f ~/.ssh/id_ecdsa
Generating public/private ecdsa key pair.
Enter passphrase (empty for no passphrase):
Enter same passphrase again:
Your identification has been saved in /home/Christine/.ssh/id_ecdsa.
[…]
$ ssh-copy-id  -i ~/.ssh/id_ecdsa Christine@192.168.0.104
[…]
Number of key(s) added: 1
[…]
$
```

When you have the key pair properly created with a passphrase on the remote system, securely transmitted, and installed on the server's authorized key file, you can employ the *ssh-agent* utility to start an SSH agent session. After the session is started, add the private ID key to the session via the *ssh-add* command. A snipped example of this is shown in Listing 10.41.

Listing 10.41: Starting an SSH agent session and adding an ID key

```
$ ssh-agent /bin/bash
 [Christine@localhost ~]$
[Christine@localhost ~]$ ssh-add ~/.ssh/id_ecdsa
Enter passphrase for /home/Christine/.ssh/id_ecdsa:
```

```
Identity added: /home/Christine/.ssh/id_ecdsa (/home/Christine/.ssh/id_ecdsa)
[Christine@localhost ~]$
[Christine@localhost ~]$ ssh Christine@192.168.0.104
Welcome to Ubuntu 18.04.1 LTS (GNU/Linux 4.15.0-36-generic x86_64)
[…]
Christine@Ubuntu1804:~$ exit
logout
Connection to 192.168.0.104 closed.
[Christine@localhost ~]$
[Christine@localhost ~]$ exit
exit
$
```

Notice in Listing 10.41 that the ssh-agent command is followed by /bin/bash, which is the Bash shell. This command starts a new session, an agent session, with the Bash shell running. After the private SSH ID key is added using the ssh-add command and entering the private passphrase, you can connect to remote systems without entering a password or passphrase again. However, if you exit the agent session and start it up again, you must readd the key and reenter the passphrase.

The ssh-add command allows you to remove ID within an agent session, if you want. Include the -d option to do so.

An SSH agent session allows you to enter the session one time and add the key, and then connect as often as needed to remote systems via encrypted SSH methods without entering a password or passphrase over and over again. Not only does this provide security, it also provides convenience, which is a rare combination.

Tunneling

Another way to provide security through OpenSSH is via *SSH port forwarding*, sometimes called *SSH tunneling*. SSH port forwarding allows you to redirect a connection from one particular network port to port 22, where the SSH service is waiting to receive it. This allows data traffic to move back and forth through a secure encrypted tunnel, similar to a virtual private network.

If you need to provide remote X11 GUI interactions, you can employ OpenSSH to use a secure tunnel. This is called *X11 forwarding*. X11 forwarding lets you interact with various X11-based graphical utilities on a remote system through an encrypted network connection (X11 forwarding is covered in Chapter 6).

First check to see if X11 forwarding is permitted in the openSSH configuration file, /etc/ssh/sshd_config. The directive *X11Forwarding* should be set to yes in the remote system's configuration file. If the directive is set to no, then you must modify it to employ X11 forwarding. In Listing 10.42, a check is performed on the configuration file for this directive on a CentOS distribution.

Listing 10.42: Checking the `AllowTCPForwarding` directive

```
# grep "X11Forwarding yes" /etc/ssh/sshd_config
X11Forwarding yes
#
```

When you have made any necessary configuration file modifications, the command to use is `ssh -X` *user@remote-host*. Similar to earlier `ssh` command uses, the *user* is the user account that resides on the *remote-host* system. The *remote-host* has the X11-based GUI utilities you wish to employ and can be designated via an IP address or a hostname. Figure 10.2 shows connecting from a remote client to a CentOS server and using a graphical utility on that server.

FIGURE 10.2 Forwarding X11

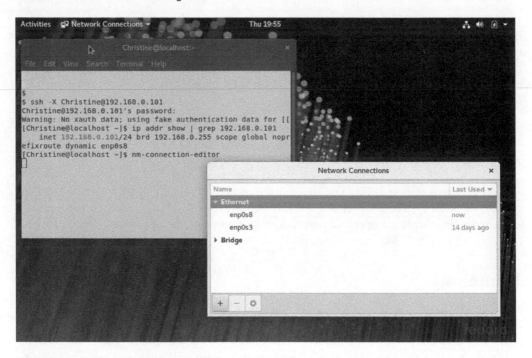

It's always a good idea to check your IP address to ensure that you have successfully reached the remote system. In Figure 10.2, the `ip addr show` command is employed for this purpose. After you have completed your work, just type in **exit** to log out of the X11 forwarding session.

WARNING   You may read about using X11 forwarding via the `ssh -Y` command, which is called trusted X11. This does not mean the connection is more secure. In fact, it is quite the opposite. When employing this command, you are treating the remote server as a trusted system. This can cause many security issues and should be avoided.

Using SSH Securely

There are a few things you can do to enhance SSH's security on your systems:

- Use a different port for SSH than the default port 22.
- Disable root logins via SSH.
- Ensure protocol 2 is in use.

One item touched upon earlier in this chapter is not using port 22 as the SSH port for any public-facing systems. You change this by modifying the Port directive in the /etc/ssh/sshd_config file to another port number. Keep in mind that there are advantages and disadvantages to doing this. It may be a better alternative to beef up your firewall as opposed to changing the default SSH port.

Another critical item is disabling root login via SSH. By default, any system that allows the root account to log in and has OpenSSH enabled permits root logins via SSH. Because root is a standard username, malicious attackers can use it in brute-force attacks. Since root is a super user account, it needs extra protection.

To disable root login via SSH, edit the /etc/ssh/sshd_config file. Set the PermitRootLogin directive to no, and either restart the OpenSSH service or reload its configuration file.

An earlier version of OpenSSH, protocol 1, is considered insecure. Most likely your system is employing protocol 2, sometimes called *OpenSSH 2*. However, it's a good idea to ensure this is true. Find the Protocol directive in the /etc/ssh/sshd_config file. If it is set to 1, then change it to 2, and restart the OpenSSH service or reload its configuration file.

OpenSSH allows secure encryption of data traveling back and forth between systems. However, if you need to encrypt a single file, then another utility is the right one to use, and it is covered next.

Using GPG

In cases where you need to employ file encryption and transfer the file beyond what scp can handle, *GNU Privacy Guard* (GPG or GnuPG) can help. Besides encrypting files, you can apply digital signatures to them, providing higher security.

Because GPG was based on the Pretty Good Privacy product, which is not open source, you'll often see it referred to as *OpenPGP* as well. It is a very popular encryption tool and often installed by default. However, if you don't find it on your system, you can install the gpg or gnupg2 package via your distribution's package tools (software installation was covered in Chapter 2).

The command to use GPG depends on your distribution; it may be gpg or gpg2. The function is similar enough, so we've used gpg in this topic's section, but you may need to replace *gpg* with gpg2 for your particular situation.

Generating Keys

To begin using GPG, you'll need to generate a public/private key pair. GPG uses the typical asynchronous keys, where the public key is available publicly but the private key is kept private. (GPG calls the private key a *secret key*.) Start the process to generate your key pair by using the following command:

gpg --gen-key

GPG will ask a series of questions, including your full name and email address, as well as a passphrase. You'll need to remember the email address and the passphrase because the address identifies your public key, whereas the passphrase allows you to use your private key.

> The key generation command needs a lot of random data in order to produce strong keys. During this process, you are asked to type on the keyboard, move the mouse, press function keys, and so on. It takes a long time to complete. An easier way is to employ the random data tool (rngd). Install it from the rng-utils or rng-tools package. Before issuing the gpg --gen-key command, use super user privileges and type **rngd -r /dev/ urandom**. After you receive the shell prompt back, issue the gpg --gen-key command. Though it will pause a moment or two at the part where the program is asking you to type on the keyboard, it will complete fairly quickly. And it is quicker than you trying to manually add random data.

After the keys are generated, they are stored in a file, which is called your *keyring* in the ~/.gnupg/ directory.

For someone to encrypt a file for you to decrypt, you'll need to make a copy of your public key for them. This is called *exporting your key*, and it will put the copy of the key into a file. The command to enact this is

gpg --export *EMAIL-ADDRESS* > *FILENAME*.pub

The *EMAIL-ADDRESS* identifies your public key on your keyring, and it was entered when you generate the key. The *FILENAME* can be anything. An example of this is shown in Listing 10.43.

Listing 10.43: Exporting a public key using the gpg --export command

```
$ gpg --export cb1234@ivytech.edu > CB_gpg.pub
$
```

After you export (copy) your public key to a file, you can give it to the people who want to encrypt files to send to you. There is no reason to keep the public key secret, so you can email it or, if you have a public web page, place it there.

The exported public key is in a binary format. If you are having trouble emailing it to someone or they cannot download it from a website, regenerate the exported public key file adding the --armor option. This will cause the key file to be in an ASCII format that may be easier to transfer.

Importing Keys

When you receive the public key file for encrypting files to someone else, you'll need to add it to your keyring before employing it. This process is called *importing*, and it uses the following command:

gpg --import *FILENAME*.pub

Of course, you'll need to substitute the file's actual name for *FILENAME*. After you have their public key added to your keyring, you can begin to encrypt files for them.

After you load a new key onto your keyring, it's a good idea to check the various keys residing there. The command to view your keyring is

gpg --list-keys

An example of loading a public key onto a keyring and then displaying the keyring's contents is shown snipped in Listing 10.44.

Listing 10.44: Importing a public key and displaying the keyring using the gpg utility

```
$ gpg --import RB_gpg.pub
gpg: key 0238[…]: public key "Richard Blum <rb4242@gmail.com>" imported
gpg: Total number processed: 1
gpg:               imported: 1
$
$ gpg --list-keys
[…]
---------------------------------
pub   rsa3072 2019-06-14 [SC] [expires: 2021-06-13]
      E4EDDC1C51638290DFDA6B90D0C94AD1415A64DB
uid           [ultimate] Christine Bresnahan <cb1234@ivytech.edu>
sub   rsa3072 2019-06-14 [E] [expires: 2021-06-13]

pub   rsa3072 2019-06-14 [SC] [expires: 2021-06-13]
      167C14E4C66FB0EBFBA5C7C60238B9C4F61CBDF7
uid           [ unknown] Richard Blum <rb4242@gmail.com>
sub   rsa3072 2019-06-14 [E] [expires: 2021-06-13]

$
```

Now that you have another person's public key on your keyring, you can encrypt a file for them to decrypt.

Gnu Privacy Guard has a secret agent. Its name is gpg-agent. Its mission is to manage the secret (private) keys separately from any protocol.

The *gpg-agent* is a daemon started automatically on demand by the gpg utility, so there's no need to use systemd or SysVinit to manage it. When GPG needs a private key, it requests it from the agent. The agent keeps any previously used keys in RAM. If the request key is not in memory, the agent loads it from your keyring but asks you for the passphrase to access it. The whole process almost sounds like a spy novel.

Encrypting and Decrypting Data

After you load the public key onto your keyring, you can start the encryption process. First create the file through a normal method, such as using a word processor or text editor. Then encrypt the file using their public key via this command:

```
gpg --out ENCRYPTED-FILE --recipient EMAIL-ADDRESS --encrypt ORIGINAL-FILE
```

Note that the *ORIGINAL-FILE* is the unencrypted file you first created and the *ENCRYPTED-FILE* is the ciphertext file. The *EMAIL-ADDRESS* is the email address of the person who will be receiving this encrypted file, and it should be the address used to identify that person's public key on your keyring. An example of this process is shown snipped in Listing 10.45.

Listing 10.45: Encrypting a file using the recipeint's public key

```
$ whoami
Christine
$
$ ls secretfile.txt
secretfile.txt
$
$ gpg --out encryptfile --recipient rb4242@gmail.com --encrypt secretfile.txt
[…]
sub   rsa3072/E3E4D21F82775FA1 2019-06-14 Richard Blum <rb4242@gmail.com>
[…]
$
$ ls encryptfile
encryptfile
$
```

The person who receives your encrypted file can then decrypt it using their private (secret) key. The command to accomplish this is

```
gpg --out DECRYPTED-FILE --decrypt ENCRYPTED-FILE
```

When you issue the preceding command, it will ask for the passphrase that identifies your private key. A snipped example of this process is shown in Listing 10.46.

Listing 10.46: Decrypting a file using the recipient's private (secret) key

```
$ ls
encryptfile  examples.desktop
$
$ whoami
rich
$
$ gpg --out CBmessage.txt --decrypt encryptfile
[…]
gpg: encrypted with 3072-bit RSA key, ID E3E4D21F82775FA1, created 2019-06-14
      "Richard Blum <rb4242@gmail.com>"
$
$ ls CBmessage.txt
CBmessage.txt
$
$ cat CBmessage.txt
Rich,
I am almost done with Chapter 10.
What shall we write about next?
The number 1138?
$
```

We find that people who are new to public/private (asymmetric) key encryption get confused concerning when to use their public key and when to use their private one. If someone wants to send an encrypted file to you, think, "It's all about me." They will be using *your* public key to encrypt the file, and you'll be using *your* private key to decrypt it. (Of course, it's all about the other person when you want to send them an encrypted file.)

Signing Messages and Verifying Signatures

While encrypting helps to protect the privacy of a document, it does not protect the document from being modified in transit. Using the example back in Figure 10.1, if a malicious actor (Evelyn) gets ahold of Helen's public key, the threat actor could encrypt a message for Helen and claim it came from Bob. Or worse, if Bob is sending Helen source code, a threat actor could modify it in some way before it reaches Helen.

Fortunately, you can digitally sign gpg encrypted files. This process creates a time stamp and certifies the file. Thus, if the file is modified in any way, the gpg utility will alert the file's receiver when checked.

To sign a file, you employ the `--sign` option, or if you need to send it as ASCII instead, use the `--clearsign` switch. The file's digital signature is encryption process is a little different. To encrypt the digital signature, the gpg utility uses your private key and will ask for the passphrase protecting this key. An example of encrypting and then signing the encrypted file is shown snipped in Listing 10.47.

Listing 10.47: Encrypting a file and digitally signing the encrypting file

```
$ cat newsecret.txt
Hi Rich,
This file came from me.
Signed,
Christine B
$
$ gpg --out tosign --recipient rb4242@gmail.com --encrypt newsecret.txt
[…]
$
$ gpg --output signed --sign tosign
$
$ ls signed
signed
$
```

When the recipient receives the encrypted and signed file, they can verify it came from the sender and that no modification occurred in the transfer via the `--verify` option:

```
gpg  --verify RECEIVED-SIGNED-FILE
```

> **NOTE**   Because the digital signature is encrypted with the sender's private key, the recipient must have the sender's public key on their keyring. If this is not true, when the recipient attempts to verify the signature, they'll receive a message similar to `Can't check signature: No public key`.

Checking the signature and decrypting the original file takes two steps. First you must decrypt and verify the signature. An example of this process is shown snipped in Listing 10.48.

Listing 10.48: Decrypting and verifying the digital signature using the gpg utility

```
$ ls signed
signed
$
$ gpg --out MessageFromCB.gpg --verify signed
```

```
gpg: Signature made Mon 17 Jun 2019 09:36:58 AM EDT
[…]
gpg: Good signature from "Christine Bresnahan <cb1234@ivytech.edu>" […]
[…]
$
```

After the signature is decrypted and verified, the original file is decrypted using the methods described earlier in this section. An example is shown snipped in Listing 10.49.

Listing 10.49: Decrypting the original file using the gpg utility

```
$ gpg --out MessageFromCB.txt --decrypt MessageFromCB.gpg
[…]
$
$ cat MessageFromCB.txt
Hi Rich,
This file came from me.
Signed,
Christine B
$
```

> If you want to digitally sign a message or file but not encrypt it, you can employ the --detach-sig option of the gpg utility. After you have created the signature file, send it along with your message or file.

Revoking a Key

If your private key has been compromised or stolen, you need to revoke your public key. The voiding process consists of the following steps:

1. Generate a revocation certificate.
2. Import the revocation certificate into your keyring.
3. Make available the revocation certificate to those who have your public key.

To generate the revocation document, you use the gpg utility with the --gen-revoke or --generate-revocation switch. You'll be asked a series of questions as to why you are voiding this particular key, and you'll be given the opportunity to include additional information concerning the issue. A snipped example is shown in Listing 10.50.

Listing 10.50: Generating a key revocation document using the gpg utility

```
$ whoami
Christine
$
```

Listing 10.50: Generating a key revocation document using the gpg utility *(continued)*

```
$ gpg --out key-revocation.asc --gen-revoke cb1234@ivytech.edu
[…]
Create a revocation certificate for this key? (y/N) y
Please select the reason for the revocation:
  0 = No reason specified
  1 = Key has been compromised
  2 = Key is superseded
  3 = Key is no longer used
  Q = Cancel
(Probably you want to select 1 here)
Your decision? 1
[…]
$
$ ls key-revocation.asc
key-revocation.asc
$
```

After you have the revocation certification, you can import it into your keyring to officially void your public/private key pair:

```
gpg --import FILENAME.asc
```

Next you need to make the revocation certificate available to others who may have your public key on their keyrings. The method you choose here depends on how you originally distributed the public key. If you used a GnuPG key server, then send the revocation certificate to it. If a website was used, publish the document to it. The holders of your public key then import the certificate using the same gpg --import command, which voids the key.

Summary

In this chapter we took a look at how to set a basic level of host security. This included how to audit your network services and disable any unneeded ones. We also explored local security topics, such as securing account passwords, limiting root account access, and locating potentially dangerous programs.

To set some foundations, we delved into basic cryptography concepts. Those concepts were then expanded into practical knowledge on using OpenSSH to secure transmissions, and GnuPGP to encrypt files.

These skills will assist you in securing your systems. As computer attacks grow, the systems in your care will be protected.

Exam Essentials

Describe the tools for auditing network services.   The nmap and netstat utilities will allow you to audit open ports and the services provided at these ports, but keep in mind the netstat command is deprecated. You can find network sockets using both the ss utility as well as via the systemctl command to view systemd managed sockets. Since Linux treats network connections and sockets as files, you may employ both the lsof and fuser utilities to audit these items as well.

Summarize super servers and TCP Wrappers.   A super server directly listens for packets containing a designated port number, and when such a packet arrives, the server starts the matching network service. The extended super daemon, xinetd, uses the /etc/xinetd .conf configuration file for its global directives and specific service configuration files stored in the /etc/xinetd.d/ directory for its managed network services' configurations.

TCP Wrappers use the /etc/hosts.allow and /etc/hosts.deny files to determine who can access a particular system service. The hosts.allow file is checked first, and if a particular system is listed in that file, then access is allowed, and no further checks are made. However, if it is not found in that file, the hosts.deny file is checked. Since access is allowed if the remote system's address is not found in either file, it is best to employ the ALL wildcard in the /etc/hosts.deny file, ALL: ALL.

Clarify how Linux secures passwords.   Linux used to store account passwords as salted hashes in /etc/passwd, but because everyone can view the data in that file, they were moved to the more locked-down /etc/shadow. In order to change your password, you must employ the passwd utility, which is able to modify the /etc/shadow file contents due to the utility's SUID settings.

Explain how to limit root account access.   Though with the su utility you can quickly log into the other account or just issue a few commands, it does not provide a nonrepudiation environment. Therefore, it's best to use the sudo command, which allows a user to issue a single command with super user privileges. The primary configuration file for this command is the /etc/sudoers file, though modifications are best made to configuration files stored in the /etc/sudoers.d/ directory for modern distributions.

Outline setting limits on a Linux system.   To protect a system from having its resources consumed by a runaway program or threat actor, it is a good idea to limit resources, such as the number of logins, processes, or memory usage per user account. The ulimit utility provides these limits and is typically configured for user account in the environment files.

Define locating SUID/SGID files.   Because SUID and SGID permissions set on a program or script can be a way for a malicious actor to cause problems on the system, it is wise to audit the files set with these permissions. The best utility to use is the find command. Search the entire virtual directory structure starting at the root directory (/), with the -perm /6000 switch and argument to find these files.

Summarize using OpenSSH. The OpenSSH utility allows you to log into a remote system through an encrypted network connection; its primary interface is the ssh command, and it employs this syntax: ssh [*OPTIONS*] *USERNAME@HOSTNAME*. It keeps track of any previously connected hosts in the ~/.ssh/known_hosts file, which contains the remote servers' public keys. Its configuration files include ~/.ssh/config (client configurations), /etc/ssh/ssh_config (global client configurations), and /etc/ssh/sshd_config (OpenSSH daemon configurations).

To manually generate the needed public/private key pair, use the ssh-keygen utility. To employ OpenSSH to copy the files to a remote system over an encrypted tunnel, use the scp command. To use password-less access, either copy over your public key to a remote system's ~/.ssh/authorized_keys file with the ssh-copy-id utility or authenticate with an authentication agent via ssh-agent and ssh-add commands. You can also tunnel X11 GUI interactions via the ssh -X *user@remote-host* command as long as tunneling is allowed.

Describe GPG concepts. The GPG utility allows you to encrypt and decrypt files using a public/private key pair. To generate the keys, you need to employ the gpg --gen-key command, which then stores the keys in a file (also called the keyring) within the ~/.gnupg/ directory. To share your public key, you must first export it from your keyring to a file via the --export option. The public key recipient then puts the key on their keyring via the --import switch. You can view the keys on your keyring by using the gpg --list-keys command. To encrypt a file, use the recipient's public key and the --encrypt option. When the encrypted file is received, the recipient decrypts the file with the private key and the --decrypt switch. There is no need to start a daemon to manage the private keys, because GPG handles its private keys via the gpg-agent daemon, which is started when needed by GPG. To protect against man-in-the-middle attacks, you can sign your encrypted files with the --sign or --clearsign option. The encrypted file recipient can then verify the signature with the --verify switch. To revoke a public key, create a revocation certificate via the --gen-revoke, import the certificate onto your keyring, and share the certificate with others who need to revoke your public key on their keyring as well.

Review Questions

You can find the answers in the appendix.

1. Which of the following utilities allows you to scan a system's network ports and see the services offered for each port, and you don't have to be logged onto the system you are scanning?

   A. fuser

   B. lsof

   C. nmap

   D. netstat

   E. ss

2. Nickie needs to scan his system to see what ports are listening for incoming TCP connections. He decides to use the netstat utility. What options should he employ? (Choose all that apply.)

   A. -l

   B. -u

   C. -s

   D. -T

   E. -t

3. Nickie knows that the netstat utility is deprecated, so he has decided to switch to the ss utility. He needs to scan his system to see what ports are listening for incoming TCP connections. What options should he employ? (Choose all that apply.)

   A. -l

   B. -u

   C. -s

   D. -T

   E. -t

4. Case is trying to lock down an older Linux system. He was surprised to find that it may be offering FTP services. He discovers in the /etc/services file that these older FTP services typically run on ports 20 and 21. What lsof command should he run to see if there are active connections to the FTP services?

   A. lsof -i UDP

   B. lsof -i 20:TCP

   C. lsof -i ftp:TCP

   D. lsof -i :ftp

   E. lsof -i 20:ftp

5. What is the main difference between using the lsof utility and the fuser utility to audit network services on your system?

   A. The lsof command utility displays open files on the system.

   B. The fuser command utility shows the port and protocol in use.

   C. The lsof command utility is deprecated.

   D. The fuser command utility shows the process PID using the port.

   E. The lsof command utility shows the port and protocol in use.

6. Hiro has completed a network service audit of his systemd systems. He now needs to disable all the unnecessary network services. What command should he use?

   A. service

   B. systemctl

   C. chkconfig

   D. update-rc.d

   E. init

7. Hiro discovered that the current systemd system he is auditing has a super server on it. He determines that there a few unneeded network services being managed by xinetd. What should he do to disable those services? (Choose all that apply.)

   A. Use the systemctl command to set the xinetd service to disabled, so it won't start on boot.

   B. Set the service's disable directive to yes in the /etc/xinetd.conf file.

   C. Use the chkconfig command to disable xinetd on all runlevels so that it won't start at boot.

   D. Set the service's disable directive to yes in its /etc/xinetd.d/ directory file.

   E. Uninstall the xinetd service.

8. Marcus is administrating a system that employs TCP Wrappers. He determines the TCP Wrapper access files are not as locked down as they should be. What can he do to improve their security?

   A. Put ALL: ALL in the /etc/hosts.allow file.

   B. Put ALL: ALL in the /etc/host.allow file.

   C. Put ALL: ALL in the /etc/hosts.deny file.

   D. Put ALL: ALL in the /etc/host.deny file.

   E. Put ALL: ALL in the /etc/host.deny file and /etc/host.allow files.

9. Which of the following is true concerning passwords on Linux? (Choose all that apply.)

   A. Passwords should be stored in the /etc/shadow file.

   B. Passwords should be stored in the /etc/passwd file.

   C. Passwords are stored as salted hashes.

D. Use the `pwconv` utility to move passwords to the `/etc/shadow` file.

E. Use the `passwd` command to change your password.

10. Yoyo is a new system administrator for Virgin Galactic. She needs to use super user privileges to perform several of her duties. What should be done?

    A. Give Yoyo the `root` account password shared by the system admin team and have her log into the `root` account via the GUI.

    B. Give Yoyo the `root` account password shared by the system admin team and have her log into the `root` account via the `su -` command.

    C. Give Yoyo the `root` account password shared by the system admin team and have her issue commands that need super user privileges via the `su -c` command.

    D. Set Yoyo up in the `/etc/sudoers` file and have her issue commands that need super user privileges via the `sudo` command.

    E. Set Yoyo up in the `/etc/sudoers` file and have her issue commands that need super user privileges via the `su -c` command.

11. Which command provides the most information concerning users who are currently logged into the system?

    A. `who`

    B. `w`

    C. `last`

    D. `who am i`

    E. `whoami`

12. Wade needs to set the number of processes each virtual reality game player can start on his gaming server. What `ulimit` option should he use in their environment files?

    A. `-a`

    B. `-l`

    C. `-t`

    D. `-u`

    E. `-v`

13. The OpenSSH application keeps track of any previously connected hosts and their public keys in what file?

    A. `~/.ssh/known_hosts`

    B. `~/.ssh/authorized_keys`

    C. `/etc/ssh/known_hosts`

    D. `/etc/ssh/authorized_keys`

    E. `/etc/ssh/ssh_host_rsa_key.pub`

14. Which of the following are OpenSSH configuration files? (Choose all that apply.)

    A. ~./ssh/config

    B. /etc/ssh/ssh_config

    C. /etc/ssh/sshd_config

    D. /etc/sshd/ssh_config

    E. /etc/sshd/sshd_config

15. Which of the following files may be involved in authenticating with SSH keys?

    A. /etc/ssh/ssh_host_rsa_key

    B. /etc/ssh/ssh_host_rsa_key.pub

    C. ~/.ssh/id_rsa_key

    D. ~/.ssh/id_rsa_key.pub

    E. ~/.ssh/id_rsa

16. Wade's OpenSSH private key was compromised, so he needs to create himself a new public/private key pair. Using super user privileges, what command should he use?

    A. ssh-keygen -t rsa -f /etc/ssh/ssh_host_rsa_key

    B. ssh-keygen -t rsa -f /etc/ssh/ssh_host_ecdsa_key

    C. ssh-keygen -t rsa -f ~/.ssh/id_rsa_key

    D. ssh-keygen -t rsa -f ~/.ssh/id_ecdsa_key

    E. ssh-keygen -t rsa -f /etc/ssh/ssh_host_rsa_key.pub

17. DeAndre wants to use password-less authentication while employing OpenSSH to reach a remote system. He has generated the needed public/private key pair and is ready to copy over the public key to store it in the ~/.ssh/authorized_keys file. What is the best utility he should use to do this securely?

    A. scp

    B. ssh-keygen

    C. scp-id-copy

    D. scp-copy-id

    E. ssh-copy-id

18. Aleena has generated her public/private key pair and put her public key in the appropriate places. She now wants to use an OpenSSH agent session so that she does not have to enter her password multiple times. What is the next command she should enter?

    A. gpg-agent

    B. ssh-copy-id

    C. ssh-add

    D. ssh-agent /bin/bash

    E. ssh

19. A system administrator, Reagan, has recently imported the public key of her friend, Aleena, using the gpg --import zer0es.pub command. Where is that key now? (Choose all that apply.)

   A. On Reagan's keyring

   B. In the zer0es.pub file

   C. In the gpg-agent

   D. In the reagan.pub file

   E. In a ~/.gnupg/ file

20. Wade wants create a digital signature. Which gpg option could he employ to do this? (Choose all that apply.)

   A. --sign

   B. --clearsign

   C. --verify

   D. --detach-sig

   E. --out

Appendix

Answers to Review Questions

Chapter 1: Exploring Linux Command-Line Tools

1. D. The /bin/sh file on Linux now typically points to a shell program, such as /bin/bash. Therefore, option D is the correct answer. The other options are all shell programs. Thus, options A, B, C, and E are incorrect choices.

2. C. The uname -r command will display only the current Linux kernel version (revision). Thus, option C is the correct answer. The uname command will display only the current operating system name, Linux, and therefore option A is a wrong answer. The echo $BASH_VERSION command will show the current version of the Bash shell. Thus, option B is also an incorrect answer. The uname -a command will display the current Linux kernel version but additional information as well, so option D is a wrong choice. The echo $SHELL command shows the current shell program being used. Therefore, option E is also an incorrect choice.

3. D. The echo \^New \^Style command will display ^New ^Style, because the backslash is a form of shell quoting that protects a single character after it. Thus the caret (^) symbol is protected and displays before each word in the output. Therefore, option D is correct. Options A, B, C, and E are incorrect answers, because these commands will not display those outputs.

4. A, C, D. The which fortytwo.sh command will search the directories listed in the $PATH environment variable for the fortytwo.sh program. If it is found, it will display the program's absolute directory reference. Thus, option A is a correct answer (and the best one too). If you already know the directory location of the fortytwo.sh program, then displaying the directory names stored in the $PATH variable via the echo $PATH command will work as well. Therefore, option C is also a correct answer. Attempting to run the program by issuing the fortytwo.sh command will also determine if the program is stored within a $PATH directory, because if it is, the program will run. On the other hand, if it is not stored in a $PATH directory, you'll receive a not found error message. Thus, option D is a correct answer as well. Displaying the file via the cat fortytwo.sh command will not help determine if the program is stored in a $PATH directory, and thus option B is a wrong answer. Attempting to run the program from a directory named /usr/bin/ also will not help you in this determination, because it is not stated as being located there. Therefore, option E is an incorrect choice as well.

5. A, C, D, E. The three modes of the vim editor are command (also called normal mode), insert (also called edit or entry mode), and ex (sometimes called colon commands) mode. Therefore, options A, C, D, and E are correct answers. The only incorrect choice for this question is option B.

6. C. The head command can use either the -n 15 switch or the -15 switch to display a file's first 15 lines. Therefore, option C is the correct answer. To display all but the last 15 lines of the file, you would need to employ the -n -15 switch, so option A is incorrect. To display all but the first 15 lines, you need to use the tail command, instead of the head

command, so option B is a wrong answer. Also, you need to use `tail` to display the last 15 lines of the file, so option D is also an incorrect answer. Option D is a wrong choice, because the command will not generate an error message in this case.

7. B. A pager utility allows you to view one text page at a time and move through the text at your own pace. Therefore, option B is the correct answer. A utility that allows you to view only the first few lines of a file would not be useful in this case, and these utilities are not called pagers. Therefore, option A is a wrong answer. While the less utility is a pager and will allow you to search through the text file, the co-worker mentioned pagers, which includes the more utility. With the more utility you cannot search through text, so option C is an incorrect choice. You do not need to filter out text in the file, and filter utilities are not called pagers, so option D is a wrong answer. A utility that allows you to view only the last few lines of a file would not be useful in this case, and these utilities are not called pagers. Therefore, option E is an incorrect choice.

8. E. You need to use the q key to exit from the less pager utility; therefore, only option E does not describe less and is the correct answer. Option A is a wrong answer, but less does not read the entire file prior to displaying the file's first page. You can also employ the up and down arrow keys to traverse the file, as well as the spacebar to move forward a page and the Esc+V key combination to move backward a page, so options B, C, and D are incorrect answers.

9. C. A text file record is considered to be a single file line that ends in a newline linefeed that is the ASCII character LF. You can see if your text file uses this end-of-line character via the `cat -E` command. Therefore, option C is the correct answer. The text file may have been corrupted, but this command does not indicate it, so option A is an incorrect choice. The text file records end in the ASCII character LF, and not NUL or $. Therefore, options B and D are incorrect. The text file records may very well contain a $ at their end, but you cannot tell via the situation description, so option E is a wrong answer.

10. E. To properly use some of the cut command options, fields must exist within each text file record. These fields are data that is separated by a delimiter that is one or more characters that create a boundary between different data items within a record. Therefore, option E best describes a delimiter and is the correct answer. Option A is made up and is a wrong answer. Option B describes an end-of-line character, such as the ASCII LF. Option C is made up and is a wrong answer. While a single space and a colon can be used as a delimiter, option D is not the best answer and is therefore a wrong choice.

11. C, D. Recall that many utilities that process text do not change the text within a file unless redirection is employed to do so. The only utilities in this list that will allow you to modify text include the text editors, vim and nano. Therefore, options C and D are the correct answers. The cut, sort, and sed utilities gather the data from a designated text file(s), modify it according to the options used, and display the modified text to standard output. The text in the file is not modified. Therefore, options A, B, and E are incorrect choices.

12. A, C. The first item output by the wc utility is the number of lines within a designated text file. Therefore, option A is correct. Option C is also correct, because the second item output by the wc utility is the number of words within a designated text file. Option B is a wrong answer, because the file contains 2,020 lines and not characters. Option D is an incorrect choice, because you do not know whether or not the Unicode subset of ASCII is used for the text file's encoding. You should always assume the last number is the number of bytes within the file. Use the -m or --chars switch on the wc command to get a character count. Therefore, the file could have 11,328 bytes in it instead of characters. Option E is also a wrong choice, because the file has 2,020 lines in it.

13. D. Option D is the best answer because a regular expression is a pattern template you define for a utility, such as grep, which uses the pattern to filter text. While you may use a series of characters in a grep *PATTERN*, they are not called regular expressions, so option A is a wrong answer. Option B is describing end-of-line characters and not regular expression characters, so it also is an incorrect answer. While the ? is used in basic regular expressions, the * is not (however, .* is used). Therefore, option C is a wrong choice. Quotation marks may be employed around a *PATTERN*, but they are not considered regular expression characters, and therefore Option E is an incorrect answer.

14. A, B, C, E. A BRE is a basic regular expression that describes certain patterns you can use with the grep command. An ERE is an extended regular expression, and it requires the use of grep -e or the egrep command. Options A, B, C, and E are all BRE patterns that can be used with the grep command, so they are correct choices. The only ERE is in option D, and therefore it is an incorrect choice.

15. E. To meet the search requirements, option E is the ERE to use with the egrep command. Therefore, option E is the correct answer. Option A will return either a record that ends with Luke or a record that ends with Laura. Thus, option A is the wrong answer. Option B is an incorrect choice, because it will return either a record that begins with Luke or a record that begins with Laura and has one character between Laura and the "Father is" phrase. Option C has the Luke and Laura portion of the ERE correct, but it allows only one character between the names and the "Father is" phrase, which will not meet the search requirements. Thus, option C is a wrong choice. Option D tries to return either a record that ends with Luke or a record that ends with Laura and ends in the "Father is" phrase, so the egrep command will display nothing. Thus, option D is an incorrect choice.

16. B. A file descriptor is a number that represents a process's open files. Therefore, option B is the correct answer. An environment variable is a variable that affects the user's environment, such as the shell prompt ($PS1). Therefore, option A is a wrong answer. Option C is also wrong, because it is a made-up answer. Option D is incorrect, because it describes only STDOUT, which has a file descriptor number of 1, and is only one of several file descriptors. A file indicator code is a symbol that indicates the file's classification, and it is generated by the ls -F command. Therefore, option E is also a wrong choice.

17. A, B. To sort the data.txt file numerically and save its output to the new file, newdata.txt, you can either use the -o switch to save the file or employ standard output redirection via the > symbol. In both cases, however, you need to use the -n switch to properly enact a numerical sort. Therefore, both options A and B are correct. Option C is a wrong answer, because the command has the newdata.txt and data.txt flipped in the command's syntax. Options D and E do not employ the -n switch, so they are incorrect answers as well.

18. D. By default, STDOUT goes to your current terminal, which is represented by the /dev/tty file. Therefore, option D is the correct answer. The /dev/ttyn file, such as /dev/tty2, may be your current terminal at a particular point in time, but /dev/tty always represents your current terminal, so option A is a wrong answer. Option C is incorrect, because it is the symbol used at the command line to redirect STDOUT away from its default behavior. The pwd command displays your present working directory, so option E is a wrong choice.

19. A. The command in option A will both display the SpaceOpera.txt file to output as well as save a copy of it to the SciFi.txt file. Therefore, Option A is the correct answer. Option B is a wrong answer, because it will only put a copy of SpaceOpera.txt into the SciFi.txt file. Option C is an incorrect choice, because this will display the SpaceOpera.txt file to output, and put any error messages into the SciFi.txt file. The cat command in option D will display only one text file after another. It will not save a copy of the original file, so option D is a wrong answer. Option E is a wrong choice, because it will put a copy of SpaceOpera.txt into the SciFi.txt file and include any error messages that are generated.

20. D. The /dev/null file is also called the black hole, because anything you put into it cannot be retrieved. If you do not wish to see any error messages while issuing a command, you can redirect STDERR into it. Thus, option D is the correct answer. Options A through C are wrong answers because they perform redirection to a file called BlackHole, instead of /dev/null. Option E is also incorrect, because it redirects STDOUT to the /dev/null file, and any error messages will be displayed.

Chapter 2: Managing Software and Processes

1. A, B, D, and E. A systems package manager database typically contains information on application files as well as their directory locations, software versions, and any library dependencies. Thus, options A, B, D, and E are all correct answers. The database does not track which username installed the software. Therefore, option C is an incorrect choice.

2. E. The CentOS Linux distribution uses the Red Hat package management system, which uses .rpm files, so option E is correct. The .deb filename extension is used to identify Debian-based package management files, so option A is a wrong answer. ZYpp is a package manager but not a file extension. Therefore, option B is also an incorrect answer. dpkg is a command-line utility for installing and managing .deb package files, so option C is a wrong choice. And yum is a utility for installing RPM packages from a Red Hat repository. Thus, option D is also an incorrect choice.

3. C, E. The yum and dnf programs are used to install .rpm packages from Red Hat–based repositories, so options C and E are correct answers. The dpkg and apt-get programs are used for installing .deb files on Debian-based package management systems, so options A and D are incorrect. The zypper program is used to install .rpm packages from openSUSE repositories. Therefore, option B is an incorrect choice.

4. A. Red Hat–based package management systems use the yum program to retrieve packages from repositories, so Scott needs to add the third-party URL configuration to the /etc/yum.repos.d/ directory, making option A correct. The /etc/apt/sources.list file is used by Debian-based package management systems to define repository locations, not Red Hat–based systems, so option B is incorrect. The /usr/lib/ folder is used for storing shared library files on a Linux system, so option C is incorrect, whereas the /bin/ directory is used for storing binary application files, so option D is also incorrect. While the /etc/ folder is typically used to store configuration files, it is not used to configure repository locations, so option E is incorrect.

5. C, D. Both the rpm2cpio and cpio utilities are needed to extract the files from an .rpm package file. Therefore, options C and D are the correct answers. The cpio2rpm command is made up, and thus option A is a wrong answer. The rpm and yum commands are not involved in this process. Therefore, options B and E are incorrect choices.

6. D. The dpkg program is used to install .deb package files on Debian-based systems, so option D is correct. The rpm, yum, dnf, and zypper programs are all tools used for Red Hat–based package management systems, not Debian-based systems, so options A, B, C, and E are all incorrect.

7. A. To list currently installed packages with missing dependencies, Tony should issue the apt-cache unmet command. Therefore, option A is the correct answer. The apt-cache stats command will display package statistics, so option B is a wrong answer. The apt-cache showpkg command lists information about a package passed to it as an argument, so option C is also an incorrect answer. The apt-cache search command displays packages that match the specified argument. Thus, option D is a wrong choice. The apt-cache depends will display dependencies required for a package but not whether or not they are unmet. Therefore, option E is an incorrect choice.

8. C. You can go through the configuration process again via the dpkg-reconfigure utility and fix your mistakes. Thus, option C is the correct answer. While you could purge or uninstall the package and then reinstall it, those are not the best choices. Therefore, options A and B are incorrect answers. The debconf-show utility allows you to view a package's configuration but not change it. Thus, option D is an incorrect answer. You cannot reconfigure the package via the dpkg or apt-get utilities, so option E is a wrong answer as well.

9. B. Steve should use the ldconfig command to update the system's library cache. Thus, option B is the correct answer. The ldd utility will display any libraries used by the program name passed to it as an argument, but it does not update the cache. Therefore, option A is a wrong answer. The ldcache utility is made up. Thus, option C is also an incorrect answer. The ld.so and ld-linux-x86-64.so.2 are both dynamic linker/loaders, but they do not update the library cache. Therefore, options D and E are both incorrect choices.

10. C, D, E. The /etc/ld.so.conf.d/ directory, LD_LIBRARY_PATH environment variable, and the /lib* and /usr/lib*/ folders are all potential locations where library file locations may be stored. Thus, options C, D, and E are correct answers. The /usr/bin*/ directories do not hold library file locations. Therefore, option A is a wrong answer. The

/ld.so.conf file does not exist, though the /etc/ld.so.conf file does and it also holds library file locations. Because the wrong directory name was used for the file, option B is an incorrect choice.

11. A, C, D. The GNU ps command in Linux supports parameters that were supported by the legacy BSD and Unix ps command, along with new options created by GNU, so options A, C, and D are correct. There are no Linux style options used by the ps command, so option B is incorrect. The ps command doesn't support numeric options, so option E is also incorrect.

12. D. With no command-line options, the GNU ps command displays only processes run by the current shell, so option D is correct. To display all processes running on a specific terminal, you need to add the -t option, so option A is incorrect. To display all active processes, you must add the -A option, so option B is incorrect. To display the sleeping processes, you need to use the -ef option, so option C is incorrect. To display all processes run by the current user account, you need to add the -x option, so option E is incorrect.

13. A. The top command displays the currently running processes on the system and updates every 3 seconds, so option A is correct. The ps command displays currently running processes but doesn't update in real time, so option B is incorrect. The lsof command displays files currently opened by processes but not the processes themselves, so option C is incorrect. The free utility only shows memory statistics. Therefore, option D is a wrong answer. The uptime command shows system load but not CPU utilization. Thus, option E is an incorrect answer as well.

14. E. The S command displays the processes based on the cumulative CPU time for each process, so option E is correct. The l command displays the processes based on the load average, so option A is incorrect. The F command allows you to select the field used to sort the display, so option B is incorrect. The r command reverses the sort order of the display, so option C is a wrong choice. The y command highlights running tasks, so option D is an incorrect answer as well.

15. D. The GNU Screen utility employs the screen commands, and the screen -ls command will display any detached windows belonging to Natasha along with their window IDs. Therefore, option D is the correct answer. The screen command by itself creates a new screen window, so option A is a wrong answer. The tmux ls command is associated with tmux windows and not GNU Screen windows, so option C is also an incorrect answer. The Ctrl+A key combination followed by the D key will detach you from a screen window you are currently using. Therefore, option E is an incorrect choice as well.

16. B. The ampersand character (&) tells the shell to start the command in background mode from the console session, so Option B is correct. The greater-than sign (>) redirects the output from the command to a file, so option A is incorrect. The pipe symbol (|) redirects the output from the command to another command, so option C is incorrect. The double greater-than sign (>>) appends the output from the command to a file, so option D is incorrect. The percentage sign (%) is used for identifying background jobs by their number. Therefore, option E is incorrect.

17. A. The Ctrl+Z key combination pauses the job currently running in foreground mode on the console session, so option A is correct. The Ctrl+C key combination stops the job currently running in foreground in the console session, not pause it, so option B is incorrect. The nohup command disconnects a job from the console session, but doesn't pause the job, so option D is incorrect. The ampersand sign (&) runs a job in background mode in the console session, so option D is incorrect. The fg command resumes a stopped job in foreground mode, so option E is incorrect.

18. B. Scott should first employ the jobs -l command to see all his current background jobs. Therefore, option B is the correct answer. The ps -ef command will show him his background processes, but it will show all the other processes on the system as well and make it more difficult than necessary to find the information he needs to stop his background job. Thus, option A is a wrong answer. The kill %1 command should not be issued until Scott confirms that the program is indeed running with the job ID of 1. Thus, option C is also an incorrect answer. The kill commands in options D and E would not kill Scott's job, because they are not using a percent sign, which tells the system to attempt to stop the process with the PID of 1 (and, if successful, this would be a bad thing). Thus, options D and E are incorrect choices.

19. C. The nice command allows you to specify the niceness level for an application, which modifies its priority, so option B is correct. The renice command allows you to change the niceness level of an application that's already running, but not one that hasn't started yet, so option A is a wrong answer. The bash utility is not for changing niceness levels, so option B is a wrong choice as well. The nohup command prevents a job from processing the hang-up signal but has nothing to do with niceness levels, so option D is an incorrect answer. The lower command is made up, so option E is an incorrect choice as well.

20. D. The kill command allows you to stop an application that's already running by specifying its process ID, so option D is correct. The killall command allows you send a signal to all the processes you own running a particular utility, so option A is a wrong answer. The pkill command allows you to stop an application, but not by specifying its process ID, so option B is an incorrect choice. TERM is a signal that is sent by default by these utilities and not a command. Therefore, option C is a wrong answer. The pgrep command allows you to display running applications based on a search term for the application name but not stop them, so option E is an incorrect choice.

Chapter 3: Configuring Hardware

1. A. The workstation firmware looks for the boot loader program to load an operating system. The fsck program (option B) is used to check and repair damage to hard drives, so it isn't useful until after the Linux system has started. The Windows operating system only starts after a Windows boot loader program can run, so option C is incorrect. The mount program is a Linux tool for attaching a partition to the virtual directory, which isn't available until after the Linux system starts, so option D is also incorrect. The mkinitrd program is used to create an initrd RAM disk used for booting, but it isn't run when the workstation starts up, so option E is incorrect.

2. B. The workstation firmware looks at the first sector of the first hard drive to load the boot loader program. This is called the MBR, so option B is correct. The boot loader program itself can use the chainloader feature to look for another boot loader in a boot partition, but the firmware can't do that, so option D is incorrect. Option A specifies the configuration directory used to store the GRUB configuration file and the kernel image file, but the actual GRUB boot loader program can't be stored there. Option C specifies the common log file directory, but that doesn't contain the GRUB boot loader program. Option E also specifies a common Linux configuration file directory, but it's not used to store the GRUB boot loader program that the firmware can access.

3. A, B, C, D, and E. The BIOS firmware can look in multiple locations for a boot loader program. Most commonly it looks at the internal hard drive installed on the system; however, if none is found, it can search other places. Most workstations allow you to boot from an external hard drive or from a DVD drive. Modern workstations now also provide the option to boot from a USB memory stick inserted into a USB port on the workstation. Finally, many workstations provide the PXE boot option, which allows the workstation to boot remotely from a network server.

4. A. The master boot record (MBR) is located in only one place: on the first sector of the first hard drive on the workstation; thus option A is the only correct answer. The boot partition in any hard drive may contain a boot loader, but it is not the MBR, which is run first by the firmware; thus option B is incorrect. The other locations are not valid locations for the MBR, so options C, D, and E are all incorrect.

5. D. The ESP is stored in the /boot/efi directory on Linux systems. The UEFI firmware always looks for the /boot/efi directory for boot loader programs, so option D is correct. The /etc directory is used to store application and system configuration files, not boot loader programs, so option B is incorrect. The /var directory is used to store variable files such as log files, not bootable files, so option C is incorrect. Option E, the /boot/grub file, is used in GRUB Legacy and GRUB2 to store the boot loader configuration files, as well as the kernel image files. However, it is not used to store the boot loader files themselves, so option E is incorrect.

6. B. The UEFI firmware method has replaced the BIOS in most IBM-compatible computers, so option B is correct. FTP, PXE, NFS, and HTTPS are not firmware methods but methods for loading the Linux boot loader, so options A, C, D, and E are all incorrect.

7. A. The solid-state drive (SSD) storage device uses an integrated circuit to store data, so option A is correct. SATA, SCSI, and PATA are drive connection types and not storage device types, so options B, C, and E are all incorrect. The hard disk drive (HDD) storage devices use disk platters and a read/write head to store data, not an integrated circuit, so option D is incorrect.

8. B. Linux creates files named sdx in the /dev directory for SCSI devices. For the second SCSI device, Linux would create the file /dev/sdb, so option B is correct. The /dev/hdb file would represent the second HDD drive connected to the system, so option A is incorrect, and /dev/sda would represent the first SCSI device connected to the system, so option E is incorrect. Options C and D both represent partitions and not entire drives, so they are both incorrect.

9. C. The lvcreate program creates a logical volume from multiple partitions that you can use as a single logical device to build a file system and mount it to the virtual directory, so option C is correct. The mkfs program creates a filesystem on a partition but doesn't create a logical volume, so option A is incorrect. The pvcreate program identifies a physical volume from a partition but doesn't create the logical volume, so option B is incorrect. The fdisk program creates and modifies physical partitions, not logical volumes, so option D is incorrect. The vgcreate program creates a volume group for grouping physical partitions but doesn't create the logical volume, so option E is incorrect.

10. B, C, D, and E. RAID 4, RAID 5, and RAID 10 all use disk striping with parity, allowing them to recover from a single disk failure, whereas RAID 1 utilizes disk mirroring to recover from a single disk failure, so options B, C, D, and E are all correct. RAID 0 utilizes disk striping across multiple disks for increased performance but can't recover if one of those drives fails, so option A is the only incorrect answer.

11. B. The GNU gparted program provides a graphical window for managing device partitions, so option B is correct. The gdisk, fdisk, and parted programs are all command-line partitioning tools, so options A, C, and D are all incorrect. The fsck program is a tool to repair filesystems, not create or modify partitions, so option E is incorrect.

12. D. The p command displays the current partition table for the hard drive, so option D is correct. The v command verifies the partition table but doesn't display it, so option A is incorrect. The n command creates a new partition; it doesn't display the current partition table, so option B is incorrect. The m command displays the help menu; it doesn't display the current partition table, so option C is incorrect. The d command deletes an existing partition; it doesn't display the current partition table, so option E is incorrect.

13. A. Linux uses mount points to insert a filesystem on a storage device to the virtual directory, so option A is correct. Unlike Windows, Linux doesn't assign drive letters to storage devices, so option B is incorrect. The /dev files are used as raw devices for storage devices; they don't access the filesystem, so option C is incorrect. The /proc and /sys directories are used by the kernel to display and change storage device information, not to add the filesystem to the virtual directory, so option E is incorrect.

14. D. The ext filesystem was the original filesystem used in Linux, and ext4 is the latest version of it, so option D is correct. This makes option C incorrect. The reiserFS and btrFS filesystems are specialty filesystems created separate from the ext filesystem, so options A and B are also incorrect. The nfs filesystem was created to allow sharing files and directories across networks and wasn't the original Linux filesystem, so option E is incorrect.

15. B. The mkfs program allows you to create a new filesystem on a partition, so option B is correct. The fdisk, gdisk, and parted programs are used to create or modify partitions, not to work with the filesystem installed on them, so options A, D, and E are all incorrect. The fsck program repairs filesystems but can't create them, so option C is incorrect.

16. C. The swap filesystem type creates a virtual memory swap area for the Linux kernel to use to create virtual memory, which augments the physical memory on the system, so option

C is correct. The ext3, btrfs, and ext4 filesystems are all Linux storage filesystems, not memory filesystems, so options A, B, and D are all incorrect. The NTFS filesystem is used for Windows compatibility, not memory storage, so option E is incorrect.

17. B. The mount program allows you to insert the filesystem on a partition into the virtual directory, so option B is correct. The fsck program repairs filesystems but doesn't insert them into the virtual directory, so option A is incorrect. The umount program removes filesystems from the virtual directory and does not insert them, so option C is incorrect. The fdisk program partitions devices but doesn't create filesystems or insert them into the virtual directory, so option D is incorrect. The mkfs program creates filesystems but doesn't insert them into the virtual directory, so option E is also incorrect.

18. B. The umount command allows you to specify either the partition or the location in the virtual directory to remove from the virtual directory, so option B is correct. The mount command is used to add a new mounted partition, not to remove an existing one, so option A is incorrect. Option C, the fsck command, is used to fix a hard drive that is corrupted and can't be mounted; it doesn't actually mount the drive itself. The dmesg command in option D is used to view boot messages for the system, which may tell you where a hard drive is appended to the virtual directory, but it doesn't actually do the appending. Option E, the mkinitramfs command, creates an initrd RAM disk and doesn't directly handle mounting hard drives to the virtual directory.

19. A. The fsck program repairs corrupted filesystems, so option A is correct. The mount program inserts filesystems into the virtual directory, but it can't repair them, so option B is incorrect. The umount program removes filesystems from the virtual directory but can't repair them, so option C is also incorrect. The fdisk program creates and modifies partitions, but it doesn't work with filesystems, so option D is incorrect. The mkfs program creates filesystems but doesn't repair them, so option E is incorrect.

20. C. The du command displays the disk usage by directory, allowing you to easily check the HOME directories of all user accounts and determine which user has the most disk space, so option C is correct. The df command displays total disk usage by partition, not directory, so it wouldn't work for singling out a specific user, making option A incorrect. The iostat, lsblk, and blkid commands display disk information based on partitions and blocks, not users, so options B, D, and E are all incorrect.

Chapter 4: Managing Files

1. A, B, and D. When choosing a filename to create on a Linux system, shell metacharacters such as an asterisk (*) and an ampersand (&), as well as spaces, should be avoided. Thus, options A, B, and D are correct choices. You can employ without worry a dash (-) or an underscore (_), so options C and E are incorrect choices.

2. E. Due to wildcard expansion, the ls *data*.txt command will list all the filenames that contain the word data and have the .txt file extension in the present working directory. Thus, option E is the correct answer. The ls data*.txt and ls data?.txt commands will list only filenames that *start* with the word data and have the .txt file extension in the present working directory. Therefore, options A and B are wrong answers. The ls *data .txt command will list only filenames that *end* with the word data and have the .txt file extension in the present working directory. Thus, option C is a wrong choice. The ls ?data?.txt command will list only filenames that have one alphanumeric character before the word data and one after (as well as have the .txt file extension in the present working directory). Therefore, option D is an incorrect choice as well.

3. C. Using a bracketed wildcard, the ls File[0-9] command will list all the filenames that start with the word File, end with a single number, and have no file extension. Therefore, option C is the correct answer. The ls File? command will list all the filenames that start with the word File, end with a single number or letter, and have no file extension. Thus, option A is a wrong answer. The ls File* command will list all the filenames that start with the word File and end with anything. Therefore, option B is also an incorrect answer. The ls File[^0-9] command uses the caret symbol (^), which negates the bracket wildcard, and thus will find the files that start with the word File but end with anything but a single number. Thus, option C is a wrong choice. The ls File[a-z] command will find the files that start with the word File but end with a letter. Therefore, option E is also an incorrect choice.

4. C. Option C will append an indicator code of / to every directory name, and therefore it is the best choice. The mkdir -v command creates a directory and lets you know whether or not it was successful, but it does not indicate directories, so option A is a wrong answer. The ls command only displays file and directory names, so option B is also a wrong answer. The ls -i command will display filenames along with their inode number, but it does not indicate directories, so option D is incorrect. While option E will work on some distributions to produce a long listing that can indicate directories, this command is not aliased to ls -l on every distribution, and therefore it is not the best command to use.

5. B. The -d switch on the ls command will allow you to view a directory file's metadata instead of seeing metadata for the files that exist within that directory. Therefore, option B is the correct choice. Option A is a wrong answer because the -a switch forces the ls command to display hidden files, which are files starting with a dot (.). The -F switch will append an indicator code to each file but not allow you to view a directory's metadata, so option C is a wrong choice. The -l option is already being employed because you are viewing metadata, so it does not need to be added. Therefore, option D is an incorrect answer. The -R switch allows you to view file information recursively through a directory tree, and thus option E is also a wrong choice.

6. A. The mkdir -v command creates a directory and lets you know whether or not it was successful, so option A is the correct answer. The touch command creates blank and empty files, so option B is incorrect. The cp -R command will recursively copy an entire directory full of files to another directory. Since you do not know if the directory TheDir is empty or not, you most likely did not use this command. Option C is a wrong answer. The mv -r command will rename a directory to a new directory name. Again, you do not know if the directory TheDir is empty or not, so you most likely did not use this command, and thus, option D is also a wrong answer. Option E is an incorrect answer because the rmdir command deletes empty directions.

7. E. The `rm -rI` command will recursively delete the files in the /home/Zoe directory tree, and it will ask before it starts, so you know you are deleting the correct tree. Therefore, option E is the best answer. Option A is incorrect because the `cp` command simply copies files. It does not remove them. Option B is incorrect because not only is part of the directory name using the wrong case, but there is no verification the correct directory is being moved to the black hole device, /dev/null/. The `rm -Rf` command would work, but it is not the best command to use because it does not ask before it starts, so you do not know if you are deleting the correct tree. In fact, the `-f` option suppresses error messages, so option C is wrong. Option D would also work, but it is not the best answer because it employs the `-i` option. If Zoe has years of files in her home directory, you may be sitting there for a long time deleting files due to the fact that you must confirm each file before it is deleted. Therefore, option D is an incorrect answer.

8. E. The `tar` options `-cJvf` will create a tarball using the highest compression utility, `xz`, and allow the administrator to view the files via the verbose option while they are being copied into the compressed archive. Thus, option E is the correct answer. The switches in options A and B perform extracts (`-x`) and do not create, so they are wrong answers. The only thing wrong with option C is that it employs `gzip` compression via the `-z` switch, so it is an incorrect choice. Option D leaves out the verbose switch, so it too is an incorrect choice.

9. A. The `dd` command in option A will accomplish the job correctly. Therefore, it is the correct answer. The `dd` commands in options B through D have the input and output files flip-flopped, so they would destroy the data on the /dev/sdc drive. Therefore, options B, C, and D are wrong answers. The `dd` command in option E would wipe the /dev/sdc drive using zeros. Therefore, option E is also an incorrect choice.

10. B, C, E. The `zip`, `tar`, and `dd` utilities all can be used to create data backups. Therefore, options B, C, and E are correct answers. The `gzip` utility can be used after a backup is created or employed through `tar` options to compress a backup, so option A is a wrong answer. The `bzcat` utility allows you to temporarily decompress a file that had been compressed with the `bzip2` command and display the file's contents to STDOUT. Thus, option D is also an incorrect choice.

11. B. Option B is the correct answer because the hard links will prevent the three other command-line interface users from accidentally deleting the data. If they delete their link's name, they will not delete the data. Option A is an incorrect choice because hard-linked files must reside on the same filesystem together. Option C is also an incorrect choice because if you do not provide the symbolic links to the other three data users, they will have to access the data file directly and could delete it. While creating symbolic links will protect the data by letting it reside on a different filesystem, if it is mission-critical data the filesystem employed should be rigorous enough to protect the data, and therefore your only threat would be human. Thus, option D is an incorrect answer. Symbolic linked files do not share an inode number. Therefore, option E is an incorrect choice.

12. B. The `chown` command allows you to set both the owner and group assigned to a file, so option B is correct. The `chmod` command allows you to change the permissions for the file but not the owner of the file, so option A is incorrect. The `ln` command creates hard links (soft links if you add the `-s` option) but not owners of files, so option C is incorrect. `owner` is a category of permissions (also called *world*) but not a command. Therefore, option D is incorrect. The chgrp command allows you to change the group assigned to a file but not the owner, so option E is also incorrect.

13. C, D. Notice that the only permission to remove is in the owner (u) permissions and it is the execute (x) permission. To achieve the desired permission string, you could employ octal mode (664) or symbolic mode (u-x or u=rw). The chmod u-x endgame.txt and chmod 664 endgame.txt commands will set the endgame.txt file's permission string from rwxrw-r-- to rw-rw-r-- Thus, options C and D are the correct answers. The umask command deals with a file's permissions before it is created, so option A is a wrong answer. The chmod o-x endgame.txt command is using symbol mode and it would take away the execute permission from the other permissions, not the owner permissions. Thus, option B is an incorrect answer. The chmod o=rw endgame.txt command would have the exact same effect as the command in option B, so option E is an incorrect choice as well.

14. B. By default, directories are created with octal mode 777, which gives them a permission string of rwxrwxrwx. The umask setting takes away permissions. Its first number is for special permissions (SUID, SGID, and sticky bit). Its next three numbers correspond to the standard permission categories—owner, group, and other. Thus, to end up with a directory that has a permission string of rwxrwxrw (776), umask needs to be set to 0001. Thus, option B is the correct answer. The 0007 setting would end up with a permission string of ---------. Thus, option A is a wrong answer. The 0776 setting would result in a permission string for directories of --------x. Thus, option C is a wrong choice. The 7770 umask setting would end up with a ------rwx permission string, so option D is also an incorrect answer. The 1000 setting would result in an rwxrwxrwx permission string for created directories. Therefore, option E is also an incorrect choice.

15. B. The Set User ID bit (SUID) allows all users to run applications as the root user account, so option B is correct. The sticky bit doesn't allow users to run the file with root privileges, so option A is incorrect. The SGID bit doesn't allow users to run files as the root user account, so option C is incorrect. The Execute and Write bits set those permissions for the standard category of users, groups, or others. They don't allow users to run files as the root user account, so both options D and E are incorrect.

16. C. The sticky bit assigned to a directory restricts all of the files in that directory so that only the file owner can delete the file, even if a user account is in the group that has write permissions, so option C is correct. The SUID bit allows a standard user to run an application with the file owner permissions but doesn't block users from deleting shared files, so option A is incorrect. The SGID bit is used on a directory to ensure all files created in the directory have the same group as the directory, but it doesn't prevent users in that group from deleting files, so option B is incorrect. The Read and Write standard permission bits control access to read to a file or write to a file, but they don't block users from deleting a file, so options D and E are both incorrect.

17. E. By default, the locate command uses file globbing, which adds wildcards to the pattern you enter. Thus, conf is turned into *conf*. Therefore, option E best explains the results and is the correct answer. The locate command will search for both file and directory names for specified patterns unless options are provided to modify this behavior. Therefore, option A is an incorrect answer. The locate command does not use the -d skip switch (the grep command does use it, though), and thus option B is a wrong answer. Because the command operated normally, there is not a problem with the locate database, so option C is an incorrect choice. Also, a regular expression switch was not used in the locate command, so option D is also a wrong choice.

18. D. When using the locate command, the *path* argument is listed first, which is a starting point directory. The find utility will search through that directory and all its subdirectories (recursively) for the file or files you seek. Also, the -name switch allows you to search for a file by name, so option D is the correct answer. Option A is incorrect because there is no -r switch, and no need for one. Option B is not the best command to use in this case because the starting directory is /, which is the root of the virtual directory structure. It is much better to start at the /etc directory, since the file is most likely located somewhere in that directory tree. Using the -maxdepth switch may hamper the search because it sets the subdirectory level to stop the search. Therefore, option C is a wrong answer. Option E is an incorrect choice, because the *path* and file name are flip-flopped and the -name switch is missing.

19. E. The find / -nouser command will search through the entire virtual directory structure looking for any files that do not have a username associated with them. Since Michael's account and home directory were deleted, any files he owned out in the virtual directory structure will not have a username associated with them—only a user ID (UID). Thus, option E is the best answer. Option A is incorrect because the -name switch is for filenames, not usernames. Option B is also an incorrect answer, because the -user switch is used to search for files owned by a particular account. Since Michael's account was deleted, his username would no longer be associated with any files. Option C is a wrong answer because you do not know when his files may have experienced data changes, as indicated by the -mmin switch, and thus this is a bad method for trying to identify them. Option D is an incorrect choice because the find command is starting the search process in the user's home directory instead of the root (/) of the virtual directory structure.

20. B. The whereis command displays a command's program binaries, manual pages, as well as source code files. Therefore, option B is the correct answer. The which command will display only a command's program location, so option A is a wrong answer. The locate command will search based on a pattern, but if the command's source code file doesn't contain the command's name, then it will not work. Thus, option C is also an incorrect answer. Depending on the search metadata you employ with the find command, you may or may not find the command's source code files. The whereis command is much faster for this search. Therefore, option D is a wrong choice. The type utility can show how the shell will interpret the stonetracker command but not find its source code files. Thus, option E is also an incorrect choice.

Chapter 5: Booting, Initializing, and Virtualizing Linux

1. E. The kernel ring buffer is an area in memory reserved for storing output messages as the Linux system boots, so option E is correct. BIOS is firmware, not an area in system memory. Therefore, option A is a wrong answer. The GRUB boot loader is a program, not a memory area. Thus, option B is a wrong choice. The MBR is a location on a hard drive, so option C is incorrect. The initrd RAM disk is an area in memory, but it doesn't store the boot messages as the system starts. Therefore, option D is also an incorrect answer.

2.   B, C, D, E. Typically Debian-based systems store the boot messages in the /var/log/boot file, whereas Red Hat–based systems store them in the /var/log/boot.log file. Therefore, options B and C are correct answers. The kernel ring buffer, which you can view shortly after boot time via the dmesg command, contains boot messages from the kernel. Thus, option D is also a correct answer. The jounrnalctl utility, if available on your system, will display boot messages as well. Therefore, option E is an additional correct answer. The /var/log/kernel.log is a made-up filename, so option A is the only wrong choice.

3.   A. A system's firmware looks for the boot loader program in order to load an operating system. Thus, option A is the correct answer. BIOS is firmware (and it may be the firmware looking for the boot loader program), so option B is a wrong answer. UEFI is a firmware interface (and it also may be the one looking for the boot loader program), so option C is also an incorrect answer. There is no command named *POST*, though you may be thinking of the Power-On Self-Test that the firmware conducts prior to searching for a boot loader. Thus, option D is a wrong choice. The init program is run by the loaded Linux kernel, so the system firmware, so option E is also an incorrect choice.

4.   B. The BIOS firmware looks at the first sector of the first hard drive to load the boot loader program. This is called the master boot record, so option B is correct. The /boot/grub/ directory is the configuration folder used to store the GRUB (or GRUB2) configuration file and the kernel image file, so option A is a wrong answer. The /var/log/ directory is the common log file folder, but that doesn't contain the GRUB boot loader program. Thus, option C is also a wrong choice. The boot loader program itself can use the chainloader feature to look for another boot loader in a boot partition, but the firmware can't do that, so option D is incorrect. The /etc/ directory is a common Linux configuration file folder, but it's not used to store the GRUB boot loader program that the firmware can access. Thus, option E is also an incorrect choice.

5.   D. The ESP is stored in the /boot/efi/ directory on Linux systems, so option D is correct. The /boot/grub/ directory is used by GRUB Legacy and GRUB2 to store the boot loader configuration files, as well as the kernel image files. Thus, option B is a wrong answer. The /boot/grub2/ directory is sometimes used by GRUB2 to store the boot loader configuration files and kernel image files. Therefore, option C is a wrong answer as well. The /boot/esp/ directory is made up, and thus option E is also an incorrect choice.

6.   E. The UEFI specification doesn't require a specific extension for UEFI bootloader files. However, it has become somewhat common in Linux to use the .efi file extension to identify them. Thus, option E is the correct answer. Option A and option D specify file extensions used to identify GRUB2 (option A) and GRUB Legacy (option D) configuration files, not UEFI boot loader files, so they are both incorrect. Option C specifies the .lst file extension, which is also used for GRUB Legacy configuration files, so it too is incorrect. The .uefi file extension is not used in Linux, so option B is incorrect.

7.   A. The GRUB Legacy configuration files are stored in the /boot/grub directory, so option A is correct. The /boot/grub2 directory is sometimes employed by GRUB2, if GRUB

Legacy is also installed on the system. However, the system admin would not find her GRUB Legacy configuration files in that directory, so option B is incorrect. Option C, the /boot/efi directory, is used to store UEFI bootloader programs, not GRUB configuration files, so it is incorrect. Even though configuration files are often stored in the /etc directory tree, boot loader configuration files do not reside there. Therefore, options D and E are incorrect choices.

8. C. For GRUB Legacy the configuration line he should change will start with the title word. This line sets the boot menu choice displayed, so option C is the correct answer. The hiddenmenu is a global GRUB Legacy directive that prevents the menu choices from displaying. Thus, option A is the wrong answer. The line starting with kernel defines the kernel image to load in GRUB Legacy file, so option B is also an incorrect answer. While the line starting with menuentry does set the boot menu choice displayed, it is used in a GRUB2 configuration file. Therefore, option D is also a wrong choice. The rootnoverify is used in a GRUB Legacy configuration file, but it is used to define non-Linux boot partitions. Thus, option E is an incorrect choice.

9. D. The grub-install command installs GRUB Legacy into MBR, so option D is correct. The grub-mkconfig and grub2-mkconfig commands are used in GRUB2 systems to create an updated configuration file, but not in GRUB Legacy systems, so options A and B are incorrect. The update-grub utility is used to call grub-mkconfig on Ubuntu distros. Therefore, option C is also a wrong choice. After making changes to the GRUB Legacy configuration file, you don't need to reinstall GRUB Legacy in the MBR, because it reads the configuration file each time it runs. However, initially GRUB Legacy must be installed, so option E is an incorrect answer.

10. B. The set root=(hd1,2) line properly specifies in a GRUB2 configuration that the root partition, the /boot directory, is on /dev/sdb2. Therefore, option B is the correct answer. The root line is used in a GRUB Legacy configuration file, so options A and D are wrong answers. The root partition is the location of the /boot directory and not the location of the root of the filesystem (/), so option C is a wrong choice. The set root=(hd1,1) line would indicate that the /boot directory was on /dev/sda2 and not /dev/sdb2, so option E is also an incorrect choice.

11. C. To enable kernel debugging, after Rey reaches the GRUB2 boot menu, she should edit the appropriate boot menu entry, find the line starting with linux*, go to the end of the line, add a space, and then type **debug** to pass the kernel parameter, which will start debugging mode. Finally, she needs to press Ctrl+X to start booting the system with the modified entry. Therefore, option C is the correct answer. Option A has everything correct, except for pressing Ctrl+C, which would put Rey into the GRUB2 command line, so option A is a wrong answer. Option B uses a science fiction ability, instead of a real set of Linux steps, so it is also a wrong choice. Options D and E are incorrect, because the kernel line is in GRUB Legacy configurations and not in GRUB2 menu entries. Thus, they are incorrect choices as well.

12. A, B, C, D, E. This is a tricky question, because all of these statements are true concerning systemd service units. Therefore, options A, B, C, D, and E are correct choices. It makes you realize that systemd managed systems are very flexible.

13. A. There is no `runlevel7.target`. The legitimate systemd targets, which provide backward SysVinit compatibility, go from `runlevel0.target` through `runlevel6.target`. Therefore, option A is the correct answer. The `emergency.target` is a special systemd target unit used to enter emergency mode. When your system goes into emergency mode, the system only mounts the root filesystem and mounts it as read-only. Therefore, option B is a systemd target unit and not a correct answer. The `graphical.target` is a legitimate systemd target, which provides multiple users with access to the system, via local terminals and/or through the network and offers a GUI. Thus, option C is an incorrect choice. The `multi-user.target` is also a legitimate systemd target, just like the `graphical.target`, except it does not offer a GUI. Therefore, option D is also a wrong answer. The `rescue .target` is like `emergency.target`; however, it mounts the root filesystem for reading and writing. Therefore, option E is an incorrect choice.

14. C. Any modified systemd service unit configuration file should be stored in the `/etc/systemd/system/` directory. This will prevent any package upgrades from overwriting it and keep the directory precedence from using the unmodified service unit copy, which may reside in the `/usr/lib/systemd/system/` directory. Therefore, option C is the correct answer. The directories in options A and B are made up, and therefore those options are wrong answers. The `/usr/lib/systemd/system/` directory should store only unmodified unit files, which are provided by default, and thus option D is an incorrect answer. The `/run/system/systemd/` directory is made up, and therefore option E is also an incorrect choice.

15. A. The best command to make the modified file take immediate effect for the openSSH service is `systemctl reload`. This command will load the service configuration file of the running designated service without stopping the service. Therefore, option A is the best answer. A `daemon-reload` command will load the unit configuration file and not the service configuration file. Thus, option B is a wrong answer. The `restart` command will stop and immediately restart the service. Although this will load the modified service configuration file, it will also disrupt the service for current service users. Therefore, option C is not the best answer and a wrong one. The `mask` command prevents a particular service from starting. Thus, option D is a wrong choice. The `unmask` command undoes the mask command's effects, and thus option E is also an incorrect answer.

16. B. To change the system's default target, you need to employ the `systemctl set-default` command, passing the target name as an argument and using super user privileges. Therefore, option B is the correct answer. The `get-default` command will show you the system's current default target. Thus, option A is a wrong answer. The `isolate` command is used to jump to new targets and not set default targets. Thus, option C is an incorrect choice. The `is-enabled` command displays `enabled` for any service that is configured to start at system boot and `disabled` for any service that is not configured to start at system boot. It deals only with services, and therefore option D is a wrong choice. The `is-active` command also deals only with services, and therefore option E is also an incorrect answer.

17. C, E. Debian-based Linux distributions that use SysVinit use only runlevels from 0 through 2. The `runlevel` command shows the previous runlevel, or N for newly booted. Therefore, the only options that this `runlevel` command would show on an older Debian-based Linux distribution system, which uses SysVinit, are options C and E. Therefore, those options are correct. Option A is incorrect, because it shows 5 as the current runlevel, and Debian-based distros don't use that runlevel. Option B is also incorrect, because it shows 5 as the current runlevel. Option D is incorrect because it shows 3 as the current runlevel, and the Debian-based distros do not use that runlevel either.

18. A. For SysVinit systems, the default runlevel is stored within the /etc/inittab file within the initdefault record. Therefore, option A is the correct answer. /etc/rc.d is a directory and not a file. Thus, option B is a wrong answer. The rc file is a script that can reside in either the /etc/init.d/ or the /etc/rc.d/ directory. It runs the scripts that start the various system services when jumping runlevels or booting the system. However, this script does not contain any information concerning the default runlevel. Therefore, options C and D are incorrect choices. The /etc/rc.local file allows you to issue certain commands or run any scripts as soon as system initialization is completed. However, this script also does not contain any information concerning the default runlevel. Thus, option E is an incorrect answer.

19. D. The wall command will only send a message to users who are currently logged into the system, using a tty terminal or terminal emulator, and have their message status set to "yes." The who -T command fits the need, because it will display all the currently logged-in users and their terminal ID as well as provide a + by their username if their message status is set to yes. Thus, option D is the correct answer. The systemctl reboot command will reboot the system, not demonstrate who will receive a wall message, so option A is a wrong answer. The shutdown command will override the message status of users, so it is not a good choice for determining who receives wall communications. Therefore, option B is also an incorrect answer. The reboot command also reboots the system, but it does not demonstrate who will receive a wall message, so option C is a wrong choice. The mesg command allows you to view and/or set your message status. While it does help to determine whether individual users can receive wall messages, it is not as efficient as the who -T command. Thus, option E is an incorrect answer.

20. A, C, E. The new cloned VMs should have their NIC MAC address, host name, and machine ID check and modified if necessary, in order for them to be able to run together on the same local network segment. Thus, options A, C, and E are correct answers. A VM template is similar to a VM clone (except you cannot boot it), and its primary purpose is to guide the creation of VMs. Thus, option B is a wrong answer. CPU extensions are related to physical hosts of the VMs and not the VMs themselves. Thus, option D is also an incorrect choice.

Chapter 6: Configuring the GUI, Localization, and Printing

1. C. A desktop environment is a series of components that work together to provide the graphical setting for the user interface. Therefore, option C is the correct answer. A graphical user interface (GUI) is a set of programs that allow a user to interact with the system via icons, windows, and various other visual elements. Thus, option A is a wrong answer. A display manager operates the screen where you choose a username and enter a password to gain system access. Therefore, option B is an incorrect choice. A file manager is the program that allows you to perform file maintenance activities graphically. Thus, option D is also a wrong choice. A windows manager is a set of programs that determine how the windows are presented on the desktop. Therefore, option E is also an incorrect choice.

2. A, B, C, E. A favorites bar, file manager, icons, and a system tray are all part of a graphical UI. Therefore, options A, B, C, and E are correct choices. A command line is a location to enter text-based commands, and though you can reach it from the GUI using a terminal emulator, it is not considered part of the graphical UI. Therefore, option D is the only incorrect choice.

3. A. KDM is the default display manager for the KDE Plasma desktop environment. Therefore, option A is the correct answer. Files, also called GNOME Files, is the file manager within the GNOME Shell desktop environment. Therefore, option B is a wrong answer. Mutter is the GNOME shell windows manager, and thus option C is an incorrect answer. GDM stand for the GNOME Display Manager. Therefore, option D is a wrong choice. Doc is another name for the GNOME Shell Dash, which is the favorites bar within GNOME Shell. Thus, option E is also an incorrect choice.

4. C. The KDE Plasma's file manager is named Dolphin. Therefore, option C is the correct answer. Nautilus is the file manager on the Unity desktop environment, making option A an incorrect answer. Plasmoid is another name for a KDE Plasma widget. Thus, option B is an incorrect answer. Kwin is the KDE Plasma's windows manager, and therefore option D is a wrong choice. Nemo is the default file manager on the Cinnamon desktop environment. Thus, option E is an incorrect choice.

5. A. The sounds keys accessibility setting provides beeps whenever Caps Lock or Num Lock key is turned on or off. Therefore, option A is the correct answer. A program that reads the GUI aloud, such as Orca, is a screen reader, making option B a wrong answer. The cursor blinking setting modifies the cursor blink rate to make it easier to locate the cursor on the screen. Therefore, option C is also an incorrect answer. Output to a refreshable braille display is provided by the Orca screen reader. Thus, option D is a wrong choice. Zoom settings allow the screen or a screen portion to be amplified to different magnification levels. Therefore, option E is also an incorrect choice.

6. D. The braille display device would be using the `brltty` service. The proper `systemctl` command to restart the services is in option D. Therefore, option D is the correct answer. Options A, B, and C all use incorrect names for the braille service and are wrong answers. The command in option E would reload any modified `brltty` configuration files but not restart the service. Therefore, option E is also an incorrect choice.

7. A. Slow keys are a keyboard option that modifies the how long a key must be pressed down to acknowledge the key. Therefore, option A is the correct answer. Sticky keys are a keyboard option that sets keyboard modifier keys, such as Ctrl and Shift, to maintain their pressed status until a subsequent key is pressed. Thus, option B is a wrong answer. Repeat keys are a keyboard option that modifies how long a key must be pressed down as well as a delay to acknowledge the key repeat. Therefore, option C is also a wrong choice. Simulated secondary click is actually a mouse option, and it sets a primary key to be pressed along

with a mouse click to emulate secondary mouse clicks. Thus, option D is an incorrect answer. A screen keyboard is a keyboard option that displays a visual keyboard on the UI that can be manipulated by a mouse or other pointing device to emulate keystrokes. Therefore, option E is also an incorrect choice.

8. E. The display server uses a communication protocol to transmit the desires of the UI to the operating system, and vice versa. Therefore, option E is the correct answer. A window manager is a program that communicates with the display server on behalf of the UI. Thus, option A is a wrong answer. A display manager controls the desktop environment's login screen where you choose a username and enter a password to gain system access. Therefore, option B is also a wrong choice. A windows server is another name for a window manager, and thus, option D is also an incorrect answer.

9. B, D. Wayland does use the $WAYLAND_DISPLAY environment variable, so option B is a correct answer. Also, X11Wayland supports legacy X11 programs. Therefore, option D is an additional correct answer. Wayland is a replacement for the X11 display server, and it is designed to be more secure. Thus, option A is a wrong answer. Wayland's compositor is swappable, and there are several other compositors, besides Weston, available for use with Wayland. Therefore, option C is wrong choice. In order to disable Wayland in GNOME Shell, you edit the /etc/gdm3/custom.conf file and set WaylandEnable to false. Thus, option E is also an incorrect answer.

10. C. The loginctl command will help you determine your current GUI session number. You can then employ the loginctl command again along with your session number to determine if your GUI session is Wayland or X11. Thus, option C is the correct answer. While you can issue the command echo $WAYLAND_DISPLAY to help determine if your GUI session is Wayland or X11, $WAYLAND_DISPLAY by itself does nothing. Therefore, option A is a wrong answer. AccessX is a program that originally provided many universal access settings. There is no environment variable used by Wayland or X11 called $AccessX, and thus, option B is an incorrect answer. The $X11 environment variable is made up, so option C is a wrong choice. The runlevel command allows you to determine your system's current runlevel and is not used in determining display servers. Therefore, option E is also an incorrect choice.

11. B, C, E. The X.Org Foundation does develop an X server, called X11. Thus, option B is a correct answer. The X server is being replaced by Wayland, so option C is also a right choice. X is short for X Window System, which is a display server, so option E is another correct answer. XFree86 was the dominant server implementing X until 2004. Now the dominant server is the X.Org Foundation's X11 server, so option A is a wrong answer. The X.Org's server implements the X Window System version 11, and that is why it is sometimes called X11. It is not due to the number of graphical sessions a particular use can have. Therefore, option D is also an incorrect choice.

12. A, D. The xwininfo and xdpyinfo commands provide information about the X server, including the different screen types available, the default communicate parameter values, protocol extension information, and individual window information. These two utilities would be the best ones to start diagnosing the problem. Therefore, options A and D are correct answers. The Xorg -configure command creates a new X11 configuration file for your perusal, which may be useful later in the troubleshooting process. However, this is not the best command to start diagnosis. Therefore, option B is a wrong answer. The xcpyinfo command is made up. Therefore, option C is also an incorrect answer. The loginctl command can help you determine whether the user is using X11 or Wayland, but since you already know that the X display server is running, this command will not help. Thus, option E is an incorrect answer as well.

13. A, B, C, D. Spice (sometimes written as SPICE), NX, Xrdp, and VNC are all remote desktops. Therefore, options A, B, C, and D are correct answers. Caja is the file manager in the MATE desktop environment and not a remote desktop. Thus, option E is the only incorrect answer.

14. A, D. Spice and VNC are the remote desktops typically used with virtual machines. By default, VNC is used with KVM virtual machines. However, you can replace VNC with Spice. Thus, options A and D are the correct answers. NX and Xrdp are not typically used with virtual machines, and thus, neither options B, C, or E is correct.

15. E. The Xrdp remote desktop software uses the Remote Desktop Protocol (RDP). Thus, option E is the correct answer. The Remote Frame Buffer (RFB) protocol is used by VNC. Thus, option A is a wrong answer. The Wayland protocol is used by the Wayland display server. Therefore, option B is also a wrong choice. Option C is also an incorrect answer, because the NX technology protocol is used by the NX remote desktop. The Simple Protocol for Independent Computing Environments (SPICE) is used by the Spice remote desktop. Thus, option D is also an incorrect choice.

16. B. You need to employ X11 forwarding. To properly and securely access the remote Linux system and run an X11-based application, using the -X command is the best choice. Thus, option B is the right answer. The command in option A uses the trusted X11 via the -Y switch, which is not secure. Therefore, option A is a wrong answer. The command in option C also uses the -Y switch, so option C is also an incorrect answer. Option D uses the correct command switch but sends the connection to the laptop instead of the rack-mounted Linux server. Thus, option D is a wrong answer. The option E command is using the -L switch, which is for local SSH port forwarding, uses the wrong syntax for that switch, and attempts to send the connection to the laptop. Thus, option E is an incorrect answer.

17. E. The Unicode character set uses 3 bytes to store characters, which provides enough space to represent all of the characters in the known world languages, so option E is correct. The ASCII character set supports only English language characters, so option A is incorrect. The LC_ALL environment variable defines a character set to use for the Linux system but isn't a character set in itself, so option B is incorrect. Both the UTF-8 and UTF-16 character sets are a subset of the Unicode character set, so they can't represent all of the language characters in use in the world, so options C and D are incorrect.

18. E. The locale command displays all of the LC_ environment variables and their values, so option E is correct. The date command displays only the time and date, not the localization information, so option A is incorrect. The time command displays the amount of time an application uses on the system, not the localization information, so option B is incorrect. The hwclock command displays the hardware clock time, not the localization information, so option C is incorrect. The LANG environment variable allows you to set all of the LC_ environment variables in one place, but it doesn't display all of their settings, so option D is incorrect.

19. C and E. The LANG and LC_ALL environment variables control all of the localization environment variable settings, so options C and E are correct. The LC_MONETARY, LC_NUMERIC, and LC_CTYPE environment variables each control a single category of localization environment variables, but not all of the localization environment variables, so options A, B, and D are all incorrect.

20. D. The cupsreject command rejects the queuing of print requests to a specific print queue, so option D is correct. The cancel command cancels just an individual print request, but it does not block other print jobs from going to the print queue, so option A is incorrect. The cupsaccept command enables sending print jobs to the queue, not blocking them, so option B is incorrect. The cupsenable command enables a specific printer to process queue jobs, but it does not block jobs from entering the queue, so option C is incorrect. The lpq command is a legacy BSD command for displaying the status of a print queue, but it does not allow you to block jobs from entering the queue, so option E is incorrect.

Chapter 7: Administering the System

1. A, B, E. The user account's username, password (though it typically only contains an x), and UID are all legitimate fields within a /etc/passwd file record. Therefore, options A, B, and E are correct answers. The password change date and special flag are fields within the /etc/shadow file. Thus, options C and D are incorrect choices.

2. A, B, C. The maximum password age, account expiration date, and password are all legitimate fields within an /etc/shadow file record. Therefore, options A, B, and C are correct answers. The comment and default shell are fields within the /etc/passwd file. Thus, options D and E are incorrect choices.

3. B, D, E. Though not very efficient, the cat /etc/passwd command would allow you to view the NUhura account's record within the /etc/passwd file. The grep NUhura /etc/passwd and getent passwd NUhura commands also would allow you to see the NUhura record. So options B, D, and E are correct choices. The getent command in option A has got the username and file name flip-flopped, so it is an incorrect choice. Also, the passwd NUhura attempts to change the account's password instead of display its file record, so option C is also an incorrect answer.

4. C. If the CREATE_HOME directive is not set or it is set to no, then when a user account is created, no home directory will be created by default. Most likely this caused the problem, so option C is the correct answer. The HOME directive determines what base directory name is used when creating home directories for new accounts, so option A is a wrong answer. If you did not employ super user privileges, you would not have been able to even create the account, so option B is a wrong choice. The INACTIVE directive pertains to when an account will be considered inactive, so option D is also an incorrect answer. The EXPIRE directive is involved with account expiration and not home directory creation. Therefore, option E is also an incorrect choice.

5. B. The newgrp command will let you switch temporarily from your account's default group to another group with whom you have membership. Therefore, option B is the correct answer. The usermod command could make that switch, but it is not best for temporary situations, so it is an incorrect choice. The groups command allows you to display group information but not change groups, so it also is a wrong answer. The groupadd and groupmod commands deal with group management but not with temporarily switching an account's default group. Therefore, options D and E are also incorrect choices.

6. C. The usermod -aG NCC-1701 JKirk command would add JKirk to the NCC-1701 group as a member and not remove any of the account's previous group memberships. Therefore, option C is the correct answer. The usermod -g NCC-1701 JKirk command would change the JKirk account's primary group membership, so option A is a wrong answer. The command in option B would add the JKirk account as a member to the NCC-1701 group, but it would remove any of the account's previous group memberships. Thus, option B is an incorrect answer. The groupadd NCC-1701 command would only add the NCC-1701 group. Therefore, option D is a wrong answer as well. The groupmod command is for modifying groups, and so the command in option E would have undesirable results. Thus, option E is an incorrect choice.

7. B, D. The getent group NCC-1701 and grep NCC-1701 /etc/group commands would both allow you to see the various NCC-1701 group members. Therefore, options B and D are correct answers. The groups command is for viewing an account's various group memberships. Therefore, option A is a wrong answer. It is always tempting to add an s to the /etc/group filename because of the groups command. However, it is the group file and *not* the groups file. Thus, options C and E are incorrect choices.

8. B, D. To view your mail queue, you use either the sendmail -bp or the mailq command, so options B and D are the correct answers. The systemctl sendmail status is a systemd service unit status command and does not show mail queues, so option A is incorrect. Option C is close, but the correct command is sendmail -bp not -bq. Therefore, option C is also a wrong answer. Option E will show you the various directories within /var/spool, not the email queue, so it is an incorrect choice as well.

9. E. When aliases are properly configured, any email addresses sent to the email with an alias is received by the alias account. Therefore, option E, wesley, is the correct answer. support would not receive the email, because the alias is set to wesley, and so option A is a wrong answer. None in option B is an incorrect choice, because the wesley account will receive the email. The ~/.forward file is associated with email forwarding, not aliases. Therefore, option C is a wrong choice. There is no reason for root to receive this email, so option D is also an incorrect choice.

10. A. The cron application schedules jobs on Linux systems, so the cron facility keyword represents event messages received from the job scheduler, so option A is the right answer. The user keyword represents events received from users, so option B is a wrong answer. The kern keyword represents events received from the kernel, so option C is incorrect. The console keyword represents events received from a console on the system, so option D is incorrect. The auth keyword represents security or authentication events, not job scheduling, so option E is also an incorrect choice.

11. C. The emerg severity level has a priority of 0, the highest level in syslog, so option C is correct. The crit severity level is at level 2, so it's not the highest level, making option A incorrect. The alert keyword is assigned level 1, but it's not the highest level, so option B is incorrect. The notice keyword is assigned level 5, and that is not the highest level, so option D is incorrect. The err keyword is assigned level 3, and that is not the highest level, so option E is incorrect as well.

12. A. The rsyslogd application uses the rsyslog.conf configuration file by default, so option A is correct. Options B and C are configuration files for other logging applications, not rsyslogd, so they are incorrect. Option D, rsyslog.d, is commonly used as a folder for storing additional rsyslogd configuration files, but that isn't the default configuration filename, so it is incorrect. Option E is not a valid logging application configuration filename, so it too is an incorrect choice.

13. C. The -r option displays the journal entries in reverse order, so the most recent entry will appear first. Thus, option C is correct. The -a option displays all of the data fields but in the normal order, so option A is incorrect. The -l option displays all printable data fields but in the normal order, so option B is incorrect. The -e option jumps to the end of the journal file but displays the remaining entries in normal order instead of reverse order, so option D is incorrect. The -n option displays a specified number of entries but in normal order, so option E is incorrect.

14. C. The systemd-cat command will allow you to manually add an entry to the system's active journal, so option C is the correct answer. The journalctl utility does not allow the addition of journal entries, so option A is a wrong answer. The journalctl-cat and journalctl -logger are made-up commands, so options B and E are wrong choices. The systemd-journal is a group to which an account may belong in order to view all the journal entries. However, it does not allow manual journal entries to be added, so option D is an incorrect choice.

15. A, B, C, E. A hardware clock (also called a real-time clock) and a software clock (also called system time) can be viewed or modified on a Linux system. Therefore, options A, B, C, and E are correct. An atomic clock is a very accurate type of hardware clock often employed in the NTP clock stratum at level 0. However, it cannot be typically viewed or modified on a Linux system, so option D is the only incorrect choice.

16. A. The hwclock utility will allow you to change the Linux system's hardware clock, so option A is the correct answer. The date command displays or allows you to modify the software clock. Therefore, option B is a wrong answer. The timedatectl command will allow you to change whether the hardware clock is using the localtime or UTC standard but not the time, so option C is an incorrect choice. The ntpdate command can change the system time if the ntpd service is being used but not the hardware clock's time. Thus, option D is a wrong choice. rtsync is a directive you can use with chronyd to change the hardware clock's time automatically, but it is not a utility, so option E is an incorrect choice as well.

17. C. The timedatectl command will display your system's time in both its current time zone as well as UTC, so option C is the correct answer. The hwclock -r command displays the hardware clock's time. Thus, option B is an incorrect choice. The date command will display your system's time only in its current time zone format. Therefore, option B is a wrong answer. The `ntpq -p` and `chronyc sources` are commands used with the NTP daemons (`ntpd` and `chronyd`) to view the system's time sources. Thus, options D and E are incorrect choices as well.

18. D. This is a tricky question, because only one option is correct. The `server 0.pool.ntp.org iburst` line is a correct configuration line in the `/etc/ntp.conf` file for the ntpd service, assuming you will be using the `pool.ntp.org` time servers. Thus, option D is the correct answer. Option A is incorrect, because the preceding 0 is missing on the `pool.ntp.org` designation. Option B is incorrect, because it uses the `pool` directive (used for `chronyd`; not `ntpd`). Options C and D are wrong, because it uses `service` instead of `server`.

19. B. The `ntpstat` command is the best command to use in this case, because Geordi will be provided a quick status on whether his software clock is synchronized as well as how often polling is taking place. Therefore, option B is the correct answer. The `ntpdate` utility allows you to manually set the software clock, but not see if the time is synchronized, so option A is a wrong answer. The `ntpq -p` command will let you see the servers that `ntpd` is polling and when the last synchronization took place, but it provides a great deal more information than is needed, so option C is not the best answer. The `date` command will show Geordi only the current system time and not whether the software clock is now synchronized. Thus, option D is a wrong choice. Finally, the `hwclock -w` command will set the hardware clock to the system time stored in the software clock, but it will not show whether the software clock is now synchronized. Therefore, option E is an incorrect choice as well.

20. D, E. The `chrony.conf` file is the chrony configuration file, and it may reside in the `/etc/` or `/etc/chrony/` directory, depending on the distribution Miles is using. Therefore, options D and E are the correct answer. The other filenames are made up, so options A, B, and C are all incorrect choices.

Chapter 8: Configuring Basic Networking

1. D. The netmask value determines the network portion of the IP address, which identifies what network the system is connected to. Thus, option D is correct. The default router is another IP address on the network, but it doesn't indicate the network portion of the address and so can't be used to determine the network address, making option B incorrect. The IP address by itself doesn't define the network address without the netmask, so option A is incorrect. The host name doesn't indicate the network address, so option C is incorrect. The DNS server maps host names to IP addresses, but if you only know the IP address you still won't know the network portion of the address, so option E is incorrect.

2. B. Starting with version 17.04, Ubuntu has switched to using the Netplan tool to set network address information, so option B is the correct answer. The `netstat` command doesn't set network information, but instead displays active network connections, so option A is incorrect. The `iwconfig` command sets wireless network parameters, but not network address information, so option C is incorrect. The `route` command sets default router information, but not network address information, so option D is incorrect. The `ifconfig` command does set network address information, but it isn't used by the newer versions of Ubuntu, so option E is incorrect.

3. A. The `ethtool` command displays features and parameters for network cards, so option A is the correct answer. The `netstat` command displays network statistics and connections, so option B is incorrect. The `iwconfig` and `iwlist` commands are used to set wireless network parameters and not Ethernet card settings, so options C and D are incorrect. The `route` command sets or displays routing information and not Ethernet card settings, so option E is incorrect.

4. E. The `ss` command displays a list of the open ports on a Linux system, along with the processes associated with each port, so option E is correct. The `iwconfig` command sets wireless network information, not open ports, so option A is incorrect. The `ip` command displays or sets network information on a network interface but doesn't display open ports, so option B is incorrect. The `ping` command sends ICMP messages to a remote host, but it doesn't display any open ports, so option C is incorrect. The `nmtui` command allows you to configure network parameters for a network interface but doesn't display the open ports on the system, so option D is incorrect.

5. A and C. The `nmcli` and the `ip` commands both allow you to set and change network settings from the command line, so options A and C are correct. The `iwconfig` command only sets wireless network information, so option B is incorrect. The `netstat` command displays open ports and doesn't change any network settings, so option D is incorrect. The `ping` command sends ICMP packets to remote hosts for testing and also doesn't set any network settings, so option E is incorrect.

6. A. The default router is used to send packets from the local network to remote networks, so to communicate with a remote host you need to define the default router address, making option A correct. The netmask defines only the local network and doesn't define what to do with packets for remote hosts, so option B is incorrect. The host name and IP address define features of the local host only, so options C and D are incorrect, whereas the DNS server defines how to retrieve the IP address of a host based on its domain name, so option E is incorrect.

7. E. The DNS server maps the host name to an IP address, so you must have a DNS server defined in your network configuration to be able to use host names in your applications. Thus, option E is correct. The default router defines how to send packets to remote hosts only and doesn't map the host name to the IP address, so option A is incorrect. The netmask value defines the local network but not how to map host names to IP addresses, so option B is incorrect. The host name and IP address define features of the local host, so options C and D are incorrect.

8. B. The Dynamic Host Configuration Protocol (DHCP) is used to assign dynamic IP addresses to client workstations on a network, so option B is correct. The default router can't assign addresses to devices, so option B is incorrect. The ARP table maps the hardware address of the network card to IP addresses, but it doesn't assign the IP addresses, so option C is incorrect. The netmask value determines the network address but not the IP address of the host, so option D is incorrect. The `ifconfig` command can set the static IP address of the host but doesn't automatically assign the IP address, so option E is incorrect.

9. **B.** The private address is a special network address range assigned to the local networks outside of the Internet so that devices can communicate with one another on a local network, making option B the correct answer. Dynamic and static IP addresses are assigned to network interfaces but can be either public or private addresses, so options A and C are incorrect. The host name identifies the local host for remote connections, not for local applications, so option D is incorrect. The MAC address identifies the network card hardware address, but it isn't used by local applications, so option E is incorrect.

10. **A.** The `dig` command can display individual host records for a domain, which you can use to find the MX mail host for the domain, so option A is correct. The `host` command displays host IP address information only and can't determine the server type from the DNS records, so option D is incorrect. The `netstat` and `ss` commands display active network connections, but not the remote host types, so options B and E are both incorrect. The `ping6` command sends IPv6 ICMP packets to test remote hosts but can't tell if the remote host is a mail server, so option C is incorrect.

11. **B.** The `ss` command can display both open ports and the applications that own them, so option B is correct. The `ip` and `ifconfig` commands just display or set network settings, so options A and E are incorrect. The `host` and `dig` commands display host name information only, so options C and D are also incorrect.

12. **A.** Red Hat–based systems use separate files to store the IP address and router information. Those files are stored in the `/etc/sysconfig/network-scripts` folder, making option A correct. Option B is where Debian-based systems store the interfaces file, which contains the network configuration settings. The `ifcfg-eth0` is a file used to store the configuration, not a folder, so option C is incorrect. The `ifconfig` and `iwconfig` are commands and not folders, so options D and E are incorrect.

13. **B.** Option B is the correct format to set a dynamic IP address for the interface. The Debian system uses the `iface` setting to set features for an interface, so options C and E are incorrect. Option A sets a static IP address for the interface and not a dynamic address, so it's incorrect. Option D sets a link local IPv6 address and not a dynamic IP address, so it's incorrect.

14. **B.** The DNS servers are listed in the `/etc/resolv.conf` configuration file using the nameserver setting, so option B is correct. The `/etc/dhcpd.conf` file defines configuration settings for a DHCP server, so option A is incorrect. The `/etc/nsswitch.conf` file defines the order in which the system searches for a host name, not the list of DNS servers used, so option C is incorrect. The `/etc/network/interfaces` file defines the network interfaces for a Debian-based system, not the list of DNS servers, so option D is also incorrect. The `/etc/sysctl.conf` file defines kernel network parameters and not a list of DNS servers, so option E is incorrect.

15. **A.** Option A is the only option that uses the correct values in the correct order. The `ifconfig` command must specify the network interface, the IP address, and then the `netmask` option before the netmask address. You can use the up or down option to place the network card in an active or inactive state by default, but it's not required. Option C is close but fails to specify the network interface. Option B is not in the correct format, and options D and E fail to list the necessary configuration settings.

16. A. The `iwlist` command displays the available wireless network access points detected by the wireless network card, so option A is correct. The `iwconfig` command configures the network card to connect to a specific access point but doesn't list all of the detected access points, making option B incorrect. Option C specifies the `ifconfig` command, which is used to assign an IP address to a wireless network card but doesn't list the access points. The `ip` command specified in option D likewise can be used to set the IP address of the card but doesn't list the access points. Option E, the `arp` command, maps hardware addresses to IP addresses so that you can find duplicate IP addresses on your network, but it doesn't list the wireless access points.

17. D. The SSID value defines the access point name, and it is set using the `essid` option in the `iwconfig` command, making option D the correct answer. The key specifies the encryption key required to connect to the access point but not the access point name, making option A incorrect. The netmask and address values aren't set by the `iwconfig` command, so options B and C are incorrect. The `channel` defines the radio frequency the access point uses, not the access point name, so option E is also incorrect.

18. E . The `ip` command allows you to both display and set the IP address, netmask, and default router values for a network interface, so option E is correct. The `ifconfig` command can set the IP address and netmask values but not the default router. The `iwconfig` command is used to set the wireless access point settings, and the `router` command is used to set the default router but not the IP address or netmask values. The `ifup` command only activates the network interface—it can't set the address values.

19. A. The netmask value sets the network portion of the IP address to 1s and the host portion of the IP address to 0s. Thus, the netmask value must have consecutive 1s in the address at the start of the value. Option A, 255.255.255.0, indicates that the first 24 bits of the address are 1s, so it represents a proper netmask value and is the correct option. In option B the 1s values aren't consecutive, so it is not a proper netmask value and is thus incorrect. Option C shows a network address but not the netmask address, and option D shows a host address but not the netmask address, so they are both incorrect. Option E shows an address that uses consecutive 1s values, but they are at the end of the address and not at the beginning, so it is incorrect.

20. B. The aggregation, or mode 0 method of bonding, combines the network interfaces to create a single, larger network pipe, so option B is correct. The active/backup, or mode 1, method keeps one interface in passive background mode, so it doesn't increase the network bandwidth of the server, making option C incorrect. All of the load balancing methods, modes 0, 5, and 6, divide traffic between separate network interfaces, so they don't create a single interface. Thus options A, D, and E are all incorrect.

Chapter 9: Writing Scripts

1. B. The `#!` character combination defines the shebang, which tells the Linux shell what shell to use to run the shell script code, so option B is correct. The `>>` character combination appends the output of a command to a file, so option A is incorrect. The `|` character pipes

the output of a command to another command, so option C is incorrect. The > character redirects the output of a command to a new file, so option D is incorrect. The 2> character combination redirects error messages from a command to a file, so option E is incorrect.

2. D. The > character redirects all of the output from a command to a new file, so option D is correct. The >> character combination appends all of the output from a command to an existing file, so option A is incorrect. The #! Character combination defines the shell to use, so option B is incorrect. The | character pipes output from one command to another command, so option C is incorrect. The 2> character combination redirects only error messages from a command to a new file, not all of the output, so option E is incorrect.

3. C. The u+x chmod permissions assigns execute permissions to the file owner so that you can run the file at the command prompt, which makes option C correct. The 644 octal permissions assigns only read and write permissions to the file owner, not execute permissions, so option A is incorrect. The u+r permission assigns read permissions, so option B is incorrect. The u+w permission assigns only write permissions, so option D is incorrect. The u=wr permission assigns both read and write permissions but not execute permissions to the file owner, so option E is incorrect.

4. A. The $USER environment variable contains the text username of the user account that started the shell, so option A is correct. The $UID environment variable contains the numeric user ID, not the text username, so option B is incorrect. The $HOME environment variable contains the home directory location of the user account, so option C is incorrect. The $BASH environment variable contains the location of the Bash shell executable file, so option D is incorrect. The $1 variable is a positional variable, not an environment variable. It's used to retrieve data from the command-line command that launched the shell, not to identify the user who started the shell, so option E is incorrect.

5. C. To assign a value to a variable, you use the equal sign, but no spaces must be used between the variable name, the equal sign, and the value, so option C is correct. Option A uses the command substitution format, which assigns a value to the output of a command, so option A is incorrect. Option B places spaces between the variable name, equal sign, and the value, so option B is incorrect. Option D places quotes around the value, making it a string value and not a numeric value, so option D is incorrect. Option E uses backtick characters around the value, which attempts to run it using command substitution, which is incorrect.

6. B. The -f file test checks if the specified object exists and if it's a file, so option B is correct. The -e file test only checks if the object exists, not the object type, so option A is incorrect. The -d file test checks if the object exists but is a directory, not a file, so option C is incorrect. The -x file test checks if the current user account has execute permissions for the file, so option D is incorrect. The -w file test checks if the current user account has write permissions for the file, so option E is incorrect.

7. C. The bar character (|) pipes the output of one command to the input of another command, so option C is correct. The >> character combination appends the output of a command to an existing file, not to another command, so option A is incorrect. The shebang (#!) identifies the shell to use to run the script, so option B is incorrect. The > character redirects the output of a command to a new file, not to another command, so option D is incorrect. The 2> character combination redirects the error messages from a command to a new file, so option E is incorrect.

8. D. The exit command allows you to return a specific error status when the shell script exits, so option D is correct. The #! shebang defines the shell to use to run the shell script, not the exit status, so option A is incorrect. The $? character combination displays the exit status from the last command—it doesn't return a specific exit status—so option B is incorrect. The $1 variable contains the first command-line parameter used when the shell script is launched from the command line, so option C is incorrect. The while command allows you to iterate through a set of commands until a specific condition is met, so option E is incorrect.

9. E. The $() command assigns the output of a command to a specified variable in the shell script, so option E is correct. The > character redirects the output of a command to a file, not to a variable, so option A is incorrect. The >> character combination appends the output of a command to an existing file, not to a variable, so option B is incorrect. The #[] command performs integer mathematical operations in the Bash shell, so option C is incorrect. The | character redirects the output of a command to another command, not to a variable, so option D is incorrect.

10. C. The $[] command performs simple integer mathematical operations in the Bash shell, so option C is correct. The > character redirects the output of a command to a new file, so option A is incorrect. The >> character combination appends the output of a command to an existing file, so option B is incorrect. The | character redirects the output of a command to another command, so option D is incorrect. The #() command redirects the output of a command to a variable in the shell script, so option E is incorrect.

11. B. The ampersand character (&) tells the shell to start the command in background mode from the console session, so option B is correct. The greater-than sign (>) redirects the output from the command to a file but doesn't run the command in background mode, so option A is incorrect. The pipe symbol (|) redirects the output from the command to another command, so option C is incorrect. The double greater-than sign (>>) appends the output from the command to a file, so option D is incorrect. The nohup command disconnects the session from the console session, so option E is incorrect.

12. E. The nohup command disconnects the shell script from the current console session, so option E is correct. The greater-than sign (>) redirects the output from the command to a file, so option A is incorrect. The ampersand sign (&) runs the shell script in background mode, so option B is incorrect. The pipe symbol (|) redirects the output from the command to another command, so option C is incorrect. The double greater-than symbol (>>) appends the output from the command to a file, so option D is incorrect.

13. C. The Ctrl+C key combination stops the job currently running in foreground mode on the console session, so option C is correct. Starting a command with the nohup command disconnects the job from the console session, so you can't stop it from the console with a key command, making option A incorrect. Starting a job with the ampersand (&) command places the job in background mode, so option B is incorrect. The pipe symbol redirects the output from a shell script to another command, so option D is incorrect. The kill command will stop a running shell script, but if the shell script is running in your console session you won't be able to submit the kill command from the command prompt, so option E is incorrect.

14. A. The Ctrl+Z key combination pauses the job currently running in foreground mode on the console session, so option A is correct. The Ctrl+C key combination stops rather than pauses the job currently running in foreground mode in the console session, so option B is incorrect. The nohup command disconnects a job from the console session but doesn't pause the job, so option D is incorrect. The ampersand sign (&) runs a job in background mode in the console session but doesn't pause it, so option D is incorrect. The fg command resumes a stopped job in foreground mode but doesn't pause the job, so option E is incorrect.

15. C. When you list the current jobs using the jobs command, there will be a plus sign next to the default job number, so option C is correct. The minus sign next to a job number indicates the job that is next in line to become the default job, so option D is incorrect. Neither the PID nor job number indicate the default job, so options A and B are both incorrect. The ps command lists the running jobs but doesn't indicate the default job in a console session, so option E is incorrect.

16. B. The fg command allows you to change a currently running or stopped job to run in foreground mode on the current console session, so option B is correct. The bg command changes a currently running or stopped job to run in background mode, not foreground mode, so option A is incorrect. The nohup command disconnects a job from the console session, so option C is incorrect. The ampersand sign (&) places a job in background mode, not foreground mode, so option D is incorrect. The at command runs a job in background mode at a specific time but doesn't place the job in foreground mode, so option E is incorrect.

17. C. The at command allows you to schedule a job to run at a specific time, so option C is correct. The nohup command disconnects a job from the console session, so option A is incorrect. The ampersand sign (&) runs a job in background mode, so option B is incorrect. The pipe symbol (|) and the greater-than symbol redirect the job output to either a command or a file, so options D and E are both incorrect.

18. D. The cron program checks the cron tables for each user account and runs any scheduled jobs automatically, so option D is correct. The at command runs a specified command only once at a scheduled time, not for multiple times, so option A is incorrect. The nohup and ampersand (&) commands do not schedule jobs to run, so both options B and C are incorrect. The atq command displays the jobs already scheduled to run from the at command but doesn't run the commands multiple times, so option E is incorrect.

19. E. The time specified in the cron table is listed in minute, hour, day of month, month, and day of week order. The hour is in 24-hour format, so the specified entry would run the job at 5:10 a.m. every day, making option E correct. Options A, B, C, and D are all incorrect times based on the specified entry.

20. C. The crontab command allows you to list or edit the cron table for your own user account, so option C is correct. The cron command is what reads the cron tables for each user account and runs the specified jobs—it doesn't list the jobs—so option A is incorrect. The at command allows you to schedule a job to run at a specific time, so option B is incorrect. The jobs command allows you to view the currently running or stopped jobs in your console session, so option D is incorrect. The nohup command disconnects the job from the console session, so option E is incorrect.

Chapter 10: Securing Your System

1. C. The nmap utility allows you to scan a system a system's ports and see what services are offered for each port, and you don't have to be currently logged onto the system (in fact, you can scan entire subnets of systems). Therefore, option C is the correct answer. The fuser, lsof, netstat, and ss utilities all can be used to audit a system's offered network services, but you must be logged into the system you are auditing. Thus, options A, B, D, and E are incorrect choices.

2. A, E. In order for the netstat utility to display what ports are listening for incoming TCP connections, Nickie should use the -lt options. (He could also use --listening and --tcp, if desired.) Therefore, options A and E are the correct answers. The -u switch listens for UDP and not TCP connections, so option B is a wrong answer. The -s switch shows statistics, but this is not what Nickie desires, so option C is an incorrect answer. The -T switch keeps long addresses from being trimmed instead of displaying TCP connections. Therefore, option E is an incorrect choice as well.

3. A, E. Just like the netstat utility, for ss to display what ports are listening for incoming TCP connections, Nickie should use the -lt options. Therefore, options A and E are the correct answers. The -u switch listens for UDP and not TCP connections, so option B is a wrong answer. The -s switch shows summary statistics, but this is not what Nickie desires, so option C is an incorrect answer. The ss utility does not have a -T switch. Therefore, option E is an incorrect choice as well.

4. D. Case can use the command in option D to see all active FTP service connections (ftp represents both ports 20 and 21). Therefore, option D is the correct answer. The lsof -i UDP command will only show UDP connections (and FTP is a TCP connection), so option A is a wrong answer. The commands in options B and C have their ports and protocols flip-flopped, so they are incorrect choices as well. The command in option E puts a port number instead of nothing or TCP, so it is an incorrect choice too.

5. D. The main difference between using the lsof utility and the fuser utility to audit network services on your system is that the fuser utility will display the process PID using the protocol and port on your system (if you use the right switches). Therefore option D is the correct answer. The statements in options A, B, and E are true for both utilities (depending on what switches you employ), so they are wrong answers. Neither fuser nor lsof is deprecated, so option C is an incorrect choice as well.

6. B. The systemctl command will allow Hiro to disable any of the network services that are not needed on his system (for example, systemctl disable SnowCrash). Thus, option B is the correct answer. The rest of the options contain SysVinit commands, so they are incorrect choices.

7. B, D. Because services that are managed by xinetd may have their configurations within the /etc/xinetd.conf file or within their own file in the /etc/xinetd.d/ directory, and because you need to set their disable directive to yes (disable = yes) in order to disable them, options B and D are the correct answers. You do not want to disable xinetd entirely, because only a few services being managed by the super server are unneeded. Thus, options A and E are wrong answers. In addition, since the system is a systemd system, the

chkconfig command would not disable xinetd (and you don't want to do that anyway), so option C is also an incorrect choice.

8. C. TCP Wrappers use the /etc/hosts.allow and /etc/hosts.deny files to control access to services that employ TCP Wrappers. Because /etc/hosts.allow is checked first, if an incoming packet's source address and destination service matches a record in that file the /etc/hosts.deny file is skipped. However, if a record does not match an incoming packet's information, the /etc/hosts.deny file is checked and if a matching record is *not* found in it, access is *allowed*. Therefore, it is best to put the ALL: ALL record in the /etc/hosts.deny file to improve security so that all packets with unmatched records in the /etc/hosts.allow file are denied. Thus, option C is the correct answer. Option A would make security worse, because it would give anyone from anywhere access to all the system's services. Thus, option A is a wrong answer. Options B, D, and E all have the wrong filenames, so they are incorrect choices as well.

9. A, C, D, and E. All the statements in options A, C, D, and E are true, so they are correct answers. Passwords should not be stored in the /etc/passwd file due to its file permissions, which allow anyone to read the file. Even though the passwords are salted hashes, rainbow tables could be employed to determine the plaintext passwords. Thus, option B is a *really* wrong answer.

10. D. The best answer is in option D—set Yoyo up in the /etc/sudoers file, and have her issue commands that need super user privileges via the sudo command. The root account password should not be shared among multiple people (and many distributions are not disabling the root account), because it sets up a repudiation environment, which is not secure. Therefore, options A, B, and C are wrong answers. If Yoyo is set up in the /etc/sudoers file, she should be using the sudo command, not the su -c command, so option E is an incorrect choice.

11. B. The w command provides the most information concerning users who are currently logged into the system, so option B is the correct answer. The who command provides almost as much information as the w command, but its data does not surpass the w utility's output. Therefore, option A is a wrong answer. The last command is primarily for displaying the last time a particular user logged into the system as well as if that user is currently on the system, and while useful, it also does not provide as much information as the w command, so option C is a wrong choice. The who am i and whoami commands show information about the current user only, so options D and E are incorrect choices as well.

12. D. For Wade to set the number of processes each virtual reality game player can start on his gaming server, the ulimit option he should use is -u. Therefore, option D is the correct answer. The -a switch shows the current user's settings, so option A is a wrong answer. The -l switch sets the maximum amount of memory that can be locked by the user, so option B is a wrong choice. The -t switch sets the maximum amount of CPU time the user account is allowed, so option C is a wrong answer. The -v switch sets the maximum amount of virtual memory that can be allocated by the user, so option E is an incorrect choice as well.

13. A. The OpenSSH application keeps track of any previously connected hosts and their public keys in each user's ~/.ssh/known_hosts file. Therefore, option A is the correct answer. The ~/.ssh/authorized_keys file is used on an SSH server to keep track of authorized public keys used for password-less authentication. Therefore, option B is a

wrong answer. Options C and D are made up and therefore incorrect choices. Option E is an RSA public key that could be created by the ssh-keygen utility, so it is a wrong choice as well.

14. A, B, C. The ~./ssh/config, /etc/ssh/ssh_config, and /etc/ssh/sshd_config files are all OpenSSH configuration files. Therefore, options A, B, and C are correct choices. The files listed in options D and E are made up and therefore incorrect answers.

15. E. The only correct answer is option E. These identity keys are created with the filenames of id_*type* for the private key and id_*type*.pub for the public key. The key in option E is a private key using the RSA algorithm. Option A's key is an RSA private key used in establishing a password authenticated SSH connection, so it is a wrong answer. The key listed in option B is a public version of option A's key, so it too is a wrong choice. The keys listed in options C and D are made up, and thus they are wrong choices as well.

16. A. The command in option A is the correct answer. The ssh-keygen -t rsa -f /etc/ssh/ssh_host_ecdsa_key command designates the key pair type to be rsa and designates the wrong filename for -t rsa, so option B is a wrong answer. Options C, D, and E also use the wrong filenames, so they are incorrect as well.

17. E. The ssh-copy-id command will not only copy over DeAndre's public key to the remote system, but it will also add it to his account's ~/.ssh/authorized_keys file on the remote system. Therefore, option E is the correct answer. The scp command will work, but it does not store the key in the ~/.ssh/authorized_keys file and should only be used if the scp-copy-id utility is not available. Therefore, option A is a wrong answer. The ssh-keygen command is for generating keys, not copying them to remote systems, so option B is also a wrong choice. The scp-id-copy and scp-copy-id commands are made up; thus, options C and D are also incorrect choices.

18. D. Aleena should enter the ssh-agent /bin/bash command to start the agent session, so option D is the correct answer. The gpg-agent command is used with GPG file encryption, so option A is the wrong choice. Aleena probably used ssh-copy-id to put her key in the appropriate places, but since she already accomplished that task, option B is the wrong answer. After an agent session is open, then the ssh-add command adds the key to the session, but since Aleena has not opened a session, option C is also an incorrect answer. The ssh command is used to make the connection to a remote system, not to start an OpenSSH agent session, so option E is also an incorrect choice.

19. A, B, E. The gpg --import zer0es.pub command will import the public key stored in the zer0es.pub file and store it on the user's keyring, which is actually a file within the ~/.gnupg/ directory. It does not remove the public key from the zer0es.pub file. Therefore, options A, B, and E are all correct answers. The gpg-agent daemon is involved only with private keys, not public keys, so option C is a wrong answer. Reagan could export the public key to a reagan.pub file but has not done so; thus, option D is also an incorrect choice.

20. A, B, D. The --sign, --clearsign, and --detach-sig switches will all create digital signatures. Therefore, options A, B, and D are correct. The --detach-sig switch is used to verify a digital signature, not to create one, so option C is a wrong answer. The --out switch is used in various gpg commands, but not necessarily one that creates digital signatures. Thus, option E is also an incorrect choice.

Index

S

Online Test Bank

Register to gain one year of FREE access to the online interactive test bank to help you study for your LPIC-1 certification exams—included with your purchase of this book! All of the chapter review questions and the practice tests in this book are included in the online test bank so you can practice in a timed and graded setting.

Register and Access the Online Test Bank

To register your book and get access to the online test bank, follow these steps:

1. Go to bit.ly/SybexTest (this address is case sensitive)!
2. Select your book from the list.
3. Complete the required registration information, including answering the security verification to prove book ownership. You will be emailed a pin code.
4. Follow the directions in the email or go to www.wiley.com/go/sybextestprep.
5. Find your book on that page and click the "Register or Login" link with it. Then enter the pin code you received and click the "Activate PIN" button.
6. On the Create an Account or Login page, enter your username and password, and click Login or, if you don't have an account already, create a new account.
7. At this point, you should be in the test bank site with your new test bank listed at the top of the page. If you do not see it there, please refresh the page or log out and log back in.